D0197421

NOTE:

See 1997 UPDATE
following index

Dedicated to James Charles Jenkins

1952–1979

Coauthor of the first three editions of this book

THE
PACIFIC CREST

Volume 1: California

TRAIL

Jeffrey P. Schaffer
Ben Schifrin
Thomas Winnett
Ruby Johnson Jenkins

 Wilderness Press
Berkeley

Acknowledgments

Each author was responsible for a particular length of trail, and hence each wishes to acknowledge different people.

Schifrin (Sections A–E): Various help, including continued updates on trail construction, plans and priorities, from Phil Horning and John "Skip" Noble of Cleveland National Forest; Bob Snyder, Pam Elliott, Dan Banks and Steven Nelson of the Bureau of Land Management; Karen Fortus, Karen Snigowski, Kim Vandehar and Ed Medina of Angeles National Forest; and Thomas Horner, Joe Astleford and Bob Ota of San Bernardino National Forest. Special thanks go to the PCT Association, especially Alice Krueper, the Southern Califonia Regional Coordinator: she is clearly the number one force in PCT development and maintenance in southern California. Nancy Kerr and Todd Fitzgibbon gave unselfish help and companionship; Chris Landa, Bruce Gilbert and Bill Webster offered repeated, accurate corrections.

Jenkins (Sections F and G): An elderly man in failing health due to his age was responsible for a freeway accident that took the life of J. C. Jenkins, the former author of these sections. Jenkins' mother, Ruby, assumed the field work and update of his work to honor his memory; his father, Bill, mapped the Piute Mountains area. While Ruby rehiked these sections for this edition, she was often accompanied by Roberta Abbe, Vonnie Diggles, Anita Hall, Rod Middleworth, Bill Whities, and Sandey and Ron Yurinak.

Winnett (Section H, Mt. Whitney to Devils Postpile): Jason Winnett rehiked parts of the John Muir Trail section of the Pacific Crest Trail. Kathy Morey did the same.

Schaffer (Devils Postpile, in Section H, through Section R): In addition to the people I've acknowledged in the first three editions, I would like to mention some of those who have written us with helpful comments since then. Particularly helpful have been detailed notes by William McCanna, Jr., Bruce Ohlson, David Shimek, and Thomas Zurr. Some others who have offered useful information are Scott Anderson, Bob Ellinwood, Bruce and Sharon Gilbert, John Olley, Steve Queen, Linda Spaulding, Jeff Stone, Gary Suttle, Taylor Wind Set, and Ben York. I have not had the time to check every detail all these fine folks have mentioned, but where I have, their notes have been quite accurate. Some useful information on my section has been forwarded to me by Wilderness Press, but only as parts of letters that lacked name and address. I apologize to anyone who has sent me constructive comments but was not acknowledged here. Finally, I would like to thank Ray Jardine for his comments on various parts of the book.

Photo credits:
Bureau of Land Management 213
Haber, Lyn 238, 239
Jenkins, J. C. 234
Jenkins, Ruby Johnson 186, 189, 212, 205, 212, 220, 221, 230, 240
Schaffer, Jeffrey P. 286 through 516
Schifrin, Ben 58 through 181
Winnett, Thomas 247 through 281

First Edition June 1973
Rev. second printing August 1975
Second Edition September 1977
Second printing July 1979
Third Edition June 1982
Second printing April 1985
Fourth Edition January 1989
Second printing April 1990
Fifth Edition July 1995
Second printing September 1997

Cover: Mt Ritter and Banner Peak above Ediza Lake, photo © 1995 by Ed Cooper
Title page: Backpackers on the PCT just north of Mt. Etna

Copyright © 1973, 1977, 1982, 1989, 1995 by Wilderness Press
Topographics maps revised by Jeffrey P. Schaffer and Bruce Appleyard
Section maps by Barbara Jackson
Design by Thomas Winnett and Kathy Morey
Cover Design by Larry Van Dyke

Library of Congress Card Catalog Number 95-9325
International Standard Book Number 0-89997-178-4
Manufactured in the United States of America
Published by **Wilderness Press, 2440 Bancroft Way, Berkeley, CA 94704**
        Write for free catalog, or phone (510) 843-8080

Library of Congress Cataloging-in-Publication Data

The Pacific Crest Trail. — 5th ed.
    p.   cm.
    Includes bibliographical references and index.
    Contents: v. 1. California / Jeffrey P. Schaffer ... [et al.]
    ISBN 0-89997-178-4 (v. 1)
    1. Hiking—Pacific Crest Trail—Guidebooks. 2. Hiking—California—Guidebooks. 3. Pacific Crest Trail—Guidebooks. 4. California—Guidebooks. I. Schaffer, Jeffrey P.
GV 199.42.P3P3 1995
796.5'1'0979—dc20   95-9325
                                        CIP

Contents

Introductory Chapters

Trail Chapters

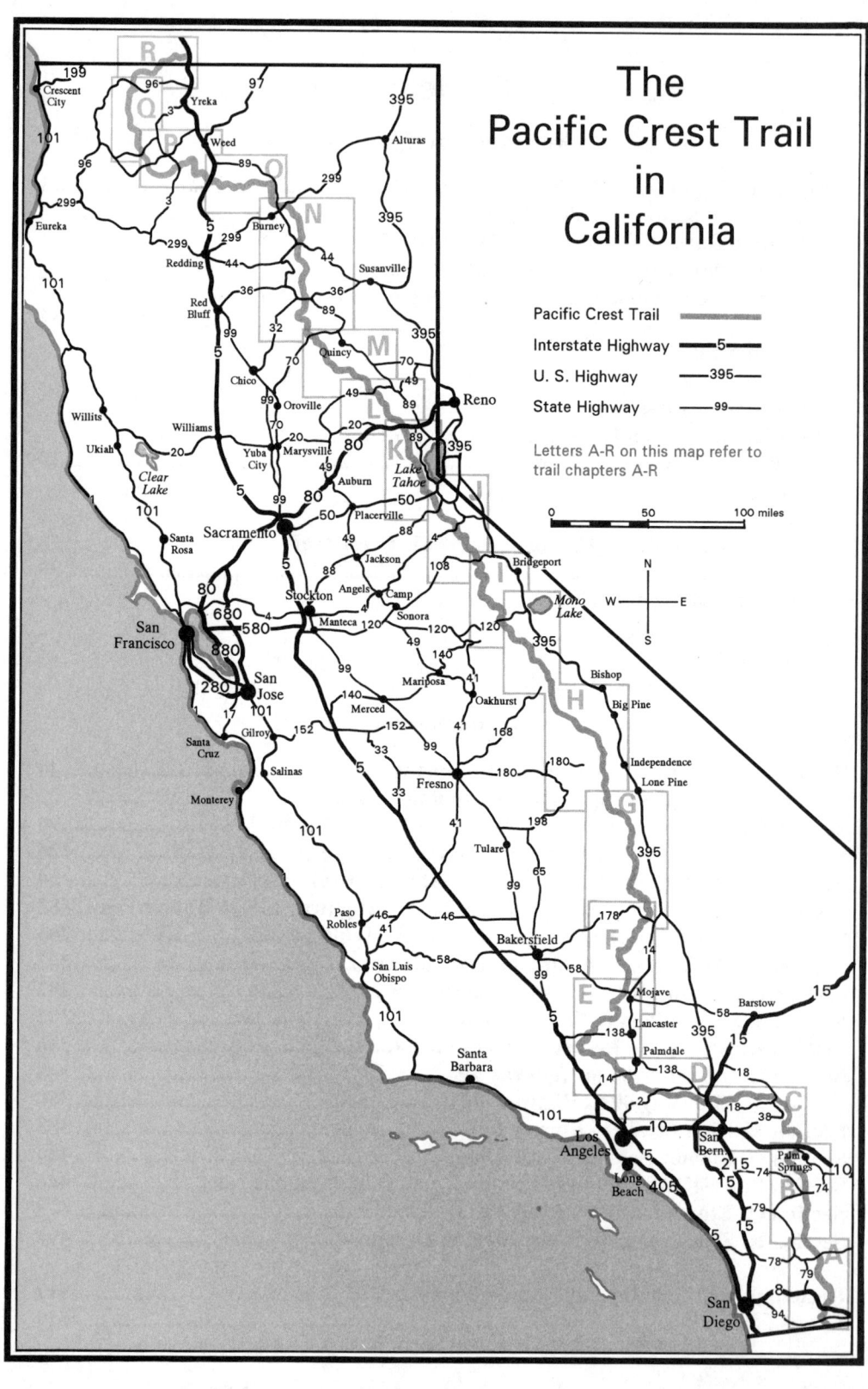

The
Pacific Crest Trail
in
California

Pacific Crest Trail
Interstate Highway ━5━
U. S. Highway ─395─
State Highway ─99─

Letters A-R on this map refer to trail chapters A-R

0   50   100 miles

Chapter 1
The PCT, Its History and Use

The first proposal for the creation of a Pacific Crest Trail that we have been able to discover is contained in the book *Pacific Crest Trails*, by Joseph T. Hazard (Superior Publishing Co.). He says that in 1926 a Catherine Montgomery at the Western Washington College of Education in Bellingham suggested to him that there should be:

"A high trail winding down the heights of our western mountains with mile markers and shelter huts—like those pictures I'll show you of the 'Long Trail of the Appalachians'—from the Canadian Border to the Mexican Boundary Line!"

To go back six years in time, the Forest Service had by 1920 routed and posted a trail from Mt. Hood to Crater Lake in Oregon, named the Oregon Skyline Trail, and with hindsight we can say that it was the first link in the PCT. (For brevity in this book, we refer to the Pacific Crest Trail as the "PCT." Technically the official name is the Pacific Crest National Scenic Trail, abbreviated as the PCNST. However, this abbreviation is more cumbersome, and essentially no one uses it.)

Hazard says that on that very night, he conveyed Miss Montgomery's suggestion to the Mt. Baker Club of Bellingham, which was enthusiastic about it. He says that soon a number of other mountain clubs and outdoor organizations in the Pacific Northwest adopted the idea and set about promoting it. Then, in 1928, Fred W. Cleator became Supervisor of Recreation for Region 6 (Oregon and Washington) of the U.S. Forest Service. Cleator proclaimed and began to develop the Cascade Crest Trail, a route down the spine of Washington from Canada to the Columbia River. Later, he extended the Oregon Skyline Trail at both ends so that it too traversed a whole state. In 1937 Region 6 of the Forest Service developed a design for PCT trail markers and posted them from the Canadian border to the California border.

But the Forest Service's Region 5 (California) did not follow this lead, and it remained for a private person to provide the real spark not only for a California segment of the PCT but indeed for the PCT itself. In the early Thirties the idea of a Pacific Crest Trail entered the mind of Clinton C. Clarke of Pasadena, California, who was then chairman of the Executive Committee of the Mountain League of Los Angeles County. "In March 1932," wrote Clarke in *The Pacific Crest Trailway*, he "proposed to the United States Forest and National Park Services the project of a continuous wilderness trail across the United States from Canada to Mexico. . . .The plan was to build a trail along the summit divides of the mountain ranges of these states, traversing the best scenic areas and maintaining an absolute wilderness character."

The proposal included formation of additional Mountain Leagues in Seattle, Portland and San Francisco by representatives of youth organizations and hiking and mountaineering clubs similar to the one in Los Angeles. These Mountain Leagues would then take the lead in promoting the extension of the John Muir Trail northward and southward to complete a pathway from border to border. When it became evident that more than Mountain Leagues were needed for such a major undertaking, Clarke took the lead in forming the Pacific Crest Trail System Conference, with representatives from the three Pacific Coast states. He served as its President for 25 years.

As early as January 1935 Clarke published a handbook-guide to the PCT giving the route in rather sketchy terms ("the Trail goes east of Heart Lake, then south across granite fields to the junction of Piute and Evolution Creeks"—this covers about nine miles).

In the summer of 1935—and again the next three summers—groups of boys under the sponsorship of the YMCA explored the PCT route in relays, proceeding from Mexico on June 15, 1935, to Canada on August 12, 1938. This exploration was under the guidance of a YMCA secretary, Warren L. Rogers, who served as Executive Secretary of the Pacific Crest Trail System Conference from 1932 until 1957, when Clarke died (at age 84), and the conference disappeared. (Rogers was an enthusiastic hiker—and mountaineer—which is remarkable considering that he limped because as a child he had been stricken with polio.) On his own Rogers more or less kept the idea of the PCT alive until hiking and trails were receiving national attention in the sixties. He stayed active in promoting the trail and its joys almost to the time of his death in 1992 (at age 83).

In 1965 the Bureau of Outdoor Recreation, a federal agency, appointed a commission to make a nationwide trails study. The commission, noting that walking for pleasure was second only to driving for pleasure as the most popular recreation in America, recommended establishing a national system of trails of two kinds—long National Scenic Trails in the hinterlands and shorter National Recreation Trails in and near metropolitan areas. The commission recommended that Congress establish four Scenic Trails—the already existing Appalachian Trail, the partly existing Pacific Crest Trail, a Potomac Heritage Trail and a Continental Divide Trail. Congress responded by passing, in 1968, the National Trails System Act, which set the framework for a system of trails and specifically made the Appalachian and the Pacific Crest trails the first two National Scenic trails.

Meanwhile, in California, the Forest Service in 1965 had held a series of meetings about a route for the PCT in the state. These meetings involved people from the Forest Service, the Park Service, the State Division of Parks and Beaches, and other government bodies charged with responsibility over areas where the trail might go. These people decided that so much time had elapsed since Clarke had drawn his route that they should essentially start all over. Of course, it was pretty obvious that segments like the John Muir Trail would not be overlooked in choosing a new route through California. By the end of 1965 a proposed route had been drawn onto maps. (We don't say "mapped," for that would imply that someone actually had covered the route in the field.)

When Congress, in the 1968 law, created a citizens Advisory Council for the PCT, it was the route devised in 1965 which the Forest Service presented to the council as a "first draft" of a final PCT route. This body of citizens was to decide all the details of the final route; the Forest Service said it would adopt whatever the citizens wanted. The Advisory Council was also to concern itself with standards for the physical nature of the trail, markers to be erected along the trail, and the administration of the trail and its use.

In 1972 the Advisory Council agreed upon a route, and the Forest Service put it onto maps for internal use. Since much of the agreed-upon route was cross-country, these maps were sent to the various national forests along the route, for them to mark a temporary route in the places where no trail existed along the final PCT route. This they did—but not always after field work. The result was that the maps made available to the public in June 1972 showing the final proposed route and the temporary detours did not correspond to what was on the ground in many places. A common flaw was that the Forest Service showed a temporary or permanent PCT segment following a trail taken off a pre-existing Forest Service map, when in fact there *was no trail* where it was shown on that map in the first place.

Perfect or not, the final proposed route was sent to Washington for publication in the Federal Register, the next step toward its becoming official. A verbal description of the route was also published in the Federal Register on January 30, 1973. But the material in the register did not give a precise route which could be unambiguously followed; it was only a *general* route, and the details in many places remained to be settled.

As construction on PCT trail segments began, many were optimistic that the entire trail could be completed within a decade. Perhaps it could have were it not for private property located along the proposed route. While some owners readily allowed rights-of-way, many others did not, at least not initially, and years of negotiations passed before some rights were finally secured. While negotiations were in progress, the Forest Service sometimes built new trail segments on both sides of a parcel of private land, expecting to extend a trail segment through it soon after. At times this approach backfired, such as in the northern Sierra Nevada in the Gibraltar environs (Map M3). The owners of some property never gave up a right-of-way, and so a new stretch of trail on Gibraltar's south slopes had to be abandoned for a snowier, costlier stretch on its north slopes, completed in fall 1985. But at least the stretch was built, which was not true for a short stretch northwest of Sierra Buttes (Map M1, Section 7), where the PCT route is a road.

The major obstacle to the trail's completion had been the mammoth Tejon Ranch, which began in Civil War days as a sheep ranch, then later became a cattle ranch, and in 1936 became a public corporation that diversified its land use and increased its acreage. This "ranch," about the size of Sequoia National Park, straddles most of the Tehachapi Mountains. An agreement between the ranch's owners and government representatives finally was reached, and in 1993 this section of the PCT was completed. However, rather than traversing the length of the Tehachapi Mountains, the PCT for the most part follows miles of roads along the west side of desert-like Antelope Valley before ascending to ranch property in the north part of the range.

Finally, there is another stretch in northern California (the end of Section Q and the start of Section R), where a trail will not replace existing roads. Private property was part of the problem, but also building a horse bridge across the Klamath River proved economically unfeasible. Consequently, one still treads 7.3 miles along roads, which is a blessing in disguise, for if the trail and bridge had been built, you would have by-passed Seiad Valley, a very important resupply point.

Dedication

The Pacific Crest National Scenic Trail officially was dedicated on Nationals Trails Day, June 5, 1993, a lengthy 25 years after Congress passed the National Trails System Act that had mandated it. The dedication was touted as the "Golden Spike" Completion Ceremony, in which a "golden" spike was driven into the trail, a reenactment of the 1869 ceremony at Promontory, near Ogden, Utah, where the converging Central Pacific and Union Pacific railroad companies joined to complete the transcontinental railroad. For the PCT, there were no competing trail crews, and the completion site should have been in the Tehachapi Mountains. However, the public was (and is) not welcome on the Tejon Ranch, and since that area is out of the way, a PCT site closer to metropolitan southern California was chosen: a flat at the mouth of a small valley on the north side of Soledad Canyon (Map D13). Protected under a canopy to shelter them from the unseasonably cold, windy, drizzly weather, Secretary of the Interior Bruce Babbitt and others spoke to an unsheltered audience of about three hundred hearty souls (and a dozen or so others protesting various unrelated environmental issues). The trail was proclaimed to be 2638 miles long officially, though the *accuracy* of this mileage may be questionable, since this number existed as early as 1990, which was *before* the completion of several stretches in southern California and in the southern Sierra Nevada, and *before* the major relocation of the Hat Creek Rim stretch north of Lassen Volcanic National Park. Future relocations are likely, and so the authors of this book, for better or for worse, have used mileages that they have measured either directly along the trail or indirectly along the route they accurately drew on topographic maps.

Some Who Walked and Rode

No doubt hikers did parts of the Pacific Crest Trail in the 19th century—though that name for it didn't exist. It may be that someone walked along the crest from Mexico to Canada or vice versa many years ago. But the first person to claim he did the whole route in one continuous journey—in 1970—was Eric Ryback, in *The High Adventure of Eric Ryback*. Actually, he accepted rides for some of the approximately 2500-mile route, and so his claim was not quite true. Nevertheless, he hiked *most* of the route, which was quite an accomplishment for a 130-pound 18-year-old hiking solo in the more difficult north-to-south direction *sans* guidebook or detailed maps. His 1971 book focused attention on the PCT, and other people began to plan end-to-end treks.

The year after his book appeared was a momentous one on the trail. The first person to hike the entire PCT (as it then existed) was Richard Watson, who finished it on September 1, 1972. He was the first *through-hiker*, as backpackers who did the trail in one continuous, multi-month effort would come to be called. Barely behind him, finishing four days later, were Wayne Martin, Dave Odell, Toby Heaton, Bill Goddard and Butch Ferrand. Very soon after them, Henry Wilds went from Mexico to Canada solo. In 1972 Jeff Smukler did the PCT with Mary Carstens, who became the first woman to make it. The next year, Gregg Eames and Ben Schifrin set out to follow the official route as closely as possible, no matter whether trail or cross country. Schifrin had to drop out with a broken foot at Odell Lake, Oregon (he finished the route the next year), but

Eames got to Canada, and is probably the first person to have walked the official route almost without deviation.

In 1975, at least 27 people completed the PCT, according to Chuck Long, who was one of them and who put together a book of various trekkers' experiences. Perhaps as many as 200–300 hikers started the trail that year, intending to do it all. In 1976, one who made it all the way was Teddy Boston, the first woman to solo the trail, so far as we know. Teddy, then a 49-year-old mother of four, like Eric made the trek the hard way, north to south.

Fascination with the trail steadily dropped, so that by the late 1980s perhaps only a dozen or so through-hikers completed the entire trail in a given year. However, as completion of the trail approached, interest in it waxed, and some notable hikes were done. Perhaps some day a trekker's PCT anthology will be written, and in it many can be given due credit for their accomplishments. However, in a trail guide, space is limited, so we will mention only a (subjectively) select few who set "higher" goals. In the past we recommended that the through-hiker allow 5–6 months for the entire PCT. No more, thanks to ultralight backpacking espoused by Ray and Jenny Jardine. In 1991 this couple completed the entire trail (their second through-hike) in only three months and three weeks, and Ray subsequently wrote a how-to book (see the next chapter) based on this accomplishment. This was comparable to the length of time taken by Bob Holtel (in his mid-50s), who over the summers of 1985, '86, and '87 ran the PCT at the pace of a marathon a day, and he also wrote a book about it (see the next chapter). A few through-hikers not only did the PCT, but also did the two other major north–south national scenic trails, the CDT (Continental Divide Trail) and the AT (Appalachian Trail). The first man to have accomplished this task may have been Lawrence Budd, who did all three in the late 1980s. Starting earlier but finishing later was Steve Queen, who hiked the PCT in 1981, the AT in 1983, and the CDT in 1991. The first woman may have been Alice Gmuer, who hiked the PCT in 1987 and '88, the AT in 1990, and the CDT in 1993. Close behind was Brice Hammack, who over eight summers completed the last of the three trails in 1994—at a very respectable age of 74. Also notable in 1994 was through-hiker Ted Derloshon, who wore sandals the entire way, including over miles of snow. Will someone ultimately do the whole trail barefoot?

While there have been hundreds of successful through-hikers on the PCT, very few equestrians have matched this feat. Perhaps the first equestrians to do the trail were Barry Murray and his family, who rode it in two summers in the early 1970s. Much later, in 1988, Jim McCrea became the first "through-equestrian," completing the entire trail in just under five months. Very few through-hikers actually do every foot of the trail, and for through-equestrians this feat so far has proved to be unfeasible, due to icy snowfields impassable to stock.

Chapter 2
Planning Your PCT Hike

Trekking Days or Weeks versus Trekking Months

On the basis of our limited research we have concluded that approximately 90% (or more) of those who buy this book will do parts of the trail as a series of short excursions, each lasting about two weeks or less. For those people, little planning is necessary; you should be able to carry enough food in your pack. You need not worry about mailing supplies to post offices along or near the trail. Furthermore, you can hike the desired stretch in its optimal season, and not need the additional clothing and gear that through-hikers must carry for when they traverse miles of snow and confront many cold-weather storms.

At the other end of the spectrum of PCT trekkers are the several dozen each year who will start at the Mexican border and will attempt to do the entire trail in one multi-month, Herculean effort. Before the early 1990s there was a rather high attrition rate among these hikers, but this need not be true today, thanks to *The PCT Hiker's Handbook* by Ray (and Jenny) Jardine (AdventureLore Press, Box 804, LaPine, OR 97739). Although we authors do not agree with every suggestion in this book, we nevertheless think that if you plan to hike the entire route—or hike for just a month—you definitely should read it. Even if you plan to hike only two weeks, we recommend it. As the back cover of their handbook states, it is "a compendium of trail tested information and instruction, addressing all the aspects of planning, preparing for, and of hiking the PCT. It is also an instructive in the art and skills of long-distance powerhiking, whatever trails the reader's feet are eager to tread. . . . Author Ray Jardine and his wife Jenny have hiked the Pacific Crest Trail twice. The wealth of knowledge they used to through-hike the trail the second time in 3 months and 3 weeks will help you succeed." Covered in this handbook are pitfalls, training regimes, pack checklists, clothing, footwear, equipment, food, injury prevention, animal hazards, creek fording, dehydration, inclement weather, stealth camping, 4-, 4½-, 5-, and 5½-month hiking itineraries, resupply stations, hiking philosophy, and other topics. However, if you follow Ray and Jenny's advice, you will have the time and energy to "stop and smell the flowers." By hiking ultralight, meeting your daily mileage quota need not be a chore.

A book in a different vein is Bob Holtel's *Soul, Sweat and Survival on the Pacific Crest Trail* (Bittersweet Publishing Company, Box 1211, Livermore, CA 94551; phone: 510/455-4826). It is not a handbook on how to hike the trail, but rather a personal account of Holtel's experiences as he *ran* it at the pace of about a marathon a day for 110 running days. Actually, when one considers his *46 rest days*, he averaged a mere 16.5 miles per day, which is less than the average, heavily laden through-hiker will do. A resurging theme is the pain, and probably his 50-something body would have been better off had he walked about 20 miles per day rather than running marathons. (Ray Jardine was pushing 50 when he did his record-pace hike.) But a habitual cross-country runner must run, and since you cannot run any significant distance with a backpack, he traveled ultralight, carrying all his necessities in a fanny pack. In addition to being quite enjoyable reading, the book gives a feel for the trail, its conditions, the hardships, the hazards, and the weather, which at times was miserable, and yet Holtel survived with minimal clothing and gear. This motivational book also lists his equipment, food, methods, and itinerary.

The books have a common theme: travel light. Obviously, a trekker can hike faster and cover more miles per day in jogging shoes with a 20-pound pack than in heavy boots with a 60-pound pack—a weight that used to be common in the early days along the PCT. (Indeed, some hikers carried packs that varied between 60 and 100+ pounds.) A lighter pack is easier on your joints and muscles, making the excursion more pleasurable. Furthermore, by traveling light you are less likely to have an injury because: 1) your body won't be overly stressed; 2) you'll be less likely to fall; 3) and if you do, the impact won't be as great. Traveling light, you'll perspire less water, which is a plus on the long dry stretches. Additionally, you'll burn fewer calories and hence can get by with less food (and less weight). Traveling light is not mastered overnight. These two books set you on the right track, but you should master traveling light *through practice* before you attempt to do it for a lengthy stretch on the PCT. Learn what you as an individual need to bring along or leave behind under various conditions of terrain, vegetation, and weather. Attempting to do the PCT "cold turkey" (that is, without any realistic experience) may be the prime reason for failure. A two-week backpack trip does *not* qualify you for a 4–5½-month excursion.

Given that few equestrians attempt most or all of the PCT, it is not surprising that a how-to book for them does not exist. However, Ben and Adeline York have self-published their notes on the whole trail, which are quite useful for potential PCT equestrians. To obtain a copy of their publication, *PCT by 2 in 1992*, write them at 1363 Peaceful Place, Alpine, CA 91901. For horse use in the mountains, they recommend you obtain *Horses, Hitches and Rocky Trails: "The Packers Bible,"* by Joe Back (Johnson Books, Boulder, CO). You will encounter more problems than do backpackers, and so the following caution is even more important: a short horseback trip does *not* qualify you for a lengthy excursion on the PCT.

Halfway between hikers and equestrians are those who walk the trail but pack with llamas. Like horses, llamas were native to western North America before going extinct there. Unlike horses, llamas are native to *high mountains*, and on erodible tread their foot pads have less impact than horses' hooves. David Harmon and Amy S. Rubin have written a llama-packer's guide, which stresses minimum-impact in the wilderness. This book and others on stock-packing are mentioned in the "Backpacking, Packing, and Mountaineering" section of "Recommended Reading and Source Books."

Organizations Relevant to the Pacific Crest Trail

The previously mentioned books should answer most of your questions about hiking or riding the PCT. But if questions linger, they may be answered by contacting one or more of the following organizations.

Pacific Crest Trail Association (PCTA). Those planning a long trek can write or phone this organization for advice that is either timely (e.g., current snowpack conditions) or expert (e.g., providing specific answers tailored to each individual). If those in the office cannot answer your questions, they will attempt to find one of their directors or members who can. Since this organization has both hikers and equestrians as members, they should be able to answer questions for either type of travel.

The organization is part of the legacy of Warren Rogers (the PCT is the other part). After the demise of the Pacific Crest Trail System Conference with the death of Clinton Clarke, Rogers in 1971 formed the Pacific Crest Club to be a "world-wide fellowship of persons interested in the PCT," as his son, Don, put it. Then in 1977 he founded the Pacific Crest Trail Conference, which addressed the needs of both the trail and its users. But old age eventually interfered with running these organizations, so in 1987 the club was merged with the conference, and for several years Larry Cash was its chief officer. The conference campaigned against trailside clearcutting and against mountain bikes, and for additional water sources along the drier stretches and for volunteer trail maintenance. In 1992 the organization changed its name to the Pacific Crest Trail Association. The 1995 address is 5325 Elkhorn Blvd., Suite 256, Sacramento, CA 95842-2526; phone: 800/817/2243. Increasingly this organization has become active in coordinating volunteer trail maintenance. For example, in 1994 the PCTA coordinated trail crews that donated an estimated 17,000 hours of their time. For this reason alone the organization deserves support and you should consider becoming a member. Most hikers and equestrians on any trail—not only on the PCT—give little thought to trail maintenance. Indeed, many PCT trekkers complain about sections being not up to snuff. But without the volunteers, there would be far more to complain about, since in these years of tight government budgets, trail maintenance has got to be among one of the lowest priorities. (Trail maintenance is ongoing: erosion locally erodes parts of the trail; fallen trees and rolling boulders may obstruct it; and brush continually attempts to bury it.)

What services does the PCTA provide the potential trekker? In addition to answering your PCT letters, phone calls, and faxes, it publishes a quarterly newsletter, *The Communicator*. This addresses general issues and timely matters as well as giving informative accounts of those who have hiked or ridden much or all of the PCT. *The Communicator* also has a section on trip partners in which people can write a paragraph about their background and experience and about what kind of partner they would like to have. Finally, the PCTA maintains registers along or near the trail. These provide the organization with a list of who did what, of relative degree of trail use, and of yearly and seasonally changing trail conditions and special problems. The trekker, by signing these registers, over time develops a camaraderie with other trekkers. Although you may never catch up to trekkers ahead of you, by trail's end you may feel that you've come to know them. The locations of these registers are not always obvious, so here is a list (subject to change), as they existed in the early 1990s.

Pacific Crest Trail Association Registers in California, South to North

Unless otherwise designated, the register is located in a post office (which at some places is just a tiny room in a store or a resort).

Campo	Mojave	Echo Lakes, Echo Lake
Mount Laguna	Onyx	Resort
Julian, Banner Store	Kennedy Meadows,	Soda Springs
Warner Springs	Kennedy Meadows	Sierra City
Anza	Store	Belden
Idyllwild	Lone Pine	Old Station
Cabazon	Independence	Cassel
Big Bear City	Mono Hot Springs	McArthur–Burney Falls
Fawnskin	Mammoth Lakes	State Park, Burney Falls
Wrightwood, Mountain	Tuolumne Meadows,	Camper Services
Hardware	concessionaire's store	Castella
Agua Dulce, Agua Dulce	Lee Vining	Seiad Valley, Seiad Valley
Business Center	Bridgeport	Store
Lake Hughes	Markleeville	Ashland (southern Oregon), Youth Hostel

American Long Distance Hikers Association-Western States Chapter (ALDHA-West). In 1993 Ray Jardine founded the Western States Chapter and also began publishing *The Distance Hiker's Gazette*, a quarterly newsletter. To join the association (and to receive its newsletter), contact Ray and Jenny Jardine at Box 804, LaPine, OR 97739. As the association's name implies, it is aimed at long-distance backpackers only. Although the association's emphasis is on the Pacific Crest Trail, it also addresses relevant backpacking matters on the Continental Divide Trail and other long trails of western North America. The newsletter carries extremely useful information for backpackers, and it has stimulating letters from trekkers that entice you to become a through-hiker. If you are seriously considering doing all (or even some) of the PCT, you should attend their annual meeting, which typically is held in October near a central part of the Oregon PCT. This weekend meeting will give you an opportunity to talk to some of those who have just completed the PCT and to participate in seminars and discussions about long-distance hiking. Nowhere else will you find so many people willing and able to answer all your questions.

Backcountry Horsemen of America. This organization can be reached at Box 597, Columbia Falls, MT 59912. It has chapters that are active in California, Oregon, and Washington. The chapter relevant for the California PCT is the following.

Backcountry Horsemen of California. This organization can be reached at Box 520, Springville, CA 93265 (phone: 209/539-3394). It offers clinics that show you how to pack with a horse and/or mule in the mountains. Besides teaching the fundamentals of packing, they stress low-impact use, courtesy, and common sense. Available from them is a pamphlet, "Gentle Use: A Pocket Guide for Backcountry Stock Users," which explains how to be "gentle" on trails, campsites, stock, wildlife, and vegetation.

Mailing Tips

As was stated at the beginning of this chapter, most hikers will not be on the trail long enough to bother with resupply points, which are mostly post offices. For those who will, we have included the following section. Although Jardine's book also has this information—and in more detailed form—a few of you will be doing a relatively short trek—and therefore won't need his book—but nevertheless will be counting on one or more resupply points.

You can mail yourself almost any food, clothing or equipment. Before you leave home, you should have a good idea of your rate of consumption of food, clothing, and fuel for your stove. You can arrange for mailings of quantities of these things, purchased at home, where they are probably cheaper than in the towns along the way. Address your package to:

> Yourself
> General Delivery
> P.O., STATE ABBR.   ZIP CODE
> HOLD UNTIL (date)

Post Offices Along or Near the Route, South to North

* = recommended for use

Some stations are seasonal. The best pickup time is weekdays 1–4 P.M. Hours of most are 9–12 and 1–5 or longer. Some are open Saturday mornings. Plan your trip schedule accordingly in order to avoid waiting two or three days in town because a post office was closed for the weekend (don't forget about the three-day weekends: Memorial Day, Fourth of July, Labor Day). Additionally, some resorts or concessionaires may accept mailed or U.P.S. parcels so check the introductory section in each of the trail-description chapters (Sections A–R).

*Campo 92006	Mojave 93501	Tahoma 95733
*Mount Laguna 92048	*Tehachapi 93561	Olympic ("Squaw")
Julian 92036	*Onyx 93255	Valley 95730
Borrego Springs 92004	Kernville 93238	*Soda Springs 95728
*Warner Springs 92086	*Kennedy Mdws. Gen. Store	Truckee 95734
*Terwilliger:	P.O. Box 3A-5	*Sierra City 96125
The Valley Store	Inyokern, 93527	La Porte 95981
Star Rte. 1, Box 243	*Lone Pine 93545	Meadow Valley 95956
Anza 92306	Independence 93526	Quincy 95971
Anza 92306	Cedar Grove 93633	*Belden 95915
*Idyllwild 92549	Big Pine 93513	Chester 96020
Cabazon 92230	*Bishop 93514	*Old Station 96071
Palm Springs 92263	Mono Hot Springs 93642	Cassel 96016
*Big Bear City 92314	*Lake Edison:	Burney Falls Camper
*Fawnskin 92333	Vermilion Valley Resort	Services, McArthur–
*Cedar Glen 92321	c/o Rancheria Garage	Burney Falls State Park
Lake Arrowhead 92352	Huntington Lake Road	Rte. 1, Box 1240
Crestline 92325	Lakeshore, CA 93634	Burney 96013
Hesperia 92340	*Mammoth Lakes 93546	Burney 96013
*Wrightwood 92397	June Lake 93529	*Castella 96017
Acton 93510	*Tuolumne Meadows 95389	Dunsmuir 96025
Saugus 91350	Lee Vining 93541	Sawyers Bar 96027
*Agua Dulce 91350	Bridgeport 93517	Callahan 96014
Green Valley 91350	Markleeville 96120	Etna 96027
*Lake Hughes 93532	*Echo Lake 95721	*Seiad Valley 96086
Lancaster 93534	Tahoe Paradise 96155	*Ashland, OR 97520

Water

There are two concerns about water: its availability and its purity. Hikers who are used to the High Sierra or the Cascades may be out of the habit of worrying about water, since it is seldom far away, even in late summer. But dehydration can be a problem along parts of the PCT. The trail description mentions water sources, and the Introduction to Section E discusses water needs when hiking in the desert. Of course, some years are drier than others, and so you should be prepared—some usually reliable springs and creeks may go dry. Also be aware that campgrounds and picnic areas with tap water often have their water turned off in the cold months to prevent water freezing in the system's pipes.

Water purity is an equally serious concern. Streams, springs and lakes may contain cystic forms of *Giardia lamblia* microorganisms, which can give you a case of giardiasis (jee-ar-dye-a-sis). Although this disease can be incapacitating, it is not usually life-threatening. Symptoms, which can develop a week or two after infection, usually include diarrhea, gas, loss of appetite, abdominal cramps and bloating. Weight loss may occur from nausea and loss of appetite. These discomforts may last up to six weeks. If not treated, the symptoms may disappear on their own, only to recur intermittently over a period of many months. Other diseases can have similar symptoms, but if you drank untreated water, you should suspect giardiasis and so inform your doctor. If properly diagnosed, the disease is curable with medication prescribed by a physician.

To play it safe, you can avoid risking giardiasis and other diseases by several methods. The traditional, most effective way to make the water safe is to bring it to a boil. You can avoid the wait if you carry two water bottles, so you can drink from one while you're boiling water to fill the other. This method has two significant drawbacks: time expended in heating the water and then waiting for it to cool (not a problem at campsites), and significant consumption of fuel (not a problem for short-distance backpackers).

A second, long-used method is to use chemical disinfectants, such as iodine and chlorine, which are not as reliable as boiling unless you use them for a long time—say, an hour. But if you carry two water bottles, then while you're drinking from one, the second can be sitting in your pack, with the disinfectant working in it. Like the previous method, this one takes time, so you need to plan ahead by treating your water well before you need it. The main disadvantage is the bad taste—why go to the mountains if you can't drink its "pristine" water? One chemical product gets around the bad taste because it has, in addition to germicidal tablets, taste-neutralizing tablets. It is advertised as being for "emergency drinking water," and given its price—over a dollar a day for the serious long-distance, water-guzzling backpacker—it most certainly is. The two-bottle package weighs only 3 ounces, and it is an acceptable solution for those planning to be on the trail for a week or less. (One package treats about 50 quarts/liters.)

The third method, which seems to have become the trekkers' choice, is a portable water filter. These range from below $20 to over $200. Not all water filters are created equal, and the more expensive ones are not necessarily better. (One of the lightest and cheapest is by Ray Jardine, who used his design on his second through-hike.) Don't wait until the last moment to acquire a filter. Ask knowledgeable and trustworthy people which designs have worked best for them. Once you purchase one, use it for some time to see how well it holds up. Schaffer went through three of one brand that tended to break easily and/or have its filter clog up too rapidly. Competition is stiff, and so hopefully the poorer ones will either disappear from the market or else be improved. If you rely on a water filter, take a small bottle of water-purifying tablets for emergency backup. Don't let water-borne microorganisms sabotage your trip of a lifetime.

Hypothermia

Every year you can read accounts of hikers freezing to death in the mountains. They die of hypothermia, the #1 killer of outdoor recreationists. You too may be exposed to it, particularly if you start hiking the PCT in April in order to do all three states. Because it is so easy to die from hypothermia, we are including the following information, which is endorsed by the Forest Service and by mountain-rescue groups. Read it. It may save your life.

Hypothermia is subnormal body temperature, which is caused outdoors by exposure to cold, usually aggravated by wetness, wind and exhaustion. The moment your body begins to lose heat faster than it produces it, your body makes involuntary adjustments to preserve the normal temperature in its vital organs. Uncontrolled shivering is one way your body attempts to maintain its vital temperature. *If you've begun uncontrolled shivering, you must consider yourself a prime candidate for hypothermia and act accordingly.* When this happens, cold reaches your brain, depriving you of judgment and reasoning power. You will not realize this is happening. You will lose control of your hands. Your internal body temperature is sliding downward. Without treatment, this slide leads to stupor, collapse and death. Learn the four lines of defense against hypothermia.

Your first line of defense: avoid exposure

1. Stay dry. When clothes get wet, they lose much of their insulating value. Cotton is the worst when wet, wool is intermediate, and synthetics generally the best in this respect.

2. Beware of wind. A slight breeze carries heat away from bare skin much faster than still air does. Wind drives cold air under and through clothing. Wind refrigerates wet clothes by evaporating moisture from the surface.

3. Understand cold. Most hypothermia cases develop in air temperatures between 30° and 50°. Most outdoorsmen simply can't believe such temperatures can be dangerous. They fatally underestimate the danger of being wet at such temperatures. But just jump in a cold lakelet and you'll agree that 50° water is unbearably cold. The cold that kills is cold water running down neck and legs, cold water held against the body by sopping clothes, cold water flushing body heat from the surface of the clothes.

4. Continue to eat and drink. It is very hard for fit outdoors persons to develop hypothermia, unless they become dehydrated and run out of energy.

Your second line of defense: terminate exposure

If you cannot stay dry and warm under existing weather conditions, using the clothes you have with you, *terminate exposure.*

1. Be brave enough to give up reaching your destination or whatever you had in mind. That one extra mile might be your last.

2. Get out of the wind and rain. Build a fire. Concentrate on making your camp or bivouac as secure and comfortable as possible.

3. Never ignore shivering. Persistent or violent shivering is clear warning that you are on the verge of hypothermia. *Make camp.*

4. Forestall exhaustion. Make camp while you still have a reserve of energy. Allow for the fact that exposure greatly reduces your normal endurance. You may think you are doing fine when the fact that you are exercising is the only thing preventing your going into hypothermia. If exhaustion forces you to stop, however briefly, your rate of body heat production instantly drops by 50% or more; violent, incapacitating shivering may begin immediately; you may slip into hypothermia *in a matter of minutes.*

5. Appoint a foul-weather leader. Make the best-protected member of your party responsible for calling a halt before the least-protected member becomes exhausted or goes into violent shivering.

Your third line of defense: detect hypothermia

If your party is exposed to wind, cold and wetness, *think hypothermia*. Watch yourself and others for hypothermia's symptoms:
1. Uncontrollable fits of shivering.
2. Vague, slow, slurred speech.
3. Memory lapses; incoherence.
4. Immobile or fumbling hands.
5. Frequent stumbling; lurching gait.
6. Drowsiness—to sleep is to die.
7. Apparent exhaustion, such as inability to get up after a rest.

Your fourth and last line of defense: treatment

Victims may deny being in trouble. Believe the symptoms, not the patient. Even mild symptoms demand immediate, drastic treatment.
1. Get the victim out of the wind and rain.
2. Strip off *all* wet clothes.
3. If the patient is only mildly impaired:
   a. Give them warm drinks.
   b. Get them into dry clothes and a warm sleeping bag. Well-wrapped, warm (not hot) rocks or canteens will hasten recovery.
4. If the patient is semiconscious or worse:
   a. Don't give hot drinks unless they are capable of holding a cup and drinking from it. Forcing drinks on semiconscious persons could cause them to gag and *drown* (unfortunately, this is quite common with inexperienced would-be rescuers)!
   b. Leave them stripped. Put them in a sleeping bag with another person (also stripped). If you have double bag or can zip two together, put the victim between two warmth donors. *Skin-to-skin contact* is the most effective treatment. Never leave victims as long as they are alive. To do so is to kill them—it's just that simple!
5. Build a fire to warm the camp.

Other notes on avoiding hypothermia

1. Choose rainclothes that are effective against *wind-driven* rain and cover head, neck, body and legs. Gore-Tex and other PTFE laminates are best, but won't last as long as some other materials.

2. Take clothing that retains its insulation even when wet, such as polypropylene, capilene or dacron fabrics. These hold even less water than the traditional wet-weather favorite, wool, and so make it easier for your body to keep warm. Always carry a two-piece underwear set, and a heavier pair of pants, plus a sweater or pullover (the new "fleece" and "pile" designs are rugged and perform well). Never forget a knit wool or fleece headpiece that can protect the neck and chin. Cotton underwear and down-filled parkas are worse than useless when wet, as are cotton shirts and pants. As early Americans long ago discovered, one stays warmer in a cold rain when stark naked than when bundled up in wet clothes.

3. Carry a stormproof tent with a good rain fly and set it up *before* you need it.

4. Carry trail food rich in calories, such as nuts, jerky and candy, and keep nibbling during hypothermia weather.

5. Take a gas stove or a plumber's candle, flammable paste or other reliable fire starter.

6. Never abandon survival gear under any circumstances. If you didn't bring along the above items, stay put and make the best of it. An all-too-common fatal mistake is for victims to abandon everything so that, unburdened, they can run for help.

7. "It never happens to me. I'm Joe Athlete." Don't you believe it.

Outdoor Courtesy

Traveling a wild trail, away from centers of civilization, is a unique experience. It brings intimate association with nature—communion with the earth, the forest, the chaparral, the wildlife, the clear sky. A great responsibility accompanies this experience—the obligation to keep the wilderness as you found it. Being considerate of the wilderness rights of others will make the mountain adventures of those who follow equally rewarding. As a wilderness visitor, you should become familiar with the rules of wilderness courtesy outlined below.

Trails. Never cut switchbacks. This practice breaks down trails and hastens erosion. Take care not to dislodge rocks that might fall on hikers below you. Improve and preserve trails, as by clearing away loose rocks (carefully) and removing branches. Report any trail damage and broken or misplaced signs to a ranger or mention them in a PCTA register.

Off trail. Restrain the impulse to blaze trees or to build ducks where not essential. Let the next fellow find the way as you did.

Campsites. This guidebook mentions campsites you will find along the trail, but you perhaps will not use them. Indeed, in his handbook Ray Jardine argues against their use and instead promotes "stealth camping," which is camping away from both trail and water, and leaving minimal evidence that you were there. Most hikers probably prefer a scenic lakeside campsite, and if it is beside the PCT, so much the better. Jardine, however, does make a legitimate point: many existing campsites have degraded the local environment. Minimize your impact at any campsite by not building a fire, even if it is legal. Defecate and urinate well away from water, not in a convenient, close-by spot perhaps used by many who have camped before you. The widespread giardiasis problem seems to stem more from poor bathroom habits than from anything else. (We cannot blame the horses and cattle for this problem.) The campsite should be left in as good condition as you found it, or even better.

Environmentally conscious equestrians need to choose carefully the location of each campsite, since evidence of their visit will be hard to miss, given all the urine, manure, and feed that will accumulate during the stay. Ideally, equestrians should make every effort to camp outside the wilderness, but that is not always possible and generally not desirable. Equestrians need to make an extra effort to clean up their campsites, partly to avert the wrath of irate backpackers who have become increasingly anti-horse (due in no small measure to real or perceived localized heavy environmental impact in the mountains by professional packers).

Litter. Along the trail, place candy wrappers, raisin boxes, orange peels, etc. in your pocket or pack for later disposal; throw nothing on the trail. Pick up litter you find along the trail or in camp. More than almost anything else (with the possible exception of abundant, fresh manure), litter detracts from the wilderness scene. Remember, you *can* take it with you.

Noise. Boisterous conduct is out of harmony in a wilderness experience. Be a considerate hiker and camper. Don't ruin another's enjoyment of the wilderness.

Good Samaritanship. Human life and well-being take precedence over everything else—in the wilderness as elsewhere. If a hiker or camper is in trouble, help in any way you can. Indifference is a moral crime. Give comfort or first aid; then seek help.

Land-Use Regulations

The California portion of the PCT passes through national parks, national forests, state parks, land administered by the Bureau of Land Management and private land. All these areas have their own regulations, which you ignore only at your risk—risk of physical difficulty as well as possibility of being cited for violations.

On private land, of course, the regulations are what the owner says they are. The same is true on Indian lands. In particular, don't build a fire on private land. Generally on such land, camping is prohibited.

Regulations on U.S. Bureau of Land Management land are not of major consequence for users of this book, since the route passes through only short stretches of it, mostly in the Tehachapis and southeast of San Gorgonio Wilderness.

The Forest Service and the Park Service, for good reason, have more regulations. These are not uniform throughout the state, or between the two services. We list below the Forest Service and Park Service regulations that are uniform along the trail, plus some that are peculiar to the Park Service. Special regulations in particular places are mentioned in the trail description when it "arrives" at the place.

1. Wilderness permits, which also serve as fire permits are required to enter a few of the wildernesses, for overnight stays in other wildernesses, and for the backcountry of the national parks. In the less-used wildernesses, wilderness permits usually aren't required. Where one is required, this information will be mentioned in the introductory material in the book's appropriate trail section. Addresses and phone numbers for agencies that dispense permits and information are given at the end of this chapter.

If you are hiking though several national-forest and/or national-park wildernesses along the PCT, you do not need a separate permit for each. Write only to the one you will begin in. Hikers planning to walk all of California southbound should get a permit from Klamath National Forest headquarters. Those hiking California northbound should get a permit from Cleveland National Forest headquarters. State that you are going to hike along the PCT beginning in Place A on X date and ending in Place B on (roughly) Y date, and you want a Joint-Use Permit. Such a permit is good only for one continuous trip along the PCT—but we don't think it would be revoked if, say, you went out to Bishop to resupply.

2. If you are not hiking in wildernesses that require a wilderness permit, you will still need a *campfire permit*. In northern California these are issued for the entire year. They may be obtained free at offices or stations of the U.S. Forest Service, U.S. Bureau of Land Management and California Division of Forestry.

In southern California within the Cleveland, San Bernardino and Angeles national forests, a special campfire permit is necessary for each visit. Obtain this permit free from an office or station in the national forest you are visiting.

Campfire permits require each party to carry a shovel. If you don't build any fires but use only gas stoves, then you can leave the shovel behind but you'll still need the permit. We strongly recommend that you not build fires, but rather use a stove. For one thing, it's hard to erase all traces of a fire; and for another, rotting wood left on the ground enriches the soil and hosts organisms that larger animals feed on.

3. A California *fishing license* is required for all persons 16 years old or older who fish. The limit is 10 trout per day, with some exceptions, given in the state Department of Fish and Game regulations.

4. *Destruction*, injury, defacement, removal or disturbance in any manner of any natural feature or public property is prohibited. This includes:

    a. Molesting any animal, picking flowers or other plants;

    b. Cutting, blazing, marking, driving nails in, or otherwise damaging growing trees or standing snags;

    c. Writing, carving or painting names or other inscriptions anywhere;

    d. Destruction, defacement or moving of signs.

5. *Collecting specimens* of minerals, plants, animals or historical objects is prohibited without written authorization, obtained in advance, from the Park Service or Forest Service. Permits are not issued for personal collections.

6. *Smoking* is not permitted while traveling through vegetated areas. You may stop and smoke in a safe place.

7. Pack and saddle *animals* have the right-of-way on trails. Hikers should get completely off the trail, on the downhill side if possible, and remain quiet until the stock has passed.

8. *Cutting switchbacks* is prohibited, since it can lead to the trail's erosion and possibly to dangerous footing.

9. Use *existing campsites* if there are any. If not, camp away from the trail and at least 100 feet from lakes and streams, on mineral soil or unvegetated forest floor—never in meadows or other soft, vegetated spots.

10. Construction of improvements such as rock walls, large fireplaces, bough beds, tables, and rock-and-log stream crossings is prohibited.

11. Soap and other pollutants should be kept out of lakes and streams. Use of detergents is not recommended, since they affect the water detrimentally.

12. *"Toilets"* should be made in soft soil away from camps and preferably 50+ yards away from any surface water. Dig a hole about 6+ inches deep, and after use fill it with soil and camouflage the ground to make the site invisible. In particular, stock should not be allowed to defecate near water, not so much because of potential dangerous contamination as because of aesthetics and to prevent adding nutrients to the water.

13. You are required to clean up your camp before you leave. Tin cans, foil, glass, worn-out or useless gear, and other unburnables must be carried out.

14. National parks but not forests prohibit dogs and cats on the trail and prohibit carrying or using firearms.

Federal Government Agencies, South to North

Bureau of Land Management
333 S. Waterman Avenue
El Centro, CA 92243
(619) 352-5842

Cleveland National Forest
10845 Rancho Bernardo
Road
San Diego, CA 92182

Bureau of Land Management
1695 Spruce Street
Riverside, CA 92507
(909) 276-6394

San Bernardino National Forest.
1824 S. Commercenter Circle
San Bernardino, CA 92408
(909) 383-5588

San Jacinto Wilderness
contact:
Idyllwild Ranger Station
P.O. Box 518
Idyllwild, CA 92549
(909) 659-2117

Angeles National Forest
701 N. Santa Anita Avenue
Arcadia, CA 91006
(818) 574-5200

Sheep Mountain Wilderness
contact Angeles Nat. For.

Bureau of Land Management
3801 Pegasus Drive
Bakersfield, CA 93308-6837
(805) 391-6000

Kiavah, Owens Peak, Dome Land (east)
contact BLM, Bakersfield

Sequoia National Forest
480 N. Henrahan St.
Porterville, CA 93257
(209) 784-1500

Dome Land (west), South Sierra and Golden Trout wildernesses
contact Sequoia Nat. For.

Sequoia and Kings Canyon National Parks
Backcountry Permits
Three Rivers, CA 93271
(209) 565-3341

Inyo National Forest
873 N. Main Street
Bishop, CA 93514
(619) 873-2400

John Muir Wilderness
contact Inyo Nat. For.
Sierra National Forest
1600 Tollhouse Road
Clovis, CA 93612
(209) 297-0706

Ansel Adams Wilderness
contact:
Mammoth Ranger District
P.O. Box 148
Mammoth Lakes, CA 93546
(619) 924-5500

Yosemite National Park
Wilderness Office
P.O. Box 577
Yosemite, CA 95389
(209) 372-0310

Toiyabe National Forest
1200 Franklin Way
Sparks, NV 89431
(702) 355-5300

Stanislaus National Forest
19777 Greenley Road
Sonora, CA 95370
(209) 532-3671

Emigrant Wilderness and Carson-Iceberg Wilderness, Sonora Pass trailhead
contact:
Summit Ranger District
#1 Pinecrest Lake Road
Pinecrest, CA 95364
(209) 965-3434

Carson-Iceberg Wilderness, Ebbetts Pass trailhead
contact:
Carson Ranger District
1536 S. Carson Street
Carson City, NV 89701
(702) 882-2766

Mokelumne Wilderness
contact Carson Ranger District (above)

Eldorado National Forest
Information Center
3070 Camino Heights Drive
Camino, CA 95709
(916) 644-6048

Desolation Wilderness
Lake Tahoe Basin Mgt.
870 Emerald Bay Road
S. Lake Tahoe, CA 95731
(916) 573-2600

Tahoe National Forest
Hwy. 49 and Coyote Street
Nevada City, CA 95959
(916) 265-4531

Granite Chief Wilderness
contact Tahoe Nat. For.
Plumas National Forest
P.O. Box 11500
Quincy, CA 95971
(916) 283-2050

Bucks Lake Wilderness
contact Plumas Nat. For.

Lassen National Forest
55 S. Sacramento Street
Susanville, CA 96130
(916) 257-2151

Lassen Volcanic Nat. Park
P.O. Box 100
Mineral, CA 96063
(916) 595-4444

Shasta-Trinity National Forest
2400 Washington Avenue
Redding, CA 96001
(916) 246-5222

Castle Crags and Trinity Alps wildernesses
contact Shasta-Trinity N. F.

Klamath National Forest
1312 Fairlane Road
Yreka, CA 96097
(916) 842-6131

Russian and Marble Mountain wildernesses
contact Klamath Nat. For.

Rogue River National Forest
Federal Building
P.O. Box 520
Medford, OR 97501
(503) 776-3600

Red Buttes Wilderness
contact Rogue River N. F.

Chapter 3
PCT Natural History

Geology

It is very likely that the California section of the Pacific Crest Trail is unequaled in its diversity of geology. Many mountain trails cross glacial and subglacial landscapes, but which ones also cross arid and semi-arid landscapes? Some parts of your trail will have perennial snow; others are always dry. Precipitation may be more than 80 inches per year in places, less than 5 inches in others. In each of the three major rock classes— igneous, sedimentary, and metamorphic—you'll encounter dozens of rock types. Because the PCT provides such a good introduction to a wide spectrum of geology, we have added a liberal dose of geologic description to the basic text. You start among granitic rocks at the Mexican border, and then we inform you of almost every new major rock outcrop you'll encounter along your trek northward. We hope that by the end of your journey you'll have developed a keen eye for rocks and that you'll understand the relations between the different rock types. Since we assume that many hikers will have only a minimal background in geology and its terminology, we'll try to cover this broad subject for them in the next few pages. Those wishing to pursue the subject further should consult the list of references at the end of this book.

Rocks

First, you should get acquainted with the three major rock classes: igneous, sedimentary, and metamorphic.

Igneous rocks

Igneous rocks came into being when the liquid (molten) rock material (*magma*) solidified. If the material solidified beneath the earth's surface, the rock is called *intrusive*, or plutonic, and a body of it is a *pluton*. If the material reached the surface and erupted as *lava*, the rock is called *extrusive*, or volcanic.

Intrusive rocks. The classification of an igneous rock is based on its texture, what minerals are in it, and the relative amounts of each mineral present. Since intrusive rocks cool more slowly than extrusive rocks, their crystals have a longer time to grow. If, in a rock, you can see an abundance of individual crystals, odds are that it is an intrusive rock. These rocks may be classified by crystal size: fine, medium, or coarse-grained, to correspond to average diameters of less than 1 millimeter, 1–5, and greater than 5.

Some igneous rocks are composed of large crystals (*phenocrysts*) in a matrix of small crystals (*groundmass*). Such a rock is said to have a *porphyritic* texture. The Cathedral Peak pluton, which is well exposed on Lembert Dome at the east end of Tuolumne Meadows in Yosemite National Park, has some feldspar phenocrysts over four inches long. High up on the dome these phenocrysts protrude from the less resistant ground-mass and provide rock climbers with the holds necessary to ascend the dome.

The common minerals in igneous rocks are quartz, feldspar, biotite, hornblende, py-roxene, and olivine. The first two are light-colored minerals; the rest are dark. Not all are likely to be present in a piece of rock; indeed, quartz and olivine are never found together. Intrusive rocks are grouped according to the percentages of minerals in them. The three common igneous groups are *granite, diorite*, and *gabbro*. Granite is rich in quartz and potassium feldspar and usually has only small amounts of biotite. Diorite is poor in quartz and rich in sodium feldspar, and may have three dark minerals. Gabbro, a *mafic* rock (rich in magnesium and iron), lacks quartz, but is rich in calcium feldspar and pyroxene, and may have pyroxene and olivine. You can subdivide the granite–dior-ite continuum into granite, quartz monzonite, granodiorite, quartz diorite and diorite. These rocks, which are usually called "granitic rocks" or just plain "granite," are com-mon in the Sierra Nevada and in most of the other ranges to the south. If you start your hike at the Mexican border, you'll begin among granitic rock known as Bonsall tonalite. *Bonsall* refers to the location where this rock is well exposed. *Tonalite* is the name given to diorite with quartz, or quartz diorite. In PCT Section D you'll encounter another intrusive rock with an unusual name: anorthosite. This rock, usually found with gabbro, is overwhelmingly composed of calcium-rich feldspar crystals.

Since it is unlikely that you'll be carrying a polarizing microscope in your backpack, let alone a great deal of mineralogical expertise in your head, your best chance of iden-tifying these granitic rocks lies in making educated guesses based upon the following table.

Rock	Color	% Dark Minerals
Granite	Creamy white	5
Quartz Monzonite	Very light gray	10
Granodiorite	Light gray	20
Quartz diorite	Medium gray	30
Diorite	Dark gray	40
Gabbro	Black	60

At first you'll probably estimate too high a percentage of dark minerals, partly be-cause they are more eye-catching and partly because they show through the glassy light minerals. If the intrusive rock is composed entirely of dark minerals (no quartz or feld-spar), then it is an ultramafic rock. This rock type, which can be subdivided further, is common along the trail from Interstate 5 at Castle Crags State Park northwest to the Oregon border.

Extrusive rocks. Extrusive, or volcanic, rocks are composed of about the same min-erals as intrusive rocks. *Rhyolite, andesite*, and *basalt* have approximately the same chemical compositions as granite, diorite, and gabbro, respectively. As with the intru-sive rocks, the three volcanics can be subdivided into many groups, so it is possible to find ordinary rocks with intimidating names like "quartz latite porphyry"—which is just a volcanic rock with quartz phenocrysts and a composition in between rhyolite and andesite.

Texture is the key feature distinguishing volcanic from plutonic rocks. Whereas you can see the individual crystals in a plutonic rock you'll have a hard time finding them in a volcanic one. They may be entirely lacking, or so small, weathered and scarce that they'll just frustrate your attempts to identify them. If you can't recognize the crystals, then how can you identify the type of volcanic rock? Color is a poor indicator at best, for although rhyolites tend to be light gray, andesites dark gray, and basalts black, there is so much variation that each can be found in any shade of red, brown or gray.

One aid to identifying volcanic rock types is the landforms composed of them. For example the high silica (SiO_2) content of rhyolite makes it very viscous, and hence the hot gases in rhyolite magma cause violent explosions when the magma nears the surface forming *explosion pits* and associated rings of erupted material (*ejecta*). For the same reason, a rhyolite lava flow (degassed magma) is thick, short, and steep-sided and may not even flow down a moderately steep slope. The Mono and Inyo craters, north of Devils Postpile National Monument, are perhaps the best examples of this volcanic rock in California. You will find very little of it along the trail.

The landform characteristically associated with andesite is the *composite cone*, or stratovolcano. Mt. Shasta and some of the peaks in the Lassen area, including Brokeoff Mountain, are examples. These mountains are built up by alternating flows and ejecta. In time *parasitic vents* may develop, such as the cone called Shastina on Mt. Shasta; and the composition of the volcano may shift to more silica-rich *dacite* rock, an intermediate between rhyolite and andesite, which gives rise to tremendous eruptions, like several at Lassen Peak.

The least siliceous and also the least explosive of volcanic rocks is basalt. A basaltic eruption typically produces a cinder cone, rarely over 2000 feet high, and a very fluid, thin flow. When in Lassen Volcanic National Park, take the alternate route up to the rim of the Cinder Cone. From this vantage point you can see what an extensive, relatively flat area its thin flows covered. Contrast this with Lassen Peak, to the west, with its steep-sided massive bulk armed with protruding dacite domes.

Sedimentary rocks

We often think of rocks as being eternal—indeed, they do last a long time. But even the most resistant polished granite eventually succumbs to the effects of weathering, although on broad, unglaciated ridges and gentle slopes the rate of removal (denudation) is about a foot or less per million years. Granite rocks solidified under high pressures and rather high temperatures within the earth. At the surface, pressure and temperature are lower and the rock's chemical environment is different, and in this environment it is unstable. The rocks weather, and the pieces are gradually transported to a place of deposition. This place may be a lake in the High Sierra, a closed basin with no outlet such as the Mono Lake basin, an open structure such as the great Central Valley, or even the continental shelf of the Pacific Ocean. The rocks formed of the sediment that collects in these basins are called sedimentary rocks.

Most sedimentary rocks are classified by the size of their particles: clay that has been compacted and cemented forms *shale*; silt forms *siltstone*, and sand forms *sandstone*.

Sandstone derived from granitic rock superficially resembles its parent rock, but if you look closely you'll notice that the grains are somewhat rounded and that the spaces between the grains are usually filled with a cement, usually calcite. Pebbles, cobbles and boulders may be cemented in a sand or gravel matrix to form a *conglomerate*. If these particles are deposited on an *alluvial fan* and then gradually cemented together to form a hard rock, collectively they become *fanglomerate*. Alluvial fans are usually formed where a stream debouches from the mouth of a canyon and drops its sedimentary load, or alluvium, over a fan-shaped area. Alluvial fans are seen along the south edge of the Mojave Desert, where it abuts the north base of the San Bernardino and the San Gabriel mountains. If the larger particles in a conglomerate or fanglomerate are angular rather than rounded, the sedimentary rock is called a *breccia*.

Limestone, another type of sedimentary rock, is formed in some marine environments as a chemical precipitate of dissolved calcium carbonate or as cemented fragments of shells, corals and foraminifers. The individual grains are usually microscopic. If the calcium in limestone is partly replaced by magnesium, the result is *dolomite*.

Since the PCT attempts to follow a crest, you'll usually find yourself in an area being eroded, rather than in a basin of deposition, so you'll find very ephemeral sediments or very old ones. The young ones may be in the form of alluvium, talus slopes, glacial moraines, or lake sediments. The old ones are usually resistant sediments that the intruding granitic plutons bent (*folded*), broke (*faulted*) and changed (*metamorphosed*).

Metamorphic rocks

A volcanic or a sedimentary rock can undergo enough alteration (metamorphism) due to heat, pressure, and superhot, corrosive fluids that it loses its original characteristics and becomes a *metavolcanic* or a *metasedimentary* rock. Metamorphism may be slight or it may be complete. A shale undergoing progressive metamorphism becomes first a *slate*, second a *phyllite*, then a *schist*, and finally a *gneiss*. The slate resembles the shale but is noticeably harder. The schist bears little resemblance and is well-foliated, with flaky minerals such as biotite or other micas clearly visible. The gneiss resembles granite, but has alternating layers of light and dark minerals.

Hornfels is a hard, massive rock, common in parts of the High Sierra, formed by contact of an ascending pluton with the overlying sediments. It can take on a variety of forms. You might find one that looks and feels like a slate, but it differs in that it breaks across the sediment layers rather than between them.

Quartzite is a metamorphosed sandstone and resembles the parent rock. The spaces between the grains have become filled with silica, so that now if the rock is broken, the fracture passes through the quartz grains rather than between them as in sandstone. Metamorphism of limestone or dolomite yields *marble*, which is just a crystalline form of the parent rock. Check out Marble Mountain, in northern California, when you reach it.

Geologic Time

You cannot develop a feeling for geology unless you appreciate the great span of time that geologic processes have had to operate over. A few million years' duration is little more than an instant on the vast geologic time scale (see following Geologic Time Scale). Within this duration a volcano may be born, die and erode away. Dozens of major "ice ages" may come and go.

A mountain range takes longer to form. Granitic plutons of the Sierra Nevada first came into being about 240 million years ago, and intrusion of them continued until about 80 million years ago, a span of 160 million years. Usually there is a considerable gap in the geologic record between the granitic rocks and the older sediments and volcanics that they intrude and metamorphose—often more than 100 million years.

Geologic Time Scale

Era	Period	Epoch	Began (years ago)	Duration (years)
Cenozoic	Quaternary	Holocene	10,000	10,000
		Pleistocene	2,480,000	2,470,000
	Tertiary	Pliocene	5,200,000	2,720,000
		Miocene	23,300,000	18,100,000
		Oligocene	34,000,000	10,700,000
		Eocene	56,500,000	22,500,000
		Paleocene	65,000,000	8,500,000
Mesozoic	Cretaceous	*Numerous*	145,000,000	80,000,000
	Jurassic	*epochs*	208,000,000	63,000,000
	Triassic	*recognized*	245,000,000	37,000,000
Paleozoic	Permian		286,000,000	41,000,000
	Carboniferous	*Numerous*	360,000,000	74,000,000
	Devonian	*epochs*	408,000,000	48,000,000
	Silurian	*recognized*	438,000,000	30,000,000
	Ordovician		505,000,000	67,000,000
	Cambrian		570,000,000	65,000,000
Precambrian	No defined periods or epochs; oldest known rocks are about 4.2 billion years old; Earth's crust solidified about 4.6 million years ago.			

Derived from latest sources available in the early 1990s. Most earth scientists still recognize the Tertiary-Quaternary boundary at 1,600,000 years, which is a poor choice except in Italy (where the boundary was so defined). The 2,480,000-year date is that of the Gauss-Matuyama reversal of the earth's magnetic poles, and this date is virtually synonymous with the commencement of the dozens of cycles of major glaciations in the northern hemisphere; and it also marks the approximate date of earliest man (origin of genus *Homo*). Thus it accommodates the two classic concepts of the Quaternary, this period originally being the Ice Age and the Age of Man.

Geologic History

With the aid of a geologic section, like the one on the next page, we can reconstruct the geologic history of an area. Our example represents an idealized slice across the Sierra Nevada to reveal the rocks and their relations.

Through dating methods that use radioactive materials, geologists can obtain the absolute ages of the two granitic plutons, the andesite flow, and the basalt flow, which respectively would likely be Cretaceous, Pliocene, and Holocene. The overlying, folded sediments intruded by the plutons would have to be pre-Cretaceous. The metabasalt could be dated, but the age arrived at may be for the time of its metamorphism rather than for its formation. A paleontologist examining fossils from the marble and slate

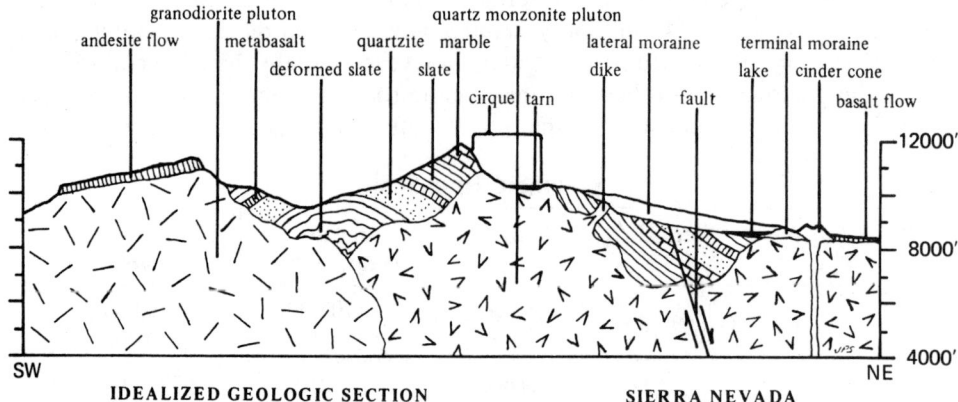

IDEALIZED GEOLOGIC SECTION   SIERRA NEVADA

might conclude that these rocks are from the Paleozoic era.

Before metamorphism the Paleozoic slate, quartzite, metabasalt, and marble respectively would have been shale, sandstone, basalt, and limestone. The shale–sandstone sequence might indicate marine sediments being deposited on a continental shelf, then on a coastal plain. Lack of transitional rocks between the shale and the sandstone leads us to conclude that they were eroded away, creating a gap in the geologic record. We then have an *unconformity* between the two *strata* (layers), the upper resting on the *erosional surface* of the lower. The basalt, shale, and limestone sequence indicates first a localized volcanism, followed by a marine and then a shallow-water environment.

These Paleozoic rocks remained buried and protected from erosion for millions of years until the intrusion of granitic plutons and associated regional volcanism. Radiometric dating would show that the quartz-monzonite pluton was emplaced before the granodiorite pluton. Field observations would verify this sequence because the latter intrudes the former as well as the overlying sediments. During the Mesozoic period, plutonism and volcanism were at times accompanied by mountain building. This occurred when large pieces of continental crust, which were riding atop a plate that generally was diving eastward beneath the edge of the continent, were transported toward the range. Being relatively low in density, this continental crust did not descend with the rest of the plate, and so was forced against the range. The resulting compression caused uplift, and the Paleozoic rocks became folded, metamorphosed, and often faulted. Until plutonism ceased about 80 million years ago, the Mesozoic Sierra Nevada was just a small part of a much longer range that extended continuously along the western coasts of North America and South America. The climate was mostly tropical, and both weathering and erosion were intense; so as uplift occurred, these processes removed much of the Paleozoic rocks.

After plutonism ceased in California, late-Cretaceous faulting broke up the longer range and the Sierra Nevada became separated from the Klamath Mountains on the north and the Coast, Transverse, and Peninsular ranges on the south. About this time, plate-transported continental crust collided with southern California, impacting near the southern end of the Sierra Nevada to cause massive uplift. Farther north along the range, uplift was correspondingly less, and the northern Sierra Nevada may not have been affected at all, judging by the accumulation there of voluminous, largely Eocene-epoch river gravels. (Westward tilting had already occurred and together with this new northward tilting, the Sierran river drainages developed their interesting, asymmetrical patterns.) By the time the dinosaurs went extinct at the end of the Cretaceous period 65 million years ago, the Sierra Nevada had achieved a largely granitic landscape, and it would have been during that time when the stepped topography so prominent in the southern part (from the Fresno River south) first began to develop. Also by this time there existed early forms of the Owens Valley and the Kern River Canyon (which developed along a late-Cretaceous fault). Like the Sierra Nevada, the Peninsular Ranges (PCT Sections A–B) had also experienced a similar postplutonic history of uplift and erosion. This also may have been true for the Coast Ranges (no PCT) and the central and eastern Transverse Ranges (PCT Sections C through most of E), but they have been so disrupted by faulting, especially over the last 30 million years, that we can only speculate on their prefaulted history.

Thirty million years ago was an important time. Roughly about then the climate began changing from one that was somewhat tropical to one that was drier and more seasonal. In the northern half of the Sierra Nevada the range was in part buried by extensive rhyolite-ash deposits. Furthermore, the San Andreas fault system was born, west of the modern coast of southern California. By 15 million years ago, California had acquired an essentially modern summer-dry climate; the northern half of the Sierra Nevada was buried under even larger amounts of andesitic deposits (burying the old, granitic river canyons); and the fault system was beginning to migrate eastward onto existing lands, thereby disrupting them. As today, lands west of any fault segment moved northward with respect to those on the east (*right-lateral* faulting).

Most of the volcanic deposits in the northern Sierra Nevada were readily eroded, but the new canyons cut in such deposits were inundated by additional sediments. About 10–9 million years ago several massive outpourings of lava flowed westward from faults near the present Sierran crest. These faults were created by extension of the Great Basin lands, which before widespread down-faulting had been a rugged, mountainous highland. The floor of the Owens Valley sank, but the already high Sierra Nevada *did* not rise; the opposite-direction arrows along the fault in the idealized geologic section indicate only relative movement, not absolute up or down. Note that the fault cuts the bedrock but not the *lateral moraine* (an accumulation of debris dropped off the side of a glacier), and this indicates that no faulting has occurred since the moraine was deposited (or else it too would have been disrupted).

Significant parts of these lava flows still remain, and the remnants best preserved are those that lie directly atop old bedrock, as does the remnant of an *andesite flow* in the idealized geologic section. Such remnants stand high above the floor of today's granite-walled canyons, which had been mostly exhumed of volcanic deposits before glaciation commenced. From this relation, geologists have concluded—incorrectly according to Schaffer—that major postflow uplift raised the flows to their present high positions, and that the steepened rivers then cut through thousands of feet of granite to their present low positions. According to this view, glaciers aided in the excavation, but misinterpretation of the field evidence has led geologists to infer major glacial erosion in some canyons, such as Yosemite Valley, and very little in others, such as the Grand Canyon of the Tuolumne River—two adjacent drainages both in Yosemite National Park.

The Sierra Nevada first experienced major glaciation about two million years ago, although it could have had episodes of minor glaciation long before that. These first large glaciers eroded the layer of rough, fractured, weathered bedrock, then retreated to leave behind much smoother surfaces. Where the bedrock floor was highly fractured and/or deeply weathered (in Yosemite Valley, the most extreme example, tropical weathering had penetrated some 2000 feet down), glaciers could excavate quite effectively, leaving behind bedrock basins that quickly filled with water each time the glaciers retreated, creating a bedrock lake, or *tarn*. (In some canyons a lake formed behind a *terminal moraine*, although such a lake exists not so much because of a moraine dam, but rather because of impervious bedrock that is buried by the moraine.) On the resistant, smoothed and polished bedrock, succeeding glaciers could do very little, despite a century of claims by glaciologists.

Some of the evidence for lack of major glacial erosion lies along or close to the PCT. In Section G you reach the South Fork Kern River in Rockhouse Basin (Map G6). This basin and lands around it have changed so little in the last 15 million years—only a few feet of erosion—that back then you could use today's topo maps. The ridge separating the basin from Tibbets Creek canyon (Section 15, Map G6) provides a particularly instructive view. From it you can look west across the canyon and see a splendid glacial landscape: straight, hanging tributary canyons that are U-shaped in cross section. The only problem is that there was no glaciation! This is a relict tropical landscape. Farther north, in Section J, you start a descent from the Wolf Creek Lake saddle north into the deep, glaciated East Fork Carson River canyon. After about two trail miles, before you cross the river's second tributary on Map J1, you should note remnants of volcanic deposits on the west slopes, which descend to within 200 feet of the canyon floor. These remnants are dated at about 20 million years old, indicating that back then—before any supposed uplift and before any glaciation—the canyon was about as wide as it is today and almost as deep.

Returning to the idealized geologic section, we see both a lateral and a terminal moraine on the east side of the crest, these usually being massive deposits left by a former glacier. (However, some lateral moraines are thin, merely a veneer atop an underlying bedrock ridge.) If glaciers do not erode, then why are moraines so large? Rockfall is the answer. It can occur at any time, but it is especially prevalent in late winter and early spring (due to cycles of freeze and thaw that pry off slabs and blocks). During and after a major earthquake, a tremendous amount of rockfall occurs, as noted in the 1980 Mammoth Lakes earthquake swarm, which was centered near the town along the east base of the range. Rockfall was greatest along and east of the crest, and so perhaps it is good that the PCT lies a few miles west of it. The greatest amount of local rockfall along the PCT route was from the ragged southeast face of Peak 11787, north of Purple Lake (Map H16). What glaciers do best is haul out a lot of rockfall, from which moraines are constructed and with which rivers are choked. Over the last two million years there were 2–4 dozen cycles of major glacier growth and retreat, and the glaciers transported a lot of rockfall. At the head of each canyon, where physical weathering was extremely pronounced, there usually developed a steep-walled half-bowl called a *cirque*. Before glaciation these already existed in a less dramatic form, as can be seen in the unglaciated lands west of Rockhouse Basin.

In the idealized geologic section, the last significant change was the eruption of lava to produce a *cinder cone*, which partly overlapped the terminal moraine, thereby indicating that it is younger. A *basalt flow* emanated from the cinder cone during or immediately after its formation. A carbon-14 date on wood buried by the flow would verify the youthfulness of the flow. Weathering and erosion arc oh-so-slowly attacking the range today, at a rate much slower than in its tropical past, but nevertheless are seeking to reduce the landscape to sea level. This will not occur. Future PCT hikers in the distant geologic future can expect a higher range, for eventually the Coast Ranges of central California should be thrust across the Great Central Valley and onto the Sierra Nevada, the crust-crust compression generating a new round of mountain building.

For now, PCT hikers can study the existing landscape. When you encounter a contact between two rocks along the trail, you might ask yourself: which rock is younger? Which older? Has faulting, folding, or metamorphism occurred? Is there a gap in the geologic record? When you can begin to answer these questions, you'll feel a great satisfaction as you slowly solve this great geologic puzzle.

Biology

One's first guess about hiking the Pacific Crest Trail—a high adventure rich in magnificent alpine scenery and sweeping panoramas—turns out to be incorrect along some parts of the trail. The real-life trail hike will sometimes seem to consist of enduring many repetitious miles of hot, dusty tread, battling hordes of mosquitoes, or slogging up seemingly endless switchbacks. If you find yourself bogged down in such unpleasant impressions, it may be because you haven't developed an appreciation of the natural history of this remarkable route. As there is a great variety of minerals, rocks, landscapes and climates along the PCT, so also is there a great variety of plants and animals.

Even if you don't know much about basic ecology, you can't help noticing that the natural scene along the Pacific Crest Trail changes with elevation. The most obvious changes are in the trees, just because trees are the most obvious—the largest—organisms. Furthermore, they don't move around, hike, or migrate in their lifetimes, as do animals. When you pay close attention, you notice that not only the trees but the shrubs and wildflowers also change with elevation. Then you begin to find latitudinal differences in the animal populations. In other words, there are different *life zones.*

Life zones. In 1894 C. Hart Merriam divided North America into seven broad ecosystems, which he called "life zones." These zones were originally based primarily on temperature, though today they are based on the distribution of plants and animals. The zones correspond roughly with latitude, from the Tropical Zone, which stretches from Florida across Mexico, to the Arctic Zone, which includes the polar regions. Between these two are found, south to north, the Lower Sonoran, Upper Sonoran, Transition, Canadian and Hudsonian zones. All but the Tropical Zone are encountered along the California PCT.

Just as temperature decreases as you move toward the earth's poles, so too does it decrease as you climb upward—between 3° and 5.5°F for every 1000-foot elevation gain. Thus, if you were to climb from broad San Gorgonio Pass for 10,000 feet up to the summit of San Gorgonio Mountain, you would pass through all the same zones that you would if you walked from southern California north all the way to Alaska. It turns out that 1000 feet of elevation are about equivalent to 170 miles of latitude. Although the California PCT is about 1600 miles long, the net northward gain in latitude in only about 650 miles—you have to hike 2.5 route-miles to get one mile north. This 650-mile change in latitude should bring about the same temperature change as climbing 3800 feet up a mountain. On the PCT you enter Oregon at a 6000-foot elevation, finding yourself in a dense, Canadian Zone pine-and-fir forest. Doing your arithmetic, you would expect to find an equally dense fir forest at the Mexican border 3800 feet higher—at a 9800-foot elevation. Unfortunately, no such elevation exists along the border to test this prediction. However, if we head 85 miles north from the border to the Mt. San Jacinto environs, and subtract 500 feet in elevation to compensate for this new latitude, what do we find at the 9300-foot elevation? You guessed it, a Canandian Zone pine-and-fir forest. Ah, but nature is not quite that simple, for the two forests are unmistakably different.

Plant geography. Every plant (and every animal) has its own *range, habitat* and *niche*. Some species have a very restricted range; others, a very widespread one. The sequoia, for example, occurs only in about 75 groves at mid-elevations in the western Sierra Nevada. It flourishes in a habitat of tall conifers growing on shaded, gentle, well-drained slopes. Its niche—its role in the community—consists in its complex interaction with its environment and every other species in its environment. Dozens of insects utilize the sequoia's needles and cones, and additional organisms thrive in its surrounding soil. The woolly sunflower, on the other hand, has a tremendous range: from California north to British Columbia and east to the Rocky Mountains. It can be found in brushy habitats from near sea level up to 10,000 feet.

Some species, evidently, can adapt to environments and competitors better than others. Nevertheless, each is restricted by a complex interplay of *climatic, physiographic* (topography), *edaphic* (soil) and *biotic* influences.

Climatic influences. Of all influences, temperature and precipitation are probably the most important. Although the mean temperature tends to increase toward the equator, this pattern is camouflaged in California by the dominating effect of the state's highly varied topography. As was mentioned earlier, the temperature decreases between 3° and 5.5°F for every 1000-foot gain in elevation, and the vegetational changes reflect this cooling trend. For example, the vegetation along San Gorgonio Pass in southern California is adapted to its desert environment. Annuals are very ephemeral; after heavy rains, they quickly grow, blossom and die. Perennials are succulent or woody, have deep roots, and have small, hard or waxy leaves—or no leaves at all. Only the lush cottonwoods and other associated species along the dry streambeds hint at a source of water.

As you climb north up the slopes of San Gorgonio Mountain, not only does the temperature drop, but the annual precipitation increases. On the gravelly desert floor below, only a sparse, drought-adapted vegetation survives the searing summer temperatures and the miserly 10 inches precipitation. A doubled precipitation on the mountainside allows growth of chaparral, here a thick stand of ocean spray, birchleaf mountain mahogany, Gregg's ceanothus and great-berried manzanita. By 7000 feet the precipitation has increased to 40 inches, and the moisture-loving conifers—first Jeffrey pine, then lodgepole pine and white fir—predominate. As the temperature steadily decreases with elevation, evaporation of soil water and transpiration of moisture from plant needles and leaves are both reduced. Furthermore, up here the precipitation may be in the form of snow, which is preserved for months by the shade of the forest, and even when it melts is retained by the highly absorbent humus (decayed organic matter) of the forest soil. Consequently, an inch of precipitation on the higher slopes is far more effective than an inch on the exposed, gravelly desert floor. Similar vegetation changes can be found wherever you make dramatic ascents or descents. In northern California significant elevation and vegetation changes occur as you descend to and then ascend from Highway 70 at Belden, Interstate 5 at Castle Crags State Park, and Highway 96 at Seiad Valley.

Physiographic influences. As we have seen, the elevation largely governs the regime of temperature and precipitation. For a *given* elevation, the mean maximum temperature in northern California is about 10°F less than that of the San Bernardino area. Annual precipitation, however, is considerably more; it ranges from about 20 inches in the Sacramento Valley to 80 inches along the higher slopes, where the snowpack may last well into summer. When you climb out of a canyon in the Feather River country, you start among live oak, poison oak and California laurel, and ascend through successive stands of Douglas-fir and black oak, incense cedar and ponderosa pine, white fir and sugar pine, then finally red fir, lodgepole, and western white pine.

The country near the Oregon border is one of lower elevations and greater precipitation, which produces a wetter-but-milder climate that is reflected in the distribution of plant species. Seiad Valley is hemmed in with forests of Douglas-fir, tan oak, madrone and canyon live oak. When you reach Cook and Green Pass (4750′) you reach a forest of white fir and noble fir. To the east, at higher elevations, you encounter weeping spruce.

A low minimum temperature, like a high maximum one, can determine where a plant species lives, since freezing temperatures can kill poorly adapted plants by causing ice crystals to form in their cells. At high elevations, the gnarled, grotesque trunks of the whitebark, limber, and foxtail pines give stark testimony to their battle against the elements. The wind-cropped, short-needled foliage is sparse at best, for the growing season lasts but two months, and a killing frost is possible in every month. Samples of this subalpine forest are found on the upper slopes of the higher peaks in the San Jacinto, San Bernardino, and San Gabriel mountains and along much of the John Muir Trail. Along or near the High Sierra crest and on the highest southern California summits, all vestiges of forest surrender to rocky, barren slopes pioneered only by the most stalwart perennials, such as alpine willow and alpine buttercup.

Other physiographic influences are the *location, steepness, orientation*, and *shape of slopes*. North-facing slopes are cooler and tend to be wetter than south-facing slopes. Hence on north-facing slopes, you'll encounter red-fir forests which at the ridgeline abruptly give way to a dense cover of manzanita and ceanothus on south-facing slopes. Extremely steep slopes may never develop a deep soil or support a coniferous forest, and of course cliffs will be devoid of vegetation other than crustose lichens, secluded mosses, scattered annuals, and a few drought-resistant shrubs and trees.

Edaphic influences. Along the northern part of your trek, at the headwaters of the Trinity River and just below Seiad Valley, you'll encounter outcrops of serpentine, California's official state rock. (Technically, the rock is serpentinite, and it is composed almost entirely of the mineral serpentine, but even geologists use "serpentine" for the rock.) This rock weathers to form a soil poor in some vital plant nutrients but rich in certain undesirable heavy metals. Nevertheless, there are numerous species, such as leather oak, that are specifically or generally associated with serpentine-derived oils.

There is a species of streptanthus (mustard family) found only in this soil, even though it can grow better on other soils. However, experiments demonstrate that it cannot withstand the competition of other plants growing on these soils. It therefore struggles, yet propagates, within its protected environment. Another example is at Marble Mountain, also in northern California, which has a local assemblage of plants that have adapted to the mountain's limey soil.

A soil can change over time and with it, the vegetation. If a forest on a slope is burned, the organic layer on the forest floor is destroyed, leaving only charred stumps as tombstones. With no protective cover, the rest of the soil is soon attacked by the forces of erosion. This mute landscape may still receive as much precipitation as a neighboring slope, but its effective precipitation is much less; it will take years to make a recovery. Herbs and shrubs will have to pioneer the slope and slowly build up a humus-rich soil again.

Biotic influences. In an arid environment, plants competing for water may evolve special mechanisms besides their water-retaining mechanisms. The creosote bush, for example, in an effort to preserve its limited supply of water, secretes toxins which prevent nearby seeds from germinating. The result is an economical spacing of bushes along the desert floor.

Competition is manifold everywhere. On a descending trek past a string of alpine lakes, you might see several stages of plant succession. The highest lake may be pristine, bordered only by tufts of sedges between the lichen-crusted rocks. A lower lake may exhibit an invasion of grasses, sedges and pondweeds thriving on the sediments deposited at its inlet. Corn lilies and Lemmon's willows border its edge. Farther down, a wet meadow may be the remnant of a former shallow lake. Water birch and lodgepole pine then make their debut. Finally, you reach the last lake bed, recognized only by the flatness of the forest floor and a few boulders of a recessional moraine (glacial deposit) that dammed the lake. In this location, a thick stand of white fir has overshadowed and eliminated much of the underlying lodgepole. Be aware, however, that lake-meadow-forest succession is very slow, the lakes being filled with sediments at an average rate of about one foot per thousand years. At this rate, about 20–30,000 years will be required to fill in most of the lakes, and Tenaya Lake, between Tuolumne Meadows and Yosemite Valley, will take over 100,000 years. However, barring significant man-induced atmospheric warming, California's climate should cool in a few thousand years, and another round of glaciation should commence.

When a species becomes too extensive, it invites attack. The large, pure stand of lodgepole pine near Tuolumne Meadows has for years been under an unrelenting attack by a moth known as the lodgepole needle-miner. One of the hazards of a pure stand of one species is the inherent instability of the system. Within well-mixed forest, lodgepoles are scattered and the needle-miner is not much of a problem. But species need not always compete. Sometime two species cooperate for the mutual benefit, if not the actual existence of both. That is true of the Joshua tree and its associated yucca moth, which are discussed in the Antelope Valley portion of PCT Section E. Another most important association goes unseen. Nearly all the plants you'll encounter have roots that form a symbiotic relationship with fungi. These mycorrhizal fungi greatly increase the roots' efficiency of water and nutrient uptake, and the roots provide the fungi with some of the plants' photosynthesized simple sugars.

Unquestionably, the greatest biotic agent is people. (They are also the greatest geomorphic agent, directly or indirectly causing more erosion—and therefore more habitat degradation—than any natural process.) For example, people have supplanted native species with introduced species. Most of California's native bunchgrass is gone, together with the animals that grazed upon it, replaced by thousands of acres of one-crop fields and by suburban sprawl. Forests near some mining towns have been virtually eliminated. Others have been subjected to ravenous scars inflicted by people-caused fires and by clearcutting logging practices. The Los Angeles basin's smog production has already begun to take its toll of mountain conifers, and Sierra forests may experience a similar fate. Wide-scale use of pesticides has not eliminated the pests, but it has greatly reduced the pests' natural predators. Through forestry, agriculture and urban practices, people have attempted to simplify nature, and by upsetting its checks and balances have made many ecosystems unstable. Along the Pacific Crest Trail, you'll see areas virtually unaffected by people as well as areas greatly affected by them. When you notice the difference, you'll have something to ponder as you stride along the quiet trail.

The role of fire. Fires were once thought to be detrimental to the overall well-being of the ecosystem, and early foresters attempted to prevent or subdue all fires. This policy led to the accumulation of thick litter, dense brush and overmature trees—all of them prime fuel for a holocaust when a fire inevitably sparked to life. Manmade fires can be prevented, but how does one prevent a lightning fire, so common in the Sierra?

The answer is that fires should not be prevented, but only regulated. Natural fires, if left unchecked, burn stands of mixed conifers about once every 10 years. At this frequency, brush and litter do not accumulate sufficiently to result in a damaging forest fire; only the ground cover is burned over, while the trees remain intact. Hence, through small burns, the forest is protected from flaming catastrophes.

Some pines are adapted to fire. Indeed, the relatively uncommon knobcone pine, growing in scattered localities particularly in the Klamath Mountains (PCT Sections P, Q, and R), requires fire to survive: the short-lived tree must be consumed by fire in order that its seeds be released. The lodgepole pine also will release its seeds after a fire, although a fire is not necessary. Particularly adapted to fires, if not dependent on them, are plants of southern California's chaparral community, which is discussed in the introductory matter of PCT Section B. But in the Sierra and other high ranges, fire is important, too. For example, seeds of the genus *Ceanothus* are quick to germinate in burned-over ground, and some plants of this genus are among the primary foods of deer. Hence, periodic burns will keep a deer population at its maximum. With too few burns, shrubs become too woody and unproductive for a deer herd. In like manner, gooseberries and other berry plants sprout after fires and help support several different bird populations.

Without fires, a plant community evolves toward a *climax*, or end stage of plant succession. Red fir is the main species in the climax vegetation characteristic of higher forests in California's mountains. A pure stand of any species, as mentioned earlier, invites epidemic attacks and is therefore unstable. But even climax vegetation does not last forever. Typically the climax vegetation is a dense forest, and eventually the trees mature, die, and topple over. Logs and litter accumulate to such a degree that when a fire does start, the abundant fuel causes a crown fire, not a ground fire, and the forest burns down. Succession over time will result in an even-age stand of trees, and the cycle will repeat itself. In the past, ecologists believed that stable climax vegetation was the rule, but we now know that unstable, changing vegetation is more common, even where man is not involved.

Fire also unlocks nutrients that are stored in living matter, topsoil, and rocks. Vital compounds are released in the form of ash when a fire burns plants and forest litter. Fires also can heat granitic rocks enough to cause them to break up and release their minerals. Even in a coniferous forest the weathering of granitic rock often is due primarily to periodic fires. This may be true even in the high desert. For example, in Anza-Borrego Desert State Park a large fire ravaged many of its granitic slopes, and a post-fire inspection revealed that the fire was intense enough to cause thin sheets of granite to exfoliate, or sheet off, from granitic boulders.

Natural, periodic fires, then, can be very beneficial for a forest ecosystem, and they should be thought of as an integral process in the plant community. They have, after all, been around as long as terrestrial life has, and for millions of years have been a common event in California plant communities.

Plant communities and their animal associates. As you can see, plant communities are quite complex, and the general Life Zone system fails to take into account California's diverse climates and landscapes. Consequently, we'll elaborate on the biological scenario by looking at California's plant communities. Philip Munz, in his day California's leading native-plant authority, used the term *plant community* "for each regional element of the vegetation that is characterized by the presence of certain dominant species." Using this criterion, we devised our own list of California plant communities, which differs somewhat from the list proposed by Munz. We found that for the PCT, the division between Red Fir Forest and Lodgepole Pine Forest was an artificial one. True, you can find large, pure stands of either tree, but very often they are found together and each has extremely similar associated plant and animal species. For the same reason we grouped Douglas-Fir Forest with Mixed Evergreen Forest. Finally, we've added two new communities that were not recognized by Munz, though they are recognized by other biologists: Mountain Chaparral and Mountain Meadow, each being significantly different from its lowland counterpart. Certainly, there is overlapping of species between adjacent communities, and any classification system can be quite arbitrary. Regardless of how you devise a California plant community table, you'll discover that along the PCT you'll encounter over half of the state's total number of communities—only the coast-range and eastern-desert communities are not seen.

As mentioned earlier, each species has its own range, which can be very restricted or very widespread. Birds typically have a wide—usually seasonal—range, and therefore may be found in many plant communities. In the following table we've listed only the plants and animals that have restricted ranges; that is, they generally occur in only one-to-several communities. Of the thousands of plant species we reviewed for this table, we found most of them failed to serve as indicator species since they either inhabited too many plant communities or they grew in too small a geographic area. Terrestrial vertebrates pose a similar classification problem. For example, in the majority of the PCT plant communities you can find the dark-eyed junco, robin, raven, mule deer, coyote, badger and Pacific treefrog, so we didn't include them in the table.

The following table of plant communities will be useless if you can't recognize the plants and animals you see along the trail. Our trail description suggests plant communities, such as "you hike through a ponderosa-pine forest." This would clue you into plant community #11, and by referring to it, you could get an idea of what plants and animals you'll see in it. But then you'll need a guidebook or two to identify the various plants and animals. We have a few suggestions. If you can spare the luxury of carrying 12 extra ounces in your pack, then obtain a copy of Storer's *Sierra Nevada Natural History*, which identifies over 270 plants and 480 animals. Although it is dated and long overdue for revision, it is the only general book on the subject. Not only does it provide identifying characteristics of plant and animal species, but also it describes their habits and gives other interesting facts. Its title is misleading, for it is generally applicable to about three-fourths of the California PCT route: Mt. Laguna, the San Jacinto, San Bernardino, and San Gabriel mountains, and from the Sierra Nevada north almost continuously to the Oregon border. To better appreciate southern California, read Jaeger's much smaller book, *Introduction to the Natural History of Southern California*. For a 4-ounce pocket book, take Keator's *Sierra Flower Finder*. Finally, if you're doing all three states, bring Niehaus and Ripper's *Pacific States Wildflowers*, which has almost 1500 species. This certainly beats carrying the 4-pound authoritative reference, *The Jepson Manual*.

Plant Communities of California's Pacific Crest Trail

1. Creosote Bush Scrub

Shrubs: creosote bush, bladderpod, brittle bush, burroweed, catclaw, indigo bush, mesquite
Cacti: Bigelow's cholla, silver cholla, calico cactus, beavertail cactus, Banning prickly pear, desert barrel cactus
Wildflowers: desert mariposa, prickly poppy, peppergrass, desert primrose, spotted langloisia, desert aster, Mojave buckwheat
Mammals: kit fox, black-tailed jackrabbit, antelope ground squirrel, Mojave ground squirrel, desert kangaroo rat, Merriam's kangaroo rat, cactus mouse, little pocket mouse
Birds: roadrunner, Gambel's quail, Le Conte's thrasher, cactus wren, phainopepla, Say's phoebe, black-throated sparrow, Costa's hummingbird
Reptiles: spotted leaf-nosed snake, coachwhip, western blind snake, Mojave rattlesnake, western diamondback rattlesnake, chuckwalla, desert iguana, collared lizard, zebra-tailed lizard, long-tailed brush lizard, desert tortoise
Amphibian: red-spotted toad
Where seen along PCT: base of Granite Mountains, southern San Felipe Valley, San Gorgonio Pass, lower Whitewater Canyon, Cajon Canyon, L.A. Aqueduct in Antelope Valley, lower Tehachapi Mountains

2. Shadescale Scrub

Shrubs: shadescale, blackbush, hop sage, winter fat, bud sagebrush, spiny menodora, cheese bush
Mammals: kit fox, black-tailed jackrabbit, antelope ground squirrel, desert wood rat, desert kangaroo rat, Merriam's kangaroo rat
Bird: black-throated sparrow
Reptiles: gopher snake, Mojave rattlesnake, zebra-tailed lizard
Where seen along PCT: L.A. Aqueduct in Antelope Valley

3. Sagebrush Scrub

Shrubs: basin sagebrush, blackbush, rabbit brush, antelope brush (bitterbrush), purple sage, Mojave yucca

Mammals: kit fox, white-tailed hare, pigmy rabbit, least chipmunk, Merriam's kangaroo rat, Great Basin pocket mouse
Birds: green-tailed towhee, black-chinned sparrow, sage sparrow, Brewer's sparrow
Reptiles: side-blotched lizard, desert horned lizard, leopard lizard
Where seen along PCT: Doble Road, Soledad Canyon, southern Antelope Valley, terrain near Pinyon Mountain

4. Valley Grassland

Grasses, native: bunchgrass, needle grass, three-awn grass
Grasses, introduced: brome grass, fescue, wild oats, foxtail
Wildflowers: California poppy, common muilla, California golden violet, Douglas meadow foam, Douglas locoweed, whitewhorl lupine, Kellogg's tarweed, redstem storksbill (filaree), roundleaf storksbill
Mammals: kit fox, Heermann's kangaroo rat, California meadow mouse
Birds: horned lark, western meadowlark, burrowing owl, Brewer's blackbird, savannah sparrow
Reptiles: racer
Amphibians: western spadefoot toad, tiger salamander
Where seen along PCT: Buena Vista Creek area, Big Tree Trail near Sierra Pelona Ridge, Dowd Canyon, Seiad Valley (manmade grassland)

5. Chaparral

Trees: big-cone Douglas-fir, digger pine, interior live oak
Shrubs: chamise, scrub oak, birch-leaved mountain mahogany, chaparral whitethorn, Gregg's ceanothus, bigpod ceanothus, hoaryleaf ceanothus, bigberry manzanita, Eastwood's manzanita, Mexican manzanita, Parry's manzanita, pink-bracted manzanita, toyon, ocean spray, holly-leaf cherry, California coffeeberry, redberry, coyote brush (chaparral broom), poison oak
Wildflowers: California poppy, fire poppy, Parish's tauschia, charming centaury, Cleveland's monkey flower, Fremont's monkey flower, scarlet bugler, Martin's paintbrush, foothill penstemon, Coulter's lupine, buckwheat spp.
Mammals: gray fox, brush rabbit, Merriam's chipmunk, dusky-footed wood rat, nimble kangaroo rat, California mouse, California pocket mouse
Birds: turkey vulture, California quail, scrub jay, California thrasher, green-tailed towhee, brown towhee, rufous-sided towhee, orange-crowned warbler, Lazuli bunting, blue-gray gnatcatcher, wrentit, bushtit
Reptiles: striped racer, western rattlesnake, western fence lizard, southern alligator lizard, coast horned lizard
Where see along PCT: Mexican border, Hauser Mountain, Fred Canyon, Monument Peak, Chariot Canyon, Agua Caliente Creek, Combs Peak, Table Mountain, upper Penrod Canyon, middle Whitewater Canyon, Crab Flats Road, west slopes above Silverwood Lake, west of Pinyon Flats, Fountainhead Spring, North Fork Saddle, Soledad Canyon, Leona Divide, Spunky Canyon, Sawmill and Liebre mountains, Lamont Canyon to north of Kennedy Meadows

6. Joshua Tree Woodland

Trees: Joshua tree (tree-like stature, but really a yucca), California juniper, single-leaved pinyon pine
Shrubs: Mojave yucca, Utah juniper, box thorn, bladder sage, saltbush
Wildflowers: wild buckwheat, rock echeveria, rock five-finger, heart-leaved jewel flower, coiled locoweed, pigmy-leaved lupine, Parish's monkey flower, mouse-tail, Mojave pen-

nyroyal, two-colored phacelia, tetradymia
Mammals: kit fox, antelope ground squirrel, desert wood rat, Merriam's kangaroo rat, white-eared pocket mouse
Birds: pinyon jay, loggerhead shrike, Scott's oriole, Bendire's thrasher
Reptiles: Mojave rattlesnake, California Lyre snake, desert night lizard, desert spiny lizard, desert tortoise
Amphibian: red-spotted toad
Where seen along PCT: middle Whitewater Canyon, Nelson Ridge, Antelope Valley, western Mojave Desert, Walker Pass

7. Pinyon-Juniper Woodland

Trees: single-leaved pinyon pine, California juniper
Shrubs: Utah juniper, scrub oak, Mojave yucca, basin sagebrush, blackbush, box thorn, curl-leaved mountain mahogany, antelope brush, ephedra
Wildflowers: rock buckwheat, Wright's buckwheat, golden forget-me-not, adonis lupine, yellow paintbrush, Hall's phacelia
Mammals: black-tailed jackrabbit, California ground squirrel, Merriam's chipmunk, southern pocket gopher, pinyon mouse
Birds: pinyon jay, rock wren, poorwill, California thrasher, gray vireo, black-throated gray warbler, ladder-backed woodpecker
Reptiles: speckled rattlesnake, Mojave rattlesnake, leopard lizard, sagebrush lizard, western fence lizard, desert spiny lizard, coast horned lizard, Gilbert's skink
Amphibian: red-spotted toad
Where seen along PCT: just south of Burnt Rancheria Campground, Onyx Summit, Camp Oakes, Van Dusen Canyon, West Fork Mojave River, Highway 58 to Kennedy Meadows

8. Northern Juniper Woodland

Trees: western juniper, single-leaved pinyon pine, Jeffrey pine
Shrubs: basin sagebrush, antelope brush, rabbit brush, curl-leaved mountain mahogany
Wildflowers: sagebrush buttercup, ballhead ipomopsis, three-leaved locoweed, Humboldt's milkweed, western puccoon, sagebrush Mariposa tulip
Mammals: least chipmunk, Great Basin kangaroo rat, sagebrush vole
Birds: sage grouse, pinyon jay, sage thrasher, northern shrike, gray flycatcher, sage sparrow
Reptiles: striped whipsnake, sagebrush lizard, short-horned lizard
Amphibian: Great Basin spadefoot toad
Where seen along PCT: Kennedy Meadows, Little Pete and Big Pete meadows, upper Noble Canyon, much of the volcanic landscape between Highways 108 and 50, Hat Creek Rim, Buckhorn Mountain

9. Southern Oak Woodland

Trees: coast live oak, Englemann oak, interior live oak, California juniper, Coulter pine, digger pine, big-cone Douglas-fir, California black walnut
Shrubs: sugar bush, lemonade-berry, gooseberry, bigberry manzanita, fremontia, squaw bush, poison oak
Wildflowers: elegant clarkia, slender eriogonum, wild oats, California Indian pink, golden stars, wild mountain sunflower, Kellogg's tarweed, Douglas locoweed, Douglas violet
Mammals: gray fox, raccoon, western gray squirrel, dusky-footed wood rat, brush mouse, California mouse
Birds: California quail, acorn woodpecker, scrub jay, mourning dove, Lawrence's goldfinch, common bushtit, black-headed grosbeak, plain titmouse, Nuttall's woodpecker, western wood-peewee, band-tailed pigeon, red-shouldered hawk

Reptiles: California mountain kingsnake, Gilbert's skink, western fence lizard, southern alligator lizard

Amphibians: California newt, California slender salamander, arboreal salamander

Where seen along PCT: Lake Morena County Park, Cottonwood Valley, Flathead Flats, Barrel Spring, Cañada Verde, Warner Springs, Tunnel Spring, Vincent Gap, Three Points, upper Tie Canyon, Mt. Gleason, Big Oak Spring, San Francisquito Canyon

10. Douglas-Fir/Mixed Evergreen forest

Trees: Douglas-fir, tanbark-oak, madrone, bay tree, big-leaf maple, canyon oak, black oak, yew, golden chinquapin

Shrubs: Pacific blackberry, California coffeeberry, Oregon grape, poison oak, wood rose, salal, Fremont's silk-tassel

Wildflowers: California pitcher plant, Indian pipe, striped coralroot, American pine sap, sugar stick, giant trillium, long-tailed ginger, one-sided wintergreen, wedge-leaved violet, California skullcap, grand hounds-tongue, Bolander's hawkweed

Mammals: black bear, porcupine, long-eared chipmunk, Townsend's chipmunk, red tree mouse

Birds: winter wren, hermit thrush, golden-crowned kinglet, purple finch, brown creeper, chestnut-backed chickadee

Reptiles: rubber boa, northern alligator lizard, western pond turtle

Amphibians: northwestern salamander, rough-skinned newt

Where seen along PCT: Middle Fork Feather River canyon, North Fork Feather River canyon, Pit River canyon, Sacramento River canyon, lower Grider Creek canyon, lower slopes around SeiadValley, Cook and Green Pass, Mt. Ashland Road 20

11. Ponderosa Pine Forest

Trees: ponderosa pine, sugar pine, Jeffrey pine, incense-cedar, white fir, Douglas-fir, black oak, mountain dogwood, grand fir

Shrubs: deer brush, greenleaf manzanita, Mariposa manzanita, mountain misery, western azalea, Scouler's willow, spice bush

Wildflowers: elegant brodiaea, spotted coralroot, draperia, rigid hedge nettle, Indian hemp, slender iris, leopard lily, grand lotus, dwarf lousewort, Sierra onion, Yosemite rock cress, shy Mariposa tulip

Mammals: black bear, mountain lion, mountain beaver, porcupine, western gray squirrel, golden-mantled ground squirrel, yellow-pine chipmunk, mountain pocket gopher

Birds: Steller's jay, hairy woodpecker, white-headed woodpecker, western tanager, band-tailed pigeon, pigmy nuthatch, western bluebird, flammulated owl

Reptiles: rubber boa, California mountain kingsnake, western rattlesnake, western fence lizard

Amphibians: foothill yellow-legged frog, ensatina

Where seen along PCT: Laguna Mountains, upper West Fork Palm Canyon, Apache Spring, upper Whitewater Canyon, much of the Big Bear Lake area, most of the San Gabriel Mountains, Piute Mountain, Haypress Creek, Chimney Rock, Burney Falls, lower Rock Creek, Castle Crags, lower slopes of Lower Devils Peak

12. Mountain Chaparral

Trees: Jeffrey pine, sugar pine, western juniper

Shrubs: huckleberry oak, snow bush, tobacco brush, greenleaf manzanita, bush chinquapin

Wildflowers: showy penstemon, dwarf monkey flower, hounds-tongue hawkweed, pussy paws, mountain jewel flower, golden brodiaea

Mammals: bushy-tailed wood rat, brush mouse

Birds: mountain quail, dusky flycatcher, fox sparrow, green-tailed towhee

Reptiles: western rattlesnake, sagebrush lizard

Where seen along PCT: near Tahquitz Peak, near Strawberry Cienaga, in small areas from north of Walker Pass to Cow Canyon, above Blaney Hot Springs, slopes north of Benson Lake, upper North Fork American River canyon, Sierra Buttes, Bucks Summit, slopes west of Three Lakes, lower Emigrant Trail, upper Hat Creek Valley, Pigeon Hill, above Seven Lakes Basin, slopes south of Kangaroo Lake, South Russian Creek canyon, upper Right Hand Fork canyon, south slopes of Lower Devils Peak and Middle Devils Peak, between Lily Pad Lake and Cook and Green Pass, Mt. Ashland Road 20

13. Mountain Meadow

Shrubs: arroyo willow, yellow willow, mountain alder

Wildflowers: California corn lily, wandering daisy, elephant's head, tufted gentian, Douglas knotweed, monkshood, swamp onion, Lemmon's paintbrush, meadow arnica, mountain carpet clover, California cone flower, Gray's lovage, Kellogg's lupine, meadow monkey flower, tall phacelia, Jeffrey's shooting star, Bigelow's sneezeweed

Mammals: Belding's ground squirrel, California meadow mouse, long-tailed meadow mouse, deer mouse, ornate shrew

Birds: northern harrier, Lincoln's sparrow, white-crowned sparrow, Brewer's blackbird

Amphibians: mountain yellow-legged frog, Yosemite toad

Where seen along PCT: Little Tahquitz Valley, Vidette Meadow, Grouse Meadows, Evolution Valley, Tully Hole, Tuolumne Meadows, Grace Meadow, upper Truckee River canyon, Benwood Meadow, Haypress Meadows, Corral Meadow, Badger Flat, Shelly Meadows, Donomore Meadows, Sheep Camp Spring area, Grouse Gap

14. Red Fir/Lodgepole Pine Forest

Trees: red fir, Shasta red fir, noble fir, lodgepole pine, western white pine, Jeffrey pine, aspen, mountain hemlock, weeping spruce

Shrubs: pinemat manzanita, bush chinquapin, snow bush, red heather, Labrador tea, mountain spiraea, caudate willow, MacKenzie's willow, Scouler's willow, black elderberry, thimbleberry

Wildflowers: snow plant, pine drops, nodding microseris, broadleaf lupine, western spring beauty

Mammals: black bear, red fox, mountain beaver, porcupine, yellow-bellied marmot, golden-mantled ground squirrel, lodgepole chipmunk, mountain pocket gopher

Birds: blue grouse, great gray owl, mountain chickadee, red-breasted nuthatch, dusky flycatcher, olive-sided flycatcher, Williamson's sapsucker, three-toed woodpecker, ruby-crowned kinglet, Cassin's finch

Where seen along PCT: upper Little Tahquitz Valley, upper San Bernardino Mountains, Mt. Baden-Powell, Kern Plateau, lower portions of John Muir Trail, much of northern Yosemite, most of the stretch from Yosemite to central Lassen Volcanic National Park, Bartle Gap, Grizzly Peak, most of the trail from Seven Lakes Basin to Mt. Ashland

15. Subalpine Forest

Trees: whitebark pine, foxtail pine, limber pine, lodgepole pine, mountain hemlock

Shrubs: Sierra willow, Eastwood's willow, white heather, bush cinquefoil

Wildflowers: Eschscholtz's buttercup, Coville's columbine, mountain monkey flower, Suksdorf's monkey flower, Sierra penstemon, Sierra primrose, mountain sorrel, cut-leaved daisy, silky raillardella, rock fringe

Mammals: red fox, yellow-bellied marmot, pika, Douglas squirrel (chickaree), alpine chipmunk, heather vole, water shrew

Birds: Clark's nutcracker, mountain bluebird, mountain chickadee, Williamson's sapsucker

Amphibian: Mt. Lyell salamander
Where seen along PCT: Mt. Baden-Powell summit, much of the Sierra Nevada (above 10,000 feet in the southern part, above 8,000 feet in the northern part), higher elevations in Marble Mountain Wilderness

16. Alpine Fell-Fields

Shrubs: alpine willow, snow willow
Wildflowers: alpine gold, Sierra pilot, alpine paintbrush, alpine sandwort, ruby sandwort, dwarf lewisia, dwarf ivesia, Muir's ivesia, Brewer's draba, feeble saxifrage, Sierra primrose
Mammals: pika, alpine chipmunk
Birds: rosy finch, mountain bluebird, rock wren
Where seen along PCT: at and just below the following passes: Forester Pass, Glen Pass, Pinchot Pass, Mather Pass, Selden Pass, Silver Pass, Donohue Pass; high traverse along Leavitt Peak ridge

A final word. Plant communities aren't the final word in plant-animal classification, since each community could be further subdivided. For example, Edmund Jaeger divides the desert environment into even more compartments than Munz does, including Desert Sand Dunes, Desert Wash, Salt Water Lake (Salton Sea), Desert Canal, Colorado River Bottom, Desert Urban, and Desert Rural. Farther north, in a glaciated basin near Yosemite's Tioga Pass, Lionel Klikoff has identified eight vegetational patterns within the subalpine forest plant community, each distribution pattern the result of a different set of microenvironmental influences. Once you start looking and thinking about organisms and their environments, you'll begin to see that all is not a group of random species. There is continual interaction between similar organisms, between different organisms, and between organisms and their environment. They are there because they fit into the dynamic ecosystem; they currently are adapted to it; they belong.

Chapter 4
Using This Guide

Our Route Description

The bulk of this guide is composed of route description and accompanying topographic maps of the Pacific Crest Trail. In 18 section chapters this guide covers the California PCT from the Mexican border north to Interstate 5 in southern Oregon. We have divided the route description into sections because the vast majority of PCT hikers will be hiking only a part of the trail, not all of it. Each section starts at or hear a highway and/or supply center (town, resort, park) and ends at another similar point. The one exception is the end of Section G and start of Section H, which occurs where the Pacific Crest Trail joins the John Muir Trail near Crabtree Meadows. From this point most PCT hikers will go east to climb Mt. Whitney and perhaps descend to Lone Pine to resupply. We also chose this break point because many hikers skip southern California and start their PCT hiking on the John Muir Trail—this guide's Section H. This section is the only one that is too long for *most* hikers to do without resupplying. All of the other sections are short enough to make comfortable backpack trips ranging from 3 to 10 days. Even so, most of these have resupply points along or close to the actual route, thereby allowing you to carry a little less food.

At the beginning of each section is an introduction that mentions: 1) the attractions and natural features of that section, 2) the declination setting for your compass, 3) a mileage table between points within that section, 4) supply points on or near the route, 5) wilderness permits (if required), 6) special problems, and 7) the 7½′ topographic maps that cover the trail in the chapter, arranged south to north. (The maps can be ordered from The Map Center, 2440 Bancroft Way, Berkeley, CA 94704; phone: 510/ 841-MAPS.) Attractions and natural features will help you decide what part of the trail you'll want to hike—very few hikers do all of California. The declination setting for your compass is important if you have to get a true reading. The declinations vary from 14½°E near the Mexican border to 20°E in southern Oregon. If your compass does not correct for declination, you'll have to add the appropriate declination to get the true bearing. For example, if your compass indicates that a prominent hill lies along a bearing of 75°, and if the section you're hiking in has a declination of 15°E, then you should add 15°, getting 90° (due east) as the true bearing of that hill. If you can identify that *hill* on a map, then you can find where *you* are on the PCT by adding 180°, getting 270° (due west) in this example. By drawing a line due west from the hill to the PCT route, you'll determine your position. *No one* should attempt a *major* section of the PCT without a thorough understanding of the compass and of map interpretation.

Each mileage table lists distances between major points found within its PCT section. Both distances between points and cumulative mileages at points are given. We list cumulative mileages south to north and north to south so that no matter which direction you are hiking the PCT, you can easily determine the mileages you plan to hike. Many of the points listed in the tables are at or near good campsites. If you typically average 17 miles a day—the on-route rate you'll need to do to complete the tri-state PCT in 5+ months—then you can determine where you should camp to maintain this rate, and you can estimate when you should arrive at certain supply points. Of course, in reality your time schedule may turn out to be quite different from your planned schedule.

At the end of this short chapter we've included a mileage table for the entire California PCT, Any two adjacent points represent the start and end of one of this book's 18 section chapters. By scanning this table's distance between points, you can easily see how long each section is. Then you can pick one of appropriate length, turn to that section's introduction, and see if it sounds appealing. Of course, you need not start at the beginning of any section, since a number of roads cross the PCT in most sections. (Sections H and I are exceptions, having only a few access points.)

Supply points on or near the route are mentioned, as well as what you might expect to find at each. You will realize, for example, that you can't get new clothes at Old Station, but can at Burney, the next major settlement. Many supply points are just a post office and/or small store with minimal food supplies. By "minimal" we mean a few odds and ends that typically cater to passing motorists, e.g., beer and potato chips (which nevertheless are devoured by many a trail-weary trekker).

Finally, the introduction mentions special problems you might encounter in each section, such as desert thirst, snow avalanches and early-season fords. If you are hiking all of the California PCT, you will be going through some of its sections at very inopportune times and will face many of these problems. Backpackers hiking a short stretch can pick the best time to hike it, and thereby minimize their problems.

When you start reading the text of a PCT section, you will notice that a pair of numbers follows the more important trail points. For example, at Highway 120 in Tuolumne Meadows (end of Section H) this pair is (8595-0.8), which means that you cross this highway at an elevation of 8595 *feet* and at a distance of 0.8 *miles* from your last given point. In our example this is at a junction by Tuolumne Meadow Lodge. By studying these figures along the section you are hiking, you can easily determine the distance you'll have to hike from point A to point B, and you can get a good idea of how much elevation change is involved. Along this guide's *alternate routes*, which are set aside by asterisks, there are occasional second mileage figures, which represent the distance along the alternate route to that point.

In the trail description, numbers below the columns indicate what maps to refer to. This description of the route also tells something about the country you are walking through—the geology, the biology (plants and animals), the geography, and sometimes a bit of history.

In the descriptions, an *alternate route* is a trail segment that the authors think is worth considering given certain circumstances. *Water access* is just that, as is *resupply access*. All these have a line of asterisks to begin them, and another at the end.

Within the trail descriptions, text printed in *italic type* and bracketed by black rectangles, ▮ *like this* ▮, is not part of the trail description, but rather is about something like geology or biology, and can be skipped if you want to read only the trail description. Exception: if material that would otherwise be in italic type occurs between a pair of asterisk lines, it is printed in roman type (for example, an embedded book title).

Following the Trail

The route of the PCT is mostly along trail tread, but occasionally it is along a stretch of road. Except where the trail tread may momentarily die out, there is no cross-country, although early-season hikers may go miles on snow, when accurate route finding becomes imperative. Quite naturally, you want to stay on the route. For that purpose, we recommend relying on the route description and maps in this book. To be sure, there are various markers along the route—PCT emblems and signs, California Riding and Hiking Trail posts and signs, metal in the shape of diamonds and discs nailed to tree trunks, plastic ribbons tied to branches, and blazes and ducks. (A blaze is a place on a tree trunk where bark has been removed. Typically a blaze is about 4–6 inches in its dimensions. A duck is a small rock placed on a very large boulder or a pile of several small rocks whose placement is obviously unnatural.)

Our route descriptions depend on these markers as little as possible because they are so ephemeral. They get destroyed by loggers, packers, motorbikers, hikers, wilderness purists, bears and other agents. Furthermore, the blazes or ducks you follow, not having any words or numbers, may or may not mark the trail you want to be on.

One way to find a junction is to count mileage from the previous junction. If you know the length of your stride, that will help. We have used yards for short horizontal distances because one yard approximates the length of one long stride. Alternatively, you can develop a sense of your ground speed. Then, if it is 2 miles to the next junction and your speed is 3 miles and hour, you should be there in ⅔ hour, or 40 minutes. Be suspicious if you reach an unmarked junction sooner or later than you expect. We go to great lengths to describe the terrain so that you can be alerted to upcoming junctions. For example, along Lake Aloha in Section K, we mention a pond found 150 yards before a trail junction. Without this visual clue you could easily miss the junction in early season, when snow still obscures many parts of the trail.

The Maps

Each section contains all the topographic strip maps you'll need to hike that part of the California PCT. All these maps are at a scale of 1:50,000, or about 0.8 mile per inch, and all are aligned with north at the top. On the maps the PCT route appears as a solid black line where it exists as a trail and as a dashed black line where it exists along roads. The legend below lists most of the symbols you'll see on this guide's topographic maps.

At the end of the introductory material for each chapter is a list of the 7½′ U.S.G.S. topographic maps that cover the section.

LEGEND FOR TOPOGRAPHIC MAPS

Heavy-duty road	▬▬▬	PCT route along trails	▬▬▬
Medium-duty road	▬▭▬	PCT route along roads	▬ ▬ ▬ ▬
Improved light-duty road	══════	Year-round streams	▬▬▬
Unimproved dirt road	========	Seasonal streams	▬ ⋯ ▬
Jeep road or trail	--------		
Railroad: single track	⊢—⊢—⊣		
Railroad: multiple track	⫢═⊣═⊣	Scale of maps 1:50,000	

I ———————— O ———————— I MILE

LEGEND FOR SECTION MAPS

PCT route	▬▬▬	Mountain peak	△
Other trail	- - - - -	Pass	)(
Paved road	▬▬▬	Ranger Station	⸸
Secondary road	▬▬▬	Spring	℺
Park/wilderness boundary	▬·▬·▬··	Structure	▲
River/creek	〜	Town	■
Topographic map page	H10		

California PCT Mileage Table

Start/*Section*/End	S→N	Section Length	N→S
Mexican border near Campo 0.0			1723.3
Section A 110.6			
Highway 79 southwest of Warner Springs 110.6			1612.7
Section B 101.4			
near Interstate 10 in San Gorgonio Pass 212.0			1511.3
Section C 132.7			
Interstate 15 near Cajon Pass 344.7			1378.6
Section D 110.2			
Agua Dulce near Antelope Valley Freeway 454.9			1268.4
Section E 108.8			
Highway 58 near Tehachapi Pass 563.7			1159.6
Section F 84.1			
Highway 178 at Walker Pass 647.8			1075.5
Section G 113.5			
John Muir Trail junction 761.3			962.0
Section H 177.2			
Highway 120 in Tuolumne Meadows 938.5			784.8
Section I 76.4			
Highway 108 at Sonora Pass 1014.9			708.4
Section J 76.2			
Echo Lake Resort near Highway 50 .... 1091.1			632.2
Section K 63.7			
trailhead-parking lateral near Interstate 80 .... 1154.8			568.5
Section L 38.4			
Highway 49 near Sierra City 1193.2			530.1
Section M 91.7			
Highway 70 at Belden Town bridge 1284.9			438.4
Section N 134.4			
Burney Falls in Burney Falls State Park 1419.3			304.0
Section O 82.9			
Interstate 5 near Castle Crags State Park 1502.2			221.1
Section P 99.8			
Somes Bar-Etna Road at Etna Summit 1602.0			121.3
Section Q 56.8			
Highway 96 at Seiad Valley 1658.8			64.5
Section R 64.5			
Interstate 5 near Mt. Ashland Road 20 .... 1723.3			0.0

18 Trail Chapters

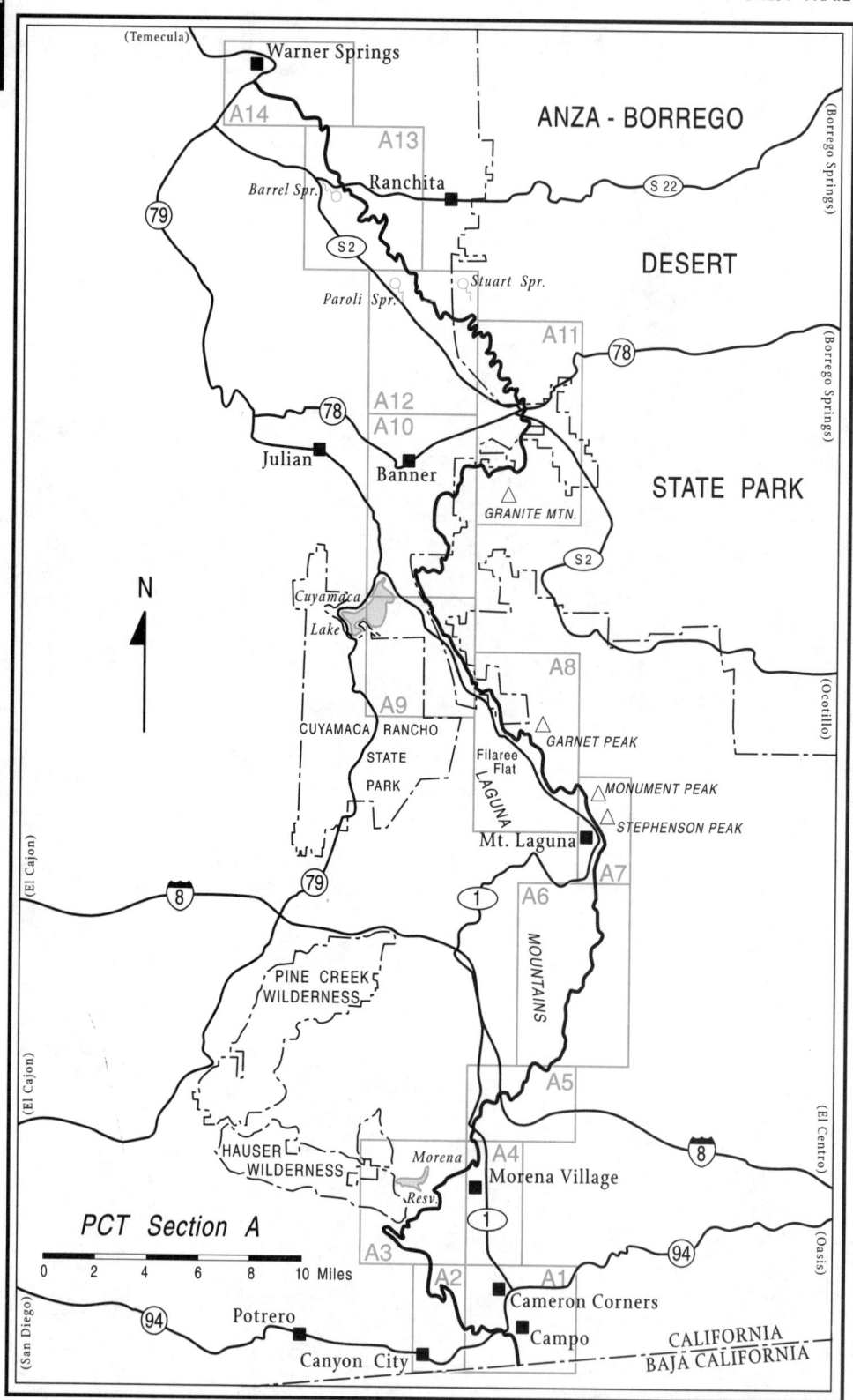

(Temecula)
Warner Springs
A14
A13
ANZA - BORREGO
S 22
(Borrego Springs)
Barrel Spr.
Ranchita
79
S 2
DESERT
Stuart Spr.
Paroli Spr.
A11
78
(Borrego Springs)
A12
78
A10
Julian
Banner
STATE PARK
GRANITE MTN.
S 2
N
Cuyamaca
Lake
(Ocotillo)
A8
A9
GARNET PEAK
CUYAMACA RANCHO
Filaree
Flat
STATE
MONUMENT PEAK
(El Cajon)
PARK
LAGUNA
STEPHENSON PEAK
Mt. Laguna
A7
8
79
A6
1
(El Cajon)
MOUNTAINS
PINE CREEK
WILDERNESS
A5
(El Centro)
8
HAUSER
A4
Morena
WILDERNESS
Resv.
Morena Village
94
PCT Section A
1
(Oasis)
A3
A2
A1
0   2   4   6   8   10 Miles
Cameron Corners
(San Diego)
94
Potrero
Campo
CALIFORNIA
Canyon City
BAJA CALIFORNIA

Section A
Mexican Border to Warner Springs

Introduction: Belying later grandeur, the Pacific Crest Trail begins in scraggly, rather unimpressive chaparral that ill fits most Americans' mental images of our southwest borderlands. Although cacti and sand are encountered often, and late-spring and summer temperatures frequently rise above 100°, the PCT in this section does not traverse true desert, but rather keeps just west of the searing Colorado Desert—which you often glimpse—passing through an area influenced by moist Pacific Ocean air. In fact, at the time when most long-distance hikers will be traversing the southernmost part of the PCT, in April and May, they are quite likely to encounter late-season snowstorms while climbing into the Laguna Mountains. In the Lagunas, which are a fault-block range of granitic rock closely related to the Sierra Nevada geologically, walkers might forget sun and thirst while walking beneath shady oaks and pines also similar to those found in the Sierra. But the next day, as they swoop down to San Felipe Valley, the stifling heat returns as the route enters Anza-Borrego Desert State Park and the Colorado Desert. The furnace breath of this arid land above the Salton Sea follows you as you traverse the San Felipe Hills to Warner Springs.

Declination: 13°E

Points on Route	S→N	Mi. Btwn. Pts.	N→S
Mexican border	0.0		110.6
		1.3	
Campo, near Border Patrol station	1.3		109.3
		18.9	
Lake Morena County Park	20.2		90.4
		5.9	
Boulder Oaks Campground	26.1		84.5
		6.7	
Fred Canyon Road to Cibbets Flat Campground	32.8		77.8
		4.2	
Long Canyon	37.0		73.6
		4.6	
Burnt Rancheria Campground	41.6		69.0
		1.3	
Stephenson Peak Road to Mt. Laguna	42.9		67.7
		4.8	
Sunrise Highway near Laguna Campground	47.7		62.9
		5.3	
Pioneer Mail Picnic Area	53.0		57.6
		8.6	
jeep track to Cuyamaca Reservoir	61.6		49.0
		2.4	
detour to water in upper Chariot Canyon	64.0		46.6
		4.9	
Rodriguez Spur Truck Trail: detour to spring	68.9		41.7
		9.2	
Hwy 78 in San Felipe Valley, near Sentenac Cienega	78.1		32.5
		23.8	
Barrel Spring	101.9		8.7
		8.7	
Highway 79 southwest of Warner Springs	110.6		0.0

Supplies: Last-minute supplies may be bought in Campo, 1.2 miles along the walk. It has a small store, a laundromat and a railroad museum. Sophisticated camping items still needed must be bought in San Diego before starting out. You can reach Campo via public transit by first taking a city bus from San Diego to El Cajon, then taking a Southeastern Rural Bus, which runs daily, to Campo. Morena Village, with a small store and cafe, lies 0.3 mile off route at Lake Morena County Park, 20 miles into the journey. Mount Laguna, a tiny mountain community with a store, post office, restaurants and motels, is the next opportunity, about 43 miles into the hike. The tourist-oriented, apple-growing ex-mining town of Julian, with stores, restaurants, lodging and post office, lies 12.5 miles west of the PCT where it strikes Highway 78 in San Felipe Valley. Julian is a welcome respite for the PCTer sporting a first set of desert-induced blisters. Borrego Springs is a desert resort community with complete supplies, motels, laundromat, and the Anza-Borrego Desert State Park headquarters, with camping and a delightful natural history museum. It is reached from two points along the PCT. From Scissors Crossing, about 78.3 miles into your journey, find Borrego Springs by hitchhiking about 5 miles east on Highway 78 to Highway S3, then heading north about 10 miles. From Highway S22 where the PCT strikes it, just north of Barrel Springs, at the 102.2-mile point of this section, hitchhike 15 miles east on S22. Warner Springs, at the end of this section, is the last supply point. This little resort community, clustered around a rejuvenating hot spring on the Aguanga Fault, has a post office and private spa but no supplies.

Water: Ground water in the dry mountains of Southern California dries up rapidly after winter's snows melt. Especially from late May through summer, hikers should not count on any water away from civilization—in Section A, this will certainly require some waterless camps and, probably, some long detours for water. Carry at least 8 liters of water per person, for each day!

In dry years, the southern California PCT's meager accompaniment of streams and springs begins to disappear. During repeated dry years, some smaller water sources remain dry, even in spring. During drought years in Section A, expect to find water only in Campo, Lake Morena County Park, Boulder Oaks Campground, Burnt Rancheria Campground, Laguna Campground and Warner Springs. Expect Hauser Creek, Cottonwood Creek, Long Canyon Creek, Chariot Canyon, Rodriguez Spur Truck Trail well, San Felipe Creek and Barrel Spring to be dry!

Conversely, years with normal or heavy precipitation will deposit heavy snows on the San Jacintos, San Bernardinos, and San Gabriels. These often pose a problem through mid-May. The higher Tehachapis, as well, routinely have over a foot of snow on northern slopes. Hence, the springtime PCT traveler must have a flexible resupply strategy, ready to load up tents, gaiters, warm parka and ice ax when needed, and to jettison them in favor of extra water bottles through the dry spells.

Walkers should carry lots of water from Mount Laguna, for it is a long, blistering 23.9 miles (including a 1.8-mile detour) to springs in Chariot Canyon. When the water tank at Pioneer Mail Trailhead Picnic Area is in operation, it will deduct 10.1 miles from this leg. An alternative to Chariot Canyon is the well on Rodriguez Spur Truck Trail, 28.1 miles beyond Mount Laguna (including a 1.3-mile detour). In either case, carry a big water container, since the next stretch to water at Barrel Springs is a mind-broiling 37.9 miles from Chariot Canyon, and 33.0 miles from Rodriguez Spur Truck Trail!

Permits: Wilderness permits are usually required for both day and overnight visits to Hauser Wilderness, through which you briefly pass early in this section. PCT trekkers, however, are exempt. Still, if you'll be heading into future wildernesses on your northward trek, then you should get a permit at the Cleveland National Forest's office—see Chapter 1's "wilderness permits" and "Federal Government Agencies."

Rattlesnakes: Few animals are more unjustly maligned in legend and in life than the western rattlesnake, and no other animal, with the possible exception of black bears (see Section I), causes more concern among walkers and riders along the California PCT.

Frequenting warmer climes generally below the red-fir belt (although they have been seen much higher), rattlers will most often be encountered basking on a warm rock, trail or pavement, resting from their task of keeping the rodent population in check. Like other reptiles, rattlesnakes are unable to control their internal body temperature (they are "cold blooded"), and therefore can venture from their underground burrows only when conditions are suitable. Just as rattlers won't usually be seen in freezing weather, it is also no surprise that they are rarely seen in the heat of day, when ground temperatures may easily exceed 150°—enough to cook a snake (or blister human feet, as many will learn). One usually will see rattlers toward evening, when the air is cool but the earth still holds enough heat to stir them from their lethargy for a night of hunting. They naturally frequent those areas where rodents feed—under brush, in rock piles, and at streamsides.

It is their nocturnal hunting equipment that has inspired most of the legends and fears concerning rattlesnakes. Rattlers have heat-sensitive pits, resembling nostrils, in their wedge-shaped heads that can sense nearby changes in temperature as subtle as 1°F. Rattlers use these pits to locate prey at night, since they do not have well-developed night vision. More important perhaps is their sensitivity to vibrations, which can alert a rattler to footfalls over 50 feet away. With such acute organs to sense a meal or danger, a rattler will usually begin to hurry away long before a hiker spots it. Furthermore, if you do catch one of these reptiles unawares, these gentlemen among poisonous snakes will usually warn you away with buzzing tail rattles if you get too close for comfort.

Like many of man's pest-control projects, his efforts to quell rattlesnake populations have been to his detriment—rattlers are invaluable controllers of agricultural pests, and fewer people are hurt each year by rattlers than by household pets. One unsuccessful program carried out in the 1960s eliminated the conspicuous, noisy rattlers and left the silent ones to breed. A population developed in which the snakes would strike without buzzing. Luckily, most rattlers encountered along your PCT way will gladly move aside without incident.

The easiest way to avoid a snake bite is to avoid snakes. Over 50 percent of rattler bites are in people who are handling a snake, and over 80 percent of all bites are on the hand. The lessons: don't catch snakes, and look before you put your hands under rocks or logs, or into tall grass. Snakes will usually graciously depart as you approach, if you make enough noise—a good reason to carry a walking stick.

If bitten, get to a hospital immediately. The only truly useful treatment for rattlesnake bite is intravenous antivenin, which can be administered in most emergency departments in southern California. The sooner it is given, the better, even if you must hike a distance for help. If you are part of a group, have the victim rest, while another hiker goes for help. Antiquated first-aid measures such as cold packs, tourniquets and incision are dangerous, and should never be used. Modern suction devices may help to remove some of the venom, but are no substitute for rapid evacuation to a hospital. Never use your mouth for suction—it won't work, and will cause infection.

Finally, some special mention should be made of one of the West's most feared vipers, the Mojave "Green" Rattlesnake. This desert denizen may be encountered in many places along the southern California PCT. Thankfully, it, like other rattlers, is not aggressive. Its real danger is the lack of early symptoms of envenomation in its victims. These are delayed for the first 6–12 hours after a strike. This quiescent period may be followed by severe neurologic symptoms and shock, too late for treatment. Hence, all victims of rattler bite are urged to get immediate medical attention. No special treatment is needed for a Mojave Rattler bite—one type of antivenin treats all North American pit viper cases.

Maps: *Campo*   *Julian*
        Potrero   *Earthquake Valley*
        Morena Reservoir   *Tubb Canyon*
        Cameron Corners   *Ranchita*
        Mount Laguna   *Hot Springs Mountain*
        Monument Peak   *Warner Springs*
        Cuyamaca Peak

The Route

State Highway 94 leads 50 miles east from San Diego to Campo, where one turns south on Forrest Gate Road, which in one block passes a U.S. Border Patrol station, where hikers should check in. The pavement ends beyond Rancho del Campo, and you continue south up the graded road. It jogs east at Castle Rock Ranch, turns south at a **T** junction with a poorer road, then climbs moderately along a telephone line. After passing under a 500 KV powerline, you reach a junction with a good dirt road that parallels the Mexican border. This road is used nightly by Border Patrol officers to scout for footprints of illegal aliens. Now look uphill to the left, southeast, to see the gray PCT monument atop a low knoll at the edge of the wide, defoliated border swath. This swath has a welter of paralleling roads which run alongside the barbed-wire border fence. Walk up a short jeep road to the monument, an eight-foot-high gray wooden affair constructed of five 12x12 posts, and capped with the soon-to-be familiar delta-shaped PCT emblem. An inscription reads, SOUTHERN TERMINUS PACIFIC CREST NATIONAL SCENIC TRAIL. ESTABLISHED BY ACT OF CONGRESS ON OCTOBER 2, 1968. MEXICO TO CANADA 2627 MILES. 1988 A.D. ELEVATION 2915 FEET. Sign the register on the back of the monument, then turn north and start your adventure (2915-0.0).

▌ *Your first vistas north show the steep southern flanks of the Laguna Mountains on the northern horizon, while the low green dome of Hauser Mountain stands in the northwest. The prominent orange buttresses of Morena Butte overlook its northern shoulder.* ▌

To find the start of the PCT, look due north, downhill from the monument to a lone 12-foot-high scrub oak, just left (west) of the road you just came up, and immediately north of the grassy defoliated border strip. Next to it is a gray sign at the actual start of the trail tread. It announces: PACIFIC CREST TRAIL: LAKE MORENA 19.5 MILES. The PCT's obvious trail tread starts, heading north, downhill into high brush. A sandy descent curves to parallel the access road. In a few minutes, you pass under the San Diego Gas and Electric powerline and walk northeast across a poor road (2810-0.4) that subserves the line. Continue gently down, just east of the access road, in a low, arid chaparral of chamise, sagebrush, ribbonwood and yucca, which is punctuated with protruding boulders of bonsall tonalite—a light gray granitic rock—and white popcorn flowers. In minutes, descent ends as you cross another dirt road (2710-0.3), then, the way marked by 4x4 posts, swing west on the edge of a large dry meadow, dotted with mustard and large canyon live oaks. Look for

See map A1

posts to indicate the way, since the tread is poorly defined. Just west of the entrance to Castle Rock Ranch, you step across Forrest Gate Road (2710-0.1) to its west side, where you wind and undulate easily above the now-paved road through stands of feathery, stringy-barked ribbonwood and around granitic blocks. Soon, you note the buildings and exercise yards of Ranchos del Campo and del Rayo—cavalry camps in World War I but now San Diego County boys' camps. Marked by a post, the path dips to merge with the paved road shoulder across from their entrances. Walk along the road's west shoulder, going north for 250 yards, past a cluster of tan-pink bungalows. Just across from Rancho del Reyo's entrance, and just up Forrest Gate Road from the Border Patrol Station, trail tread resumes and veers left, northwest, away from the roadside (2600-0.5), via three old concrete steps.

* * * *

Resupply access: Before heading off on the PCT, be sure you are adequately provisioned, since the next certain water is at Lake Morena County Park, 18.9 miles away. A post office lies only 2 blocks north, in sleepy, agricultural Campo. A good store lies 0.3 mile north, at the junction of Forrest Gate Road and Highway 94. The next supply point is in Mount Laguna, about 41.6 miles away.

* * * *

Now turning your attention to the trail, you climb gently from the road, pass a lone live-oak tree, momentarily reach a terrace and then cut obliquely across a road serving the bunga-lows. Beyond, the sandy path climbs minimally across a brushy slope, then swings southwest at an overlook of Highway 94 and Campo Valley. Paralleling the highway, the PCT undulates over a string of low ridges, comes close to a descending jeep road, then descends easily to a PCT-posted crossing (2475-1.0) of two-lane Highway 94. North of it, the PCT leads coun-terclockwise around a low hill, then descends into a grove of cottonwoods alongside Campo Creek. Just before crossing that attractive, but seasonal, stream on a log telephone-pole bridge built in spring 1994 by PCT Association vol-unteers, you ignore a jeep road climbing south.

Instead, you follow PCT posts to the northwest bank, then traverse southwest on an alluvial terrace for a few minutes. Presently the route veers uphill, soon to find the abandoned San Diego & Arizona Eastern Railroad's tracks (2475-0.6). You have a gentle ascent as you continue over the tracks and wind westward over the nose of a low ridge. Now in a maze of small gullies and waist-high chamise chapar-ral, the tread descends gently to a larger ravine, which is just north of the tracks. Here the cool shade of willows and cottonwoods, with an un-derstory of mint and cattails, makes a pictur-esque lunch spot. Alas, the creeklet here flows only in winter and early spring.

After momentarily coming close to the tracks again, you undertake a longer but still easy climb northwest to a low gap. A minute's walk beyond it, you strike a poor jeep road (2550-2.2), which descends in a south-trending val-ley. Now climbing more in earnest, you swing southwest on Hauser Mountain's broad, sunny slopes, then switchback to find a north-ascend-ing line. The well-built, alternately sandy and rocky path soon rises high enough to afford fine, clear vistas southeast back to the border, and east over a lovely ranch that lies below Hauser Mountain's eastern escarpment. Pleasant walk-ing leads northwest, more or less level, then the trail abruptly switchbacks up to the south to gain a canyon rim. Here the steep slopes yield to the chaparral-covered summit dome of Hauser Mountain. The path continues south, ascending gently and then passing through a pipe gate to a little-used road (3350-3.7). Be-yond it you climb only minutes more before striking a second jeep road (3400-0.2). Next you undertake a contour north, and you can see your trail snaking ahead for over a mile. Ump-teen hillside ravines later, you step across an east-descending jeep road (3345-2.0) before winding up to a viewful point (3400-0.5) low on the northeast ridge of Hauser Mountain. ∎ *To the north and west, an impressive panorama of Hauser Canyon unfolds. On the northern can-yon wall stand orange granitic pillars of Morena Butte. This area now lies in one of California's smallest wilderness areas, Hauser Wilderness, created in 1984.* ∎

The trail now descends in a northwestern di-rection along the north face of Hauser Moun-tain, making a long traverse down-canyon. Presently, you note a road below you and con-

See maps A1, A2, A3

see MAP A3

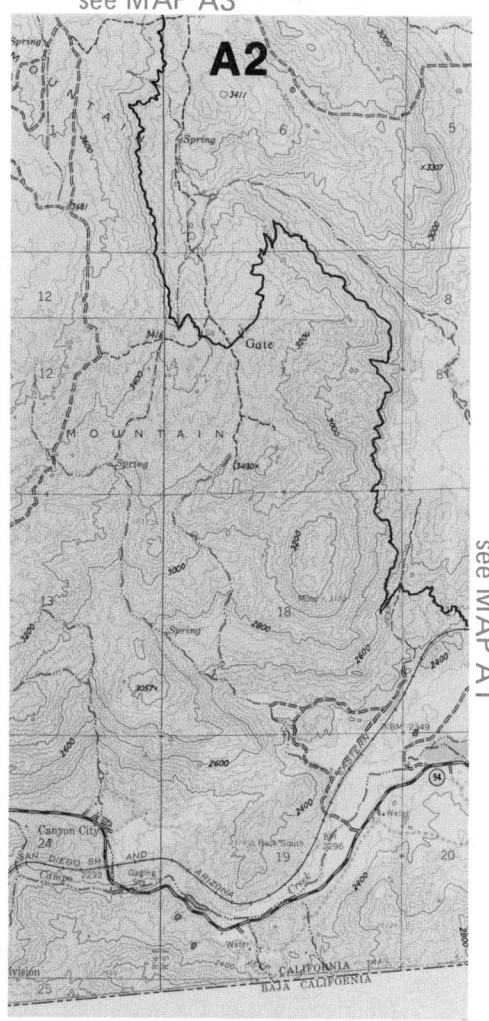

see MAP A1

tinue out onto the nose of a low ridge to meet it—South Boundary Road 17S08 (2910-2.7). The PCT route heads southeast on this little-traveled road, first climbing gently and then descending likewise to a junction (2810-0.8) with a 1988-vintage trail segment. This branches left, east, dropping rapidly from the road where it begins to bend north on a rocky hillside. To stay on public lands, but to avoid unnecessary elevation loss, the trail makes a willy-nilly, rocky descent northwestward across the canyon wall, via five switchbacks. Finally, the grade moderates to reach a pleasant glade of live oaks and sycamores. In it, the PCT crosses Hauser Creek (2320-0.7), which is usually flowing in winter and early spring, but probably dry by April of drought years. A small flat just downstream could offer the best first night's camp north of the Mexican border for those who are disinclined to make the 1,000-foot climb to reach Lake Morena County Park. However, beware of cattle pollution of the stream and of plentiful poison oak.

Just across Hauser Creek you find Hauser Creek Road, then cross it to begin an earnest, sweaty ascent of the southern slopes of Morena Butte. The first leg of this climb lies in the southeastern corner of Hauser Wilderness, and it consists of a moderate-to-steep grade through straggly chaparral. As the climb progresses, vistas unfold down-canyon to meadows and to sky-blue Barrett Lake, which is framed by the bluffs of nearby Morena Butte. Switchbacks long and short eventually bring you to a saddle (3210-1.3) on the granitic southeastern spur of Morena Butte. Now the PCT undertakes a traversing descent north, shortly joining and then leaving a jeep trail (3150-0.2), which climbs more directly up from Hauser Canyon. Beyond it, you wind for a minute or two along a dry creek bed, then step across its sandy wash to climb moderately north, then east, through lush mixed chaparral. In spring, the heavy perfume of startling lilac-blue ceanothus shrubs hangs heavy in the air, while a number of red-and-yellow-flowered globe mallows line the trailside. After reaching a low ridgecrest, you climb southeast a bit to a fair viewpoint (3495-1.0), which gives panoramas north over the southern Laguna Mountains.

Now you drop gently east to find a good jeep road in a saddle (3390-0.3). Walk right, east, on

the jeep road for 50 yards, then leave it to angle first northeast and then north along a viewful, outcrop-strewn ridge. Eventually the route veers northwest down a chaparral-cloaked nose, then leaves the heights for a descending traverse east to an oak grove and a gate in a barbed-wire fence at the corner of Lake Morena Road and Lakeshore Drive (3065-1.7). Just north is the entrance to Lake Morena County Park. This large facility offers, for a fee, 90 campsites with showers, water, picnic areas, and angling for bass, bluegill and catfish in Morena Reservoir. A trailhead parking area and a lateral trail ½ mile west to primitive camping are planned for the

See map A3

see MAP A4

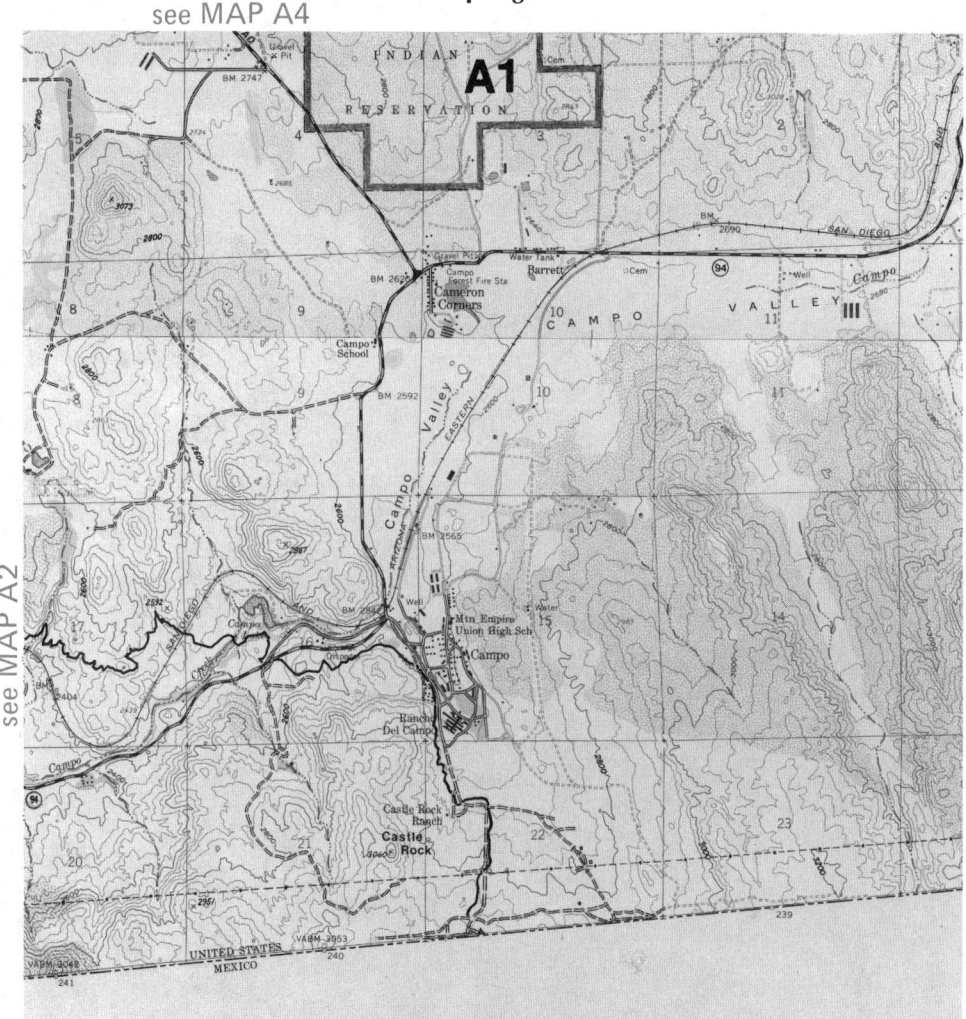

see MAP A2

future. Just 0.3 mile southeast on Lake Morena Road is a malt shop and grocery store.

The PCT continues from the corner of the two paved roads, following Lakeshore Drive north 80 yards to where one steps through a fence to follow a dirt road that traces the campground's perimeter. Beyond the camp area the route becomes trail and continues north to an oak-shaded overlook of Morena Reservoir and its chaparral-cloaked basin. Now walk levelly east and north around the lakeshore. Only 0.1 mile from the campground, ignore some prominent but rapidly fading paths that fishermen use to continue along the lakeshore. Rather, just after

passing below the last house built in an adjacent cul-de-sac to the east, head right, northeast, uphill through a gated barbed-wire fence, onto a sandy rolling upland, clothed in waist-high chemise scrub. The route next crosses many jeep tracks in the open chamise chaparral as it turns east, then northeast, climbing gently to a low ridgetop (3220-1.5). Now the way drops northeast into a nearby secluded, oak-shaded canyon, hops its seasonal creek, and climbs moderately east, then southeast, to gain a 3375-foot ridge with expansive vistas west over the reservoir, Morena Butte and Hauser Mountain. The Laguna Mountains are seen on

See maps A3, A4

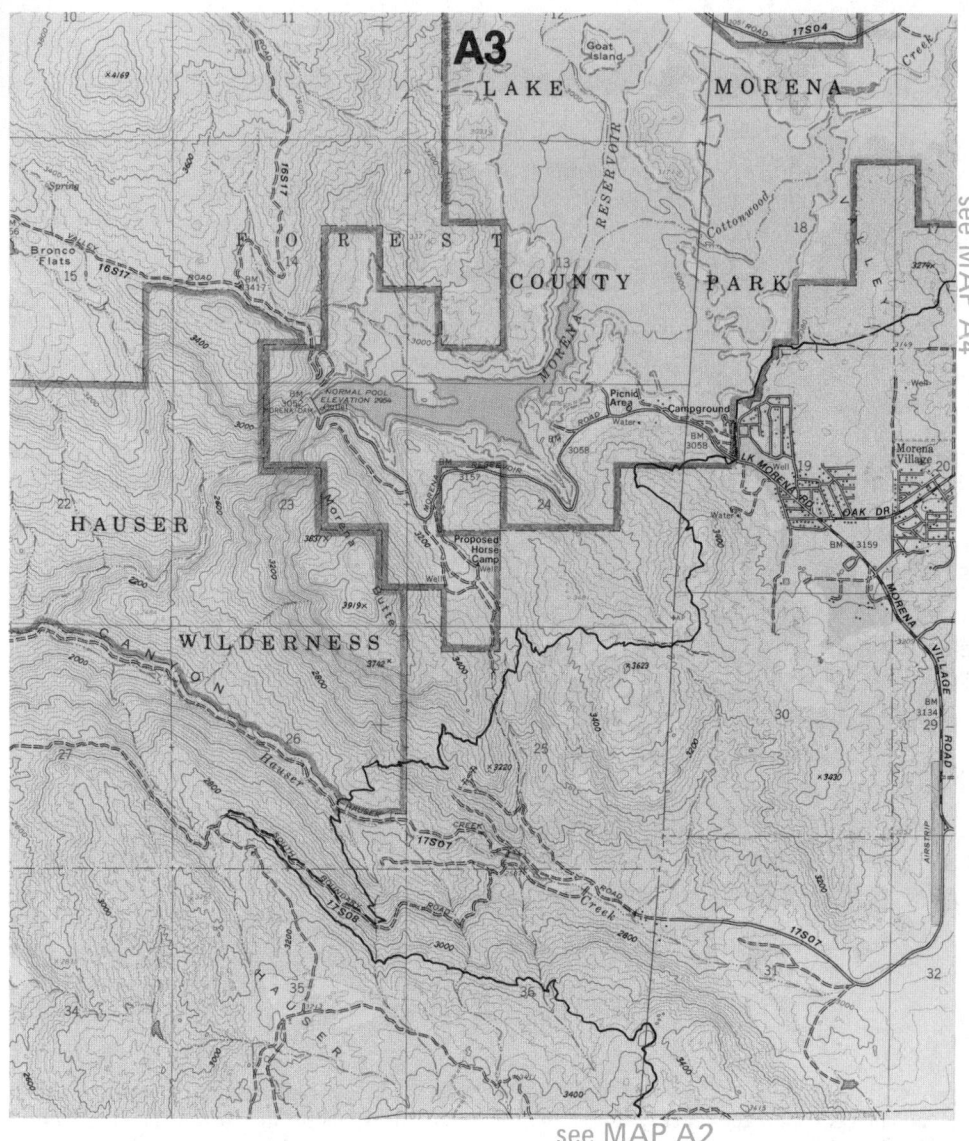

see MAP A4

see MAP A2

the northern skyline. You romp easily north on the spine of the ridge in mixed chaparral. After a mile the route makes a traversing descent along the ridge's west flank to a switchback, then to a gate on the ridge's northern nose. You quickly reach Buckman Springs Road S1, which you parallel briefly to its bridge over Cottonwood Creek (3065-2.6), which may be dry by April of drought years. The PCT's ford of the seasonally swollen creek may be too deep. If so, use the road's bridge and drop off

its west end to find the PCT—an abandoned road. You can camp here, although grazing cattle may have contaminated the creek.

Continuing north, PCT trail tread soon diverges from the roadbed to wind through a pleasant mile of oak stands and dry meadows, always within earshot of Buckman Springs Road. Abruptly the route then veers east and descends to the 0.1-mile wide, sandy-gravelly bed of Cottonwood Creek (3105-1.4). Dry most of the year, the creek in winter and spring may

See maps A4, A5

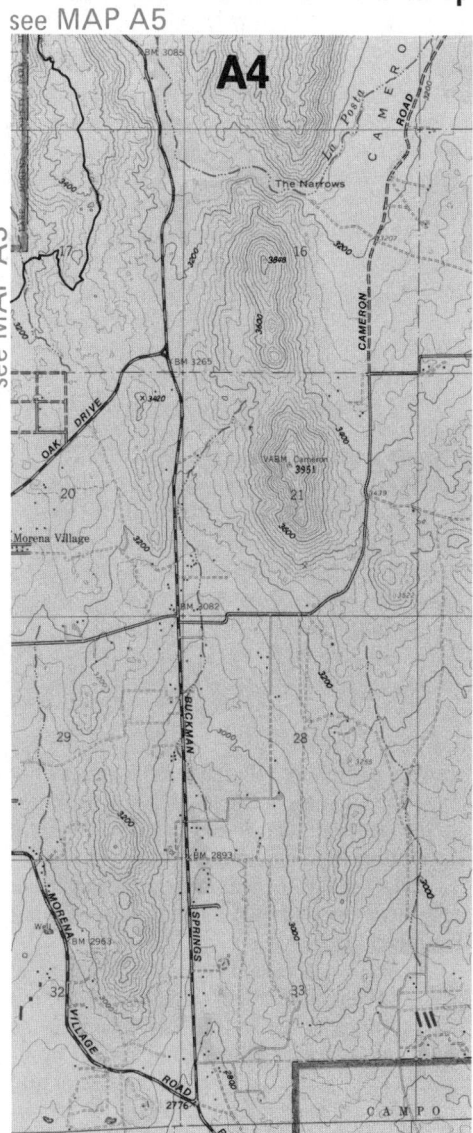

see MAP A3

2-lane Boulder Oaks Road (3165-0.1) just south of the campground's entrance. Now walk north along the road's west shoulder to small Boulder Oaks Store (3150-0.3), which offers snack items and limited supplies. (The US Forest Service is currently locked in a court battle with the owners of the Boulder Oaks complex. The store and adjacent mobile-trailer park may close in the future.)

The PCT resumes opposite the store, leading east. Soon the route leads north and then east under two concrete spans of Interstate Highway 8. Just beyond the second bridge, switchbacks climb south to an ascending traverse that heads to a brushy gap. Here the route turns northeast for a long, traversing climb on open, sometimes rocky slopes, eventually finding a position some 100 feet above the cool, pooling early-season flow of Kitchen Creek. Arcing north around Peak 4382, you then switchback up, east, to find paved Kitchen Creek Road (3990-3.8) on a viewful pass.

The northbound PCT from atop the pass is found beyond a firebreak east of the pavement. Panoramas expand back to the Mexican border and to Cameron Valley as one ascends gently-to-moderately along slopes composed of foliated, red-stained gneiss, colored in season with blossoms of white forget-me-nots. After leveling off momentarily on a 4310-foot saddle, the trail drops, flanked by nodding, brown-flowered peonies and mixed chaparral, to a glade of oaks beside the usually dry creek of Fred Canyon (4205-1.9). Now on the west side of the canyon, the trail ascends to Fred Canyon Road 16S08 (4410-0.6), which descends 0.8 mile northwest to Cibbets Flat Campground with toilets, tables and water.

Now the path climbs moderately in heavy ceanothus/ocean spray/chamise cover, switchbacking once around a nose and then climbing to a traverse past Peak 5036 over to the dry headwaters of Fred Canyon. Next the PCT gains 500 feet, passes a jeep trail east to Fred Canyon Road, and then makes an undulating traverse and a gentle descent into Long Canyon (5230-4.2), where a camp could be made beside a seasonally trickling creek near wild roses. A gentle ascent in this pretty, meadowed canyon, dotted with black oaks, finds a ford (5435-0.8) of Long Canyon creek, followed by switchbacks and two crossings of a jeep road

be flowing and may be a couple of yards wide. Across it the trail heads east up a ravine, then joins a steadily improving and climbing jeep road that leads through a gate and over a low ridge to reach the equestrian section of Boulder Oaks Campground (3170-0.4). This pleasant and little-used facility offers picnic tables, piped water, toilets and horse corrals among boulders and shady live oaks. Marked by posts the PCT winds east across the campground, then momentarily goes north to reach paved,

See maps A5, A6

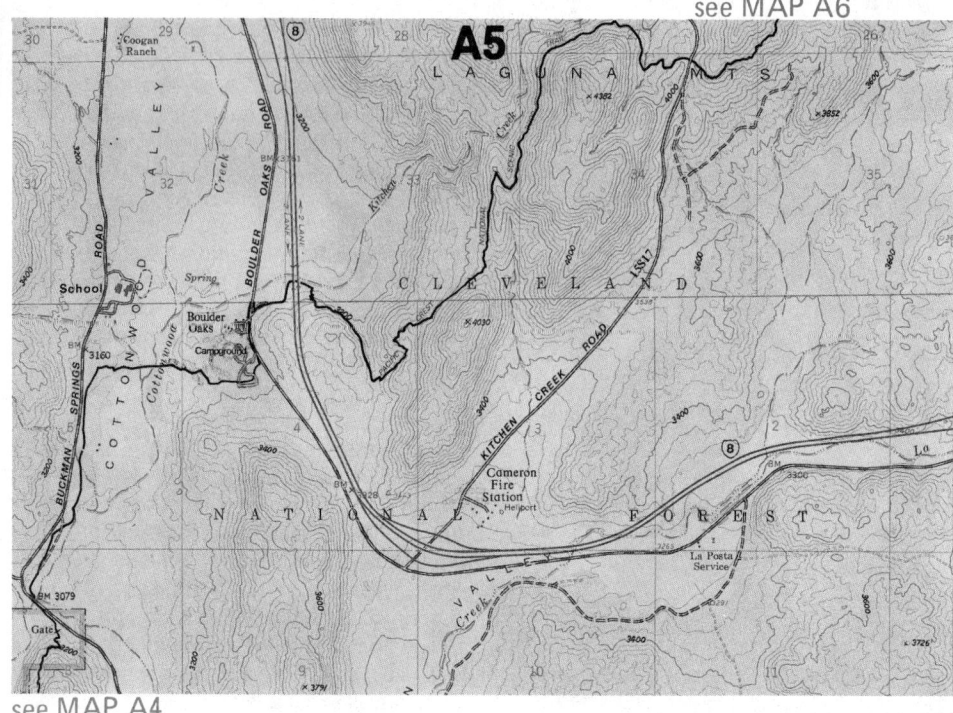

see MAP A4

from Horse Meadow. At the second crossing (5900-1.1) you could follow the jeep road northwest 0.3 mile to pretty Lower Morris Meadow, which has a horse-trough spring and a cozy cluster of Jeffrey pines—the best camp so far. The USFS plans an equestrian/backpacker trail camp here in the future.

Climbing still into the relatively cool Laguna Mountains proper, you alternate between mountain mahogany and Jeffrey-pine/black-oak forest to cross a saddle, then descend slightly to a crossing of Morris Ranch Road (6005-1.2). A few minutes north of the crossing of Morris Ranch Road, the undulating duff-treaded path intersects, then for 80 yards ambles along, a jeep road under open cover of Jeffrey pines and black oaks, before clearly branching away to descend. A few minutes' walk leads you to cross a much better road (5825-0.7) beside shaded La Posta Creek. ∎ *Here you'll see outstanding examples of acorn-woodpecker food caches—custom-built niches for individual black-oak and interior-live-oak acorns in Jeffrey pine bark. When tasty insect larvae hatch in the stored acorns, the birds return to feast!* ∎ Leaving La Posta Creek, the route contours

above a pumphouse that in the future may become the site of a backpacker camp. Trekkers should be aware that in the Laguna Mountain Recreation Area camping is restricted to designated sites. The recreation area stretches from near this site north 10.4 miles to Pioneer Mail Trailhead Picnic Area.

Your trail ascends into the recreation area, passing abandoned wood-rat nests and the first pinyon pines of the trail before reaching the south boundary of Burnt Rancheria Campground (5950-0.8). This has toilets, water and tables. ∎ *Cattlemen invaded the Laguna Mountains in the later 1800s, fattening their herds to the displeasure of the natives, called "Dieguenos" by the Spanish padres. The natives attested to their dislike of the white man's invasion by burning down a seasonal ranch house—whence the name "Burnt Rancheria."* ∎ Northbound hikers should know that the next water lies in Chariot Canyon, a 1.8-mile detour from the PCT after a long, usually too warm, 22.4-mile trek. Less reliable water is found at Pioneer Mail Trailhead Picnic Area, 10.1 miles north.

Climbing away from the campground, the

See maps A6, A7

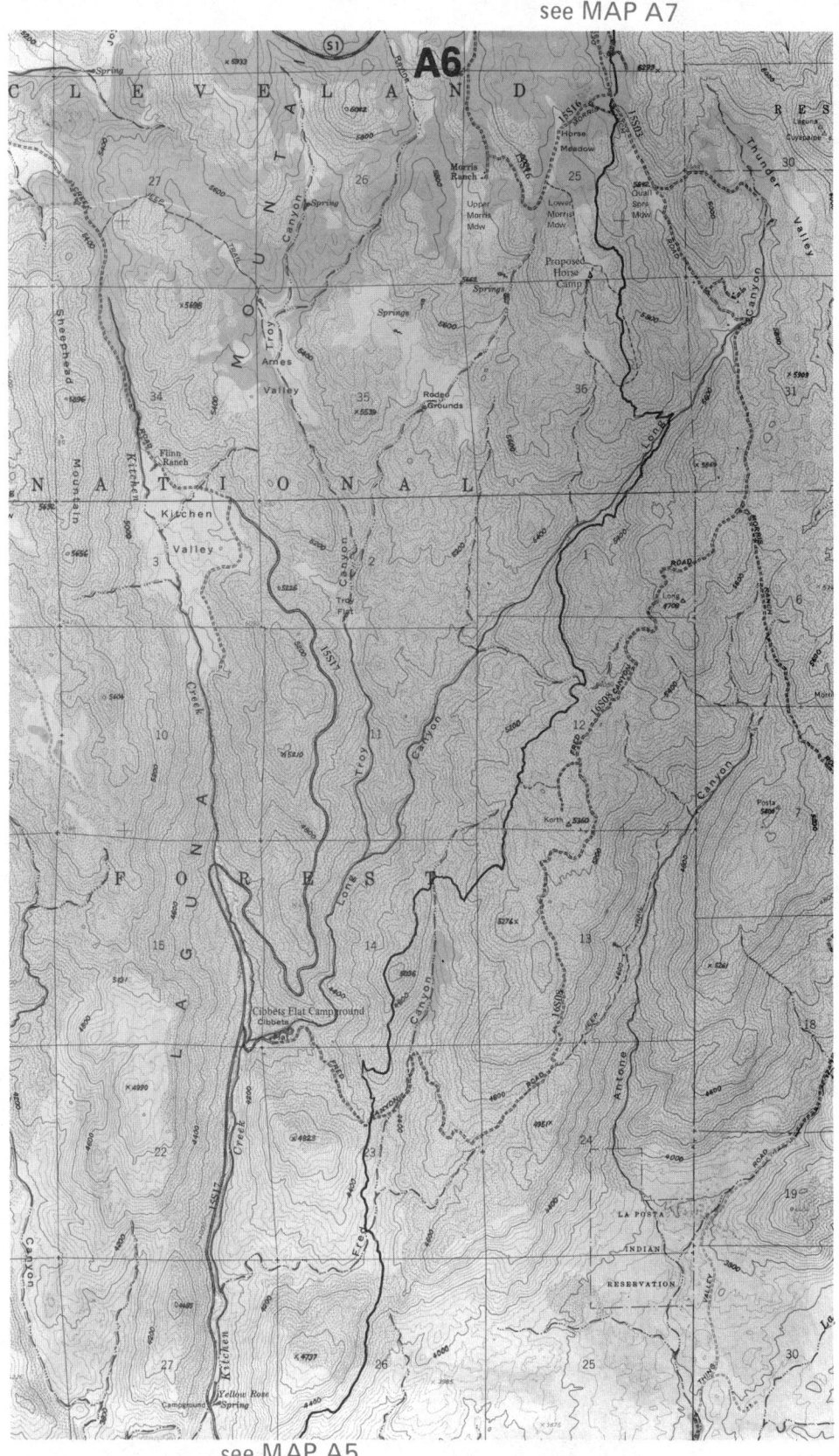

see MAP A9

see MAP A7

PCT does double-duty as the Desert View Nature Trail, passing live-forever, pearly everlasting, thistle, yerba santa and beavertail cacti, all of them xeric (drought-tolerant) plants that reflect your proximity to the searing Colorado Desert to the east. Bending north and passing numerous, poorer side trails, your now nearly level path leads back into restful forest, joins dirt Desert View Road, and passes a dirt-road spur leading southwest to Burnt Rancheria Campground (5970-0.6). A concrete culvert horse trough and faucet were installed here in 1993 by a group of local PCT advocates. Travelers should rely on it only during seasons when Burnt Rancheria Campground is open, from mid-May thru late October.

From here the PCT climbs north along the Desert View Nature Trail, reaching a spectacular overlook of arid Anza-Borrego Desert State Park, its floor—Vallecito Valley—lying 4400 feet below you in the rain shadow of the Laguna Mountains. *The rocks you stand on are now-familiar banded Mesozoic intrusive rocks: just to the east, a contact separates these from well-foliated pre-Cretaceous metasediments blotched with yellow lichens—a cliff on the east face of Stephenson Peak, to the north, is a good example. To your east Vallecito Valley is bedded in Pleistocene sediments, and beyond it the Tierra Blanca Mountains are composed of intrusive tonalite and the Vallecito Mountains of several-million-year-old nonmarine sediments.*

Leaving this overlook, the PCT descends into cooler black-oak forest, passes below tables of the Desert View Picnic Area, now with toilets and a faucet, and then switchbacks up to a paved road (5980-0.7), which leads to Stephenson Peak and the abandoned Mount Laguna USAF Western Air Defense Network Station.

*　　　*　　　*　　　*

Resupply access: Hikers in need of supplies can turn left on the road and walk 70 yards west to Sunrise Highway S1, and thence south 0.4 mile to Mount Laguna Post Office, a store, phones, restaurants and motels, and a Forest Service station. The next supply point along the PCT is Warner Springs, 67.7 miles away.

*　　　*　　　*　　　*

Continuing on the PCT, you have an easy traverse through high scrub and forest that lie below the golf-ball radar domes on Stephenson Peak. The traverse then ends at a second paved road (5895-0.6) climbing to the summit. Iris, snowberry, yellow violets and baby blue eyes lend springtime color to the forest floor as the route skirts north around the Air Force station's boundary. Then it crosses a succession of jeep roads, and rises moderately in huckleberry-oak, manzanita and ocean-spray chaparral below Monument Peak before dropping easily to a saddle (5900-2.0) where some jeep roads terminate.

A startling contrast of vegetation is presented when the PCT tops the next small ridge. To the east nothing but drought-tolerant, clumped shrubbery survives, while on the Laguna Mountains' summits to the west, a nearly uniform Jeffrey-pine and black-oak forest stretches from North, Cuyamaca and Stone-

see MAP A8

A7

see MAP A6

See map A7

wall peaks, in Cuyamaca Rancho State Park, over to hazy mountains above San Diego. A disparity of rainfall maintains these two different life zones, caused by the Laguna Mountains' geography. Warm, moisture-laden air sweeping inland from the Pacific Ocean cools as it rises over the obstructing Lagunas. This cooling causes moisture in the air to condense, bringing rain to nurture pine forests, and leaving parched, water-absorbing air to blast down desert slopes in the mountains' lee. ∎

Leaving this instructional vista, the PCT descends, perhaps vaguely, through a small burn, crosses bulldozer tracks that encircle it, and then turns west, descending easily into oak-shaded Flathead Flats (5715-0.9). Here an obvious patchwork of poor roads leads west for 75 yards at the head of Storm Canyon. If the tread has been vague, it will become obvious here, as the trail ascends just under a northwest-trending road, crossing that road in a moment to emerge from shade onto a chaparral-covered nose. Merging with the road, your thoroughfare narrows as it descends viewfully northwest past rock and chaparral, then turns south to switchback down to a ravine and resume a gently undulating traverse below the Sunrise Highway. In just a moment you reach a dirt spur (5440-1.3) descending from the highway.

*   *   *   *

Water access: To get water, head west up the road to the highway and take it south 0.2 mile to Laguna Campground. This is the last certain source close to your route until Cuyamaca Reservoir, 13.9 miles farther along the PCT and then 1.7 miles along a lateral. Closer but less certain water may be had during late spring and summer at Pioneer Mail Trailhead Picnic Area, in 5.3 miles. Possibly more convenient to some northbound travelers are the year-round springs in Chariot Canyon, a 1.8-mile detour from the PCT in 16.3 miles, or the well on Rodriguez Spur Truck Trail, a 1.3-mile detour from your path in 21.2 miles.

*   *   *   *

Back on route, a few minutes' walk leads to a lone switchback that raises you to a ridgetop pole-line road, which you cross westward to descend to a quiet draw and a better dirt road (5430-0.5) that descends north to Oasis Spring. After you leave this road, live and black oaks, scattered pines and mountain mahogany line the viewful way around the spectacular furnace-breathed head of Storm Canyon to reach G.A.T.R. Road (5440-0.9), on cooler, forested

See map A8

Vallecito Valley and Mountains, from south of Oasis Spring

see MAP A10

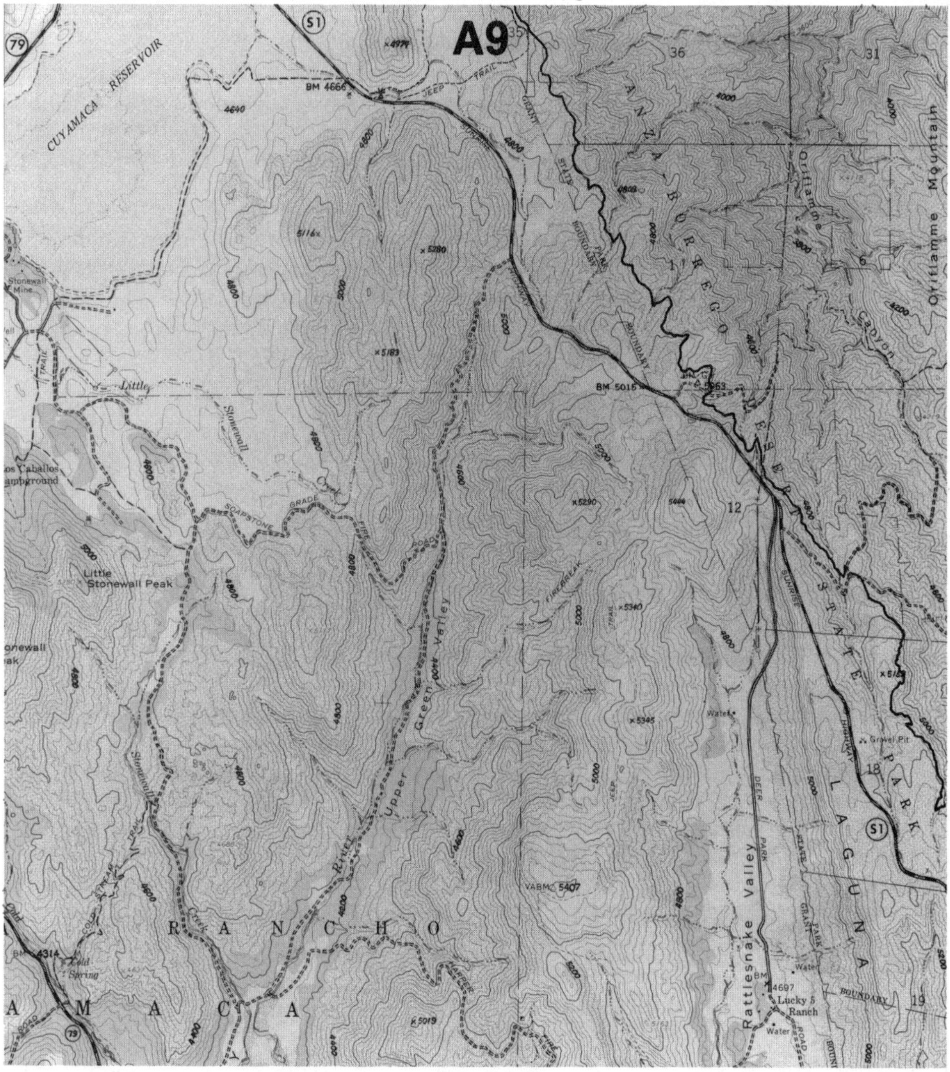

land. For many years a trailhead parking area, with water, has been planned to go here.

North across the road, the PCT soon veers east, recrossing the road to climb easily under the Lagunas' steep eastern scarp to a saddle with the end of a jeep road (5540-0.5). From it the route undulates northwest on scrub-bound slopes while keeping just above the rough jeep track. Your path crosses jeep spurs to the summits of Peak 5663 and Garnet Peak and then strikes another spur at a saddle (5495-1.6) west of Garnet Peak. The PCT next traverses around Peak 5661, passing through hoary-leaved ceanothus brush and providing excellent vis-

tas of Oriflamme Mountain to the north. Beyond, the route drops first south and then west to a sandy saddle with a grass-floored pine forest. The route then heads northwest before winding west to shaded Pioneer Mail Trailhead Picnic Area (5260-1.8), which lies at the end of a parking spur coming from Sunrise Highway. Here the PCT is signed as Laguna Rim Trail 5E08. In 1994 the USFS placed a 6-foot-in-diameter, 4-foot high aboveground 1000-gallon water tank in low brush just 50 feet beyond the trailhead information sign. It is filled only during late May and summer and only with untreated water. Find it just uphill of

See map A8

the trail. Please conserve water, and don't promote vandalism by advertising the tank's presence!

The PCT's continuation north from the picnic area follows the old, unpaved alignment of Sunrise Highway gently up across a cliff at the head of Cottonwood Canyon to meet the end of paved Kwaaymii Point Road (5450-0.7). Northbound tread recommences a few yards up this road, only 40 yards south of a defunct jeep road climbing Garnet Mountain. Now you contour on the mountain's eastern declivity and enter Cuyamaca Rancho State Park. At the mountain's north end, you drop briskly north on sunny slopes to a jeep road (5250-1.4) that descends into Oriflamme Canyon. ∎ *Oriflamme ("golden flame") Mountain, whence the canyon derives its name, received its appellation from numerous sightings, since the 1880s, of "burning balls" or "spirit lights" on the mountain's east side. These led to insistent prospecting for gold over the years, but scientists have at least one more-interesting theory—that the lights are static electricity, discharged when dry desert winds blow sand against quartz boulders on the hillside.* ∎ The next leg meanders northwestward along steep hillsides of light-colored granodiorite—weathered to futuristic knobs—and affords excellent panoramas of seemingly sterile Vallecito Valley. But these views hardly compensate for the shadeless, monotonous trail.

∎ *Vallecito Valley was once the site of a Butterfield Overland Mail Stage station. Following an old Spanish trail from Fort Yuma, stages ran from St. Louis to California from 1858 to 1861. The first Europeans to traverse this part of the Colorado Desert, however, were Spanish forces led by Lieutenant Pedro Fages from the San Diego Presidio, who marched through in search of deserters in 1772. Two years later Captain Juan Bautista de Anza, for whom the park is named, scouted this area for a life-line trail from Mexico to impoverished Alta California settlements.* ∎

Presently the route descends to meet a second road to Oriflamme Canyon (4875-2.8). Across it you climb through brush on a trail that soon closely parallels Sunrise Highway. ∎ *The rocks lining your route from here to Chariot Canyon are Julian schist—metasediments of Paleozoic age. This particular schist (a rock, once a shale, that now breaks along paper-thin parallel planes) shows abundant flecks of reflective, glassy mica, and it weathers to a rusty brown containing frequent mineral-stain bandings.* ∎ Presently you cross a ridgetop jeep road, and then another (5025-1.3).

∎ *A sweeping vista unfolds to the north; green forested Volcan Mountain stands above your unfortunate route down to arid San Felipe Valley and the brown San Felipe Hills. Beyond, Combs Mountain, Thomas Mountain and the Desert Divide rise to the rugged subalpine splendor of San Jacinto Peak. Over its west shoulder, the bald white alpine cap of San*

See maps A8, A9

Oriflamme Mountain, from west of Garnet Peak

Cameron Valley, view south from Peak 4737

Gorgonio Mountain thrusts its height—your next two weeks' work is displayed! ■ Continuing, the PCT undulates above Oriflamme Canyon to reach a faint jeep track (4770-2.4) at a low gap.

*　　*　　*　　*

Water access: Here thirsty hikers may opt to follow that track west for 1.0 mile through a verdant meadow to Sunrise Highway. There is a horse trough at the barbwire gate here, which may afford a water gift in springtime, but must not be relied on. From the highway, follow California Riding and Hiking Trail (CRHT) posts 0.7 mile west to Cuyamaca Reservoir, where long-overdue draughts of water are available. Los Caballos Campground, in Cuyamaca Rancho State Park, is 1.6 miles farther along the well-marked CRHT. It is reserved for horsemen only. Cuyamaca Rancho State Park (from the Indian "Ah-ha-kwe-ah-mac", meaning "the place where it rains") is a recommended layover spot, having cool forests, seasonally chortling streams, and campgrounds with showers. An excellent Indian cultural exhibit and the old Stonewall Mine could round out the visit.

*　　*　　*　　*

Returning to your trek, you follow the PCT as it winds north along chaparral-clothed summits to the Mason Valley Truck Trail (4690-1.1), just east of a locked gate. Northbound travelers here turn right and curve 100 yards east to a junction with Chariot Canyon Road, now barely distinguishable as a road. Emergency water is sporadically available 75 yards east of this junction, where a spigot juts out of the hillside below a concrete-box water tank used by fire crews. Don't count on it! Back on route, the PCT leads north down rocky Chariot Canyon not-a-road, on a bone-jarring descent, which ends at a lupine flat holding the canyon's seasonal creek. Fair but waterless camping may be found here, by a road junction (3860-1.3).

*　　*　　*　　*

Water access: If you are low on water, you should detour here, and continue north down Chariot Canyon Road in search of that precious desert commodity. But check upstream from the PCT before heading down-canyon to the springs—water is sometimes found there. Otherwise, walk north down the gently sloping sandy, sunny wash, passing, in a few yards, a set of native American mortars ground in a large boulder near the creek bed. Presently, you pass in and out of stands of cottonwoods and live oaks and leave Anza-Borrego Desert State Park (3700-0.6). Beyond, you begin to encounter tailings, mine tunnels and shacks of some of the many gold mines that dot Chariot Canyon. One commonly finds water in the streambed in the next quarter mile, relieving the hiker of the

See maps A9, A10

A

Mexico-
Warner Spgs.

A10

JULIAN 3 MI.

MOVOLCAN MOUNTAIN

NER CANYON

Banner

BM 2760

Banner Queen Trading Post
BM 2601

Banner

Warlock Mine Group

Pioneer Mine
McMadden Mine
Cincinnati Belle Mine
Kentucky Mine Group
Gold Cross Mine

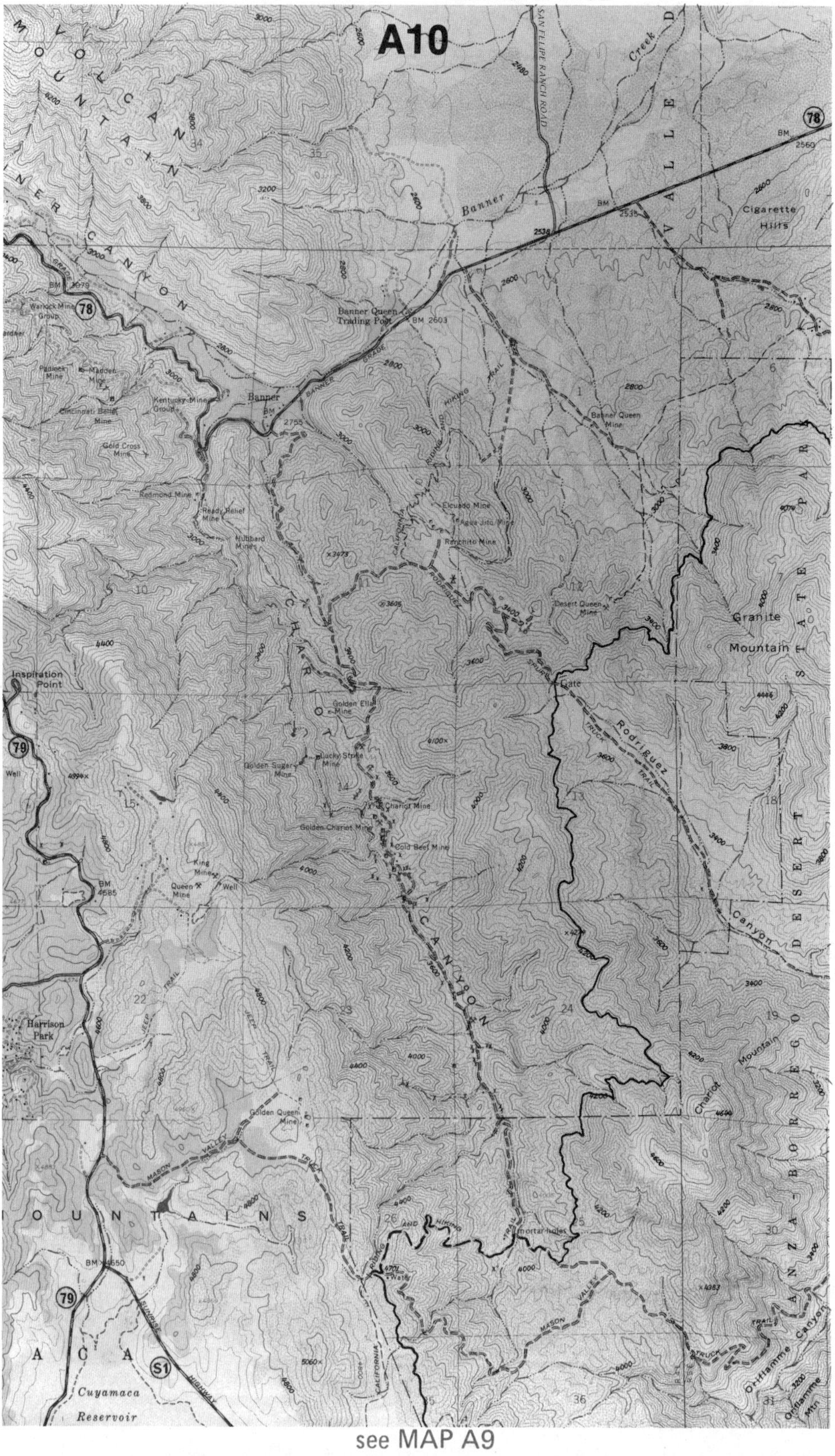

Redmond Mine
Ready Relief Mine
Hubbard Mines

Inspiration Point

Well

King Mine
Queen Mine
BM 4585

Well

Golden Ella Mine

Golden Sugar Mine

Bucky State Mine

Golden Chariot Mine
Cold Beef Mine

Harrison Park

Golden Queen Mine

MOUNTAINS

BM 4650

Cuyamaca Reservoir

SAN FELIPE RANCH ROAD

Creek

VALLEY

BM 2560

Cigarette Hills

Banner Queen Mine

Elevado Mine
Magno Jim Mine
Ranchito Mine

Desert Queen Mine

Granite Mountain

Gate

Rodriguez Canyon

ANZA BORREGO DESERT STATE PARK

Chariot

mortar holes

VALLEY

Oriflamme Canyon

see MAP A12

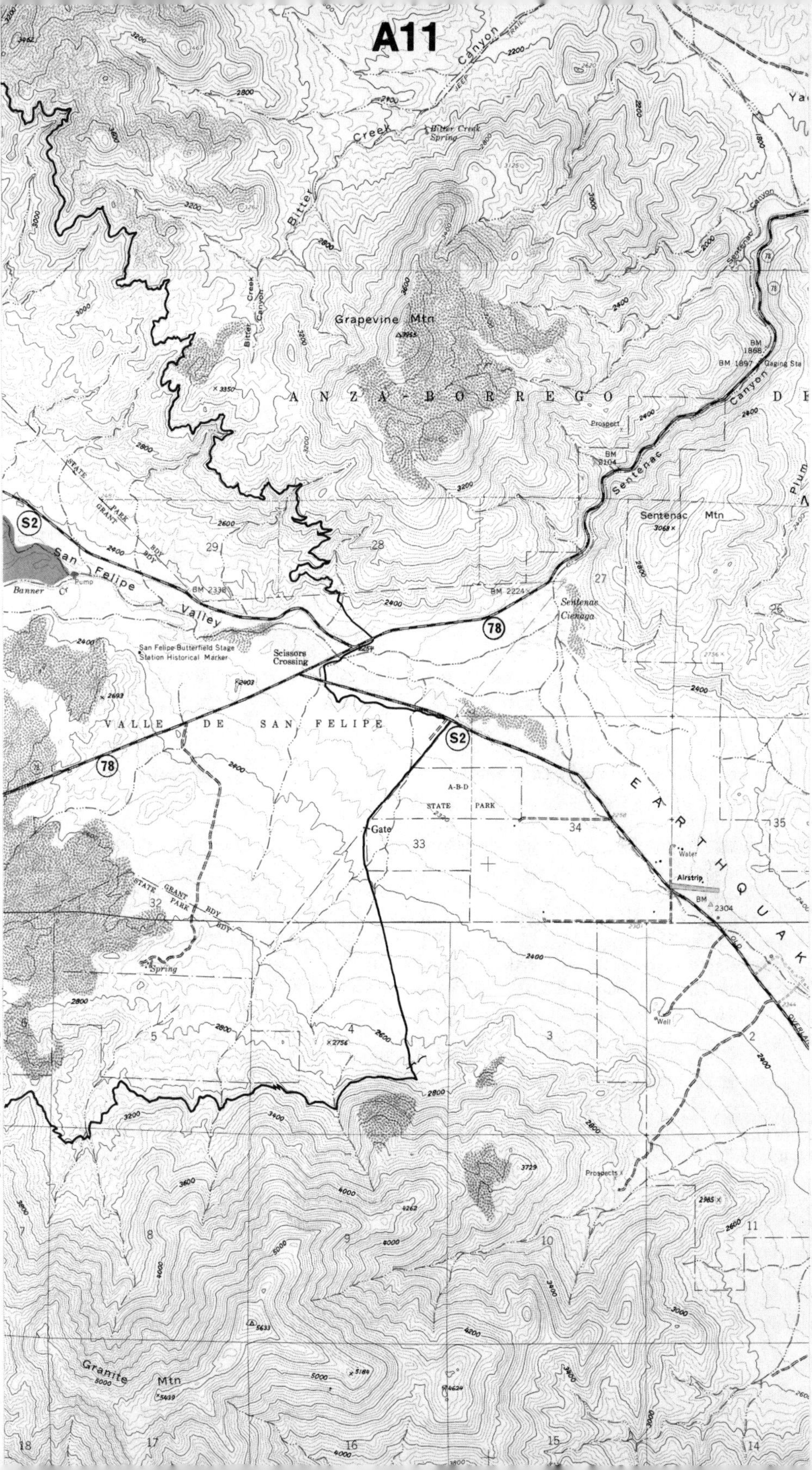

see MAP A10

full trek down to the main springs. If not, continue north, cross to the east bank, and presently find a short dirt spur road (3565-0.6). It branches right, east, uphill for 75 yards to an 18-foot-diameter, buried concrete water tank set in the hillside. This road is marked near its junction by a square concrete valve box. Water can be had from the tank by way of a 4'x18" iron plate set in its top. Camping is adequate, nearby. If water or accommodations here aren't to your liking, continue down-canyon farther, recrossing Chariot Canyon creek twice in quick succession to find permanent springs (3490-0.6), just short of dirt Ben Hur Mine Road. In severe drought years, the springs have become very close to dry.

*   *   *   *

Water access: If they are dry, continue down-canyon to one of a half-dozen active gold-mining claims, and ask for water. If that is futile, continue out to the road's end on Highway 78 at Banner (2755-3.2), a small resort with a store, restaurant, phones and camping. From there it is 7.5 miles west on Highway 78 to beautiful Julian, with complete supplies and delicious apple pie. The northbound traveler could get back on route by heading east from Banner to the PCT near Scissors Crossing, in 5 miles.

Those who return to the PCT in upper Chariot Canyon should note that their watery treasure must last a while: the well on Rodriguez Spur Truck Trail is the next near-route water for the northbound, a 1.3-mile detour from the PCT in 4.9 miles. Barrel Spring, 33.0 blistering hot miles ahead from the junction, has the next on-route water. Heading south, the next completely reliable water is at Laguna Campground, 16.3 long miles, up in the Laguna Mountains.

*   *   *   *

From the road junction in upper Chariot Canyon you climb steeply east up the Mason Valley cutoff road to a resumption of PCT trail tread (4075-0.3). This branches left, northeast, the junction perhaps marked with a brown and white state park sign. Now, a well-built tread snakes gently uphill around the western and northern slopes of rounded Chariot Mountain. Eventually the path skirts briefly northwest

along a crest saddle, veers left, and then soon veers northeast across a gap (4240-2.6). Just beyond it you get vistas southeast, down desertlike Rodriguez Canyon and into the mirage-wavering, incandescent heart of Anza-Borrego Desert State Park. Thankfully, your way continues north and skirts the hottest regions. A businesslike descent now leads down to the head of Rodriguez Canyon, where you cross Rodriguez Spur Truck Trail (3650-2.0).

*   *   *   *

Water access: Here you can detour north to an important water source: Follow Rodriguez Spur Truck Trail left, west, for a brisk descent northward. Make two big switchbacks, then turn right, east, on a dirt road spur (3410-0.9) leading in just a minute to a cream-colored clapboard house in grove of poplars. Ask for water, from a small spring and pond just uphill of the house. Alternatively, one may continue down Rodriguez Spur Truck Trail for a few minutes more to find a well (3270-0.4) just 40 feet below the road. It is 12 feet high, capped with a blue plastic barrel. A circular concrete horse trough in a small patch of irrigated grass lies just to the northwest, only yards below the road. The vicinity is private property, so no camping is allowed hereabouts.

*   *   *   *

Immediately beyond good dirt Rodriguez Spur Truck Trail, you pass through a pipe gate and angle across an east-curving jeep track, then you too swing east. A graded but persistent descent next leads northward on the steep, rocky, barren slopes of Granite Mountain, offering impressive panoramas. ∎ *North over arid San Felipe Valley, look carefully for the next leg of the PCT, which traverses along the San Felipe Hills, low on the northern horizon. In the far distance, green San Jacinto Peak and glistening, bald San Gorgonio Mountain rear above 2-mile heights. Closer by, the rusty headframes of a few old gold mines—part of the once rich Julian mining complex which caused excitement in 1869-70—lie in ravines below you.* ∎

After winding down a succession of dry slopes, the PCT turns more east and almost lev-

See maps A10, A11

els just above the gentle, brushy alluvial fans at the foot of Granite Mountain. Unfortunately, a logical, direct PCT route from here—northeast to the southern San Felipe Hills—was blocked by uncooperative landowners, who denied right-of-way to trail construction. Hence your route now makes a frustrating, hot, time-consuming detour east to remain on public lands.

First you ascend to a rocky gap (3390-3.2) on Granite Mountain's north ridge. Next you descend to cross a succession of bouldery washes, then undulate east some more to a second gap (3130-1.9) behind a prominent light-colored granitic knob. A final descent is begun on four small switchbacks, followed by a descending traverse eastward. Abruptly, near the base of a cluster of pinnacles below Granite Mountain's northeast ridge, you veer north, debouching onto a sandy alluvial plain. After quickly crossing a jeep track, you proceed almost arrow-straight across northern Earthquake Valley, imperceptibly descending through an open desert association of low buckwheat, rabbitbrush and teddy-bear cholla shrubs, these sprinkled with larger junipers and graceful agave. You eventually pass through a gate in a barbed-wire fence, then swing northeast, tracing an old jeep road that is immediately west of the fenceline. This stretch ends at busy, 2-lane Highway 52 (2245-2.9) at a spot just west of a white, wooden cattle guard.

Now locate a faint trail that turns left, west, near the south shoulder of Highway S2 just south of a 4-strand green barbed-wire fence. It winds fairly level past low shrubs, many of them equipped with murderously efficient, thigh-slashing, clothes-grabbing spines. Nearing a junction with Highway 78, find a red metal pipe gate and cross Highway S2 (2275-0.8), safe from attack by menacing vegetables, but now exposed to a considerable traffic of desert-bound vacationers. This was the route of the Butterfield Stage Line, which carried mail across the western US, passing this way in the 1850s. Now walk directly north, at first paralleling a wooden-post fence, then drifting vaguely away to the left through cat-claw shrubs, beyond which trail tread peters out as you walk down to cross a dry sandy wash. Momentarily, you emerge on a low terrace, just beneath the south shoulder of Highway 78.

Now head right, northeast, along the shrubby terrace, close beside Highway 78, to find another cattle gate adjacent to the concrete bridge where the highway spans San Felipe Creek (2250-0.2). This stream almost always runs well into summer, even during drought years, but should not be counted upon. Even when present, it is usually heavily contaminated by cattle. Just to the north of the bridge is a large cottonwood tree which could afford a fair camp. Continuing, step across San Felipe Creek's sandy bed, then resume a parallel course to Highway 78, again on a low terrace, where trail tread is often overgrown by tumbleweeds, mustard and baccharis. It was cleared of brush by PCT Association volunteers in late 1994, but the riparian shrubbery will no doubt grow back quickly. If it is too dense, simply step north onto the road shoulder, instead. In just a few minutes, we cross Highway 78 to find a resumption of PCT tread (2252-0.2). It climbs northwest, up from the highway at a junction that may be marked with a CHAINS REQUIRED sign.

* * * *

Water access: Northbound hikers should be reminded that Barrel Spring, the next possible (but not certain) waterhole, is still 23.8 potentially scorching miles away. If your water reserves are low, consider walking one mile northeast on Highway 78 to Sentenac Cienaga, a marsh along San Felipe Creek. Water is usually found here all spring. Better yet, hitchhike 5 miles southwest to Banner to refill. Southbound hikers will find water in Banner too, or near-route at Rodriguez Canyon Truck Trail, in 9.2 miles, or in Chariot Canyon, 14.1 miles hence. This is also a reasonable spot to detour for supplies as well as water—delightful and cool Julian is 12.5 miles west up Highway 78, while Borrego Springs is about 15 miles east on Highway 78.

* * * *

Commencing a long, exposed traverse of the San Felipe Hills, the PCT ascends briefly across a cobbly alluvial fan to the southern foot of Grapevine Mountain. Here you cross into Anza-Borrego Desert State Park and, now on rotten

See map A11

see MAP A13

A12

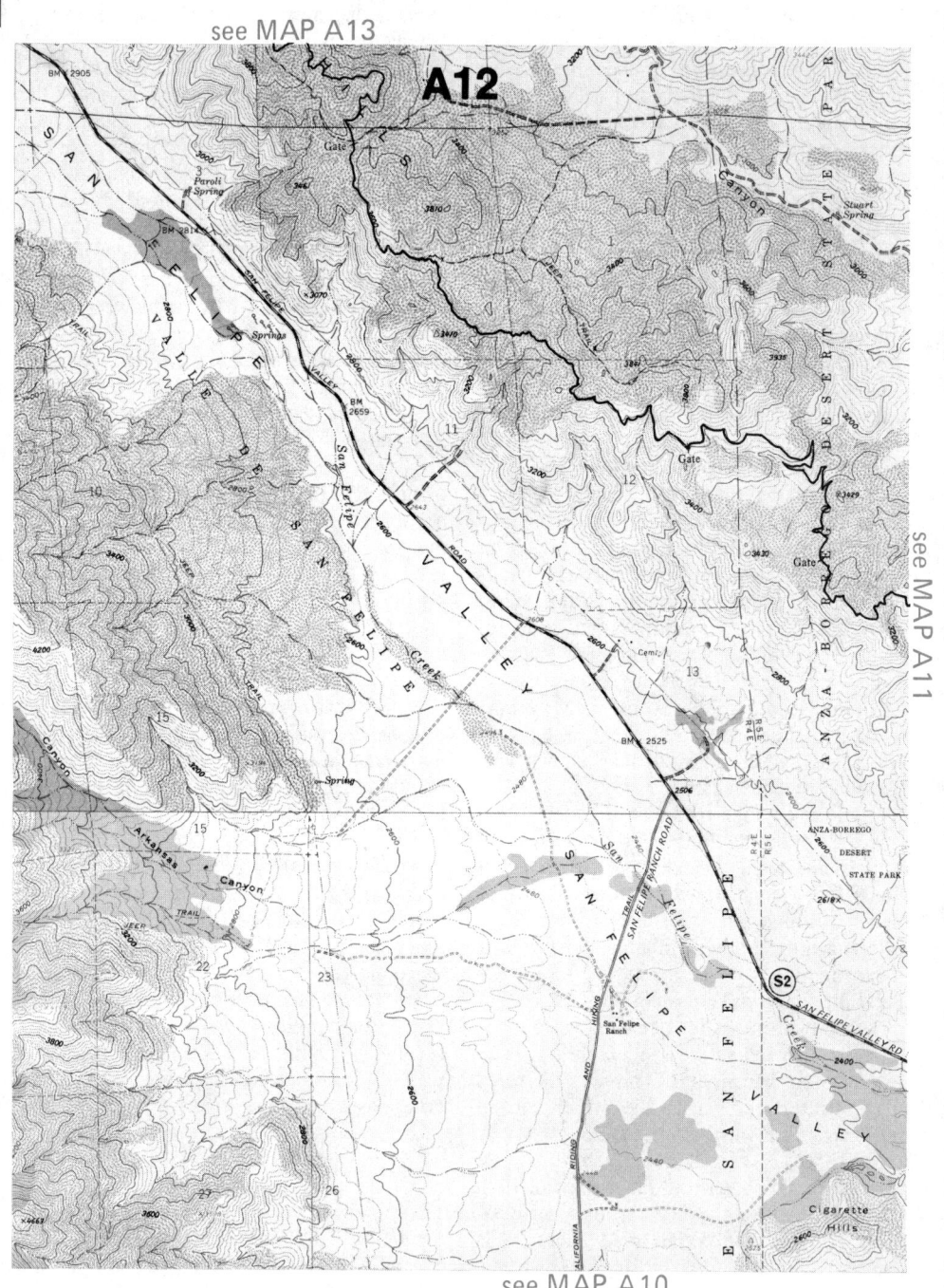

see MAP A11

see MAP A10

granite footing, begin to climb Grapevine Mountain's truly desertlike southwestern flanks. Even in springtime PCT hikers would do well to attack this ascent in the very early morning, since temperatures over 100° are commonplace, and most of the next 24 miles are virtually shadeless. Hikers trying to walk the length of the San Felipe Hills in one hot day will be either gratified or frustrated by the extraordinarily gentle grade of the route, which adds many extra switchbacks and a few unnecessary miles to the task. ∎ *Early on the walk, however, the easy grade allows one to marvel at the "forest" of bizarre ocotillo shrubs. Standing 10–15 feet tall and resembling nothing more than a bundle of giant, green pipe cleaners, ocotillos are perfectly adapted to their searing desert environment. Much of the year, ocotillos' branches look like spiny, lifeless stalks. But within just 2–3 days after a rainstorm, the branches sprout vibrant green clusters of delicate leaves along their entire length, allowing renewed growth. Almost as quickly, the leaves wither and die as groundwater becomes scarce. In this manner ocotillos may leaf out 6–8 times a year.* ∎

The PCT continues to climb imperceptibly in and out of innumerable small canyons and gullies, none of which holds running water except during a rainsquall. Still in a very desertlike association of agave, barrel cactus and teddybear cholla, you eventually reach the crest of the San Felipe Hills, and cross to their northeastern slopes at a pipe gate (3360-8.5). Now the path descends gently into a small, sandy valley where a sparse cover of scrub oak and juniper would make for adequate but waterless camping. Your trail tread becomes indistinct for a moment as you cross a dry, sandy wash (3210-0.6) which drains the valley, but you can see the trail's switchbacks on the slopes ahead, so navigation is easy.

An ascent of those switchbacks leads gently back to the ridgecrest (3600-1.6). The next leg of your journey stays high on the San Felipe Hills' steep southwestern slopes on an undulating course ranging between 3400 feet and 3600 feet. Just below a ridge saddle you pass a junction (3485-2.1) with an east-branching jeep road, and then your path crosses the next saddle to the north, bisecting another, poorer jeep road (3550-0.8) just beyond a pipe gate. Either of

these roads may be followed east, down into Grapevine Canyon. There, approximately 2½ miles from the PCT, travelers who are desperately short of water will find a ranch at permanent Grapevine Spring.

Pressing on, you begin a long ascent, again on the eastern slopes of the San Felipe Hills, climbing now past dense chamise. An excruciatingly gentle, time-consuming switchback finally brings you back to the ridgetop and a cattle gate (4155-2.7). A more interesting trail then traverses the headwalls of two treacherously steep canyons, these plummeting 1200 feet to linear San Felipe Valley. ∎ *Across that valley the Volcan Mountains rise in pine-green splendor, an enviable cool contrast to your scorched environs. The San Felipe Hills are dry and brown for the same reason that the Volcan Mountains are lush and green: a rain-shadow situation causes moisture-laden Pacific storms to dump their rain on the higher Volcan Mountains, leaving little for the San Felipe Hills. Volcan Mountain is the logical location of the PCT, and in fact was Congress' designated route. Unfortunately, the USFS took the easy way out, and so condemned hikers and horses to a truly dangerous, waterless, desert path on the non-Pacific crest of the San Felipe Hills, rather than wrangle with land owners for right-of-way over the better location. The author urges all PCT users to write their Congressperson and demand a safer relocation of the PCT to Volcan Mountain.* ∎

Presently you veer northeast through a gap (4395-1.9), back into dense chaparral on the east side of the San Felipe Hills. Beginning a long, gentle downgrade, the route winds infuriatingly around minor ridges and into nooks, crannies and (it seems) every gully in sight. After a few miles of such mistreatment, most hikers will yearn for a more direct, if steeper, route. But slowly the PCT loses elevation as it circumnavigates a branch of Hoover Canyon, and you gain vistas northeast over sparsely populated Montezuma Valley to San Ysidro Mountain. After only a short eternity you pass through three gates in quick succession, then just a few minutes later, descend under live-oak cover to join a poor road. Now, perhaps marked by a PCT post, your route goes left, west, just a few yards on the road to find Barrel Spring (3475-5.6). Here, after the first ma-

See maps A11, A12, A13

see MAP A14

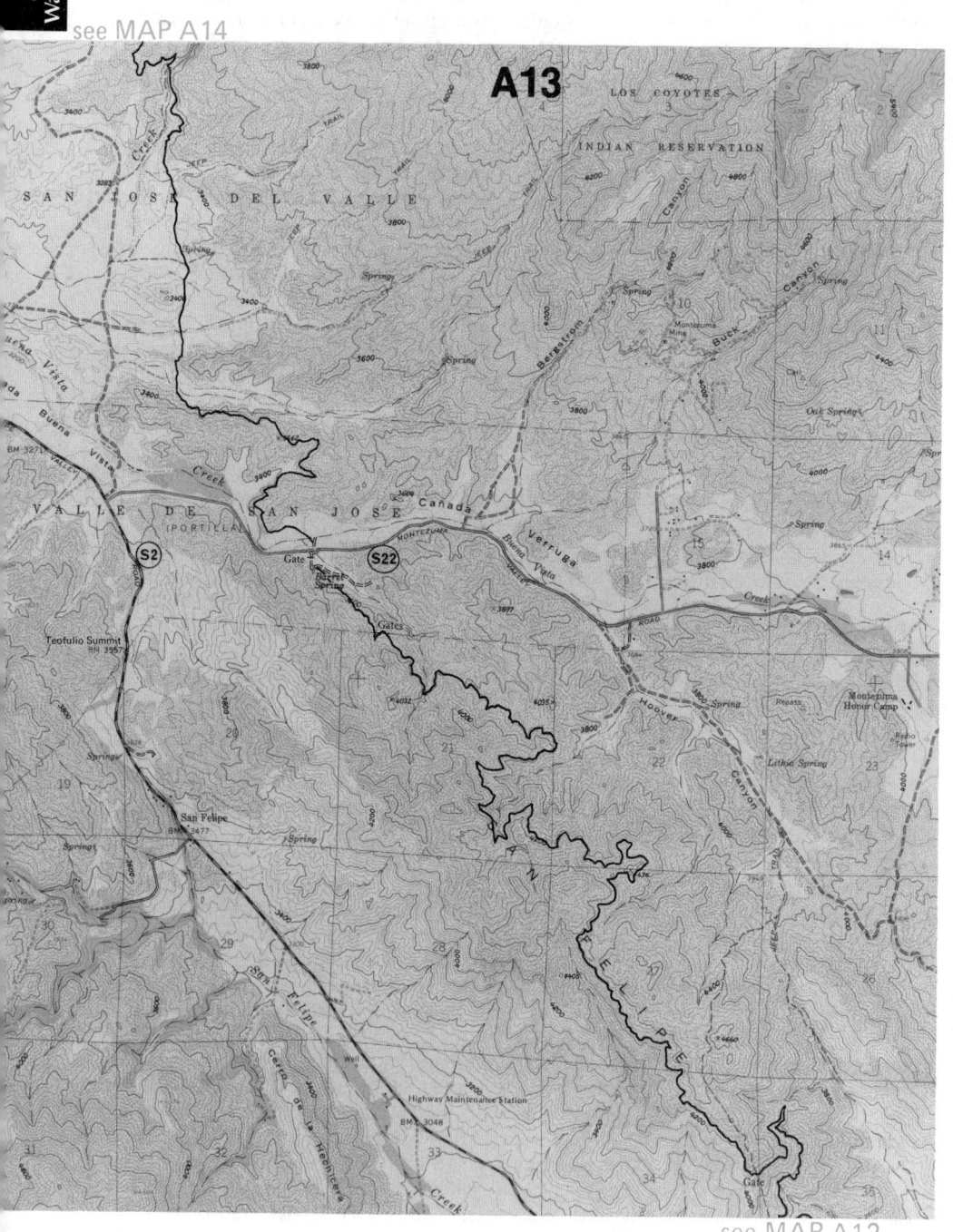

A13

see MAP A12

jor spring rains, cool water is piped into a concrete trough. Adjacent litter notwithstanding, this good waterhole and a pleasant, shady stand of canyon live oaks make a hospitable campsite, which the Forest Service may improve. If water is not flowing in the trough, follow the PCT and the feeder pipe back southeast for about 100 yards to an old dirt road that angles uphill to the spring's source. Northbound hikers can be assured of reliable water in 8.7 miles at Warner Springs Fire Station.

*   *   *   *

Water and supply access: Southbound hikers have a longer walk to water—23.8 miles to springtime off-route water at Sentenac Cienega, 33.0 miles to off-route water on Rodriguez Spur Truck Trail, or 37.9 miles to off-route springs in Chariot Canyon. If no water is available at Barrel Spring, hitchhike 4.5 miles east on Montezuma Valley Road S22 to Ranchita, which is a small village. One may continue east on S22 15 miles from the PCT to Borrego Springs, for resupply. On the way, the village of Ranchita, with a single small minimarket, is passed, in about 4 miles.

*   *   *   *

Resuming your northward trek, you follow the dirt road from Barrel Spring, down through a gate to a dirt-road pullout just south of paved Montezuma Valley Road S22 (3445-0.1). Just across the highway is a poor dirt road, on which you head north just 50 yards to a barbed-wire cattle gate. Just beyond it PCT posts indicate a treadless route leading left, northwest, which quickly crosses the sandy wash of usually dry Buena Vista Creek. The poorly defined way continues northwest across a sagebrush flat to the southern foot of a ridge. As the trail turns west at the ridge's base, the tread becomes well-defined, soon contouring north into a small canyon. Then the trail begins to climb easily, and you are treated to pleasant views west as you ascend to a 3550-foot ridgetop. The trail next drops easily west along its northern slope and, nearing the southern margin of a narrow, grassy, west-trending valley, the tread abruptly ends. But looking north across the pasture, you'll hopefully spot a PCT post marking the

crossing of a jeep road (3285-2.1). You'll then note tread immediately to the north, ascending north along the next low ridge. Climb it, then drop northeast to its base on the edge of another, much larger rolling grassland where, again, tread simply ceases. This time, however, far too few PCT posts show the way, so, with compass in hand, follow a bearing of 355° quite level for almost 0.2 mile to a PCT post, then a bearing of 5° for another 0.2 mile to the crest of a gentle ridge northeast of hill 3406. Here, ignore a much-better-defined cattle trail descending northwest, and instead proceed along an average bearing of 350°, arcing down and across a hillside under a trickling spring seep where cattle often congregate. At the crest of the next rise, another PCT post reaffirms your route. The route from here is more difficult, at a bearing of 340°, but lasts only about 0.1 mile, and is marked by two PCT posts. But get your bearings before proceeding: look north across a smaller grassland, with a cattle-cum-jeep trail ascending it. There is chaparral upslope to our right (east) and the sandy bed of San Ysidro Creek descending obliquely to our left (northwest). Our route, which is quite difficult to follow precisely, goes almost levelly across the grassland toward the mouth of San Ysidro Creek, and then traverses along the hillside east of San Ysidro Creek. If you lose your way, walk upstream along the creek's east bank, and look uphill for trail tread. Alternatively, look almost due west to an 8-foot-diameter concrete cattle trough at a well, below the mouth of San Ysidro Creek. Go to it, then walk upstream, looking east for the trail, just above a fringe of good-size live oaks. Here, actual PCT trail tread resumes among scrub oaks at the edge of the eastern hillside. This path contours north along the canyon's east slopes, but soon drops to cross San Ysidro Creek (3355-1.7), which usually flows in spring. Like other key points on this frustrating, poorly constructed trail segment, this crossing is confused by a jeep track just north of the creek but is now marked by a large PCT sign. Anticipate the crossing where San Ysidro Creek first bends northeast, up-canyon, under the first white-barked sycamore tree to shade your path. A fair camp could be made here.

Across San Ysidro Creek, head straight uphill for 20 yards to find the path, which contin-

See map A13

see MAP B1

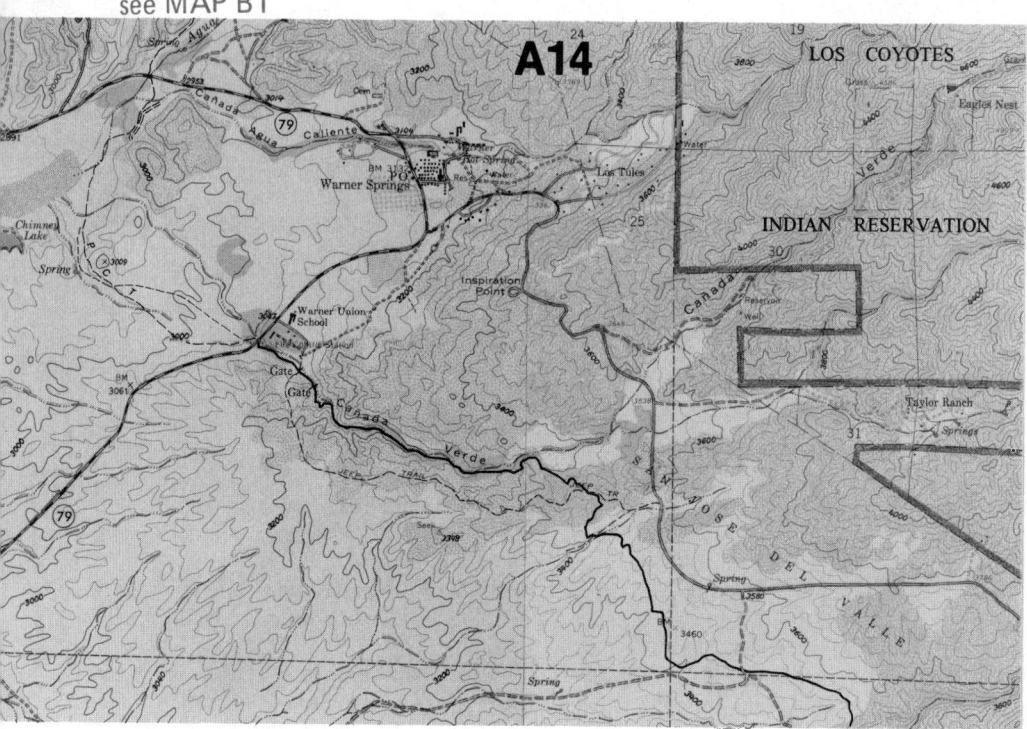

see MAP A13

ues up-canyon for only a moment before switchbacking west moderately up out of the shade onto an open hillside. Ineptly built and poorly maintained, the tread ascends from San Ysidro Creek, soon turning north to attain the canyon's rim. ▮ *Here you have views west over Warner Valley to Lake Henshaw, a sag pond along the Elsinore Fault, and to famous Mount Palomar Observatory, on the horizon.* ▮ After a brief course north the trail turns west and re-enters grassland. This time, however, tread is visible. It leads gently up, then down, to cross a good dirt road (3495-1.2), then soon it adopts a more northern course as it rolls across a corrugation of ridgelets and dry washes. After crossing a poor jeep trail in one such ravine, the trail climbs through low chaparral and soon crosses a ridgetop jeep road (3510-1.6), which served as part of the temporary PCT route for many years.

From the ridge you descend gently past shady canyon live oaks and cottonwoods which line the pretty valley called Cañada Verde (Spanish for "Green Ravine"). Soon the PCT closely par-

allels the southern banks of a small stream that flows until late spring of most years. A fine camp can be made almost anywhere along the next mile of creek, in grassy flats adorned with pink wild roses. The Forest Service may develop a formal camping area here. You follow the canyon bottom for almost a mile, and then, near Cañada Verde's mouth, pass through two pipe gates, the second one at a jeep road. Across the jeep road you continue northwest just south of Cañada Verde's banks, and in ¼ mile find the concrete bridge of two-lane Highway 79 (3040-2.0), just west of Warner Springs Fire Station. Although the PCT actually heads under the highway, the bridge clearance is too low for horses, so a pipe gate allows access to the highway. Warner Springs Post Office lies 1.2 miles northeast along the highway. Water is available at the fire station. The next water for northbound hikers lies in Agua Caliente Creek, in 5.3 miles, while for the southbound, water is next obtained at Barrel Spring, 8.7 miles away.

See maps A13, A14

Laguna Rim view of Anza-Borrego Desert State Park and the Santa Rosa Mountains

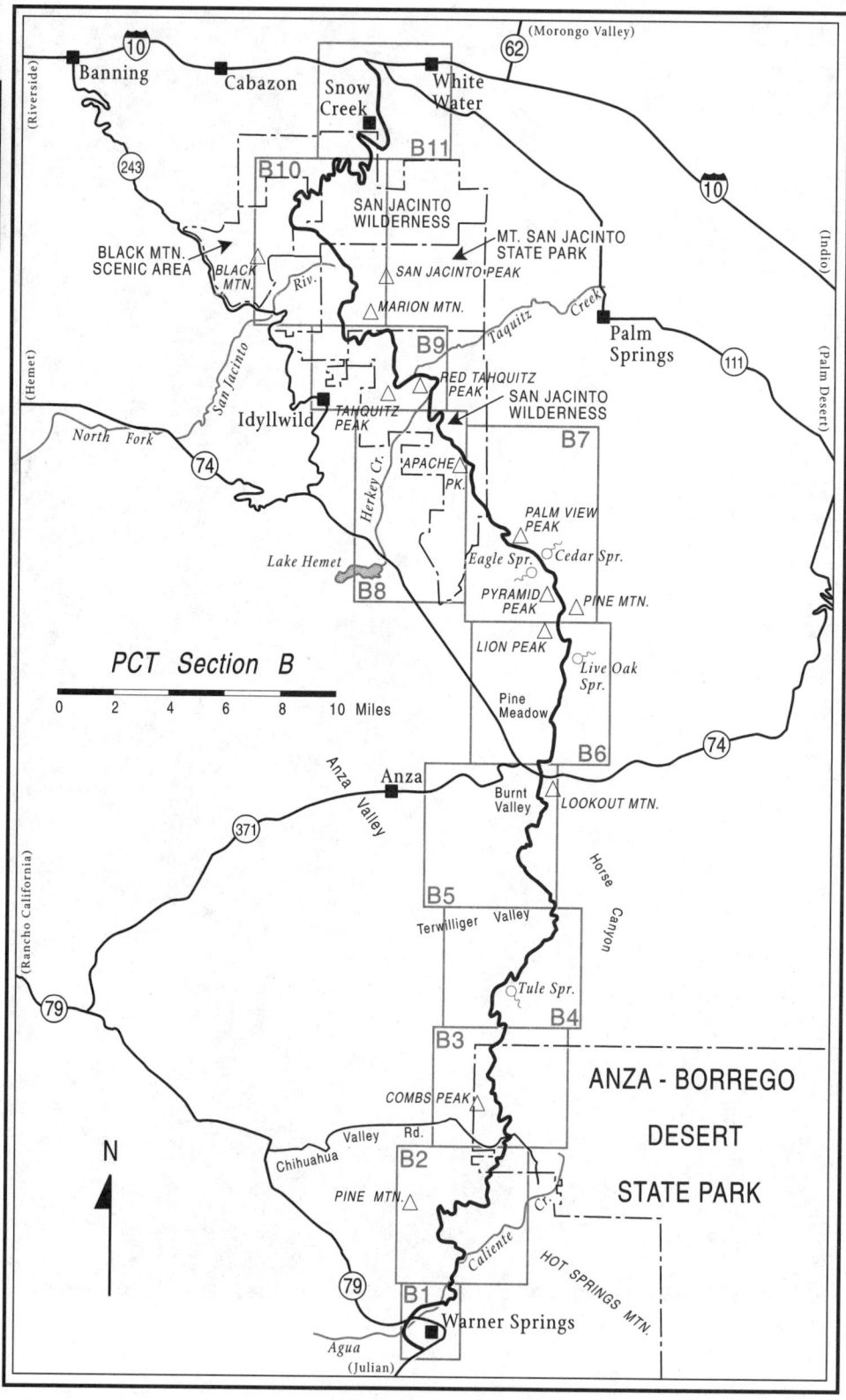

Section B
Warner Springs to San Gorgonio Pass

Introduction: The San Jacinto Mountains are the high point—and the highlight—of the Pacific Crest Trail's excursion through the northern Peninsular Ranges, and they afford the first true high-mountain air and scenery of your journey. But this section of trail also includes many miles of walking under shady live oaks and through the shadeless chaparral community (see below). On the Desert Divide, where you have your first taste of the San Jacinto Mountains, you find an interesting combination of pine forest, chaparral and desert species. Leaving the San Jacintos, the PCT plunges almost 8000 feet down to arid San Gorgonio Pass, and in so doing passes through every life zone in California save for the alpine zone.

The Peninsular Ranges stretch from the southern tip of Baja California, paralleling the coastline, some 900 miles north to San Gorgonio Pass, which truncates the range along the Banning Fault and lesser faults. The ranges' core, forming the Laguna Mountains, the Anza Upland and the San Jacinto Mountains, where the PCT winds, is made of crystalline rocks—granite and its relatives—which were first intruded in a liquid state several miles beneath the surface and then later solidified. These rocks are similar in age and kind to the granitic rocks of the Sierra Nevada.

Your walk from Warner Springs to San Gorgonio Pass treads mostly upon these rocks, which are usually fine-grained, gray-to-creamy in color, and strongly resistant to weathering, as demonstrated by obdurate monoliths around Indian Flats and Bucksnort Mountain, by outcrops jutting from the alluvium of Terwilliger and Anza valleys, and by the jagged, saurian spine of the San Jacinto Mountains, as on Fuller Ridge. The remainder of the terrain you tread is across either sand and gravel weathered from the granite, found in basins, or metamorphic rocks. These rocks are seen in Agua Caliente Creek's canyon and along much of the Desert Divide.

Section B ends at San Gorgonio Pass, a broad, cactus-dotted trough running eastwest, flanked by the San Bernardino and San Jacinto mountains to the north and south respectively. Once a major corridor of Indian traders, San Gorgonio Pass is bounded by faults on either side. It lies some 9000 feet below the summits of San Jacinto and San Gorgonio, each standing just a few air miles to one side.

Proof that awesome geologic processes are at work today can be seen right at the start of this section, at Warner Springs. Now a tourist spa, but used for centuries past by neighboring Cahuilla and Cupeño Indian tribes, the hot springs here bubble up from deep within the earth's crust and escape along the Aguanga Fault, which cuts just yards behind this small resort community. Warner's hot spring also served Kit Carson in 1846, and was an overnight stop on the Butterfield Stage Line from 1858 to 1861.

Declination: 13°E

Points on Route	S→N	Mi. Btwn. Pts.	N→S
Highway 79 southwest of Warner Springs	0.0		101.4
Highway 79 west of Warner Springs	1.8	1.8	99.6
Agua Caliente Creek ford in Section 13	5.2	3.4	96.2
Lost Valley Road to Indian Flats Campground	8.8	3.6	92.6
Chihuahua Valley Road to water	17.7	8.9	83.7
Tule Canyon Road to Tule Spring	27.7	10.8	73.7
jeep road to Terwilliger	34.2	6.5	67.2
Pines-to-Palms Highway to Anza	43.1	8.9	58.3
Live Oak Spring Trail	49.7	6.6	51.7
Cedar Spring Trail	53.8	4.1	47.6
Apache Spring Trail	59.9	6.1	41.5
Tahquitz Valley Trail	67.7	7.8	33.7
Saddle Junction and trail to Idyllwild	69.6	1.9	31.8
North Fork San Jacinto River	75.8	6.2	25.6
Fuller Ridge Trailhead Remote Campsite	81.6	5.8	19.8
Snow Canyon Road	97.8	16.2	3.6
near Interstate 10 in San Gorgonio Pass	101.4	3.6	0.0

Water: Water remains scarce in the southern reaches of Section B. Except high in the San Jacinto Wilderness, or at springs where wells have been dug for livestock, do not expect to find water away from civilization. Once you reach the cooler, higher Desert Divide, however, water becomes more plentiful. In fact, many would-be PCT through hikes have been ended prematurely by thigh-deep spring snows on the southern flanks of the San Jacinto Mountains. Keep a weather eye out, and be prepared for rough going.

Supplies: The Warner Springs spa and facilities are now a private club, and public access is not allowed. Camping food may be mailed to Warner Springs Post Office, located 1.2 miles northeast of the start of this section on Highway 79. The next possibility for resupply is in the mobile-home community of Terwilliger, a 4.4-mile detour from the PCT, 34.3 miles along this section's stretch. There, the Valley Store, open 7 days from 8:30 A.M. to 6:00 P.M., has limited supplies, precious water, a PCT register and a telephone. They will cash money orders and hold food parcels, but request two weeks prenotification of any package, and you must use a package-delivery service, not the USPS. The larger town of Anza, a 6.0-mile detour from the route 43 miles beyond the section's start, boasts a post office, stores and restaurants. At Saddle Junction, high in the San Jacinto Wilderness and 69.6 miles from the start of Section B, most trailers choose to descend the historic Devil's Slide Trail to Idyllwild. This restful mountain resort community has a complete range of facilities, including Nomad Ventures, a mountaineering supply shop, with a very knowledgeable staff and everything for the PCT trekker.

Ending this section in West Palm Springs Village, a tiny community without any supplies, you have a choice of supply stations. Here, about 102 miles from the start, you can hitchhike east 12.5 miles via Interstate 10 and Highway 111 to revel in the fleshpots of Palm Springs, that famous movie-star and golf-course-studded desert oasis. It offers complete facilities, including a not-to-be-missed tour for PCTers fresh from their conquest of the first major mountain range on the trail: an aerial-tram ride from Palm Springs up 6000 feet to the subalpine shoulder of San Jacinto Peak, for a lavish dinner at the viewful summit tram station!

Alternatively, hikers may elect to hitchhike west on Highway 10 from West Palm Springs Village. From the Verbenia Avenue exit you go 4.5 miles on Highway 10 to the Main Street exit of Cabazon, a small town with a post office and store. It also boasts The Wheel Inn, a good restaurant complete with life-size concrete models of a brontosaurus and a tyrannosaurus. Hadley's, a backpacker's dream market, lies 2 miles farther west on Highway 10 (Apache Trail exit), and it sells an astounding variety of dried fruits and nuts. Cabazon Ranch Outfitters, located at 50150 Esperanza Avenue, offers professional pack-animal support and guiding in the San Jacintos and San Bernardinos. Horse feed is available. Also, free of charge, are corrals, water, hot showers, camping and package holds for riders and hikers. Contact: Barbara Gronek, POB 876, Cabazon, CA 92230, or phone (909) 849-2528.

Permits: The San Jacinto Wilderness consists of two units—the national-forest wilderness and the state-park wilderness. If you are camping in only one of these, you need a permit only for it; if you are camping in both, you need two permits. Obtain the national-forest permit by writing Idyllwild Ranger Station, Box 518, Idyllwild, CA 92549. You can also pick one up at the station, at 25925 Village Center Drive in Idyllwild, which is open between 8 A.M. and 4:30 P.M. Monday through Friday until about June 1, and then 7 days a week through summer. Obtain the state-park permit by writing Mt. San Jacinto Wilderness State Park, Box 308, Idyllwild, CA 92349, or by going to the station at the north edge of Idyllwild on the highway to Banning between 8 and 5 o'clock 7 days a week.

The Chaparral: Hikers along the California PCT cannot help but become familiar with the chaparral, that community of typically chest-high, tough, wiry, calf-slashing shrubs and small trees that you meet first by the Mexican border. Draped like a green velvet blanket over most of that part of Southern California reached by ocean air, and extending from close beside the sea up to about 5000 feet, where it mingles with conifers and oaks, chaparral lines most of the PCT south of the Sierra. Chaparral surrounds Warner Springs, at the beginning of this section.

Named by early Spanish Californians, who were reminded of their "chaparro," or live-oak scrub from Mediterranean climes, the California chaparral is a unique assemblage of plants—mostly shrubs—that find this region's long, rainless summers and cooler, wet winters ideal for growth. Chamise, also known as "greasewood" because of its texture and its almost explosive flammability, is the most widespread species, but several species of ceanothus (mountain lilac, buckbrush, tobacco brush and coffee brush), plus ribbonwood, ocean spray, sumac, sagebrush, mountain mahogany, holly-leaf cherry and yerba santa also rank as major members of chaparral, depending on topographic and soil conditions.

All true chaparral plants have small, evergreen, thick, stiff leaves and many have leaves with waxy outer surfaces. The plants' roots are long, to reach deep into rocky subsoil for scarce water. Chaparral plants are suited to survive not only the protracted rainless, hot months, but also a low annual rainfall and a rapid runoff from the thin, poorly developed soils. The plants' main defense against loss of precious water is near-dormancy during the hot, dry summer spells. Almost all photosynthetic activity ceases during this time, but the stiff evergreen leaves are ready to resume photosynthesis within minutes of a rainfall, unlike those plants which lose their leaves or wilt in the face of heat. The small size of the leaves themselves, with the addition of a waxy coat or a hairy insulating cover, plus the presence of relatively few evaporative stomata, greatly reduces water losses.

Not only can chaparral plants vie successfully for, and conserve, scant water resources, but they also win out by thriving in the face of fire. All of the most widespread species are adapted to reproduce well in the aftermath of fast-moving range fires that are a hallmark of Southern California wildlands. In fact, fires actually benefit these species, and most of them contain highly flammable volatile oils, which promote fires. Before the advent of white people, wildfires burned the Southern California chaparral every 5 to 8 years! Not only does fire exterminate encroaching species, but it returns valuable nitrogen to the soil, thus promoting growth. Some of the species, like scrub oak and ceanothus, need fire to weaken their seeds' coatings to allow germination. Most of the other chaparral plants circumvent the ravages of fire by resprouting—in as little as 10 days—from tough root crowns or by putting out so many seeds that at least some will survive any fire. Chaparral is also unusual in that it succeeds itself right after a fire, unlike other plant communities, such as pine forests, which after a major fire pass through one or more vegetational stages before returning to the final, climax stage.

Maps: *Warner Springs*	*Butterfly Peak*
Hot Springs Mountain	*Palm View Peak*
Bucksnort Mountain	*Idyllwild*
Beauty Mountain	*San Jacinto Peak*
Anza	*White Water*

The Route

Before leaving Warner Springs, northbound hikers must be sure to stock up on water. The next certain source along the route, barring the seasonal flow of Agua Caliente Creek (reached in 5.2 miles), is Tule Spring, a long, usually hot, 27.7-mile trek away.

Pedestrians can start north on Section B's PCT by simply ducking under Highway 79 via Cañada Verde's streambed, but equestrians must climb through the gate onto the highway shoulder. Then they should follow the highway northeast 200 yards to the entrance to Warner Union School. Across the street from this entrance, a short dirt road along a fence heads left, northwest, 100 yards to a short spur trail that turns south back to Cañada Verde's wash and to the PCT. Your trail departs west away from the wash, quickly crosses a jeep road, and curves gently down into spring-wildflower meadows. Well marked by posts and having a refreshingly well-defined tread, the PCT soon recrosses the jeep road (2960-0.7).

Next your trail skirts the flanks of low knob

3009, then turns north across sandy flats speckled with mature canyon live oaks to cross the usually dry bed of Agua Caliente Creek (2910-0.6). In just a minute or two, your deep-sand trail recrosses the creek to its east bank and then climbs east a few yards into a cozy oak grove and to a privately operated campground (2925-0.2), which is closed to public use. Here the PCT momentarily joins the dirt road that gives access to the campground's sites, and then it turns northward before branching left to cross another usually dry streambed in Cañada Agua Caliente. Moments later, the PCT passes under Highway 79 (2930-0.3) via a concrete bridge, while simultaneously crossing Agua Caliente Creek, which often flows lazily here.

*   *   *   *

Water access: Warner Springs Post Office and sure water can be found 1.3 miles east along Highway 79.

*   *   *   *

See map B1

Opuntia **cactus in bloom**

and coming slowly closer to the cut banks of Agua Caliente Creek. In a short while, the trail strikes the dirt road at its end, where a large campsite (2975-0.3) is found. This pleasant, sunny spot has a number of picnic tables and metal fireplaces, a pair of hooks for hanging packs out of the reach of squirrels and raccoons, and an outhouse, all just a few feet from the cool, trickling stream. Trail resumes at the upstream end of the camp, and descends momentarily to cross via rocks 15-foot-wide Agua Caliente Creek, here burbling among baccharis shrubs, sycamores and cottonwoods. Across the stream, the route climbs north and east away from the creek.

Chia, white forget-me-not and beavertail cacti line the moderate ascent across the Cleveland National Forest border to a terrace, along which the sandy path winds north through ribbonwood chaparral. Then you soon descend to cross Agua Caliente Creek (3195-2.3), where tall grasses, squaw brush, brodiaea and forget-me-nots grow below screening oaks, sycamores and willows in the narrow, usually watered canyon—a refuge for mourning doves and horned lizards. Particularly in winter and spring, ticks also inhabit the grasses and shrubs, and travelers should check their legs often. You cross Agua Caliente Creek four more times in the next mile, alter-

North of the highway the PCT leaves the western margin of Agua Caliente Creek's sandy bed just beyond a sandbag-reinforced slope. The trail clambers up to pass through a gate, then, ignoring a right-branching path back down to the stream, climbs from a fringe of trees onto a nearly level alluvial terrace covered with sagebrush and dotted with massive live oaks. Follow the terrace northeast, up-canyon, staying some 30 feet above Agua Caliente Creek, which usually flows in this vicinity, if only as a trickle. The PCT dips momentarily in a north-trending wash (ignore a prominent trail down to the creek), then shortly merges with a wider path (an old jeep road) (2960-0.6) that continues eastward, up-canyon, well-marked by PCT posts. A few minutes' walk leads to a junction (2965-0.2) with a dirt road that crosses from the southwest. Beyond this junction the trail, indicated by PCT posts, continues ahead, now paralleling the aforementioned road to its right,

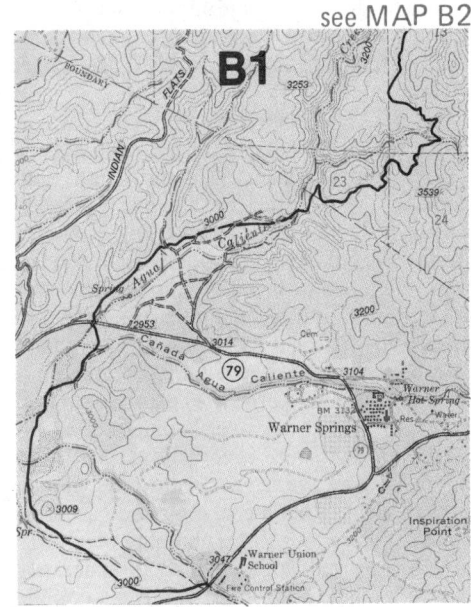

see MAP B2

see MAP A14

See maps B1, B2

nating shady, cool creekside walking with hot, yucca-dotted Paleozoic Julian schist hillsides. Unfortunately, heavy rains in Spring 1993 washed out the trail where it made each crossing of Agua Caliente Creek. This does not confuse the hiker so much as it makes traversing the canyon a chore. The USFS plans to rebuild the trail higher on the slope. Camping possibilities are frequent. A final, shaded traverse north of the seasonal stream leads to a switchback (3520-1.5) in a side canyon, after which the moderately ascending route winds northwest in chaparral laced with deer brush and white sage. Soon the grade eases to contour west, then north, below Peak 4844 and above Indian Flats Road. Here the trail affords good views southwest across Warner Valley to Lake Henshaw, a large sag pond on the Elsinore Fault, and northwest to weathered tonalite outcrops near Indian Flats.

*   *   *   *

Water access: Upon striking Lost Valley Road (4170-2.1), trekkers may opt to detour left (west) to Indian Flats Campground for oak-shaded camping and fresh water. This is reached by first walking south 0.5 mile down the dirt road—now closed to vehicles—to oiled Indian Flats Road, both part of Road 9S05. Turn right on the latter and go 2.6 miles to Indian Flats Campground, which is nestled among oaks and boulders on the site of an old Cahuilla Indian camp.

*   *   *   *

Continuing north, the PCT turns right onto poor Lost Valley Road and ascends it to reach a spur road (4450-1.1). From here Lost Valley Road descends north 0.2 mile to reach vandalized, often dry Lost Valley Spring, while the PCT climbs northeast along a 0.3-mile spur—an overgrown jeep track—to reach a continuation of trail tread where the spur ends in a ravine. You ascend briskly to the south to find excellent views back over boulder-dotted Indian Flats and south over Valle de San Jose. Soon the way swings eastward on a gentle, sandy ascent through chaparral and past scattered Coulter pines. After climbing over three low, fire-scarred ridges, you drop moderately east to a saddle (4945-3.2) that lies along the

northwest-trending Hot Springs Fault. To the southeast, Hot Springs Mountain's lookout tower rises above tree-lined Agua Caliente Creek.

The PCT ascends east a bit, then turns north to undulate through dry brushland—often sparingly shaded by oaks and Coulter pines—to the east of a boulder-castellated ridge. After about 2 miles from the saddle you pass into Anza-Borrego Desert State Park, then cross a gap to the sunnier west slopes of the ridgeline. With vistas west over Chihuahua Valley, you contour generally north to yet another gap, then descend quickly east, cross a ravine, and traverse northwest to strike nearby Chihuahua Valley Road (5050-4.6), which drops west into Chihuahua Valley.

*   *   *   *

Water access: Detour here for water: walk east 0.2 mile to a left-branching 0.1-mile dirt spur that descends to a private home. A 20-foot-high, silver water tank with a valve at its base is the source. Descend first to the house (beware of the dogs!) to ask permission.

*   *   *   *

Directly across the dirt road the PCT starts a sustained, moderate ascent along Bucksnort Mountain's east slopes. The climb ends at the east shoulder of Combs Peak (5595-1.9), where a grove of Coulter pines, now sadly burned, outstanding vistas, and the first level spot for miles combine to make a nice, if waterless, campsite.

▌ *The 180° panorama here encompasses a sizable chunk of Southern California real estate. To the north, distant, seasonally snow-capped San Gorgonio Mountain peers over the west shoulder of nearer, sometimes snowy San Jacinto Peak. Closer in the north, Thomas Mountain stands behind sprawling Anza and Terwilliger valleys. The rocky spine descending right (southeast) from San Jacinto Peak is the PCT-traversed Desert Divide. To the east-northeast, the dry summits of the Santa Rosa Mountains loom above desert-floored Coyote Canyon, while you spy to the east the vast Salton Sea beyond Anza-Borrego Desert State Park. The park and the town of Anza to the*

See maps B2, B3

see MAP B3

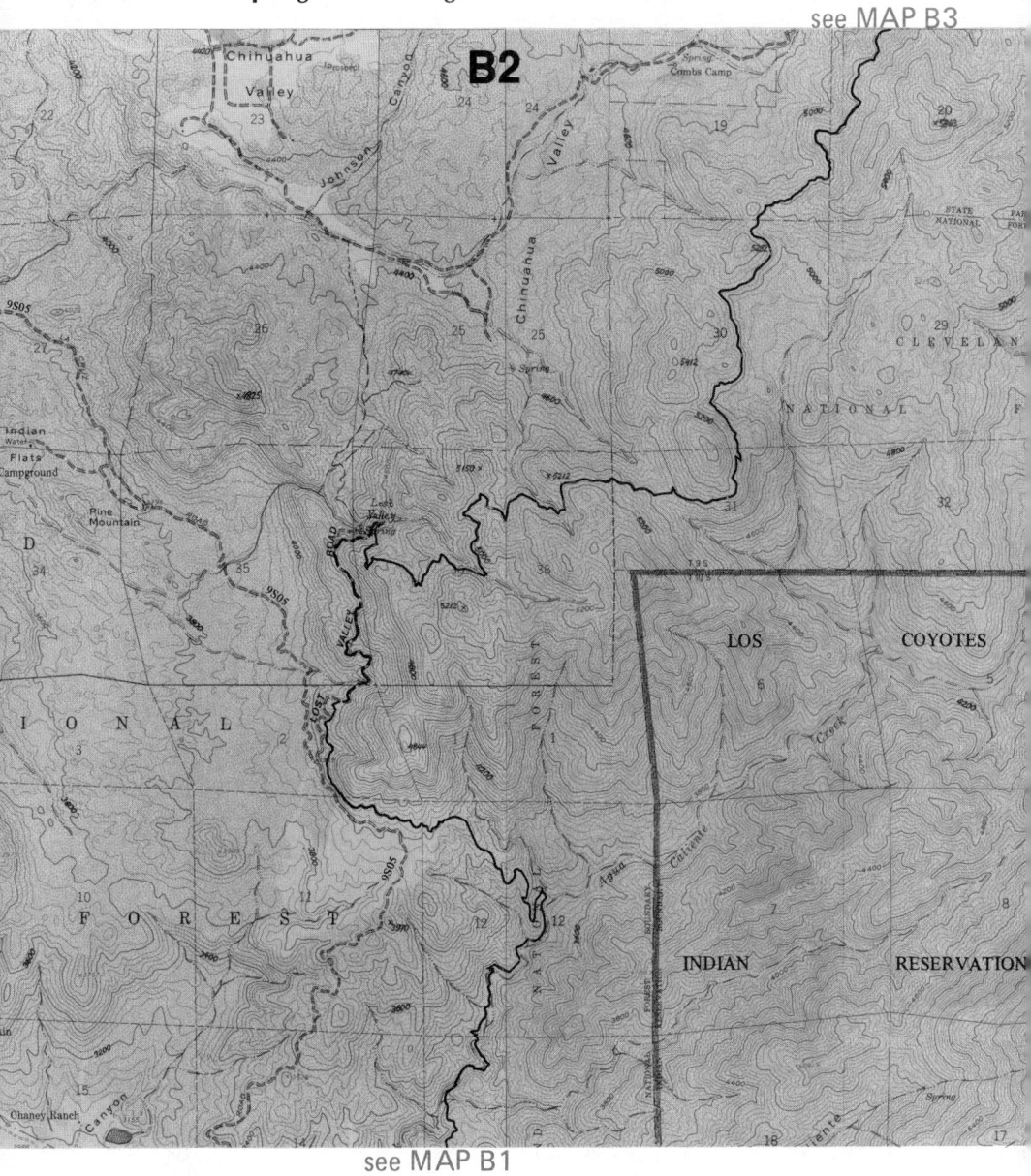

see MAP B1

north both commemorate Captain Juan Bautista de Anza, who in 1774 rejoiced upon entering the valley now bearing his name. He had struggled through the Borrego Desert and Coyote Canyon with a couple dozen men— mostly soldiers—while scouting a route from Sonora, Mexico, to San Francisco. He returned a year later, leading more than 200 settlers and many cattle. ∎

Continuing on, the northbound PCT contours across the steep east face of Bucksnort Mountain, then begins to descend in earnest, on rocky, sandy tread in low chaparral. You eventually cross a usually dry creekbed at the head of Tule Canyon (4710-2.4), just south of where some level spots offer waterless camping. From here your way becomes less steep and rolls northward into a tall brushland dominated by

See map B3

see MAP B4

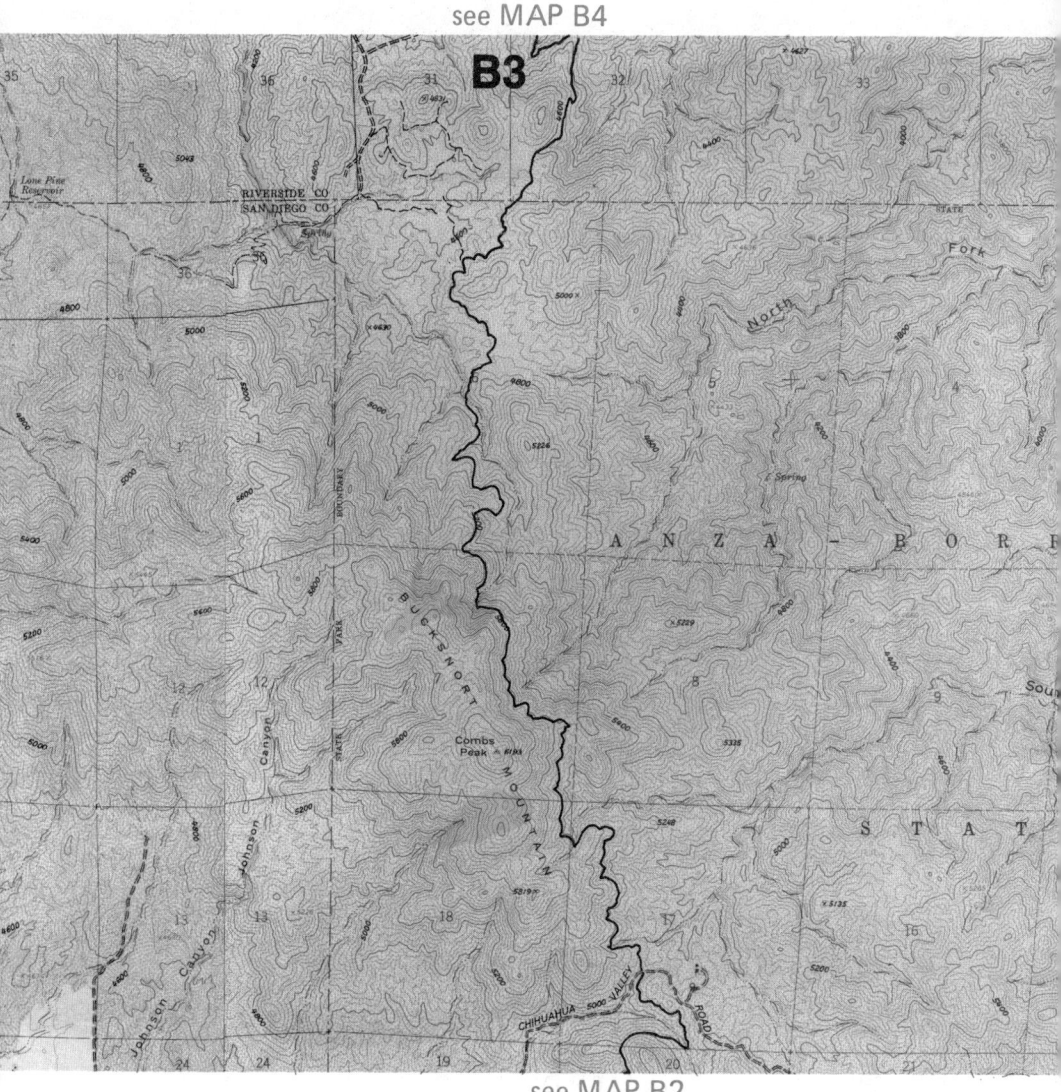

see MAP B2

ribbonwood and chamise. The PCT rounds the canyon's eastern slopes, drops easily to a broad saddle, then climbs gently north to gain the west end of a low ridge. A few minutes' gentle downhill walk leads to a trail junction (4675-0.9). The north-descending old, temporary-PCT route heads left for 0.3 mile before deadending. You take the newer, 1987-vintage tread, which first contours east and then drops moderately across the nearby Riverside County line on a northward tack. After traversing east-facing slopes, the PCT descends across to the west side of a small saddle, next descends southwest, and then soon levels to momentarily strike a fair dirt road (4110-2.3) at the Anza-Borrego Desert State Park boundary. Northwest across it the path resumes, making an easy but shadeless descent through Section 30. After an unneces-

See maps B3, B4

sary switchback the way bends north, still descending. ∎ *Some hikers may wonder about the logic of the PCT's route between the county line and the Pines-to-Palms Highway. In order to avoid conflicts with local landowners, the PCT is forced to traverse a checkerboard of public-land parcels. Hence the PCT crosses each section near one of its corners to essentially avoid treading on private property.* ∎ Ponder this situation as you continue north, past a white-pipe post marking a section's corner. You then drop for a moment to a shallow, hop-across ford of Tule Canyon Creek (3590-2.1). Water usually flows here, sometimes merely at a trickle, for most of the year. It is more reliable downstream at Tule Spring. Due to land-ownership constraints the PCT is forced to climb very steeply up the sandy hillside north of Tule Canyon Creek. Afterward it side-hills gently northeast, down-canyon, soon to cross good Tule Canyon Road (3640-0.4).

* * * *

Water and resupply access: Just ¼ mile southeast down this dirt road is year-round Tule Spring, the only reliable waterhole on the PCT for miles. Thanks to work of the PCT Association and CDF, water is now easily available from a metal-handled spigot found 50 feet below the 10,000-gallon water tank, on the edge of Tule Canyon creek's high cut bank. Should the water tank or spigot not be operational for some reason, check in the high grass to the left of the tank—a seep is always present, even during the late 1980s' drought years. Floods in Spring 1993 caused destruction of most of the lovely cottonwoods and flat areas hereabouts, but camping is still possible. In the morning quiet, one may see desert bighorn sheep watering here, having escaped the scorching heat of the Borrego Sink. Everyone should fill water bottles here. Northbound hikers have 22.0 usually hot miles until the short detour to Tunnel Spring, on the Desert Divide, while southbound hikers have an even hotter 22.5 miles to Agua Caliente Creek in Section 13. One may also choose to resupply at Terwilliger or Anza from Tule Springs. Ascend Tule Canyon Road past the PCT, reaching a locked gate 0.3 mile west of the trail, at the boundary of Anza-Borrego Desert State Park. Continue up the sandy, rut-ted road, which steadily improves, past a home or two to a junction with larger dirt Terwilliger Road (4045-2.5), where the road is signed, "Tule Canyon Truck Trail". Turn right, north, and follow this busier way past numerous smaller junctions and a handful of homes to a T-junction with larger dirt Ramsay Road (3921-1.3). Now swing right, east, to the paved continuation of Terwilliger Road (3920-0.2). Swing left, again due north, on the shoulder of Terwilliger Road to paved Bailey Road (3859-0.2). Kamp Anza Kampground (3990-1.6) is farther north on Terwilliger Road. Find the town of Anza (3920-5.1) beyond Kamp Anza as described in more detail in the next "water & supply access" paragraph.

* * * *

After refreshing yourself, return to the PCT's northward continuation. It starts a sandy, hillside traverse, undulating through rocky ravines, first overlooking the environs of Tule Spring, then bending northeast. After dipping to a broad valley, the easy trail climbs slightly to a small pass with an interesting self-replenishing wildfowl "guzzler" water tank, then drops on sandy, indistinct tread to nearby Coyote Canyon Road (3500-2.9). Across it you continue down a ravine to a single switchback leading to the pleasant grassy floor of Nance Canyon. Step across its seasonal creeklet (3350-0.5) to find some small flat spots that offer potential dry camping. Ignore a spur trail going right, downstream, after crossing the creek. Instead, go left, upstream. Beyond, a moderate grind leads up around a low knob, then across a rugged bluff where the trail was unnecessarily routed, at the expense of much dynamite and at least one badly injured trail-crew worker. This route does, however, offer panoramas south and east over Anza-Borrego Desert State Park's wild, northern canyons, which are visible through a haze of heat waves and salt particles from the Salton Sea. After pausing momentarily, you continue the ascent, which eventually makes two small switchbacks and passes a faint use-trail through a chain link fence to reach a chamise-covered gap (4185-2.4) on the southern end of Table Mountain. Now you wind north and descend gently to a narrow, very sandy jeep road (4075-0.7), which comes down

See map B4

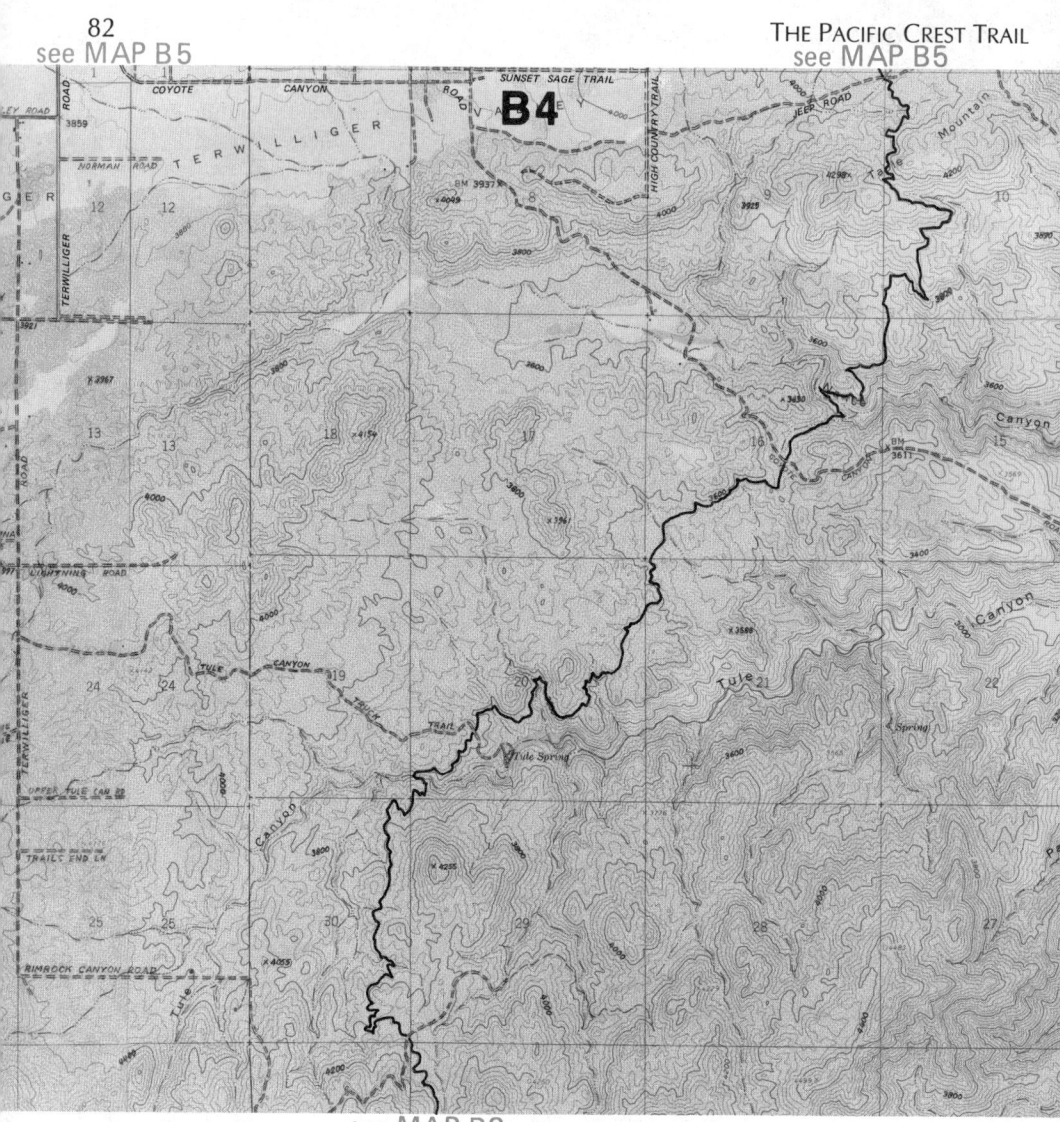

see MAP B3

from a saddle to the east. This hard-to-spot junction occurs where the road is obscured in a broad white-sand wash draining a far eastern part of Terwilliger Valley. Look for this junction a few yards south of a prominent 10-foot-tall plastic post.

*   *   *   *

Water & resupply access: The reason this jeep road is so important is that it leads out to the community of Terwilliger and on to Anza—both logical resupply sites for long-distance

PCT travelers. To reach Terwilliger, turn left, west, and gently descend the road, which rapidly becomes more distinct. After 1.1 miles it ends with a slight ascent to a good dirt road, signed HIGH COUNTRY TRAIL. Turn right onto it, and walk north ¼ mile easily up to a broad road, Sunset Sage Trail, which branches left, west. Take this dirt road ¾ mile easily down past numerous north-branching dirt roads and past a few homes to its end at Yucca Valley Road (3925-2.1). Turn left and follow this dirt road south for just a minute to a four-way junction, from where larger Coyote Canyon Road heads

See map B4

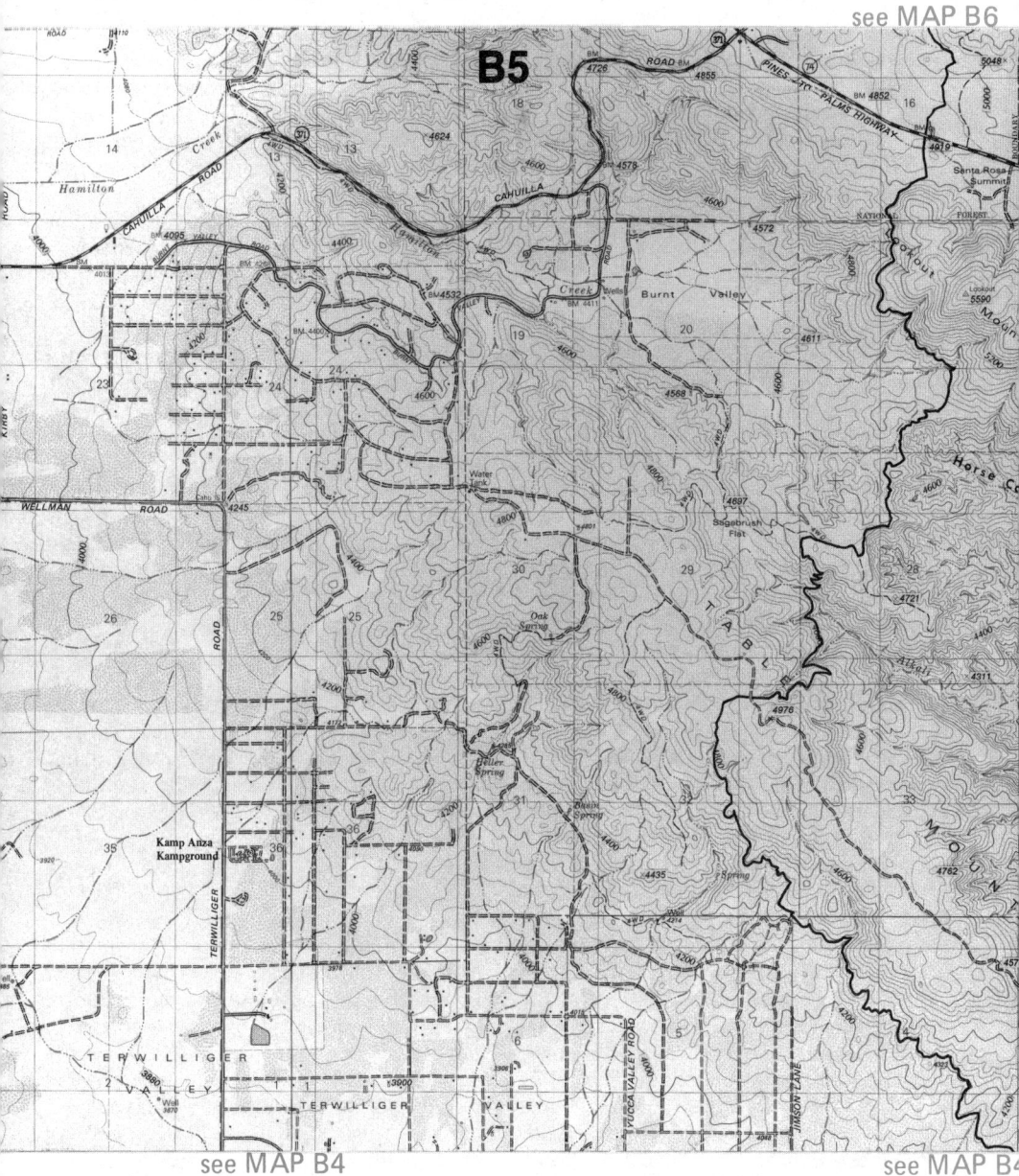

see MAP B6

see MAP B4

see MAP B4

both south and west. Follow this road right, west, across the arid, level grassland, finally making a small dogleg before ending at paved Terwilliger Road (3870-1.8).

Terwilliger Road may be followed south just 0.3 mile, to paved Bailey Road. Just 250 yards west on it is the Valley Store, with water and a warm welcome for PCT hikers. From Coyote Canyon Road's junction with Terwilliger Road,

hikers can walk north to Kamp Anza Kampground (3990-1.3), with phones, a surprisingly good grocery selection, laundry, hot showers and campsites available at a very reasonable cost. Hikers who are intent on an Anza resupply can continue north past the trailer park to Wellman Road (4245-1.5). Take it west to Kirby Road (3935-1.0), then take that road north to Cahuilla Road (Highway 371) (3970-

See maps B4, B5

1.0-8.7). Now turn left, west, and head over to the small town of Anza (3920-1.6-10.3), which has a post office, well-stocked grocery stores, restaurants and a laundromat.

If you don't want to backtrack from Anza to the PCT at the far eastern part of Terwilliger Valley, walk east back along Cahuilla Road, passing Kirby Road and later crossing a 4855-foot summit just before reaching a junction with Pines-to-Palms Highway 74 (4790-6.0). Then go southeast on this highway, which starts southeast and then climbs gently through a grassy valley to reach the PCT just short of a dirt parking turnout (4919-1.0-17.3).

*   *   *   *

From the obscure jeep-road junction at the far eastern part of Terwilliger Valley, the PCT ascends indistinctly northwest for a moment before good tread resumes. It leads moderately and persistently uphill, in an ascending traverse along the granitic, boulder-strewn southwestern flanks of Table Mountain. Soon you gain excellent vistas over Terwilliger Valley and south to your PCT's route along Bucksnort Mountain. On a breezy day this stretch is quite enjoyable, particularly in spring when it's likely to be flanked by clusters of California poppy, purple chia, baby-blue-eyes, and feathery green ribbonwood shrubs among white boulders. At one point, you pass a side trail that leads a few yards south to a dirt road serving some hillside homes. Beyond, your climb continues, eventually rising to top Table Mountain's shoulder and cross a dirt road (4910-3.9) at a point just northeast of the long mountain's highest point.

Now the route drops and leads you into a narrow ravine, switchbacks once to cross it, then descends to the bottom of the dry head of Alkali Wash (4540-1.2). A steep, rocky and sometimes hot quintet of switchbacks accomplish the ensuing ascent of the far slope. They lead to atop a chaparral ridge, where your trail swings east over a low saddle into a grassy flat. Now the path winds north, right along the raw, precipitous lip of Horse Canyon. ∎ *Uplifting of the area with each passing earthquake is making the course of Horse Canyon's stream steeper, and it is responding by aggressively eroding into the red and white strata of the surrounding uplands. This has resulted in a badland of*

tortuous ravines and ridgelets, which you see stretching east to Vandeventer Flat, at the foot of Toro Peak. Eventually this erosive process will result in a drainage rearrangement in Burnt Valley, to your northwest, as Horse Canyon's stream advances headward into that valley. ∎

You walk along a narrow divide, enjoy instructional views, then push on, moderately up across the flanks of Lookout Mountain. Eventually the trail finds a low pass (5070-3.3) on the peak's northwestern shoulder, and you have a delightful panorama north over the entire length of the San Jacinto Mountains. In the leftmost distance the rounded form of lofty San Jacinto Peak reigns, usually with a regal coat of snow in spring. Leaving the gap you descend into San Bernardino National Forest. The trail levels and then turns north across a sandy, sagebrush-matted valley to quickly strike 2-lane Pines-to-Palms Highway 74 (4919-0.5) at a point just west of Santa Rosa Summit.

*   *   *   *

Water access: Water may be obtained by detouring left, northwest, for 1.0 mile to a restaurant at the junction of Highway 74 and Cahuilla Road (Highway 371). For supplies, one could walk 6.0 miles farther west on Highway 371 to Anza.

*   *   *   *

Across Pines-to-Palms Highway 74, you skirt a dirt trailhead parking area and ascend gently in a recently burned brushland. Just a minute up the trail is a mileage sign and a 6-foot stone monument that diagrams the PCT's route through the San Jacintos and commemorates the death of a trail worker. Beyond, you walk north to a ridgetop, then switchback once down on its north side. You are soon engaged in a sandy, fitful ascent into and out of numerous small ravines and around picturesque blocky cliffs of crumbling granite. You pass close along the western face of a low ridge, then descend short switchbacks to hop across the usually dry creek (5040-3.7) that drains Penrod Canyon. Here, a comfortable waterless camp could be made under Coulter pines and live oaks. The track winds up-canyon, crossing the stream bed

See maps B5, B6

see MAP B7

see MAP B5

twice more before climbing to sunnier chamise and oak chaparral for a contour of the canyon's eastern slopes. The PCT eventually strikes Road 6S01A (5700-2.0), ascending from the west to reach an open-pit limestone quarry just above your trail. Your way proceeds directly across the road to resume the ascent, now steeper, along Penrod Canyon's east wall. Excellent vistas west over the shoulder of Thomas Mountain and south to Bucksnort Mountain are obtained on this stretch, just before you swing east around a nose to abruptly

See map B6

see MAP B9

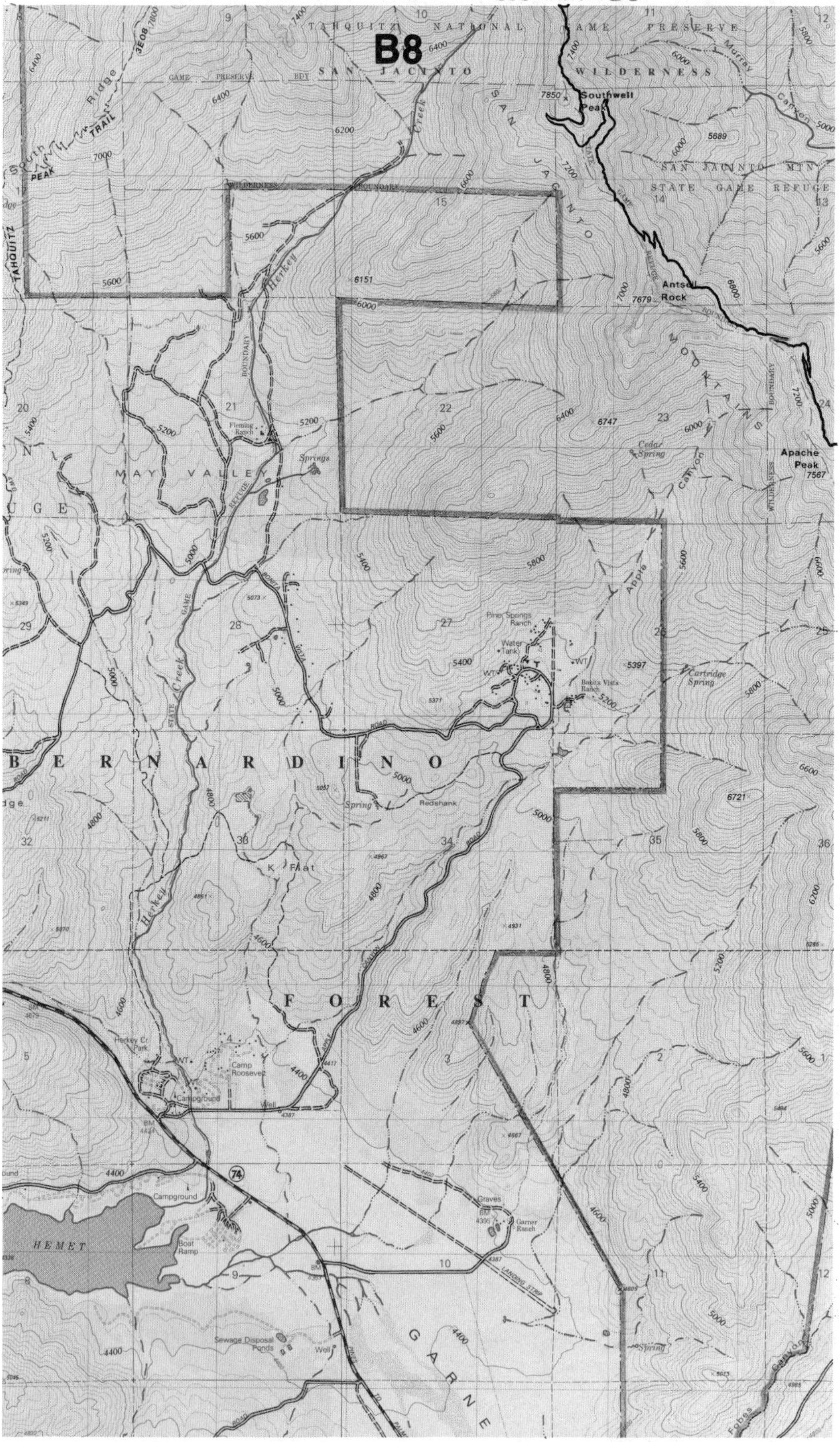
B8
TAHQUITZ NATIONAL GAME PRESERVE
SAN JACINTO WILDERNESS
Southwell Peak
7850
SAN JACINTO MTN STATE GAME REFUGE
Antsel Rock
7679
SAN JACINTO MOUNTAINS
Apache Peak
7567
Murray Canyon
South Ridge TRAIL
3E08
TAHQUITZ PEAK
WILDERNESS BOUNDARY
Herkey Creek
6151
6747
Ceda Spring
Canyon
Fleming Ranch
Springs
MAY VALLEY
REFUGE
Apple
Pine Springs Ranch
Water Tank
Bonita Vista Ranch
5397
Cartridge Spring
BERNARDINO
Redshank
Spring
K Flat
6721
FOREST
Herkey Cr Park
Camp Roosevelt
Campground
Well
74
HEMET
Boat Ramp
Graves
Garner Ranch
LANDING STRIP
Sewage Disposal Ponds
GARNE
Fobes Canyon

see MAP B7

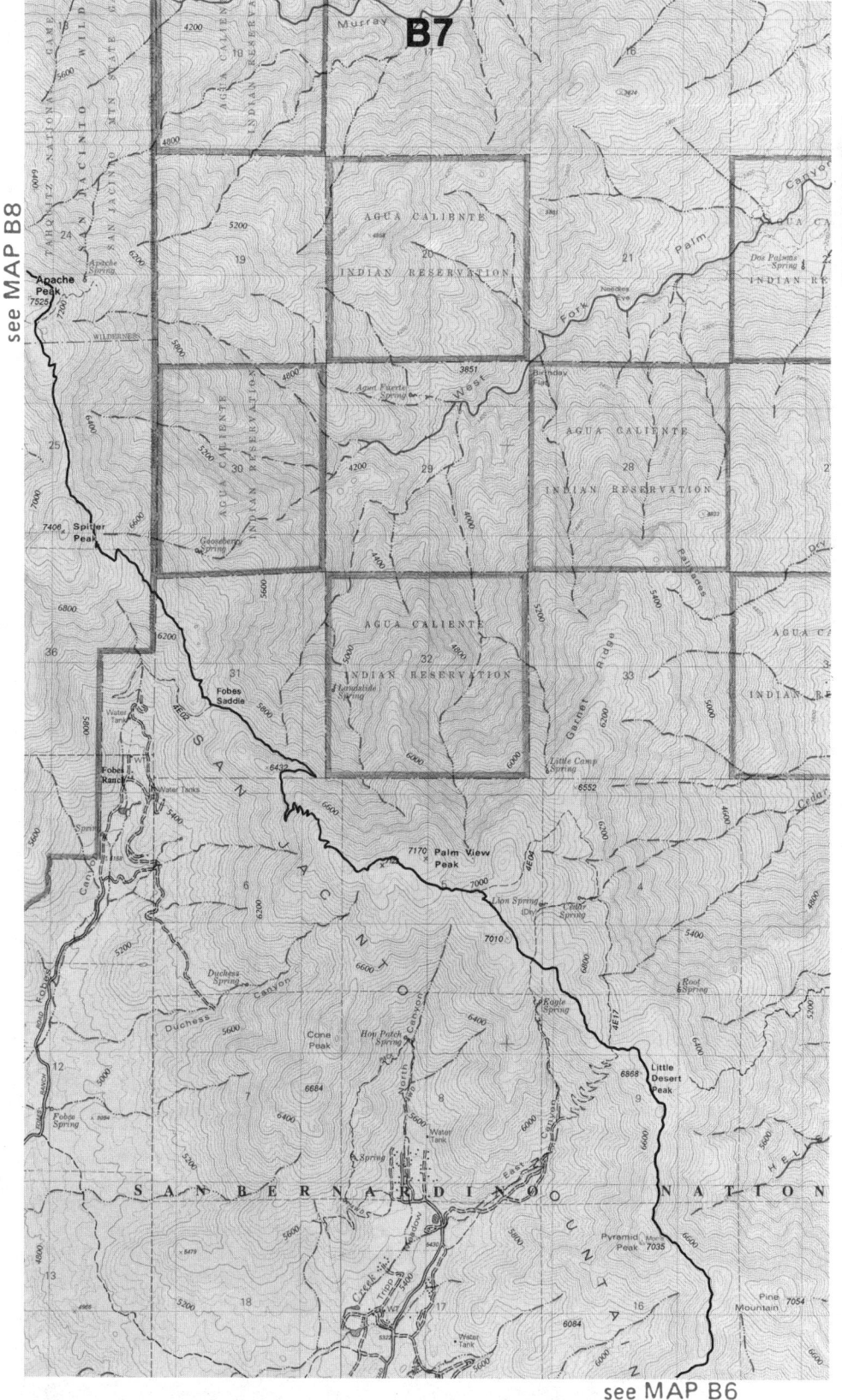

see MAP B8

see MAP B6

encounter marble bedrock. The first leg of the PCT's climb into the San Jacinto Mountains ends soon, as you first go through a stock gate, then pass southeast-traversing Trail 3E15 to Bull Canyon, and in 50 yards top out at a saddle on the Desert Divide (5950-0.9). Here are junctions with Live Oak Trail 4E03, right, and the Tunnel Spring Trail, left.

*   *   *   *

Water access: Travelers low on water are advised to go to Live Oak Spring, if they also plan camping or lunch, but to Tunnel Spring—half the distance—for emergency water only. Live Oak Spring is reached by a sunny 1-mile, well-graded path that descends east from the saddle, eventually finding two nice campsites under an enormous gold-cup oak and box elders. It has much better camping than Tunnel Spring, and delightful clean water in a circular concrete trough.

The Tunnel Spring Trail descends southwest from the PCT atop the gap. Steep, rocky tread leads down 0.3 mile to where the trail moderates in a grove of oaks and four tall Coulter pines, which have scattered their huge, clawed cones on the ground. Now look right, north, to a shallow stream bed and a faint trail along a black PVC pipe. This goes up a few yards to the metal cattle trough at Tunnel Spring, shaded by box elders. Poor camping is the best that can be found nearby.

*   *   *   *

Resuming your northbound trek, you turn north along the east face of the Desert Divide. Shady interior live oaks and Coulter pines alternate with xeric chaparral areas (look for shaggy Mojave yuccas) as the trail ascends gently across Julian schist to the east slopes of Lion Peak. You get sporadic vistas down Oak Canyon to subdivided upper Palm Canyon, then a rough switchback leads to the ridgetop north of Lion Peak. For the next 2 miles the route remains on or near the divide, traversing gneiss, schist, quartzite and marble bedrock and skirting past low chaparral laced with rabbitbrush and cacti. Little Desert Peak (6883') offers panoramas east and north to the Coachella Valley and Palm Springs, and west to coniferous Thomas Mountain and pastoral Garner Valley.

Moments later, a short descent ends at a saddle where you cross the Cedar Spring Trail 4E17 (6780-4.1), which descends southwest to Morris Ranch and north a short mile to Cedar Spring Camp (6330')—the best camp and the only permanent water along the southern Desert Divide.

*   *   *   *

Alternate route: In the face of high snowpack or early-spring snowstorms on the Desert Divide, northbound hikers should consider leaving the PCT via the Cedar Spring Trail, exiting south to the Pines-to-Palms Highway, then going north to Idyllwild and Cabazon. The Tunnel Spring Trail down to Penrod Canyon may also be used for the same purpose. In the face of severe storms, another option would be to go east on the Pines-to-Palms Highway to Palm Springs, and thence northwest to White Water.

*   *   *   *

The route, however, steeply ascends the ridgecrest, then it briefly descends to another saddle with a junction (6945-0.6). A very rough trail, which descends steeply south to Morris Ranch, passes a polluted cattle trough at Eagle Spring, while a similar trail, which descends north ¾ mile to Cedar Spring Camp, passes often-dry Lion Spring.

Continuing northwest, you soon pass Trail 4E04 (7080-0.5), which starts east from near Palm View Peak, then drops north toward Garnet Ridge. Then, past a 7123-foot summit, you descend, often steeply, on a rocky, nebulous tread back into a cooler environment of white firs growing at the head of the spectacular West Fork Palm Canyon. Presently the route emerges on brushy Fobes Saddle and meets Fobes Ranch Trail 4E02 (5990-2.4), which descends west. Thirsty hikers may choose to go west down this overgrown trail to reach a spring in ½ mile (poor camping), but must respect private property and descend no farther.

The PCT north from this saddle ascends steeply to the upper slopes of Spitler Peak, where one encounters a charred forest of black oak, white fir, incense-cedar and Jeffrey pine, gloomy mementos of a massive 1980 blaze that blackened almost the entire upper West Fork Palm Canyon and Murray and Andreas can-

See maps B6, B7

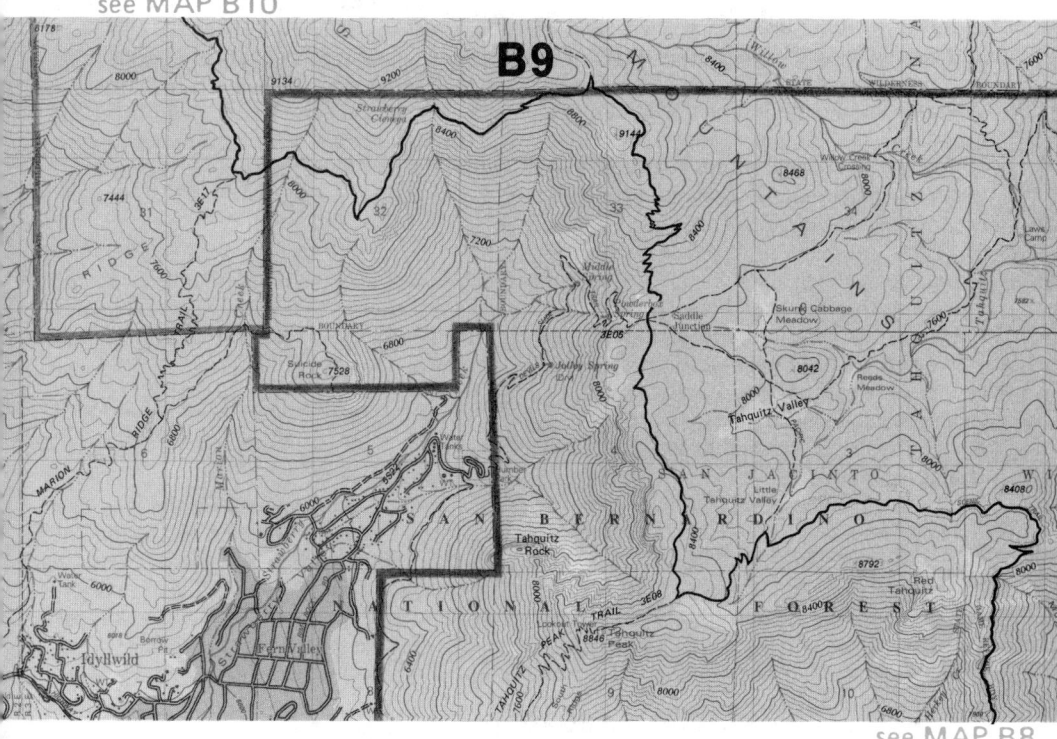

see MAP B10

B9

see MAP B8

yons. One will find evidence of it all the way to Red Tahquitz. Along your climb you enter San Jacinto Wilderness and then beyond some very steep pitches the PCT levels to wind around to the north of Spitler Peak. It then descends just east of the rocky spine that forms the ridge between Spitler and Apache peaks. Gaining this knife-edge col, where the PCT was widened by fire fighters to form a fuelbreak, the trail wastes no time in attacking the next objective: Apache Peak. Steep rocky-sandy tread leads up its southern slopes to emerge on a black, burned summit plateau. Here you find a sign marking the Apache Spring Trail (7430-2.6), which descends steeply east ½ mile to poor camps at burned-over, usually flowing Apache Spring. From your junction too, a short use trail ascends northwest to the viewful, if ugly, summit of Apache Peak.

The PCT now begins to descend gently along the eastern flanks of Apache Peak, passing through a ghost forest of immense, burned manzanitas. After a useless 0.2-mile-long switchback you reach a fine overlook of the northern Coachella Valley and of Joshua Tree National Monument, which lies well beyond the valley in the Little San Bernardino Mountains. A well-constructed stretch next leads west along a cliff face to a gap, where one can dry-camp, at the head of Apple Canyon. To circumvent the granitic ramparts of Antsell Rock, the PCT's next leg follows a dynamited path under its sweeping northeast slopes, which are thankfully shaded by conifers spared from the 1980 fire. Once north of Antsell Rock's major buttresses, you take switchbacks for a 400-foot elevation gain to reach the San Jacinto's crest at a pleasantly montane gap (7200-2.9). Big-cone spruce, a close relative of Douglas-fir, plus white fir and mountain mahogany provide pleasant cover as the often-dynamited path ascends another 400 feet, first on the east and then on the southwest slopes of Southwell Peak. Notice Lake Hemet, lying just east of the active Thomas Mountain Fault, at the head of Garner Valley, to your southwest.

North of Southwell Peak the rocky PCT is dynamited to traverse under precipitous, granitic gendarmes, and the ascending hiker can gaze northwest to Tahquitz Peak and north to Red Tahquitz, or east down rugged Murray Canyon. The ascent ends (8380-3.4) above

See maps B7, B8, B9

Andreas Canyon's deep gorge, where your route turns west to descend gently on duff and sand and eventually to cross South Fork Tahquitz Creek in a forest, and then join, moments later, the Tahquitz Valley Trail (8075-1.5). This trail descends north ⅓ mile to good camps and water in Little Tahquitz Valley, and then traverses to Tahquitz and Skunk Cabbage meadows.

From your junction the PCT climbs southwest through dense groves of lodgepole pines to manzanitas and western white pines, which grow on gravelly slopes of decomposed granite. Presently you come to a junction with the Tahquitz Peak Trail 3E08 (8570-0.6), which offers a side trip ½ mile up to the peak's airy summit lookout.

*   *   *   *

Side route: This trip is well worthwhile, for from the 8846-foot summit you can get an idea of how steep canyons, such as Strawberry Valley below, are eroding back into the high, roll-ing landscape that lies between Red Tahquitz and San Jacinto Peak. Tahquitz Peak commemorates a legendary Cahuilla Indian demon who lived hereabouts, dining on unsuspecting Indian maidens and, when displeased, giving the weather a turn for the worse.

*   *   *   *

Those who need to press on will turn north and ease down the PCT to Saddle Junction (8100-1.3), the crossroads for an array of trails into the San Jacinto Wilderness.

*   *   *   *

Resupply access: From the saddle Devils Slide Trail 3E05 descends 2.5 miles west past three springs to Fern Valley Road 5S22. The mountain-resort community of Idyllwild—a good place to resupply and take a layover day—lies 2 miles down this road. Also leaving the saddle are two more trails, one branching northeast to Long Valley, and another one southeast

See map B9

Tahquitz Peak and Tahquitz Rock, from near Wellman Divide Trail

to Tahquitz Valley.

*　　*　　*　　*

The PCT continues north, soon switchbacking out of the forest to slopes that offer excellent over-the-shoulder vistas toward Tahquitz (Lily) Rock, a magnet for Southern California rock climbers. Almost 1000 feet higher than Saddle Junction, the PCT levels to turn left from a junction with the Wellmans Cienaga Trail (9030-1.8), just within the confines of Mount San Jacinto Wilderness State Park.

*　　*　　*　　*

Side route: This trail arcs about 2 miles northeast to Round Valley Trail Camp and beyond to 10,804-foot San Jacinto Peak, a recommended side trip.

*　　*　　*　　*

From the junction the PCT immediately leaves the state park and descends on a generally westward bearing above Strawberry Valley's steep headwall to Strawberry Cienaga (8560-0.9), a trickling sphagnum-softened freshet and a viewful lunch stop. "Cienaga" is a Spanish word, often seen in Southern California, meaning "swamp" or "marsh." Further descent leads to a forested junction with Marion Ridge Trail 3E17 (8070-1.4). Just before this junction, Marion Ridge/Strawberry Junction Trail Camp is found on a small ridge south of the trail. This makes a very pleasant and viewful, but unfortunately, waterless camp. There may be some trickles of water until mid-summer in heads of canyons nearby.

*　　*　　*　　*

Side route: As an alternative to the Devil's Slide Trail, one can use the Marion Ridge Trail to descend 4.3 miles to Highway 243, just ½ mile west of downtown Idyllwild. Multiple dry flats in open pines and firs 2–3 minutes below the PCT's junction with the Marion Ridge Trail could also offer dry camping.

*　　*　　*　　*

Now out of the Federal wilderness and back in Mount San Jacinto State Park, the PCT turns north to ascend Marion Mountain's pleasant mixed-conifer slopes, and eventually passes two closely spaced trail junctions.

*　　*　　*　　*

Side route: The first, the Marion Mountain Trail, descends west-southwest to the environs of Marion Mountain and Fern Basin campgrounds. The second, the Seven Pines Trail, descends generally northwest, then west to a saddle, from which Road 4S02 switchbacks almost 2 miles down to Dark Canyon Campground.

*　　*　　*　　*

Soon after the second lateral your trail heads heads up along a marshy dank creek: the reliable North Fork San Jacinto River, which you cross (8830-2.1), below Deer Springs. This used to be a campsite, but is now closed to allow revegetation. Before leaving, hikers should restock their water bottles, since the next water along the route is from Snow Creek, at the northern base of the San Jacinto Mountains, a punishing 25-mile descent away.

A minute beyond the infant San Jacinto River, you climb to a nearby junction with the San Jacinto Peak Trail, which is the return route of the recommended side trip to the peak's summit. From the junction you switchback down to Fuller Ridge (8725-1.9), a rocky, white-fir-covered spine separating the San Jacinto and San Gorgonio river drainages. ■ *Here the northbound trekker gets his first good view of the San Bernardino Mountains' 11,499-foot San Gorgonio Mountain, to the north, which is Southern California's highest point. Separating that range from ours is San Gorgonio Pass, 7000 feet below you, lying between the Banning Fault and other branches of the great San Andreas Fault (also known as the San Andreas Rift Zone).* ■

The PCT's route along Fuller Ridge is a tortuous one, composed for the most part of miniature switchbacks, alternately descending and climbing, which wind under small gendarmes and around wind-beaten conifers. In a little over 2 miles, though, the route takes to north-facing slopes, and, exchanging state wilderness for a brief stint in the Federal wilderness, it gently descends to a small dirt-road parking circle at Fuller Ridge Trailhead Remote Campsite

See maps B9, B10

see MAP B1

B10

see MAP B9

(7750-3.9). Pleasant but waterless, the sites lie in open stands of ponderosa pine and white fir. The PCT, marked by a post, resumes on the west side of the road loop, heading due north past a site. It rounds northwest above, then drops to cross, well-used Black Mountain Road 4S01 (7670-0.2).

*   *   *   *

Water access: Those low on water may opt to follow this road left, descending 1.3 miles to Black Mountain Group Campground.

*   *   *   *

The trail leaves the road on a gentle-to-moderate descent north along a ridge clothed in an open stand of mixed conifers. You switchback down three times across the nose of the ridge separating Snow Creek from chaparral-decked Brown Creek. ∎ *More-open conditions on the west side of the ridge allow for sweeping vistas: hulking San Gorgonio Mountain looms to the north, above the desert pass that bears its name, while, stretching to the northwest, the San Bernardino and San Gabriel valleys, flanked by the lofty summits of the San Gabriel Mountains, extend toward the Los Angeles basin. On a clear day in winter or spring, snow-flecked Mount San Antonio (Mount Baldy) and Mount Wilson are both visible in that range.* ∎ You re-enter San Jacinto Wilderness and presently your sandy, lupine- and penstemon-lined path meets a switchback in a dirt road (6860-1.9), which winds eastward into a shallow basin. Marked by large ducks the trail leaves the northwest side of the open gap containing the road, but soon your route turns south to descend alongside and just below that road. After a bit your course veers from the road and winds east down dry washes and under the shade of low scrub oaks to a narrow gap (6390-1.3) in a sawblade ridge of granodiorite needles. Four long switchbacks descend the east face of this prominent ridge, depositing us in noticeably more xeric environs. ∎ *Initially, Coulter pines replace other montane conifers, and then, as the way arcs north in continual descent, you enter a true chaparral: yerba santa, buckwheat, holly-leaf cherry, scrub oak, manzanita and yucca supply the sparse ground cover, while scarlet gilia and yellow blazing star add spring*

color. Unlike chaparral communities moistened by maritime air, the desert-facing slopes here force these species to contend with much more extreme drought conditions. As a result, many more of the plants growing here are annuals, which avoid drought by lying dormant as seed, while others, such as yerba santa, wilt and drop their soft leaves to prevent water loss during sustained dry periods. ∎

A continued moderate downgrade and another set of long switchbacks soon allow you to inspect the awesome, avalanche-raw, 9600-foot north escarpment of San Jacinto Peak, which rises above the cascades of Snow Creek. ∎ *To your northeast the confused alluvial terrain beyond San Gorgonio Pass attests to recent activity along the San Andreas Fault. Beyond, suburban Desert Hot Springs shimmers in the Coachella Valley heat, backdropped by the Little San Bernardino Mountains.* ∎

Inexorably, your descent continues at a moderate grade, presently switchbacking in broad sweeps across a dry ravine on slopes north of West Fork Snow Creek. After striking a small saddle (3200-8.6) just west of knob 3252, the trail, now taking an overly gentle grade, swings north, then northwest down a boulder-studded hillside. You note the small village of Snow Creek lying below you at the mountain's base before your way makes three small switchbacks and then heads back southeast toward Snow Canyon. After winding your way through a veritable forest of 20-30-foot high orange, granitic boulders, you negotiate a final set of switchbacks before dropping to cross a dry creekbed on the western edge of Snow Canyon. Soon after, you strike narrow, paved Snow Canyon Road (1725-4.2). Here a sign points northeast, across the road, indicating a mile-long deadend segment of PCT tread that has been abandoned in favor of an eventual alignment west of Snow Canyon Road. Snow Canyon is both a game refuge and a water supply for Palm Springs, so camping here is not allowed. Additionally, most of Snow Creek's water is carried east in a pipeline, and no water is available here, so continue a bit farther to reach water.

Doing this, you make a moderate descent along narrow Snow Canyon Road, which winds north down Snow Canyon's rubbly alluvial fan, often near a small, usually flowing western branch of Snow Creek. This stream may be dry by April of drought years. If so, the closest

See maps B10, B11

water is available from homes in Snow Creek village, but there is no camping currently allowed thereabouts. The PCT Association and the BLM are working with the Desert Water Agency to develop formal water access for the PCT somewhere nearby. Eventually the road simultaneously leaves San Bernardino National Forest and its San Jacinto Wilderness at a Desert Water Agency gate, and then it veers northwest to hop across the western branch. Just beyond, your route joins paved Falls Creek Road (1225-1.0) at the outskirts of the small village of Snow Creek. Southbound hikers should note that this community is their last certain water source until North Fork San Jacinto River, a grueling 24 miles and a 7600-foot climb away high in the San Jacintos. For the northbound, the next

water is at Mesa Wind Station, 6.5 miles (an emergency source only), or better, at the Whitewater River, a long, hot 13.3 miles away.

Now you briefly follow Falls Creek Road northwest to a junction with Snow Creek Road 3S01 (1230-0.2). From here the permanent PCT route starts a contour northwest. Constructed by Sierra Club volunteers and the Bureau of Land Management, the next 2 miles of PCT are not really trail at all. Because of shifting sands and the possibility that off-road-vehicle enthusiasts might abuse an actual trail, they decided not to build an actual trail across broad San Gorgonio Pass. Instead, the PCT route is indicated by a row of 5-foot-tall 4x4 posts, some metal, some redwood, each emblazoned with the triangular PCT shield and with white

See map B11

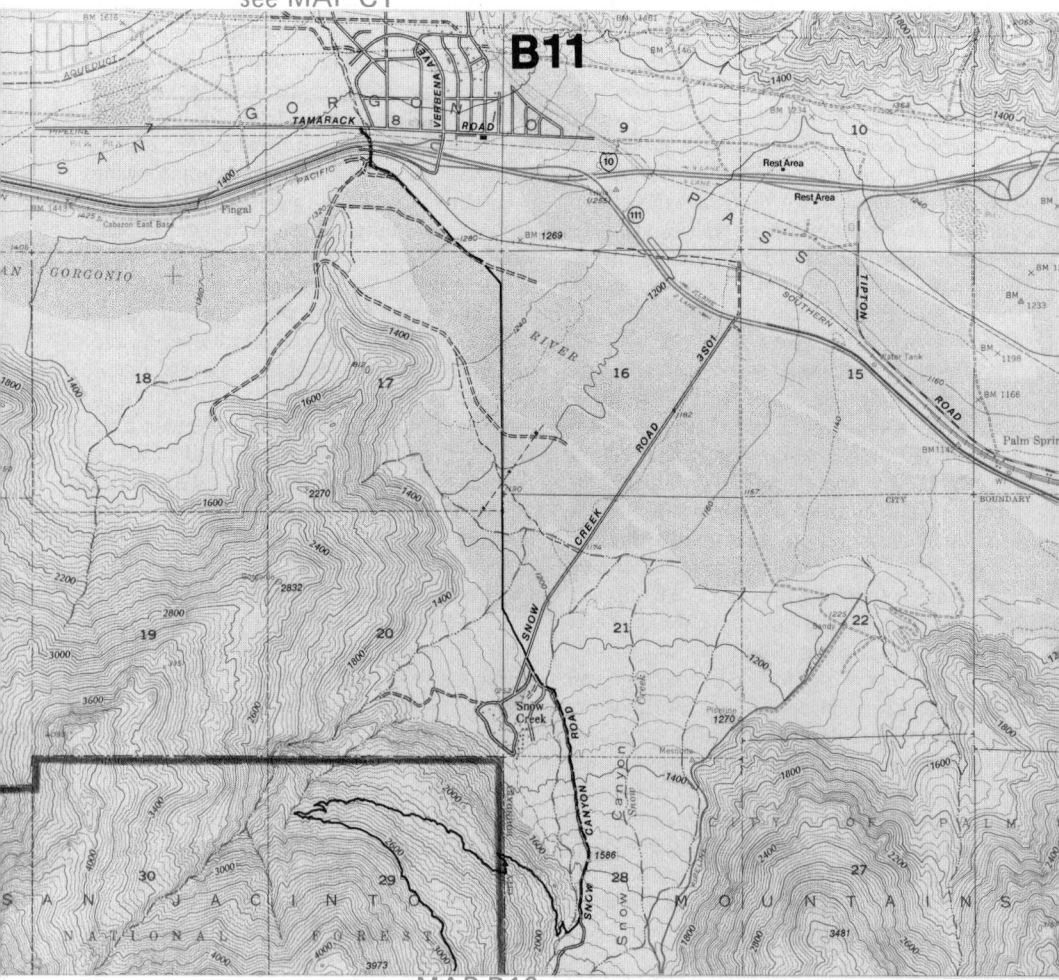

see MAP C1

see MAP B10

directional arrows. Standing beside one post, you can usually see the next one without much difficulty. The first metal post stands a few yards northwest of Snow Creek Road, in a field of foxtails. It indicates the way (330° bearing) to the first of a long line of redwood posts that march due north along a section boundary.

The actual route is somewhat more tortuous, winding through well-spaced head-high yellow-flowered creosote bushes on a very gentle descent. A few minutes' walk leads across a sandy wash, which at about 1188 feet elevation is the PCT's lowest point south of the Columbia Gorge on the Oregon-Washington border. Another few minutes finds your not-a-trail intersecting a pair of crossing jeep roads (1195-0.7) under a high-tension powerline. Beyond, the wooden posts continue north, now across a more cobbly desert floor with mixed shrubbery. You cross a good gravel road (1210-0.2), then proceed across numerous sandy washes that constitute the ephemeral San Gorgonio River. Usually no water at all is to be found, but often there is a strong westerly wind, which throws stinging sand in your face. Also it sets hundreds of power-generating wind turbines flapping like alarmed sea gulls, these standing to the north, across Interstate 10. In the rainy season, look for purple-flower clus-ters of sand verbena hereabouts.

Eventually, metal posts indicate a bend northwest in the route to soon join a good dirt road (1265-0.7). This you trace left, northwest, keeping just south of a 20-foot-high alluvial bank upon which runs the busy Southern Pacific Railroad. You soon diverge from the good road to a poorer one, well-marked by posts, which leads obviously to a tangle of roads at the mouth of Stubbe Canyon Creek (1320-0.7). Here the route emerges from three concrete bridges, one of Southern Pacific Railroad and two of Interstate 10. Now you follow a dirt road that goes north under the bridges, then clamber up a road bank to paved Tamarack Road (1360-0.1).

*　　　*　　　*　　　*

Resupply access: A slowly dying suburb, West Palm Springs Village, is centered ⅓ mile east along Tamarack Road, at Interstate 10's Verbena Avenue offramp. Although water might be obtained in an emergency from a few homes there, the village has no other resources for PCT travelers. To resupply, hitchhike, as recommended under "Supplies," 12.5 miles east to Palm Springs or 4.5 miles west to Cabazon.

*　　　*　　　*　　　*

See map B11

Mt. San Jacinto, from slopes above West Fork Snow Creek

San Gorg. Pass -I-15

C

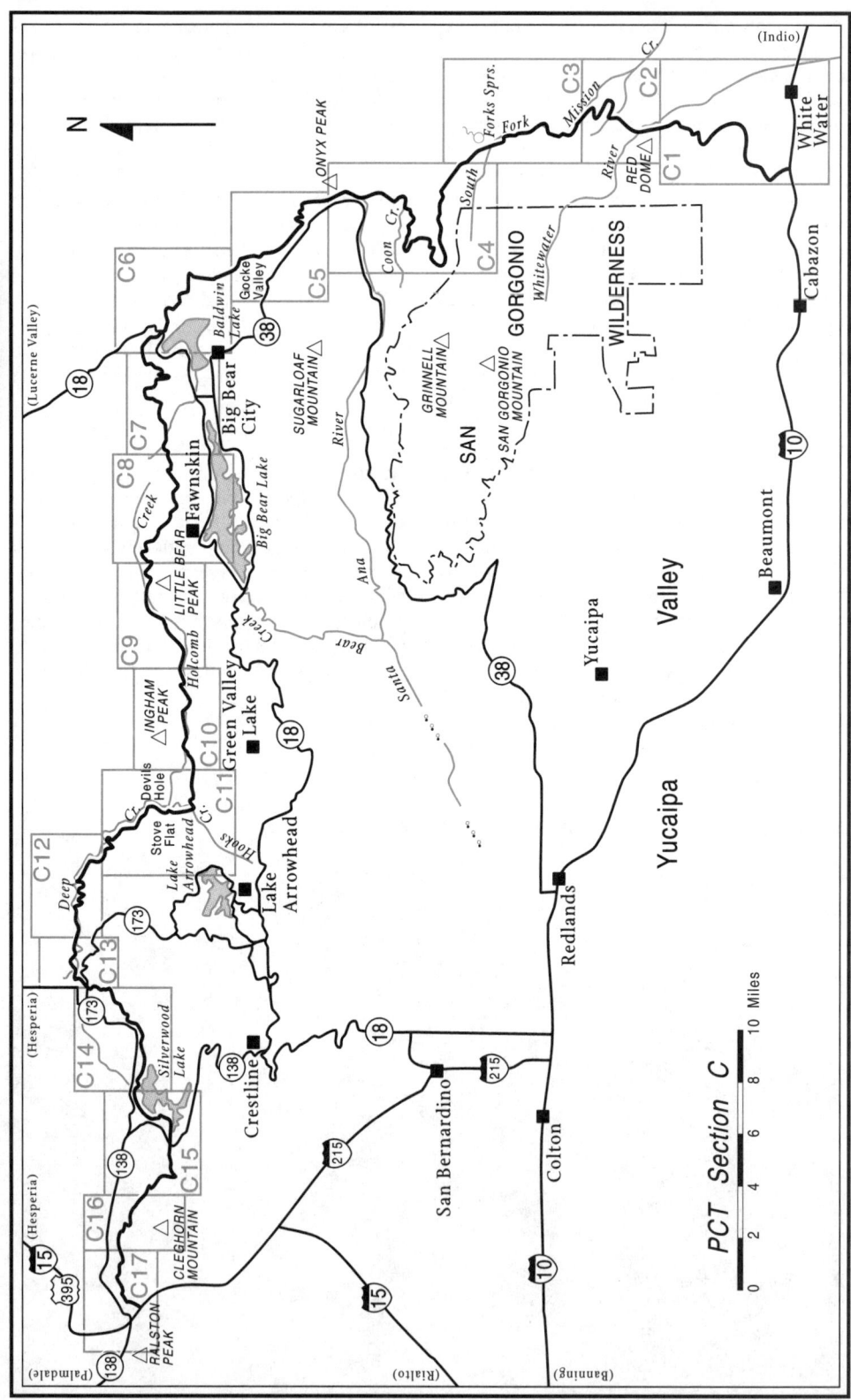

PCT Section C

Section C
San Gorgonio Pass to Interstate 15 near Cajon Pass

Introduction: Running the entire length of the San Bernardino Mountains, this long trail section samples most of the diverse ecosystems found there. Beginning in San Gorgonio Pass in the sweltering heat of a typical Colorado Desert (Lower Sonoran Zone) ecosystem, the Pacific Crest Trail crosses the San Andreas Fault and then climbs through a sparse, drab chaparral of bayonet-sharp cacti and thorny scrub along the Whitewater River and Mission Creek. Though sprung from subalpine snowbanks high in the San Gorgonio Wilderness, these streams almost all evaporate or sink beneath desert gravels before reaching the foothills.

As you climb higher, small drought-tolerant pinyon pines, favored food source of Indians and various animals, soon border the trail, heralding your passage through the Upper Sonoran Zone. These trees gradually mingle with Jeffrey pines and incense-cedars until, at about 7000 feet, you find ourselves in the crisp air and enveloping forests of the Transition Zone. Just north of Coon Creek, at the 8750-foot apex of the PCT in the San Bernardino Mountains, the route touches the Canadian Zone, where isolated snow patches might linger into early summer. Hikers traversing the high San Bernardinos in April or May should expect possible hail or snow and nightly subfreezing temperatures. Bring warm clothing and carry a tent. From the high point, one can turn southwest to scan the San Gorgonio Wilderness' high summits, where hardy subalpine conifers huddle below gale-screening ridges. The PCT was routed around the wilderness because its backpacker population was already excessive.

Nearing dammed Big Bear Lake, a popular resort area, the PCT alternates between Jeffrey-pine and pinyon forest. In this northern rainshadow of the San Bernardinos, plant and animal life is much more influenced by proximity to the high Mojave Desert, stretching northward, than by the terrain's elevation, which would normally foster a uniform montane Jeffrey-pine-and-fir forest. Instead, Joshua trees, cacti, mountain mahogany and sagebrush share the rolling hillsides with dry pinyon-pine groves, and drive Jeffrey pines, incense-cedars and white firs away to higher summits or to the cold-air microclimates of stream beds.

North of Big Bear Lake the PCT begins to trend west, following the main axis of the San Bernardino Mountains. A part of the Transverse Range Province, which includes the San Gabriel Mountains and other mountain chains stretching west to the Channel Islands, the San Bernardinos cut conspicuously across the lay of other California physiographic features, which trend northwest-southeast. Long before being intruded by molten rock that solidified to form granitic plutons, the region now straddled by the San Bernardinos had been alternately low land and shallow sea floor. Evidence of this lies in two rock types you will encounter often: the Furnace marble—derived from marine carbonates that became limestone—and the Saragossa quartzite—derived from sand that became sandstone. The limestone and sandstone were then altered under heat and pressure, perhaps several times, to reach their present metamorphic states.

Near Lake Arrowhead, another reservoir originally constructed to store water to irrigate foothill orange groves, the PCT again veers north, now down Deep Creek, a permanent stream feeding the ephemeral Mojave River. The floral composition of the Mojave Desert, seen here and also later as the PCT skirts Summit Valley, differs strikingly from the lower Colorado Desert flora seen farther south. Bitter-cold, windy winters here account for many of the differences.

Section C ends unremarkably under 6-lane Interstate 15 in Cajon Canyon, overshadowed by massive workings of humanity—the freeway, the powerlines from the Colorado River, and the multiple railroad tracks. These in turn are dwarfed by an awesome artifact of nature—the cleft of the San Andreas Fault, which slashes through Cajon Canyon and bends east to demarcate the southern base of the San Bernardino Mountains.

Declination: 13°E

Points on Route	S→N	Mi. Btwn. Pts.	N→S
near Interstate 10 in San Gorgonio Pass	0.0		132.7
Mesa Wind Station	3.9	3.9	128.8
camps by Whitewater River ford	10.7	6.8	122.0
East Fork Mission Creek Road	15.9	5.2	116.8
Forks Springs	22.3	6.4	110.4
Road 1N93 and Mission Creek Trail Camp	29.5	7.2	103.2
Coon Creek Jumpoff Group Camp	36.1	6.6	96.6
dirt road just east of Onyx Summit	41.8	5.7	90.9
Arrastre Trail Camp at Deer Spring	45.9	4.1	86.8
Highway 18 near dry Baldwin Lake	55.4	9.5	77.3
Doble Trail Camp	57.9	2.5	74.8
Van Dusen Canyon Road to Big Bear City	64.3	6.4	68.4
Holcomb Valley Road to Fawnskin	67.8	3.5	64.9
Little Bear Springs Trail Camp	75.0	7.2	57.7
Crab Flats Road	81.8	6.8	50.9
Holcomb Crossing Trail Camp	83.7	1.9	49.0
Deep Creek Bridge to Lake Arrowhead	87.8	4.1	44.9
Deep Creek Hot Spring	97.2	9.4	35.5
Mojave River Forks Reservoir Dam	102.2	5.0	30.5
Hwy. 173 above Mojave River Forks Reservoir	103.7	1.5	29.0
Road 2N33 near Cedar Springs Dam	113.1	9.4	19.6
Silverwood Lake Area's entrance road	119.1	6.0	13.6
Little Horsethief Canyon's dry creek bed	126.2	7.1	6.5
Interstate 15 near Cajon Pass	132.7	6.5	0.0

Supplies: West Palm Springs Village, at the beginning of Section C, has nothing for hikers. Supplies may be purchased 4.5 miles west on Interstate 10, in Cabazon, which has limited services, or 10 miles west on that freeway, in Banning, which has all services. Cabazon Ranch Outfitters, located at 50150 Esperanza Avenue in Cabazon, offers professional pack animal support and guiding in the San Jacintos and San Bernardinos. Contact Barbara Gronek, POB 876, Cabazon, CA 92230, or phone: (909) 849-2528. Horse feed is available at their facility, and they host, free of charge: corrals, water, hot showers, camping and package holds for riders and hikers. Palm Springs lies 12.5 miles east via Interstate 10 and Highway 111. It has a dazzling array of markets, hotels and fine eateries.

Big Bear City, 3 miles south down Van Dusen Canyon Road from the 64.3-mile point on the PCT, is the next convenient provisioning stop. It boasts a post office, stores, restaurants, motels and laundromats beside shallow, picturesque Big Bear Lake. In recent years, the fire station has offered showers to PCT hikers. Fawnskin, another resort community, is located on the northwest shore of Big Bear Lake, and it is 3.7 miles off-route along Holcomb Valley Road, 67.8 miles from the start. It has a post office, stores, restaurants and motels. It is also accessible via the Cougar Crest Trail, at the 67.0-mile point of this PCT section, by way of a 2-mile detour. The next chance for supplies lies in Lake Arrowhead, 3½ miles from the PCT's crossing of Deep Creek, 87.8 miles from the start. Here you'll find post office, stores, restaurants and motels. Crestline, a similar mountain village, also offers similar accommodations for hikers who hitchhike south 10 miles on Highway 138 from the 119.1-mile point of the PCT, at Silverwood Lake State Recreation Area. Travelers with less extensive needs may avail themselves of a small store and cafe a short distance off the trail in the recreation area, or Summit Valley Store, reached via a short detour from the Mojave-scorched PCT in Summit Valley, at the 109.5-mile point.

Section C terminates at a roadend just shy of Interstate 15 in Cajon Canyon. This paved spur road leads 0.6 mile northwest to meet Highway 138 about 200 yards east of its overpass of Interstate 15 at Cajon Junction. Gas stations and a fine 24-hour restaurant lie near this cloverleaf, from where Highway 138 continues northwest 8½ miles to Highway 2, which goes 5½ miles to Wrightwood. This pleasant mountain community has a post office, stores, restaurants, motels and a laundromat. Those who don't mind a return to true civilization—smog, congestion, street lights and concrete—may go south 17 miles on Interstate 15 to San Bernardino, which has all the dubious advantages of a hectic metropolis.

Water: Be sure to carry ample water north from West Palm Springs, since the Whitewater River and the lower reaches of Mission Creek that the PCT traverses are often dry by June of drought years. The most certain water source is Fork Springs, a mind-broiling 22.3 miles into the journey. For most of the remainder of this San Bernardino Mountains section, however, water sources are encountered regularly, even if they are not numerous. This situation changes for the last leg, along the rim of the Mojave Desert, however. Be sure to leave Deep Creek and Silverwood Lake with a few liters of water per person—the stretches of dusty chaparral along Summit Valley, and over to Cajon Pass, are usually bone-dry.

Ticks: Ticks are a ubiquitous problem in the grassy fields and brushy slopes of the PCT as it traverses southern California. Bites by these blood-sucking arachnid pests cause two general problems for hikers and equestrians: 1) How to get them off and what to do to the wound; and 2) rare infections. The recognition of Lyme disease has raised the level of concern about infections from tick bites; thankfully, tick bites in California's inland mountains are more nuisance than risk.

Ticks burrow their headparts into the skin of the groin, armpits, hairline or other body areas, especially where there is a constriction created by snug clothing, such as the waistband. The trick is to get them out of you, whole, without doing further injury. Countless lore has been retold in Scouting and woodcraft manuals about the task of removing embedded ticks from the body. Home methods abound, such as to apply the tip of a hot match to the tick's derriere, or to smother it with vaseline, margarine or nail polish, or to irritate it with a dollop of gasoline or alcohol. Equal argument has arisen as to whether they should be tugged on with fingers or tweezers, or unscrewed clockwise, or the reverse. Scientific investigation has shown that *all of the above methods work*, but the most effective one is also the simplest—simply grasping the tick, with tweezers or fingers, as close to its attachment to you as possible, and pulling gently, but firmly, until the tick lets go.

Once the tick has been removed, examine its business-end to make sure that you haven't ripped its head off, and examine the skin wound for a black or brown dot that might represent a tick head left behind. If seen, remove it with tweezers. In any event, try to prevent infection: wash the wound with soap and water, apply a small amount of antibiotic ointment, and try to keep it clean. No further preventive treatment is ever necessary.

Tick-borne infections are the feared hazard of tick bites. All are sometimes difficult to diagnose, even by doctors, so prompt hospital attention is recommended for anyone who has symptoms that suggest such an infection. **Lyme disease** is exceedingly rare in any mountains of California, and particularly unlikely in the southern Sierra and southern California ranges. It is characterized by a migrating rash, fevers, flu-like symptoms, and worsening joint pains. It is easily treated by antibiotics.

Spotted Fever is marked by high fever, headache, and a red spotty rash that becomes purple over time. This very serious illness is promptly treated by antibiotics. It is quite rare throughout the Pacific West.

Tick Paralysis is a rarer condition of progressive severe weakness. It is usually completely reversed by removal of the tick.

Prevention of tick bites is the best medicine. In tick country, wear long-sleeved clothing, with cuffs tucked under sox or into boots. Insect repellent is also of some use for ticks—apply it liberally, and often, to skin and clothing.

Maps: *White Water*   *Fawnskin*
Catclaw Flat   *Butler Peak*
Onyx Peak   *Lake Arrowhead*
Moonridge   *Silverwood Lake*
San Gorgonio Peak   *Cajon*
Big Bear City

───────────────── **The Route** ─────────────────

Reach the southern terminus of Section C via Interstate 10's Verbenia Avenue exit. Head briefly north to Tamarack Road, which parallels the freeway, and follow it ⅓ mile west to the posted PCT, just west of Fremontia Road.

Easy-to-follow PCT trail tread climbs gently north from Tamarack Road, first just west of the dry bed of Stubbe Canyon Creek, then on a low levee to its east. You wind past numerous roads of a failed subdivision and then pass

See map C1

C1

under a powerline and its attendant road. Across a second such road (1475-0.5) the tread may be vague, but it is easily traced in the sandy wash, since it is marked by 4x4 PCT posts and it runs just west of a green-wire fence. Beyond it, you wind up to a dirt road over the buried Colorado River Aqueduct (1580-0.4). A minute later, you cross a better road, then veer northeast and ascend to better views south of the incredible north wall of San Jacinto Peak.

Keeping to a low bench with knee-high scrub, you traverse across a succession of jeep roads, then cross better Cottonwood Road (1690-0.6). Now the expediently routed PCT turns left, north, uphill alongside Cottonwood Road, keeping always within 10 yards of it, in a delightful, thigh-high garden of silver-flannel-leaved, yellow-flowered brittlebush, a drought-tolerant shrub of the sunflower family. Nearing the mouth of Cottonwood Canyon, the trail passes around a metal-signed Cottonwood Trailhead, a dirt parking area, then crosses two side-by-side roads (1850-0.6) then makes a slightly indistinct ford of the almost always dry stream that drains Cottonwood Canyon. Across it, the way merges with a jeep track to strike east to the mouth of Gold Canyon, whose unusual east-west orientation is due to erosion along the Bonnie Bell fault, a splinter of the great San Andreas rift.

Entering Gold Canyon, your jeep track strikes Gold Canyon Road (1845-0.2), then you wind just south of it on trail constructed by the Sierra Club. In the next long mile, your pleasant way recrosses the road, passes through a stock fence at a corral, then crosses the road, now blocked, twice more, all in desert vegetation of Mojave yucca, rabbitbrush, creosote bush and multiple species of cacti. Presently, numerous windmills of the Mesa Wind Farm come into view, and the canyon bends north. Here, a large trailside map and a list of mileages through the San Bernardinos stand beside a now-blocked spur trail (2310-1.6) to a dirt road junction near the metal headquarters shed.

*   *   *   *

Water access: The water fountain that once existed at this road junction was dismantled in November 1994, due to traces of uranium contamination found in the 400-foot-deep well.

Workers at the wind farm now bring in their own bottled water, but this author seriously doubts the health hazards of drinking a few quarts in an emergency. If you are dangerously low on water at this point, walk 100 yds east and 80 yds north, to the large metal building, and ask for water. It comes from a well that you walk past: just south of the road, at an electric control panel for the transformer station, a blue-domed cylinder sits atop the wellhead, with numerous valves and taps. Camping—in the company of range cattle—could be done anywhere nearby.

*   *   *   *

Sometimes vague, your path now leads more moderately up a small parallel ravine west of the road. Later, you come back alongside the main ravine and momentarily join a rough jeep road (2470-0.5). Now inside a BLM study area for possible inclusion in the San Gorgonio Wilderness, the way leads easily up-canyon, keeping just west of its dry wash and braiding with a network of cattle paths. After passing through a stock drift fence, the path steepens to climb the head of Gold Canyon. Mostly, the way is unrelentingly shadeless, but occasional, small laurel sumac trees do offer respite. During the wet season, a profusion of wildflowers may sprinkle the route, including many members of the sunflower family, and also white, blue and lavender phacelias, chia and popcorn flower. Lizards too numerous to count also scurry from underfoot. Finally, four small switchbacks help you gain a narrow pass (3225-1.3) between Gold and Teutang canyons. The most impressive vistas are southeast, contrasting the granite and seasonal snow of the San Jacinto massif with the Colorado desert sands of Coachella Valley.

Starting north, you descend moderately to a ridge nose, down which small, tight switchbacks descend. These bring the PCT to a dry crossing of the stream bed in Teutang Canyon (2815-0.7), just upstream of a chasm of gray granite. Next you round an intervening promontory to step across another canyon tributary, which has a seasonal spring ¼ mile up-canyon, then proceed fairly level down-canyon. When you gain a narrow ridgetop, your path doubles back on itself to climb northwest, per-

See map C1

haps indistinctly, up an open grassy slope, before resuming a traversing line high above the canyon's floor. This stretch does afford interesting panoramas east over the cleft of Whitewater Canyon to the sun-browned Little San Bernardino Mountains.

Eventually you descend, first directly along a ridgelet, then in a sweeping arc that leads to the lip of Hatchery Canyon. Now on switchbacks that are susceptible to erosion, you drop quickly to the floor of Hatchery Canyon, where you step across its dry stream bed. The trail now heads sandily downstream, soon passing through a stock gate, and then striking an old jeep road (2285-2.7) at the canyon's mouth in Whitewater Canyon, just beneath an impressive conglomerate scarp. Here you turn left, north, on sandy alluvium of the west bank of the Whitewater River, which is a raging torrent true to its name in early season, but more often is a noisesome brook. Southbound trekkers must fill their canteens here—the next safe, certain on-route water lies across desertlike San Gorgonio Pass at the west branch of Snow Creek, 14.3 long miles way. The Whitewater River usually has water throughout summer, but may be dry by early May of severe drought years. The route—essentially a jeep road—winds across sandy washes where the flanking scrub is alive with phainopeplas, which are crested silky flycatchers closely related to waxwings.

Just past red basalt outcrops of Miocene age that mark two good camps (2605-1.6), large ducks and a sign lead you northeast across the Whitewater River's bouldery granite and marble bed to a narrow canyon peppered with boulders of basalt and gneiss, among junipers, catclaws and bladderpods patrolled by collared lizards. Here the best jeep track jogs northwest, paralleling the river bed for a moment, to find a resumption of trail at an old California Riding and Hiking Trail (CRHT) sign post. From the post your path ascends moderately northeast in a terrain not unlike Death Valley, soon switchbacking to gain a ridgetop (3075-1.3) in deeply incised gneiss and fanglomerate. Ignore a short deadend trail climbing south along the ridge from here. Fiddleneck and foxtail brush against one's legs on the descent northeast from this saddle, and one soon reaches and turns north beside West Fork Mission Creek Road (2918-0.6). Just minutes later the PCT veers

north away from this dirt road (3010-0.2) in a dry, sandy wash. Look for CRHT posts and follow them east into a side canyon, then up, arcing across the north side of the small valley, across its head, and then ascending its south wall to an east-ascending nose, eroded from Quaternary and Tertiary sediments. ∎ *Atop this ridge, views are panoramic and startling. The southern horizon is dominated by 10,804-foot San Jacinto Peak, often frosted in winter and spring with snow and contrasting markedly with the red, yellow and gray hues of the desert's alluvial landscape, in the foreground. To the west, gneissic rocks support Kitching Peak, while the Whitewater River Canyon ascends as a rocky scar northwest to the Jumpoffs below barren San Gorgonio Mountain. The gully just north of the ridge that you ascended, plus West Fork Mission Creek, Catclaw Flat, and Middle Fork Whitewater River are all aligned with the north branch of the San Andreas Fault, which is partly responsible for this region's varied geology.* ∎

The PCT continues to wind northwest up the ridgetop dividing the East and West forks of Mission Creek, then the ascent gives way to a moderate descent east down a chaparralled nose, bringing you to East Fork Mission Creek Road (3060-3.1). Here you turn northwest up-canyon to cross usually flowing East Fork Mission Creek in about ½ mile, then continue along its shadeless north bank to the end of the dirt road (3360-1.4). From this point your hike up Mission Creek is often difficult, despite reconstruction efforts by C.C.C. trail crews, who in 1993 installed boulder bridges across each of the stream fords. Mission Creek's narrow gorge, incised in tortured granite gneisses, leaves little room for a trail, so washouts are frequent and the path is often vague through alluvial boulder fields and jungles of baccharis (false willow), alder, willow and cottonwood. Rattlesnakes inhabit the grassy stream margins, as do garter snakes, racers, horned lizards, antelope ground squirrels, summer tanagers and bobcats—so keep an eye open while making any of the 20+ fords of Mission Creek lying south of Forks Springs. Note too where prominent faults cross the canyon—at 3400 feet, at 3900 feet and at 4080 feet, where the Pinto Mountain Fault further tortures the banded gneisses. ∎ *Chia, yerba santa, catclaw,*

See maps C1, C2

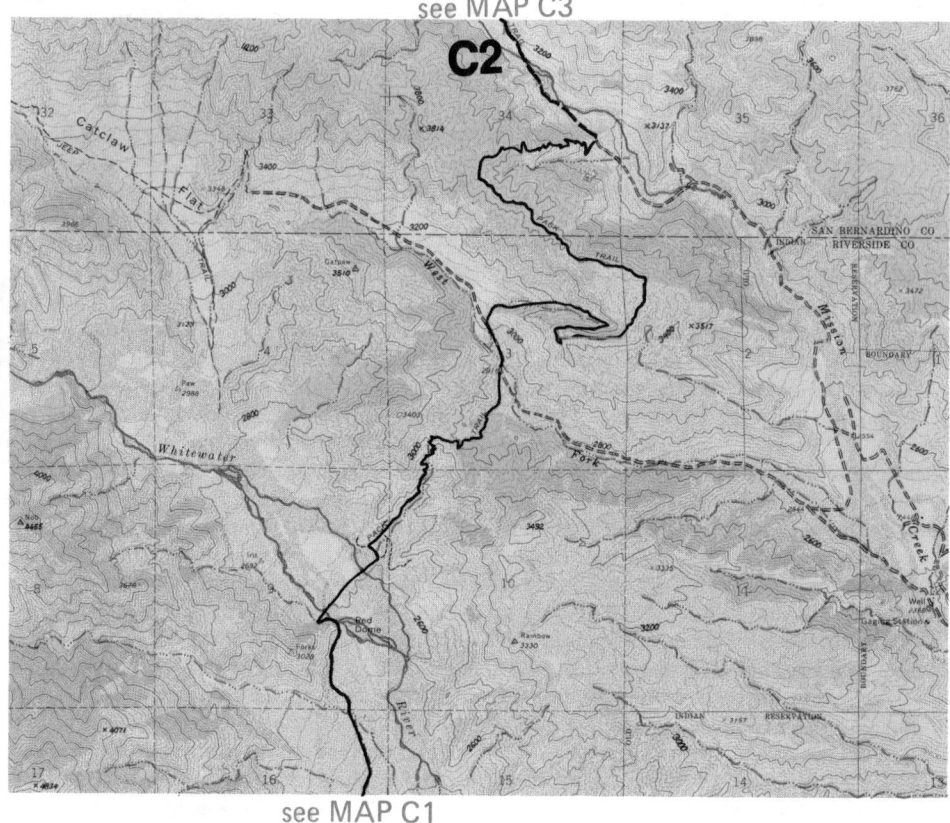

see MAP C3

C2

see MAP C1

baccharis and bladderpod are the most frequent plants, but you also see notable specimens of Joshua tree, yucca and cactus. ∎

Just below the confluence of the South and North forks of Mission Creek you pass nice campsites, then cross this major creek (4830-5.0), which is fed just up-canyon by Forks Springs. Water is generally available here year-round, but may not be elsewhere in Mission Creek due to the porous sediments of its bed. North of Forks Springs, the now discernible PCT keeps usually to northeastern banks in an ocean-spray chaparral. Near 5200 feet the path crosses granitic bedrock emplaced at the same time as Sierran granites, and later, at 5600 feet, the tread turns to sugar-white and yellowish Saragossa quartzite. Near 5900 feet the PCT veers away from Mission Creek into a side canyon and quickly reaches a pleasant creekside camp (6110-3.1) shaded by alders, incense-cedars, Jeffrey pines and interior live oaks. Eight switchbacks lead west from this spot, elevat-

ing you to atop a phyllite-and-quartzite promontory. The friability and instability of the quartzite bedrock are demonstrated both by vegetational scarcity and by a massive landslide cutting across your path as you contour a steep slope shortly after gaining this ridge. Just past this slide, you leave BLM jurisdiction for San Bernardino National Forest.

White firs and Jeffrey pines soon shade the PCT as it resumes its ascent close beside Mission Creek, which usually has flowing water near its headwaters. Tank up here, for there might not be water at Mission Creek Trail Camp. A rough jeep road, built to log the forested flats south of Mission Creek, is met at a junction (7490-3.0) which may still be marked by yellow paint-daubs on nearby trees. Follow its overgrown tracks west up along willowy creekside meadows to meet gravel Road 1N93 (7965-1.1) at a PCT marker. A sign here pretentiously announces MISSION CREEK TRAIL CAMP, which is merely a pleasant flat spot with fire

See maps C2, C3, C4

rings, located south of North Fork Mission Creek. Fill your water bottles here, since the next water on route is at Arrastre (Deer Springs) Trail Camp, in 16.4 miles.

PCT trail tread resumes here, starting north up from Road 1N93 on a well-graded trail in an open stand of pines. The route rounds northeast, with some fine backward glimpses of subalpine Ten Thousand Foot Ridge in San Gorgonio Wilderness. Soon you reach a sandy gap and cross Road 1N05 (8240-0.6). Now you have some fine views northwest to rounded Sugarloaf Mountain and its smaller western sibling, Sugarlump. Next on your agenda is a pleasant, level traverse, first northward, then southeastward, in cool forest on the north side of the divide, which here separates the Santa Ana River and the Whitewater River drainages. Eventually the trail dips easily to a post-marked crossing of Road 1N05 (8115-0.8) at a saddle. Now, the easy route leads east under a forested summit, and you have panoramas northwest to Sugarloaf Mountain. Later, dropping rockily, the PCT finds a junction (7980-0.8) with a CRHT-marked trail that descends northwest from just below a forested saddle.

*   *   *   *

Water access: Travelers low on water may trace this trail about ½ mile down to usually flowing Heart Bar Creek.

*   *   *   *

The PCT proceeds north from this junction, contouring at first, then making a sustained moderate ascent through a woodland of mountain mahogany, manzanita, pinyon and Jeffrey pines and scraggly white fir. Vistas gradually unfold southwest over to San Gorgonio Mountain and Ten Thousand Foot Ridge and west down Heart Bar Creek to lush Big Meadows and the popular Barton Flats camp area. Bending northwest, the path soon levels out atop the long west ridge of Peak 8828, and then it swings east into shady mixed-conifer forest lying north of that summit. ∎ *For a few minutes the PCT skirts across white, granular Furnace marble, and the surrounding vegetation also changes markedly: edaphic effects (see Chapter 3's "Biology") allow only hardy whitebark pines and junipers, the former normally found in higher, colder*

See map C4

Terrain in East Fork Mission Creek canyon

C4

see MAP C3

climes, to muster a scattered occupation of the crumbly slopes. ❚ Rounding to the east of Peak 8828, you descend gently to a ridgetop and join Road 1N96 (8510-2.5), where good views southeast over North Fork Mission Creek to the San Jacinto Mountains and the Coachella Val-

ley help to make a pleasant, but waterless, camp surrounded by lupine and purple sage.

You continue east down the poor dirt road to a road junction (8340-0.6) located on the ridge east of Peak 8588. From here the PCT contin- ues east along the ridgeline as Road 1N96,

See map C4

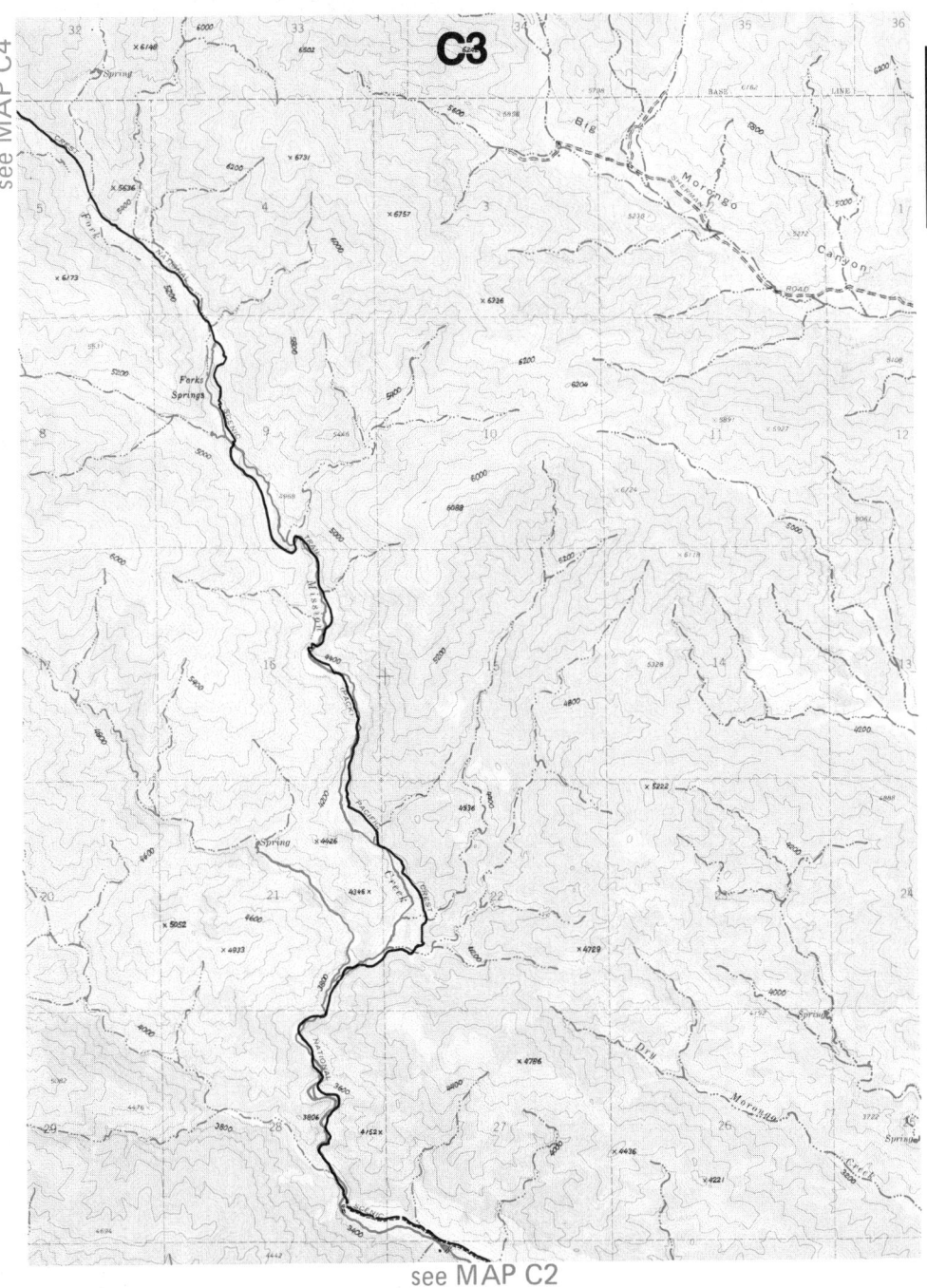

see MAP C4

see MAP C2

San Gorg. Pass
C
-J-15

while a better dirt road, 1N95, branches north-west, downhill. The route soon crosses onto north slopes, becomes a trail, and drops gently around Peak 8751 to Coon Creek Jumpoff—a spectacular, steep, granitic defile at the head of a tributary of North Fork Mission Creek. ■ *The raw scarp here points to rapid erosion east of the Jumpoff and illustrates the process of stream capture. The small stream draining the Tayles Hidden Acres basin and part of adjacent Section 20, to your northeast, used to connect with Coon Creek, to the west, but accelerated headward erosion of Mission Creek at the Jumpoff has intercepted that stream. Its waters now flow southeast, eventually to the Salton Sea, rather than west to the Santa Ana River and the Pacific Ocean.* ■

From this thought-provoking overlook, the trail climbs gently for a moment to Coon Creek Road 1N02 (8090-1.3). Coon Creek Jumpoff Group Camp, with toilets but no water, is just to the east.

*   *   *   *

Water access: Until midsummer, water may be obtained by walking as much as 1.5 miles west down the dirt road.

*   *   *   *

The way now attacks, via moderate switchbacks through scattered pines, firs and montane chaparral, the south slopes of the ridge dividing Coon and Cienaga Seca creeks. ■ *Extensive views compensate for the climb. Seasonally snowy Grinnell and San Gorgonio mountains loom in the southwest, Mounts Baldy and Baden-Powell mark your upcoming travels west, and glimpses of the Santa Rosa Mountains and Palm Springs shimmer in the southeast.* ■ Rounding north of a conifered hillock alive with mountain bluebirds, Clark's nutcrackers, white-headed woodpeckers and dark-eyed juncos, you strike a trail (8610-1.3) which cuts perpendicularly across your route and meets a jeep road immediately east of your trail. The PCT continues ascending for ⅓ mile, passing under small, granitic cliffs before reaching a viewless, forested ridgetop. This 8750-foot point is the highest spot your trail reaches in the San Bernardino Mountains.

Mt. San Jacinto, from ridge north of Coon Creek Jumpoff

Now the way drops sandily on a gentle gradient to cross a dirt road (8635-0.7), then it switchbacks down into a canyon, the path flanked by tall mountain-mahogany shrubs. At the mouth of a gully in the canyon bottom, you cross a jeep road (8390-0.6), and then the PCT momentarily parallels its northward course before routing itself onto this road. Private land in Section 18 prevents the Forest Service from constructing PCT trail tread at this time, so you continue north on the jeep road/CRHT right-of-way. Soon the jeep road yields to a better dirt road (8260-0.4), which you trace north down-canyon to a five-way junction—four roads and a trail—(8100-0.6) located beside often dry Cienaga Seca Creek. The PCT rises north from this junction out of lodgepole pine into stands of juniper and mountain mahogany, then descends west along a dirt road for 130 yards to a junction (8440-1.0). Here the trail picks up again to contour the west slope of Onyx Peak over to a dirt road (8510-1.1) that is just east of Highway 38 and Onyx Summit.

The PCT crosses the road and climbs gently-to-moderately above Road 1N01, gaining increasingly good views of Baldwin Lake and Gold Mountain, in the northwest. Presently the path levels and crosses Road 1N01 (8635-1.0), then descends, first north, then west below a ridge. Lower, the well-marked route crosses a jeep road twice in quick succession before a

See maps C4, C5

see MAP C6

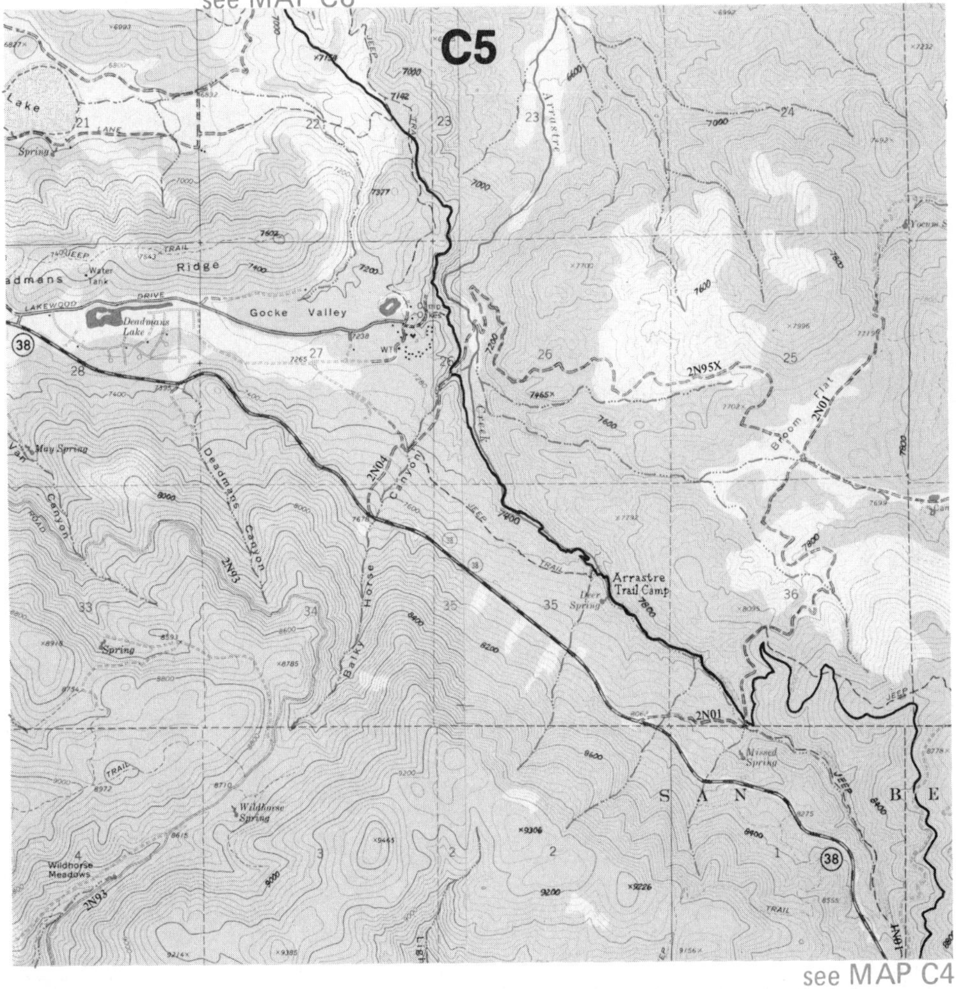

C5

see MAP C4

Baldwin Lake, Bertha Peak and Gold Mountain, from Nelson Ridge

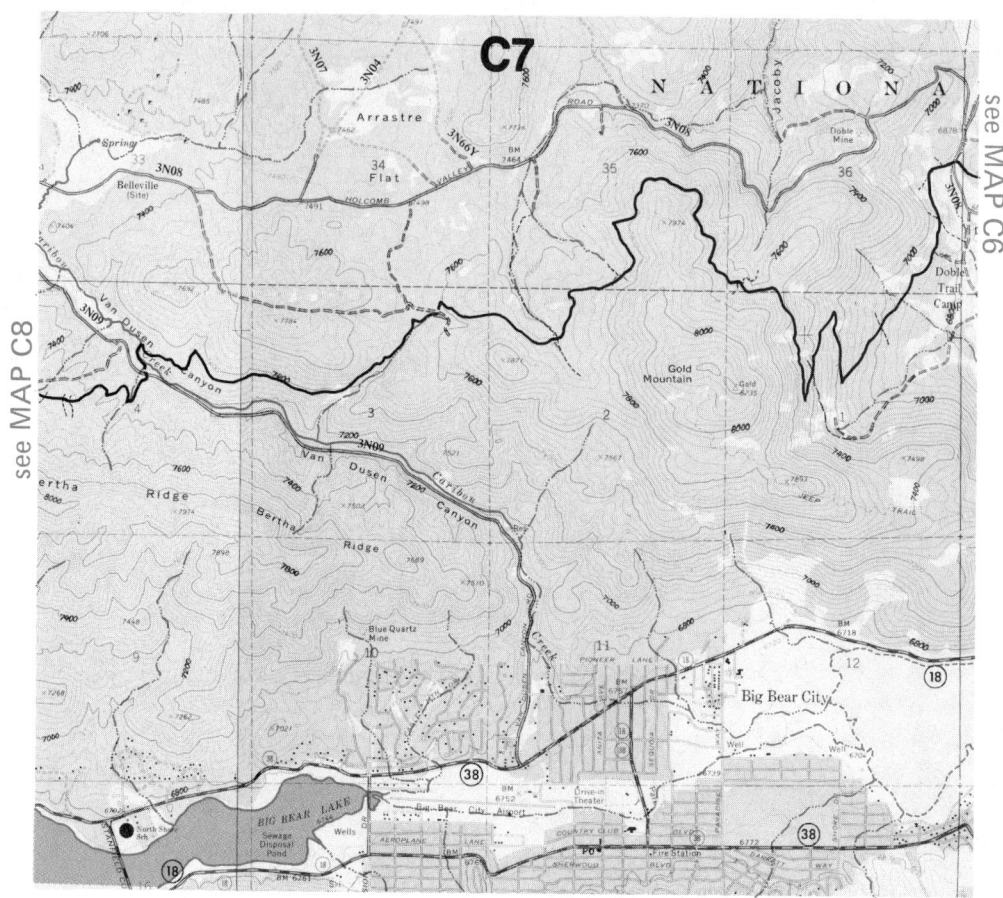

switchback drops the trail to Broom Flat Road 2N01 (7885-2.2), a good dirt road running alongside shaded Arrastre Creek. Now you enter fragrant white-fir groves to descend easily northwest along the seasonal creek, and soon find Arrastre Trail Camp at Deer Spring (7605-0.9). This has a fire pit, toilet, hitching posts, benches, and the last water until Doble Trail Camp, 12 miles away.

Two minutes onward, you turn north at a junction with a jeep road that leads to Balky Horse Canyon. The route continues down Arrastre Canyon to Balky Horse Canyon and crosses Road 2N04 (7155-1.5). ▮ *One can appreciate the subtle changes in vegetation that have occurred on the descent into this region, which are influenced more by the Mojave Desert's*

parching winds than by moisture-laden ocean breezes. ▮ Minutes later, you reach wooden berms that lead under Camp Oakes' rifle range, and then you climb gently across Saragossa quartzite in a true high-desert plant community: pinyon pines, buckwheat, and ephedra, a shiny yellow-green shrub with wiry stems called Mormon Tea—after its use by Mormon pioneers. Atop a 7240-foot shoulder, you gaze eastward and see gold mines near Tip Top Mountain's summit and also see a high-desert woodland of Joshua trees and pinyon pines.

Now paralleling an expansive, desertlike ridge, the PCT crosses two jeep roads and first gives you views west over seasonal Erwin Lake and east to the Mojave, then later views west to large, shallow, sometimes completely dry

See maps C5, C6

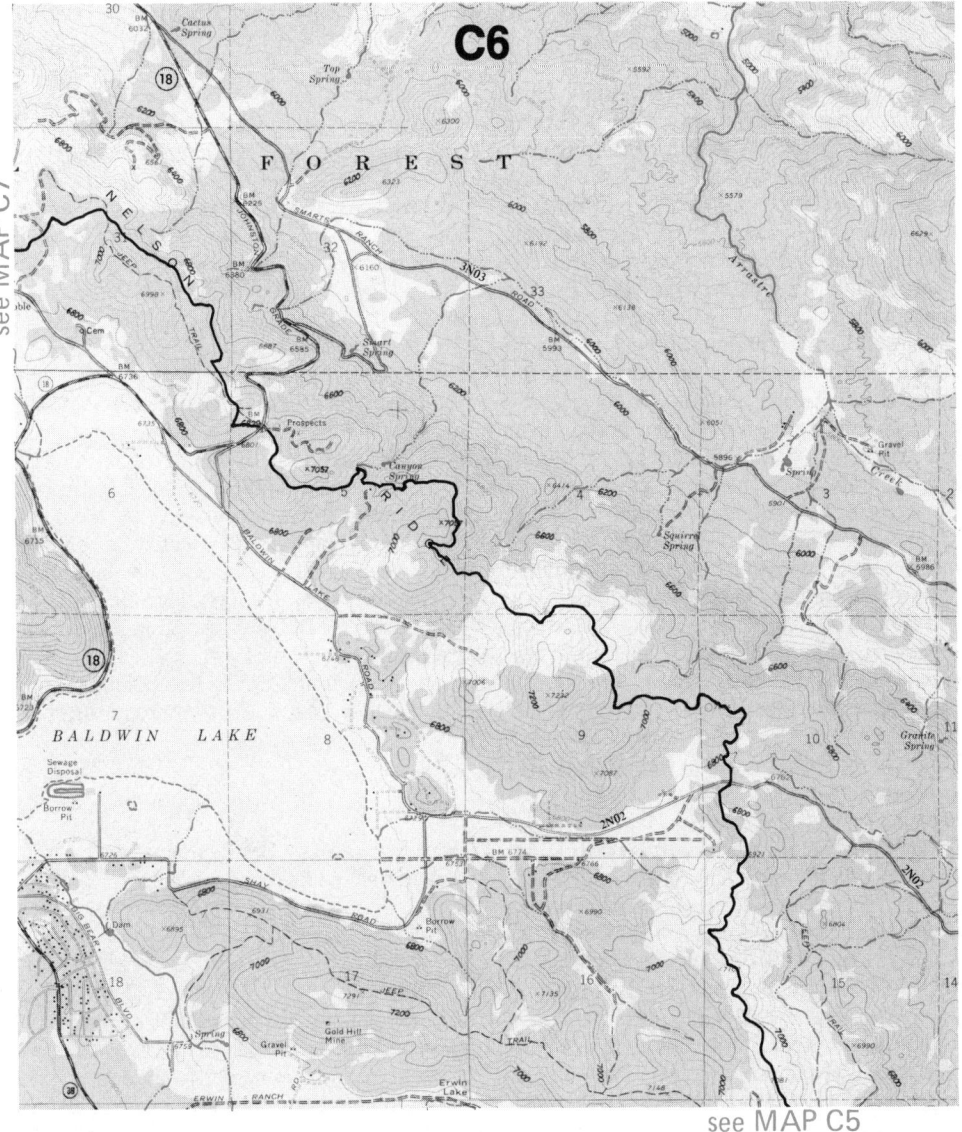

see MAP C7

see MAP C5

Baldwin Lake. Eventually the sandy path descends to cross Arrastre Creek Road 2N02 (6775-3.8) amid pinyon pines, Joshua trees and sagebrush. From that road the PCT climbs north, then contours northwest for alternating vistas of desert and mountain as it wanders among pinyon pines and crosses the Doble Fault just northeast of Peak 7057. ▮ *Here the rock underfoot abruptly changes from banded Precambrian gneiss to whitish Paleozoic quartzite. The Helendale Fault, stretching from north of Victorville southeast to Tip Top Moun-* *tain, runs parallel to Nelson Ridge, lying below you to the northeast.* ▮ Presently, with fleeting glimpses of Baldwin Lake you descend to meet Highway 18 (6829-4.2) just yards west of some interesting mining prospects.

North of the highway, find the trail angling left of a metal gate across a jeep road at the edge of a small pinyon forest, just west of a bulldozed-bare slope. The PCT next switchbacks to cross the jeep road, then contours north of Nelson Ridge before angling west down through a dense stand of pinyon pines to

See map C6

meet Doble Road 3N08 (6855-2.0) just south of the county dump. West across Doble Road the trail curves and contours south across three jeep tracks in sagebrush and rabbitbrush, affording good views of Baldwin Lake's playa surface beyond the ruins of Doble. Baldwin Lake is named for Elias J. "Lucky" Baldwin, owner of the prosperous Doble Gold Mine, located high on the slopes above you. The PCT contours low on Gold Mountain, and soon reaches a short, inobvious and unsigned spur trail (6880-0.5) down to signed Doble Trail Camp. Look for the first lush patch of rushes and iris under scattered pinyons and junipers to mark the junction. The camp has a pit toilet, corral, campfire ring and good piped water.

Continuing on, you make a gentle ascent in scrubby vegetation, crossing two jeep roads and making three switchbacks to gain a saddle on the northeast ridge of Gold Mountain. Here you leave pinyon pines behind for incense-cedars, Jeffrey pines and junipers. A gentle traverse around Gold Mountain's northern flanks bisects a jeep road and offers vistas over Arrastre and Union flats, scenes of the fevered Holcomb Valley mining excitement in the 1860s. ∎ *This gold rush began when William F. Holcomb discovered flecks of placer gold at the head of Van Dusen Canyon, one mile west of Arrastre Flat. Hired by other prospectors for his ability with a rifle, Holcomb and a companion trailed a wounded grizzly bear north from Poligue Canyon. His experience prospecting in the mines of the Sierra Nevada's Mother Lode paid off when his bear-tracking led to the alluvial flats on Caribou Creek. Soon the sagebrush-and-pine-dotted basin swarmed with prospectors, and a camp, named Belleville, was erected.*

History records that this settlement was one of the least law-abiding of the California gold camps—over 40 men died by hanging or gun battles. Causes for argument included not only the usual charges of claim-jumping and theft, but also political affiliations in the Civil War. Southern sympathizers were particularly numerous, as they had been forcibly ejected from many pro-Northern mining camps in the Mother Lode. Although the site of fevered and hectic activity for almost a decade, Holcomb Valley was relieved of most of its readily accessible placer gold by 1870, and its inhabitants moved on to greener pastures. Belleville was soon a ghost town. Interest in the region revived, how-

ever, when hard-rock mines opened to seek the local Mother Lode—the source of the Holcomb Valley placer gold. Soon shafts and their adjunct tailings dotted the land. Lucky Baldwin's Doble Mine was one of these, but, like the other hard-rock mines, it failed to locate the Mother Lode, and it is doubtful that Baldwin recouped his $6 million purchase price for the mine. ∎

The PCT veers south along Gold Mountain's flanks to strike one jeep road, then a second (7630-3.9), which leads north ⅔ mile down to Saragossa Spring. About ¼ mile beyond the next small rise you cross a better road (7560-0.7), then turn southwest down to a tributary of Caribou Creek, dotted with mining ruins. A mile-long contour then leads to Caribou Creek itself, which rarely flows later than early June, but offers good camping before then. The next water for northbound PCT hikers is not until Little Bear Springs Trail Camp, 10.8 miles; for the southbound, at Doble Trail Camp, 6.3 miles. Just 0.1 mile beyond Caribou Creek the trail bisects Van Dusen Canyon Road 3N09 (7260-1.8), which leads southeast 3 miles to Big Bear City.

          *   *   *   *

Resupply access: Big Bear City, the best resupply town in this section, is closest from this point.

          *   *   *   *

More mountain mahogany, Jeffrey pines and junipers shade the PCT as you leave Van Dusen Canyon, crossing numerous jeep tracks as you make a gentle ascent west under Bertha Ridge. Finally, a switchback leads to a saddle north of Bertha Peak, where you cross a jeep road (7720-1.6), then another (7735-0.7), leading to the summit, in excellent exposures of marble. West of the second road, sweeping vistas open up to the south across dammed Big Bear Lake to Moonridge and to the high summits of the San Gorgonio Wilderness. Just beyond these vistas, the PCT junctions with the Cougar Crest Trail 1E22 (7680-0.4).

          *   *   *   *

Resupply access: This enjoyable path starts west, then heads south 2.0 miles to Highway

See maps C6, C7, C8

see MAP C9

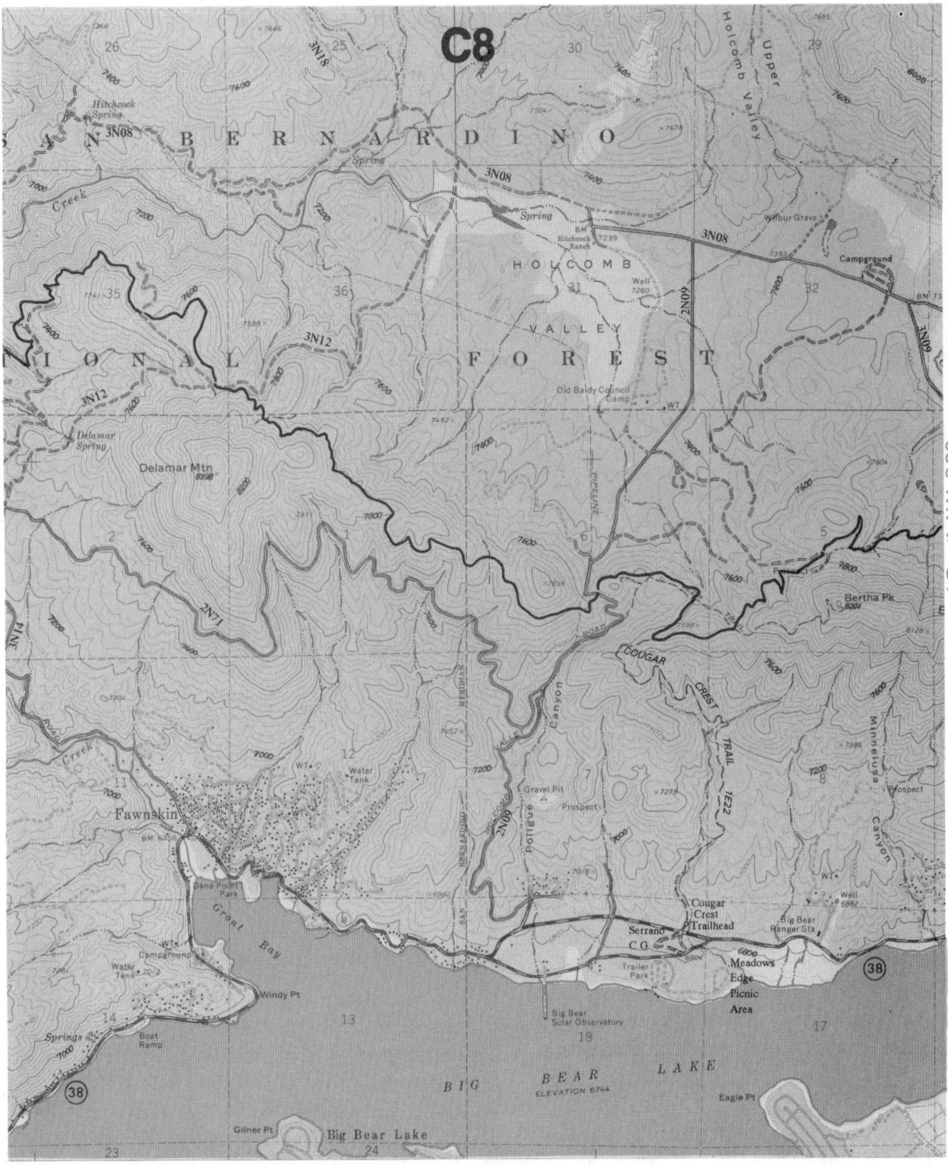

C San Gorg. Pass -I-15

see MAP C7

Big Bear Lake and the high peaks of San Gorgonio Wilderness

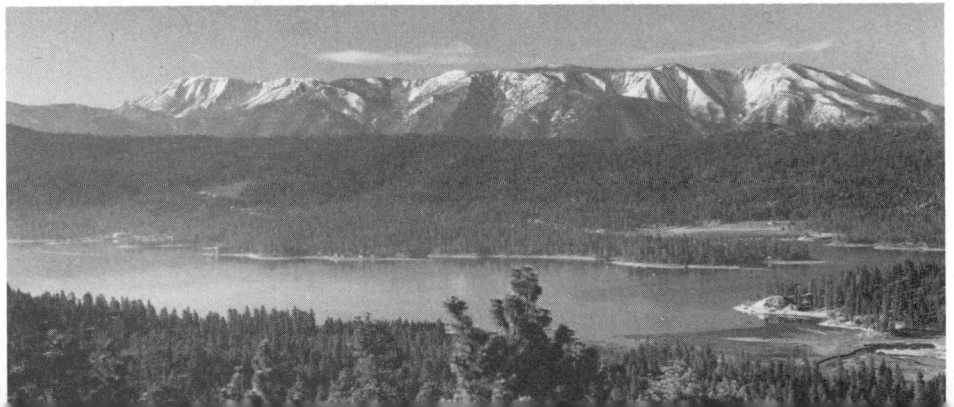

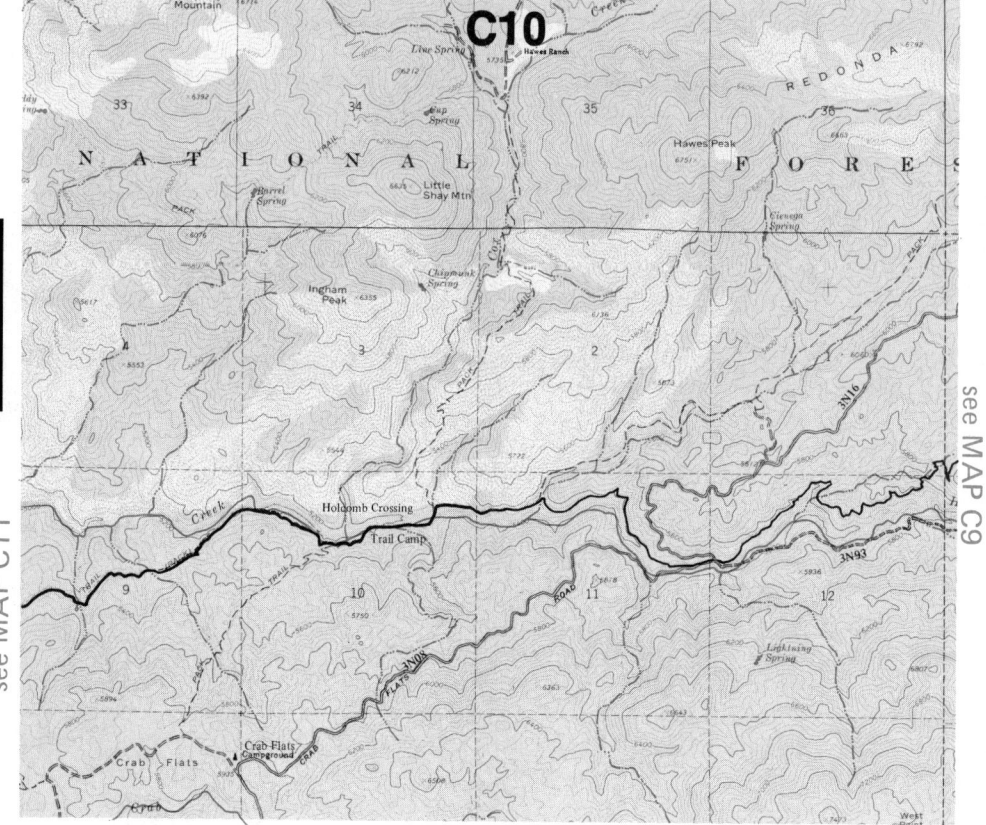

see MAP C11

see MAP C9

San Gorg. Pass
-1-15

C

38, near Serrano Campground on the north shore of Big Bear Lake—a convenient place from which to hitch-hike either west to Fawnskin, with its limited supplies, or east to Big Bear, with more complete provisions.

*   *   *   *

The PCT recrosses the last jeep road midway down to wide Holcomb Valley Road 2N09 (7550-0.8).

*   *   *   *

Resupply access: From here travelers can head 3.7 miles to Fawnskin for supplies by first walking south along the dirt road, which descends Poligue Canyon to reach Highway 38 beside Big Bear Lake, then walking west along the highway.

*   *   *   *

From Holcomb Valley Road the PCT continues its traverse of the San Bernardino Mountains' spine by continuing west, easily up along the south side of Delamar Mountain's east ridge. This pleasant and viewful walk under open conifers and oaks ends after a long mile when the route crosses to the shadier north side of the ridge to traverse past an east-ascending jeep track, then descends to Road 3N12 (7755-2.8), atop a saddle.

*   *   *   *

Water access: Delamar Spring, with poor camping nearby, lies 0.9 mile west down this dirt road.

*   *   *   *

See map C8

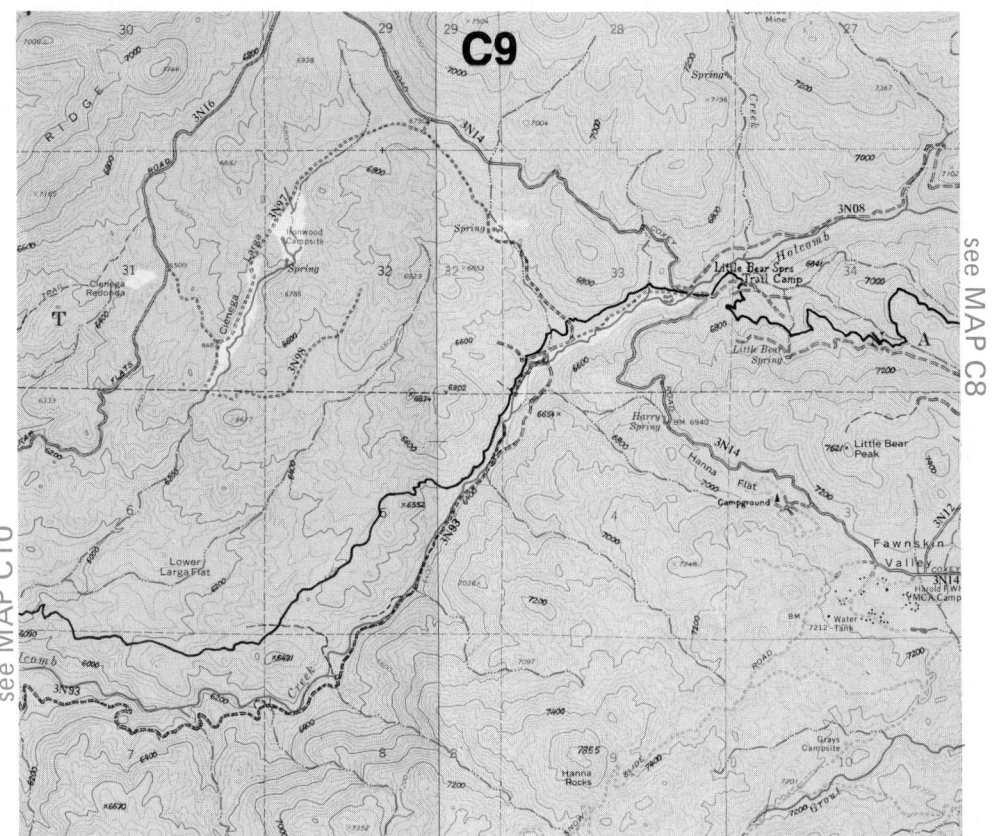

The PCT contours north from Road 3N12, then arcs west around a nose covered with mountain mahogany before crossing another good dirt road (7610-0.8). Dropping gently, the trail rounds north on a steep hillside with vistas east over Holcomb Valley, but soon turns southwest and eventually strikes a jeep road (7305-1.1), which you follow downhill for 35 yards before resuming trail tread. Next, continued descent for 0.3 mile leads into a small canyon, then northwest along its south wall, then into another, similar canyon, now just below a dirt road. Later, near the bottom of Holcomb Creek's wide canyon, the route switchbacks, crosses one poor dirt road, then another, and immediately reaches Little Bear Springs Trail Camp (6600-2.5), with corral, toilets, benches and piped water. Southbound PCTers should tank up here, since the next seasonal water is 10.8 miles away, at Caribou Creek in Van Dusen Canyon. Most wilderness lovers will likely not spend the night at this poorly sited campground, which is a haven for buzzing motocross enthusiasts, but rather will

sack out farther down Holcomb Creek.

From the trail camp the PCT turns northwest down a creek's mouth to quickly reach the willow-lined, sagebrush-dotted banks of year-round Holcomb Creek. The trail follows its south bank, crossing a jeep road leading to the trail camp, then parallels the lower shoulder of Coxey Road 3N14 as it descends west a few yards to a culvert bridge over Holcomb Creek (6510-0.3).

The PCT resumes above Holcomb Creek's north bank, 35 yards up Coxey Road, and proceeds gently down-canyon in an open ponderosa-pine forest, staying just above canyon-bottom dirt Road 3N93, which is repeatedly drowned under beaver-dammed pools. The trail passes two dirt roads and a jeep track, and then about ½ mile later it turns west up a side canyon, climbing moderately to a saddle (6485-2.1). From it a gentle descent southwest in warm groves of conifers and black oaks leads across a dirt road (6350-0.9), beyond which the route follows a sunny, rock-dotted divide north of Holcomb Creek. Drier conditions prevail as

See maps C8, C9

Holcomb Creek near PCT junction with Hawes Ranch Trail

the easy descent continues, eventually leading to a rock-hop crossing of the Cienega Larga fork of Holcomb Creek. From it the trail parallels some 50 feet above shaded, bouldery Holcomb Creek, soon passing some nice campsites and dropping to cross it via boulders. Moments later the streamside canopy of willows and cottonwoods opens where wide Crab Flats Road 3N16 (5465-3.5) has a junction with rough Road 3N93.

The PCT now continues on Holcomb Creek's south bank, via very rocky tread under white alders. You soon enter a sandy flat with adequate camps and again cross Holcomb Creek (5430-0.2). The trail now winds northwest above it in a dry chaparral of mountain mahogany, buckwheat, and yellow, fleshy-petalled flannelbush. Turning more westward, the way

drops once again alongside Holcomb Creek, traverses the perimeter of a bouldery sand flat with a good camp, and then crosses the permanent Cienega Redonda fork of Holcomb Creek to find the north-branching Cienega Redonda Trail (5325-1.0). Many horned lizards might be seen as the trail continues its gentle descent west on rotting granitic rock along Holcomb Creek and soon enters a grassy flat to reach a junction with the Hawes Ranch Trail (5230-0.4), just shy of the PCT's bouldery fourth ford of Holcomb Creek. Minutes later, one finds Holcomb Crossing Trail Camp (5190-0.3), with firepits and a toilet under large Jeffrey pines.

Just 300 yards after Holcomb Camp, the Crab Flats Trail climbs southwest, but the PCT stays near Holcomb Creek's alder- and cedar-shaded banks a while longer before gently ascending, alternately in forest and in high chaparral. In a mile the trail begins to descend, and eventually heads northwest, dropping via four oak-shaded switchbacks to a beautiful 90-foot steel and wood bridge (4580-4.1) spanning Deep Creek. Here the beautiful stream drops between large granitic boulders, and harbors a good population of rainbow trout.

*   *   *   *

Resupply access: Just beyond the bridge, a good, signed trail strikes left, back upstream, briefly to cross diminutive Bear Creek and hit the end of dirt Hooks Creek Road 3N34C. This road leads west, up-canyon 0.5 mile to cross Road 3N34, then later becomes paved and designated 2N26Y, climbing 3½ miles in all past numerous homes and cabins to Lake Arrowhead. Here you find the Cedar Glen Post Office and supermarkets just before meeting Highway 173 near the lakeshore.

*   *   *   *

After crossing Deep Creek the PCT briefly climbs northeast, then contours under live oaks and near crumbling granitic parapets. After ½ mile the path descends gently, matching the gradient of Deep Creek, which is flanked by spruces and pines 140 feet below. The way presently becomes hot and exposed near ocean spray and holly-leaf cherry, and many will wonder why the trail wasn't routed lower, along

See maps C9, C10, C11

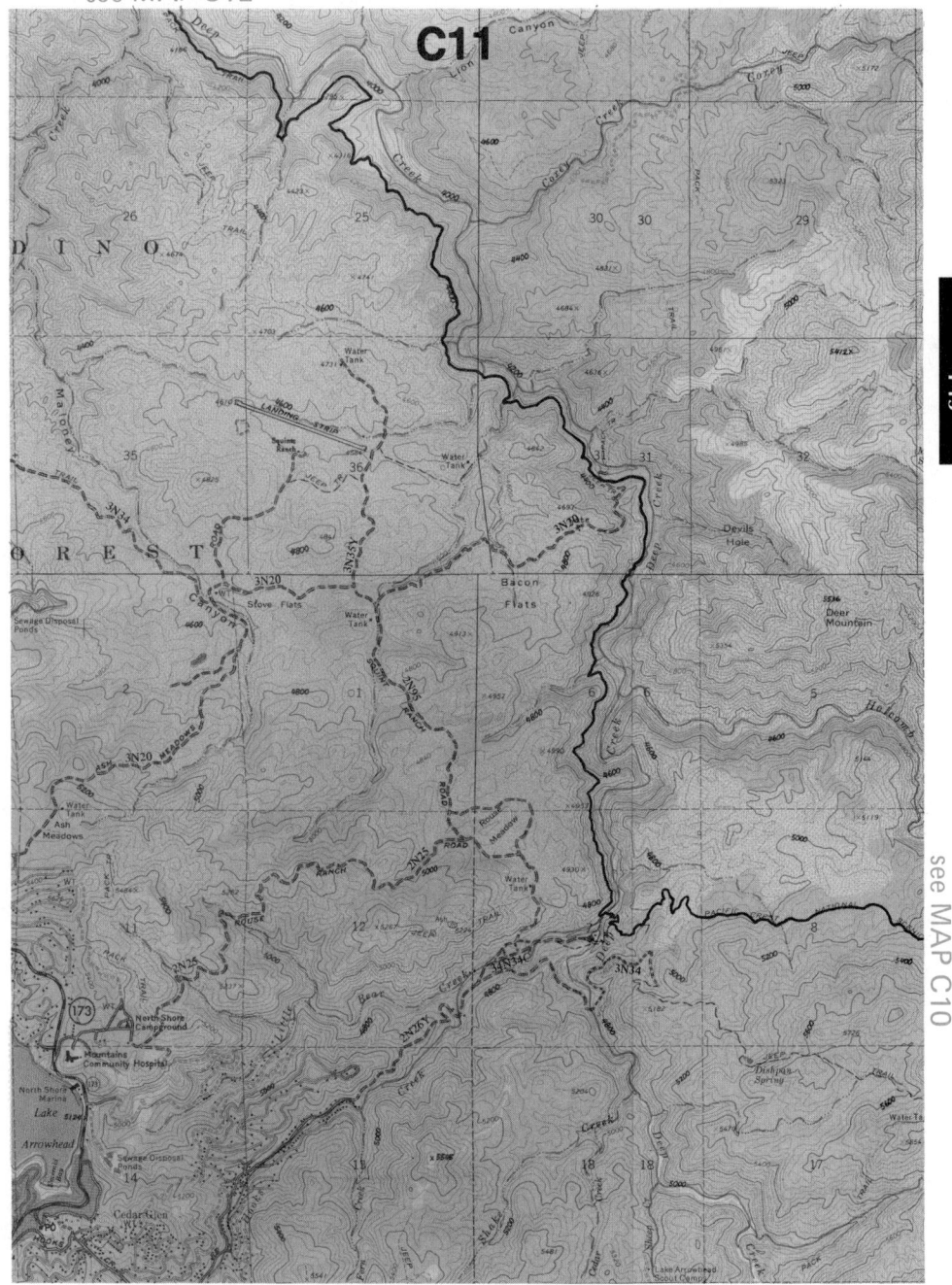

see MAP C12

C11

see MAP C10

C San Gorg. Pass -I-15

the cool streamside. Soon you get your answer, in the form of steep, friable bluffs, above which the PCT must skirt. Later, the route bends west and strikes Bacon Flats Road 3N20 (4255-2.6),

which offers the last chance to head out to Lake Arrowhead to resupply.

Across Bacon Flats Road the PCT winds along the canyon walls, well above quietly

See map C11

flowing Deep Creek and its streamside willows, cottonwoods and alders. One mile north of Bacon Flats Road, 40 yards of trail have been washed out by erosion due to a forest fire in the Bacon Flats drainage. The Forest Service is planning to build a bridge or to construct a major reroute here. Walkers may now scramble carefully across, but equestrians must either retrace their route to descend to the creekbed and lead their horses downstream for a considerable distance before regaining the trail, or detour via Bacon Flats Road out to Hwy 173, and thence north down to Mojave River Forks Reservoir to rejoin the trial. Though sometimes shaded by steep, granitic bluffs, your route soon becomes more exposed to sun and seasonally stifling heat. ∎ *Your proximity to the Mojave Desert is reflected in both the shimmering heat and in the flora and fauna. Coarse chamise chaparral, harboring flitting phainopeplas and somnolent horned lizards, lines your way, while scurrying insects and pursuant roadrunners share your sandy path. Rattlesnakes are also seen, although not in the heat of day—their cold-blooded metabolism cannot stand extreme ground temperatures, but they love to bask when shadows are long.* ∎

Soon after passing a streamside terrace where the Forest Service plans an equestrian camp, your undulating descent alters its northwestward course to a more westward one. Shortly thereafter, it passes a jeep road that rolls ½ mile east to Warm Spring, and then it drops ¼ south to Deep Creek Hot Spring (3535-6.8), which is situated on a prominent northeast-southwest fault. The hot spring, with its bubbling water, high-diving rocks, warm sunbathing, and green grass, is a surprisingly popular and crowded spot at almost any time of the year. Trail-dusty would-be swimmers should heed this caution, however: a very rare, microscopic ameba living in the hot water has caused deadly amebic meningoencephalitis by invading a few swimmers' bodies through their noses. Swimming may cut your hike short!

Taking leave of the skinny-dippers, you eventually cross Deep Creek via an arched bridge (3315-2.0), and then start a traverse west along the almost barren north wall of Deep Creek canyon, tracing the route of an old aqueduct. This walk ends at the spillway of the Mojave River Forks Reservoir dam (3131-3.0). This

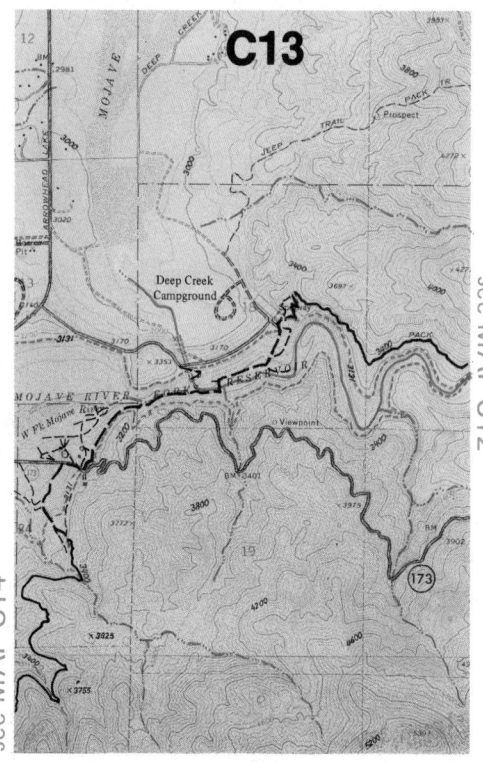

mammoth flood-control dam, over a mile long, is an example of overkill, since West Fork Mojave River and Deep Creek don't have that much flow. Fair camping exists below the dam's spillway.

*   *   *   *

Resupply access: From the foot of the dam, one could walk north on Deep Creek Road, eventually striking good paved Arrowhead Lake Road, which leads north to Hesperia, about 7 miles from the PCT. Hesperia is a good-sized town with full services, but difficult access to and from the PCT limits its utility to most trailers.

*   *   *   *

The next morning, rejoin the PCT atop the dam and drop south from its spillway along a route marked by 4x4 posts, which connect the myriad jeep roads leading to its base. Walk more or less levelly west along the dam's base

See maps C11, C12, C13

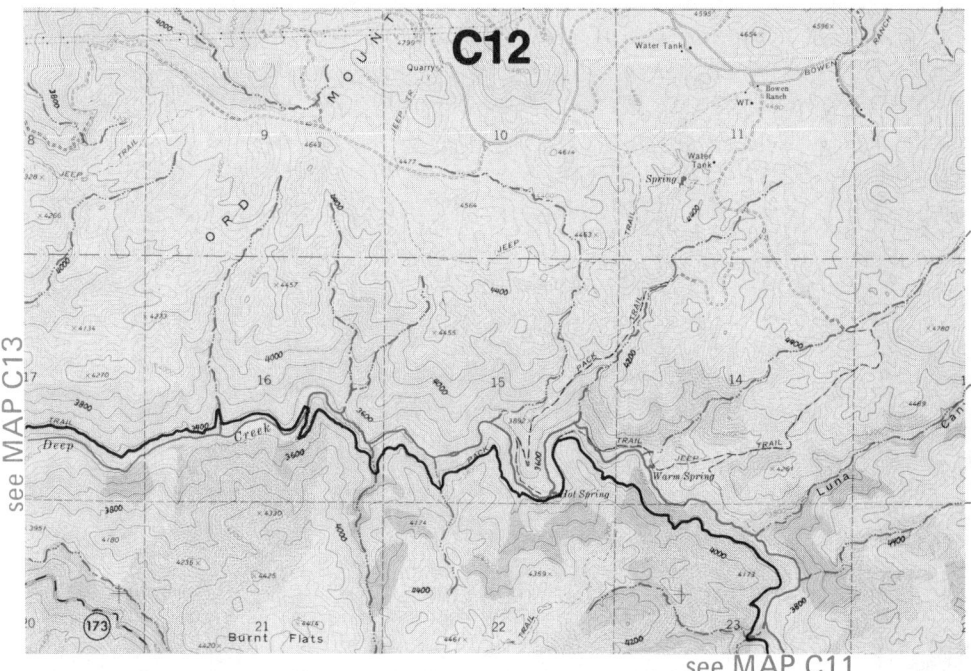

see MAP C11

on a well-used jeep road, staying north of shallow, pooling Deep Creek. Shaded flats hereabouts make for potentially pleasant camping, but pick your site with care since 2-, 3- and 4-wheeled off-road vehicles can be everywhere. Just west of a small canyon's mouth on the opposite bank, your posted PCT route makes a usually shallow but wide and rocky ford (2990-0.5) to the south side of Deep Creek. For a few minutes you trace another jeep track west above a fringe of baccharis and willows before dropping again to the creekside. Here, Deep Creek is sucked north through the dam, down a massive, iron-gated outlet tunnel.

From here, you're back on a trail, which winds west in a thicket of willows and cottonwoods that show evidence of beaver cuttings. These trees are just south of another sandy arroyo, this one draining ephemeral West Fork Mojave River. Presently you cross the base of a narrow ravine, where your trail begins to trace the grade of an abandoned, torn-up paved road (3010-0.6). This is followed moderately uphill, southwest, giving you a fair overlook of the "reservoir." Soon you level out on a terrace to strike a wide turnout on a curve of Highway 173 (3190-0.4).

Across Highway 173, pick up a new segment of signed PCT and follow it almost levelly south along a fence line in open chaparral. After a bit, the path begins an easy, sandy ascent, soon striking the end of a little-used jeep road (3205-0.4). Now the path climbs briefly south into a small canyon, then ascends around several ridges on a southward, winding course, soon leveling in the process to undulate at about 3500 feet. Just after heading around a north-dropping ridge, you reach a small canyon that spawns a trailside spring (3470-1.7). This flows through late spring of most years, but has no nearby camping. Turning more westward, the route traverses hillsides clothed in an open, desert-dry low chaparral of chamise, buckwheat and flannelbush, with panoramas northwest over the broad expanse of Summit Valley to the aberrant alluvial scarp forming its northern limit. ▌ *This long, steep-faced ridge is actually the upslope edge of an early Pleistocene alluvial fan, whose sediments originally came from canyons of the San Gabriel Mountains, seen far to the west. However, subsequent right-lateral movement along the San Andreas Fault displaced the range northwest, thereby cutting off the fan's source of sediments. Continuing lateral and vertical movement along the San Andreas Fault and associated parallel faults not only altered the landscape but also brought about drastic changes in the stream-drainage pattern.* ▌

See maps C13, C14

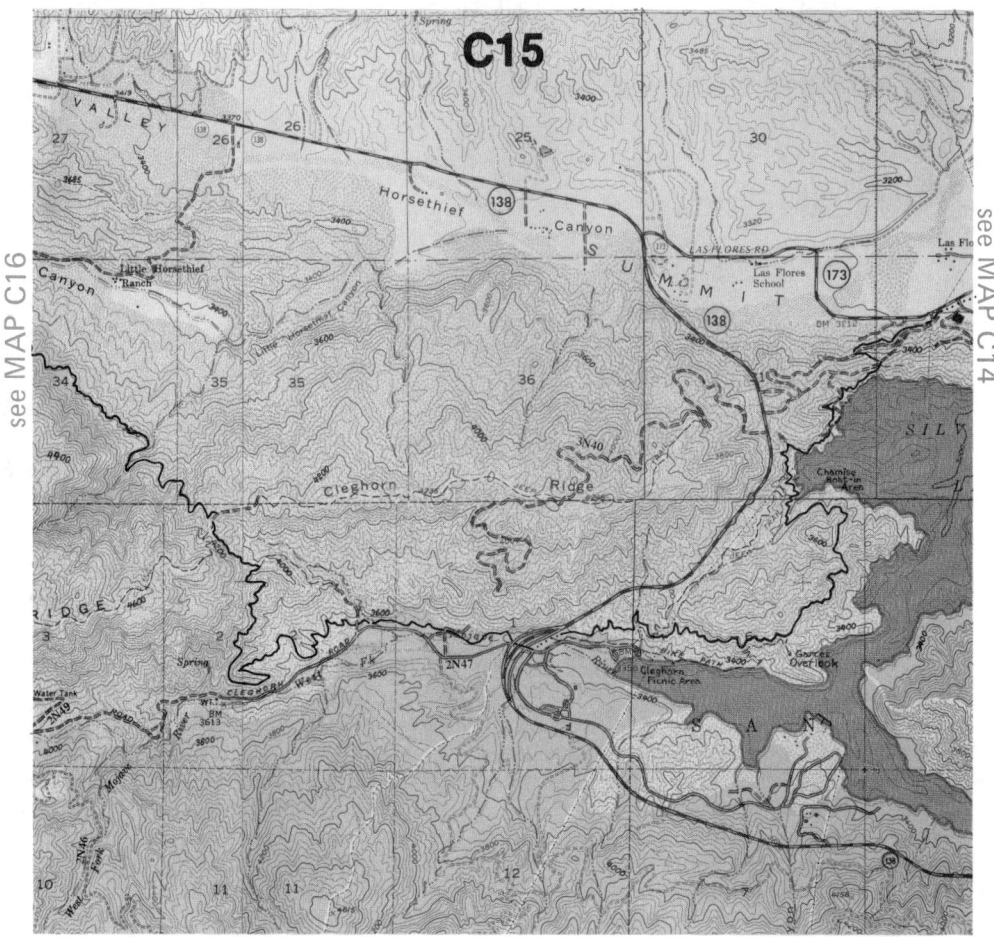

The PCT drops slightly as it winds south into a broad valley, then climbs to a ridgetop saddle where it joins a jeep road (3430-1.5) serving a powerline. You follow this road south down to an easy ford of Grass Valley Creek (3330-0.3), which flows most summers. Unfortunately, private lands prohibit camping here. The trail resumes just across the stream, on the jeep road's east (left) side, and momentarily it crosses a second, poor jeep track before climbing northwest. Around a nose, the trail hairpins south across another steep jeep road (3480-0.7), then undulates interminably west in and out of gullies and ravines in shadeless chaparral. About halfway to Silverwood Lake, you cross another north-descending jeep road (3480-2.6).

*   *   *   *

Resupply access: This road can be followed 0.2 mile north down to two-lane, paved Highway 173, clearly visible along the south margin of arid Summit Valley. Follow Highway 173 left, west, 0.1 mile to Summit Valley Country Store, with a good selection of snacks, well-deserved cold drinks, and camping foods, and a telephone. The store sits 1.7 miles east of where the PCT later strikes Highway 173 at the spillway of Cedar Springs Dam.

*   *   *   *

Back on the PCT and refreshed by a cool

See map C14

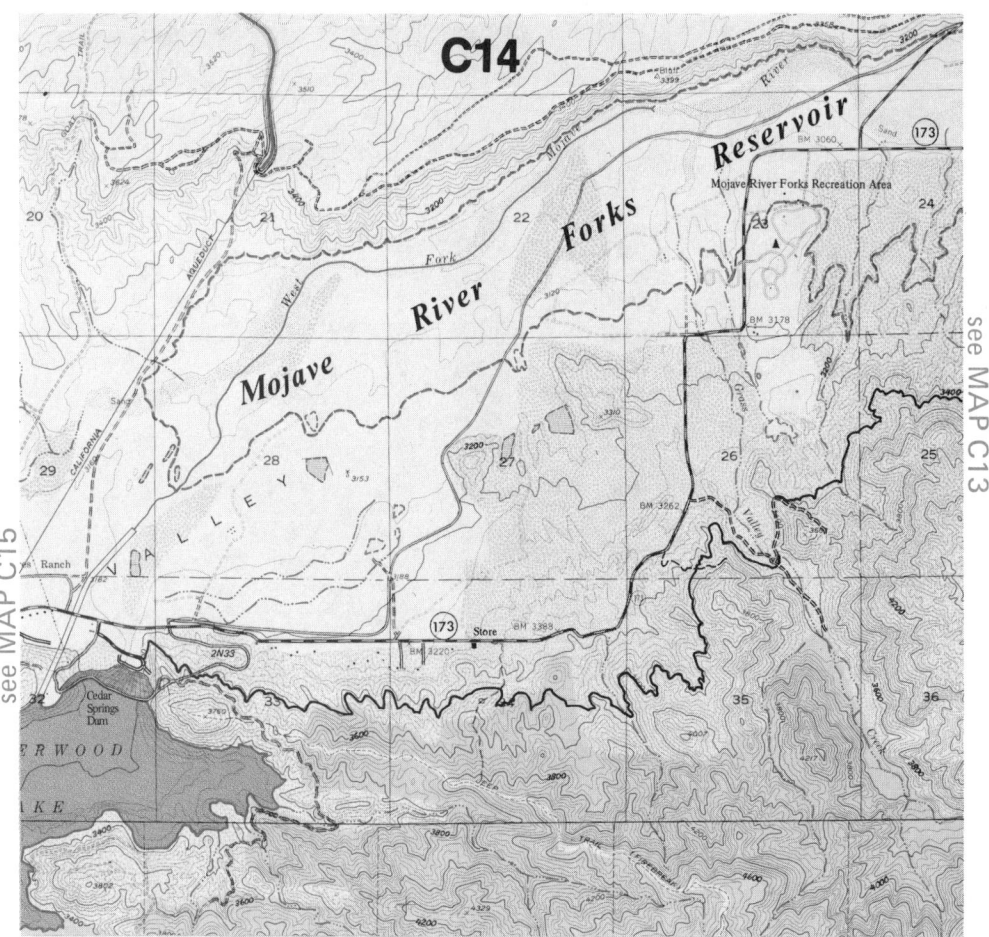

drink, you continue winding almost levelly west. Eventually the way strikes Road 2N33 (3400-2.2), a paved road ascending west to the nearby east end of Cedar Springs Dam. Walking a few minutes up to that end will give you vistas over giant Silverwood Lake, which is part of the California Aqueduct system. From Road 2N33 the PCT descends steeply, then turns south around a sharp ridge and joins a west-branching dirt road close under the base of 249-foot high, rockfill Cedar Springs Dam. ∎ *PCT travelers lacking a fast mode of transportation might be less than enthused to learn that the active Cleghorn Mountain Fault lies not far south of the damsite: the reservoir's northern east-west arms lie along the fault.* ∎

Now, possibly with a brisker stride, you turn west down the dirt road for a few yards to the end of a poorly paved road (3170-0.4) that bridges the canyon bottom and continues northwest to some dam-maintenance facilities. Follow the poor road left, gently up onto a sandy flat, to a paved road just east of the large maintenance sheds. Turn right, north, along that short road's west shoulder, through a hurricane fence and out to two-lane paved Highway 173 (3175-0.3) at a line of junipers. Now walk left, west, on the highway shoulder, crossing a bridge that straddles the concrete spillway flume of Cedar Springs Dam. Pass dirt Las Flores Ranch Road and an access road to new Mojave Siphon Power Plant, to the next road on the south

See maps C14, C15

C17

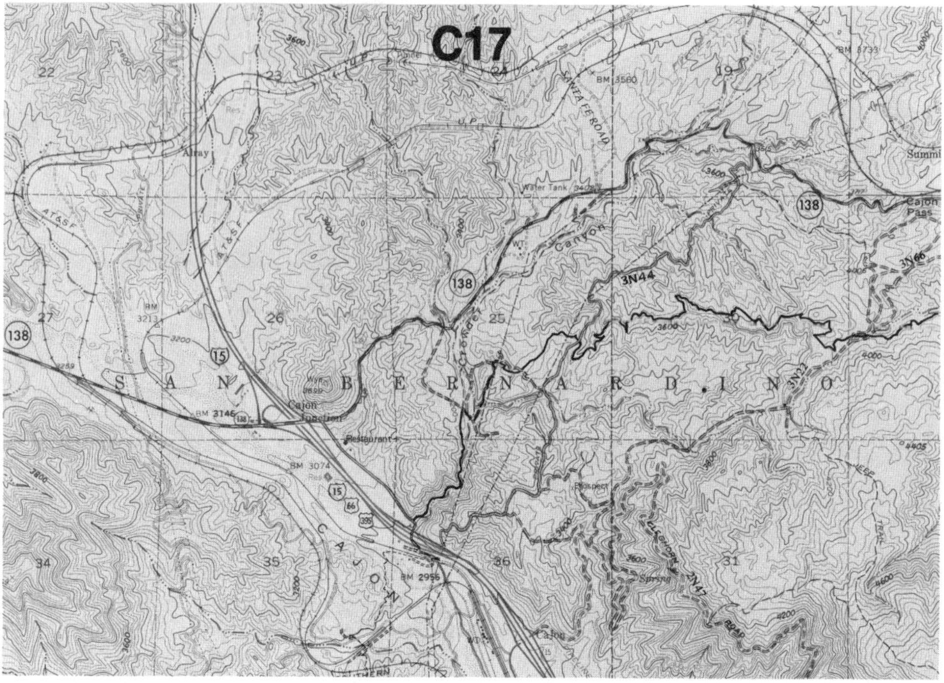

see MAP C16

see MAP D1

Silverwood Lake, from Garces Overlook

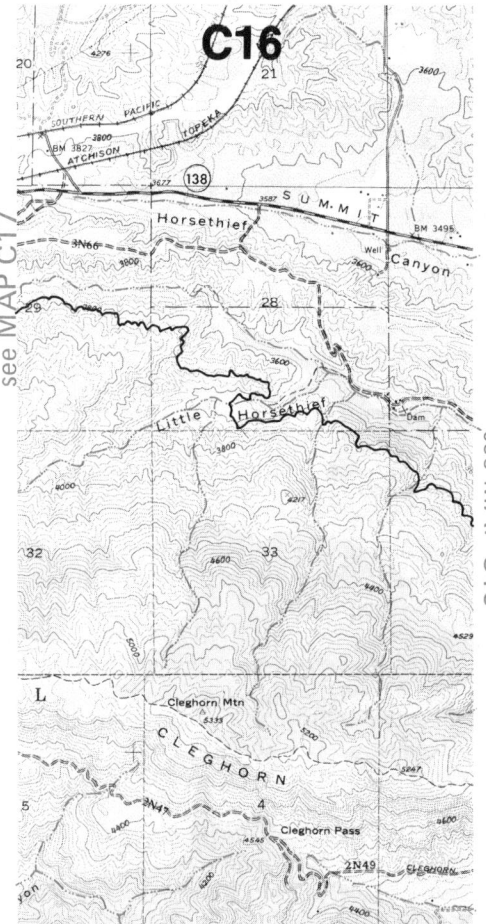

the reservoir's western shoreline. Twice you follow jeep roads for 60 yards as the route winds through sparse chaparral, crossing many gullies. North of the westernmost arm of northern Silverwood Lake, a meager spring wets the trail, then the path meanders south before climbing moderately east above the Chamise Boat-in Picnic Area, which lacks running water. Now 200 feet above the reservoir, you pass onto a hillside scorched by a fire that started at the picnic area, then the trail bends south to an unsigned spur trail (3580-2.5) that drops south to another trail and to Garces Overlook—an octagonal hilltop gazebo—which makes a fine, albeit waterless, picnic spot.

Back on the PCT, you descend easily west across a jeep road (3455-0.8) and eventually come to a paved, two-lane bike path (3390-0.7) next to a paved road leading east to Cleghorn Picnic Area, which has water, tables, bathrooms and telephones. This junction is not signed, but is easy to spot, coming southbound on the PCT, if you look carefully: It is 80 yards east of where the infant, usually dry West Fork Mojave River passes under the bike path via a cattle grate. The trail leaves from a curve in the path that is farthest from the paved road to the picnic area. Heading toward Oregon on the PCT, walk southwest across the Mojave River's wash and slightly up to a signed junction (3380-0.1) with another paved bike path that leads west, towards the group-camp complex. Follow the path up to the paved Silverwood Lake State Recreation Area's entrance road (3390-0.1).

*   *   *   *

Resupply access: This road may be traced south to the entrance station and then 1.7 miles east beyond it for camping, water, showers, telephones and a small store and cafe at the reservoir's marina. Northbound hikers must note that the next certain water lies in lower Crowder Canyon, 13.2 miles west of the SRA, while, except for the reservoir, the next water for those southbound flows in Grass Valley Creek, 11.5 miles east.

*   *   *   *

Continuing on the PCT route from the SRA entrance, you first walk west under the High-

(3200-0.5), a very poor dirt road angling southwest, up the brushy hillside. Here the PCT's overgrown trail tread resumes, climbing parallel to the dirt road, which is immediately above it. Many hikers have complained that the start of this trail segment is indistinct, and it is, though it is marked by a PCT post at the roadside. The segment is also quite overgrown with brush farther on, as is much of the route around Silverwood Lake.

Entering Silverwood Lake State Recreation Area, the PCT continues below the road for a bit, then crosses it and switchbacks southeast to a nearby saddle (3460-0.6), on which it crosses a similar road. Here northbound hikers gain their first vistas over windy Silverwood Lake. The warm water will likely prove irresistible to most, as the PCT route traverses near

See map C15

see MAP C17

see MAP C15

way 138 overpass to its offramp (3395-0.1). From here one may hitchhike southeast to Crestline for supplies at its post office and stores. Here too, the trail resumes at the offramp's junction with the SRA's entrance road. PCT posts and ducks lead northwest from a concrete culvert across a small grassy field to five sycamores, clustered against the northern hillside. Here tread becomes more distinct. The PCT leads gently up-canyon, then dips into West Fork Mojave River's sandy wash for a moment before crossing a dirt road that serves a small picnic area (3440-0.4). From it the route continues up along the base of a canyon wall cloaked in chamise, buckwheat and pungent yerba santa. The trail's tread is interrupted as you follow the paved group-camp access road for 25 yards, then it resumes to strike a narrow paved road (3530-0.4) that climbs steeply to a water tank. Three lavish group camps lie just down this road, in Silverwood Lake State Recreation Area.

Now you leave the SRA and begin climbing in earnest, winding southwest up numerous dry gulches, then around an east-jutting nose, and finally turning north up to join a jeep road (4040-2.2) at a small promontory. Here the PCT turns west, following the track which climbs moderately to its junction with a road (4160-0.3) atop viewful Cleghorn Ridge. ∎ *Eastward gazes take in the Lake Arrowhead region, Miller Canyon, Silverwood Lake and West Fork Mojave River, the last three aligned along the east-west Cleghorn Fault, which separates Mesozoic granitic rocks, found here, north of the fault, from older Precambrian metamorphic rocks south of the fault.* ∎

Resuming your trek, you follow the ridge road north 100 yards down to where the trail's tread resumes. The way descends moderately northwest across hillside gullies, presently reaching a deeper canyon with a small stream (3830-0.9), which usually flows through late spring. No camping is possible, however. The next leg winds northwest across numerous similar ravines while it contours above ranches in Little Horsethief Canyon. ∎ *This canyon and Horsethief Canyon to its north commemorate Captain Gabriel Moraga's pursuit of an Indian band suspected of horsethievery in 1819. The first known crossing of nearby Cajon Pass occurred in 1772, and this key pass was heavily* used by the Mormon Battalion and Death Valley borax teams. ∎ Eventually the route drops into the canyon's head, where PCT posts show the way through a grassy flat. The Forest Service plans to build a trail camp with well water here.

Your trail turns north across Little Horsethief Canyon's dry creek bed (3570-2.8), ignoring a use-trail that continues up-canyon, then climbs again, up to a narrow ridgecrest, which you traverse in low, bedraggled chamise chaparral—an impoverished indicator of your proximity to the Mojave Desert. The PCT then proceeds west up into another draw, and near its head strikes a road (3840-2.5) under a huge power-transmission line. You walk across the road, then west along a spur beneath a mammoth power pylon. Trail tread continues west from here, vaguely at first along a gravelly wash, then more obviously as it climbs to an overlook of spectacularly eroded badlands above Cajon Canyon. ∎ *The Pliocene sediments here were eroded from the infant San Gabriel Mountains, then shifted east, relatively speaking, along the San Andreas Fault, which now cuts through Cajon Canyon, below. Because these sediments have been removed from their source of rejuvenating alluvium, stream flow has easily incised their once gently sloping surfaces into a dramatic series of razorback ridges.* ∎

The path climbs to top the most spectacular of these ridges, then winds tortuously down, west, along it, giving you superb vistas of the San Gabriel Mountains' crown, Mount San Antonio, and of Lytle Creek Ridge, which you will climb on the PCT one day hence. Presently you cross Road 3N44 (3355-2.4) and minutes later you pass through a burnt gate on a saddle, and then descend easily southwest. You quickly cross another road (3300-0.4), from which well-marked trail tread resumes to lead west, momentarily passing under power-transmission pylon #63 to strike the previous descending dirt road (3265-0.2). Here the PCT turns left, south, down the road as it drops steeply into quiet Crowder Canyon, dotted with baccaris and willows. There, just shy of a hop-across ford of sandy, always-flowing-a-little Crowder Canyon creek, you end the descent at a post-marked merger with a better dirt road (3140-0.3), which goes briefly down-canyon

See maps C15, C16, C17

to another power pylon.

A cluster of cottonwoods and baccharis, teeming with birds, at this three-way junction would make the best camp since Silverwood Lake. You follow the PCT, which proceeds right, northwest, directly across the cress-decked creekbed, then leads 90 yards uphill across a buried gas pipeline to a wood PCT post, which marks the resumption of trail heading left, south, onto an alluvial bench.

This pleasant path winds along the narrow, shady gorge of lower Crowder Canyon, where pools and trickles of water (3045-0.3) afford the last on-route water until Guffy Campground, a long 23 miles away. The trail ends abruptly at six-lane Interstate 15 (3000-0.4) in Cajon Canyon, just south of a roadend memorial to Santa Fe Trail pioneers.

*   *   *   *

Resupply access: No facilities are available here (save for a weighing station on the freeway if your backpack loads are "over gross"), but they are found in Wrightwood and San Bernardino, as described in the introduction to this section. Just 0.5 mile northwest up the access road to the trail's terminus, just 0.1 before the Route 138 cloverleaf, is a fine 24-hour restaurant. If no palatable water is available in lower Crowder Canyon, this restaurant is a recommended detour. Just west of the cloverleaf are a gas station-minimart and a motel.

*   *   *   *

See map C17

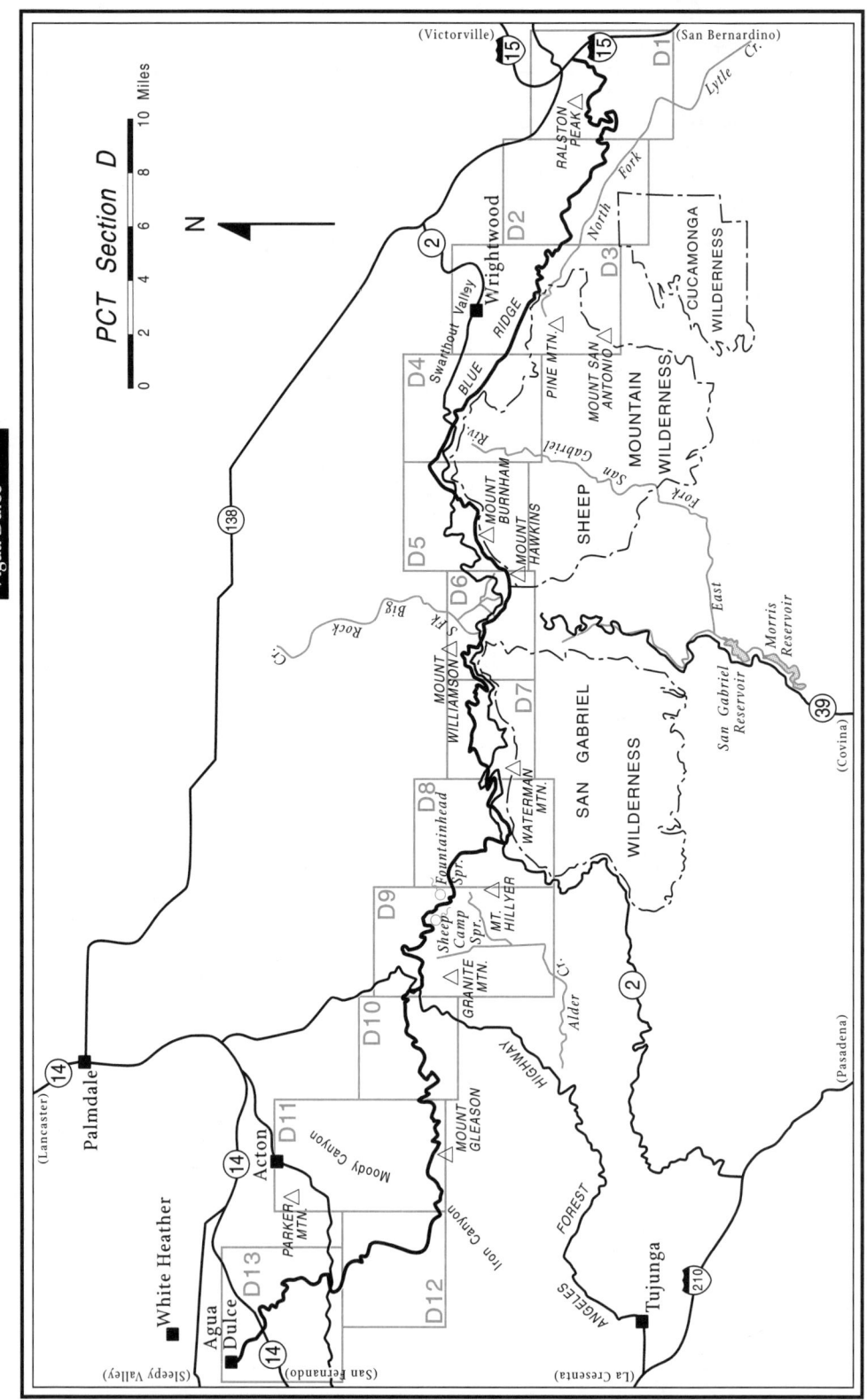

Section D
Interstate 15 near Cajon Pass to Agua Dulce

Introduction: True to its name, the Pacific Crest Trail through the San Gabriel Mountains remains on or close to the watershed dividing streams that flow into the Pacific Ocean from those that run north, losing themselves in the sand or evaporating from muddy playas in the Mojave Desert. The PCT climbs quickly from smoggy, arid Cajon Canyon to the subalpine reaches of the San Gabriel Mountains, and soon ascends its Southern California apex—wind-torn, 9399-foot Mt. Baden-Powell. Most of the PCT's winding route lies between these two extremes, treaded in pine-needle duff under groves of shading, hospitable Transition Zone forest trees: Jeffrey pine, incense-cedar, black oak, sugar pine, white fir and water-loving white alder.

Except for frequent roads and resorts that the PCT skirts, much of the trail route traverses country unchanged, at first glance, by the encroachment of modern man. But on closer inspection, the San Gabriels are seen to be no longer the wild and remote range that moved legendary mountaineer John Muir to call them "more rigidly inaccessible than any other I ever attempted to penetrate." Man has tamed the San Gabriels' clawing chaparral and steep-walled gorges with miles of highway, and has prevented once-devastating floods with dams and catchment basins. Bears and bighorn sheep, which once roamed the range, have been driven by thousands of hikers, skiers, picnickers, hunters and loggers into the most remote and forbidding canyons. The forests, however, show the most insidious and far-reaching effects of California's burgeoning population. Smog, that yellow pall that has made Los Angeles infamous, now rises well into the surrounding mountains, and the pollutants are severely damaging timber—yellowed needles on thousands of acres of dying pines and firs are mute testimony.

A part of the Transverse Ranges geologic province, the San Gabriels are thought to be rather young, at least in their present stature. Despite their relative youth, geologists state that some of California's oldest rocks lie in the San Gabriels. Precambrian anorthosite (a light-colored, plutonic rock composed almost entirely of plagioclase feldspar and high in aluminum content) and gabbro estimated to be 1.22 billion years old both line the PCT route in the vicinity of Mt. Gleason. These rocks are much older than most of the rocks along the San Gabriel Mountains segment of the PCT. Most of the trail tread lies in familiar granitic rocks of Mesozoic age; these were intruded at the same time as similar rocks in the Sierra, San Bernardino and San Jacinto mountains, and in Baja California. Other rocks, like the Pelona schist, which you first encounter on Upper Lytle Creek Ridge as you enter the San Gabriels, are metamorphic rocks, once volcanic and ocean-bottom sediments, which may have been altered by the intruding granites.

The present-day San Gabriels are a complex range, cut by and rising along numerous faults that occur along their every side. The major San Andreas Fault is the most famous, and it bounds the San Gabriels on their northern and eastern margins. This great fault stretches from near Cape Mendocino southeast about 1000 miles into the Gulf of California. Geologists now know that hundreds of miles of horizontal shift along the fault (with the western side moving north) have occurred in the last 30 million years, since about the time the fault first formed. Where the San Andreas Fault slashes through Cajon Canyon, at the start of this section, one can see an example of long-term motion along the fault: the bizarre Mormon Rocks and Rock Candy Mountains, all sedimentary rocks, lie northeast of the fault about 25 miles east of related rocks at the Devils Punchbowl, on the fault's southwest side. The Punchbowl and the trace of the San Andreas Fault can be seen easily from atop Mt. Williamson, a short side hike from the PCT.

Declination: 13½°E

Points on Route	S→N	Mi. Btwn. Pts.	N→S
Interstate 15 near Cajon Pass	0.0		110.2
		5.5	
Swarthout Canyon Road	5.5		104.7
		4.4	
Sharpless Ranch Road 3N29	9.9		100.3
		11.3	
Acorn Canyon Trail to Wrightwood	21.2		89.0
		0.9	
Guffy Campground	22.1		88.1
		6.1	
Grassy Hollow Family Campground	28.2		82.0
		1.3	
Jackson Flat Group Campground	29.5		80.7
		4.0	
Lamel Spring Trail	33.5		76.7
		5.7	
Lily Spring Trail	39.2		71.0
		2.0	
Little Jimmy Campground	41.2		69.0
		7.2	
Rattlesnake Trail	48.4		61.8
		4.1	
Cooper Canyon Trail Campground	52.5		57.7
		6.4	
Three Points	58.9		51.3
		3.3	
Sulphur Springs Campground	62.2		48.0
		12.3	
Mill Creek Summit Picnic Area	74.5		35.7
		11.8	
Messenger Flats Campground	86.3		23.9
		5.5	
North Fork Saddle Ranger Station	91.8		18.4
		8.7	
Soledad Canyon Road	100.5		9.7
		7.0	
Antelope Valley Freeway at Escondido Canyon	107.5		2.7
		1.9	
Vasquez Rocks County Park entrance	109.4		0.8
		0.8	
Agua Dulce	110.2		0.0

Supplies: No supplies are available at the start of Section D, save for snack items from a gas station-minimart at the freeway overpass 0.6 mile north of the trail's beginning. A complete selection of needed items may be purchased in San Bernardino, 17 miles south on Interstate 15. Be sure to restock on water before leaving Cajon Canyon, since the next water won't be found until Guffy Campground, high in the San Gabriels, about 22 miles away. Wrightwood, a ski-resort community with a post office, stores, restaurants, and motels, is the next possible supply point. In the past, a PCT register has been kept at the pharmacy. Check with the Methodist Church camp—they sometimes offer bunks, showers and laundry facilities. Wrightwood is a 4.4-mile round-trip detour down from the PCT via the Acorn Canyon Trail, 21 miles from Interstate 15.

Cajon Pass area near Sullivans Curve

Acton, a small town with a post office, grocery stores and motel, lies 5.8 miles east off the PCT route in Soledad Canyon, about 100 miles from Interstate 15. Saugus, a larger town with complete amenities, lies west of the PCT some 12½ miles from the same point in Soledad Canyon. Agua Dulce, at the end of Section D, is the most logical resupply point, and a long carry from Wrightwood. Now a rapidly growing ranching center, the village of Agua Dulce boasts a post office, three restaurants, an equestrian feed store and two markets—one is a large supermarket. The post office also keeps an official PCT register and listings of local families who will host PCT walkers, and might even cache water for them in the Sierra Pelona!

Water: While generally well-watered, the San Gabriel Mountains nonetheless pose a challenge to the PCT walker in search of regular water sources. This is especially true at either end of the mountain chain, where lower elevations and the proximity to the fiery Mojave Desert create an arid chaparral, with few permanent springs or streams. Carry plenty of water for the long, hard uphill day at the start of this section, to reach water at Guffy Campground. From there, you should encounter water a few times a day, from natural sources or campgrounds. By summertime, however, don't count on stream-flowing water in most creeks. West of North Fork Saddle Ranger Station, the pickings again become slim—don't count on water, except at man-made facilities.

Poison Oak: Some botanists have claimed that there are places in the chaparral belt, stretching from Southern California's coastal plains north through Sierran foothills, where poison oak is the single most common plant! In some locations, optimal conditions allow the waist-high shrub to assume the proportions of a small tree, or a thick, climbing vine. Certainly, many PCT travelers would agree that, with the possible exceptions of flies or mosquitos, poison oak is the most consistent nuisance along the trail in California. The allergic rash it causes in most people leads, at worst, to a few days of insane itching and irritation. It may, however, completely incapacitate a luckless few.

Poison-oak dermatitis is best managed by avoidance, and avoidance is best accomplished by recognition of the plant, in all phases of its life cycle: In spring and summer, it puts forth shiny green leaves, each divided into three oval, lobed leaflets, which, even on the same plant, exhibit an unusual variety of sizes. Toward fall, the leaves and stems turn reddish, and the small whitish flowers become smooth berries. In winter and early spring, when its leaves are gone, identification is most difficult: look for gray-dusty bark on stems, with smooth green, red-tipped new growth, and possibly some white-green berries left over from the previous season.

Avoid touching any part of the plant in any season—all parts contain an oily toxin that will, in a few days, lead to an allergic reaction where it has penetrated the skin. If you do brush against the shrub, wash the area immediately. Water helps to inactivate the toxin, and alcohol helps to extract the oil from skin, as does soap. Try to avoid spreading the oil by rubbing, however, since it takes a few minutes to an hour to fully penetrate the skin, and so one might actually spread the dermatitis by rubbing the oil around, without washing. Better yet, avoid exposure entirely by wearing loose, long-sleeved clothing, tucked into boottops. But beware—poison-oak oil on clothing can, hours later, be wiped onto the skin, with toxic results. If you must wear shorts, try applying a commercial barrier cream, which catches the oil before it can reach your skin. Above all, avoid smoke from burning poison oak, and never eat any of the plant—fatal internal reactions have occurred.

If you do develop the itchy, red, blistering, weeping rash of poison-oak dermatitis, console yourself with the knowledge that it will be gone in a week or so. In the meantime, try not to scratch it—infection is the biggest hazard. Use calamine lotion, topical hydrocortisone cream and oral benadryl for itch relief. Severe allergic reactions, characterized by trouble breathing, dizziness, or swelling around the eyes or mouth, should be treated promptly by a doctor.

Maps: *Cajon*   *Waterman Mountain*
      Telegraph Peak   *Chilao Flat*
      Mount San Antonio   *Pacifico Mountain*
      Mescal Creek   *Acton*
      Valyermo   *Agua Dulce*
      Crystal Lake

--------------------------------- **The Route** ---------------------------------

The beginning of Section D is reached by taking Interstate 15 north 17 miles from San Bernardino to the "Palmdale Highway 138/ Silverwood Lake" exit. Atop the offramp, turn right and head 12 yards east along Highway 138 to paved Wagon Train Road, the frontage road that branches south. Paralleling Interstate 15, take this road down past a fine 24-hour diner, 0.6 mile to its end beside a stone monument to Santa Fe Trail pioneers. This spot is just short of narrow Crowder Canyon, the PCT's route. Just south of the memorial plaque, the Pacific Crest Trail curves south under the freeway via a boxed culvert, emerging on the other side in a verdant thicket. The author has found water running here even in midsummer of severe drought years. The route becomes a sandy-muddy jeep track paralleling the freeway. Moments later, you pass under the wooden Atchison-Topeka and Santa Fe Railroad trestle,

See map D1

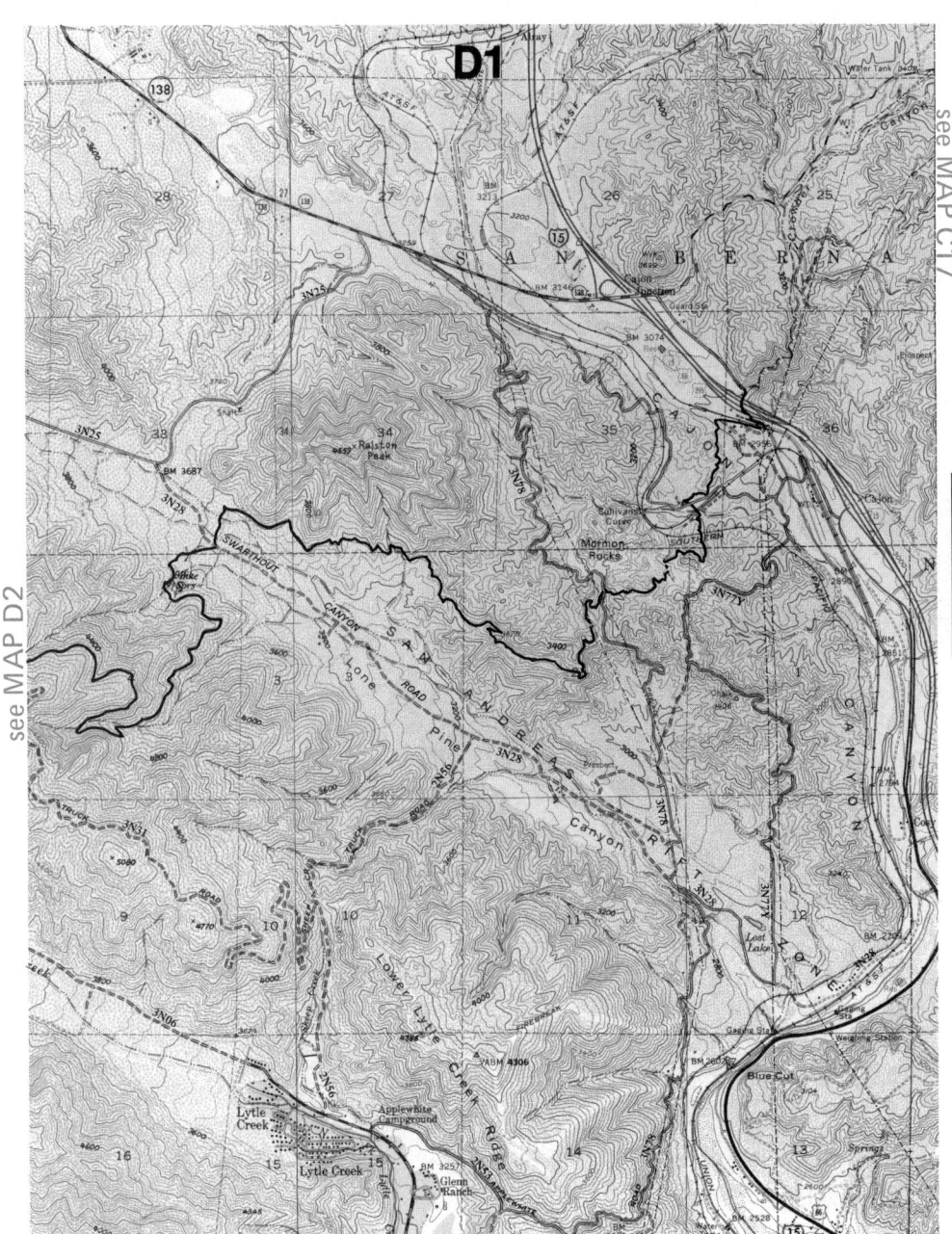

then turn right, to follow a jeep road west, just below the tracks, well-marked by PCT posts. Just north of a fenced private home, PCT trail tread resumes (2930-0.4) branching obliquely left, west-southwest, from the jeep trail, and marked by a yellow PCT post. The path winds levelly through a desert chaparral, soon to encounter a welter of faint side paths. This is San Bernardino County's Elsie Arey May Nature Center. Hikers should spend a few minutes here,

See map D1

D

I-15-
Agua Dulce

walking the trails, to learn to identify the common chaparral plant species that are here described on trailside plaques. Beyond this instructive herbarium, the PCT swings south, up and over a sandy ridge on a well-signed route, then dips to a rough dirt road that heads west to Sullivan's Curve, an historic railroad grade. Cross this road, then walk down a short trailless wash to a culvert under another AT&SF railroad track. Now walk right, southwest, up a faint path that parallels the rails, to find the PCT climbing south once again, via two small, overgrown switchbacks.

Soon the trail crosses the newer Southern Pacific Railroad tracks (3020-0.8), and then bends southwest to wind among the hills and sandstone-conglomerate outcrops of the Mormon Rocks, a badland of Miocene alluvium. At one point, you amble south along a jeep road for 100 yards. ∎ *The Mormon Rocks commemorate Mormon pioneers who were among the first Caucasians to utilize Cajon Pass, and who settled San Bernardino Valley. Pedro Fages, who on one trip discovered the Colorado Desert and the San Jacinto Mountains, crossed the mountains in this vicinity when he tired of leading a contingent to capture Army deserters, and an urge to explore captured him. The De Anza-Garces forces passed near here 4 years after Fages, in 1776, on their way north from Sonora, Mexico. By 1813 the Cajon Pass route, part of the Santa Fe Trail, was seeing frequent use by American trapper-trader Ewing Young and others. The Mormon Battalion used this route both coming from and going to the Great Salt Lake, and borax teams from Death Valley and the Santa Fe Railroad also crossed here.* ∎

Pushing on, you cross first one powerline road, Road 3N78, and then in ¼ mile cross another (3360-1.2) amid bush sunflower, chamise and scattered cacti. Next the PCT ascends to a sandy ridge dominating lower Lone Pine Canyon, eroded along the San Andreas Fault. The path traverses this ridge, which presents some striking blue clays, then cuts across sandy washes under the south face of Ralston Peak to dirt Swarthout Canyon Road 3N28 (3560-3.1). The PCT route strikes invisibly west from the road, marked by 4x4 posts in the cobbly alluvium, then turns south across a bouldery wash to a jeep road (3700-0.5). Two vandalized concrete tubs at Bike Springs are found just yards north, but they have been dry more often than

not in recent years. Even when water is running, its heavily polluted nature relegates it to emergency use only. Four white PVC pipes have been driven here in the dry wash, and will eventually be developed as a well, hopefully with a horse camp. No reliable water is available yet, as of Spring 1995.

Attacking the chaparral-clothed eastern flanks of Upper Lytle Creek Ridge, the trail swings into a canyon, then switchbacks north, up across three canyons to finally strike dirt Sharpless Ranch Road 3N29 (5150-3.9) near the ridge's crest. Now, on a segment of trail built in 1994 by PCT Association volunteers to avoid a shooting-range on the south side of Upper Lytle Creek Ridge, you round a nose and amble more-or-less levelly west on the cooler northern slopes, just yards below ridgetop Sheep Creek Truck Road. At the next gap in the ridge (5260-1.0), you find remains of the old south-side PCT tread, and might choose to walk up to the ridgetop, where cooling vistas are had of the snow-dappled Mt. San Antonio massif and the rugged Cucamonga Wilderness, to the west and southwest, above North Fork Lytle Creek. In the 1890s Lytle Creek was the setting for a spirited but short-lived gold rush.

Continuing on, your path ascends gently, keeping to the ridge's steep north side, where you parallel arid Lone Pine Canyon from a slightly cooler vantage. Eventually, you cross dirt Sheep Creek Truck Road 3N31 (6300-3.2), at an intersection where it turns northwest to drop into Lone Pine Canyon. Now your chialined path crosses to the south side of the ridge, and in a few minutes finds a small, viewful ridge-top flat (6350-0.2), where, under a cluster of shady big-cone spruce, one could make the first nice camp west of Cajon Pass. Unfortunately, the site is waterless. Beyond it, you wind south around a prominence to a roadend (6480-0.9) just east of Gobber's Knob. Above this point the way used to be more shaded, by frequent groves of big-cone spruce, mountain mahogany and some juniper. Sadly, a man-caused fire here in the early 1990s burned many of the trees.

As the route swings under Blue Ridge, both the Devils Backbone and Dawson Peak dominate the southern horizon, thrusting ridges of platy brown Pelona schist above timberline. These points mark the eastern boundary of Angeles National Forest's new Sheep Moun-

See maps D1, D2, D3

tain Wilderness, a 43,600-acre preserve which protects the rugged San Gabriel River drainage, just west of Mt. San Antonio.

Look for black-granular phyllite and outcrops of white quartz and fibrous green, shiny actinolite, a close relative of asbestos, in the schist before the PCT switchbacks east up to a jeep road (8115-4.3) atop Blue Ridge. This road climbs northwest up to a posted trailhead (8176-0.1) just north of the jeep road's intersection with Road 3N06. Here you can gaze north down to Wrightwood, across the north face of Wright Mountain, where cycles of mudflows, triggered by the melting of winter snows, have cut a spectacular, barren swath. The PCT contours south around Jeffrey-pine-forested Wright Mountain, staying just above dirt Road 3N06. ∎ *Soon Prairie Fork San Gabriel River comes into view, incised along the San Jacinto Fault. Mt. Baden-Powell dominates the western horizon, while San Gabriel Valley smog is partly screened by the Pine Mountain Ridge to the south.* ∎ West of Wright Mountain you meet the Acorn Canyon Trail (8250-1.6).

*   *   *   *

Resupply access: This path descends 2 miles north to a road that drops 1½ miles to the western edge of Wrightwood. The next possibility for reprovisioning on the route lies in Agua Dulce, about 89 miles ahead.

*   *   *   *

The PCT continues west up Blue Ridge, sometimes on Road 3N06, but often to its north on short trail segments. It enters Angeles National Forest and arrives at Guffy Campground (8225-0.9), which has water at a good spring reached by a side trail 270 yards down Flume Canyon to the north. Trekkers have frequently complained that water here, the first logical campsite west of Interstate 15, was hard to find. It can be, especially during the summer of drought years. A better strategem for throughhikers in those years would be to detour to Wrightwood, the best resupply point in this section, and avoid the uncertainty.

See map D3

Pine Mountain, from Wright Mountain

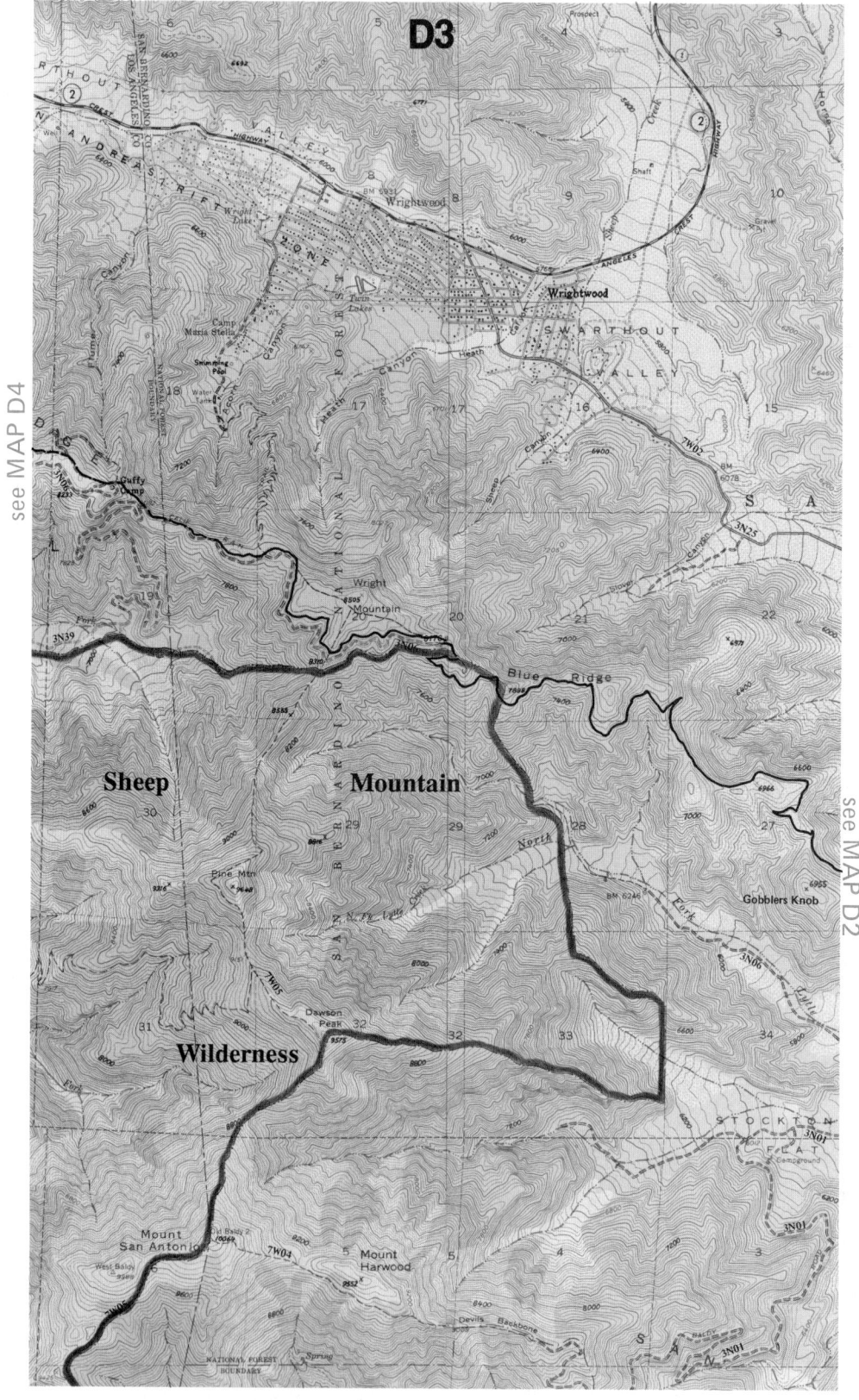

see MAP D4

see MAP D2

Wrightwood

Sheep **Mountain**

Wilderness

Mount San Antonio

Mount Harwood

Gobblers Knob

Continuing, the trail, often sited on old, narrow dirt roads, continues mostly north of Blue Ridge's crest, offering vistas to the north over Swarthout Valley and the San Andreas Fault Zone to pinyon-cloaked ridges abutting the Mojave Desert. You descend easily in fine mixed-conifer forest around Blue Ridge's high point, eventually reaching a dirt road (8115-2.3) beside an artificial lake, enclosed by a high fence. This is one of two reservoirs serving the snow-making operations of the Mountain High Ski Area, which has ski-lift terminals that you

See maps D3, D4

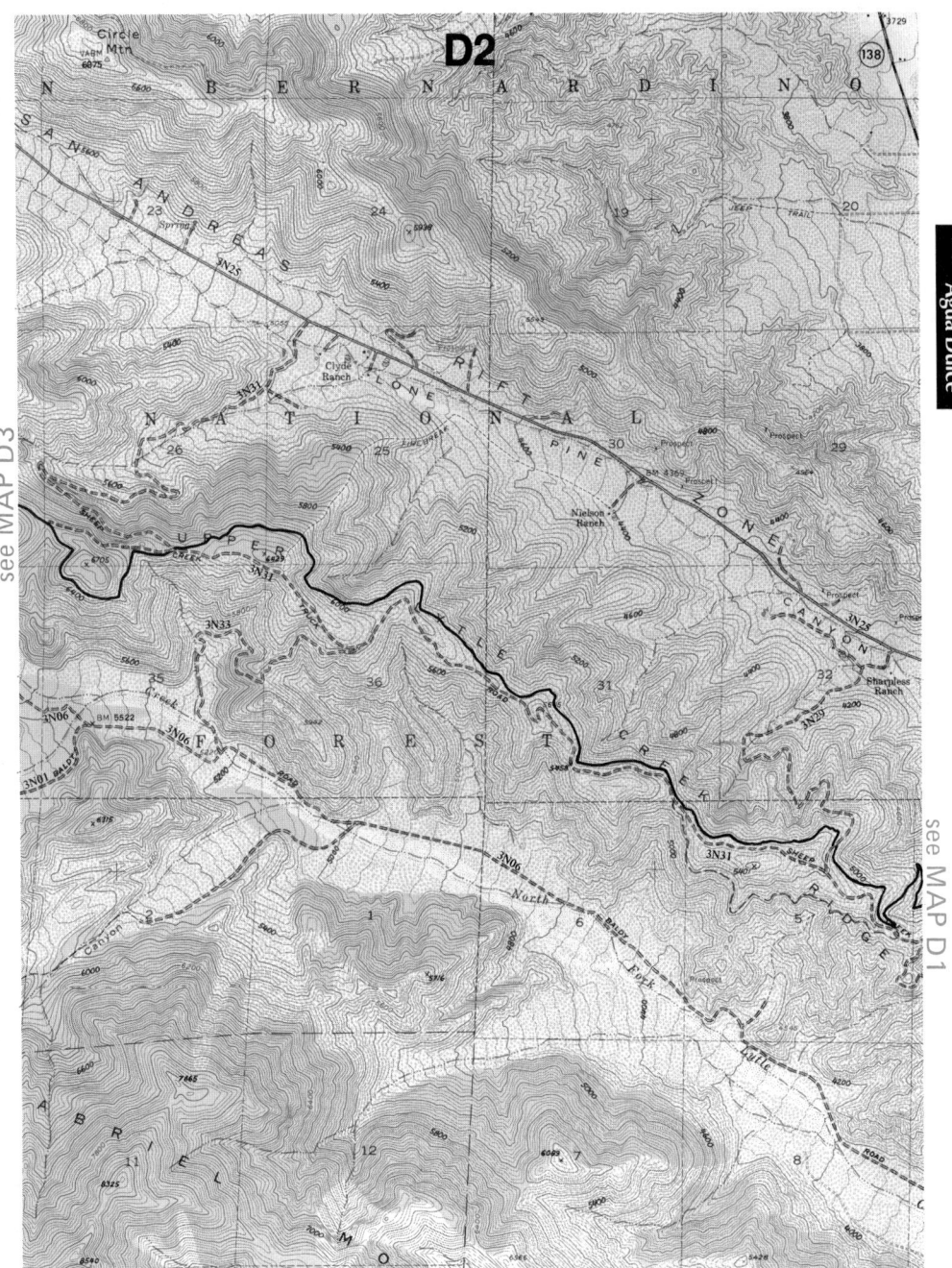

see MAP D3

see MAP D1

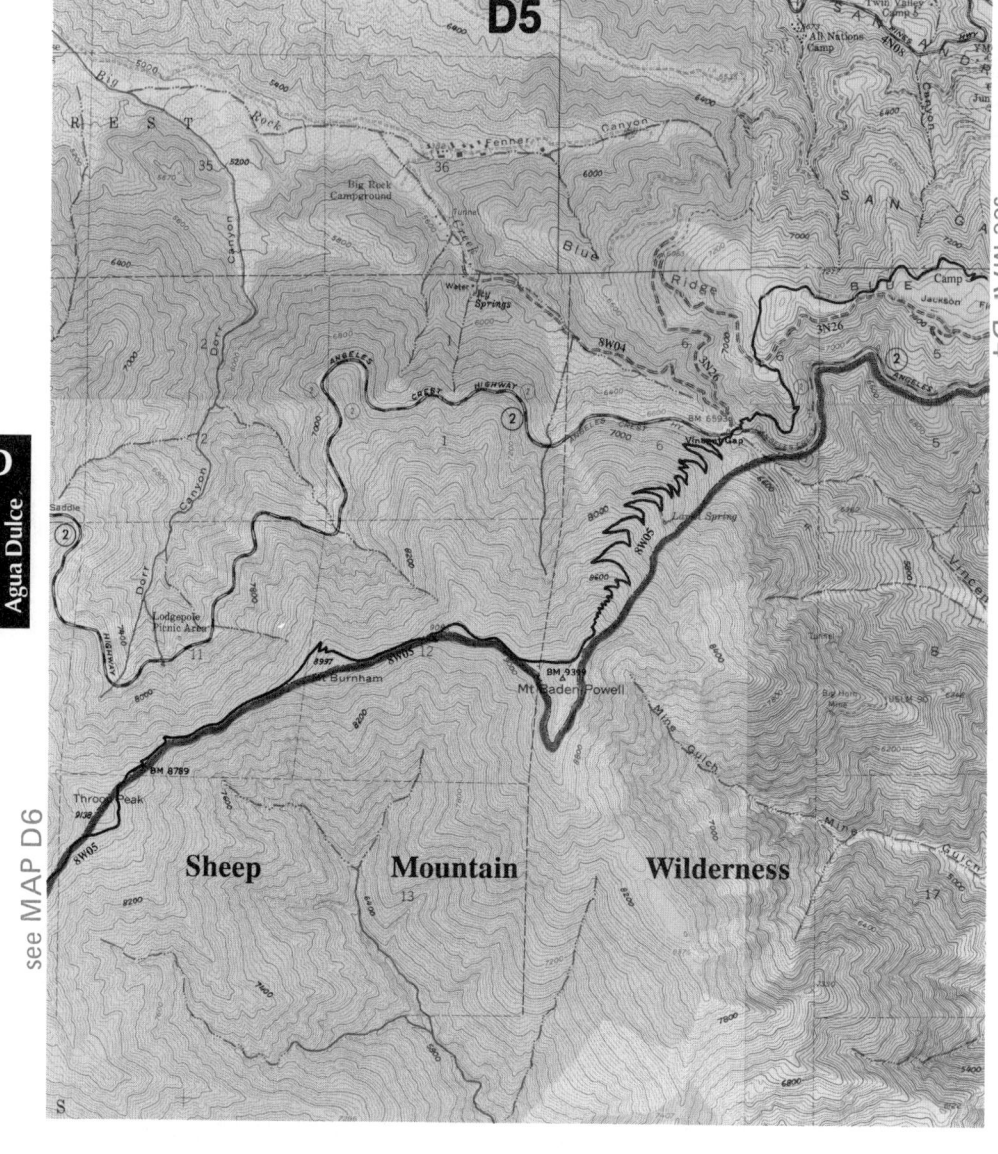

will pass in the next mile. Here, turn left, south, briefly up over the ridgecrest, through a large white pipe gate to Road 3N06, which you follow right, west, for a minute to access a resumption of PCT pathway (8120-0.1) on the west side of the reservoir. This leads back up to the ridgetop, from which you wind down in nice fir forest, beside a ski run, to again strike Road 3N06 (7955-0.4). As indicated by white

metal PCT posts, you cross the road and descend a few feet to traverse the western perimeter of pleasant but waterless Blue Ridge Campground (7910-0.1). Beyond the campground, you parallel the boundary of Sheep Mountain Wilderness, the rugged chaos of mostly trailless ridges and gorges to your southwest. Atop the second hill along your way, you find the second artificial lakelet and some more

See map D4

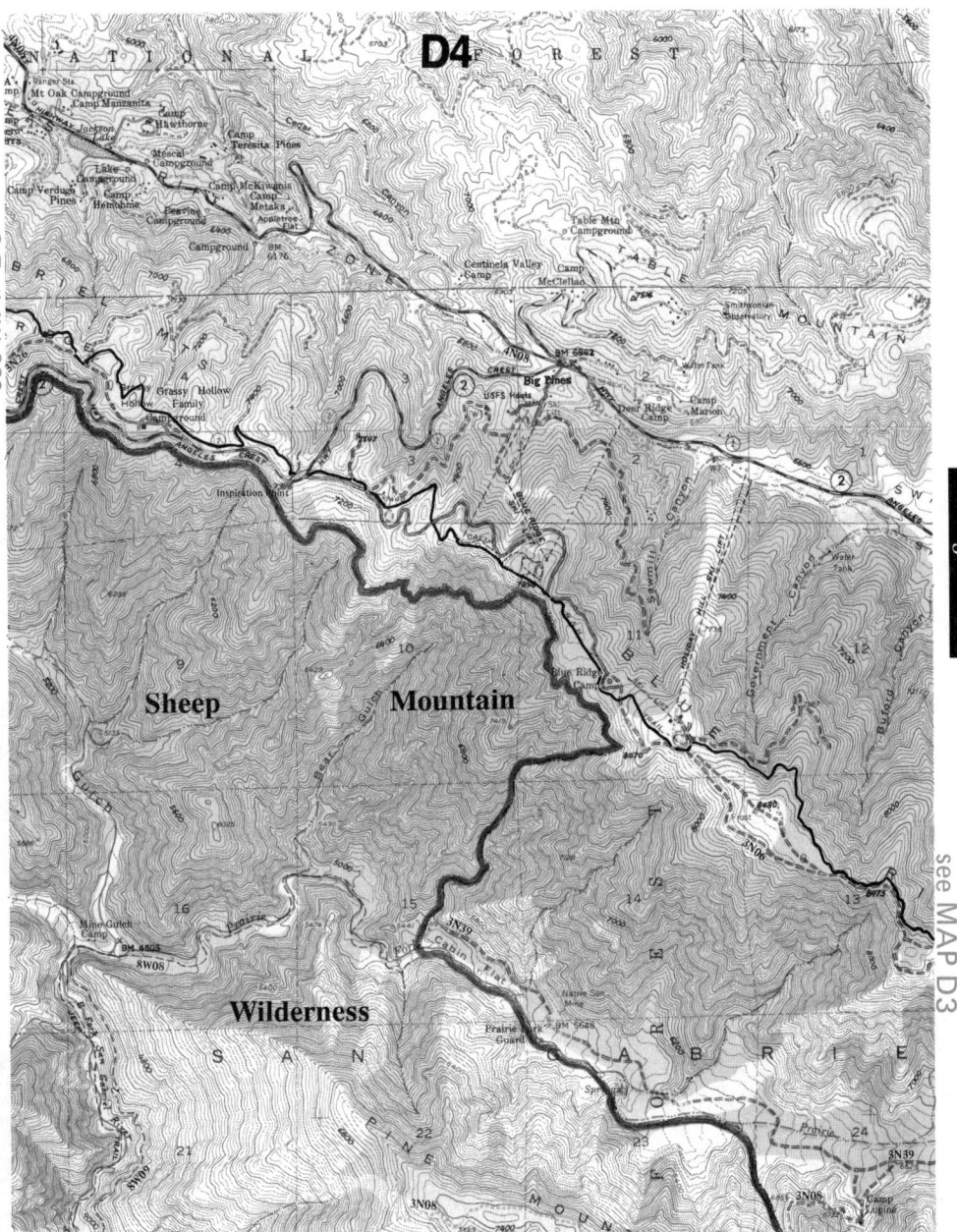

ski lifts, and the path is forced directly onto the brink of Bear Gulch's steep headwall. Beyond, you cross or swing next to now-paved Road 3N06 several more times. Black oaks and white firs join the ecosystem as you near Angeles Crest Highway 2 (7386-2.2), just east of Inspi-

ration Point, a sweeping overlook of the East Fork San Gabriel River basin.

Carefully cross the highway to a paved parking area, which has bathrooms but no water. Here a white metal PCT post marks your route, branching left, west, from short Lightning

See map D4

Ridge Nature Trail. Ascend easily, then drop west through flats of whitethorn and bitter cherry to reach forested Grassy Hollow Family Campground (7300-1.0), with water, toilets and a large new visitor center.

About ½ mile northwest of the campground the PCT route goes along Jackson Flat Road 3N26 for 100 yards before returning to trail tread on the north side of Blue Ridge. Next on the itinerary is a short spur (7480-1.3) to walk-in Jackson Flat Group Campground, in shading pines and firs. After passing north of Jackson Flat and turning Blue Ridge, the PCT drops south across Road 3N26 (7220-1.5), then switchbacks moderately down past interior live oaks and ocean spray to Angeles Crest Highway 2 at Vincent Gap (6585-0.8).

South of the highway, beside a parking area and a trail east to the interesting Bighorn Mine, is Mt. Baden-Powell Trail 8W05—a popular pilgrimage for Southern California Boy Scouts. You take this trail, which starts southwest before switchbacking gently-to-moderately up in Jeffrey-pine/white-fir groves on crunchy Pelona schist tread. After a number of switchbacks you reach a side trail (7765-1.7) that contours 100 yards south to Lamel Spring. This marks a good rest stop, and one might choose to camp at either of two level spots a minute farther along the main trail.

Above, the switchbacks become tighter, the air grows crisper, and firs give way to lodgepole pines, which yield in turn, above 8800 feet, to sweeping-branched, wind-loving limber pines. These hunched, gnarled conifers, believed by some botanists to be 2000 years old, are the only obvious living things at the Mt. Baden-Powell Spur Trail (9245-2.1).

*   *   *   *

See maps D4, D5

Mt. San Antonio, from Inspiration Point

Side route: Take this side hike to the 9399-foot summit for superlative views north across desert to the southern Sierra, west to Mt. Gleason, south down Iron Fork San Gabriel River (in Sheep Mountain Wilderness) to the Santa Ana Mountains, and east to Mts. San Antonio, San Gorgonio and San Jacinto. On the clearest days, Mt. Whitney, still 3–4 weeks to your north, and Telescope Peak, overlooking Death Valley, can be seen. A concrete monument here is a tribute to Lord Baden-Powell, founder of the Boy Scout movement. This summit marks the terminus of the Silver Moccasin Trail, Scouting's 53-mile challenge through the San Gabriel Mountains, which is congruent with the PCT until Three Points, about 23 miles away.

*　　　*　　　*　　　*

Back on the PCT, your route bears west, descending the steep ridge under Mt. Burnham, and passing a signed spur trail that heads north down the shoulder of Throop Peak to Dawson Saddle. You climb briefly in open pine-fir forest, with an understory of manzanita, whitethorn and sagebrush, to navigate Throop Peak's east and south slopes, where you briefly enter Sheep Mountain Wilderness. More descent follows, past a signed lateral to the summit of Mt. Hawkins. Then, on the sparsely conifered ridge west of that peak, you pass a lateral (8540-3.6) that drops ⅓ mile north to Lily Spring. Just a bit later, you pass another signed lateral trail, this one south to South Mt. Hawkins, before an aggressive descent ensues, bringing you to aptly named Windy Gap (7588-1.6), from where a trail drops south to campgrounds in the Crystal Lake Recreation Area. From here the PCT descends north off the ridge to Little Jimmy Spring (7460-0.2), lying just below the trail. This is the last water until Little Rock Creek, in 7.7 miles. Little Jimmy Campground (7450-0.2) is just a couple of minutes farther, with toilets, tables and firepits.

Beyond the campground you curve west on a trail that soon passes above Windy Spring. Now your route parallels dirt Road 9W03, keeping some distance below it. Presently, the road hairpins across the trail (7360-1.2), and here you should find a sign identifying the PCT route. The trail heads west moderately down to An-geles Crest Highway 2 (6670-1.0), reaching it just east of its Islip Saddle intersection with now-closed Highway 39. Just west of the parking area and restrooms on Islip Saddle, turn right on Mt. Williamson Trail 9W02 and ascend moderately northwest past white firs and whitethorn ceanothus to the Mt. Williamson Summit Trail (7900-1.6), which climbs 0.4 mile north to good views of fault-churned Devils Punchbowl. While you switchback west down from your ridgetop, you can look south down deep ravines in the friable tonalite to the San Gabriel Wilderness, which is a Southern California refuge of mountain bighorn sheep. Ending the descent, the route merges with a jeep road for 200 yards, and then crosses Angeles Crest Highway 2 (6700-1.3).

Trail resumes about 50 yards west to ascend Kratka Ridge in a heterogeneous forest of white fir, sugar and ponderosa pines, interior live oak and mountain mahogany. Soon, you descend back to Angeles Crest Highway, where you walk along the southern road shoulder, past a large tan metal highway-maintenance shed for 180 yards to waterless Eagles Roost Picnic Area (6650-0.9). At its entrance just west of the highway, turn west down a rocky, unsigned dirt road and descend to its end at Rattlesnake Trail 10W03 (6165-1.2), in a shady gully. This little-used path drops north under the stone gaze of Eagles Roost, leaves behind an older, poor path that climbs south, and crosses melodious Little Rock Creek (6080-0.3) in cedar-lined Rattlesnake Canyon. A cozy camp can be made here by the stream, but no more campsites are available as the PCT continues, contouring to Rattlesnake Spring and another spring a mile later. Past the second spring, a pleasant descent leads to several delightful camps beside Little Rock Creek, where the PCT merges with Burkhart Trail 10W02 (5640-2.3) and turns south across the stream to ascend southwest into Cooper Canyon. Past a pristine waterfall and the south-branching Burkhart Trail (5730-0.3), which climbs to Buckhorn Flat Campground, the PCT route becomes an often steep jeep road, Road 3N02. It passes Cooper Canyon Trail Campground (6240-1.2), with reliable water, as it climbs to Cloudburst Summit (7018-1.7), where you cross the Angeles Crest Highway again.

On the west side of this forested gap, the path

D

**I-15-
Agua Dulce**

See maps D5, D6, D7

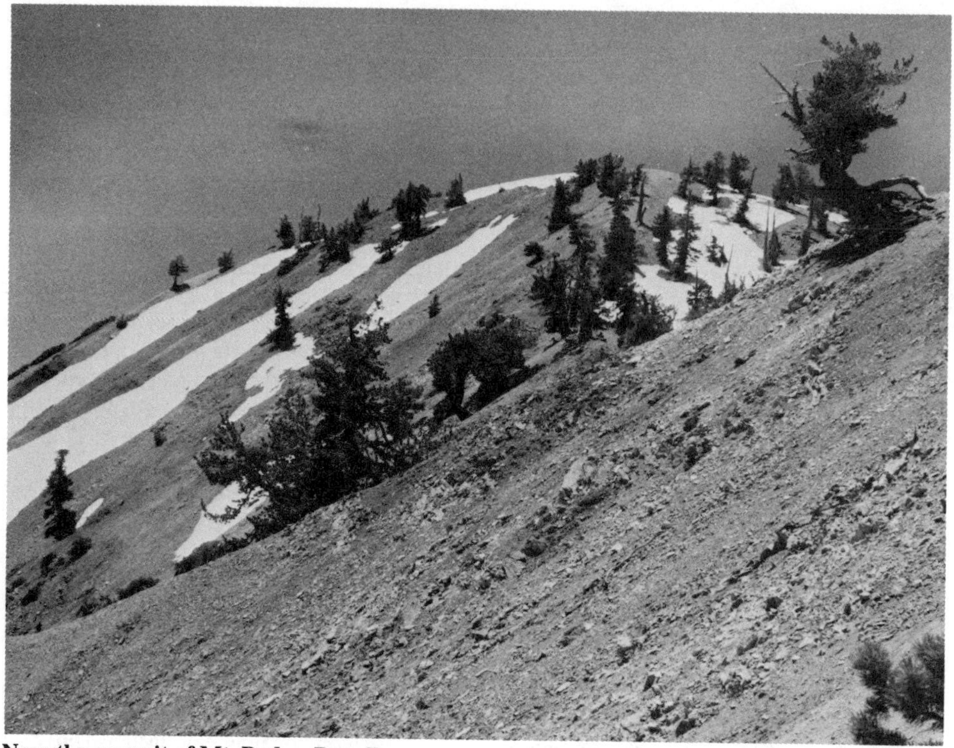

Near the summit of Mt. Baden-Powell

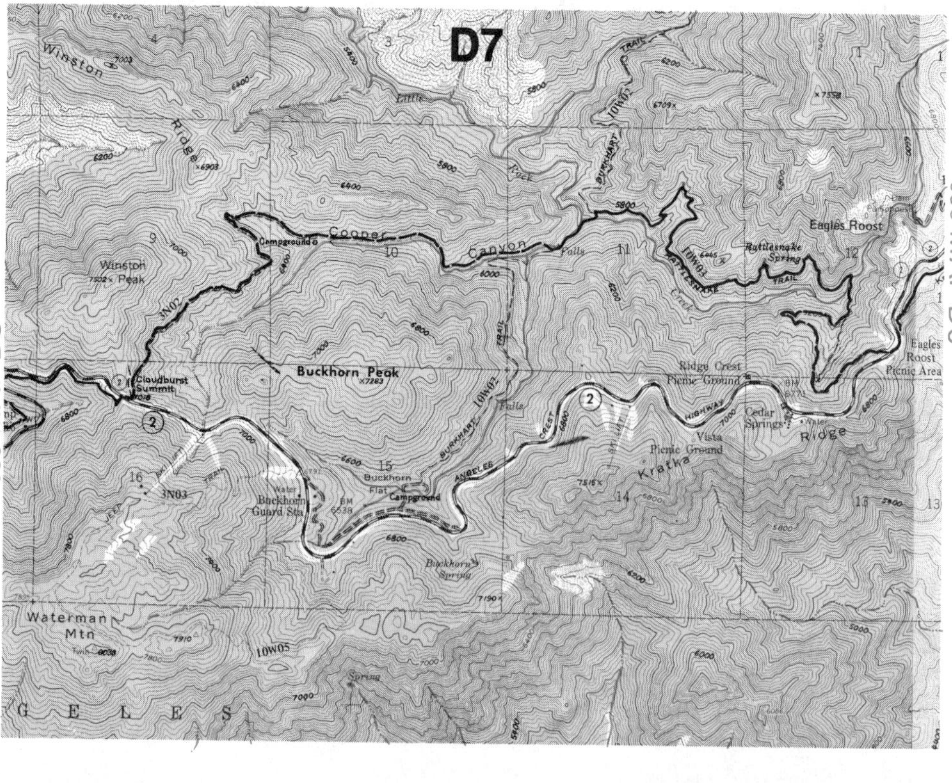

see MAP D8

see MAP D6

drops to contour just south of the highway in open forest, then crosses the highway (6735-0.9) again below a hairpin turn. Now you follow another gated jeep road, Road 10W15, which makes a switchback down into the head of Cloudburst Canyon, where you find a road junction (6545-0.6) with a dirt spur leading west down to Camp Pajarito. Here brown plastic PCT posts point your way straight ahead, contouring southwest across the dry creekbed, and below two water tanks. Easy, shaded descent carries you below the highway, soon reaching a small saddle atop which sits Camp Glenwood. Water is available here. Two minutes west of the camp's lodge, treading on the dirt access road, you pass a 14-foot-high, narrow steel water tank. Here the PCT drifts right, west-southwest, away from the road, onto a poor dirt road, indicated by plastic posts. In a moment, you dip across a culverted gully and walk up to a slightly better dirt road, which strikes left, south, for just a few yards to reach Highway 2 (6320-1.3). Now turn right, west, on the highway shoulder for 80 yards to a saddle with a large parking pull-out. Here we cross south to briefly ascend a dwindling dirt road (still Road

10W15). After a few minutes, gentle descent resumes, this time above the highway, to emerge from big-cone spruce at Three Points (5885-1.9) on the Angeles Crest Highway.

The Chilao Flat/Waterman Mountain Trail here continues southwest, but the PCT goes north across the highway. In a moment it reaches Horse Flat Road 3N17 and a trailhead parking area with restrooms and seasonal water. This is just beyond the left-branching Silver Moccasin Trail, which continues west to Bandido Campground and Chilao Flat. Across gravel Horse Flat Road, the PCT, indicated by a sign post, continues north, climbing slightly onto a granite-sand hillside shaded by interior live oaks. A northward contour on this slope soon ends as the PCT swings west through a gap, then drops gently west under big-cone spruces to an unused dirt road (5760-1.5). Turn left along this track, descending to reach, in 200 yards, a continuation of the trail, which branches right from the track. This short leg drops to another dirt road (5655-0.2) which, like the one before it, leads left to populous Pasadena Camp. The PCT here follows the gently descending dirt road north just 130 yards down

See map D8

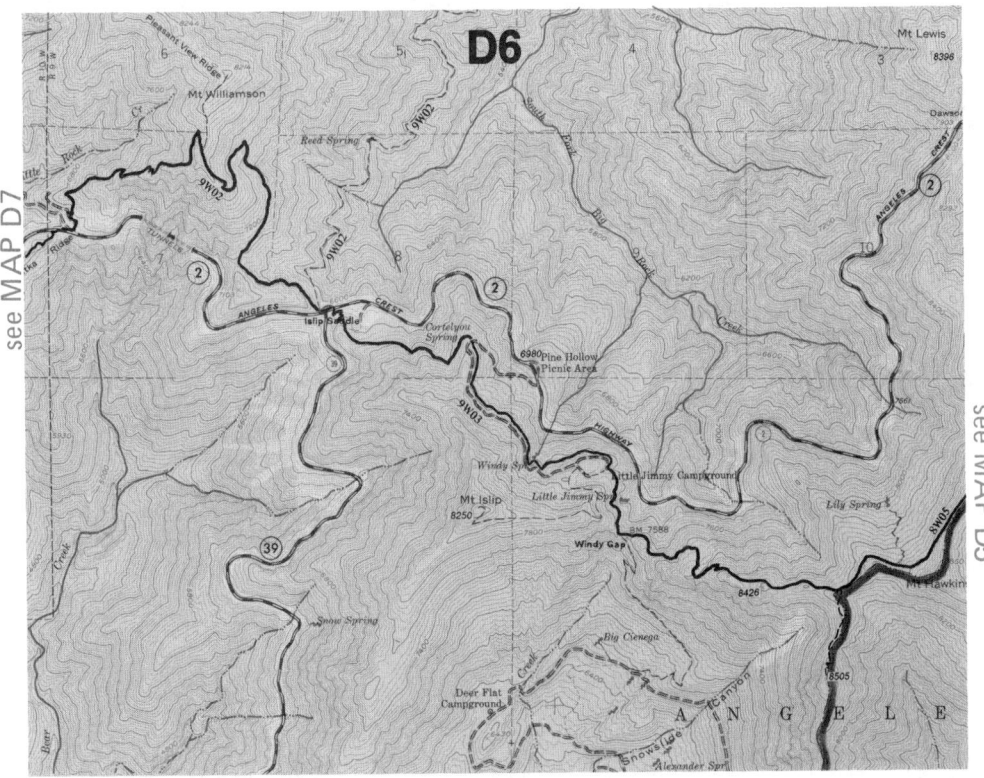

see MAP D10

see MAP 8

D

I-15-
Agua Dulce

to a resumption of trail where the road ends. Winding in and out of small, sandy ravines, the trail descends easily out onto a chaparralled ridge on a more-or-less northward tack. This descent ends at a usually dry stream bed, where the trail climbs for a moment to terminate on an old jeep road. Turn right, east, down the ravine for a moment to find a signed trail junction (5240-1.5). Here the hiker-only PCT branches left, while the signed equestrian PCT heads right, northeast, down to a dirt roadend and a stone water trough marking the

See map D8

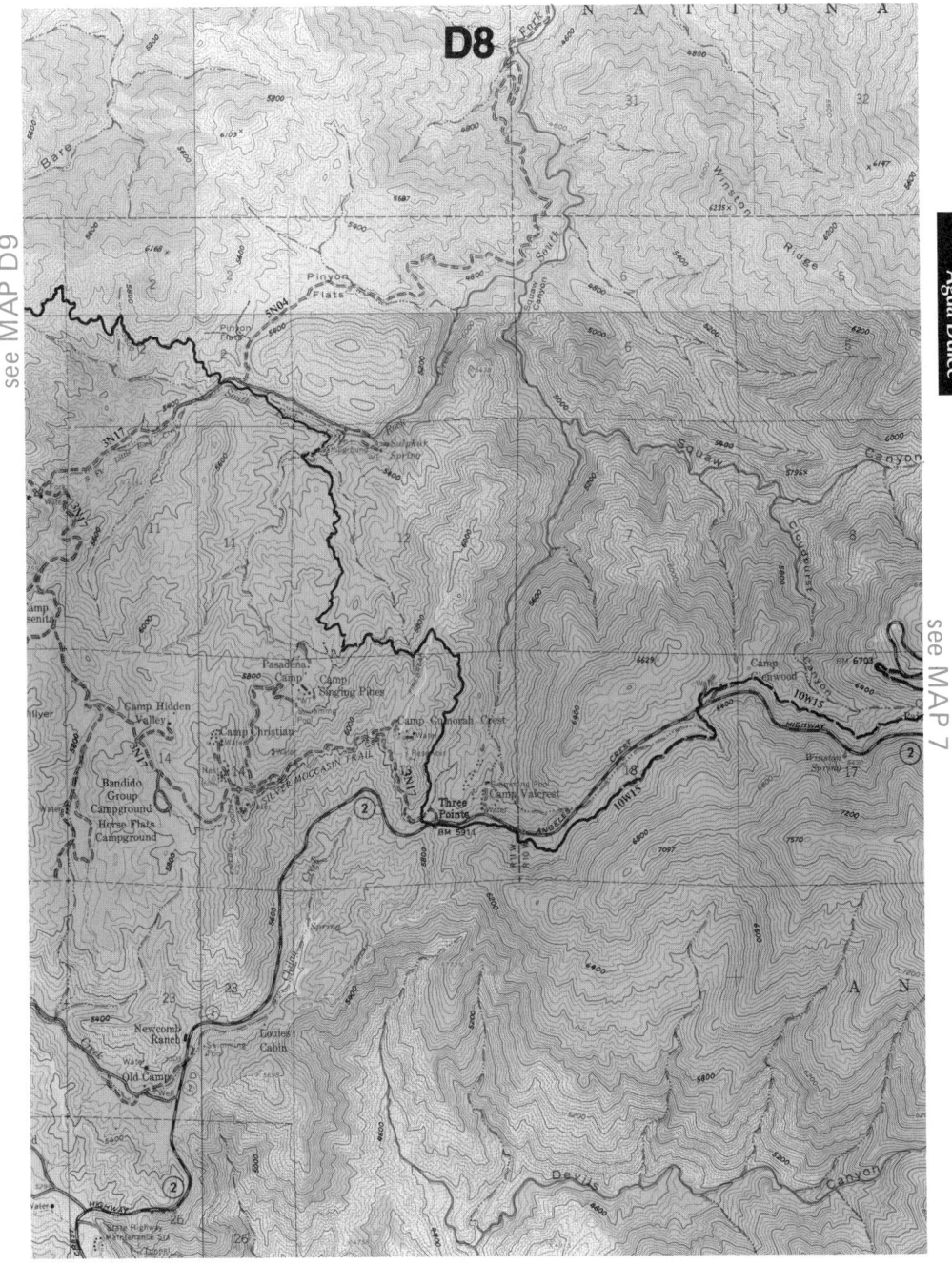

horsemen's section of lovely Sulphur Springs Campground (5200-0.1). Good water, lasting until summer, and adequate campsites are available in the main campground, 0.2 mile east down the oiled access road.

The PCT leaves the environs of Sulphur Springs Campground via two different routes. From the trail junction southwest of the equestrian camp, the foot trail contours northwest on the shaded hillside above South Fork Little Rock Creek, then gently descends to step across that spring-flowing rivulet. A minute later, you merge with the signed equestrian trail. The horse route leaves the campground at its western entrance via its previously paved access, Road 5N40H. This ambles northwest, just north of South Fork Little Rock Creek, to a resumption of trail tread, which drops left, southwest, away from the road for a few yards to merge with the foot trail (5265-0.5). Now you wind up-canyon, generally west-northwest, through sagebrush and scattered pines to clamber to the shoulder of dirt Little Rock Creek Road 5N04 (5320-0.3), just a moment west of its junction with the road to Sulphur Springs Campground. Across the road, the tread steeply ascends a brushy ravine, then circles northwest. This section was recently rerouted away from its previous location in Pinyon Flats, the second place in southern California where the PCT needed relocation to avoid gunfire from a shooting range—unfortunate reminders of our proximity to big-city violence. Continuing, you invisibly merge with the old alignment, and gently but relentlessly proceed up the brushy hillside.

Soon your path starts to zigzag in and out of numerous small ravines, sometimes shaded in their bottoms by interior live oaks, but usually a sunny mixture of ocean spray, hoary-leaved ceanothus, yellow-blossomed flannelbush, and pungent yerba santa. Eventually the PCT winds through a gap (5830-2.1) and turns southwest at the head of Bare Mountain Canyon, but not before you notice how easily the orange-rust-stained, rotting granite is quickly eroded by torrential rains into a badland of sharp-crested, barren ravines. Just below the level of a saddle at the head of Bare Mountain Canyon, the route turns northwest, then switchbacks briefly south, and ascends easily northwest to a grassy flat just shy of a shaded, seeping spring (6240-1.1) that emerges from the side of Pacifico Moun-

Eagles Roost

tain. An emergency camp may be made here, but be aware that the spring may be dry by early summer of drought years.

Leaving the spring, your path climbs north to a notched ridge, then swings west to a chaparral-and-boulder-choked canyon dampened by Fountainhead Spring, 140 feet above you. Like the previous spring, it may be waterless by early summer of dry years. No camping is afforded here. Next your trail leads into and out of many small gulches clothed in 10-foot-high greenbark ceanothus, but these are soon left behind for a gentle amble up in an open forest of Jeffrey pine floored with rabbitbrush. After gaining Pacifico Mountain's north ridge, the trail swings southwest to a bare ridgetop vista point (6760-1.9), giving panoramas north down Santiago Canyon to Little Rock Reservoir, Soledad Pass, and the environs of Lancaster and Palmdale in the Antelope Valley.

From here the PCT begins a gentle descent southwest on steep, sparsely shaded slopes, passing above Sheep Camp Spring, where a

See maps D8, D9

planned side trail and camping area will eventually serve PCT users. Where the trail turns north in a shady gap (6645-0.8), trekkers may leave the PCT and walk south a few yards to a dirt road that can be ascended east to Pacifico Mountain Campground (no water) for outstanding sunrise views, or one may descend south on the road and then east on Road 3N17 to a water fountain 0.9 mile from the PCT.

Returning to the PCT, you descend gently northwest, then west under shading interior live oaks and big-cone spruces to a jeep road (6380-1.7), which is followed north down to its end and a resumption of trail (6210-0.5). Now the path gently descends the head of spruce-mottled Tie Canyon, named for the railroad ties that were lumbered here in the late 1800s. Lower, you swing west through a Forest Service tree nursery and under the first of a pair of high-tension powerlines, where you find a signed spur trail (4980-3.2). It climbs left, south, for just a few feet to Pacifico Mountain Road 3N17 and a paved PCT trailhead, with toilets, a water fountain and hitching rails. If the fountain is turned off, walk northwest down the paved road for just a minute to the Forest Service's Mill Creek Summit Ranger Station for water. Be sure to tank up here, since the next absolutely certain water on the northbound PCT is at North Fork Saddle, 17.5 miles away.

The PCT itself rounds down below the ranger station and a highway-maintenance yard, soon making tiny switchbacks to reach Angeles Forest Highway at Mill Creek Summit (4910-0.2). ▌*Cut by the Mill Creek Fault, which is the cause of this saddle, the Mill Creek/Big Tujunga Wash area was the scene of a considerable mining rush in the 1880s, with men searching for the legendary Los Padres gold mines.* ▌

*   *   *   *

Water access: Aliso Spring, which is never dry, is found 0.7 mile east down Angeles Forest Highway, should no water be available around Mill Creek Summit.

*   *   *   *

North across Angeles Forest Highway, the PCT begins to climb close alongside paved Mt. Gleason Road 3N17, then leaves yerba-santa

scrub as it turns west, just north of the ridgetop, in shading interior-live-oak stands. Frequent glimpses north include the shimmering Antelope Valley and the barren Sierra Pelona (Spanish for "a bald range—or ridge—devoid of trees"). The PCT dips to cross Mt. Gleason Road (5590-2.6), then keeps north of and below that road. An undulating traverse at about 5600 feet soon turns south to more-open slopes and switchbacks down to a narrow dirt road in a small northeast-trending canyon. Your route follows this track 0.1 mile southwest gently down to dirt Road 4N24 (5500-3.7). Across the road, trail resumes and interior live oaks, ponderosa and Coulter pines, brodiaea and lush grasses line the cooler parts of the way north of the Mt. Gleason Young Adult Conservation Corps Center—once an Army Nike missile base. Here, in a deep, shady ravine, a flat just below the trail constitutes Big Buck Trail Camp (5195-0.8). Water is available here only in earliest spring, but at any time the canopy of oaks, big-cone spruce and incense-cedar makes a nice stopover. Beyond the trail camp, the way begins to climb easily, first north around a ridge, then south and west. Later, the PCT switchbacks up to black oaks and Jeffrey pines surrounding a junction with a south-branching trail (6360-3.8).

Ignoring a north-branching trail, which was part of an earlier, now defunct PCT route down to Acton, you start along the south trail, which climbs for a moment to top Mt. Gleason's north ridge and cross a narrow dirt road (6410-0.1). One could ascend southeast about 300 yards along this road to Mt. Gleason's viewful 6502-foot summit. The PCT, however, crosses the road and abruptly turns downhill into the head of Paloma Canyon, sadly burned in a Fall 1985 fire. Soon you are switchbacking down on poorly maintained, heavily eroded tread in a charred woodland of oak and manzanita. The trail then quickly makes a traverse just above Santa Clara Divide Road, but after a short while you leave the burned brush behind and, at the entrance to Messenger Flats Campground (5870-0.8), come to within a few feet of that road. This delightful area, nestled in a stand of ponderosa pines, has 10 campsites plus tables, toilets and a horse corral. Piped water is usually available during the spring and summer hiking seasons. The next water is at North Fork

See maps D9, D10, D11

see MAP D12

see MAP D10

Saddle Ranger Station in 5.5 miles.

Leaving the campground, the PCT descends northwest momentarily, staying on the road's northern shoulder. This gentle descent soon becomes moderate-to-steep, however, as the trail veers from the roadside to traverse under the north rim of the Santa Clara Divide. This 1980s trail segment is narrower and more tortuous than you have become used to. It was built by Forest Service crews, local Boy Scouts and service clubs after it had become apparent that the original PCT route, northward through Acton, had to be abandoned due to private-property considerations.

Initially you are shaded by the now familiar trio of big-cone spruce, live oak and ponderosa pine, but as the route drops, a low, chamise chaparral supervenes. The otherwise monotonous scrub does, however, allow you excellent, if smog-shrouded, vistas north over Soledad Canyon and Acton, and northwest to ranks of low, seasonally green mountains, over which

the PCT will pass on its way to the High Sierra. Soon you dip into a small ravine to strike Moody Canyon Road (5320-1.4). Hikers desperately low on supplies could follow it north down to Acton, 11.6 miles away.

The PCT crosses west below Moody Canyon Road, and adopts a fairly level route, once again under open oak-and-spruce shade. This course eventually leads you to intersect a ridgeline gap and its Santa Clara Divide Road (5425-1.3). Here the PCT and the road coincide, descending gently west for just a moment to the next gap on the ridge, where PCT tread resumes (5395-0.1). Climbing west, initially beside a poor jeep road, the trail now keeps on the sunnier south side of the divide, in low, dry chaparral. Beware of the multitudes of ticks residing on the brush hereabouts, and check your legs for them often. Presently, an easy ascent yields to a gentle descent, and you pass the scattered wreckage of an airplane—its pilot missed clearing the ridge by only a few feet. Soon after, the

D
I-15-
Agua Dulce

See maps D11, D12

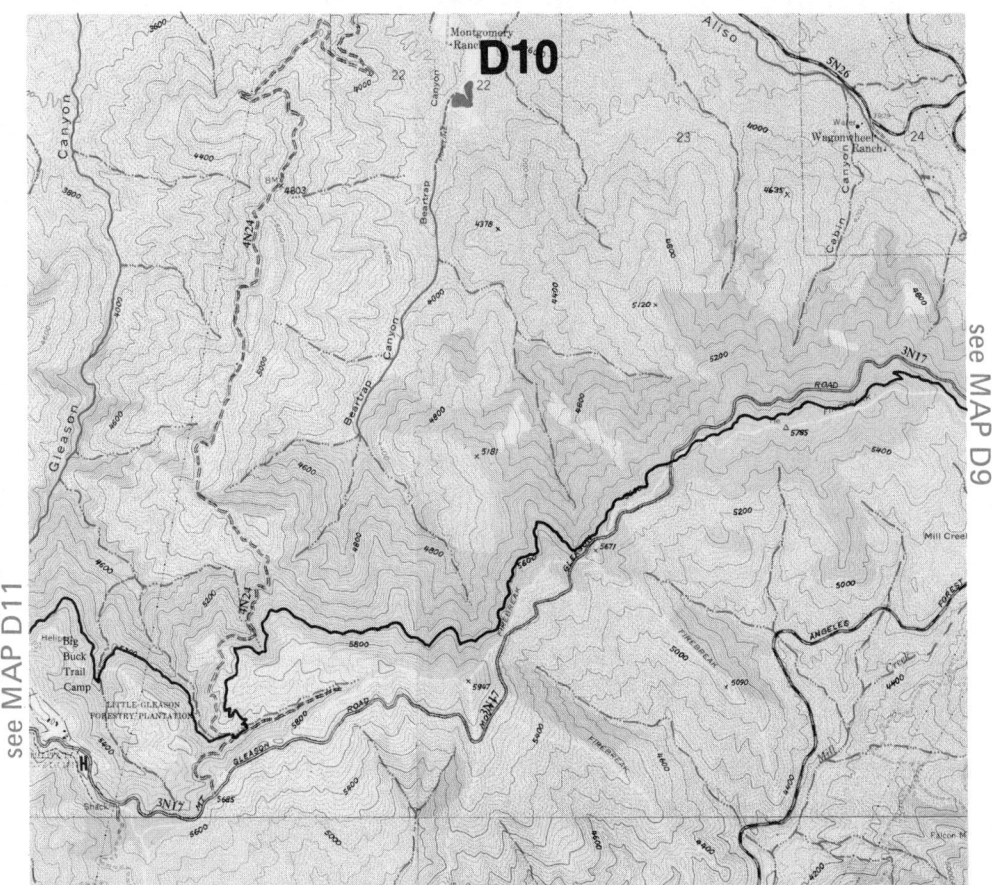

see MAP D13

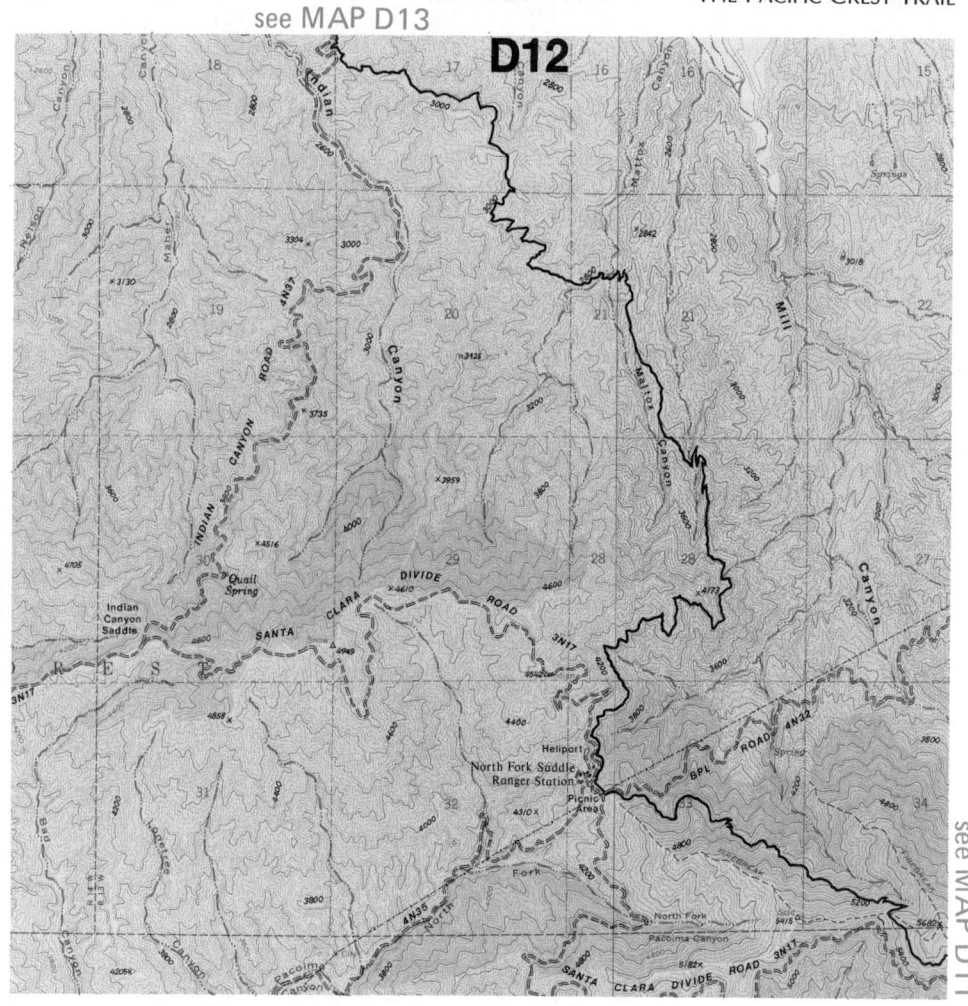

see MAP D11

PCT reaches a firebreak atop the main divide, and descends from its steeply west-descending jeep track (5395-0.7). Just a minute down the jeep track is a small flat, shaded by a single Coulter pine, which is the only nice, though waterless, campsite between Messenger Flats and North Fork Saddle.

After an initial descent northeast, the PCT turns northwest to descend moderately across the forested head of Mill Canyon. A few short switchbacks lead to a more earnest descent on often rocky tread. You get frequent glimpses down into Soledad Canyon, and later, as the tree cover thins, you can look northwest to the fantastic, red Vasquez Rocks, this assemblage being the next major point of interest on your northward agenda. Another set of small switchbacks and further bone-jarring presently deposit you at North Fork Saddle, where you find BPL Road 4N32 (4210-2.0), under a crackling high-tension powerline. On the north side of the saddle is the Forest Service's North Fork Saddle Ranger Station, which has year-round water and a picnic area with tables and toilets. No camping is allowed here, but hikers may camp anywhere along the nearby PCT. Northbound trekkers will find their next certain water in Soledad Canyon, 8.7 miles away, while southbound trekkers must carry water at least up to Messenger Flats Campground, 5.5 miles away, or possibly all the way to Mill Creek Summit, a long 17.5 miles away.

See map D12

Bound for Soledad Canyon, the PCT descends northward from the BPL road, initially just under Santa Clara Divide Road, but soon far below it, on a diagonaling descent on steep, rocky hillsides above Mill Canyon. Soon you are clambering steeply up and down across narrow ravines, on poorly constructed tread that is destined to quickly erode. In one spot, it already has, for a landslide has swept away a 50-foot stretch of trail. Later, the PCT drops at a gentler angle, but as it rounds the east side of point 4173, the path virtually plummets northward, into the head of Mattox Canyon. For the most part, your "economy model" PCT stretch steeply traces a ridgetop firebreak, but in one place, switchbacks do relieve the strain of your aching thigh muscles. When you can afford not to watch your footing, views east reveal a tree plantation in Mill Canyon. ∎ *Beside the trail in springtime, yerba santa bears fragrant blue blossoms, and chia and fiddleneck show small purple and white flowers, respectively.* ∎ Eventually, you encounter a second set of switchbacks, which deposit you at a step-across ford of Mattox Canyon creek (2685-4.3). This small stream usually flows into May, but should not be relied on for water. However, some small flats next to the trail—and a pretty line of sycamores—make this the nicest camping area between North Fork Saddle and Soledad Canyon.

Pushing on, you ascend moderately west and north through dry chaparral to gain a 3000-foot ridgecrest. A short drop from its north end leads to a contouring traverse above Fryer Canyon. From here, you can identify the PCT route, under some large pink cliffs, climbing the north slopes of Soledad Canyon. About one mile later, your path starts a swoop down to a nearby saddle, just feet above Indian Canyon Road. ∎ *This pass is formed by the Magic Mountain Fault, one of a series of southwest-northeast trending faults that transect the PCT in the next few miles. Notice how the Precambrian feldspar-rich granitic rocks have here been crushed to a fine white powder by the fault's action.* ∎ Now the PCT makes a steep initial climb, paralleling Indian Canyon Road 4N37 and staying just above it. In a few minutes you reach a pass and dip to cross this dirt road (2640-3.3), which switchbacks steeply north down into Soledad Canyon. The PCT instead continues west, traversing gently down above the mouth of Indian Canyon before rounding back east to terminate on Indian Canyon Road at a point just 35 yards above that road's signed junction with 2-lane, paved Soledad Canyon Road (2237-1.1).

*   *   *   *

Resupply access: Congratulations are in order at this time, for you have now finished walking the length of the San Gabriel Mountains! Acton, with a post office, market, restaurants and a PCT register, lies 5.8 miles east up Soledad Canyon Road. Saugus, a larger town with complete facilities, is 12.5 miles west down the road. A number of RV parks are found in nearby Soledad Canyon. They all have water, and some offer hikers and equestrians use of their campground, showers, laundromats and small stores. Northbound, the next certain water is in Agua Dulce, 12.0 miles ahead. Southbound trekkers will next get water up at North Fork Saddle, a usually hot 8.7-mile ascent into the San Gabriel Mountains.

*   *   *   *

Following the chaotic route of the northbound PCT across the Santa Clara River on the floor of Soledad Canyon can be very difficult since it is not properly signed. To achieve success, simply keep in mind that you want to attain the railroad tracks running along the north side of the canyon, and respect private property as you go.

From Indian Canyon Road 4N37, northbound PCT travelers amble east along the shoulder of Soledad Canyon Road for about 50 yards to a short, poor dirt-road spur that drops left, down-canyon, toward the riverside. Trail tread resumes from the eastern verge of this spur, marked unobtrusively by a brown plastic PCT post. Two tiny switchbacks drop 20 feet to the alluvial flat, where trail tread is already (November 1994) being obscured by a new growth of brush. A line of half-buried oil barrels points the trail north, levelly across the sandy wash, which serves as an RV parking lot. You pass a stand of Fremont cottonwoods to reach a ford of the Santa Clara River (2205-0.1). Usually, this ford is accomplished easily via a large log, amid false-willows and large ankle-high patches of watercress. ∎ *In the quiet of morning,*

See maps D12, D13

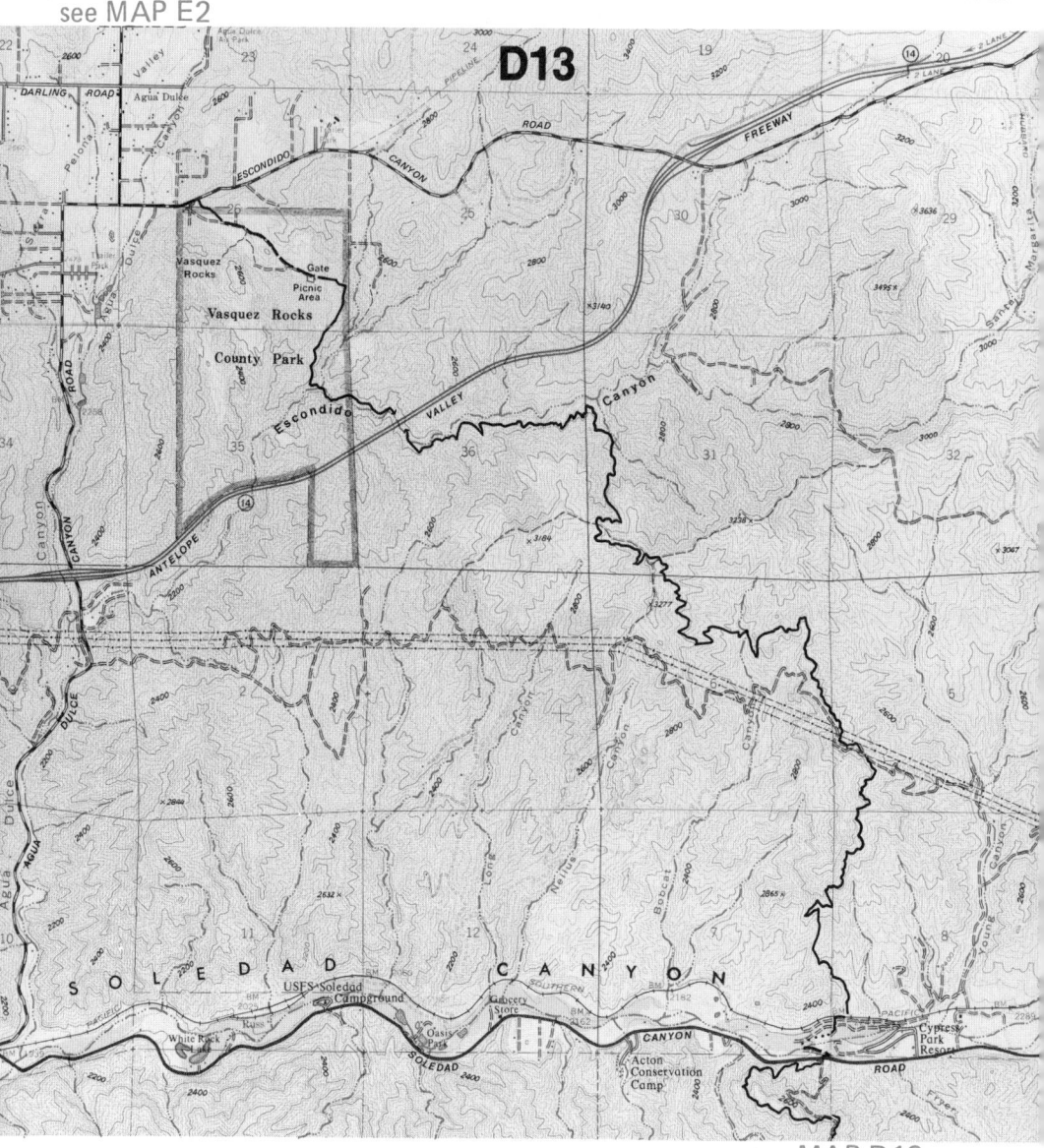

see MAP D12

one might disturb nesting mallards, or a great blue heron fishing in the clear shallow stream for a strange-looking fish, the endangered finger-long three-spine stickleback. This fish is now restricted in range primarily to Soledad and San Francisquito canyons. ∎

You emerge on the extensively bulldozed north banks of the river, just upstream of a long, 8-foot-high retaining wall constructed of rust-brown railroad-car sides. Now turn right, north-east, following a pair of brown plastic PCT posts up past a graveyard of decrepit autos to enter the west side of Fiesta Cypress Parks Resort, an RV campground. Here the route merges with a poor dirt road that almost immediately merges with another. This one turns right, east, paralleling the south side of a barbed-wire fence that separates the park's picnic tables from the Southern Pacific Railroad tracks. After a minute, a break in the fence

See map D13

marked with PCT emblems ushers you left, north, across another, better dirt road tracing the southern shoulder of the railroad tracks. This road may be followed east along a line of tables and water spigots to the main camp area of Fiesta Cypress Park Resort, or a few minutes more to its entrance station, with a convenience store and snack bar. Alternatively, one might amble west into The Robin's Nest RV Park, which also accommodates hikers and equestrians. You step north, up to a stop sign marking your crossing of the Southern Pacific Railroad tracks (2243-0.1). A 3-foot-high cobble-and-concrete obelisk stands to the left of the trail, with a brass plaque embedded in its top that commemorates completion ceremonies for the PCT held here on June 5, 1993.

Leaving the shady canyon bottom to climb briskly back onto a brushy hillside, the trail quickly gains a saddle (2485-0.4), but hardly pauses before continuing upward. Soon you pass beneath strange, pinkish cliffs—our first encounter with the Vasquez Formation, which is a conglomerate of igneous and metamorphic cobbles set in a fine-grained pink siltstone. The sometimes steep ascent finally abates as the trail rounds the east side of a summit to cross Young Canyon Road (2960-1.5), which serves a trio of parallel, humming, high-voltage transmission lines. Across the good dirt road the way swings northwest, descending gently-to-moderately below the road, soon to cross a gap (2980-0.7) near the head of Bobcat Canyon. Around here you see, to the southwest, a spectacular formation of rock-candy pink Vasquez outcrops. Next the PCT climbs a bit, then drops into Bobcat Canyon's dry wash before climbing in earnest to cross a jeep road (3160-1.6) on the divide separating Soledad and Agua Dulce canyons.

Vistas south, east to Mt. Gleason, and north to the Sierra Pelona are obtained as you catch your breath, then you descend west, quickly recrossing the jeep road once, and then again at a saddle (2960-0.5), from where the trail leaves the ridgetop. In an unusual economy of PCT construction, the trail north from this saddle wastes no time—nor does it spare your knees—in a willy-nilly, steep descent north to a narrow branch of Escondido Canyon. After a bone-jarring half mile, the incline abates as the route hops to the ravine's west side, then levels out to turn west along a terrace above Escondido Canyon's seasonal creek. White-trunked sycamores in the canyon bottom contrast starkly with the surrounding red, rocky bluffs, dappled by yellow lichens, while yerba santa and white-flowered buckwheat dot the ruddy hillside. ∎ *Across the canyon to your north is an even greater contrast—four-lane Antelope Valley Freeway 14 climbing toward Palmdale.* ∎

A gradual descent carries you down to the level of the stream bed at a side canyon and a use trail from the south (2400-2.0). Here a sunny, if often waterless and noisy, camp could be made. Now Escondido Canyon's trickling springtime stream, lined with watercress, bends more northward, and the PCT follows it, to abruptly enter a lengthy, 10-foot-high tunnel under Antelope Valley Freeway 14 (2370-0.1).

Emerging from the north end of the 500-foot passage, you find an abrupt change of scenery. Here the creekside is lined by thickets of willows and baccharis shrubs, while lush groves of squaw bush, flannelbush and poison oak stand just back from the creek's edge. The air is noticeably cooler, and myriad birds call from the underbrush. Your route proceeds directly down the shallow, sandy stream bed for a few yards, then picks up a well-traveled path near the creek's north edge. You continue down-canyon and enter Vasquez Rocks County Park. Please be aware that camping in the park is allowed only in designated areas and only with the permission of the ranger; contact him at the northwest entrance ranger station.

∎ *In the park, note how the canyon's south wall begins to steepen into pink and red cliffs of sandstone and conglomerate. These rocks are layered sediments of Oligocene and Miocene age, having a nonmarine origin.* ∎ Your path soon crosses to the canyon's south side, and then ascends slightly under a fantastic precipice of multilayered overhangs. Rounding north of this cliff, the route then drops to cross once again to the north bank (2335-0.6).

Here, at a major side canyon from the north, the southern cliff bulges into a huge, cobbled overhang. Just downstream, the northern canyon wall is also overhung by cliffs. Now, look north for a rudimentary path leading steeply up an easy slope on the far hillside. Any safe route that gets you onto the north rim of Escondido

D

I-15- Agua Dulce

See map D13

Canyon will do, and there are many of them to choose from. Once on the canyon's rim, you find a different world, an almost flat upland dotted with low buckwheat, sagebrush shrubs and head-high junipers. Lying in the northwest are the spectacular Vasquez Rocks, the 1850s hideout of famed badman Tiburcio Vasquez. If you lose your path, simply head for the rock that resembles a tilted Matterhorn, since your route eventually takes a dirt road that lies along its north base. With a bit of luck you find a little-used dirt road, hopefully still marked with a brown plastic PCT post.

On it, you start a very gentle ascent northeast as you parallel the western rim of the major tributary of Escondido Canyon, ignoring a north-branching track. Soon, across the canyon from some ridgetop homes, the route strikes a junction (2535-0.5) with another poor dirt road, descending west. This junction is marked by a yellow pipe post, and on the road, you follow a succession of similar posts west down past a cluster of picnic tables and across a large grassland to a gate (2485-0.1) at a large parking area. Amble northwest along a good dirt road, climbing gently between the two most spectacular rock outcrops. A number of tables and fire rings are scattered about, in secluded nooks, but this

park is currently designated for day use only. Now the road curves west and drops gently to a short segment of PCT trail tread (2310-0.5), perhaps signed by a lone brown plastic PCT post standing on the low rise just north of your road. This PCT segment winds northwest, around a half-dozen clifflets, to strike Escondido Canyon Road (2510-0.2) at the signed entrance to Vasquez Rocks County Park. The ranger station, where information concerning camping and water may be obtained, is just a minute's walk south down the entrance road.

Here you turn left, west, along Escondido Canyon Road, soon coming to a stop sign at larger Agua Dulce Canyon Road (2470-0.3). Turn right, north, onto it, and head into the village of Agua Dulce. Passing a cafe, you soon reach "downtown" Agua Dulce at Darling Road (2530-0.5). Here is Agua Dulce Post Office, now located in the Agua Dulce Business Center, 33336 Agua Dulce Canyon Road. It is closed on Sundays. A large new supermarket and restaurants are nearby, as is a smaller grocery and a feed and supply store for horsemen. Host homes and showers for PCT trailers are available—check in the PCT register at the post office.

See map D13

D
I-15-
Agua Dulce

Mt. San Antonio, from Throop Peak

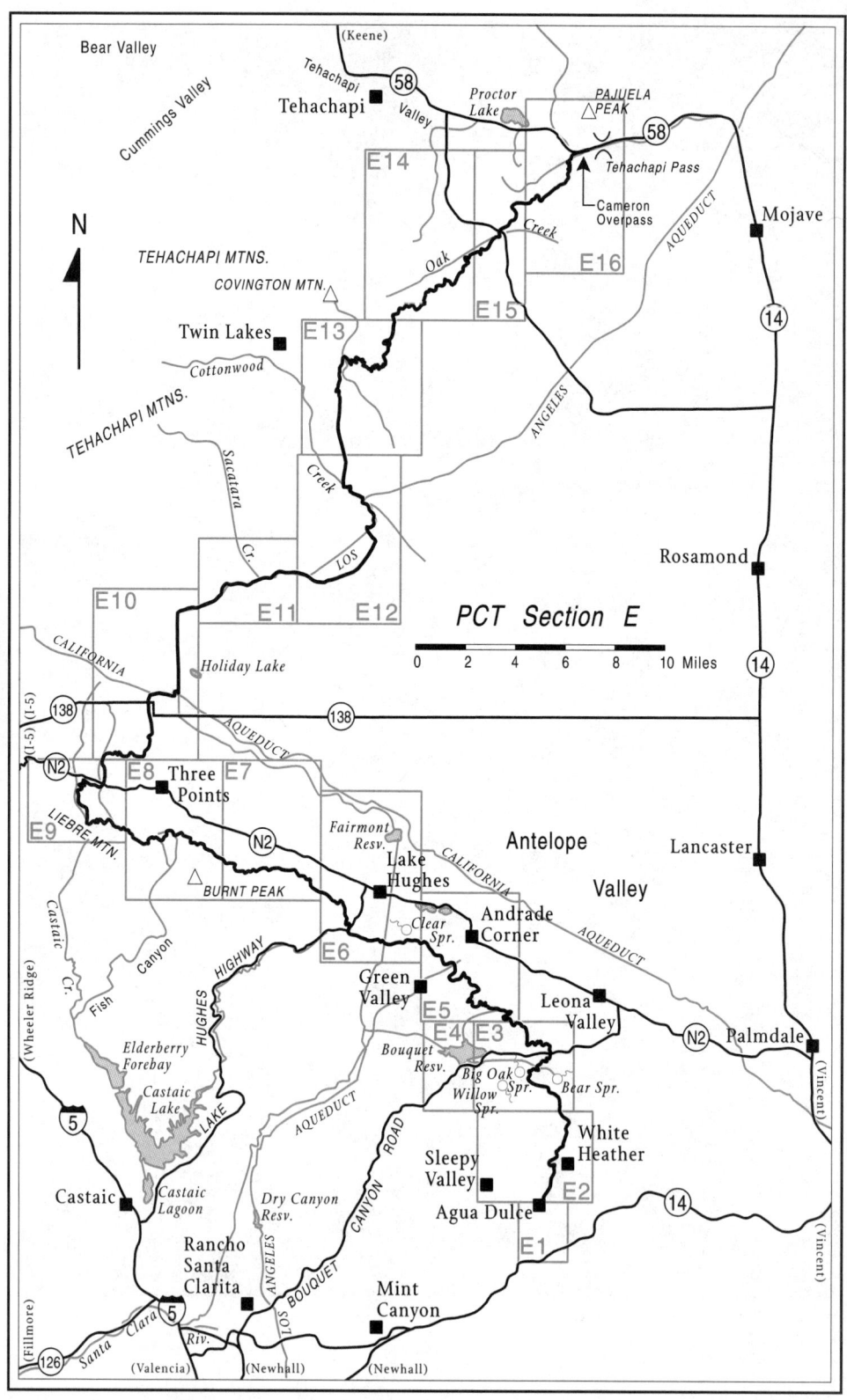

Section E
Agua Dulce to Highway 58 near Mojave

Introduction: The Mojave Desert is the arid setting for this short, least characteristic segment of the Pacific Crest Trail. Some of the route is not even really trail, but rather it follows dusty dirt roads along the Los Angeles Aqueduct. Congress's original intent was to align the PCT atop the ridge of Liebre Mountain, going all the way west to the vicinity of Quail Lake. (In fact, some of this trail was built by the Forest Service, and later abandoned.) There, it was to ascend into the western Tehachapi Mountains, the start of the Sierran chain, and follow their crest northeast. This route would have had all the necessary characteristics of the Pacific *Crest* Trail, including mountain vistas, cool black oak and pine forests, and numerous springs. The major snag in the government's plan to construct a true mountain-crest route was the refusal of the owners of the mammoth Tejon Ranch, which lies astride the Tehachapi Mountains, to allow right-of-way for the PCT. After years of wrangling and threatened litigation, the Forest Service surrendered in the contest of wills with so well-heeled an adversary. Hence, no mountain path now connects the southern California PCT with its Sierran continuation. A hot, waterless, dangerous, ugly and entirely un-Crest-like segment of trail now winds along a gerrymandered route that traces Tejon Ranch's boundaries, and entirely subverts Congress's vision of its greatest National Scenic Trail. Hopefully, future administrations will have the courage to relocate the PCT to its rightful course.

So for the time being, the PCT drops north from Liebre Mountain, abandoning any pretense of being a crest route, and strikes north across the heart of the Antelope Valley, which is the western arm of the immense Mojave Desert. The pronghorn antelopes seen by John C. Frémont when in 1844 he forced passage through Tejon Pass via this valley are gone, exterminated by hunters and later by encroaching alfalfa fields, but Antelope Valley's desert flavor remains.

Even in early spring, temperatures can soar over 100°F, and swirling dust devils can send unwary hikers sprawling or ducking for cover behind a grotesque Joshua tree. The temporary route strikes due north across the shrub-dotted desert, and then, at the alluvial stoop of the Tehachapi Mountains—a southern extension of the Sierra Nevada—you turn east beside the underground Los Angeles Aqueduct.

Beginning in the Owens Valley, on the east side of the Sierra, the Los Angeles Aqueduct was the brain child of William Mulholland, a former L.A. County Water Superintendent. It was constructed in 1913 and later extended northward to the Mono Lake basin. Bitter disputes, court battles, and even shooting wars raged when Owens Valley farmers realized that the water needs of a growing Los Angeles would turn their well-watered agricultural region into a dust bowl. Litigation continues today, as does resentment. But Mulholland is a hero to some Angelenos, for millions of Southern Californians drink Owens Valley water, and without this project Los Angeles might have remained a sleepy patchwork of orange groves.

Declination: 13¾°E

Points on Route	S→N	Mi. Btwn. Pts.	N→S
Agua Dulce	0.0		1.8
		1.8	
Old Sierra Highway	1.8		6.4
		6.3	
Bear Spring	8.1		1.9
		2.2	
Bouquet Canyon Road	10.3		6.1
		6.1	
Road 6N09 in Spunky Canyon..................................	16.4		6.3
		6.3	
San Francisquito Canyon Road to Green Valley	22.7		7.6
		7.6	
Elizabeth Lake Canyon Road to Lake Hughes	30.3		7.0
		7.0	
Upper Shake Campground Trail	37.3		6.0
		6.0	
Atmore Meadows Road 7N19..................................	43.3		4.3
		4.3	
Bear Campground	47.6		9.5
		6.8	
Pine Canyon Road to Three Points	54.4		3.1
		6.7	
Highway 138	61.1		0.8
		1.8	
California Aqueduct crossing....................................	62.9		5.3
		3.5	
Los Angeles Aqueduct; north side Antelope Valley ..	66.4		10.5
		11.1	
Cottonwood Creek bridge and water	77.5		5.0
		6.6	
Tylerhorse Canyon	84.2		5.8
		3.9	
Gamble Spring Canyon	88.0		6.2
		12.2	
Tehachapi-Willow Springs Road: Oak Creek	100.2		6.1
		8.6	
Highway 58 at Tehachapi Pass..................................	108.8		0.0

E
Agua Dulce-
Hwy. 58

Supplies: The village of Agua Dulce boasts a post office, three restaurants, an equestrian feed store and two markets, one a large supermarket. The post office also keeps an official PCT register and names of local families who will host PCT walkers, and might even cache water for them in the Sierra Pelona! Many hikers reaching this point choose to hitchhike southwest 14 miles on Highway 14 to Saugus, a large town with complete accommodations. Later, the settlement of Green Valley is a short detour from the PCT where it drops into San Francisquito Canyon, 22.6 miles from Agua Dulce. It is reached by walking southwest 1.7 miles down San Francisquito Canyon Road to Spunky Canyon Road in quiet Green Valley, then heading southeast 0.9 mile to the combined post office, grocery store and restaurant. A 2.2-mile detour to Lake Hughes, 30.3 miles into your journey, is the last chance to reprovision before facing the Mojave Desert. This small village has a post office, restaurants, stores, motels and a private campground with showers. Lancaster might seem an improbable choice for resupply: It lies in the middle of sweltering-hot Antelope Valley, fully 30 miles east of the PCT's crossing of Highway 138, some 61.1 miles into this section. However, access is surprisingly easy, since Highway 138 is very busy, and hitchhiking should not pose a problem. Also, Lancaster is the largest town in this section, and it boasts a complete array of needs for the PCT traveler, including shopping malls and specialty mountaineering and backpacking shops.

Tehachapi lies 9.2 miles west of the PCT route at the end of this section. It is more easily reached, as described later, by a 7.6-mile detour from Tehachapi-Willow Springs Road, at the 98.2-mile mark. Most hikers will make the detour, to minimize the need to carry heavy loads across the hot, dry Mojave Desert and Tehachapi Mountains segments. Tehachapi is a large and growing community, with many stores, restaurants, motels and laundromats as well as a post office. Additionally, there are limited sporting goods available, as well as bus service and a small airport. Mojave is a desert town, also 9 miles from the PCT at the end of this section, reached east along Highway 58. It is a fair-sized community, with services similar to Tehachapi. However, the town is a bit more spread out, and harder to walk around, than Tehachapi. Additionally, it is much hotter, and usually a bit harder to get to, especially if you're hitchhiking.

Water and Desert Survival: The Mojave Desert was a formidable barrier to early travelers, causing much hardship and greatly slowing Southern California's growth. That part of the Mojave traversed by the PCT is now tamed by criss-crossing roads and dotted with homes and ranches, eliminating any dangers—as imagined by the uninformed—of dying like French Legionnaires, with parched throats and watery dreams. Still, the Mojave Desert stretch of the PCT can broil your mind, blister your feet, and turn your mouth to dust—in all, an unpleasant experience—if you are not adequately prepared. With a little forethought, enough water, and the right equipment this hike can be a tolerable variation from the PCT's usual crestline surroundings.

Water is the key to all life, and enough of it will make yours more enjoyable. While planning your nightly stops or possible side hikes to water sources, you might consider the following government figures, arrived at by subjects operating under optimal experimental conditions. (They weren't carrying heavy packs!) Without water you can survive only 2 days at 120°F if you stay in one spot, 5 days at 100°F, and 9 days at 80°F. If you walk during the day, you will survive only one third as long. If you rest during the day and hike at night, then these figures become 1, 3 and 7 days, with 12, 33 and 110 miles being covered. At 100°F, the mid-figure, you would be able to hike 20 miles for every gallon of water you carried, though you would become hopelessly dehydrated in so doing, and eventually incapacitated. Actual hiking conditions require at least 2 gallons a day while hiking in 100° heat with a backpack, and most persons will function better with 2.5 gallons.

Be aware that humans are the only mammal that does not drink automatically to replace the body's lost water stores, when water is available. Even when water is plentiful, exercising humans tend to become dehydrated, since most people drink only enough to keep their mouths and throats wet! Unfortunately, however, only a small degree of dehydration will exact a considerable toll on performance and endurance, and possibly result in health problems. Hence, you must force yourself to drink enough water while exercising, and drink at frequent intervals. It is much better to drink a cup of water every 15 minutes or so, than to stop every few hours and force down 2 quarts of water.

When drinking, pick the most palatable liquid (although most hikers will have little more than plain water). The addition of a small amount of flavoring helps the chore of forced hydration, and some salts and a bit of sugar may actually help absorption of water from the stomach. Beware, though, that most instant drink mixes, including many specialty athletic drinks, contain enough sugar and salts to actually delay stomach absorption, and may lead to nausea during heavy exercise. Diluting commercial drinks to twice their volume usually prevents this problem. Otherwise, all that is necessary to make sure that vital body electrolytes are replaced during prolonged exertion is to eat a balanced diet while drinking plain water. Most hiking foods contain more than enough salts to maintain body stores.

San Gabriel Mountains above L.A. smog, from the Sierra Pelona crest

Agua Dulce-
Hwy. 58

E

The best way to conserve water is to hike at night, and night-hiking has added bonuses in the Mojave Desert: astounding star-filled skies, fewer passing cars, and the chance to observe some little-seen desert wildlife—inquisitive kit foxes sometimes play tag with hikers. Yucca night-lizards, which spend their days under fallen Joshua trees, also scurry about at night. But use a flashlight, even on moonlit nights, because rattlesnakes like to lie on the warm roads.

If you prefer to hike in daylight, start early, before sunrise, say at 5 in the morning during spring. Hike about 4 hours, perhaps getting in 12 miles, rest until evening, and then hike about another 2 hours. By day, walkers should ignore their desire to shed sweaty shirts or pants, since clothing prevents excessive moisture loss and overheating, and it also forestalls an excruciating high-desert sunburn.

It is no secret that water is a critical issue throughout arid Section E, and especially so in drought years. After about April 1, don't count on water at any sites away from human improvement. Even before then, most streams are small seasonal trickles, and likely to be polluted. Treat all water with iodine, or use a filter before drinking water from any natural sources. In an emergency, you may be forced to try to obtain water from springs or creekbeds that are barely flowing. A trick for tapping these seeps, without the frustration of scooping up mud and debris as well, is offered by PCT expert Alice Krueper: carry a 6" length of narrow-gauge aluminum tubing. It weighs next to nothing, and makes a fine straw with which to lead a trickle of clean water to your canteen.

Maps: *Agua Dulce*   *La Liebre Ranch*
      Sleepy Valley   *Neenach School*
      Green Valley   *Fairmont Butte*
      Del Sur   *Tylerhorse Canyon*
      Lake Hughes   *Tehachapi South*
      Burnt Peak   *Monolith*
      Liebre Mountain

E2

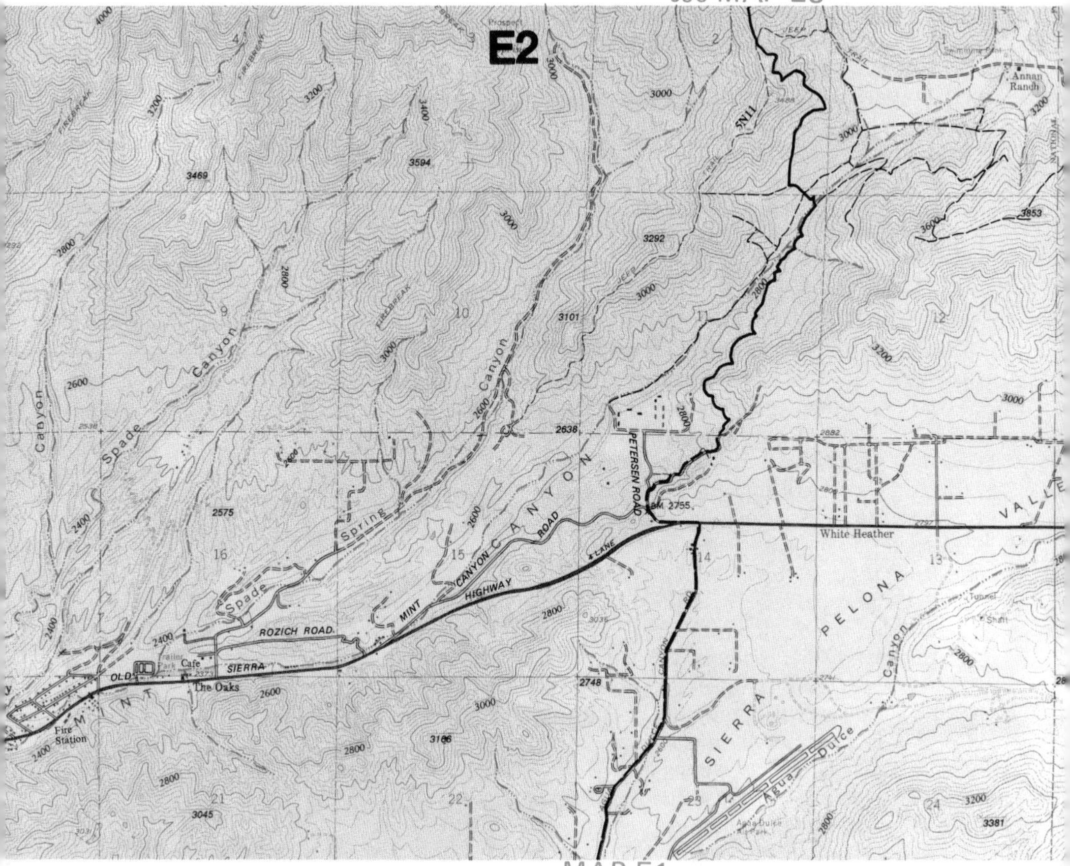

see MAP E1

see MAP E2

The Route

Agua Dulce is reached via Highway 14, 18 miles east of its junction with Interstate 5 in Sylmar or 21 miles south of Palmdale. Take Highway 14's Agua Dulce Canyon Road exit, then head north 2.5 miles up that road to east-west Darling Road, in Agua Dulce. Your first chance for camping and water north of town, discounting homes, is at Bear Spring, 8.1 miles. However, in recent drought years, Bear Spring has been quite unreliable, so plan to carry water until the next certain water, at San Francisquito Ranger Station, a long 22.7 miles away.

Leave Agua Dulce by walking northward on Agua Dulce Canyon Road very gently up grassy Sierra Pelona Valley. You pass numerous homes and side roads, a few businesses, an airfield, and finally a church before your road ends at wide, paved Old Sierra Highway (2725-1.8). Turn left and go west along its north shoulder

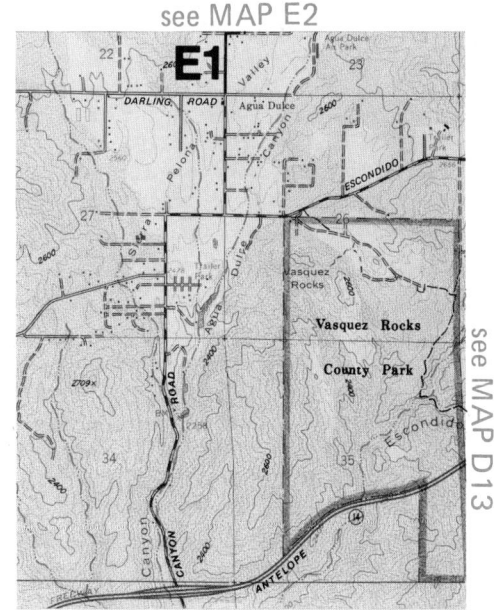

See maps E1, E2

see MAP E5

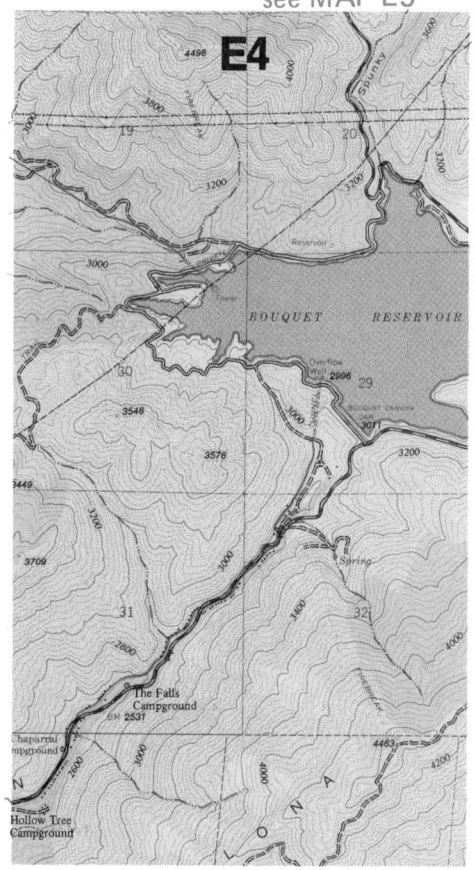

see MAP E3

for just a bit to paved Mint Canyon Road (2730-0.1). Follow that road up and right, west, shortly to a low gap where paved Petersen Road (2755-0.1) branches north. Turn right on Petersen Road and descend gently to the southern edge of a ranch-dotted bench in Mint Canyon. Here a dirt road (2750-0.1) servicing a line of high-tension electric wires, branches right.

The PCT route begins by climbing momen-tarily northeast up this road, then down, and then ascends moderately again. Quickly, the road gains exposed slopes of withered chamise on the eastern flank of Mint Canyon. Just back inside the Angeles National Forest boundary, trail tread resumes (2905-0.4), marked, hope-fully, by a large PCT emblem. Follow the tread left, northward, as it contours around a nose, then makes a long, easily descending traverse to the shadeless southeast banks of Mint Canyon's infrequently flowing stream. At a step-across ford of the creek (2865-1.3) you pass a horse trail that continues up-canyon. The PCT, however, clambers west up onto a low bench with an equestrian trail register. Beyond, you walk straight uphill on an old jeep road, passing another that runs down-canyon. You now see evidence of a brush fire that burned here in 1985. Where a jeep road climbs left along an old barbed-wire fence, you follow the obvious PCT right, ascending north. A prom-ontory overlooking large Annan Ranch is soon reached, after which the path climbs moderately northwest to survey more blackened chaparral on the headwall of Mint Canyon. By walking a few minutes more, you reach Big Tree Trail 14W02 (3330-1.1) astride a saddle.

The PCT is routed along this old path, which ascends steeply north on cobbly schist tread much abused by dirtbikers. The climb moder-ates near the top, presenting excellent vistas south to the bizarre Vasquez Rocks, purported refuge of bandit Tiburcio Vasquez, and more eastward to Mts. Gleason, Williamson and Baden-Powell. Atop Sierra Pelona Ridge, where gusts of wind have been measured at 100 miles per hour, you turn right, east, on Sierra Pelona Ridge Road 6N07 (4500-2.2), and walk gently up to a low saddle (4555-0.3). Here, PCT posts lead your way northeast via a disused jeep road, through a white pipe gate, then steeply down the hillside at the head of Martindale Canyon. The little-used path soon crisscrosses

the even more steeply descending jeep track multiple times, and is easily lost on sloping hillside meadows of foxtails and grasses. Pres-ently, you circle just above the levelest such flat, grown waist-high in yellow mustard. Hid-den in a tangle of wild grape vines at its foot is Bear Spring (4350-0.7). This waterhole often runs late into springtime, but should not be re-lied upon. Camping hereabouts is suboptimal. Continuing down with vistas north across An-telope Valley to Owens Peak in the southern Sierra, you circle the upper reaches of fault-aligned Martindale Canyon, soon reaching a ridgetop-firebreak jeep trail (3995-0.7). This you descend, continuing west, down to a junc-tion (3785-1.0) with the old PCT trail align-ment, which formerly climbed south up to Big Oak Spring. Now you turn right for a more gradual descent on chaparral-choked trail, lead-ing northeast to paved Bouquet Canyon Road

See maps E2, E3

E

Agua Dulce-
Hwy. 58

see MAP E5

E3

see MAP E4

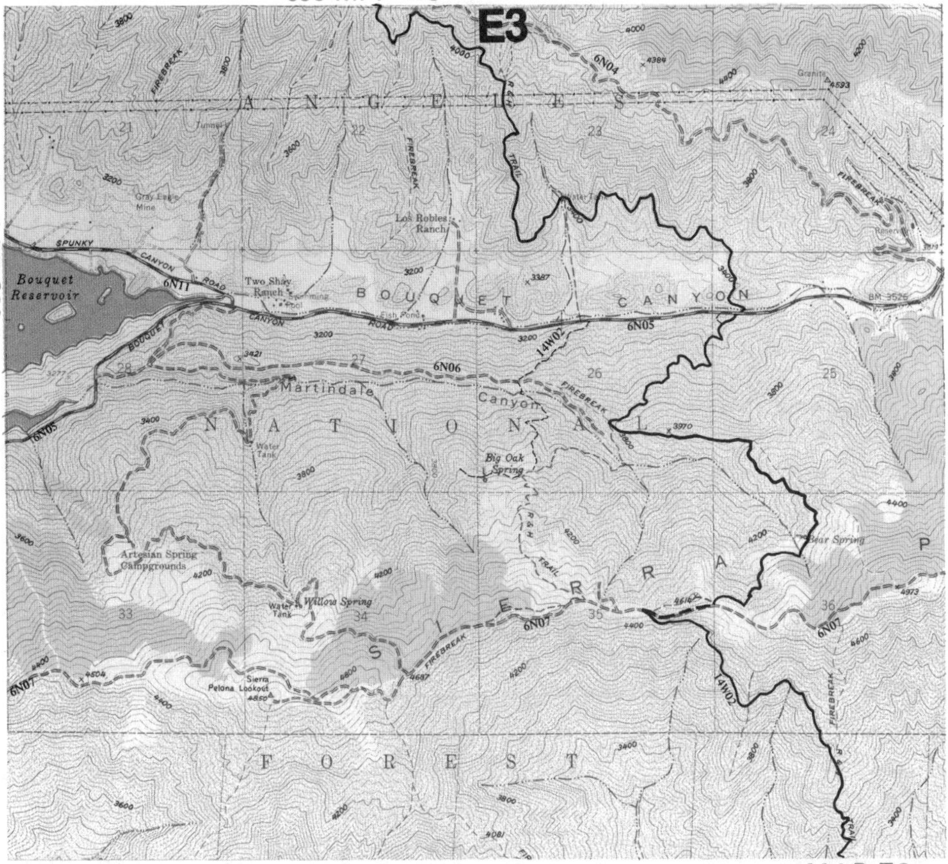

see MAP E2

Bouquet Reservoir

6N05 (3340-0.5).

■ *Merging under Bouquet Reservoir, 2¼ miles to the west, the San Francisquito and Clearwater faults run Bouquet Canyon's length and separate southern Pelona schists from granites on the canyon's north wall.* ■ The PCT drops across the dry wash draining Bouquet Canyon, then arcs easily up, northwest, to cross a jeep road near a water tank in a small canyon. Now the trail ascends moderately on coarse granitic sand to just north of a powerline, where the PCT branches northwest from the

See map E3

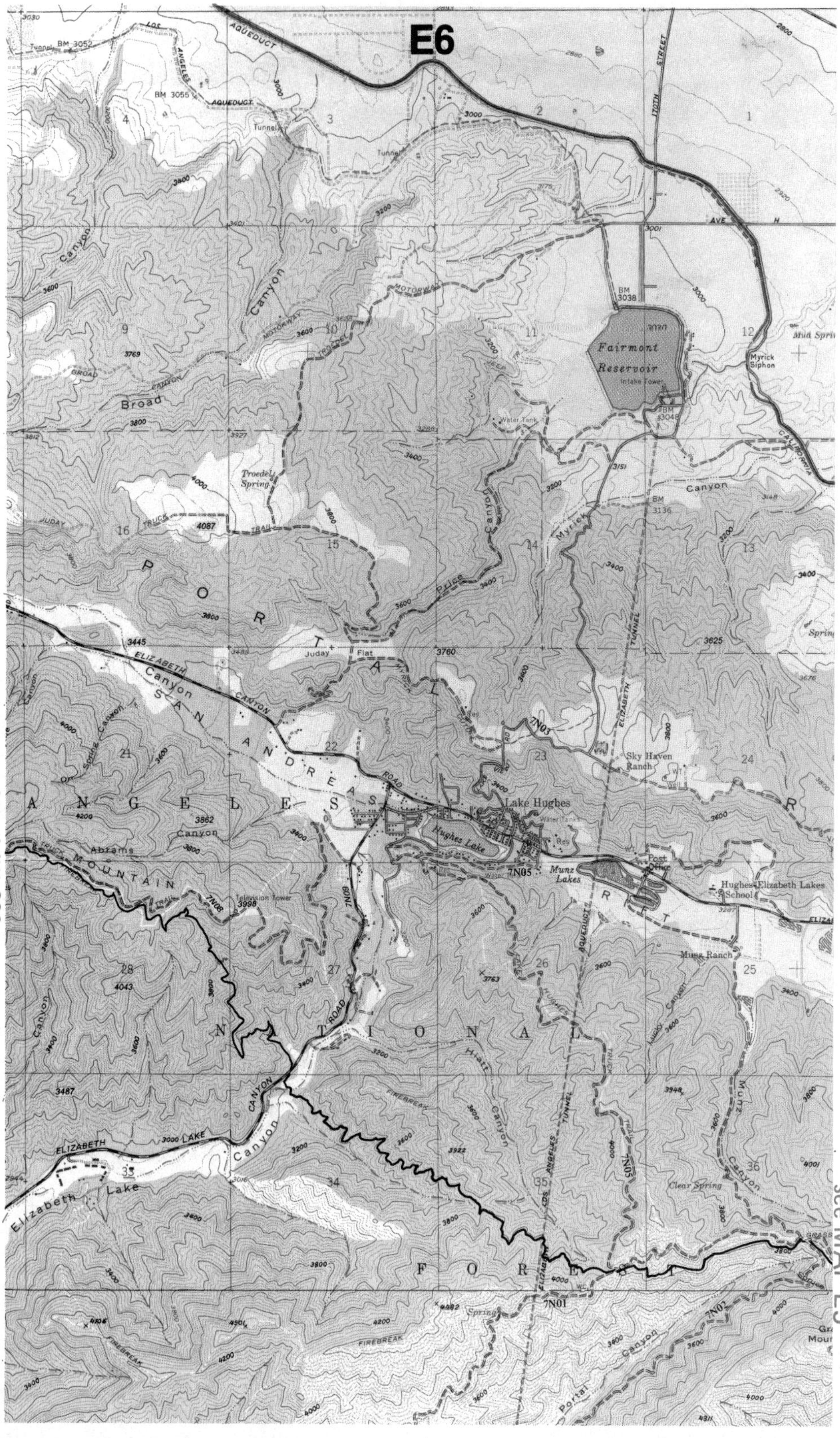

see MAP E7

see MAP E5

Agua Dulce-
Hwy. 58

E

old CRHT (California Riding and Hiking Trail) (3985-2.7), which continues north up to Leona Divide Truck Road 6N04.

The PCT climbs along the steep south-facing slope through sickly, low chamise, crosses a descending firebreak, and then veers more northward, just under the Leona Divide Road, to gain a pass (4300-1.4) with another firebreak, which tops a ridge dividing Spunky and Bouquet canyons. A gentle switchback in now-denser chaparral and occasional shading oaks drops you to the head of Spunky Canyon, where you turn west down-canyon, then climb slightly to strike Road 6N09 (3725-2.0).

*   *   *   *

Resupply access: If you're thirsty, seeking a campsite, or needing supplies, then first walk west 1.7 miles down this dirt road to paved

See maps E3, E5

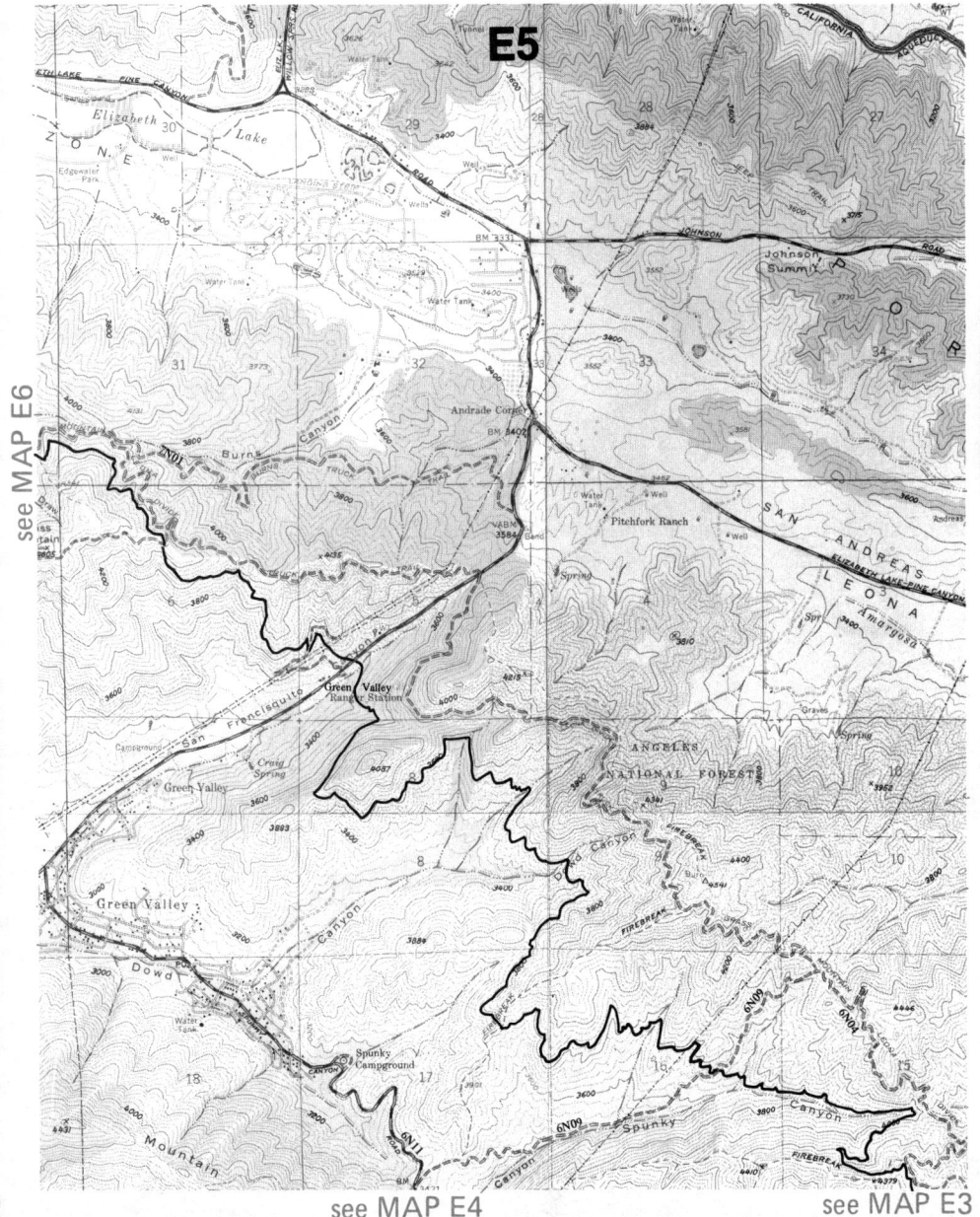

Spunky Canyon Road 6N11. On it, wind northwest 1.1 miles to Spunky Campground or 0.8 mile farther to Green Valley, with a post office, grocery store and restaurant.

*   *   *   *

The PCT climbs gently away from Road 6N09, winding in and out of small ravines on a westward bearing. Eventually the path tops a small ridge, again with a firebreak (3815-2.1), and then the trail angles northeast, through a gap and down into the upper end of Dowd Canyon. Seen from here, Jupiter Mountain looms impressively across the valley. You reach a low point of 3475 feet in Dowd Canyon, in a gully where native bunchgrasses grow, then you amble first north-northwest before heading southwest around Peak 4087 over to a ridgetop separating Dowd and San Francisquito canyons. From here a final northeastward swoop under shady interior live oaks brings the PCT to paved San Francisquito Canyon Road (3385-4.2). Green Valley Ranger Station, with water, is 250 yards southwest, just beyond tiny San Francisquito Picnic Area. San Francisquito Campground, with tables scattered amid sagebrush and under canyon live oaks, is 1.0 mile southwest down-canyon. Green Valley, which

has a combined post office, grocery store and restaurant, can be reached by continuing 0.7 mile farther down to Spunky Canyon Road.

Across San Francisquito Canyon Road the PCT begins its climb of Grass Mountain by ascending northwest into a nearby side canyon, above which it strikes a dirt road (3520-0.3) serving two powerlines. The trail follows the road north momentarily, then switchbacks west and progresses unremittingly up chaparralled slopes to Grass Mountain Road (4275-1.3), striking this dirt road just above its junction with Leona Divide Truck Trail. ❚ *Panoramas unfold northward over Elizabeth Lake—a sag pond on the San Andreas Fault—to distant Antelope Valley and the Tehachapi Mountains, and if one is enjoying a smogless spring day, Owens Peak in the southern Sierra Nevada may be seen.* ❚ You enjoy this scenery as the path contours, then descends the north slopes of Grass Mountain to a saddle (3900-1.3), where four dirt roads converge at the head of South Portal and Munz canyons.

Keeping on a steep hillside south of the ridge, the PCT contours from this gap over to another saddle, where it crosses dirt Tule Canyon Road 7N01 (3900-1.2) by its junction with Lake Hughes Truck Trail. Onward the route rolls across dry ravines in dense chaparral,

See maps E5, E6

Panorama of the Sierra Pelona highlands and the distant Tehachapi Mountains

Agua Dulce-
Hwy. 58

E

switchbacks once to pass through a gap, and then descends unhesitatingly toward misnamed Elizabeth Lake Canyon by crossing an interminable array of narrow, rocky gulches. At the bottom of this unpleasant segment, your path bursts from brush cover to traverse the broad, sandy wash of misnamed Elizabeth Lake Canyon. Southbound trekkers may lose their way here in a welter of game trails; they should head straight for the ridge's shoulder, where it strikes the canyon's bottom. Northbound hikers head for nearby, paved Elizabeth Lake Canyon Road 7N09 (3050-3.5).

The next permanent on-route water hole along the PCT is a distant 32.6 miles northwest, at the California Aqueduct, so be sure that you leave this canyon with at least three gallons. The next usually reliable water source near the northbound PCT is at Upper Shake Campground, a 0.6-mile detour that leaves the PCT in 7.0 miles.

* * * *

Resupply access: If you need water or supplies, you should detour north, 1.5 miles up-canyon along Elizabeth Lake Canyon Road to Newvale Drive, which is on the west side of the small resort community of Lake Hughes. Very small stores, a hotel, a cafe and the entrance to a private campground and picnic area are on the east shore of small Hughes Lake (great for your blistered feet!). These are reached by following Newvale Drive east 0.3 mile to Elizabeth Lake-Pine Canyon Road, then walking 0.4 mile farther east along Elizabeth Lake-Pine Canyon Road, just across from another nice campground, with showers and a small store, the best in town. The next chance to resupply on the northbound PCT is at Tehachapi, which lies west of the PCT at the end of Section E.

* * * *

Across Elizabeth Lake Canyon Road 7N09, the PCT attacks Sawmill Mountain's east flank. The trail climbs quickly northwest into a small valley, which has a sycamore-shaded flat that could serve as an adequate, though waterless, campsite. Soon the route, now back in chamise-and-oak chaparral, passes the mouth of an old graphite mine tunnel, then switchbacks to climb more steeply southwest past two more tunnels. After reaching a ridge, the trail again swings northwest to ascend moderately through yerba santa and chamise back into the canyon. Here

E
Agua Dulce-
Hwy. 58

See map E6

you find some shade in the form of interior live oaks and a cluster of disheveled big-cone spruces surrounding a trailside wet-season spring (3710-1.2). No camping is possible on the steep slope here. Continuing on, the path leads up the now-narrow ravine, then veers southwest at its head to reach a viewful intersection with the Sawmill-Liebre Firebreak (4190-0.6), just above a wide dirt road, Maxwell Truck Trail 7N08.

Now-familiar vistas north over the western part of Antelope Valley to the Tehachapi Mountains are presented here and accompany you as the PCT adopts a leisurely, traversing ascent of Sawmill Mountain's spine, always keeping

just a stone's throw south of Maxwell Truck Trail. Repeated crossings of the ridge and its firebreak in a mix of chaparral eventually lead you to Maxwell Truck Trail 7N08 (4505-1.9) in an open glade of black oaks. You walk 35 yards northwest along this road to where the trail's tread resumes, near the start of a poorer road. The PCT drops slightly, then assumes an undulating traverse in and out of gullies on the north slope of Sawmill Mountain. After a short while the PCT becomes situated just below moderately ascending Maxwell Truck Trail and maintains that arrangement through chaparral sprinkled with Coulter pines. Eventually the PCT turns south into a larger ravine to cross

See maps E6, E7

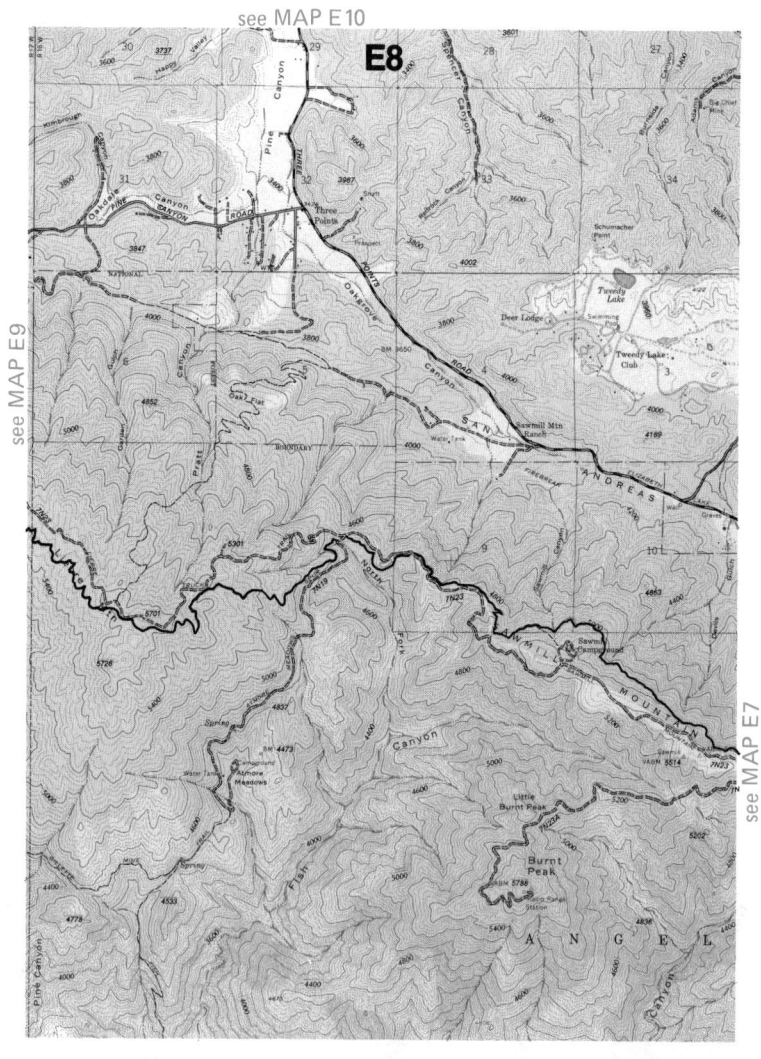

two dirt roads (4680-2.9) in quick succession. These rough access roads mark the site of a small plantation of trees, whose young Coulter pines and incense-cedars offer a potentially pleasant though waterless campsite.

Pushing on, you ascend a shadier hillside and soon reach a trail intersection (4805-0.4). The poorer branch climbs steeply southeast to strike Maxwell Truck Trail, while a good branch, descending northwest, drops via switchbacks 0.6 mile to Upper Shake Campground, which has tables, fire rings, toilets and seasonal piped water. If the campground water supply is turned off in early or late season, a small, usually flowing stream can be found in Shake Canyon, just

north of the campground. Note that this is the only campsite close to the PCT with reliable water until the California Aqueduct, still a dry 25.6 miles away.

The northbound PCT heads southwest gently up from the Upper Shake Campground trail junction, traversing the hillside first under shady oaks and big-cone spruces as it ducks into and then heads out of a small canyon. This pleasant segment crosses an abandoned jeep road dropping into the head of Shake Canyon, then continues to a ridgetop road junction (5245-2.6). From here Maxwell Truck Trail 7N08 starts south on a generally eastward traverse, Burnt Peak Road 7N23A traverses

See map E7

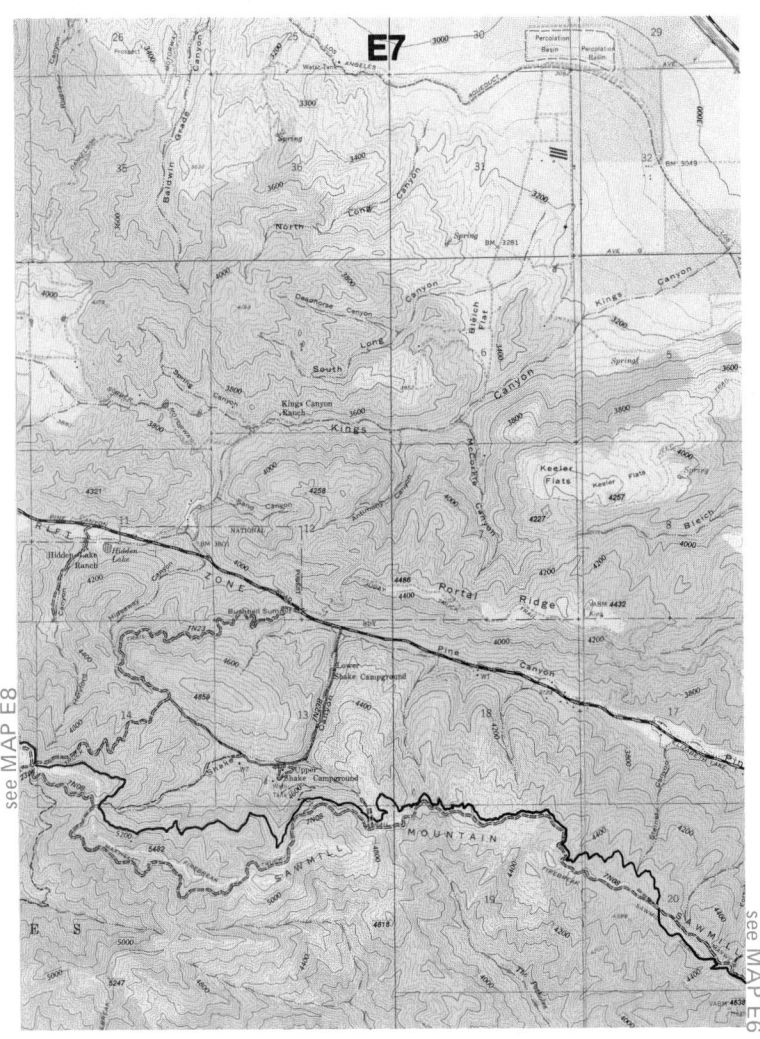

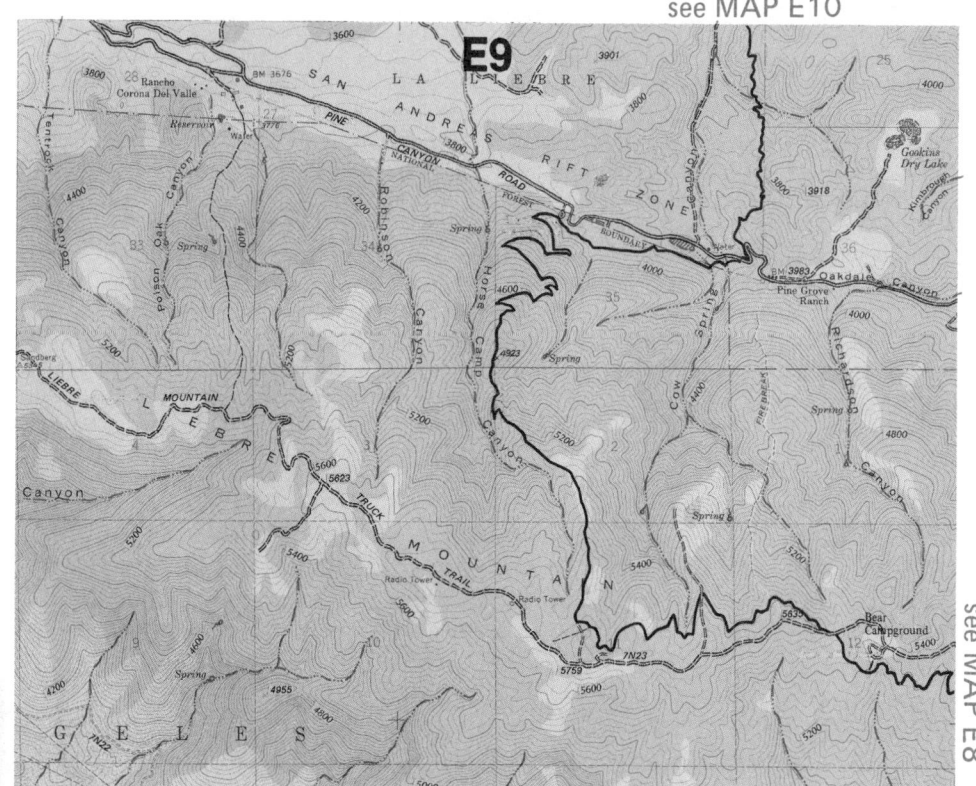

west, and Sawmill Mountain Truck Trail 7N23 traverses northwest and also descends northeast to Elizabeth Lake-Pine Canyon Road.

The PCT descends gently north under the upper branch of Sawmill Mountain Truck Trail, now in even shadier mixed forest and chaparral. Next a long, descending traverse leads across a broad black-oak-clothed ridge nose to a junction (5015-1.8). From here a spur trail ascends southeast 0.2 mile to small Sawmill Campground, which is pretty but waterless.

You first contour and then switchback twice to resume a position just north of and below Sawmill Mountain Truck Trail. Presently, you cross that road (4790-1.1) at a large turnout. Across the road, your trail drops indistinctly southwest, through a corridor of Coulter pines, then winds west around the head of wild, rugged North Fork Fish Canyon. Soon you reach a saddle junction of Sawmill Mountain Truck Trail and Atmore Meadows Spur Road 7N19 (4705-0.5). The PCT follows the latter road

southwest for 80 yards to a resumption of trail tread in a steep ravine.

*   *   *   *

Water access: Before continuing, however, hikers may wish to detour 1.7 miles farther along Atmore Meadows Spur Road to a fair spring, or another 1.0 mile beyond it down to a series of shaded glens, the site of Atmore Meadows Campground, which has water, tables and toilets.

*   *   *   *

Next on the PCT's agenda of chaparral-cloaked summits is Liebre Mountain, and the steep, seasonally hot trail that climbs from Atmore Meadows Spur Road quickly dispels any thoughts of a sedate ascent. After an effort you are high on brushy slopes, panting toward a grassy saddle (5655-2.1), which marks an end

See maps E7, E8

to the unpleasant grind. Now descending easily, zigzags lead northwest first close to Liebre Mountain Truck Trail, then into and out of interminable dry washes that alternate with brushy ridgelets. Sometimes you have good views south to the wildlands of deep Cienega Canyon. Eventually the undulating descent ceases and the grade becomes a moderate ascent. Moments later, you encounter a junction with a spur trail (5370-2.2) that climbs north a few yards to waterless Bear Campground. An additional three minutes' climb along the PCT leads to a crossing of Liebre Mountain Truck Trail 7N23 (5545-0.2).

Now on the cooler north slopes of Liebre Mountain, your way becomes much nicer, winding almost level along hillsides shaded by open groves of black oaks. In spring the grassy turf underfoot is a green sea dotted with brodiaea, baby blue-eyes and miner's lettuce. Soon you cross a north-descending dirt road (5580-0.9) on a ridge nose as the PCT winds west close to the gentle summit of Liebre Mountain. You wind over two more small, delightfully oak-clothed ridgetops, then merge with a poor jeep track, still traversing more or less levelly, for just a minute to reach another jeep road (5745-1.2) on the crest of a broad, open ridge. Here a sign points out the new alignment of the PCT, branching right, northwest, down the ridgetop on the jeep road. You ignore the older, abandoned trail alignment, which continued straight ahead along the summit of Liebre Mountain and has now been overrun by four-wheel vehicles. Either jeep track, however, continues only a minute before striking a fair dirt road (5720-0.1).

*   *   *   *

Side route: Here, take a few minutes' detour, and walk left, south, back up to the top of Liebre Mountain's ridge for its expansive vistas south to the Santa Monica Mountains, the Pacific Ocean, and the highrises of Hollywood looming over the white rollercoasters of Magic Mountain amusement park. Possibly more interesting is an eastward inventory of terrain conquered: beyond Vasquez Rocks, the San Gabriel Mountains, from Mts. Wilson and Gleason on the west, to towering Mt. Baden-Powell and Mt. Baldy on the east, are all there for inspection.

*   *   *   *

The newer PCT heads north, downhill, on this closed ridgetop road, passing through a plantation of young black oaks and their older in-laws. Soon the downgrade steepens and sagebrush replaces much of the understory. Windswept panoramas over the westernmost corner of Antelope Valley remind you that you have now ended a sweeping 250-mile skirting of the southwestern border of the Mojave Desert, which has led you west from Whitewater along the summits of the San Bernardinos, the San Gabriels, and Sawmill and Liebre mountains—a job well done!

Continuing your descent, you lose these views as you re-enter big-cone spruce, pine and oak cover below 5200 feet in elevation. Soon thereafter, the road, which has diminished to a rough jeep track, ends (5140-1.0). Switchbacks lower you gently from just beyond this point into a saddle—a good but dry camp—just short of a conifer-clad 4923-foot knob. Beyond, the enjoyable trail enters thick chaparral, descends moderately via switchbacks, and presently levels out at a dirt road spur (3995-2.5) atop a minor pass just south of paved Pine Canyon Road.

The very last segment of permanent Pacific Crest Trail was finally constructed north from here, in Summer 1993. After years of legal wrangling with the Forest Service, the massive Tejon Ranch finally allowed construction of a part of the PCT around the border of their lands. Unfortunately, the final route was clearly designed by lawyers intent on inconveniencing hikers, rather than by trail planners trying to accommodate them. The trail's actual construction was likewise amateurishly undertaken with a small bulldozer, which resulted in a road-wide, poorly laid rut which will be quickly destroyed by erosion.

This new trail segment heads right, south, away from the road spur, descending easily in a hillside stand of Coulter pines and black and scrub oaks. The trail finds a sandy traverse eastward and eventually comes upon the south banks of a small sag pond (3810-0.6) which lies on the San Andreas Fault. Here, under huge black oaks, dozens of migrating waterfowl hide in the rush-rimmed shallows. No formal campsites are found here, and the water certainly requires treating before drinking, but this locale is the last nice camping spot before the Tehachapi Mountains. It is commonly dry by

See maps E8, E9

E10

see MAP E9

fall. The PCT continues east from the pond, ascending gently past a sign notifying you that you have passed out of Angeles National Forest and onto private property, then swings close to and then crosses paved Pine Canyon Road (3845-0.3).

*　　　*　　　*　　　*

Water access: If desperately low on water, you could here continue east along Pine Canyon Road, over a low saddle and down to the hamlet of Three Points, which has a convenience store and a campground, 2.7 miles from the PCT.

*　　　*　　　*　　　*

White pipe posts mark the road crossing, which leads to a gentle ascent right alongside the switchbacking road, soon to reach a large sign diagramming the PCT's course through the Tejon Ranch's property. The sign asks that hikers not leave the path for any reason for the next 7 miles, and expresses a prohibition against camping and fires.

Now commences a tiring and annoying stretch of trail designed to keep hikers as close to the boundary of Tejon Ranch lands as possible. Up and down you march, north across hillsides of hot, dry, low chamise and manzanita scrub on shaly, loose trail tread, marked by frequent tiny, reverse-banked switchbacks. Eventually, you drop steeply down a ridge nose to the verge of a dry grassland in Cow Spring Canyon. Here the ranch boundary, marked by a four-strand barbed-wire fence, turns abruptly east, so you do, as well.

The next leg continues on an eastward bearing, ascending up and across a number of small, sunny ridges. In due time, you descend 100 feet from one of the ridges to cross a jeep road (3522-3.8) in a sandy, buckwheat-dotted wash. Beyond, you climb eastward steeply out of the wash, through a gap, then traverse a hillside with an overlook of Pine Canyon. Steep, then gentle, descent soon ensues, now turning north to bisect a broad wash. Now heading north again, you amble over a broad saddle, then descend via over-engineered switchbacks to merge with a good jeep road (3175-2.1) in a small, narrow valley. Turn right, northeast, along the gently descending road, which passes above a small ranch at the canyon's mouth.

Beyond, the road descends north, arrow-straight out onto the alluvial verge of the Antelope Valley. Pass some branching fence-line jeep roads, but continue straight ahead, soon reaching a new alignment of busy, paved Highway 138 (3040-0.8), just west of its intersection with 270th Street West. Green metal gates now allow horse and foot traffic access to the pavement. Hurry across—the highway is very busy.

*　　　*　　　*　　　*

Water access: Just a few yards east along Highway 138 is a paved driveway (address: 26803 West Avenue C-15) leading to a yellow house with a silver water tank. This is the home of Mr. Jack Fair, a concerned citizen who has generously offered water and camping to all through-travelers on the PCT—a godsend for all hikers facing the dry and daunting Mojave Desert. Please treat him and his property with the respect he deserves. Alternatively, one might choose to proceed west along newly re-aligned Highway 138 to reach a small mini-market in just over 1 mile.

*　　　*　　　*　　　*

Resuming your northward trek, you leave Highway 138, passing through a green gate to regain your fence-side dirt road-cum-trail, still descending easily on a due north bearing. In less than a half mile you find another sign announcing the special restrictions for using the PCT in the Tejon Ranch. Beyond it, you pass through two sty-gates to reach Old Lancaster Road at its junction with paved 270th Street West (2992-0.5). Walk across the former and continue north along the latter, which is the locale of Neenach Elementary School. A moment north of the school, pavement ends (2970-0.3), and arrows point the PCT right, east, through a gate and onto a sandy dirt road. This road parallels the behemoth California Aqueduct, a veritable concrete-lined river flowing in a channel hidden behind a massive earthen berm to our north. Follow the PCT-marked path or either of two firmer, more-used roads, just south of the aqueduct, levelly east to a pair of roads that bridge the aqueduct at a siphon (2965-1.0). Cross north over the aqueduct, then walk a short distance right, east, along its north-

See maps E9, E8, E10

ern bank to the historic Los Angeles Aqueduct (2965-0.3).

Here, the L.A. Aqueduct takes the form of a huge, buried pipe, and engineers were faced with the rather bizarre problem of routing the larger California Aqueduct under the smaller waterway. For the northbound, the next certain water, given the vagaries of reconstruction of the L.A. Aqueduct, lies in Cottonwood Canyon, 13.3 miles ahead. If you're heading south on the PCT, the next water is at Upper Shake Campground, a long 25.9 miles up on Liebre Mountain.

Now the northbound PCT does just that: turns left, due north, on a sandy tack just east of the buried L.A. Aqueduct. Brown plastic PCT posts redundantly indicate the route at numerous intersections with other dirt roads.

You pass a few habitations, all built in the peculiarly eccentric style of California desert residents. Later you descend to your lowest

Antelope Valley point, 2865 feet, to cross the sandy wash of a seasonal creek bed. Here the shade of a wooden trestle supporting the massive, black-tarred, 8-foot-diameter aqueduct pipe offers a rest spot amid another quintessentially California desert feature, an ad-hoc garbage dump of cans, household appliances and auto carcasses, all riddled with bullet holes.

Now the route north leads into a low, scraggly "woodland" of Joshua trees, the hallmarks of the Mojave Desert. ∎ *At one time Joshua trees, or tree yuccas, were more widely distributed, as evidenced by fossils of the extinct giant yucca-feeding ground sloth, found in southern Nevada, where Joshua trees are no longer living. These giant members of the lily family, with their unusually branched, sometimes human forms, were likened by Mormon pioneers to the figure of Joshua, pointing the route to the Great Salt Lake—whence the name. These "trees" will not branch at all unless the*

See map E10

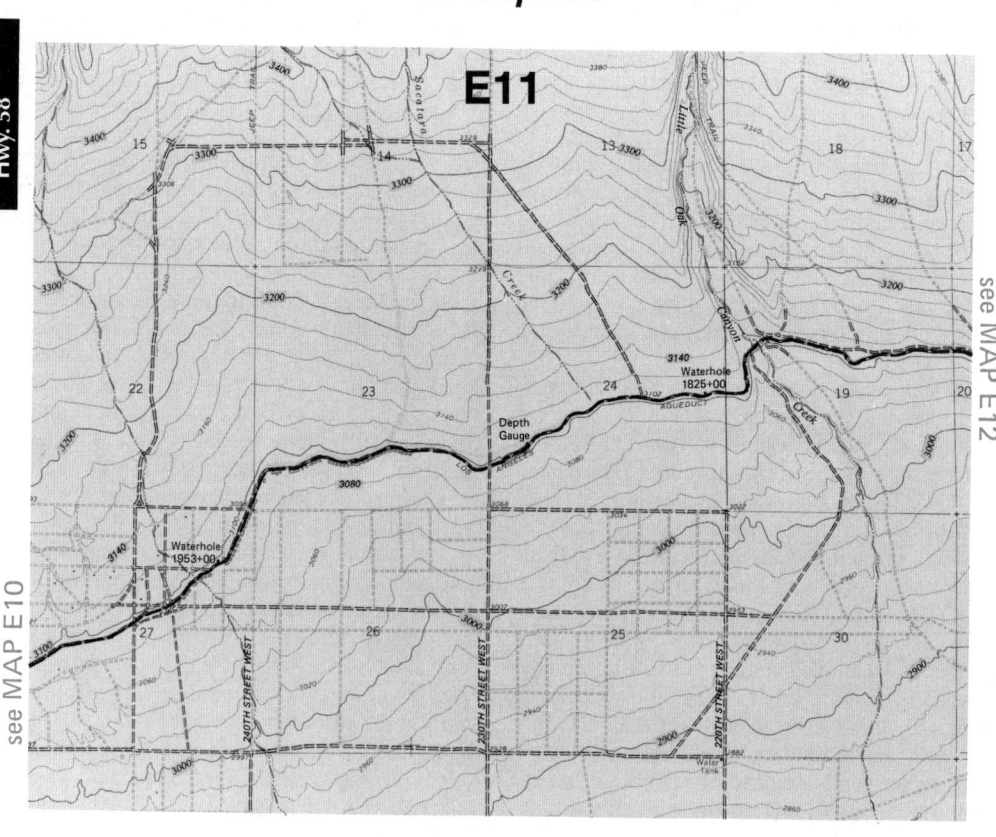

E12

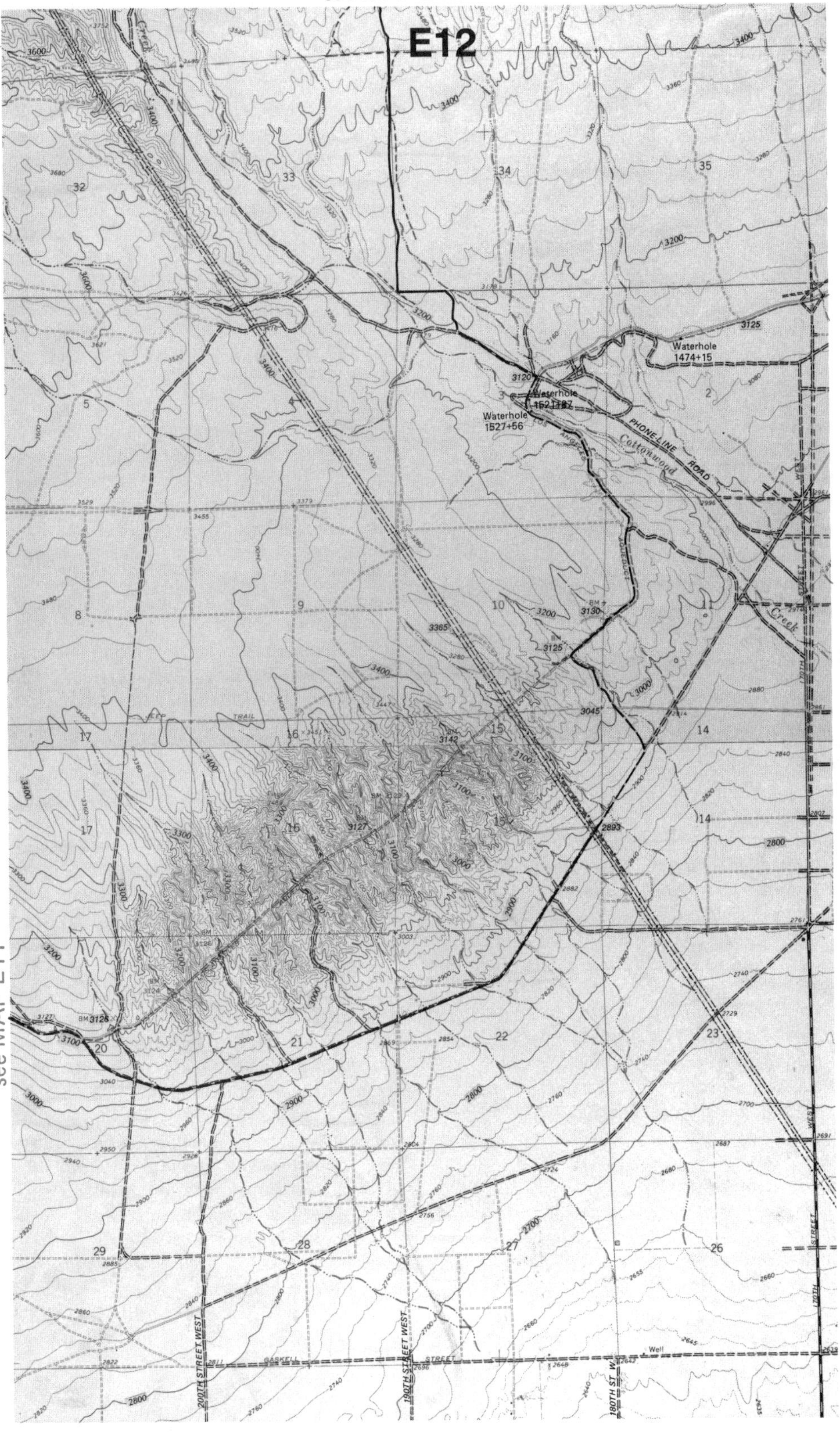

see MAP E11

E

Agua Dulce-
Hwy. 58

Waterhole
1474+15

Waterhole
1521+87

Waterhole
1527+56

PHONE LINE ROAD

Cottonwood

Creek

Joshua trees

Agua Dulce- Hwy. 58

E

trunk's tip flowers are damaged by wind or by boring beetles. Each time a Joshua tree blossoms, an event determined by rainfall or temperature, it sprouts a foot-long panicle of densely clustered, greenish-white blooms that become football-shaped fruit later in the year. But Joshua trees cannot pollinate themselves. Like that of other yuccas, their pollen is too heavy to reach another plant, even in strong desert winds, so they rely on a symbiotic relationship with female Joshua tree yucca moths, which have mouthparts adapted for carrying a ball of pollen. Unlike other insects, which may unwittingly carry pollen from one plant to another, the yucca moth makes a separate trip to carry pollen, which it stuffs deep into a Joshua tree's blossom, and then it drills a hole in the base of the flower, where it lays an egg. When the moth grub hatches, it has fruit to feed upon. Another animal that apparently can't live without Joshua trees or other yuccas is the small, mottled desert night lizard, which hides under fallen Joshua trees, feeding on termites, spiders and ants. ∎

You amble into Kern County, and then just over a mile later, your straight-north course turns east (3090-3.2) as the L.A. Aqueduct itself bends east, transforming at the same time from a black-tarred pipe to an underground channel with a broad, flat, concrete roof. (Contrary to a U.S.G.S. topo, the aqueduct actually lies just north of the main dirt access-road that the PCT route follows.) Your way leads east, climbing imperceptibly alongside the aqueduct as it traces a scalloped, contouring route across a succession of broad alluvial fans footing the Tehachapi Mountains. In the first mile, you pass through a nice grove of Joshua trees—a possible, but waterless, place to camp. Unfortunately, barbed-wire fences make it difficult to stray from the aqueduct. Even more unfortunate is the fact that, although one is walking alongside a buried river of cool, pristine High Sierra water, there is not way to get at it! The Los Angeles Department of Water and Power has undertaken a series of repairs to the roof of the aqueduct which have resulted in the cementing-over of all of the "water holes" that PCT travelers previously relied on, along this otherwise waterless stretch. The next reliable water for northbound hikers is in Cottonwood Canyon, a hot 11.1 miles away!

Forging ahead, you soon find a long stretch of aqueduct that was recently resurfaced. It winds across the broad fan of Sacatara Creek, passing innumerable branching dirt roads bound for everywhere and nowhere. ∎ *In this vicinity, the commonest large desert shrub is green, glossy-leaved creosote bush. Note how evenly spaced the shrubs are. Each one secretes a toxin, washed to the ground by rains, that poisons nearby plant growth, thereby allowing it enough root space to gather the water supply it needs. Observant walkers may note some of the creosote bushes growing in clustered rings, the bushes up to a few yards apart. Botanists have discovered that root-crown branching by one of these bushes results in a ring of plants, each one a genetically identical clone of the original colonizing plant. By radiocarbon dating and growth-rate mesaurements, scientists have found some creosote-bush clonal rings growing in the Mojave Desert with an estimated age of 11,000 years—far older than the well-known longevous bristlecone pine!* ∎

The route now turns across Little Oak Can-

See maps E10, E11

yon Creek's wide, dry wash, then winds monotonously across a gentle alluvial hillside to an intersection (3110-5.5) with a good dirt road that crosses the aqueduct via a concrete bridge. Here the PCT is signed to branch right, southeast, via brown plastic posts with emblems. This junction is just a short distance before the L.A. Aqueduct disappears altogether at the western foot of a rugged hillside. Now you amble gently down, soon curving east-northeast, then northeast, at the pediment of a fascinating badland of steep-sided ravines and ridges. Flash floods have carved the firm red and yellow sediments into a complex of narrow gullies, which has a sparse flora of low juniper trees and rabbitbrush that give color contrast. Eventually, you come to a trio of high-tension electric lines marching uphill from the southeast. Ignore the dirt road (2893-3.0) that runs along their route and instead continue straight ahead, northeast, on the better road. Very soon you strike a poorer dirt road, your first left turn, at a triangular junction (2915-0.4). It takes you gently but directly up-slope, soon coming along the southwest side of a small, shallow canyon. Quickly you once again rejoin the Los Angeles Aqueduct (3105-0.6), here underground, and turn right, northeast, along its road.

You climb over a low rise, then descend momentarily to resume a nearly level amble, curving north and then northwest into the massive, broad valley of Cottonwood Creek. There are no cottonwoods in evidence along the usually dry creek bed, but there is a nice stand of Joshua trees. Here you finally find a reliable summer-long water hole: a reinforced concrete horse trough, which is fed continuously by a pipe from the aqueduct. It sits below the southwest end of concrete Cottonwood Creek bridge (3120-1.6), just north of a small concrete maintenance structure with a walkway that overlooks the wash, and below the level of the aqueduct road. (Be aware, however, that water may not be available here year-round—L.A. Department of Water & Power may have drained the aqueduct for maintenance at any time between October 1 and May 1). Beyond the trough, the bridge carries you across the main wash. A nice flat north of the wash makes a logical campsite before you tackle the waterless Tehachapi Mountains, but be aware that this has become a noisy staging area for dirt bikers and ATV enthusiasts. Be sure to get an early morning start, and load up with water before leaving the aqueduct—the next reliable water, discounting its infrequent presence in Tylerhorse Canyon 6.6 miles away, is at the bottom of Oak Creek Canyon, a long 22.7 miles away.

Walk briefly along the aqueduct to the next dirt road (3120-0.1) branching left, northwest, up Cottonwood Creek. It is frequently signed by 4-foot-high brown plastic posts topped with PCT emblems; they are just as frequently blown to smithereens by thoughtless target-shooters. Follow it gently up through a sunny Joshua tree grove to a resumption of PCT trail tread (3160-0.4) branching right, north, up the first ravine that cuts the 50-foot-high alluvial embankment above your road. This junction and all others in the next few miles were also originally marked by brown PCT posts, but some dirt bikers have made a project of uprooting them. Ascend to the top of the slope, emerging on the bajada—a formation consisting of alluvial fans—up which your route will wind into the Tehachapis. Here, trail tread all but vanishes. In fact, here, as for the next three miles, tread was never constructed by cost-conscious USFS and BLM trail crews. Instead, you follow six-to-twelve inch wooden survey stakes across the desert floor (hoping that they remain in place until a trail is worn). It is some consolation that each leg of the trail is laid out in a straight line! At first, you walk north to the lip of another ravine, where posts indicate your turn across two prominent dirt-bike paths to head due west along the Section 3/34 line, soon finding another good bike path (3250-0.5) right on a lip overlooking Cottonwood Creek. Here is a pipe benchmark locating the adjacent corners of Sections 3, 4, 33 and 34. Now, as indicated by a brown plastic post, turn right, due north, following wooden stakes through the open desert. Soon you parallel and then leap-frog a jeep track on a hot, gentle ascent. Cross an east-west jeep road (3465-1.0) at some old fence posts, then turn a bit west of north to continue up, now with increasing numbers of low junipers and decreasing Joshua trees beside your shadeless path.

Strike more poor dirt roads at a **T** junction (3609-0.5), after which the trail is quite indis-

See maps E11, E12

E13

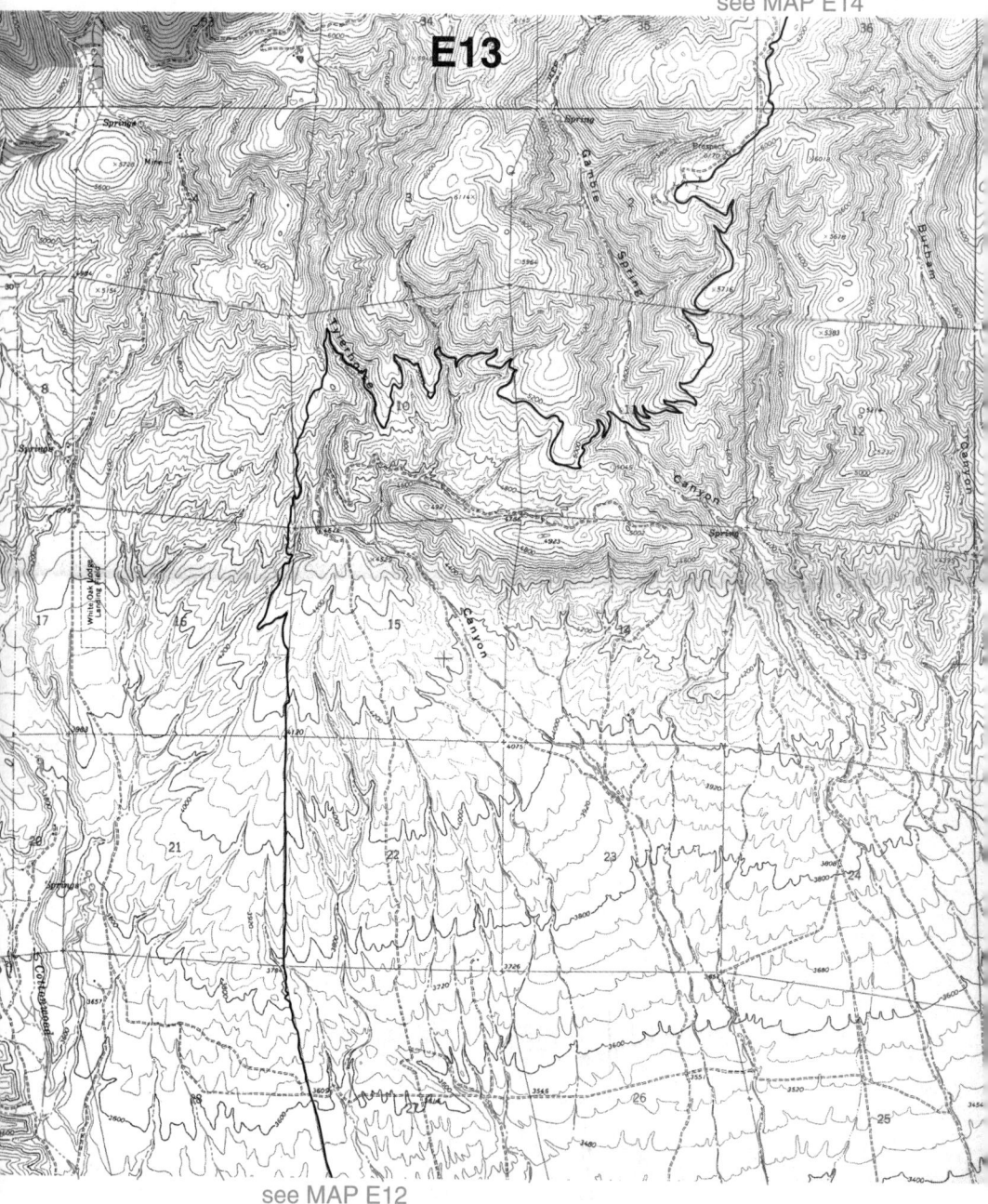

see MAP E12

tinct, but continues on the same bearing up to a viewful and breezy knoll (3800-0.4), where you take note of your progress and survey the southern flanks of the Tehachapis. Next, descend briefly across a pair of ravines to cross a poor jeep road (3790-0.2) that traces the south boundary of a barbed-wire fence. The PCT parallels the 4-strand fence, with its steel and wooden posts, as it marches due north up along the Section 21/22 boundary, in sandy, open

See map E13

grassland. Approaching the west side of a large ravine, you join with a good jeep road (4070-0.7), walk along it for 0.1 mile, then resume your fence-line position to soon find a perpendicular jeep road and the end of the fence (4120-0.3).

From here, the path takes a more logical line, and a slightly steeper one, northward to the head of the ravine, then over two low ridge noses and across a dry stream bed, now in much denser cover of sagebrush, rabbitbrush and low junipers. A brisk ascent follows, eventually reaching a wide, rough jeep/dirtbike path (4960-2.2) which climbs the ridge west of Tylerhorse Canyon. Climb momentarily north along that path to find a post marking PCT tread, which drops steeply down into often cool and shady Tylerhorse Canyon (4840-0.3). Often, within a week or two of spring rains, a trickle of water will run here, and tall junipers and Coulter pines will afford a nice quiet camp. Beware of flash floods during and after storms.

The PCT continues up into the Tehachapis by now turning generally east, making a hot but well-graded ascent across three major ravines, then descends a bit to a saddle (4960-3.2) overlooking Gamble Spring Canyon. Here you ignore the now-familiar plethora of dirtbike trails, and instead descend almost 400 feet, via sandy switchbacks, to the dry floor of Gamble Spring Canyon (4625-0.7). Above, the final 1600-foot leg of our 3000-foot climb into the Tehachapis awaits: First, eight hot switchbacks, badly abused by motocross riders, lead up to a brief respite where you traverse around a 5716-foot knob. Two more switchbacks attack the next slope, but not nearly as viciously as the dirtbikers have—a huge, rutted swath cuts directly up the ridge, obliterating the PCT in places. Near the top, you round clockwise across a breezy nose that is cut by a jeep road (6070-3.0) and pocked with prospect pits in a small outcropping of Paleozoic marine metasediments. Here, the trail swings northeast, keeping just below the ridgetop and its jeep track, soon finding the welcome shade of stands of junipers and pinyon pines which frame vistas south over Antelope Valley. ∎ *On a clear morning, Mt. San Antonio, San Gorgonio Mountain and Mt. San Jacinto can all be seen, as well as the massive buildings of the NASA space shuttle center in Palmdale.* ∎

Soon the PCT begins to undulate up and down between groves of fragrant pinyon and Coulter pines and large junipers, which clothe slopes between dry flats of sagebrush scrub and mountain mahogany brush. You stay close to, but rarely see, a good dirt road that serves a scattering of vacation cabins. Without fanfare, you reach the PCT's 6280-foot highpoint in the Tehachapi Mountains, then descend easily, winding along the pinyon-forested ridge that forms the south side of Oak Creek Canyon. Beyond a gap at the heads of Burnham and Pitney canyons (5980-2.6) you climb for a few minutes, then resume your easy descent. ∎ *Frequent vistas are had over meadow-bottomed Oak Creek Canyon, which is carved along the active Garlock Fault, whence the southern Sierra Nevada rises. Oak Creek Canyon is home to one of the last herds of wild dark brown horses that once roamed the Antelope Valley area, having descended from horses lost by Spanish explorers.* ∎

The canyon, like these slopes above, is private property, so no camping is allowed, and hikers must stay on the trail. Anyone who drops into the canyon bottom for any reason will be prosecuted. Continue winding easily down the ridge, in open groves of juniper, occasionally making well-marked crossings of vague, branching jeep trails. ∎ *Presently, the hum of electric generators and the whoosh of blades are heard, and the way descends to the edge of a vast array of wind turbines. These harvest electrical energy from the nearly incessant breezes that blow across the Tehachapis, spawned by temperature gradients between cool coastal air and the hot Mojave Desert. You will grow used to these mammoth windmills, since you will walk among them all of the way to Highway 58, but initially their incongruous presence reminds one of an enormous flock of squeaking, flapping seagulls.* ∎ The wind farms force our route to trace the lip of the canyon wall, then to switchback sandily down it, eventually reaching the streamside of Oak Creek, in a delightful open stand of white oaks. In a minute you step through a pipe gate, then cross Oak Creek (4075-6.4) via a small steel bridge at the dam of a stream-flow gauging pond, where water is almost always available through early summer. Unfortunately, this is private land and camping is not permitted.

See maps E13, E14, E15

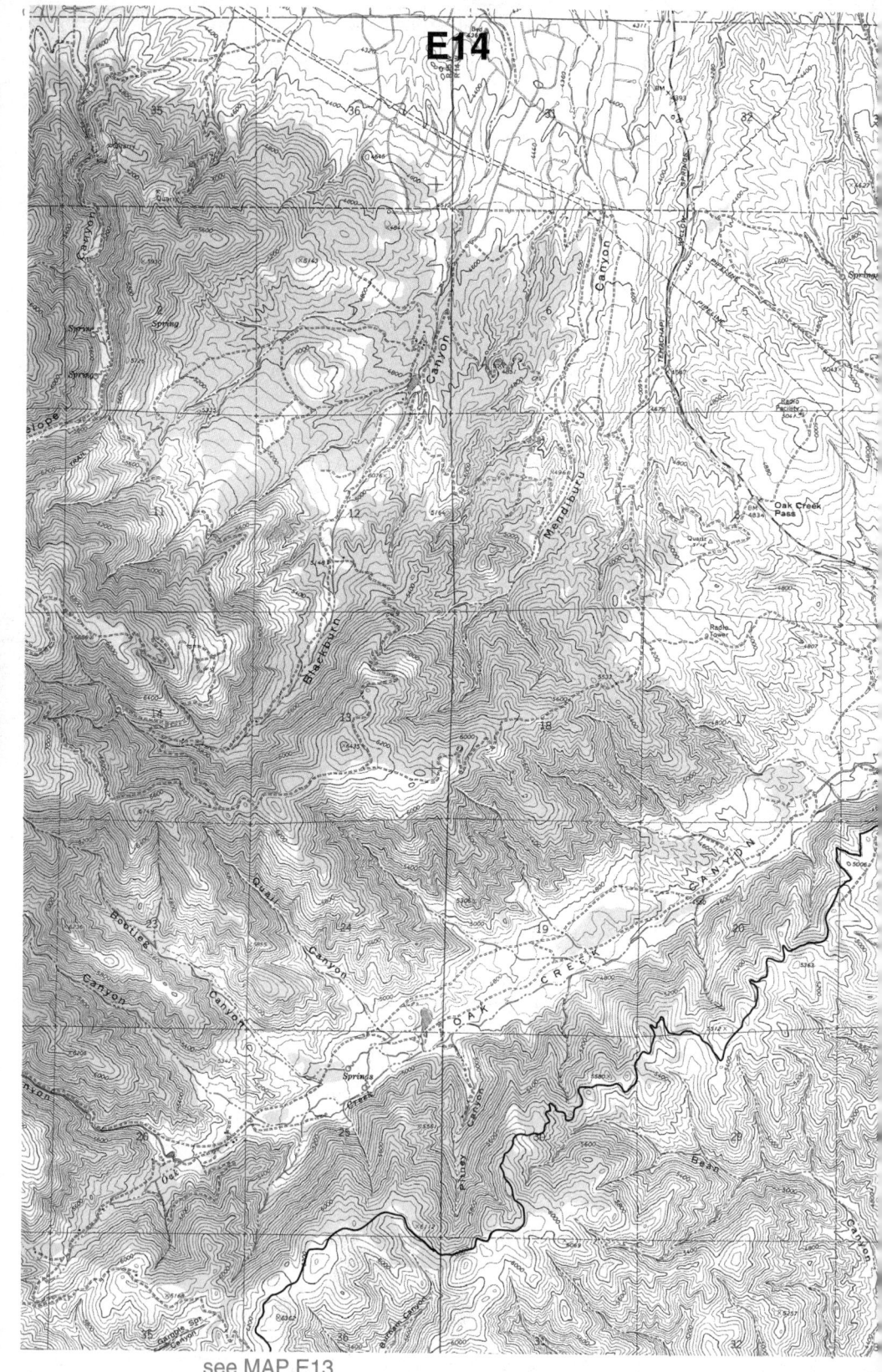

E14

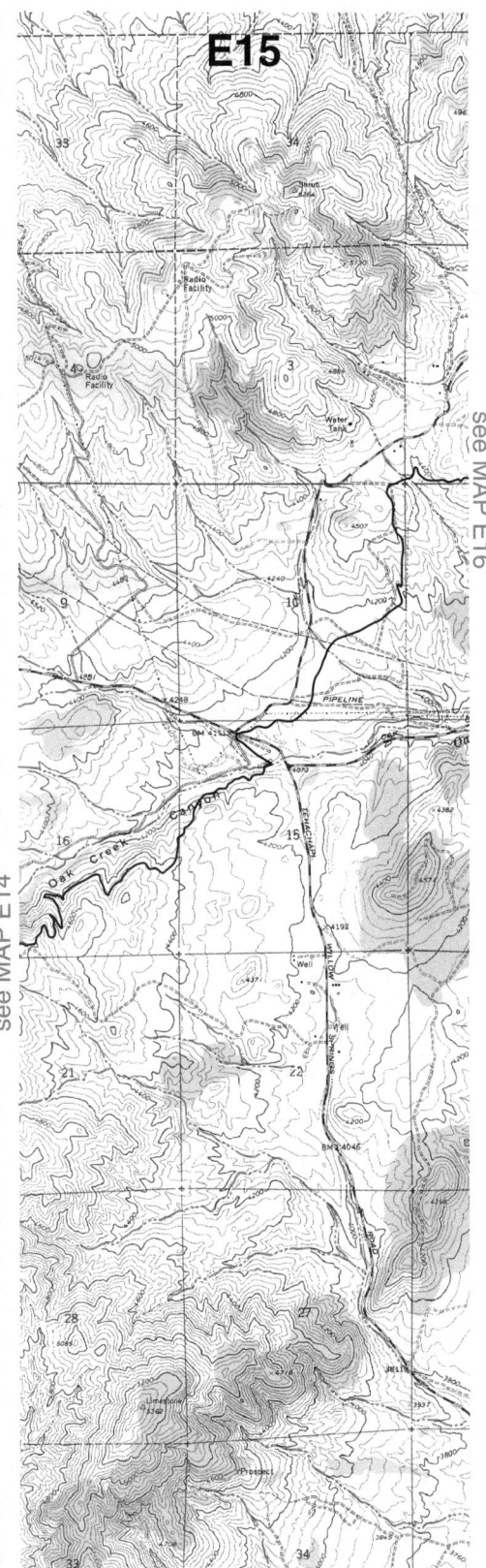

E15

see MAP E16

see MAP E14

Now, parallel the stream on its north bank for a moment, then turn northwest up across a gentle ridgetop. Soon, pass under a double-pole powerline, step across a poor dirt road, and drop a few feet to two-lane, paved Tehachapi-Willow Springs Road (4150-0.2), at its junction with paved Cameron Road.

*   *   *   *

Resupply access: Here, most Trailers will veer from the PCT to head 9.4 miles into Tehachapi for resupply. Access to Tehachapi is much easier from here than via Highway 58, at the end of this section. Go up Tehachapi-Willow Springs Road 1.8 miles to 4834-foot Oak Creek Pass, then descend north through fields of California poppies to paved Highline Road (3.6 miles). Here, one has two equidistant options—walk left, west, on Highline Road 3.0 miles to Summit Road, then right, north, 1.0 mile into the center of Tehachapi; or continue north on Tehachapi-Willow Springs Road, over Highway 58 via an overpass, 1.0 mile to Tehachapi Boulevard. Now turn left, west, 1.0 mile to cross under Highway 58 and find a very good hotel, restaurant, bar, gas station and mini-mart at Steuber Road. Continue 2.0 miles farther west on Tehachapi Boulevard to reach the center of Tehachapi, with numerous motels, large markets, laundry, restaurants, banks, pharmacies, hardware, and a hospital. Alternatively, one could also choose to detour from the PCT here and head down Tehachapi-Willow Springs Road 12 miles to Mojave instead.

*   *   *   *

Back on the PCT in Oak Creek Canyon, cross Tehachapi-Willow Springs Road and pick up slightly indistinct tread heading east, marked by a 4x4 post with a PCT emblem. Turn northward across three dirt roads in quick succession, the first two subserving polelines. Then gently ascend across a broad, dry, sandy ravine, in open grassland dotted with sagebrush and a few low junipers, to the melodious calls of flocks of meadowlarks. Reaching a hillside, you might lose trail tread momentarily where bulldozers have cut a wide swath, but plastic marker-posts show the way across one good dirt road (4165-0.8) to a second (4160-0.2), just below another large windmill plantation. Now you turn north, attacking the hillside at a mod-

E
Agua Dulce-
Hwy 58

See map E15

see MAP F1

see MAP E15

erate angle, soon crossing numerous dirt roads of varying quality which serve the windfarm and the double-pole powerline that runs along its western boundary.

The climb eventually abates at a small saddle (4495-0.6). Here you drop north for a few yards, step across a dirt road, and bend eastward. Open two pipe gates in a barbed-wire fence, drop into a gully, then climb steeply east to another gate and again gain a viewful ridgetop (4560-0.6). Wide vistas extend south over windfarms, Joshua trees and desert to the San Gabriel and San Bernardino mountains.

For the next leg, you undulate eastward under the propeller-bedecked crest of the Tehachapis on sunny, sandy trail which three times crosses dirt access roads. At a fourth, good dirt road (4485-1.6), you note a guardhouse for one of the windfarming corporations at a road junction just to your north. You pass south of that road, then cross it and ascend gently over the ridgecrest and down to a saddle, also with a poor dirt road (4600-0.5). The path from here makes its way onto the steeper northern slopes of the ridge, with sweeping panoramas over Cameron Canyon to the Tehachapi Valley and beyond to the southern Sierra. An easy ascent eventually finds a narrow ridge, where you step across a dirt road (4765-0.9) just below a heavy steel gate, then pass through a barbed-wire gate in a cluster of junipers. A single switchback leads to a steep hillside, heavily eroded by wild horses. Below, a dozen well-graded switchbacks lower you to the floor of Cameron Canyon. Reaching the bottom, you turn west momentarily to strike two-lane paved Cameron Road (3905-2.1) at a pipe gate. Now follow 4x4 PCT posts along that road's south shoulder, easily down to cross Atchison Topeka and Santa Fe and Southern Pacific Railroad tracks (3824-0.5). From here, the PCT, unmarked, follows Cameron Road east to its overpass of busy four-lane Highway 58 at Tehachapi Pass (3830-0.8). Welcome to the Sierra Nevada!

*   *   *   *

Resupply access: Tehachapi, with its extensive facilities described previously, lies 9.2 miles west on Highway 58, but is difficult to reach from this spot, due to the rarity of traffic that exits or enters via the Cameron Road offramp.

*   *   *   *

See map E15, E16

Rattlesnakes may be found almost anywhere along Section E

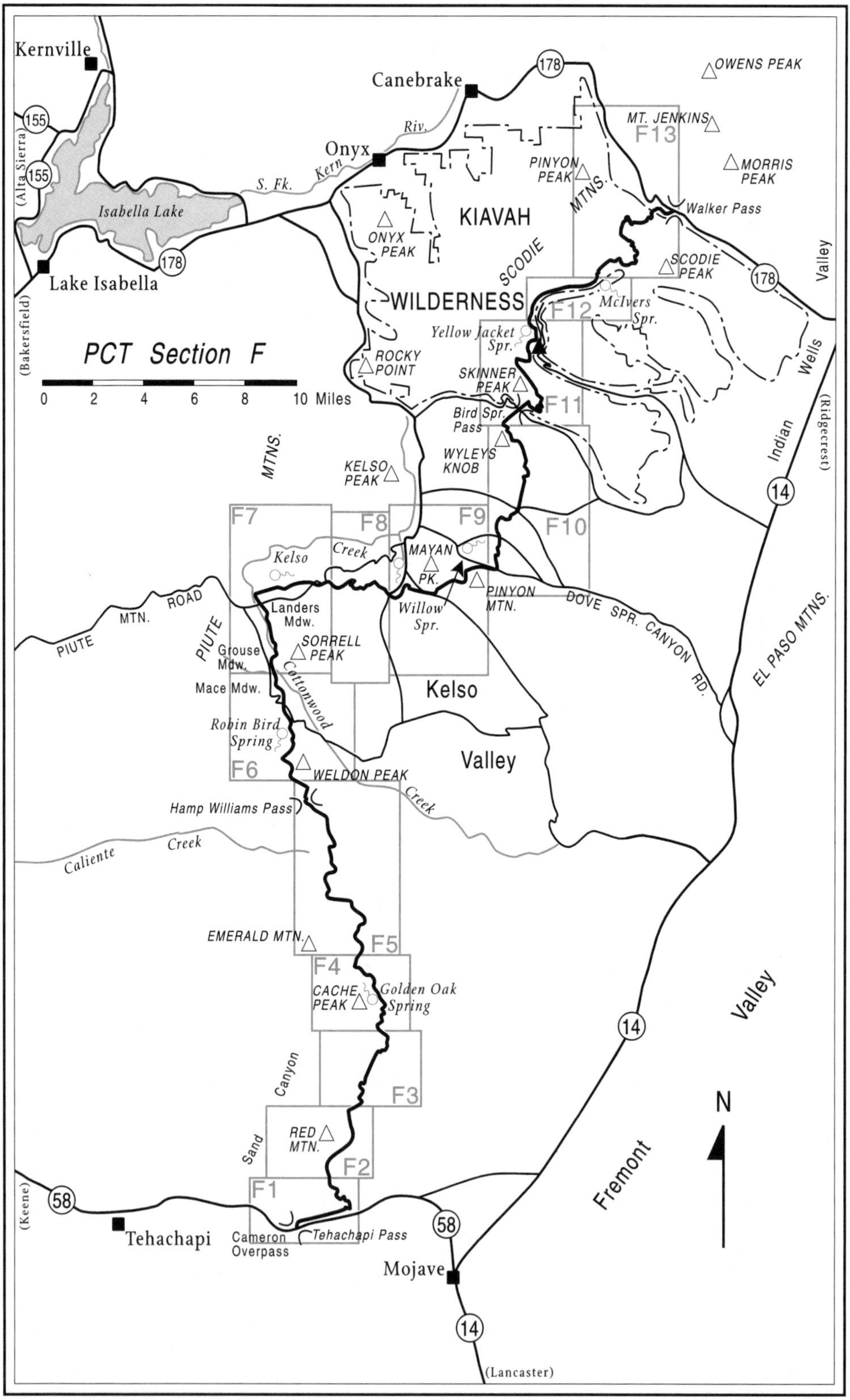

Kernville

(155)
(Alta Sierra)
(155)

(Bakersfield)

Isabella Lake

(178)

Lake Isabella

PCT Section F

0   2   4   6   8   10 Miles

Canebrake

(178)

Riv.

Onyx

S. Fk. *Kern*

*ONYX
PEAK*

ROCKY
POINT

△ OWENS PEAK

MT. JENKINS △
F13

PINYON △
PEAK

SCODIE MTNS.

MORRIS
PEAK △

Walker Pass

KIAVAH

△ SCODIE
PEAK

(178)

WILDERNESS

Yellow Jacket
Spr.

McIvers
Spr.

F12

SKINNER
PEAK △

F11

Bird Spr.
Pass

Indian

(Ridgecrest)

(14)

KELSO
PEAK △

WYLEYS
KNOB

MTNS.

Wells

F7

F8

F9

F10

Kelso
Creek

MAYAN
PK.

EL PASO MTNS.

Landers
Mdw.

Willow
Spr.

PINYON
MTN.

DOVE SPR. CANYON RD.

PIUTE   MTN.   ROAD

*SORRELL
PEAK*

Kelso

Grouse
Mdw.

PIUTE

Mace Mdw.

Cottonwood

Valley

*Robin Bird
Spring*

F6

△ *WELDON PEAK*

Creek

Hamp Williams Pass

Caliente   Creek

EMERALD MTN. △

F5

F4

*CACHE
PEAK* △

*Golden Oak
Spring*

Canyon

F3

*RED △
MTN.*

Sand

F2

F1

(Keene)

(58)

Tehachapi

Cameron
Overpass

Tehachapi Pass

(58)

Mojave

Fremont

Valley

N

(14)

(14)

(Lancaster)

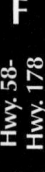

F
**Hwy. 58-
Hwy. 178**

Section F
Highway 58 near Tehachapi Pass
to Highway 178 at Walker Pass

Introduction: Surprisingly to many people, most geographers include the Tehachapi Mountains as part of the mighty Sierra Nevada, calling the range the "Sierran Tail" or the "Sierran Hook." The Sierra's southernmost tip, then, is the southwest point of the Tehachapi Mountains below the junction of the San Andreas and Garlock faults.

In the Sierra north of the Tehachapi range, the PCT immediately climbs onto the Sierra crest, where it remains for most of this section, traversing the granitic Sierra Nevada batholith, which is exposed so widely. It quickly climbs from a Joshua/juniper woodland to a pinyon pine/oak woodland, with five species of oak along the route. A cool Jeffrey-pine forest in the Piute Mountains offers a refreshing midsection change for the hiker before he drops to a desert community of plants, then progresses again to a pinyon-pine woodland.

The charm of this section lies not only in its diversity of flora, but also in the unobstructed views of rows of sharp ridges and deep valleys, of sprawling desert lands and distant peak silhouettes, of faraway pockets of populated, sometimes historic enclaves, of evidence of man's quest for riches and of his quest for energy to power his lifestyle.

Declination: 13¾°E throughout this section.

Points on Route	S→N	Mi. Btwn. Pts.	N→S
Cameron Overpass at Highway 58	0.0		84.1
		16.1	
Golden Oak Spring	16.1		68.0
		18.2	
road to Robin Bird Spring	34.3		49.8
		0.4	
Jawbone Canyon Road in Piute Mountains	34.7		49.4
		5.6	
Piute Mountain Road, first crossing	40.3		43.8
		3.0	
Piute Mountain Road, second crossing	43.3		40.8
		4.8	
Kelso Valley Road	48.1		36.0
		2.1	
Butterbredt Canyon Road	50.2		33.9
		4.1	
road to Willow Spring	54.3		29.8
		9.2	
Bird Spring Pass	63.5		20.6
		6.0	
road to Yellow Jacket Spring	69.5		14.6
		6.7	
road to McIvers Spring	76.2		7.9
		7.3	
Walker Pass Campground spur trail	83.5		0.6
		0.6	
Highway 178 at Walker Pass	84.1		0.0

Supplies: You have a choice between the rapidly growing town of Tehachapi, 9.6 miles west, and the desert town of Mojave, 9.6 miles east, both off Highway 58. Of the two, Mojave may be your better choice. It caters to the needs of travelers by offering motels (a Motel 6 was built in the 1980s), numerous fast-food franchises, and large markets. Its post office is 10.8 miles from Cameron Overpass, off Highway 58 on Belshaw Street. Highway 58 ceases to be a freeway 0.1 mile east of the overpass, which makes it easier to catch rides. Until the BLM supplies a water source nearby, you will have to obtain a supply in town, too, for your first water on the trail is 16.1 miles in.

At the end of this section, Onyx has limited groceries and supplies and a post office 16.5 miles west of Walker Pass Campground off Highway 178. A KOA Campground is 7.0 miles farther west off Highway 178. Kernville is 36 miles northwest of Walker Pass Campground: take Highway 178 and Sierra Way. It has a post office, supplies, motels, etc., and for your rest and relaxation days, kayak rentals and one-hour to multiday raft trips on the tumultuous Kern River during adequate water flow.

Permits: A fire permit is required for this section, but only if you do not already have a wilderness permit. It can be obtained from the Bureau of Land Management or Sequoia National Forest.

Special Problems

Water: Available year-round water sources are sparse in this section. During periods of extended drought, even usually reliable springs dry up. Most water sources have heavy cattle use, but boiling or filtering and maybe also adding iodine tablets should render the water suitable for you. Both the BLM and the Forest Service are upgrading the springs in this area. This will greatly improve the water quality, but the water will still need to be treated. Although there is usually a breeze on this mostly shadeless trail section, days can be hot and humidity can be low. It is advisable to hydrate yourself well at every water source and to carry a minimum of two quarts per waterless 10 miles.

Rattlesnakes: Of the many types of rattlesnakes, perhaps three species can be found along the PCT corridor in the Southern Sierra. The Speckled, 25–50 inches, appears sandy and speckled like gravel, with muted crossbar-to-diamond-shaped blotches. Ranging in elevation to 8000 feet, it is usually seen around boulders and chaparral. The greenish tinged Mojave rattlesnake, 25–50 inches, has black bands alternating with wider white bands encircling its tail next to the rattles. It lives in the desert and up to 8000 feet on arid slopes. The Western rattlesnake, 16–24 inches, has broad diamondlike markings that become rings near the rattles. It prefers rock outcrops, but is also found in grassland, chaparral and riparian areas up to 11,000 feet elevation. This rattler shows more aggressive behavior than some species, usually after emerging from hibernation.

All rattlesnakes prefer to be left alone and to leave you alone. They do not chase you. They defend themselves by striking, but only when provoked or stepped on. They usually warn you by rattling. They can strike one third to one half of their length, and can bite even after they have been killed. A bite is not fatal for most people; small children are at greater risk. Envenomation does not occur with every bite. Numbness and tingling around your mouth indicate that venom has been injected. Envenomation by any of the species affects the circulatory system, but injection by the Mojave rattlesnake affects the nervous system as well—considerably more dangerous. Do not cut the fang marks or apply a tourniquet. Try to stay calm, rest the affected area if possible, and get to a hospital. Suction devices now on the market may help to extract venom from the wound.

Ticks: These bugs rank as the most sinister and sneaky of the nuisance bugs encountered in the Southern Sierra. Ticks can cause serious diseases that, fortunately, are uncommon in this area: most notably Lyme disease and Rocky Mountain spotted fever. Lyme disease usually presents a ringlike red rash around the bite; spotted fever causes reddish-black spots. Both diseases involve flu-like symptoms. Specific antibiotics offer a cure, and should be given early in the illness.

Ticks seem most prevalent in late winter and spring. They neither jump nor fly, but transfer from grass or brush to animals or you. You hardly see them and often do not feel their bite. This eight-legged creature can be as tiny as a dot of this i (larvae) or up to ¼ inch (adult). Remove one with tweezers by gently pulling upward and outward. Try not to crush it, as doing that releases its fluid into the bite. Inspect your clothes frequently when in brushy, grassy areas.

Off-highway Vehicles (OHVs): Be forewarned that the seemingly unlimited open space along some stretches in this section attracts weekend OHVs, but very few during the week. They are prohibited on the PCT.

Maps: *Monolith*   *Claraville*
        Tehachapi NE   *Pinyon Mountain*
        Cache Peak   *Cane Canyon*
        Cross Mountain   *Horse Canyon*
        Emerald Mountain   *Walker Pass*

The Route

The BLM hopes to establish a water source nearby, south of Cameron Overpass. This is greatly needed, as the closest source north on the trail is Golden Oaks Spring, 16.1 miles ahead. Before starting this often windy, exposed section north of Tehachapi Pass, you should hydrate yourself well and carry at the very minimum two quarts of water per 10 miles. The trail passes through a crazy quilt of private and BLM lands. Because of private lands, you are asked not to stray from the trail, even for peakbagging.

You begin your trek at the south end of Cameron Overpass (3800-0.0), then cross busy Highway 58 on the overpass to the trail on the north side. Here you descend, pass through a gate, and then parallel the highway east-northeast along a fenced corridor and through another gate (3780-1.2): this one opposite the CAMERON ROAD EXIT 1 MILE sign. Next you dip through the large wash of Waterfall Canyon and turn northeast to ascend to the right of the flood-control berm next to the wash. Leaving the berm, you progress east while passing groves of juniper trees interspersed with Joshua trees and a few yuccas.

■ *While in the Tehachapi Pass area, you cross over the northeast-southwest Garlock fault, the second largest fault in California. Movement along this fault is approximately 7–8 millimeters per year. To the north there is no move-* *ment; the fault is locked. Seismologists expect a major earthquake in the locked area. These hills show the fault-zone mishmash of granitics and metamorphics. Geologists identify the rocks as mafic and ultramafic plutonic rocks and associated amphibolite, gneiss and granulite.* ■

Climbing north via three switchbacks and some curves, you arrive on a broad slope among scrubby junipers 3.0 miles into your trip—a level place for a camp if needed. ■ *From below you hear the distant chug of locomotives pulling a long chain of freight cars to and from the 17 tunnels and the famous loop at Walong, just west of the town of Tehachapi. Built in 1875–76, the loop is one of the most photographed railroad sections in the world. It is composed of a tunnel and an ascending circle where a gain of 77 feet elevation puts the locomotives over the caboose if the train is more than 4000 feet long.* ■

■ *Usually you feel the prevailing winds that race through Tehachapi Pass. They activate the forests of windmills strung on ridges seen from here. The winds are the result of cool air rushing in from the coastal west to replace hot air rising from the desert east. The flow of air increases as it compresses against the ridges, resulting in wind speeds recorded here of up to 70 miles per hour.* ■

F
Hwy. 58–
Hwy. 178

See map F1

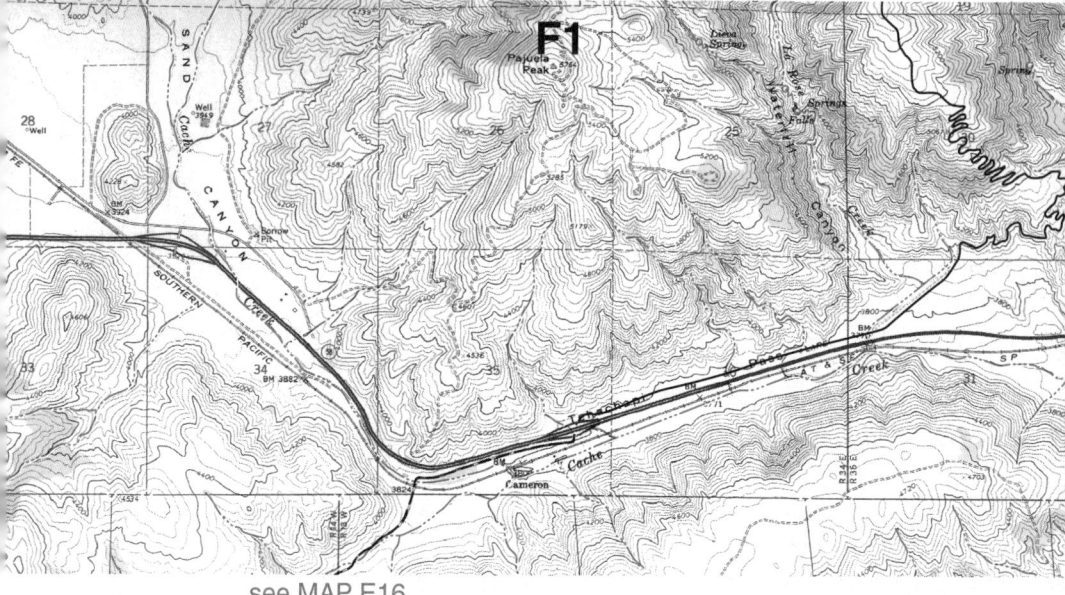

F1

see MAP E16

❚ *The wind farms you see were developed as an alternative to energy generated by air-polluting fossil fuels. Wind-energy people estimate that each turbine displaces approximately 1100 barrels of oil annually, which, in turn, reduces air pollutants by 1900 pounds. But the windmills, some claim, are esthetically polluting, the terrain disturbed during construction is subject to erosion, and the ridges become gouged with roads. The possible expansion of the Sky River wind farm ahead, and the introduction of other wind farms, has heightened concern in neighboring communities and among PCT users.* ❚

Moving on, you climb a long, tight series of switchbacks that on the map resemble a recorded earthquake on a seismograph. At length you reach gentler slopes along a broad ridge where camping is possible. ❚ *Viewing clockwise from the ridge you see the Mojave Desert*

See map F1

Campsite 3 miles north of Highway 58 on the PCT

to the east; the town of Mojave with its rows of mothballed airplanes glistening in the sun just below the Sierra to the southeast; and the isolated features of Soledad Mountain and Elephant Butte rising south of the town. Those low volcanic mountains produced millions of dollars worth of gold and silver extracted from contacts between rhyolite and granitic rock along 100 miles of tunnel. Farther southeast you view the barren expanse of Edwards Air Force Base with Rogers Dry Lake air strips, which is home base for experimental aircraft and occasionally the landing for space shuttles. To the south loom the Tehachapi Mountains, and west, their namesake town. The large scar on the north side of Tehachapi Pass resulted from excavations by Monolith Cement Company. Their product was used in the construction of the Los Angeles aqueduct, which runs along the east side of the Sierra. ∎

The PCT descends slightly to straddle a narrow ridge between steep canyons, resumes its ascent, and shortly crosses from east-facing to west-facing slopes. In time it encounters pinyon-pine trees. ∎ *From these trees, in days of yore, the Kawaiisu Indians gathered pinyon nuts. They gathered and hunted from the Tehachapi Mountains north through this area* *to the South Fork Kern River Valley. To preserve their culture, in 1994 the State of California purchased land surrounding a former village in Sand Canyon, 2.5 air miles west, for a historical park.* ∎

Now your trail seeks the crest on ascending slopes. To the right on the crest before a descent, a river of sand hidden amid pinyon pines offers wind-protected campsites. To the left colorful Waterfall Canyon dominates views. The trail next crosses a jeep road that leads to a prospect, then climbs a ridge via three switchbacks and passes a chalky white hill of tuff protruding at the head of an east-facing canyon. Soon the PCT crosses and then parallels a jeep road, crosses it again, and curves around the head of Waterfall Canyon. Abruptly, the trail ends and the route joins that jeep road (6120-7.1).

You turn left on the seldom-used jeep road, which heads generally north, descends to the east, and then heads north again. At the bottom of the descent, 2.0 miles along the road, you curve around a huge gray pine tree on a flat offering several sites for camping. Again you climb a ridge, perhaps serenaded by a mountain chickadee's clear three-note "How-are you"—the "How" a whole note, the "are you"

See maps F2, F3

see MAP F3

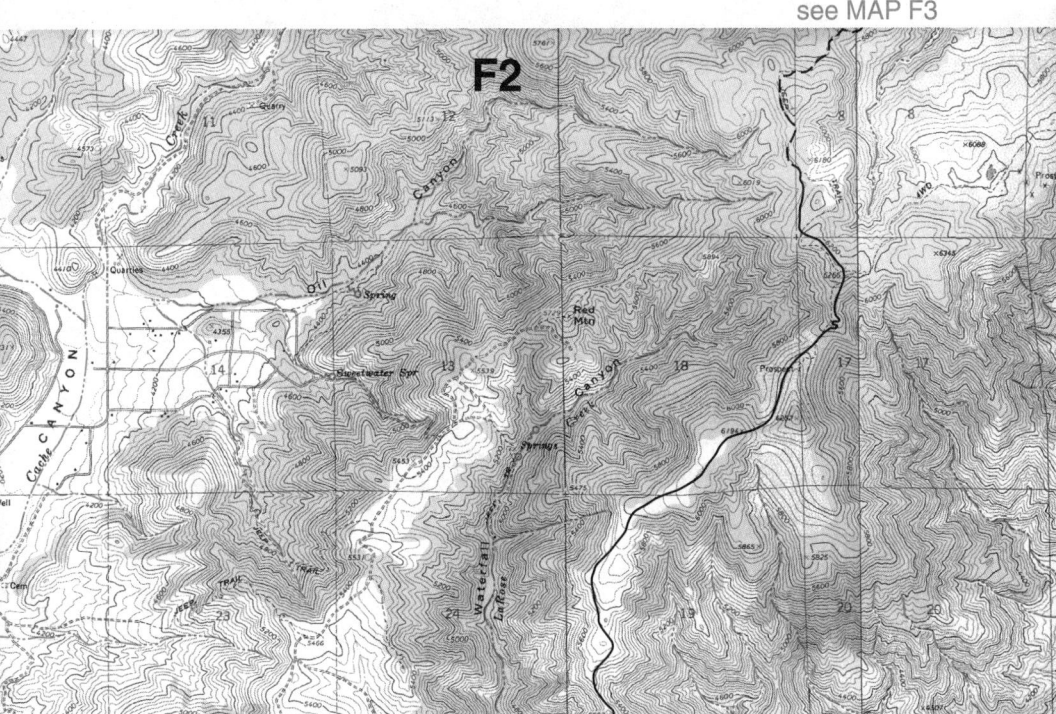

see MAP F1

see MAP F4

F3

see MAP F2

see MAP F5

F4

see MAP F3

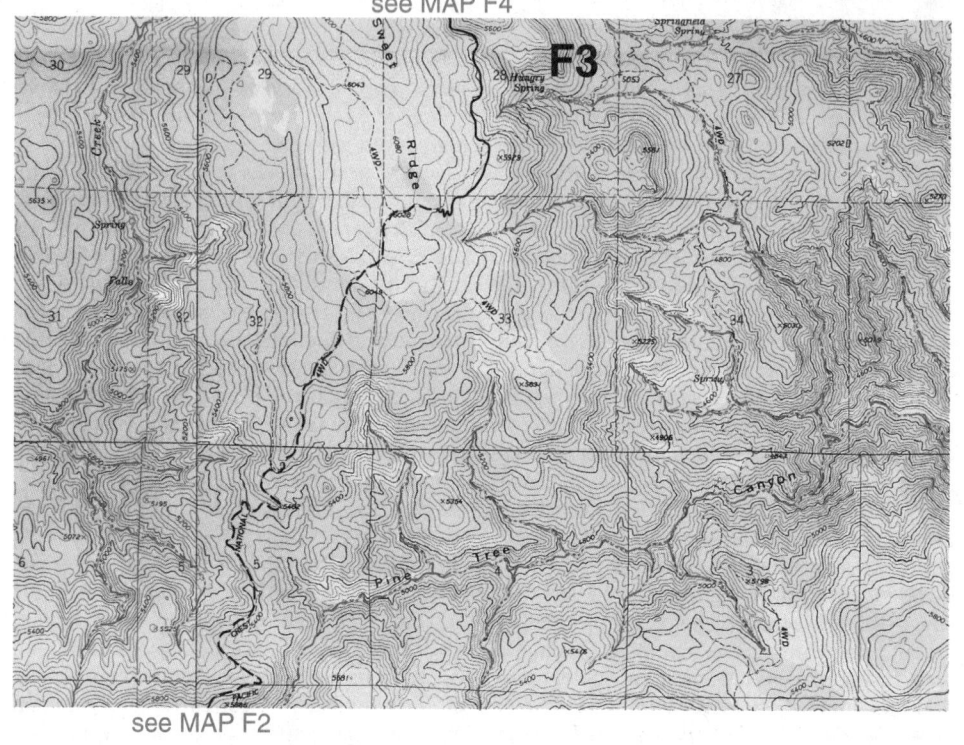

A deciduous oak arches across the PCT

two eighth notes at a lower pitch.

Ahead, as the route eventually descends into a sagebrush swale, you see the first of the 90- and 140-foot wind-turbine towers perched over 5 miles of ridgeline. ▮ *The Vestas V-27 three-blade turbines, used here in the early 1990s Sky River project, are far more efficient than the earlier versions you saw previously on ridges. Total output of Sky River exceeds 600 million kilowatt hours per year—enough to supply electricity for a residential population of 300,000. Now the twirling giant pinwheels produce a mechanical hum to accompany the chickadee's serenades.* ▮ In this hollow the course crosses a dirt road, passes a road that is returning to nature, and forks right where the sign on the locked, gated road to the left declares SKY RIVER RANCH—PRIVATE PROPERTY. In 0.2 mile from the gated road, the PCT branches right (6000-4.3), leaving the jeep road where it becomes closed and abruptly descends.

▮ *Your route ahead crosses several roads to turbines; most are mentioned in the text; none are mapped. The company asks that you not venture near the machines.* ▮

The PCT, a trail again, zigzags, turns sharply left, and crosses both a wide road to turbines and the ragged jeep road you just left. ▮ *Here you see your first view of Olancha Peak far to the north over waves of ridges. Mount Whitney*

beyond, the highest mountain in the lower 48 states, barely reaches above the waves. Pointy Owens Peak rises southeast of Olancha Peak, with Mt. Jenkins at its right. The PCT eventually passes near all of these peaks, and long-distance hikers on the trail are given many opportunities to view this scene as they progress. ▮

Your path, cut on very steep slopes, begins a long, descending traverse around the east side of turbine-bristled Sweet Ridge. It then rounds the flanks of 6698-foot Cache Peak, the highest peak in the southernmost Sierra north of Tehachapi Pass. In time, the trail, passing slender snowmelt streamlets, drops along three switchbacks, crosses a jeep road at an offset junction, and arrives at a resurfaced stone-and-cement trough catching a piped-in, year-round flow from Golden Oaks Spring (5480-3.5). In 1994 the BLM constructed a new spring box, fenced the spring to protect it from cattle contaminants, and installed a new pipe from the box to the trough. This important water source is now easily accessible to hikers and still serves the cattle and wild life in the area. The level cul-de-sac on Zond's private property above the spring and off the adjacent jeep road is no longer posted with NO TRESPASSING signs.

▮ *Springs are important to wildlife, of course, as well as hikers. The area's mule deer, bob-*

See maps F3, F4

F

Hwy. 58-
Hwy. 178

F5

cats, mountain lions and black bears will shy away from this water source while people are near. Bighorn sheep frequented this spring as well as other springs in these mountains as recently as the early 1900s. At that time domestic sheep infected with scabies were released in the area. The scabies spread to the native bighorns, resulting in their demise. In 1978 tule elk were transplanted here from Owens Valley, but most of the elk migrated to lower elevations and found their way to the alfalfa fields in Fremont Valley. ∎

With full water containers to last until Robin Bird Spring, 18.3 miles, you head generally northwest, crossing a closed road, then paralleling a wide road to turbines before crossing it. You resume on trail a few paces up the road and on it traverse steep slopes to eventually round prominent Point 5683. Next, on a pair of switchbacks, you descend below an old jeep road now used to access turbines; where the descent eases you find camping possibilities. You then cross a ravine and climb up its west side. Beyond a switchback, a turbine road and a saddle, you arc west around the extensive drainage of Indian Creek, providing good views of Cache Peak to the south. In time, after noting a white plastic pipe marking a miner's border, you reach an east-west ridge, which you cross via a green gate (5102-6.5) in a cattle fence.

Beyond the gate, the route heads generally west in shade, then swings north to follow a sunny crest, the watershed divide between Caliente Creek to the west and Jawbone Canyon to the east. ∎ *This crest affords comprehensive views of multicolored Jawbone Canyon and, to the northeast, of Kelso Valley and pyramid-shaped Mayan Peak. (The PCT eventually curves alongside distant Mayan Peak.)* ∎ The trail undulates near or on the crest, then descends a north-facing ridge to a blue-oak savannah with a large grassy area to the left nicely suited for camping. Several gleaming quartz rocks form fire rings here. Your route is crossed below the camping area by an east-west road (5010-3.0). ∎ *This road connects with other roads to offer passage from Highway 14 on the east to Highway 58 on the south, but it is a private, gated and locked road, and extremely rough to the west.* ∎

Traveling north, you ascend easily across a grassy ridge with a springtime wildflower sea of baby blue eyes, curve around a minor eastward extension, and then hike along a narrow saddle. The path north of the saddle looks ominous, and it is a steep climb by PCT standards. The curious upslope swath cut through scrub oak followed the original trail design. Grateful you are not panting up that route, you ascend north through a scrub-oak aisle. ∎ *Scrub oak resembles live oak in miniature: its growth is dense; its branches are ridged; its forest is impenetrable without the help of cutting tools.* ∎

Upon turning northwest, you leave the chaparral oak for the domain of lofty Jeffrey pines and spreading black oaks, the first appearance of these pines and oaks on this section of the PCT. If looking for campsites, you will find a shaded area off the path at the north end of the forest. Just beyond the forest you descend to traverse below Hamp Williams Pass (5530-3.3).

Once again you are faced with a steep climb by PCT standards, lined with scrub oak and relieved slightly by four switchbacks. Breaks in the oak cover offer vignettes of Jawbone Canyon Road below. You will cross that road where it winds in the mountains ahead. Here you make a traverse, a zig and a zag, and climb over a saddle to west-facing slopes, again among welcome Jeffrey pines and black oaks. Just where the Piute Mountains begin in the south is uncertain, but you are surely in the Piutes now. You descend on a traverse past two peaks and part way around Weldon Peak before the descent increases down a west-facing ridge, then decreases as you turn northeast to enter a cluster of privately owned small parcels. No camping allowed. Much of the land you crossed in this section was large blocks of privately owned land or BLM-governed land. Your PCT path ends on a curve of a private dirt road (5620-3.2).

Turning right, you proceed up the main private road, permitted for PCT use. You turn left at the first fork at 0.1 mile, pass several spur roads, ease around a locked cable crossing the road, and then meet a T junction (5996-0.8) with a west-descending, prominent unpaved road. Here you keep right, then ascend along a tight right curve, and find the PCT path resuming to the left (6160-0.4). (The road continues to Jawbone Canyon Road 0.2 mile beyond.)

Walking north, on the PCT path again, below and parallel to Jawbone Canyon Road, you

F

Hwy. 58-
Hwy. 178

See maps F4, F5, F6

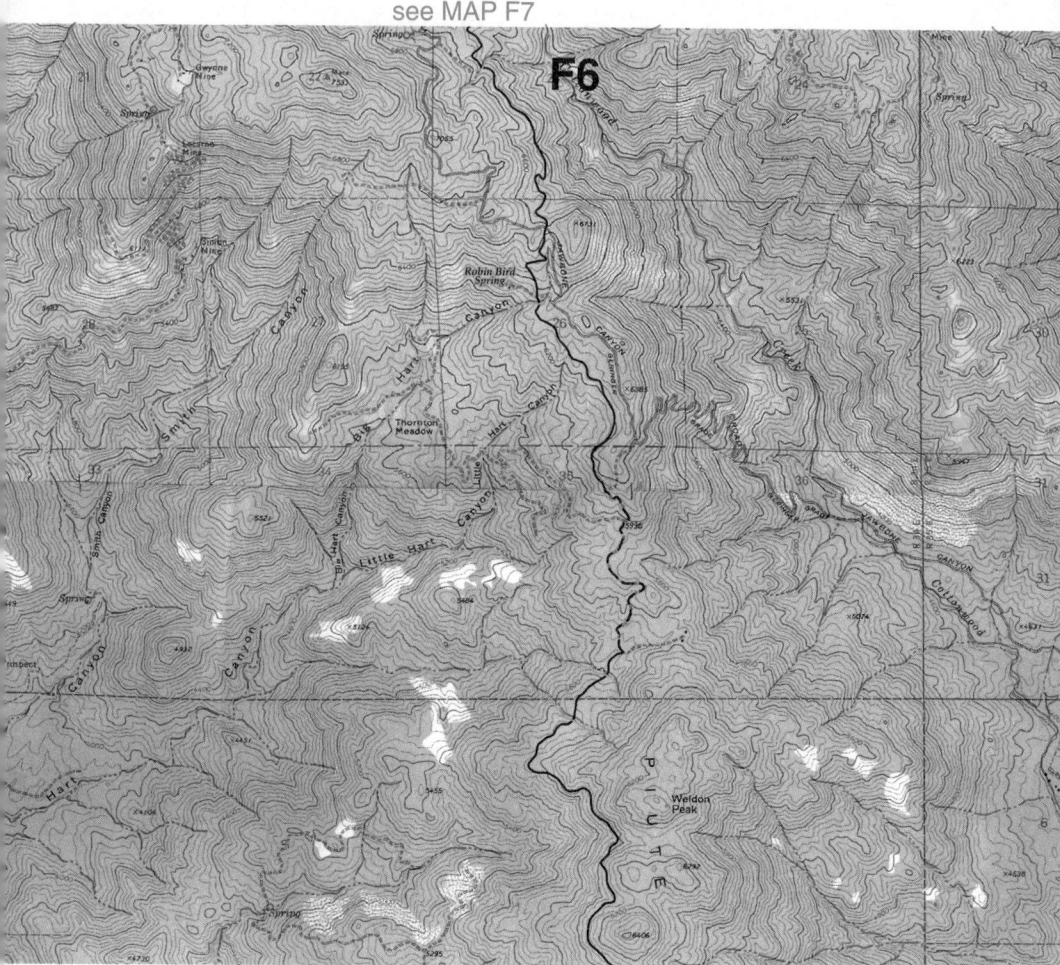

F6

see MAP F5

enter Forest Service land in 0.2 mile and soon angle across a dirt road (6360-1.0).

*　　　*　　　*　　　*

Water access: Your first water source since Golden Oaks Spring is 0.1 mile down this road. In 1994 the Forest Service developed this flowing spring, freed it from cattle contaminants, and piped the water, making it easily accessible to you. They then cleared the enormous amount of rubble of a dilapidated two-story house, leaving a flat area for camping. With a deserved sense of pride, they named this lovely area Robin Bird Spring.

*　　　*　　　*　　　*

Beyond the spring access road, the PCT

switchbacks up to unpaved Jawbone Canyon Road (6620-0.4).

*　　　*　　　*　　　*

Side route: Emergencies only. This lightly traveled PCT access road, Jawbone Canyon Road, leaves east down the Piute Mountains, crosses Kelso Valley, winds among low, exposed hills, and reaches State Highway 14, 26.4 miles later. Limited supplies and groceries are at Jawbone Canyon Store near the junction.

*　　　*　　　*　　　*

North of Jawbone Canyon Road the PCT descends among scattered Jeffrey pines, white firs and mistletoe-trimmed black and live oaks. It drops down a few switchbacks and winds along

See map F6

east-facing slopes where cascades of white-flowered spreading phlox perk up the early-season wayside scenery. In 0.5 mile the trail passes above a seasonal spring hidden by willows; a use path descends next to the spring, but easier water sources are at Cottonwood Creek ahead. The path gently undulates now, passes a magnificent golden oak to your left—a tree climber's delight—then adds gravel to the dirt tread as boulders surrounded by manzanitas appear.

In a short time the trail crosses a willow-lined branch of Cottonwood Creek with possible camping nearby: a good source of water until late summer. The stream, coming from Mace and Grouse meadows on this multi-use mountain, may be water that cows have enjoyed as well. The path briefly parallels another willow-hemmed branch of the slender creek, crosses it on a log footbridge (6480-1.8), and then proceeds above it.

The well-defined path continues to wind and dip, generally heading north. Strips of Jawbone Canyon Road appear to the west before the PCT turns up a canyon, crosses a logging road (6720-1.0) and climbs over a saddle, the watershed divide of Cottonwood and Landers creeks. Within ½ mile, watch for a spring above the trail whose water is caught by a crude cement structure. ∎ *Below the trail squat the roofless remains of a crumbling log cabin with an upright chimney. Apple trees and lilac bushes soften the clutter. This area and its short mine shaft tunneled into a creekbed are worth investigating.* ∎ Back on the trail, you walk above, then switchback down to the headwaters of Landers Creek: a trickle through a pocket meadow with nearby camping potential. In minutes you see an old sluice box sitting among the willows by the creek. Later you switchback down to cross Landers Creek (6300-1.9) and quickly cross back to the east side again.

*   *   *   *

Water access: Before recrossing the creek, you can hike 0.2 mile along the west bank where a dirt road leads to creekside Waterhole Trail Camp. (The dirt road continues to Piute Mountain Road.) The camp has a table and piped-in spring water. Since this is one of the Fire Safe areas in the Piutes, you can have a campfire here even during periods of restricted fire use. You can easily cross Landers Creek here to pick up the PCT again on the east bank.

*   *   *   *

Heading north, the trail remains in the little canyon until the canyon flares near Landers Meadow, spreading to the east. After crossing the meadow's outlet stream, the path bridges a trench and crosses Piute Mountain Road (6220-0.9). The PCT crosses this road again in 3.0 miles.

On the north side of Piute Mountain Road, the Forest Service has installed an ingenious gate across the PCT, flanked by fences. This discourages motorcyclists, but hikers and horses can easily step over it. The trail beyond gently weaves along a rolling, selectively logged pine flat inland from the creek, then meets graded, unpaved SNF Road 29S05 (6300-0.7), unsigned at the junction.

*   *   *   *

Water access: This road leads left to a tree-shaded Fire Safe Area primitive campground in 0.3 mile. A spring above the campground is captured in a tank and piped to splash into a cattle trough, the last source of water for 8.8 miles. A curious mortarless stone hut sans roof sits near the spring.

*   *   *   *

Returning to the PCT, you head east while aloof wallflowers, standing straight and single, display clusters of bright orange blossoms in season, and blue-purple lupines add a dash of contrasting color. Pinyon pines signal your approach to drier climes, and a logging road crosses your path. In time lichen-splashed boulders appear, along with golden oaks and a few dramatic yuccas. ∎ *Yuccas grow tough, daggerlike leaves a foot or more long, with sharp tips that puncture the unwary. The stalks, with massive creamy white blossoms that seem to explode in spring, reach 8–14 feet tall.* ∎ Soon you enter BLM land and meet Piute Mountain Road (6620-2.3) again, this time at the summit of Harris Grade, Piute Mountains' best access. Here you cross both the trail-protecting gate

F

Hwy. 58-
Hwy. 178

See maps F6, F7

see MAP F8

see MAP F6

and the road.

In 0.1 mile, as you begin a descent along the north and then east slopes of St. John Ridge, you again see far off to the north majestic Olancha Peak, reigning over the Kern Plateau. ▮ *To the northeast, pointed Owens Peak with curved, serrated Mt. Jenkins next to it, divides the desert from the mountains, and all three peaks delineate the Sierra crest.* ▮ While gradually losing elevation, you eventually descend by switchbacks and a long traverse across the slopes of St. John Ridge, passing en route a motorcycle path occupying a gully.

In time, and after two more switchbacks, you spot a post just below the path near a large fremontia bush. ▮ *It marks the boundary of a mining claim. Fremontias especially attract attention when frocked in large, waxlike yellow flowers.* ▮ Farther below, a jeep road climbs up a steep grade. Soon in the east the serpentine sliver of paved Kelso Valley Road appears. Mayan Peak is in the east, and, to its right, the Butterbredt Canyon road winds up to the Sierra crest. Your exposed trail descends through colonies of bitterbrush and its companion plants to meet Kelso Valley Road at a pass (4953-4.8).

*   *   *   *

Side route: Lightly traveled Kelso Valley Road leads north 19.7 miles to Highway 178, which crosses the lower Sierra from Highway 99 in Bakersfield on the west to Highway 14 on the east, along the desert. Emergency supplies are available in towns around Isabella Lake, west on 178. (A short cut to the water source described next leads 1.7 miles to the left down this road, to the stream beyond the large cottonwoods and willows. Return 0.5 mile to the Butterbredt Canyon road, SC123; hike up it 0.7 mile to pick up the PCT—total 2.9 miles.)

*   *   *   *

After crossing the summit of Kelso Valley Road where it loses its pavement, you approach two distinct paths: an OHV path and the PCT. The OHV path climbs the ridge ahead, becoming one in a web of trails that covers the transitional range you are about to hike: an OHV playground on weekends. These OHV paths cut erosively across your trail, and new ones are added periodically. Although the BLM posts signs that clearly indicate the path of the PCT and forbid OHV use of it, it nevertheless receives their heavy traffic. This use has led to ruts in the trail, to layers of loose dirt on it, and to tight, annoying undulations along its entire length in the transitional range.

You take the trail to the left that heads in a southeast direction on a crenulated course across slopes mantled with bitterbrush, sagebrush and Mormon tea—all dominant brush throughout the range. Next you curve across a gully where, downslope to the left, pepper-colored debris excavated from several claims collectively known as the St. John Mine becomes visible. ▮ *Beginning in 1867, miners extracted gold here for over 70 years. Most of them lived in the now-vanished settlement of Sageland, just a few miles north.* ▮

The route turns northeast to descend on a prominent ridge, curves across a ravine with lines of OHV tracks, traverses north-facing slopes while crossing a band of Joshua trees, and eventually meets the Butterbredt Canyon road, SC123, near the mouth of its canyon (4540-2.1).

*   *   *   *

Water access: Before continuing, check your water supply. At this intersection, year-round water is available at a spring-fed stream 0.7 mile down the Butterbredt Canyon road, then 0.5 mile down paved Kelso Valley Road; a 500-foot elevation loss. A group of cottonwood and willow trees just west of the paved road marks the spring, but the water flows freer just beyond. An unused cement cow trough lies hidden by brush near the road in this private grazing land that abounds with cows. The next dependable water is at Willow Springs, 4.1 miles from the Butterbredt Canyon road junction, then 1.8 miles down-canyon with 760 feet elevation drop.

*   *   *   *

The shadeless, often hot and windy PCT ahead continues from this offset junction at the unpaved road by climbing switchbacks up the ridge between Butterbredt Canyon to the right and an east-trending gulch to the left, then ascending

F

Hwy. 58-
Hwy. 178

See maps F7, F8, F9

on an easy-to-moderate grade just south of the gulch. The slopes of the gulch eventually flatten as the path traces the valley's elongated curve to the east. ▮ *The temple of 6108-foot Mayan Peak to your left rules out northwestward views of the Piute Mountains, but it cannot block out the ribbon of Kelso Valley Road draped on a shoulder of the Sierra crest.* ▮

The trail crosses a bike path on a south saddle of barely discernable Point 5402; the path west could confuse southbound hikers. The PCT descends to wind around two canyons, then ascends gently to contour past many lesser ravines cut in the north slope of Pinyon Mountain. The impounded waters of Willow Spring glisten like a distant mirage far below while around you a moderately dense stand of pinyon pines cloaks the north slopes, the only forest for miles. ▮ *Long-eared owls have been seen on the eastern edge of this forest. Look under the trees by the trail for their pellets, composed of bone and fur regurgitated by the bird.* ▮

As you proceed east, the ranks of the forest dwindle and trees are replaced by xerophytic brush. Still on the slopes of Pinyon Mountain, you reach a multi-road-and-path junction on a Sierra crest saddle (5283-4.1). Pinyon Mountain, a steep 0.8-mile climb of 900 feet to the southeast, has a camping area protected by boulders and pinyon trees, and offers a full view that is especially enticing when the sun hangs low in the southern sky and the shadows stretch long on the desert floor.

F
Hwy. 58-
Hwy. 178

*   *   *   *

Water access: If you need water, Willow Spring is 1.8 miles left, down-canyon, on Road SC103 to the northwest. The BLM plans to upgrade this water supply. To find the pond, where there are no willows but plenty of cows, look for a fence above the road to the right and the outlet stream that flows on the road from the spring. Road SC103 continues to Kelso Valley Road. The next reliable water is at lower Yellow Jacket Spring, 15.9 miles from the Willow Spring road junction, and 0.7 mile down-canyon with 400 feet elevation loss. Road SC103 east of the junction passes Dove Spring in 3.3 miles on its way to Red Rock Canyon State Park (no supplies) and State Highway 14.

See maps F9, F10

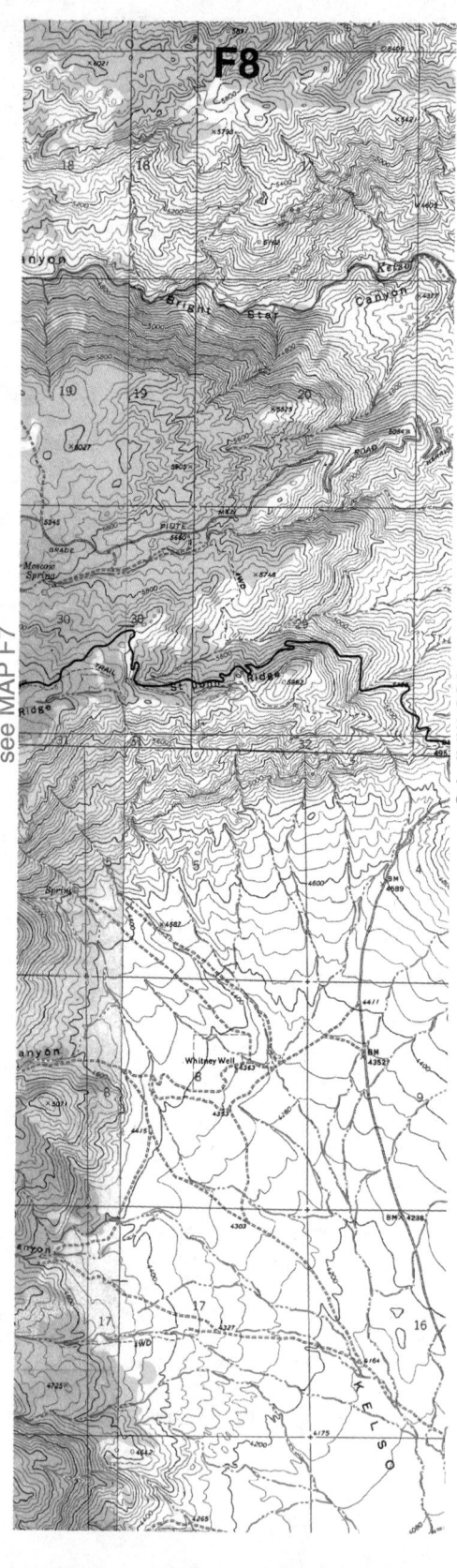

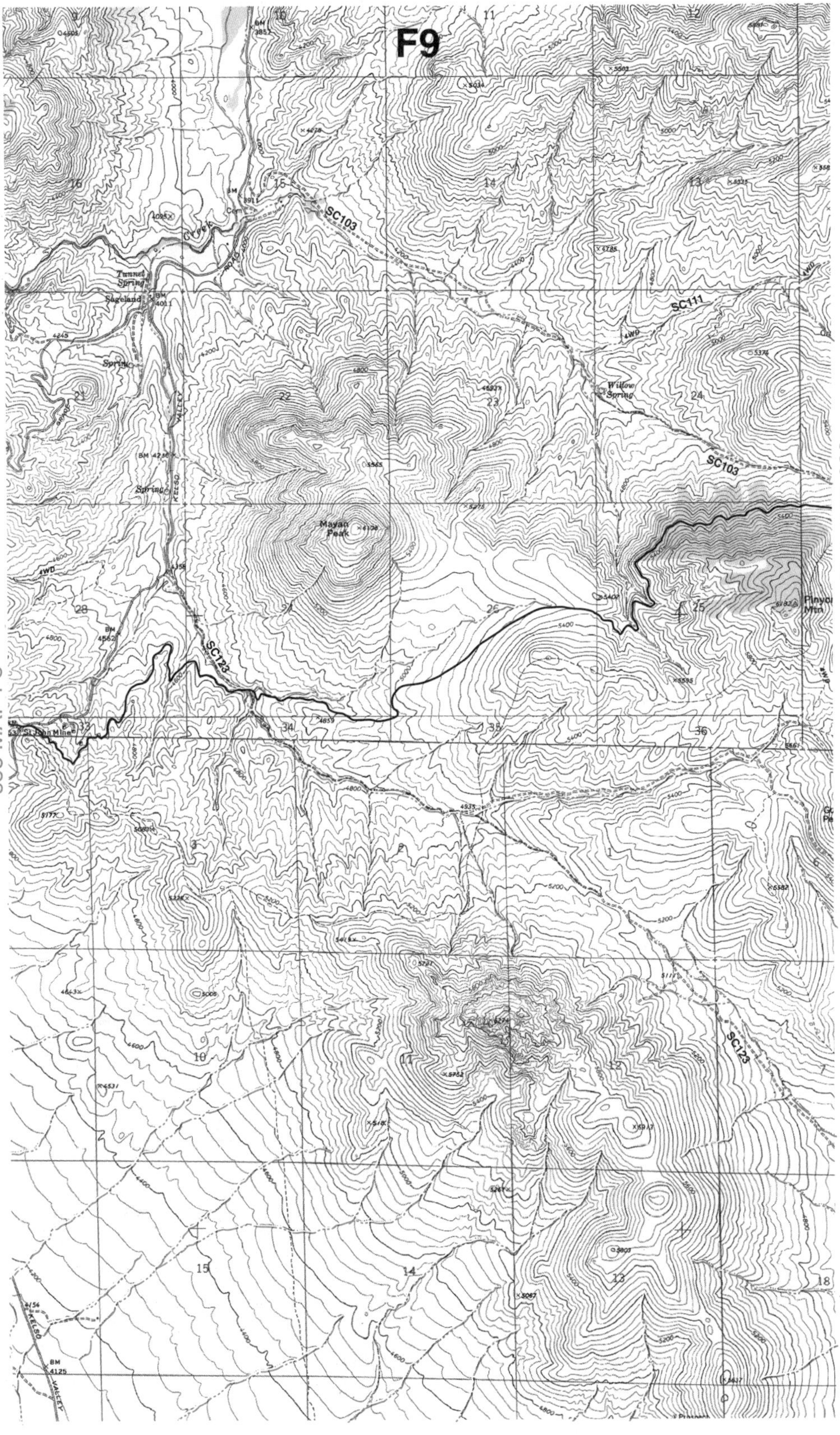

see MAP F10

see MAP F8

SC103

SC111

SC103

Tunnel Spring

Sageland

Spring

Willow Spring

Mayan Peak

Spring

4WD

SC122

Pinyon Mtn

SC123

Multi-road and cycle path junction Sierra crest saddle

Hwy. 58-
Hwy. 178

F

*   *   *   *

You leave the saddle to wind north around gullied, east-facing slopes, climbing a little at first and then contouring. Along the way Indian Wells Valley, the El Paso Mountains and Fremont Valley intercept your gaze as it sweeps the eastern horizon from north to south. Presently you arrive at another multi-road-and-trail junction (5382-1.6) on a saddle with flats for camping. Road SC111 leads west past the Sunset Mine road to connect with the Willow Spring road just below the spring and pond, and east to connect with the Dove Spring road just above its spring.

You diagonal northwest across the junction saddle, then wind gently upward, staying west of the crest. Glancing downslope you can see the rubble of Sunset Mine. ∎ *Upon closer inspection, you find two shafts about 35 feet and 70 feet deep covered with plywood held in place by iron belt-driven flywheels, patented 1916; a hulk of a rusted bus; and rails from the mine to the chute.* ∎ Then you see below the litter around two more prospects. Again you climb the slopes beside and then across a road before reaching a ridgecrest saddle (5700-1.1). ∎ *To the west, prospect digs, a prominent ore chute and, next*

to parallel concrete slabs that slash the slope, an overturned Ford, all of which indicate the past activity here at Danny Boy Gold Mine. ∎

Wyleys Knob, the 6465-foot radio-tower-crowned summit to the north, now stands as a gauge of your progress. From the saddle, the wide PCT path to the right makes a moderate descent northeast via two rounded switchbacks to intersect Road SC328 on a crestline saddle (5300-0.8). Ahead the austere journey takes you generally north over a low hill to another crestline saddle (5380-0.2), where Road SC47 crosses.

The path gains a low east-west ridge 0.2 mile beyond the saddle, where there are good campsites among the boulders to the right. Next the PCT dips to a Joshua-tree-covered gap, climbs north on a moderate grade while paralleling a gully, and then curves along a ridge. The gradient eases and the trail first winds around spur ridges emanating from the Sierra crest, then crosses a gap in the crest itself. The Scodie Mountains and the granitic outcrop of Wyleys Knob loom to the north. The trail traverses just east of the crest and passes three rounded, weathered crestline boulders that form a barely balanced stack. Below Hill 5940 a switchback shortcut by cyclists, leads you to skirt a hill on

See map F10

F10

F

Hwy. 58-
Hwy. 178

Bird Spring

Canyon

SC120

SC47

SC47

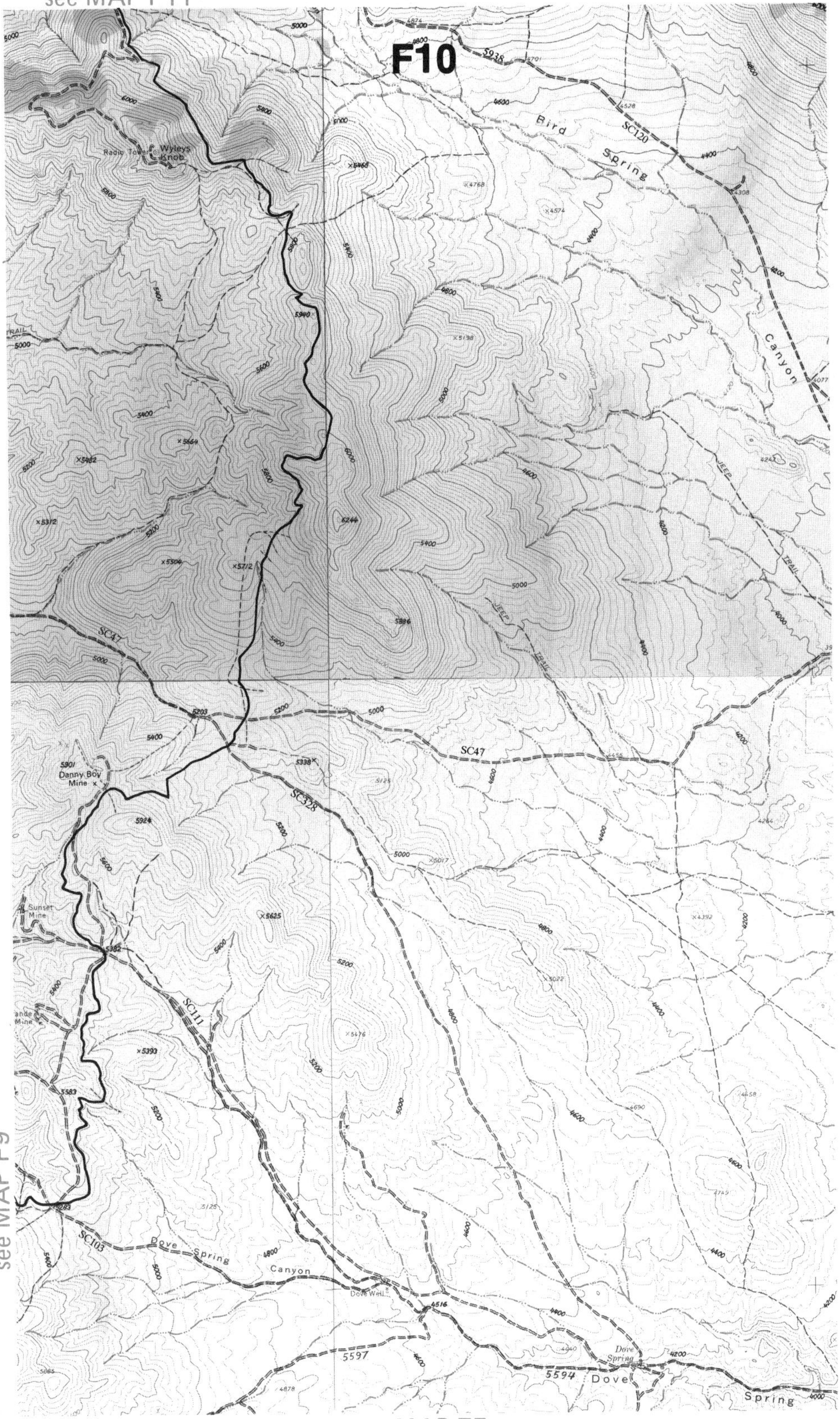

SC328

SC111

SC103

Dove Spring Canyon

Dove Well

Dove Spring

Danny Boy Mine

Sunset Mine

the crest, then to diagonal across an intersection (5740-3.0) with Road SC42.

Now your moderately ascending route curves west, passes granite bluffs and, below Wyleys Knob, begins a gentle-to-moderate descent. It first drops among pinyon pines but later crosses exposed northeast-facing slopes. The path travels just downslope from the Wyleys Knob road, SC24, and quickly reaches a junction (5355-2.5) at Bird Spring Pass, where camping is possible. ∎ *This pass was first crossed by Caucasians when in March 1854 John Charles Fremont, on his fifth expedition west, led his party through this passage.* ∎

*   *   *   *

Side route: Unpaved but maintained, the Bird Spring road, SC120, is the most used access road to the Pacific Crest Trail in the transitional mountain range. From the saddle it drops west to paved Kelso Valley Road and east to the aqueduct road, north to SC65 and east to State Highway 14.

*   *   *   *

∎ *Thanks to the sweeping California Desert Protection Act signed into law by President Clinton in 1994, you now enter an unbroken network of Congressionally mandated wildernesses that take you through the Sierra. Ahead lies the Kiavah Wilderness. Unlike the "rock and ice" areas of remarkable beauty first encompassed in the National Wilderness Preservation System established in 1964, this 88,290-acre area is designated to preserve the biota of a semiarid land. You know the area as*

See maps F10, F11

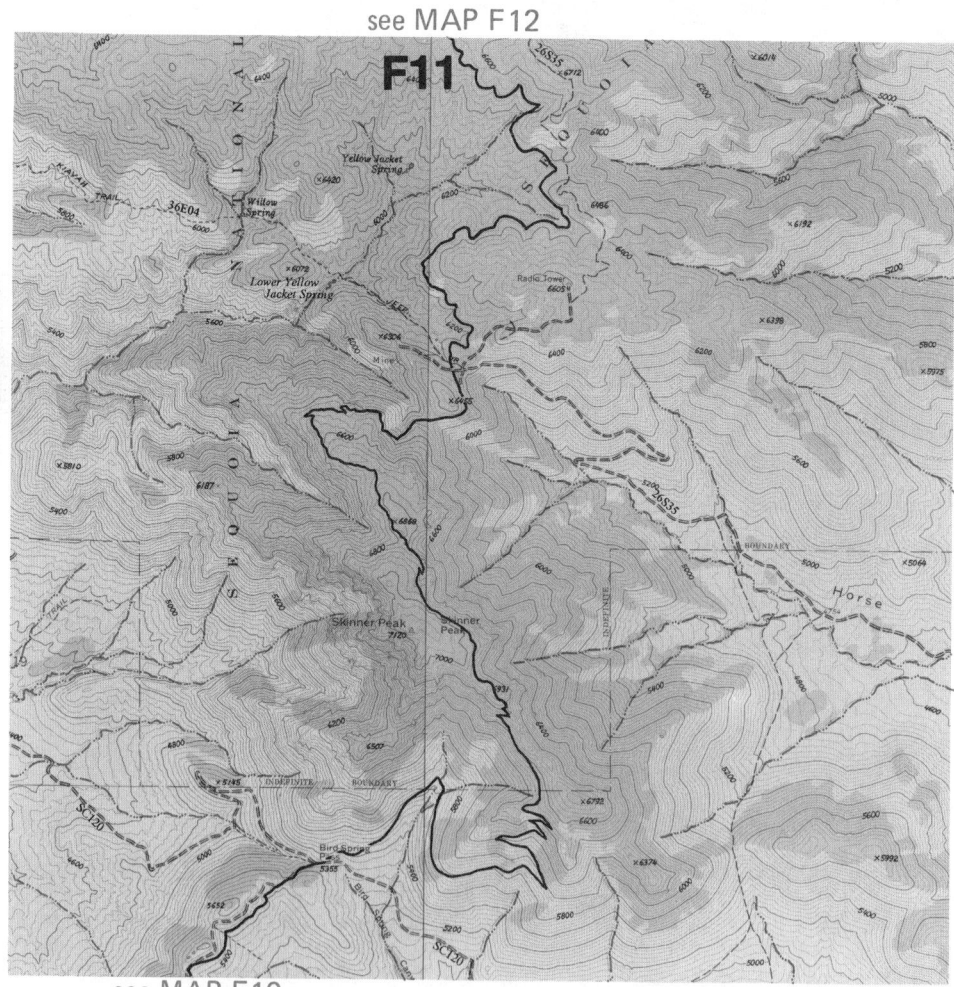

see MAP F12

see MAP F10

F

Hwy. 58-
Hwy. 178

Scodie Mountain, but the Native Americans called it Kiavah. ∎

Leaving Bird Spring Pass, you ascend on the PCT northeast into a side canyon along a sandy path ornamented with nosegays of blue penstemons—showy tubular flowers, and enter into Sequoia National Forest and Kiavah Wilderness. Ahead you pass a trail-register box and a spur road, then climb south from the canyon's wash. ∎ *The curious fenced-in square seen below is a quail guzzler constructed to catch rainwater for the local fauna—at this point you could use a PCT guzzler! An occasional Joshua tree and some straggly pinyon pines dot the slopes that abruptly slant away to the vast alluvium of Bird Spring Canyon, spreading far below.* ∎

Southwest across the pass the radio tower, its road, and the PCT slowly recede as you climb moderately up long-legged, then short-legged switchbacks, and cross over a ridge with a westward orientation (6460-2.4). You can find small flats to sleep on here. After a long ascending traverse and several short, steep switchbacks, you hike up a ridge, also with room for possible waterless camping, above the Horse Canyon watershed. ∎ *To the north, the High Sierra rises above the crests of east-west Scodie Mountain ridges, while around you manzanitas and golden oaks join the scattered pinyon pines and numerous spring wildflowers.* ∎

The PCT soon reaches its highest point (6940-1.3) in this section, then drops along a switchback and descends northwest close to the ridgecrest above a drainage of Cane Canyon. ∎ *Across the canyon the northern extension of the Piute Mountains borders the valley of Kelso Creek.* ∎

Following two quick switchbacks, your trail turns east across north-facing slopes, allowing glimpses of the eastern reaches of Isabella Lake. Lower on the path you see a mining scar gouged in creamy quartz rock across the ravine, and a telephone microwave relay tower perched on a point to the northeast. The route's descent eases at a saddle, then traverses 1/# mile across the grassy slopes of minor Peak 6455, above sprawling Horse Canyon. Heading north, the PCT cuts across a road that reaches the mine you just saw, and seconds later crosses another road (6260-2.3), both branching from the Horse Canyon road.

*   *   *   *

Side route: The maintained Horse Canyon road, SC65, also a PCT access road, serves the relay station and descends east to Highway 14. It is not a part of the wilderness, and the rutted northward extension of the road, which the PCT later uses for its route, probably is outside the wilderness as well.

*   *   *   *

Water access: A trio of springs is west, down the steep second branching road. In 1994 the Forest Service began the permit process for upgrading lower Yellow Jacket Spring, the closest to the PCT. The plan includes a spring box enclosed by fencing and a pipe to carry the water out, making it easily accessible to hikers. They promised a good flow, but, like all "wild" water, it will need to be filtered. To reach the spring, descend 0.7 mile to the first broad intersecting canyon. Lower Yellow Jacket Spring is to the left off the trail.

The Forest Service may even upgrade upper Yellow Jacket Spring—0.5 mile right, up the broad side canyon, then 0.2 mile up the left fork—and Willow Spring—0.5 mile farther down the road. The next water source near the PCT is McIvers Spring, 7.0 miles ahead of the second branching road junction.

*   *   *   *

∎ *Back on the PCT, abundant pinyon pines, the dominant tree on Scodie Mountain, supply ample shade. The distinguishing characteristics of the pinyon, which grows in high desert ranges, are the single, gray-green needle, the blackish-barked trunk, the much-branched crown and the 2x3-inch cones. You are allowed to gather the nuts of this tree for noncommercial use.* ∎

∎ *Pinyon nuts tucked beneath the scales of the pitchy pine cones ripen in early autumn. To gather pinyon nuts, collect closed cones in a brown paper bag; then, to open them, place the bag in an oven and set the heat on low. After the cones open and the nuts have been loosened, shell them, and eat them raw or roast them again in oil and a little salt.* ∎

∎ *The fall gathering season of protein-rich*

F

Hwy. 58-
Hwy. 178

See map F11

see MAP F13

F12

see MAP F11

Hwy. 58-
Hwy. 178

pinyon nuts was one of reverence and fellowship for Indian families. After a solemn ritual,
the men shook the trees or loosened the cones
with hooks fashioned on willow poles. Children
gathered the cones in woven willow baskets for
the women to roast. Some nuts were eaten
whole, but most were ground into flour. The
grinding action created the many holes (mortars) in boulders you find scattered about the
mountains. These nuts are still gathered by
Native American descendants as part of their
diet. Continuing this gathering binds today's
Native Americans to this important aspect of
their past. ∎

Below the tower, the PCT gradually gains elevation as it undulates and weaves in and around
scalloped slopes, and then below the road to
McIvers Spring. At length it reaches and joins
that road (6670-4.5), arcing east. ∎ The "Ichabod
Crane" forest of pinyon pines continues to surround you as you walk northeast along the road.
The naturally denuded lower branches, gnarled
and twisted, make contorted figurations that
awaken your imagination. ∎

Abruptly, the trees give way to a sagebrush/
buckbrush expanse, and then forest reappears.
In less than a mile after the PCT left the path, a
short road forks sharply left off your route, and
then within the next mile two spur roads fork
right. Some rills cross your road that have early-
spring water and late-spring puddles of laven-
der-flowered, inch-high "belly" plants; and, 0.3
mile before the PCT route returns to path, a
seasonal brook flows across it.

At a fork (6680-2.2) the PCT route leaves the
road and resumes as trail heading northeast.

*   *   *   *

Water access: If you need water or a campsite, you can stay on the road for 0.3 mile to
reach McIvers Spring. The next water is 7.4
miles ahead at Walker Pass Campground.

*   *   *   *

∎ Snuggled among picturesque slabs at the
spring is a batten-board hut with porch and
outhouse once owned by McIvers and Weldon,
who equipped it with the bare necessities of a
1938 rustic retreat. Although run down, it remains today. Hunters, motorcyclists and OHVers
have used it over the years, as the litter and
graffiti attest. Barring a drought, some water
issues from this spring year-round, and good
campsites abound here in this bright green oasis among the gray-green pinyons. The Forest
Service plans to upgrade this spring as well. ∎

At the junction where trail resumes, you hike
on an ascending, undulating path. ∎ Manzanita
appears along with a few stands of Jeffrey pine
and black oak. The declivitous slopes of Boulder Canyon fall away to the southeast, and vistas of the Mojave Desert and the ethereal San
Gabriel-San Bernardino mountains appear
through the haze. ∎ Soon you round some three-
story boulders, dashed with rust and chartreuse
lichen, supporting a pinyon pine tenaciously
growing from a slight crack. Leaving the gentle
tableland, you descend on north-facing slopes,
with views of the Mt. Whitney group in the distant north and, in the northeast, the top of
Olancha Peak.

See maps F11, F12, F12

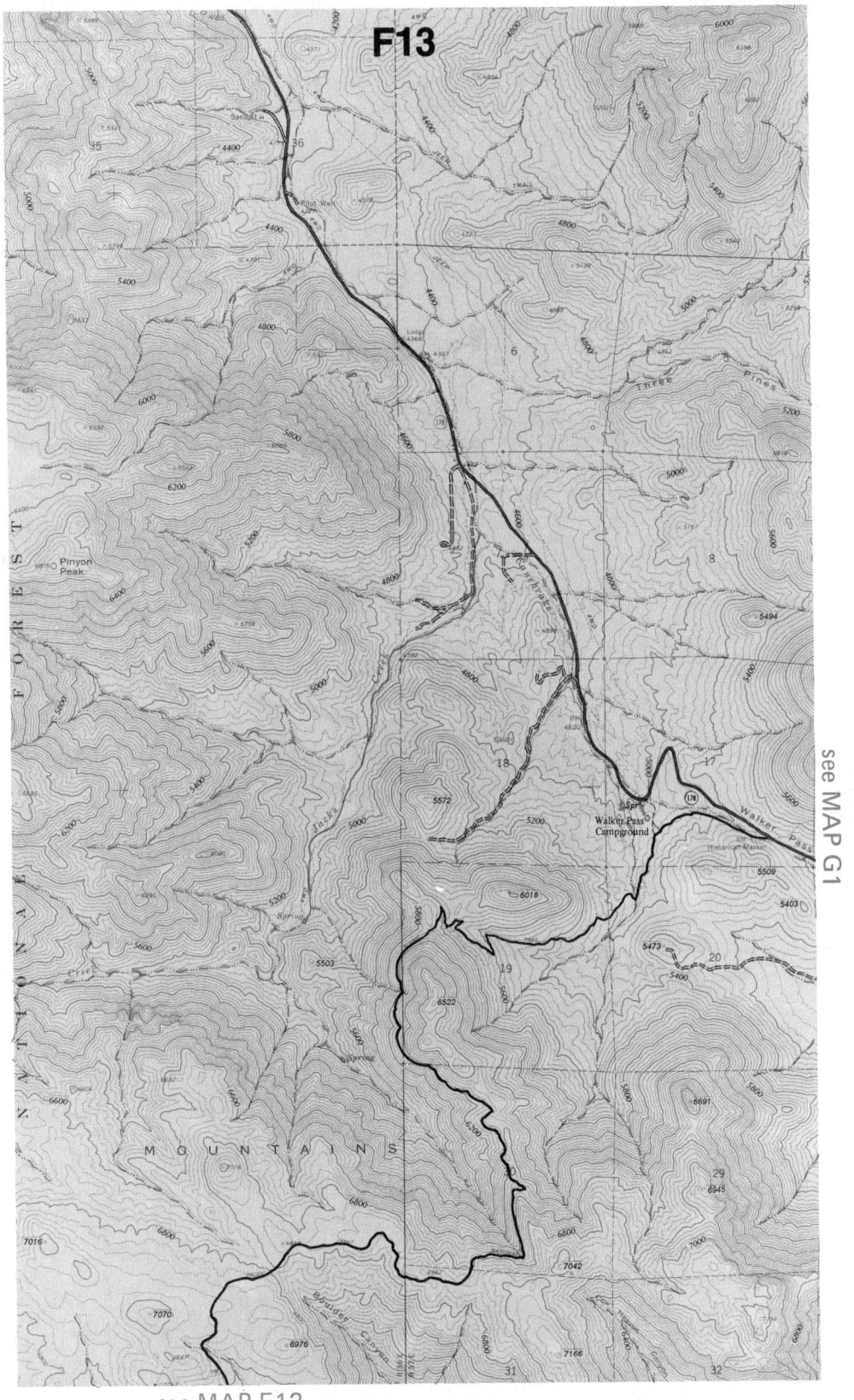

see MAP G1

see MAP F12

Next the trail curves around a sharp canyon crease (6680-3.0). Beyond, the PCT briefly reaches over the ridgetop at a switchback where you catch a fleeting glimpse of the Owens Peak group and the hairpin curve of Highway 178, with Walker Pass Campground at the south end of that curve. Far to the north, the slash of Canebrake Road cuts across slopes, and to the northeast the PCT rises above Walker Pass. The trail continues on a long descent across steep westfacing slopes high above Jacks Creek Canyon. In time it passes a use trail angling down the slope to Jacks Creek, crosses a slight ridgeline saddle (5860-2.2), and descends on the mountain's northeast-facing slopes.

After the second switchback down the mountainside, you round just below a ridgetop where, obscured from your view but easily reached, the Forest Service has placed a sub-stantial guzzler for small animals. You then skirt along the lower slopes of Peak 6018. ∎ *Among other plants along this section of the PCT, you may see an occasional large, tissue-paper-thin, white flower of a prickly poppy—resembling a fried egg, sunny side up.* ∎

Quite soon the trail crosses the usually dry bed of Canebrake Creek, leaves Kiavah Wilderness, and crosses a path (5100-2.1) leading 0.1 mile to the comfortable Walker Pass Trailhead Campground, built especially for PCT trekkers. If the camp faucets are turned off, spring water flows from a pipe into a 9-foot-square cement-enclosed "cattail garden" cow trough, to the left of Highway 178, 0.1 mile down, next to the 30 MILES PER HOUR sign.

The PCT continues to Walker Pass winding northeast and exiting at a historical marker (5246-0.6).

See map F13

F

Hwy. 58-
Hwy. 178

Pine needles soften PCT path in cool Piute Mountains

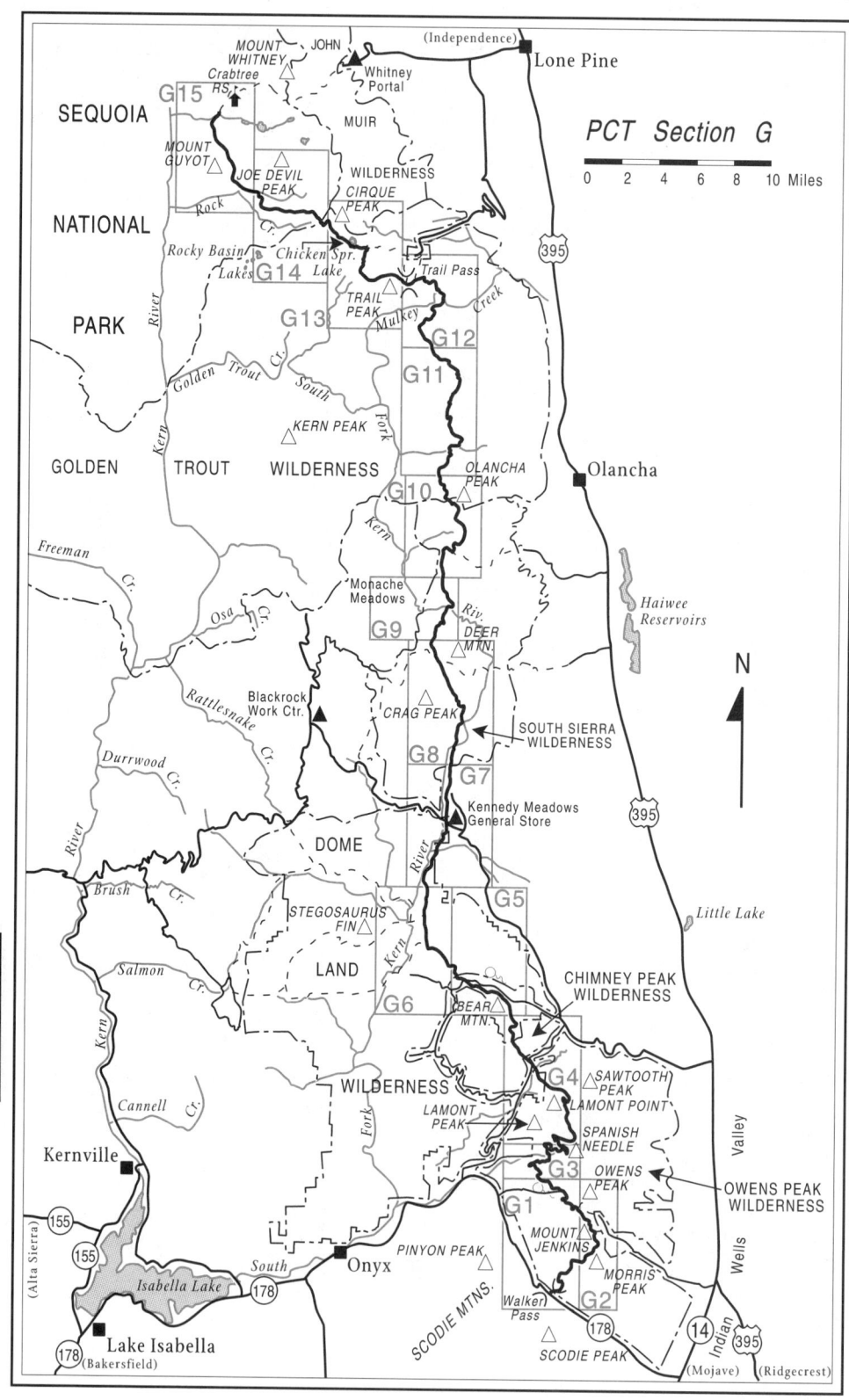

PCT Section G

0   2   4   6   8   10 Miles

N

Section G
Highway 178 to Mt. Whitney

Introduction: Near the end of this section PCT hikers reach the celebrated High Sierra, with its 14,492-foot Mt. Whitney, the highest point in the contiguous United States. Your journey there passes entirely within federally designated wildernesses on the Southern Sierra's Kern Plateau, a land of meadows and mountains. Hikers in this nearly pristine country can enjoy the sinuous South Fork Kern River, included in the prestigious National Wild and Scenic Rivers System; sprawling Monache Meadows, the largest meadow in the Sierra; groves of high-elevation, twisted, foxtail-pine trees; and vast lands of solitude where the only sounds are the serenades of nature.

As always, the PCT seeks the high crest whenever possible, and hence it traces the semiarid eastern heights of the Southern Sierra. This often-exposed country offers a series of expansive, panoramic views.

Declination: 14¼°E throughout this section.

Points on Route	S→N	Mi. Btwn. Pts.	N→S
Walker Pass at Highway 178	0.0		113.5
		11.5	
Joshua Tree Spring	11.5		102.0
		16.8	
Canebrake Road near Chimney Creek Campground	28.3		85.2
		7.9	
Long Valley Loop Road	36.2		77.3
		13.0	
Sherman Pass/Kennedy Mdws. Rd. nr. gen. store	49.2		64.3
		2.4	
Kennedy Meadows Campground	51.6		61.9
		11.5	
South Fork Kern River bridge in Monache Mdws.	63.1		50.4
		4.4	
Olancha Pass Trail	67.5		46.0
		3.6	
saddle west of Olancha Peak	71.1		42.4
		6.1	
Death Canyon creek	77.2		36.3
		14.0	
Trail Pass Trail	91.2		22.3
		4.8	
Cottonwood Pass Trail	96.0		17.5
		0.6	
Chicken Spring Lake's outlet	96.6		16.9
		10.1	
Rock Creek crossing	106.7		6.8
		6.0	
Mt. Whitney lateral/Crabtree Meadows	112.7		0.8
		0.8	
John Muir Trail junction	113.5		0.0

**G
Hwy. 178-
Mt. Whitney**

Supplies: The closest post office and groceries to Walker Pass are in Onyx, 17.6 miles west off Highway 178. The next provisions are at Kennedy Meadows General Store, 49.9 trail miles north of Walker Pass, where there are groceries, gas, and usually a Saturday night movie. The owner will pick up your packages at Inyokern P.O., east of the mountains, for a small fee. (To confirm this service, enclose SASE. See "Post Offices" section in Ch. 2 for address.)

For major resupplying at the north end of the Kern Plateau, descend 2.1 miles north from Trail Pass to the parking lot at the end of Horseshoe Meadow Road and hitchhike 22.8 miles down it and the Whitney Portal Road to Lone Pine.

Permits: Short-trip hikers will need a permit for Golden Trout Wilderness and Sequoia National Park. They will need only a fire permit, good for one calendar year, for the other wildernesses and for nonwilderness areas.

Special Problems

Bears: Though bears are not much of a problem in the Southern Sierra until you reach Sequoia National Park, rare incidents of bears seeking hikers' food have been reported. Therefore, it is best to hang your food throughout this section wherever possible. Bears are not interested in you, only your food.

Before the 1960s, a backpacker in the mountains rarely had to worry about a black bear stealing his food. But somewhere along the line, black bears learned that people carry delicious food in their packs. As backpackers increased in numbers, their food became an ever more desirable resource for hungry bears. By the start of the 1970s, the backcountry had a serious problem with marauding bears. Backpackers were urged to hang their food on a tree limb. Bears, being very intelligent animals, learned how to get most of the food, regardless of what measures were taken, and sows passed this knowledge on to their cubs.

The national parks of California now have two counters to the bear threat. At great expense, they have placed heavy metal, bearproof food lockers at the most popular camping areas and at all campgrounds. They also sell or rent to backpackers cylindrical bearproof containers weighing under three pounds, which could probably carry a five-day food supply. Lacking either of these conveniences, backpackers have to hang their food in trees. In the parks they are subject to a fine for noncompliance.

A fairly reliable method of bearbagging has evolved: the counterbalance method. First find a tree with a branch that will support the weight of your food but not of a bear or even a cub. Your food should hang at least 10 feet from the trunk and 12 feet from the ground. Put your food and anything with an odor—e.g., toothpaste, garbage—in two sacks. Tie a rock to a strong, lightweight rope and throw the rock over the branch. Next tie the heavier sack to the rope and haul it all the way up to the branch. Now tie the lighter food sack as high up on the rope as you can. Then stuff the extra rope into the bag. Finally, push the lighter bag up with a stick until both bags are at the same level. Use the stick in the morning to push up one sack, thus lowering the other.

Another method is to stuff your sack far enough into a deep crack in a rock that bears cannot get it but you can (and rodents can, too). Or hang your food over a cliff, then somehow conceal the anchored end of the rope. With either of these methods you will have to rodent-proof your sacks—try a foul-smelling spray—mosquito repellent?

If all fails and bruin gets your food, he is your guest. Do not try to retrieve it; he is bigger than you are!

Lions: This is also mountain-lion habitat, but lions have been seen so infrequently that you can consider yourself fortunate if you catch a glimpse of one. If one gets too close, face it with eye contact, do not stoop—look as big as possible, back off slowly, and fight if attacked.

Snow: At any time of year, be prepared for unexpected snow storms in the Sierra. In some years, through hikers will find ice and deep snow when they arrive in the high country. Hiking through the snow-covered Sierra with its wondrous scenery can be an incredible adventure, but it should be attempted only by very competent, strong hikers. In snow conditions an ice axe is highly recommended. It has many uses: as a walking stick for balance in snow, as a tool to chop steps in ice or hard snow, as a brake to stop a slide after a fall. Skill with compass is also recommended: few markers or signs indicate a snow-obscured trail. Proper clothing is essential, of course, and knowledge of hypothermia symptoms and treatment is a must. Snow travel is fatiguing and slow; hiking early in the day when the snowpack is firm may be helpful.

Some hikers take the bus through Owens Valley to bypass the Sierra snow, then return to travel the high country last, before the next winter's storms set in. One alternative is to experience the snow until you reach Trail Pass, and there decide whether or not to exit. If exiting, descend to Horseshoe Meadow and hope to hitchhike to Lone Pine to catch a bus. Rides may be scarce before snowmelt. However, the 22.8-mile distance down the road offers breathtaking views of Owens Valley and the distant snow-capped mountains. This plan also helps avoid crossing Sierra streams when they are swift and swollen with snowmelt, and avoids emerging swarms of mosquitoes too. Anticlimactic? Maybe, but think of finishing your PCT odyssey in the High Sierra during its most accommodating season.

Maps: *Walker Pass*
Owens Peak
Lamont Peak
Sacatar Canyon
Rockhouse Basin
Crag Peak
Long Canyon

Monache Mountain
Haiwee Pass
Templeton Mountain
Olancha
Cirque Peak
Johnson Peak
Mount Whitney

―――――――――――― **The Route** ――――――――――――

You need to hydrate yourself well before starting your hike. The next water is at Joshua Tree Spring, 11.5 miles. Since the California Clean Water Act passed in 1988, the standard for healthful drinking water has become so stringent that agencies who test their backcountry piped water seldom find it meets the high level of purity the California Act requires. At the spring in 1993 and at the Chimney Creek Campground, slightly higher than acceptable levels of uranium were found. (It is reasonable to assume that the free-flowing, untested stream water would show the same result.) The end product of uranium is lead, and it is cumulative in the body; you would not want to drink this chemical every day of your life. However, you are just passing through, and the minimal amount of impurities you would swallow seems negligible.

Because of the propensity for winter rock slides on the steep slopes of Mt. Jenkins, equestrians are urged to contact the BLM's Caliente Resource Area in Bakersfield for current conditions.

The PCT resumes north of Highway 178 opposite the Walker Pass historical marker (5246'). The trail soon enters 74,640-acre Owens Peak Wilderness. ∎ *It and Chimney Peak Wilderness ahead were mandated by Congress in 1994 by the California Desert Protection Act, designed to keep the area in its natural state and to protect its diversity of plant and animal life.* ∎

You ascend moderately northeast, where the trail makes a highly visible line across steep, sandy slopes of medium-grained granodiorite, then becomes gentle as it winds above a canyon. ∎ *A look back showcases pine-clad Scodie Mountain. Below, your gaze follows Highway 178 east to the distant El Paso Mountains. Around you in early spring of some years, the slopes are carpeted with blue chia, a sage that has two and sometimes three pompons ringing one stem. Chia seeds were roasted by Native*

G
Hwy. 178-
Mt. Whitney

See map G1

G1

CANEBRAKE ROAD 3.8 MI.

G

Hwy. 178-
Mt. Whitney

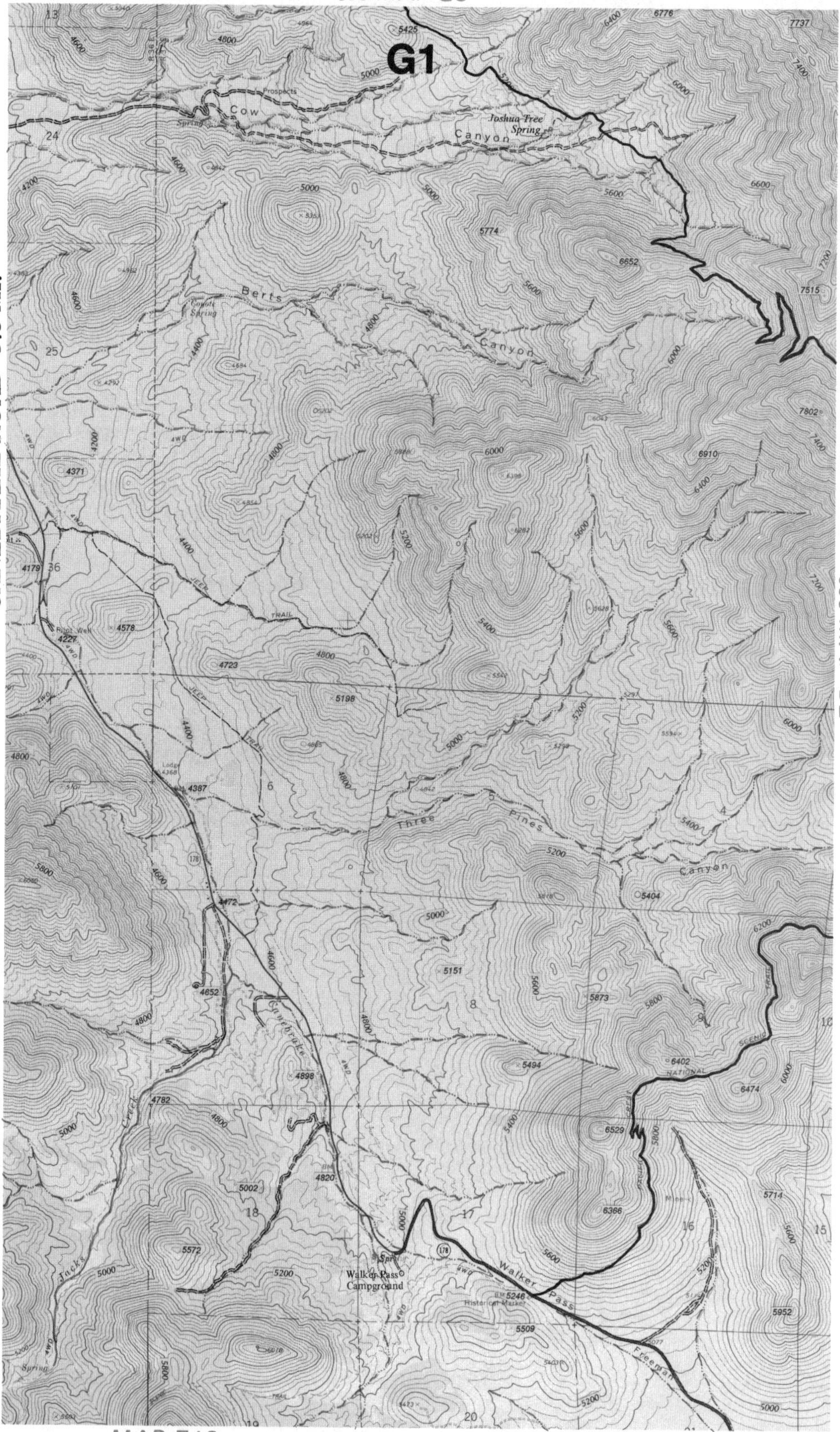

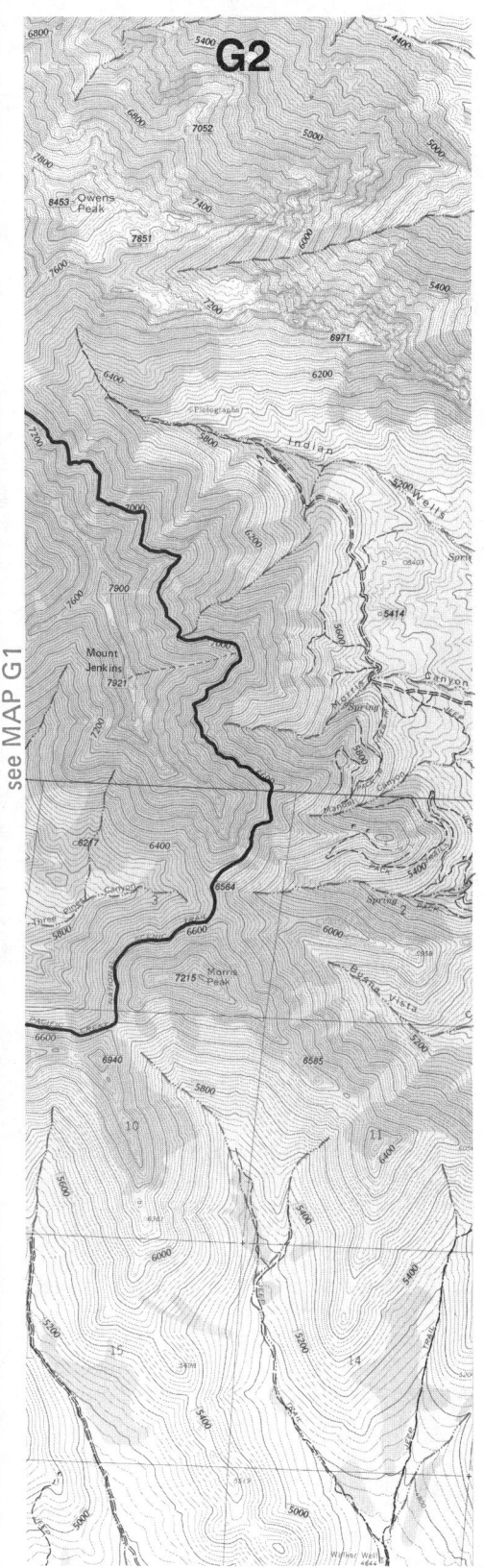

see MAP G1

Americans for food and used by Spaniards for medicinal purposes. Here, too, are lupines and tiny white forget-me-nots that perfume the air. ▮

You veer gradually north on the path, upslope from a shack and its associated rubble, then negotiate six switchbacks in the welcome shade of pinyon-pine trees. Shortly you cross the crest at a saddle and note a few golden oaks added to the pinyon forest.

The trail, now an easy grade near the crestline, crosses a south-facing slope, then regains the crest amid forest near a trailside medium-sized campsite (6390-2.1). The path proceeds on a long traverse across northwest-facing slopes, over a crestline gap and then across west- and north-facing slopes to a saddle (6585-1.8) with a small campsite southwest of Morris Peak.

After rounding Morris Peak you attain the Morris/Jenkins saddle (6500-0.8), where a campsite to the south of the small hill on the crest can accommodate several tents. Beyond the hill you cross the crest to the east side of Mt. Jenkins. Now you ascend slightly to the commemorative plaque (6580-0.3) cemented to a granite boulder, which has a small seat formed during trail construction blasting. Here you may rest, reflect and view. ▮ *Indian Wells Canyon spreads to the desert below, where the towns of Inyokern and, farther away, Ridgecrest waver in the desert sun. Vast China Lake Naval Air Weapons Station, where many sophisticated weapons have been conceived and developed, occupies the land north of Ridgecrest.* ▮

▮ *In December 1984 the United States Board on Geographic Names officially named this mountain Mount Jenkins. This sprawling, serrated 7921-foot mountain on the Sierra crest commemorates James (Jim) Charles Jenkins, who as a teenager hiked across its steep slopes while helping scout a route for this trail. He had been assigned to write the section of the PCT from the town of Mojave to Mt. Whitney for this guidebook.* ▮

▮ *Jim soon expanded his interest. In the following years he hiked over all the trails in the whole Southern Sierra, some several times, no matter how obscure; climbed most of the peaks; covered miles of cross-country; and drove on every bumpy, rutted ribbon of dirt that passed for a road. He gathered information about plants, animals, geology, weather, and the lore of gold miners, cattle ranchers, and the Native*

See maps G1, G2

Mt. Jenkins, named for former co-author of this book

Americans who preceded them. While doing fieldwork and research, he developed a deep appreciation for these mountains, which is reflected in his guidebooks: Self Propelled in the Southern Sierra *(2 volumes), now revised with a name change:* Exploring the Southern Sierra *(2 volumes).* ∎

∎ *He also became greatly involved in promoting conservation and protection for the Southern Sierra. For his contributions to this area Mount Jenkins was named in his honor, the culmination of a five-year, grassroots effort by his friends. The official record in the archives of the United States Department of Interior reads, ". . . named for James Charles Jenkins (1952–1979), noted authority on the flora, fauna and history of the southern Sierra Nevada who wrote guidebooks on the area."* ∎

∎ *While you hike along the PCT, you may see vivid deep-blue Charlotte's phacelia. This exquisite flower, found beside the plaque when the mountain was dedicated, is uncommon and should be left to propagate. In contrast to the less-than-foot-high velvety phacelia is* Nolina parryi, *reaching 10 or more feet high. This plant is indigenous in the Sierra to only this small corner. Nolina's pliant leaves are sharp-edged but not sharply tipped. Its trunk is broad, and*

its blossoms when dry resemble creamy parchment paper, lingering until late autumn and sometimes into the following year. Nolinas are often mistaken for yuccas. ∎

The path, weaving around the extensions and recesses of Mt. Jenkins, undulates slightly, passes a prominent ridge, which supports a few exposed campsites, curves deeply into the mountain scarred with slides of quartz diorite rocks, and then rounds another ridge. At the rounded point of that ridge (6950-1.3), ducks flanking the trail indicate the start of the best route to climb Mt. Jenkins.

*   *   *   *

Side trip: Climbers turn west to scramble up the ridge and follow the ducked use path to and over the sky-scraping, nontechnical Class 2+ summit rocks to the highest point, 7921 feet, where another, similar commemorative plaque rests. The views are spectacular, and the register pad in a metal box placed by Sierra Club members is fun to read and sign. Registers are found on most named peaks above 5000 feet in the Southern Sierra and on selected peaks in the High Sierra.

*   *   *   *

See map G2

Striding along the PCT, you hike over chunks of metamorphic rocks, negotiate minor rock slides, observe Jeffrey pines, sugar pines and white firs—uncommon in this high-desert environment—and proceed around another ridge where you see ahead the ragged light granites of Owens Peak. You then gradually descend while crossing more mountain creases. ∎ *Above the trail, one of these creases marked by a duck, 2.9 miles north of the trail plaque and 0.6 mile south of the Jenkins/Owens saddle, conceals scattered pieces of a Navy C-45 twin engine Beechcraft. The 1948 crash took the lives of five scientists and two pilots from China Lake Naval Air Weapons Station who were on their way to a classified symposium on the Manhattan project in Oakland. This secret project dealt with the building of the first atomic bomb.* ∎

Moving on, you reach the Jenkins/Owens saddle (7020-2.2). A small campsite is upslope on Mt. Jenkins and more space is available on the windy Sierra crest, the jumping-off point for 8453-foot Owens Peak, the highest peak fully within Kern County.

The PCT descends west from the saddle, and you see Highway 178, distant Isabella Lake, Canebrake Road, which you will cross, and the Dome Lands. Beyond four switchbacks and several small slides of diorite rock, the path contours northwest, skirts a minor knob, and reaches a lesser saddle (6300-1.3) east of conical Peak 6652. After another set of four switchbacks the trail curves around the Cow Canyon watershed. In this canyon it crosses a rough dirt road (5500-1.3), which the California Conservation Corps work crews, who built much of this section of PCT, used for access.

* * * *

Side route: This rutted road reaches Highway 178 in 3.9 miles, at a point 6.7 miles west of Walker Pass.

* * * *

Water access: Beyond the rutted road, you cross a seasonal creek, then reach a ¼-mile spur trail (5360-0.4) to year-round Joshua Tree Spring, whose water quality was mentioned above.

* * * *

At the spring, boughs of golden oak arch over several places for campsites near an elongated cattle trough. A pipe brings water from a spring box, affording easy access for hikers. The seasonal creek flows below the spring. Volunteers from the American Hiking Society helped the BLM develop the spur trail and lay the spring box. The next seasonal water is 4.4 miles ahead at Spanish Needle Creek, the next nonseasonal water 16.8 miles ahead at Chimney Creek.

* * * *

The PCT loses elevation as it tracks a northwest route around a major ridge from Owens Peak. Then after ascending to cross this ridge at a saddle (5240-1.1), it climbs, sometimes steeply, northeast up a draw before again resuming a northwest direction to still another saddle (5860-1.1). Leaving views of Highway 178 and the South Fork Valley behind, the path

Co-author Ruby Jenkins, with husband Bill on Mt. Jenkins dedication hike

See maps G2, G1, G3

see MAP G4

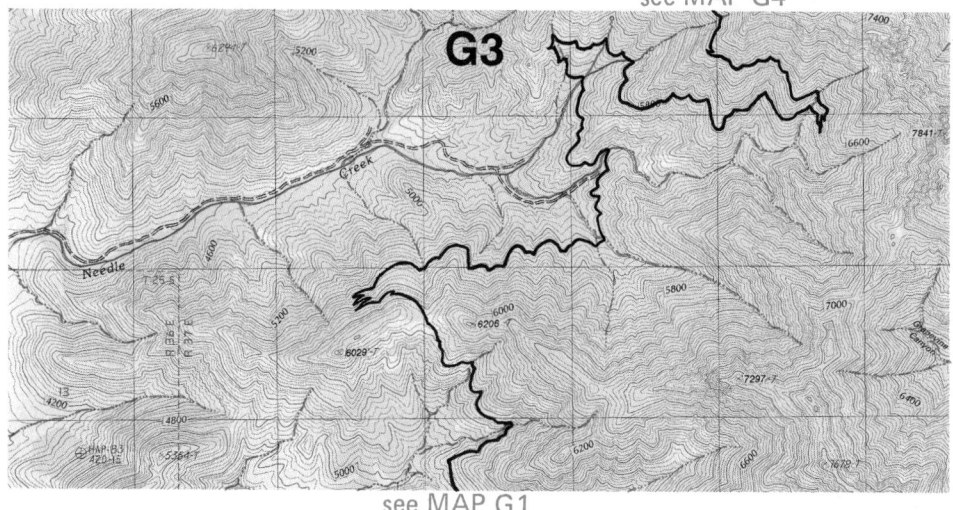

G3

see MAP G1

continues in pinyon forest and its associated understory brush. The wide, smooth PCT again loses elevation now by a series of five switches, while below and off to the west the prominent slash of Canebrake Road gains elevation via one lengthy switchback. ∎ *A summit block of Lamont Peak looms directly north of you, hiding its sheer, jagged north ridge, and Spanish Needle soon shows to your right. At your feet, sometimes in the middle of the path, arrowleaf balsam root's big yellow flowers bloom—everything is big about this sometimes 32-inch-tall plant.* ∎

Beyond the switchbacks the trail nearly levels before again descending east along the steep slopes. Within your view below, a private, gated road hugs the path of Spanish Needle Creek. After crossing a canyon with early-season runoff, your path bends north and its gradient eases. A half mile later it crosses a headwaters branch of Spanish Needle Creek (5160-2.2). A large shelf just off the trail before the creek crossing makes an ideal campsite for weary PCTers.

Usually some water trickles along the Spanish Needle Creek drainage, which is shaded by willows and cottonwoods. ∎ *While in the drainage you may look for a recently discovered species—the Spanish Needle onion,* Allium shevockii—*the tipped-back flower petals are bright maroon above and lime green below.* ∎

Leaving the trees momentarily, the trail climbs out of the canyon around exposed slopes and again enters a forest, here with a few alders added, well-watered by a spring-fed finger of Spanish Needle Creek (5300-0.7), your best source of water in this canyon. ∎ *Because water is so scarce along the crest, the PCT was routed to drop into Spanish Needle Creek canyon in order to take advantage of this series of springs. The trail's circuitous routing added several extra miles of hiking.* ∎

You next climb in a pinyon-pine woodland along a minor ridge where you are likely to startle coveys of mountain quail, seemingly abundant in these mountains. You negotiate a sharp turn in a side canyon which points you generally east to cross a spring-fed streamlet, this one frocked with wild roses (5560-0.6). Then you clamber briefly along a blasted area, cross a seep and again enter a shady canyon adorned with occasional bracken ferns. Once more you cross a finger of Spanish Needle Creek (5620-0.2); this and the previous streamlet join to form the creek you crossed below. The next reliable water is 10.9 miles away at Chimney Creek.

After a brief stretch south, the trail climbs east across the south-facing slopes of Spanish Needle Creek canyon, then contours around another ridge. Here the first of several white marbleized veins was blasted to carve the path. ∎ *On this stretch you are treated to open views of jagged peaks bracketing Spanish Needle, which looks like a rounded, protruding thumb on a clenched fist.* ∎ The trail again turns southeast, abruptly turns back, climbs a switchback

See map G3

G4

HWY. 178 6 MI.

Chimney Peak

Fox Mill Spring

Campground

Campground

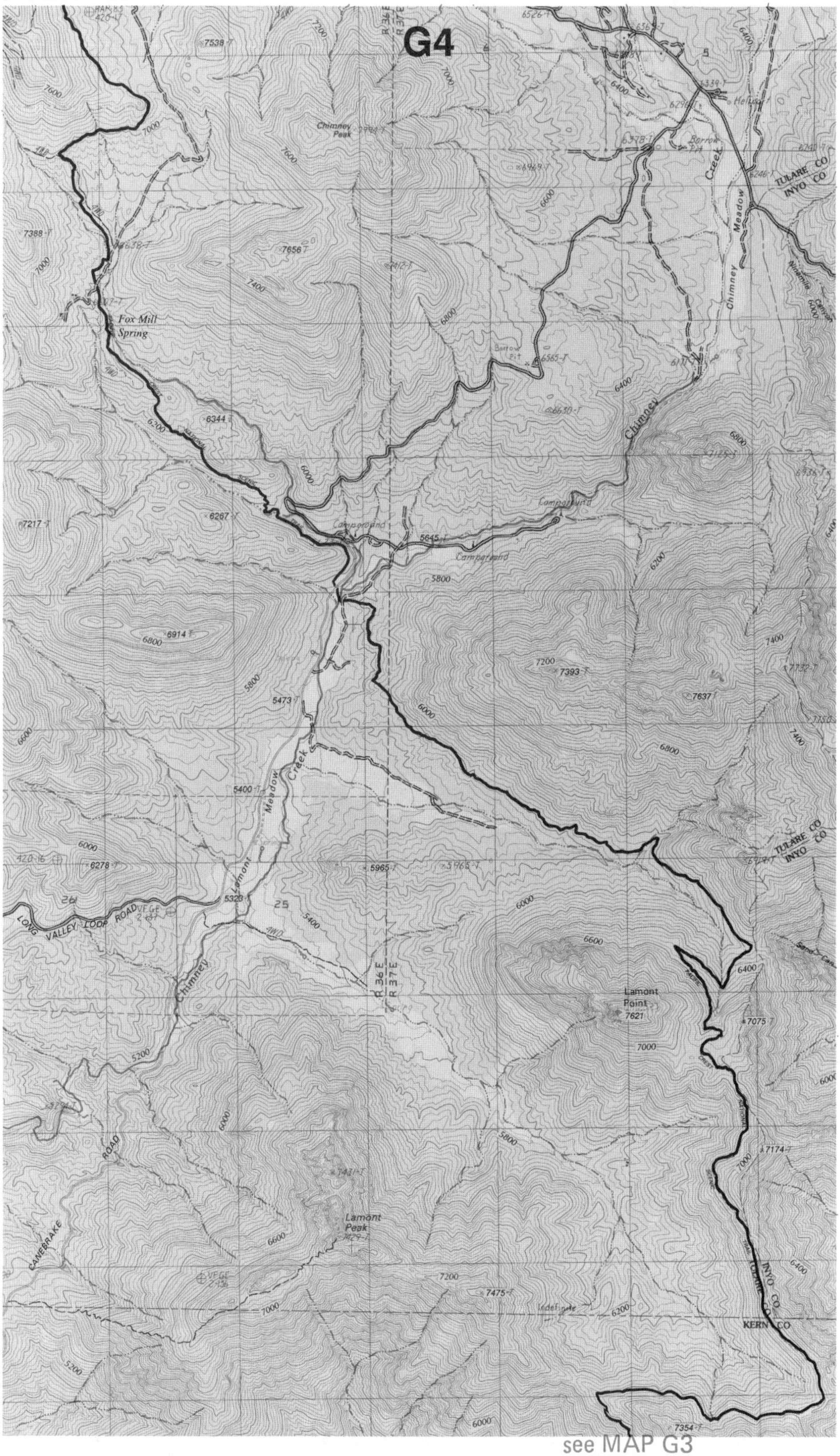

Lamont Point
7621

Lamont Peak

TULARE CO
INYO CO

TULARE CO
INYO CO

KERN CO
INYO CO

LONG VALLEY LOOP ROAD

CANEBRAKE ROAD

and ascends out of the canyon. A pair of short switchbacks, 0.3 mile apart, helps you gain elevation to reach the ridge between the Spanish Needle group and Lamont Peak (6800-3.0). Campsites were developed along the divide, to the left of the trail, to accommodate trail crews, and more have been added above the trail by PCTers.

❚ *While looking north and east at the BLM's Chimney Peak Recreation Area below, you see land favored by the Tubatulabal Native Americans and probably by prehistoric tribes before them. The area is rich in archeological sites; for instance, some bedrock mortars are within easy access of the trail. A reminder, however: since Congress passed the antiquities legislation, it is illegal to remove or disturb anything pertaining to our Native Americans' culture; even as little as pocketing an obsidian chip is unlawful.* ❚

The PCT once again curves above a canyon, but this eastward leg takes you through another break from pinyons and live oaks to north-facing slopes of Jeffrey and sugar pines, white firs and black oaks—a mix of trees found in abundance on the west side of the Kern Plateau. After gaining some elevation, the trail then curves north along the Sierra crest, where expansive eastern views unfold of Sand Canyon below and the desert beyond. Ahead on the crest a large pinyon protects a campsite from the usual ridgetop winds.

The trail cuts a nearly straight swath northwest, just below the ridgeline, taking you once again through pinyons, oaks and brush in sunny, dry country, then swings briefly east into a canyon where another small stand of Jeffrey pines and firs flourishes. ❚ *These few patches of pine and fir occur typically on north slopes where moisture lingers longer in this dry climate.* ❚ Now the trail traverses to a narrow saddle and then climbs a bit to a broader one (6900-3.3) with camping possibilities.

Now an extended descent on the PCT to Canebrake Road and Chimney Creek Campground begins. A short switchback leads you northwest to a half-mile-long leg along Lamont Point slopes. ❚ *A couple of solitary rust-brown, shreddy-barked, fragrant, scaly-needled western junipers thrive here and ahead in the most insecure places.* ❚ Rounding boulders, the path heads east before turning north onto another

Sierra crest saddle (6260-1.4), this one with limited views.

Heading in a general northwest direction again, the PCT leaves the Sierra crest not to return until Gomez Meadow, 49.3 trail miles ahead. It slowly loses elevation, but occasionally rises briefly as it heads along lower slopes of the north side of the canyon between Lamont Point and Sawtooth Peak. ❚ *Gray pine debuts as you stroll along the path of decomposed granodiorite.* ❚

Accompanied by its water-loving willows, a seasonal creek crosses the path (5950-0.8); its water tumbles down from multicolored, sheer-sided rock canyons high above. Soon Lamont Meadow and a private inholding in this BLM-administered public land called Chimney Peak Recreation Area, come into view, then Canebrake Road. Finally you dip to cross a north-south dirt road, and then to cross adjacent year-round Chimney Creek. Faucets at the campground are often turned off—best to get your water here. Immediately, you are ushered by a corridor of late-summer-blooming rabbitbrush to unpaved, maintained Canebrake Road (5555-2.4). The campground, popular during hunting season, 0.3 mile up the road, provides 37 shaded sites with tables, grills, pit toilets and sometimes faucet water. The creek, however, flows year-round across the center of the linear camping area.

The PCT leaves Owens Peak Wilderness, crosses the unpaved road, and enters 13,700-acre Chimney Peak Wilderness. Your route leaves the rabbitbrush and sagebrush behind for a short while to climb above and parallel to the road and campground amid a flurry of spring blossoms featuring the yellow, daisylike coreopsis. The path, less sandy now, dips to cross a usually dry creek, and then by small switchbacks it proceeds up the south-facing slopes of the creek's canyon.

❚ *Often you need to step carefully here lest you harm a "horney toad," blending so well with the rocks and sand. It is really a horned lizard, and with its spikes and bumps it is one of those contradictions: a creature so homely as to appear attractive.* ❚ Ahead you top out of the canyon and enter another above a stream whose chortle echoes as the precipitous granodiorite walls of the canyon close in.

Beyond the canyon, to the left of the route,

See maps G3, G4

you find a scattering of debris where the multi-level ruins of a barite mill appear. ∎ *The mineral barite, used in drilling muds, was mined hereabouts until the early 1950s. Gold and tungsten were also mined in the area.* ∎

*　　*　　*　　*

Water access: This clutter overlooks Fox Mill Spring, hidden in a sagebrush- and willow-choked meadow below. The BLM has upgraded this spring and improved its accessibility; it provides the last water, except for seasonal streams, until the South Fork Kern River, 14.4 miles ahead in Rockhouse Basin.

*　　*　　*　　*

Immediately beyond the spring the trail crosses a dirt road (6580-2.2) descending from a flat area used for camping. The path winds along slopes, passing an eroded dirt track, and gains elevation while several sagebrush meadows appear to diminish below. Chimney Peak's double points seem just a stone's throw across the canyon to the east-northeast. Don't scan the peak for a chimney—it was named for one still standing in Chimney Meadow.

Soon you cross another dirt road, round a nose about ½ mile later, then tramp through sagebrush and cross yet another road. Most of these spurs closed after the advent of wilderness status here. Now you begin a northwestward trek traversing across the steep ridges and dry furrows of 8228-foot Bear Mountain, slowly ascending over metamorphic soils and chunks of rock. ∎ *To the east, beyond the meadows below and the dirt roads that snake through them, you see Sawtooth Peak and several unnamed points that anchor the eastern Sierra.* ∎ At last you attain the trail summit of this segment (8020-3.6), atop a minor ridge suitable for camping.

You begin a descent now, bearing west and crossing a road (7980-0.2), then immediately crossing another, both leading to a large excavation sliced into the earthy-red slate to the left. Several more of these gouges attract attention as you progress down the trail. ∎ *Past that excavation, a road leads to a locked facility on the mountain, housing a seismograph. This is one instrument in an important network of many seismographs placed by the USGS to record earth tremors.* ∎

∎ *The red-brown soil hereabout enhances the gray-green pinyon forest, and an occasional juniper adds to the pleasing weave. Farther ahead the tapestry of Rockhouse Basin appears, with the stark granites of the domed lands weighting the basin's southwest border. The distant blues of Bald Mountain and other Kern Plateau peaks delineate the northwest curve of the basin, where the muted sage greens of Woodpecker Meadow are barely visible. The High Sierra silhouette stretches across the northern horizon, containing the Great Western Divide and the Mt. Whitney group.* ∎

The trail, curving northwest, crosses a road and then descends along a canyon where a sun-dappled seasonal creek glitters in the recesses and a weathered hut squats by its bank. At a bend in this canyon, the path arches over an artfully constructed culvert containing the seasonal stream, near some camping possibilities. In about 100 yards the trail crosses unpaved, maintained Long Valley Loop Road (7220-1.9). Here it leaves Chimney Peak Wilderness and enters into a 1994 extension of Dome Land Wilderness. ∎ *This 7000-acre addition and the 32,000 acres earlier added in 1984 have considerably enlarged the original "rock" wilderness, which was a "charter member" of the National Wilderness Preservation System established by Congress in 1964.* ∎

∎ *Domes, spires and obelisks rise from this semiarid wilderness, now encompassing more than 100,000 acres. Rock climbers find it an excellent place to practice their skills. Surprisingly, beside the granites, there are grassy meadows, forests and sizable fishing creeks along with the serpentine South Fork Kern River. A breeze usually moderates the heat of summer in this spacious land.* ∎

You next climb over a saddle and descend along the southwest side of a deeper canyon. In time a flat on a small northeast spur ridge (6600-2.7) offers one last place to camp before the broader lands of Rockhouse Basin. ∎ *There are better views now of Woodpecker Meadow, an area burned in the Woodpecker Fire of 1947. The trees, unable to re-establish themselves, were replaced by sagebrush and buckbrush. Stegosaurus Fin, Dome Land's resident dinosaur, which sits prominently in the wilderness interior, displays its fin and curved back. The*

G

Hwy. 178-
Mt. Whitney

See maps G4, G5, G6

see MAP G7

G6
DOME
LAND
WILDERNESS
Creek
Creek
Creek
Rockhouse
Basin
Kern
South
Fork
Mile
40
Rockhouse
Meadow
VABM
Canyon 7315
VABM
Long 7178
Water
Prospects
R 35 E
R 36 E

see MAP G5

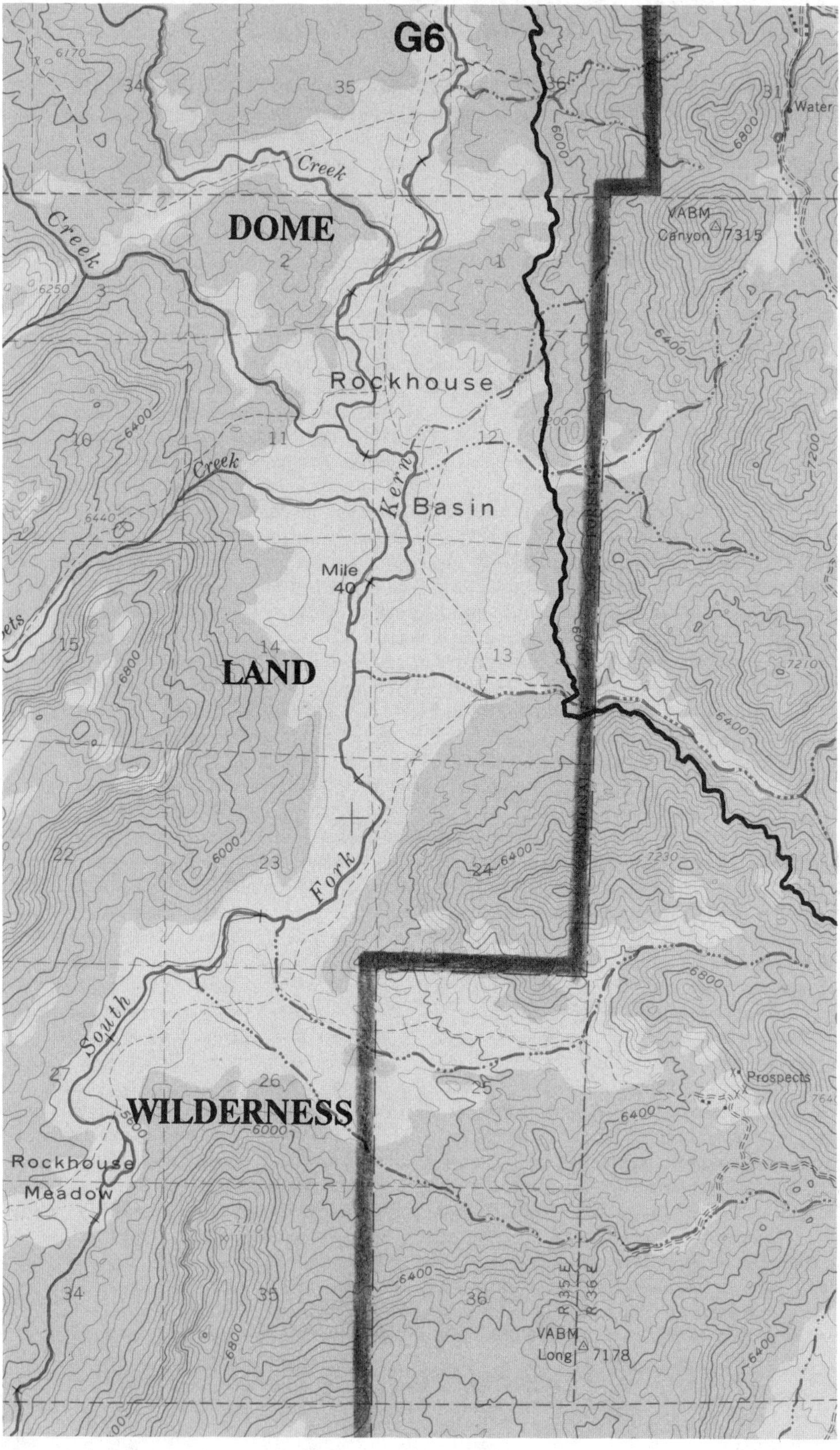

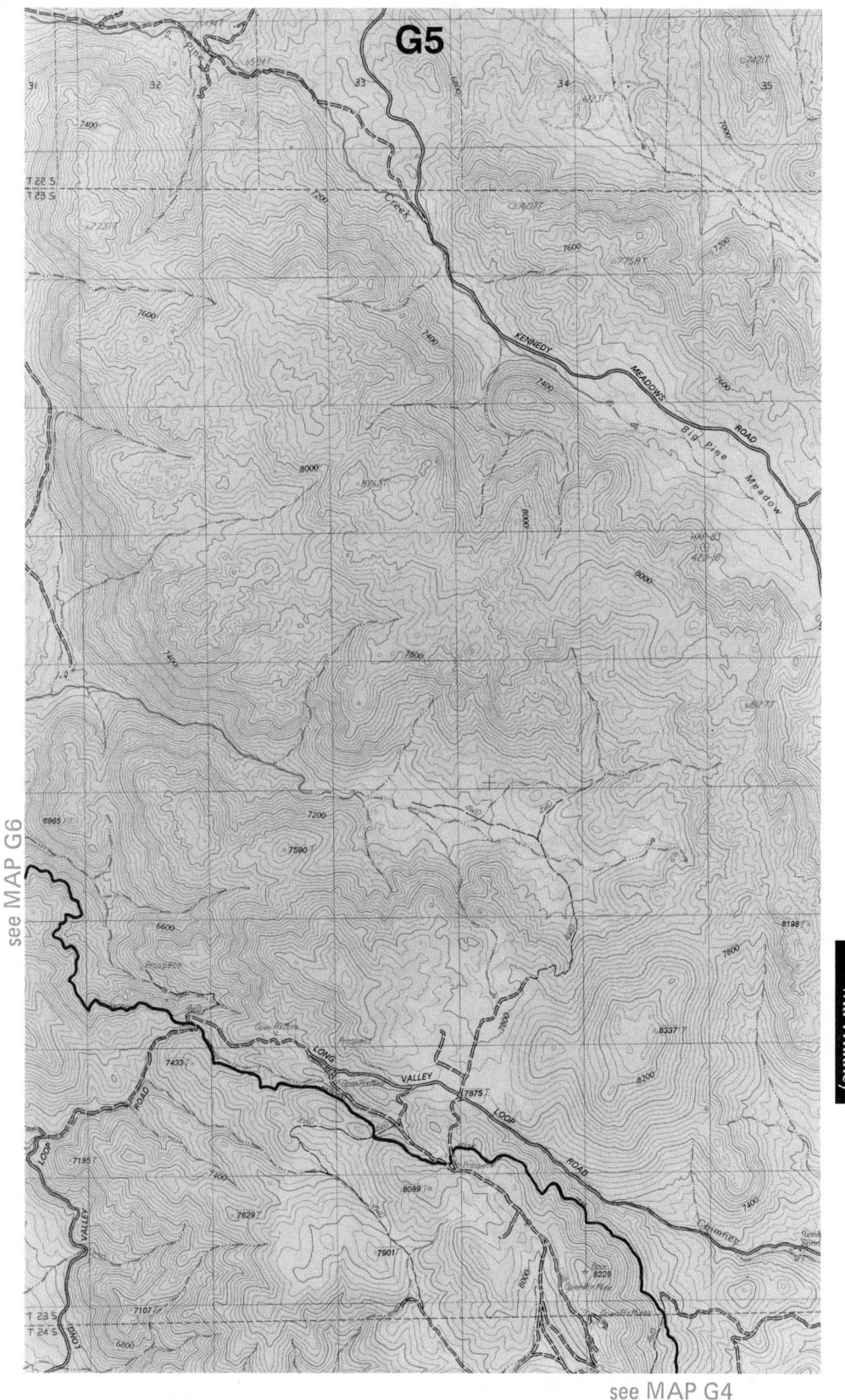

see MAP G6

see MAP G4

G Hwy. 178-
Mt. Whitney

South Fork Kern River at bedrock gateway

South Fork Kern River, weaving through the basin below, remains hidden. ❚ You continue to descend, sometimes clinking over loose, rocky slopes, then slowly plodding through sandy soils near the foot of the descent.

Now in Rockhouse Basin, you turn right and cross first a creek (5845-1.8) with exposed campsites on a sandy bank, then immediately a closed road that is returning to nature. (If water is needed and the creek is dry, follow its bed 1.1 mile to the river.) Once again in national forest, near a large campsite to the right, you head north, roughly following the South Fork, but, alas, the river is about a mile away for the next several miles. You now scuff along the sandy trail through a forest of pinyon pines. This sandy trail is subject to erosion, but if erosion has made it hard to see, just follow the corridor through the trees scarred by sawed-off branches.

You soon dip through the brushy wash of a waterless basin and later pad across a northeast-southwest-trending closed road, which descends along a gully. In a bit over a mile from the closed road you cross a willow-lined, seasonal creek (5870-3.2). A large campsite is at the end of a closed jeep road north of the creek.

❚ *In late spring, dainty funnellike white gilia flowers, fully open when the light wanes, cover these sandy grounds.* ❚ Contouring slightly northwest now, you approach a gateway of resistant metamorphic bedrock through which flows the South Fork Kern River (5760-1.0).

❚ *Beginning on the slopes of Trail Peak near Cottonwood Pass, a place you will visit as you travel north on the PCT, the South Fork Kern River flows south, wandering across the Kern Plateau, gathering much of the eastern plateau's drainage and eventually flowing into Isabella Lake, a reservoir. Most of the year it resembles a placid creek with good fishing holes and refreshing bathing pools, but during snowmelt the river becomes tumultuous, charging wildly through its banks. Then it is dangerous to cross. But during snowmelt this river, unspoiled by man, displays its most scenic value and illustrates why in 1987 it was included with the North Fork Kern River in the protective custody of the prestigious National Wild and Scenic Rivers System.* ❚

Turning north again, the path threads passages between the willow and wild-rose tangles that edge the river and the boulders composing the cliffs. The trail climbs and dips, generally fol-

G

Hwy. 178-
Mt. Whitney

See maps G6, G7

lowing the watercourse but not slavishly. ▌ *Sprinklings of flowers add an artist's touch to the captivating scenery, and the three-needled, vanilla-scented Jeffrey pines line the water's edge.* ▌

Shortly you cross spring-fed Pine Creek, and then about ½ mile later you notice that the trail melds into a closed road. In time, as you descend with views of a house below, you leave the road at a junction (5950-1.9) where it curves west toward the river, and continue on the path straight ahead (north) following the barbed-wire fence on the right. Soon you pass west of the house with its assorted vehicles and dogs, then wade through a stream garnished with sedges and watercress (5916-0.1) and cross a closed OHV road next to the stream. A vast outlier of sagebrushy Kennedy Meadows stretches ahead, and you begin hiking through it.

Just ¼ mile later the PCT approaches a fence corner, then leaves the fence and angles off to the northeast, away from the river. In the middle of this meadow, the path crosses another closed OHV road (5980-0.6). Not far north of the meadow, the PCT climbs the lower west slope of a hill, where you catch your first sight of paved Sherman Pass Road and a few buildings along it. Pressing near the river again, the trail passes through three cattle gates (please close). Between the first two gates, it rounds west of outcrops where the path is often washed out by high water or covered with tall grass. After the second gate, the path nears a large campsite under a juniper tree, and 0.4 mile later it winds

up to the paved road, just east of a bridge (6020-1.7).

*   *   *   *

Resupply Access: At this point, if you need supplies or refreshments, have a package pickup, or just wish to sign the PCT register and chat and maybe catch the Saturday night movie, continue 0.7 mile, right, generally southeast, along the highway to tree-shaded Kennedy Meadows General Store. There is no phone at the store. If faced with an emergency, try to catch a ride to the Forest Service's Black Rock Station, 12.7 miles west of the store on the highway.

This road with many names—Sherman Pass, Kennedy Meadows, Nine Mile Canyon, SNF Road 22S05, J41, M-152—reaches Highway 395 in 24.2 miles. Major supplies are available in Ridgecrest, 25 miles southeast of the junction, off Highway 178. The road reaches the Kern River to the west in 44.3 miles, and subsequently Kernville 19.5 miles farther, where there are ample supplies and accommodations.

*   *   *   *

When it is time to move along, you return to the trail where it crosses the road and amble north to Kennedy Meadows Campground. You would walk the same distance if you took the northbound road just beyond the store to reach the campground.

Across the Forest Service's paved road, you

See map G7

Bridge north of Kennedy Meadows

SOUTH SIERRA

Kennedy Meadows
Camp

WILDERNESS

Creek

Bitter

DOME LAND

Kennedy Meadows
General
Store

Windy Springs

Kennedy

Meadows

WILDERNESS

Kennedy

Meadows

Mile
46

Mile
45

Kennedy Peak

River

G8

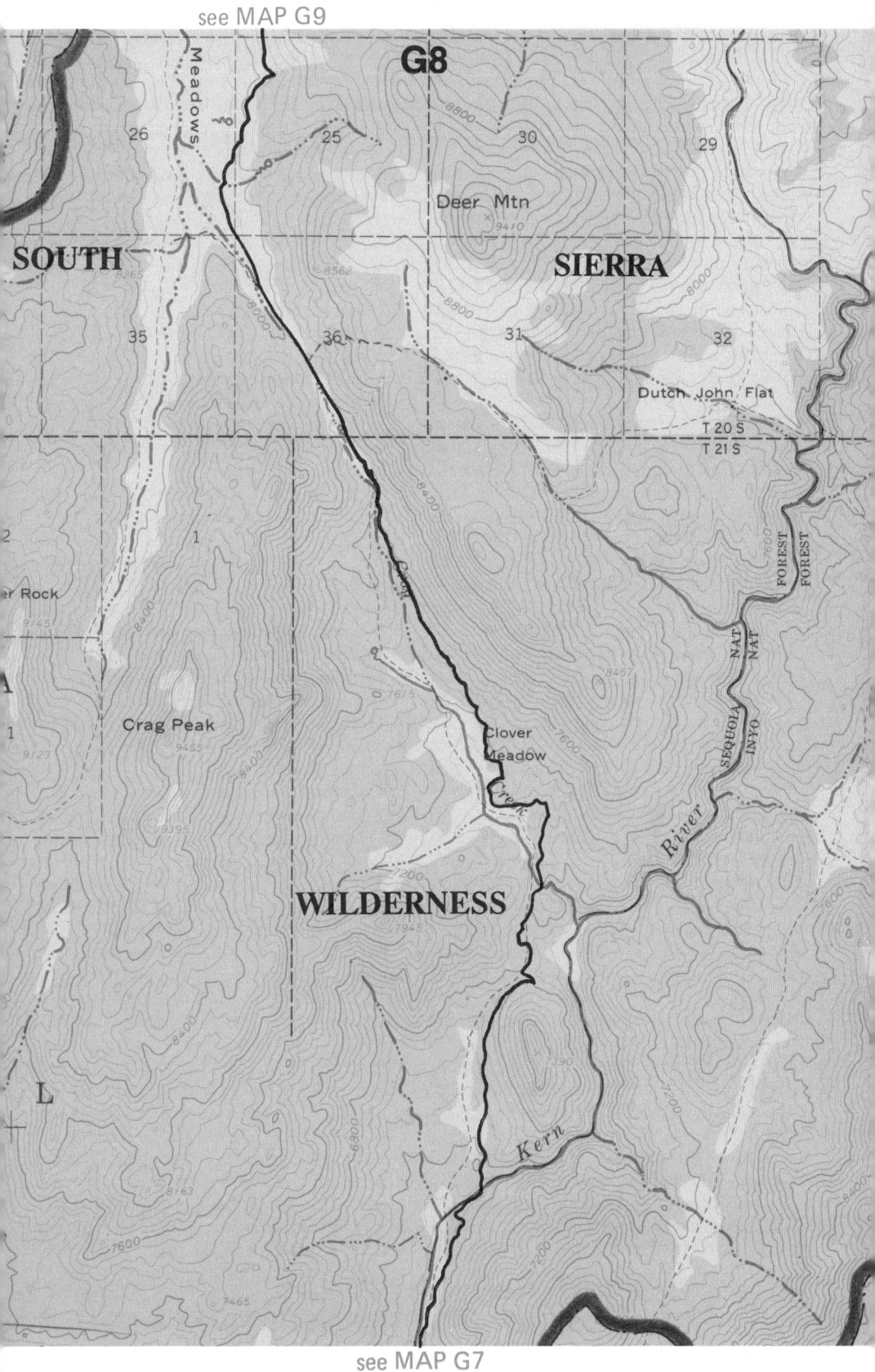

SOUTH

SIERRA

26

25

30

29

Deer Mtn
×9410

×8562

8800

35

36

31

32

Dutch John Flat

T 20 S
T 21 S

er Rock

1

Crag Peak
9455

Clover
Meadow

WILDERNESS

River

SEQUOIA NAT FOREST
INYO NAT FOREST

L

Kern

continue on sandy turf among early-season high-desert flora. Heading north, you dip through washes and cross dirt roads that lead west to riverside campsites, fishing pools, and swimming holes. Occasional junipers offer spots of shade as you pass fences, first on the right and then on the left. Then you go through one gate and soon through another. Enticing murmurs of the river increase as you reach and then hike above the musical South Fork. Slowly you leave the sagebrush meadow that is embraced by the gentle peaks of the semiarid side of the Kern Plateau and head toward a distant fire-scarred mountain, seen up the river canyon to the north.

Soon the trail crosses the road to the campground (6080-1.8) and proceeds along higher ground. Here it winds for a short time around boulders among pinyon pines and brush. Then it crosses the road again (6120-0.4) and bisects Kennedy Meadows Campground (6150-0.2).

∎ *This year-round, no-fee campground with 39 units is especially popular with anglers who fish for the colorful golden trout in the river. The camp has the usual facilities but no trash pickup—a good place to overnight while you sort through your food packages from home.* ∎

The PCT leaves the north end of Kennedy Meadows Campground and joins the old Clover Meadow Trail. Pinyon and Jeffrey pines along with juniper trees offer shade as the trail immediately dips into a side canyon, then eases through a stock-fence gate, passes several lateral paths to the river, and enters South Sierra Wilderness. ∎ *This wilderness was one of many established by the comprehensive California Wilderness Act of 1984. Its 63,000 acres closed the gap between Dome Land and Golden Trout wildernesses, giving wildlife a wide, unperturbed area to roam and wildflowers room to spread.* ∎

The PCT soon approaches the river and winds to a forked junction (6240-1.1) where it leaves the Clover Meadow Trail, which continues to a river crossing—hazardous during snowmelt. (The old path west of the river is now used as a stock driveway.) Your route, the right fork, leads to a sturdy, yet scenic, steel-girdered wooden bridge built in 1984 (6300-0.8).

Beyond the bridge, the trail climbs north of a knoll, passes a medium-sized campsite perched to the right above the river, then continues over gravelly terrain. Soon your path gains the slopes of a craggy 7412-foot mountain whose soils nurture an occasional prickly-pear cactus. ∎ *The prominent yellow-orange blossoms of this spiny plant turn pink to rose as they mature.* ∎

Past the ascent, the path switchbacks down once to reach a saddle where it crosses the old trail, and then it makes a weaving traverse above the rumble of the South Fork Kern River, sometimes heard but not seen in its canyon to the east. The PCT intersects the old trail again, then dips to cross Crag Creek (6810-2.0). Yellow monkey flowers and cinquefoil luxuriate near the banks of the creek. There are campsites here and upstream along the old trail, all of which, however, are within 100 feet of the water—easily damaged areas the Forest Service wishes to protect.

After a short ascending hike beyond the ford, you abruptly face the skeletal remains of trees burned in the 1980 Clover Meadow blaze. ∎ *Started by a PCT hiker's campfire that was set too close to tree branches and improperly extinguished, the wind-whipped fire engulfed 5000 acres before it was contained. Buckbrush ceanothus, rabbitbrush and associated xerophytic plants have replaced the forest; the pines are not regenerating. The stark grays and blacks of the burn contrast sharply with the creek's riparian expanse and the plush greens of Clover Meadow below.* ∎

You pass campsites in an unburned pocket of trees and, 1.8 miles into the burn, again reach the welcome shade of forest. ∎ *Mountain mahogany is abundant here. This woody brush with small, wedge-shaped leaves clustered near branch tips turns silvery in the fall when clad in its corkscrew, feathered plumes.* ∎

The path meets the usually dry eastern branch of Crag Creek at a junction (7560-2.5) with the old Clover Meadow Trail (stock driveway arriving on your left, which you join. In 0.1 mile the PCT passes to the right of a campsite established in 1936, according to the words on a concrete slab. ∎ *The old trail was probably built by the Civilian Conservation Corps, which was active from 1933 to 1942, during the Depression.* ∎ A spring appears in the creek's channel just before the path climbs up a narrowing, boulder-strewn slot, but a lush growth of willows and wild roses laps up most of the water, leaving a timid flow. The grade abates amid

See maps G7, G8

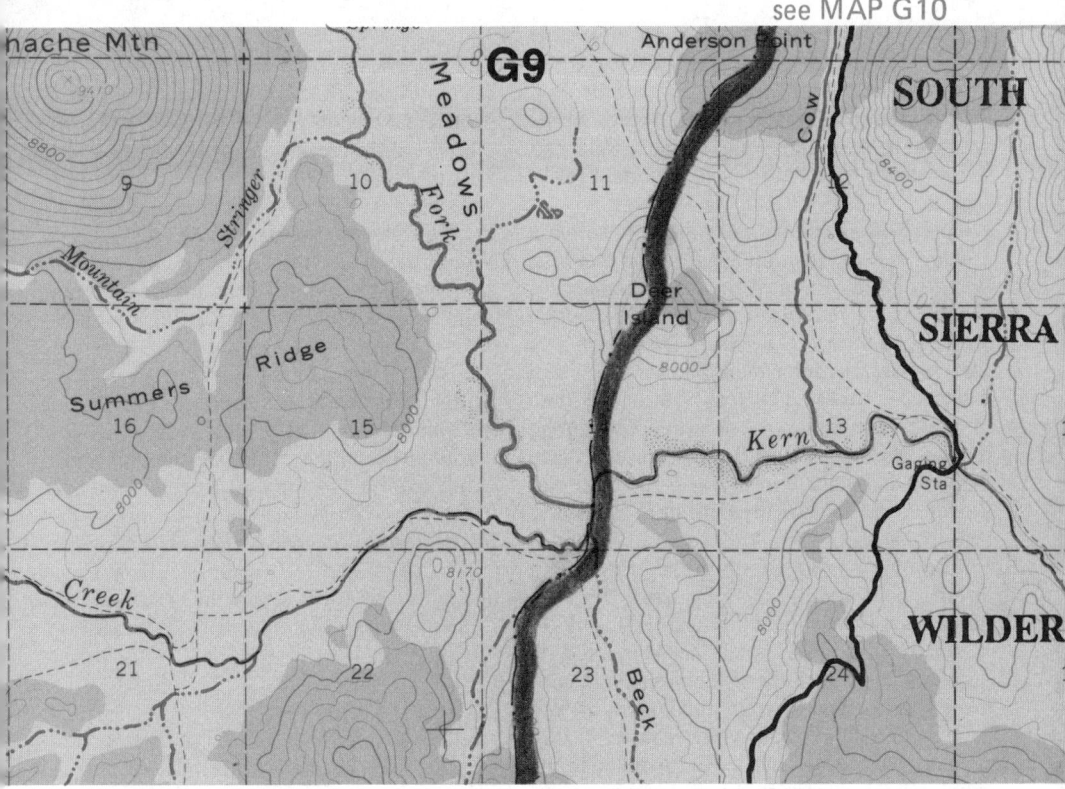

yellow-flowered bitterbrush and ends at a saddle with campsites and a **T** junction (8060-1.1) with Haiwee Trail 37E01, which follows an ancient Indian path east to the river and through Haiwee Pass to Owens Valley—a route that almost became the eastern leg of a trans-Sierra highway.

Beyond the saddle, the PCT drops gently to Beck Meadows, a sagebrush finger of Monache Meadows. Campsites can be found at the foot of the grade in the trees on either side of the trail. ❚ *A spacious view of Monache Meadows, the largest meadow in the Sierra, includes distant Mt. Whitney melding with its neighbors, peering over the plateau peaks. Among the seasonal flowers trailside, the yellow evening primrose with its heart-shaped petals makes a dramatic appearance.* ❚ The PCT veers north from northwest-leading Beck Meadows Trail 35E01 (7953-0.4), and from the all-but-gone grooves of an old jeep road that crossed the path. ❚ *Jeeps first penetrated into Monache Meadows in 1949, but long before that horse-drawn buckboards left their parallel treads.* ❚

You focus your attention on direction now,

for in 0.6 mile you leave a former section of the PCT, which is reverting to nature, and turn right (north-northeast) toward hulking Olancha Peak, to angle up the lower slopes of nearby Deer Mountain. After crossing a usually dry gulch, you climb through another gully from where you see a cow trough below at the edge of Beck Meadows. A usually dependable spring bubbles forth above the trough in the gully. You next pass through another stock-fence gate, and then Mt. Langley, framed by Brown and Olancha mountains, comes into view in the north. Its rounded backside resembles that of Mt. Whitney, with which it is often confused. After 0.7 mile from the gate, you top out on Deer Mountain's northern ridge (8390-2.2) near a dry campsite.

From there the path briefly heads southeast to a switchback, then north to drop out of the forest and cross a retired jeep road that bisects a low, broad ridge (7940-1.0). The PCT heads northeast along the ridge, turns right, and drops to an arched 1986 bridge over the South Fork Kern River (7820-0.4). Interestingly, the steel in this bridge was treated to resemble an old,

See maps G8, G9

rusted structure, rendering it less conspicuous. The bridge spans shallow water except during snowmelt, when most long-distance PCT hikers pass this way; then it is an important safety factor.

▌ *You will probably cause great commotion among the cliff swallows that return annually to raise their young in the braces under the bridge. Their mud nests are gourdlike, with a narrow, short tunnel entrance into which they dart to feed fat bugs to their families.* **▌** An ideal campsite is sheltered by trees on the slope south of the bridge, and exposed sites sprawl along the river's sandy north bank. Here you leave Sequoia National Forest and enter Inyo National Forest, but still remain in South Sierra Wilderness.

Resuming its route north of the bridge, here briefly overlapping an OHV road, the PCT passes a southeast-heading trail (7840-0.1) to Kennedy Meadows, a path that vibrated with motorcycles before the wilderness was established. Immediately your trail passes a once heavily used OHV road, which leads north into the canyon straight ahead. After paralleling the river a short way, the PCT turns right at a junction (7840-0.1) while the road/trail it was on continues to Monache Meadows.

Trail width now, the PCT climbs northwest above the meadow while jogging laterally around washes and ridgelets to stay within its required grade of 15% or less. (One can usually identify sections of PCT that overlay old trails: on old trails it plunges in and out of washes rather than curving around them.) In time the trail mounts a low ridge (8050-1.2) and heads north, leaves open slopes sparsely dotted with chartreuse-lichen-painted boulders and enters forested Cow Canyon. Midway up this canyon the trail resumes on the former PCT path that it left in Beck Meadows, and immediately crosses Cow Creek (8260-1.3), where you find the first of a spread of campsites along the creek.

The trail soon crosses the creek again, but quickly returns and ascends a canyon where Kern ceanothus debuts. **▌** *This bush has hollylike leaves and blue-to-purple pompon flowers. It is a denizen of the plateau, occurring only in a few other places.* **▌** The trail merges briefly with paths of a stock driveway angling in from the left. (North-to-south hikers take note; an accidental turn onto a drive-

way path would take you to the head of Monache Meadows.)

You ford the creek once more and look for a PCT post marking the return ford. Again on the left side of the creek, you find your trail among the multiple twining cow paths paralleling it. Where the creek turns east, almost one mile after the last junction, you continue north and quickly reach a trickle from a spring just above. After a short, winding ascent you turn right to join the Olancha Pass Trail (8920-1.2). Vegetation coils about the sometimes slack spring immediately south of this junction.

Your route on the conjoined trail runs eastward, now on a gentle ascent around the head of Cow Canyon. Along the way it passes disturbed terrain on the canyonside created by stock drives, and then it crosses Cow Creek again just 250 yards before the next trail junction (9090-0.5), where the PCT departs north.

*   *   *   *

Side route: The Olancha Pass Trail continues east over the pass, then descends to Sage Flat Road, 6.9 miles. The paved, lightly traveled road heads east 5.8 miles to Highway 395. For emergency supplies, the town of Olancha, 5.0 miles north on the highway, has a BLM fire station, restaurant, motels and a store with limited supplies.

*   *   *   *

The ascending PCT, left at the junction, switchbacks, arcs northeast up a rounded ridgelet, and then turns north where a lateral (9240-0.2) branches off to the trail you just left. Your trail runs across slopes of chinquapin and manzanita, fords Cow Creek and zigzags many times amid bush currant, a favorite berry of black bears. Now leaving the forest, the PCT continues to parallel the creek, which flows among groups of corn lilies, aptly named plants resembling cornstalks. The open tread is sandy and often very dusty, but it still supports the colorful scarlet gilia, a cluster of red flowers with tubular necks and pointed, starlike lobes. The gradient steepens, and the trail zigs sporadically as it climbs a side canyon. Then it fords a spring-fed brook and switchbacks near a large campsite among boulders by a foxtail

See maps G9, G10

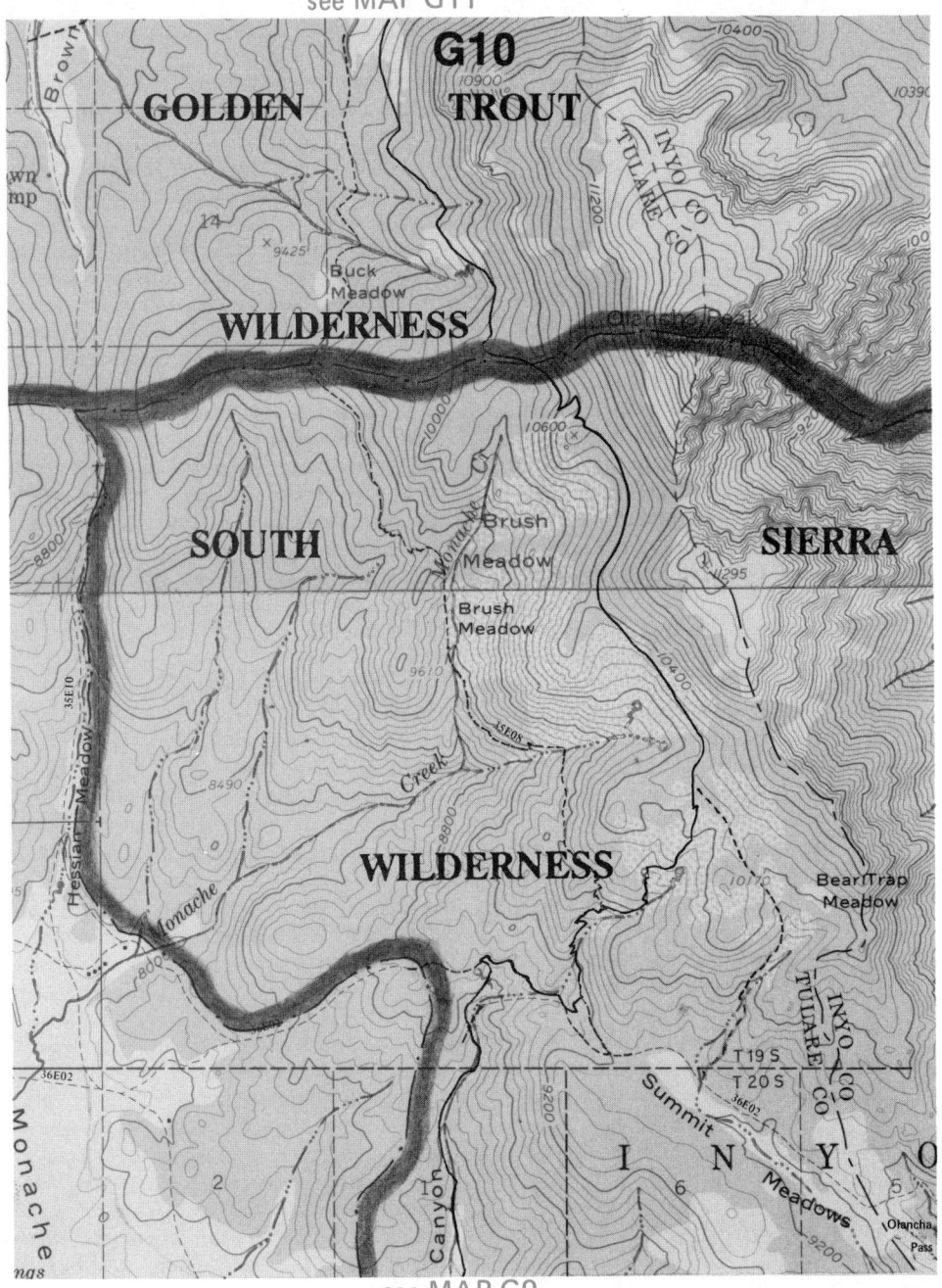

pine, with an extensive view of Monache Meadows and the sandy flood plain of South Fork Kern River.

*   *   *   *

Side trip: Minutes beyond this campsite, a short path climbs from your trail to a broad, gently sloping ridge with a packer campsite and a corral. The verdant, watered meadow there sports corn lilies, buttercups and numerous mountain bluebells, an aptly named flower that resembles tiny, hanging bells whose styles extend like clappers. Mosquitoes may make lin-

See map G10

gering there in spring or early summer a bit unpleasant.

*   *   *   *

On the PCT, the grade diminishes as the trail leads into the shade of lodgepole and occasional foxtail pines—isolated specimens of the impressive foxtail-pine groves ahead. ∎ *This tree grows in gravelly soils just below timberline along with very few understory plants. Its short, five-clustered needles surround the branches; a bristly branch end with its tip up resembles a fox's tail. Foxtail pines seem to survive nicely in the extreme weather of the high country where other trees cannot exist.* ∎

Atop a ridge, your trail proceeds past a junction signed COW TRAIL, mostly obscured by a large fallen tree. (The path connects with the Olancha Pass Trail.) North of the fallen tree your path ascends gently to moderately, curves northwest, and crosses another open slope with seasonal streamlets and seeps. The farther the trail climbs on this slope, the more remarkable are the Southern Sierra views; Dome Land is particularly prominent. In almost one mile the trail crosses a flat, forested ridge with considerable camping potential. ∎ *Provocative vignettes ahead, east to west, of Olancha Peak, Mt. Langley, the Kaweah Peaks Ridge, and Kern Peak may be seen framed by the boughs of the forest.* ∎

Continuing to climb, the path curves around a headwaters bowl of Monache Creek and then levels off on a saddle (10,540-3.4) of a ridge that juts out from the west-facing slope of Olancha Peak. This, the highest point of the trail on the side of Olancha Peak, is a good departure point for the nontechnical 1550-foot climb to the top of the most dominant peak on the Kern Plateau.

*   *   *   *

Side trip: To climb Olancha Peak, ascend northeast on a 0.6-mile cross-country route among foxtail pines to timberline, aiming for the slope north of the summit. There the rounded and gentler terrain makes for an easy final ascent, but only after you have pulled up and over scores of large boulders. Unexpectedly found among these boulders are vigorous

plants of yellow columbine. Then you scale the 12,123-foot summit. At the top stands a tall stack of rocks, a cairn, precariously perched on a slab that juts over the sheer eastern face. On the cairn is a box with a register in which you can record your ascent.

You might pause to reflect on the fate of the Indians for whom this summit was named. Olanche and Yaulanchi were spoonerisms for Yaudanchi, a tribe of Yokuts Indians who probably traded with either the Paiutes north of Owens Lake or the Kosos south of it. The decimated Yaudanchi now reside on the Tule River Indian Reservation.

An alternative to climbing Olancha Peak for plateau views is Point 10,600, west of the saddle and the trail. From there you barely see the rounded backside of Mt. Langley fronting the same part of Mt. Whitney, but you see the Kern Plateau wonderfully spread before you. If you need a campsite you can find places on the saddle.

*   *   *   *

From the saddle, the PCT drops to Gomez Meadow on a gentle-to-moderate grade. Along the way it switchbacks five times and then curves around another headwaters bowl of Monache Creek. The trail leads across a watershed divide, where it leaves South Sierra Wilderness and enters Golden Trout Wilderness.

∎ *As you saunter along this easy northern descent, you may contemplate some events that involved this area. Before the late 1940s the only way one could reach the gentle Kern Plateau was on foot, on animal, or on a breathtaking flight in a small aircraft. Then logging began in the southern part, and it slowly pushed northward. The loggers' roads opened the land to jeeps and their cousins, motorcycles. All these intrusions resulted in slope erosion, damaged meadows and silted streams. Environmentalists became alarmed and campaigned to protect the remaining land. They were eventually successful. In 1978 President Carter signed into law 306,000-acre Golden Trout Wilderness, named for the colorful trout—California's state fish— that evolved in this area. The northern third of the Kern Plateau is part of this wilderness.* ∎

∎ *But, you may ask, if land is set aside in wildernesses to preserve its natural biota, why are*

See map G10

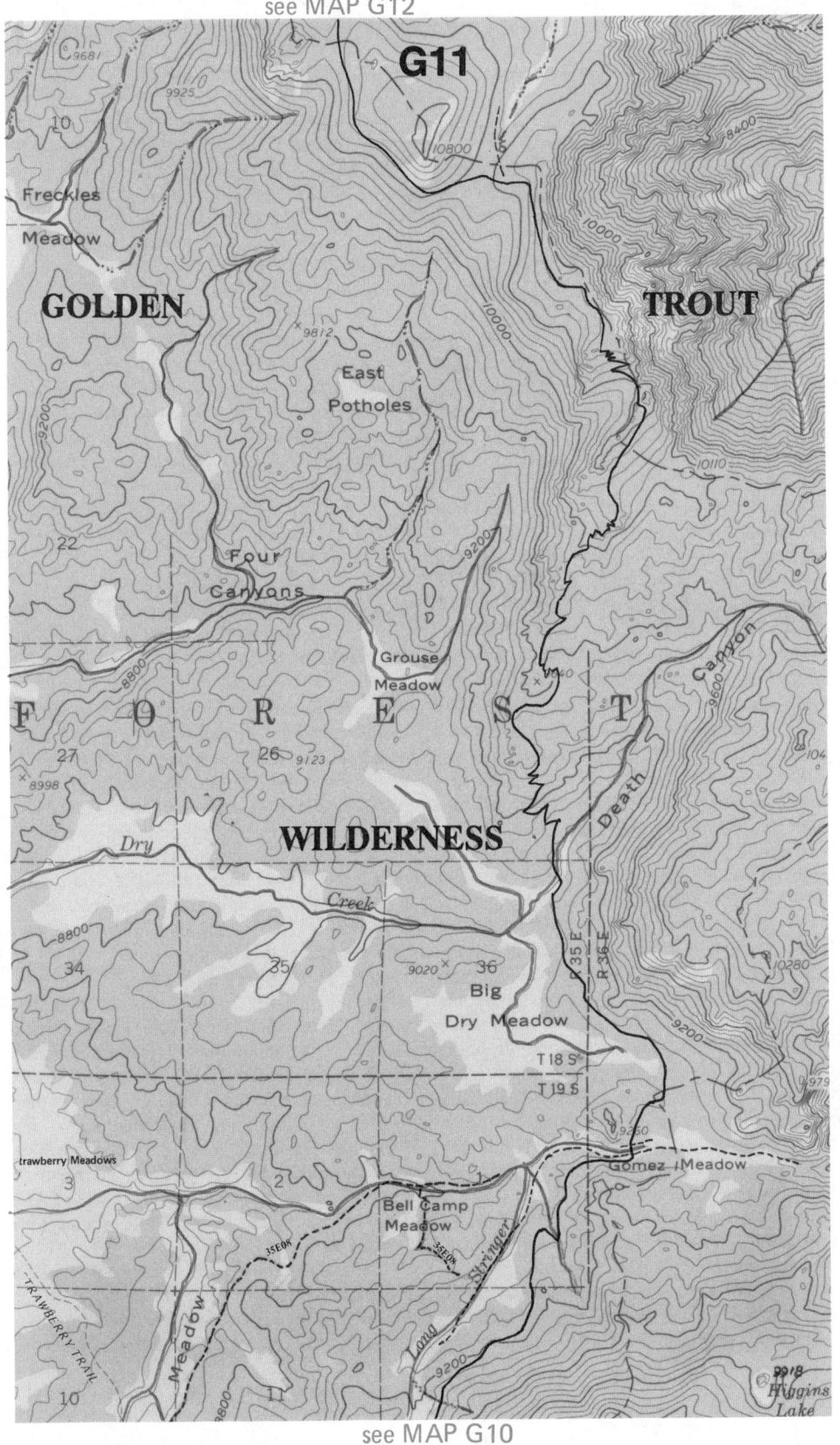

G11

TROUT

GOLDEN

Freckles
Meadow

East
Potholes

Four
Canyons

Grouse
Meadow

F O R E S T

WILDERNESS

Death Canyon

Dry

Creek

Big

Dry Meadow

Strawberry Meadows

Gomez Meadow

Bell Camp
Meadow

Higgins
Lake

Olancha Peak seen between trailside pinnacles near Trail Pass

cattle-grazing, hunting and fishing allowed? People interested in those activities would ask, "What about hiking?" The answer to the latter is that hikers seem neither to destroy nor disturb the flora and fauna as they walk along on their narrow paths and adhere to "no trace" camping. ▮

As you ponder these thoughts and this recent history, you pass above a seasonal spring while hiking across exposed slopes with views of brownish, boulder-topped Kern Peak across the Kern Plateau. This 11,510-foot peak counterbalances Olancha Peak; the two are among the highest points on the plateau.

Now the PCT meanders northwest, dropping in and out of forests, passing seeps and springs that find their way to Brown Meadow and Long Stringer. The trail gradually curves northeast, then bends southeast to cross a year-round creek (9030-3.7) with camping potential near its banks. This is a better source of water than the stringer ahead. From the creek the PCT leads north and then east on a slightly rolling course. Then it bends sharply north and crosses a meadowside trail at a causeway abutment (9010-0.7) just west of very level Gomez Meadow.

The causeway's 35-yard length elevates the path above the sodden stringer beneath. ▮ *Shooting stars seem almost airborne across the meadow. The common name of this flower is well-chosen, because its swept-back crimson/purple petals suggest flight.* ▮ The PCT resumes at the north abutment and immediately crosses another meadowside path. It then curves northeast into a dense forest of lodgepole pines, touching the inconspicuous Sierra crest, which it last crossed in Owens Peak Wilderness. The trail gradually turns northwest and soon skirts Big Dry Meadow.

Beyond this meadow you pass a creekside campsite, then ford a step-across all-year creek (8940-1.7) at the mouth of Death Canyon. To the left are several campsites; to the right, up-canyon, a path takes PCT equestrians to another in a series of corrals and camping areas built for the PCT trail crews of Inyo National Forest. The corrals are infrequently maintained. The trailside campsites are ideal places to overnight before the nearly 2000-foot steep climb out of Death Canyon.

Next, amid a fine grove of fragrant, gnarled old mountain juniper trees, you labor up 22 broadly spaced switchbacks and numerous curves on the blocky, spired ridge west of the

See maps G10, G11

canyon. You may pause occasionally to view pointed Kern Peak and the broad expanse of Big Dry Meadow. You eventually cross the crest of this ridge for the last time at a slender slot between craggy outcrops. Foxtail pines now shade you and red mountain-pride penstemons decorate your path as you descend gently to a crestline saddle (10,390-3.7) from which the eastern slope drops precipitously to Owens Lake bed. ∎ *This alkali flat is usually dry because the Los Angeles Department of Water and Power diverted its inflow into their adqueduct. The pink coloration of the lake bed is due to algae and bacteria.* ∎

Next you ascend on seven switchbacks to attain a crestline prominence, reaching an elevation of 10,700 feet. ∎ *Here you are rewarded again with grand views of Owens Lake bed and the Coso and Inyo mountains east of it. Olancha and Kern peaks dominate the southern half of the horizon.* ∎ At length you leave the ridgetop in a descending traverse of west-facing slopes, then curve west to a saddle where you meet a junction (10,425-1.5) with a faint, ½-mile-long lateral that descends north to a corral and campsites.

*   *   *   *

Water access: A spring waters a meadow polkadotted with buttercups in the crease of the canyon about 0.3 mile in on this lateral. This spring and the next off the PCT are good sources of water.

*   *   *   *

Beyond the faint junction, you ascend more or less northwest, crossing two more crestline saddles. Just east of the second saddle (10,260-1.6) is a path signed CORRAL to another corral and campsite.

*   *   *   *

Water access: A spring emerges 0.2 mile down-canyon on this path.

*   *   *   *

About ½ mile later you cross yet another saddle. ∎ *Here you leave one cattle allotment and enter another. In fact, the whole plateau is*

a patchwork of these parcels; wilderness classification here does not ban grazing. Most of the cattle people involved have been summering their animals in these allotments for several generations. ∎

The PCT curves north where Sharknose Ridge juts off to the west, then skirts the west edge of wide Ash Meadow, traversing a nearly level stretch of Sierra crest. The trail leaves the crest to make a brief, easy descent of northwest-facing slopes, where it passes a nearly obscure path (10,000-1.8) to another corral down in a ravine above Mulkey Meadows.

As the dusty PCT descends, Mt. Langley, the southernmost 14,000-foot peak in the Sierra Nevada, sinks behind the shoulder of Trail Peak while views of Mulkey Meadows improve. Your path bends east around a spur ridge where you find a rather unusual juxtaposition of foxtail pine, sagebrush and mountain mahogany. For almost a mile now the path nearly levels and then regains the Sierra crest at a low saddle (9670-1.8).

*   *   *   *

Side trip: The PCT begins to ascend, but if you need a campsite, leave the trail on a use path east, to the right of Diaz Creek, to find some open space. A spring issues forth in a side canyon just under ½ mile in on this use path.

*   *   *   *

You now climb the crest on a gentle-to-moderate grade gradually heading northwest. After a mile you curve on the crest, then leave it for a short climb north to top a broad ridge south of Dutch Meadow. (North-to-south trekkers: be alert lest you wander onto a former trail, again in use, to Mulkey Meadows. Take the left fork.) You turn sharply left at a signed CORRAL junction (9960-1.3), just below a switchback, but if you need water, a campsite, or a corral, turn right on the 0.2-mile lateral to Dutch Meadow. Your trail ascends west with two sets of switchbacks to cross the Sierra crest again. It attains a spur ridge, bends from north to west around a canyon, and then contours over to cross Mulkey Stock Driveway at Mulkey Pass (10,380-1.5). Beyond the driveway, the PCT traverses around the south side of a crestline-straddling hill to reach Trail Pass and a junc-

See maps G11, G12

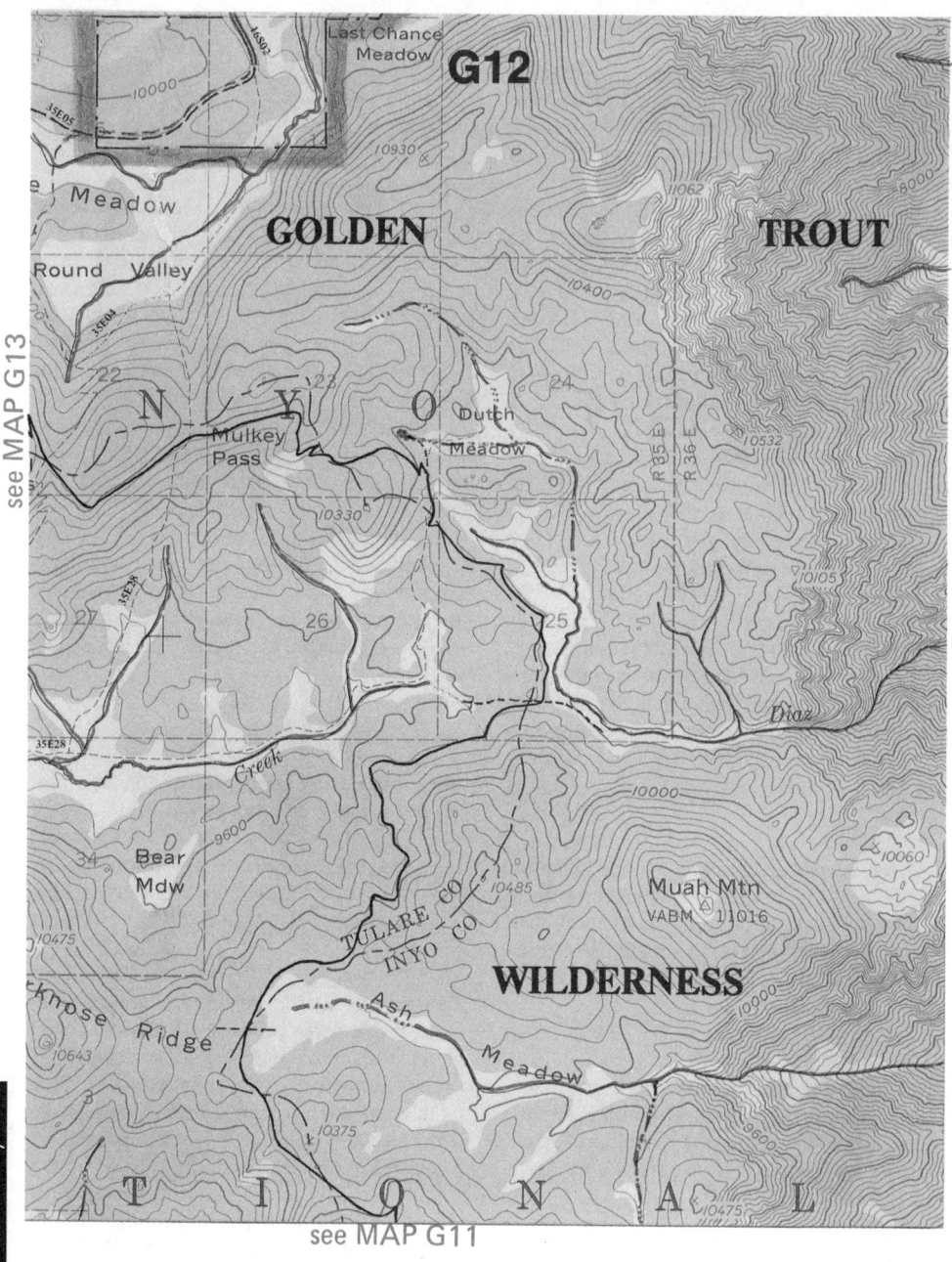

see MAP G13

see MAP G11

G12

GOLDEN   TROUT

WILDERNESS

tion (10,500-0.8) with the Trail Pass Trail.

*   *   *   *

Resupply access: If you have a package pickup in Lone Pine, need other supplies or need equipment repair, descend 2.1 miles north on Trail Pass Trail to Horseshoe Meadow Road

and an overnight campground, then hitchhike 22.8 miles to Lone Pine. During most spring weekends after snowmelt and during summer, this place buzzes with activity, but on early-season weekdays finding a ride at this parking area or the adjacent Cottonwood Lakes parking area may not be easy. Nevertheless, this is a far better place to begin a detour to Lone Pine

See map G12

G13

JOHN **MUIR**

WILDERNESS

TULARE CO.
INYO CO.

Pass
High Lake
Long Lake
Cottonwood

Cirque Peak
VABM 12900

South Fork
Lakes

Cirque
Lake

Chicken Spring
Lake

Cottonwood
Pass

Horseshoe Meadow
Ranger Station

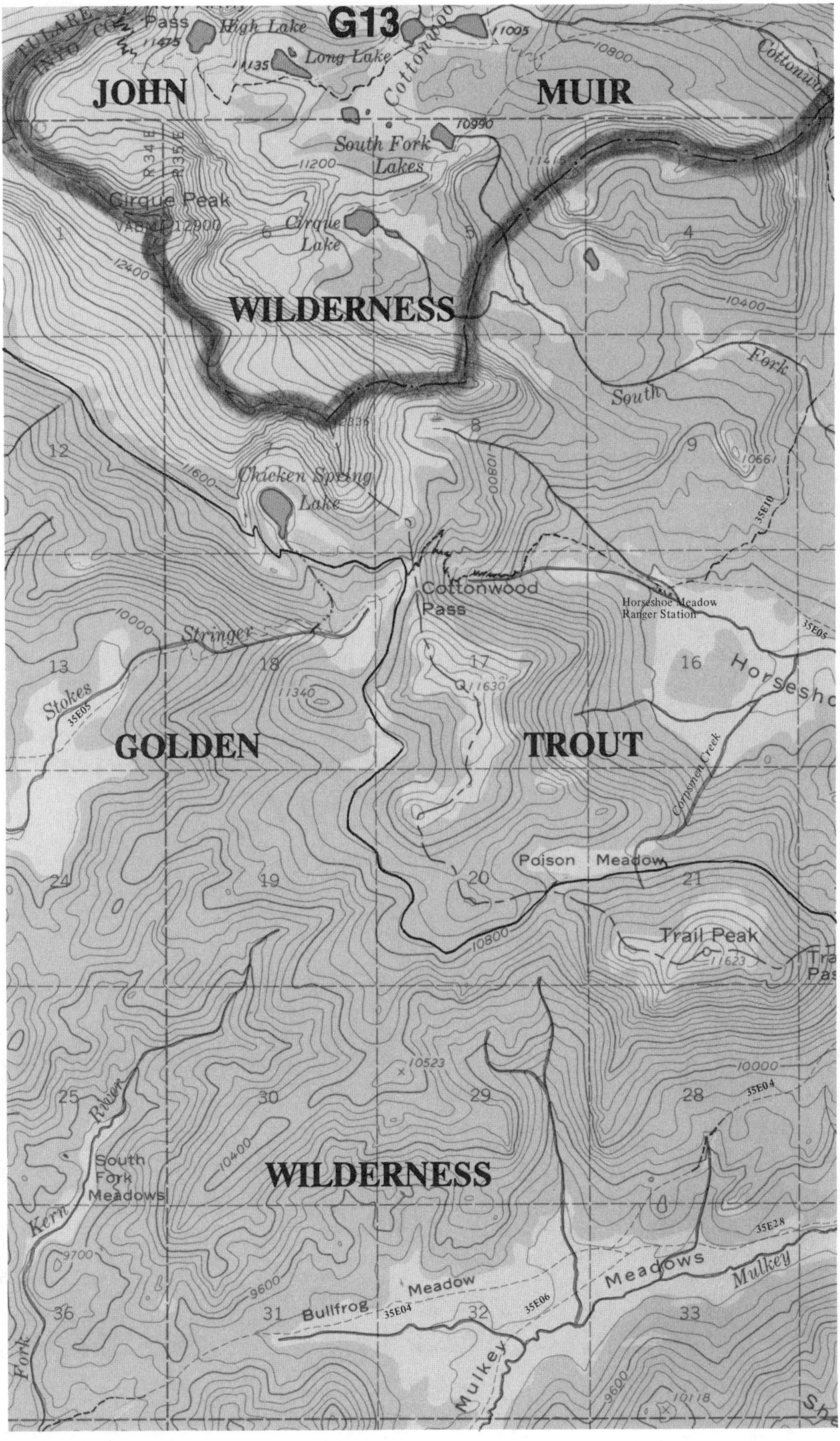

Stringer

Stokes

GOLDEN **TROUT**

Corpsman Creek

Horsesho

Poison Meadow

Trail Peak

South
Fork
Meadows

Kern River

WILDERNESS

Bullfrog Meadow

Mulkey

Meadows

Mulkey

than the detour over Trail Crest to Whitney Portal, where cars are frequent—unless returning to the PCT up Mount Whitney's steep east face toting a heavy pack is of no concern to you.

*   *   *   *

Continuing beyond Trail Pass the PCT ascends gently northwest amid foxtail pines and talus, switchbacks twice, and then rounds the north-facing slopes of 11,605-foot Trail Peak. ❚ *Portals in the forest frame the last exhilarating views of Mt. Langley seen from the PCT and the nearer views of Poison Meadow below.* ❚ Your trail winds past a path (10,740-1.3) to Poison Meadow, which descends on a westward slant, crosses Corpsmen Creek, and reaches a corral and a large meadowside campsite with spacious, pleasing views.

Now the PCT crosses the refreshing creek just beyond the meadow lateral, then soon leaves the slopes of Trail Peak to intersect the crest at a saddle (10,740-0.6) and traverse southwest along a route that offers sweeping views of Mulky Meadows below. The path then curves northward, passing several small meadows. ❚ *The meadows' seeps and springs combine to become the headwaters of South Fork Kern River, a stream that meanders through three wildernesses on the east side of the gentle plateau until it courses off the south end in a harsh area called The Roughs.* ❚

Foxtail pines shade you, parting occasionally to reveal views of the Great Western Divide. In time you round a watershed divide and pass through a west-facing, flower-flecked meadow. ❚ *This meadow's drainage finds its way into Golden Trout Creek, where it travels west to tumble off Kern Plateau's basaltic rim into the narrow, steep trench of North Fork Kern River—the river's main branch.* ❚ After ascending to a spur-ridge saddle, you descend to meet the Cottonwood Pass Trail at Cottonwood Pass (11,160-2.9). This trail also reaches Horseshoe Meadow Road and the campground to the east.

North of the junction, you climb imperceptibly around the head of an alpine meadow, turn west upon entering forest, and soon reach the outlet stream of Chicken Spring Lake (11,235-0.6). To catch shoreline views of the lake in its granite cirque, leave the trail before the outlet and stroll northwest to the shore. The lake is the last reliable water source before a tarn 2.7 miles onward or a brook that leads into Rock Creek, 9.2 miles ahead. Campsites abound at the lake, and on weekends so do people using them. On any summer day, though, you will not be alone, since Clark's nutcrackers—crow-

See map G13

Big Whitney Meadow, from the PCT above Chicken Spring Lake

sized, black, white and gray birds—will hop to your pads and caw at you for handouts.

Back on the PCT, the trail crosses the lake's sometimes-dry outlet stream, climbs, and switchbacks above the lake to gain a spur ridge, then makes a seemingly endless timberline traverse of the southwest-facing slopes below 12,900-foot Cirque Peak. Big Whitney Meadow appears intermittently far below you through the forest of foxtail pines. Your trail is at times annoyingly sandy. The PCT intersects a seasonal creek (11,320-2.5), which often flows through summer; a NO STOCK GRAZING sign is posted on a pine here.

*   *   *   *

Water access: There is no longer a lake in the little basin below the trail here; it is now a meadow where campsites may be found. Above the trail, however, a cross-country ascent of 200 feet, alongside the outlet creek, takes you to a fair-sized tarn snuggled within a cirque. This sparkling lake, its sandy, sloping beach, and a couple campsites make this an attractive stopover.

*   *   *   *

Climbing a little, the trail soon swings around a flat-topped ridge, then begins a descent that, except for some minor ups, does not end until it reaches the Rock Creek ford. The PCT passes an eye-catching "fang-toothed" rock formation, then enters Sequoia National Park (11,320-0.6), leaving Golden Trout Wilderness. Pets, firearms, grazing cattle and logging activities within the park are illegal.

▌ *On this descent, excellent views of the Great Western Divide appear across Siberian Outpost in the west.* ▌ Your downgrade first steepens somewhat, then becomes gentle as the path skirts the northeasternmost prong of Siberian Outpost. ▌ *Though named for its desolate aspect, the Outpost is surrounded by weathered foxtail-pine snags whose reddish-brown hues lend the place an impression of warmth and mellowness.* ▌ Now the PCT wanders westward, then crosses the Siberian Pass/Rock Creek trail (11,139-0.9).

You next head toward the broad, gently rolling ridgetop separating the watershed of Rock Creek to the north from that of stagnant Sibe-

rian Pass Creek to the south. The dramatic skypiercing crags of Rock Creek's headwaters basin are seen to the right, and Joe Devel Peak seems but a few steps away. After a 2-mile stroll from the last junction, you start an earnest downgrade. You descend and switchback, describing an **S** curve, then level to cross a sandy-grassy flat. Lodgepole pines, at first only scattered among foxtail pines, come to dominate the forest as you stroll northwest along a ridgetop, descend moderately via nine switchbacks northward, then hike down to a junction (9959-4.9) with the Rock Creek Trail.

Now your wanderings turn westward and zigzag several times more before crossing a brook (9840-0.3), the first reliable water since the tarn 6.5 miles back or Chicken Spring Lake, 9.2 miles. Pausing, you can easily identify the aromatic wild onions with their pinkish-purple blossoms gracing the banks upstream. Beyond, you follow the south edge of a meadow for a while, then cross it diagonally. Back in forest, you drop to a series of large campsites overlooking Rock Creek. You should bearproof your food if staying here or anywhere in the park. You can even be cited for noncompliance. A heavy metal retangular bearproof food locker has been placed at the creek crossing. You are asked to share the locker, keep it clean, close the door, and always secure the latch.

*   *   *   *

Side trip: The Rock Creek Ranger Station is 0.2 mile above (east of) the campsites. You reach it by first crossing the meadow while paralleling Rock Creek; then, finding the path among the trees, you follow it, hop across a stream, turn right immediately after, and then curve left. There it is—an ideal hideaway.

*   *   *   *

On the westbound PCT, the trail approaches Rock Creek, fords a rivulet while swerving away from the creek a bit, and finally crosses the creek on steppingstones (9550-0.9). Just downstream is a log for high-water crossings.

Your path ahead switchbacks, first north and then west-northwest, as it begins to climb a moderate-to-steep—sometimes steep—grade through stands of lodgepole pine and juniper trees. After passing cold, plant-caressed brooks

See maps G13, G14, G15

see MAP H2

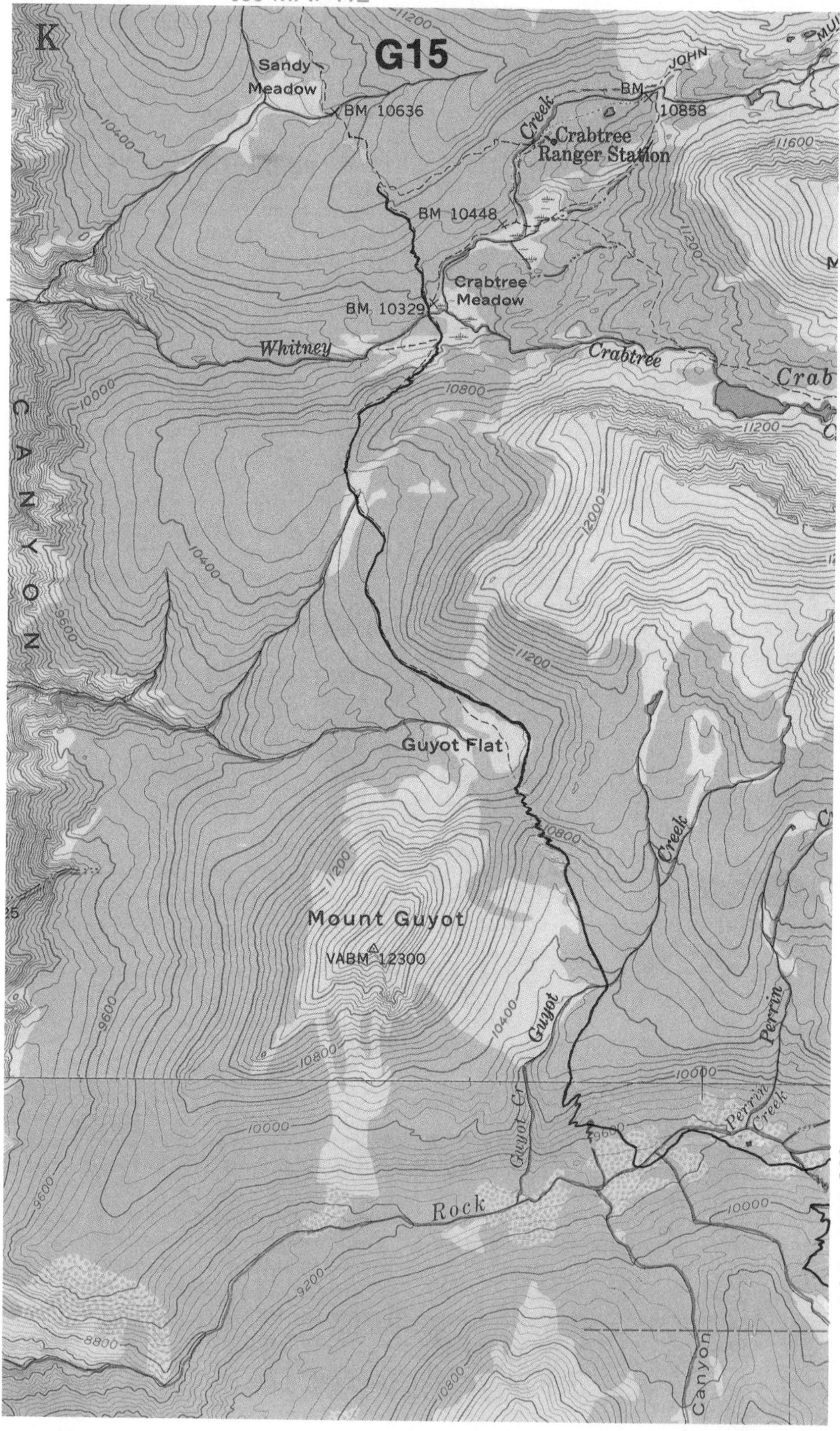
K
G15
Sandy
Meadow
BM 10636
JOHN
BM
10858
Creek
Crabtree
Ranger Station
11600
BM 10448
11200
Crabtree
Meadow
BM 10329
Whitney
Crabtree
Crab
10800
11200
10000
C A N Y O N
12000
10400
9600
11200
Guyot Flat
10800
Creek
Mount Guyot
VABM 12300
9600
10400
Guyot
Perrin
10800
10000
Guyot Cr
Perrin
Creek
10000
9600
Rock
10000
9200
8800
10800
Canyon

see MAP H1

see MAP G14

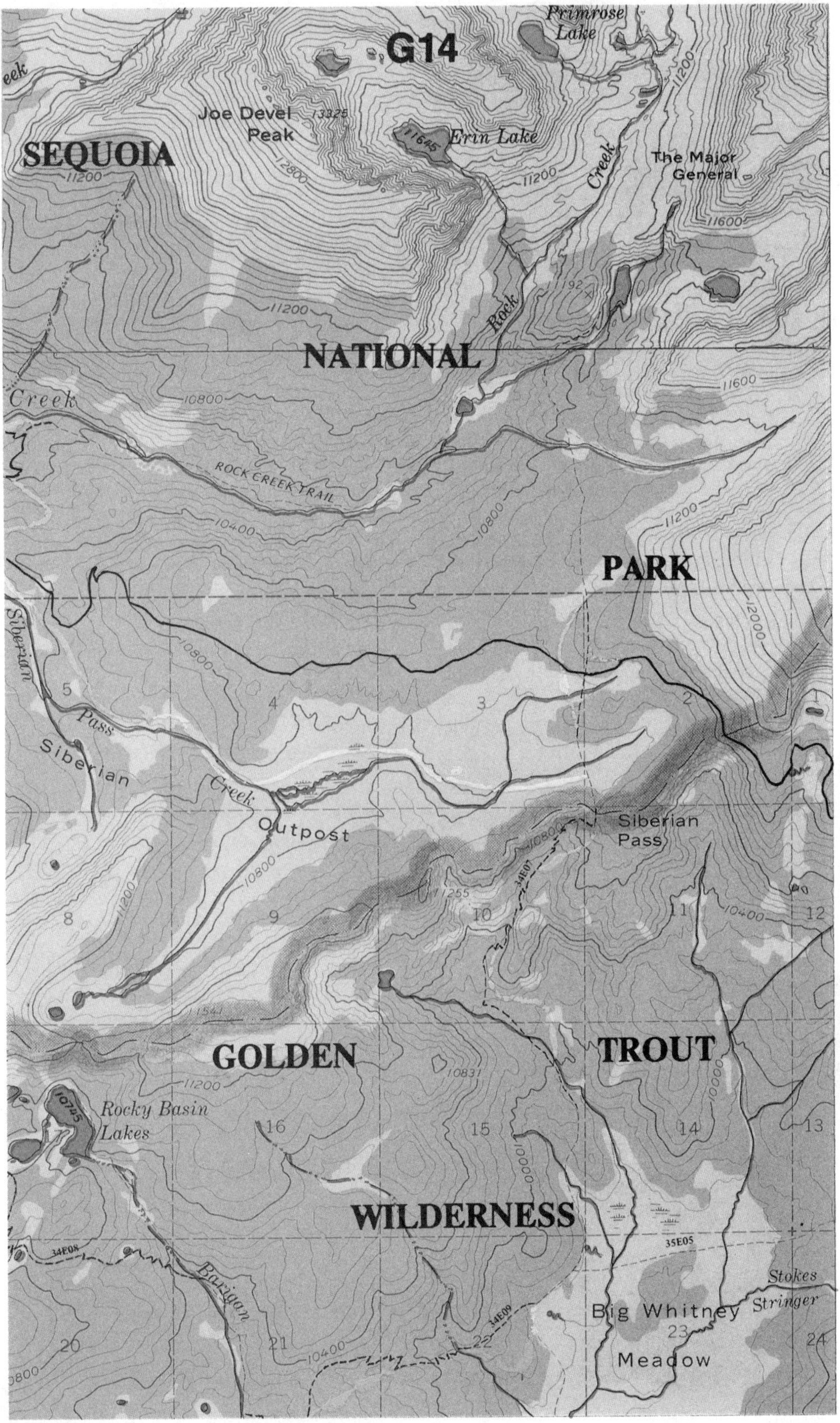

SEQUOIA

Joe Devel
Peak

13325

11645

Erin Lake

Primrose
Lake

The Major
General

11600

92 ×

NATIONAL

Rock

Creek

11200

11200

11200

11600

Creek

10800

ROCK CREEK TRAIL

10400

10800

11200

PARK

12000

see MAP G15

see MAP G13

Siberian

10800

Pass

5

4

3

2

1

Siberian

Creek

Outpost

Siberian
Pass

8

9

10800

10400

11200

265

10800

3407

3409

10

1

10400

12

G

11541

GOLDEN

10831

TROUT

10000

Rocky Basin
Lakes

10795

11200

16

15

10000

14

13

WILDERNESS

35E05

34E08

Bairigan

Stokes
Stringer

Big Whitney

Meadow

23

24

20

21

10400

3409

22

10800

Lower Rock Creek, Miter Basin rim

just below their springs, the PCT climbs a rack of 10 switchbacks, and then its grade eases. Camping areas are found here before the trail crosses Guyot Creek (10,320-1.5), the last source of water until Whitney Creek, 4.5 miles ahead.

After some easy hiking over gravelly terrain, you pass through a wreckage of mature trees on the slopes east of Mt. Guyot that were uprooted and broken by a 1986 snow avalanche. Young resilient trees survived. Beyond, you labor up and over a pass (10,920-1.0) northeast of 12,300-foot Mt. Guyot. As you descend and cross above grit-filled Guyot Flat, you have magnificent views across Kern Canyon of Red Spur and the Kaweah Peaks Ridge, then westsouthwest beyond the gap of the Big Arroyo, of the Great Western Divide peaks—notably the pointed summit of Mineral King's monarch mountain, Sawtooth Peak. Shaded by foxtail pines, you hike along the sandy trail, gradually veering north and passing another gritty flat. Next you ascend a broad, flat-topped ridge, then proceed northeast, dropping abruptly through a series of switchbacks.

Ahead of you, while descending the switchbacks, looms Mt. Young. East of it you receive your first near view of 14,491-foot Mt. Whitney, the highest mountain in the contiguous United States. *❚ PCT through-hikers have glimpsed this peak from great distances as far back as Sweet Ridge north of Highway 58. From here its furrowed backside and rounded top are partly hidden by Mt. Hitchcock. The grand mountain's most spectacular side, however, is its precipitous east face. The mountain, surrounded by other 14,000-foot peaks, lies on the granitic Sierra crest, thrust up by many grinding earthquakes.* ❚

At the foot of the descent, the PCT travels through a wooden-gated fence, levels out, and passes a use path that plummets west next to Whitney Creek and ends at the Kern River. Your path proceeds north, passing to your left a cluster of campsites and a food locker. Then it fords Whitney Creek and arrives at Crabtree Meadow, where it meets a lateral (10,329-3.5) to Mt. Whitney.

If you do not plan to climb up Mt. Whitney, proceed along the winding path north-northwest to a signed junction (10,870-0.8) with the John Muir Trail, the start of Section H.

*   *   *   *

Side trip: However, few can resist the opportunity to climb such a famous peak, so you turn northeast to ramble along the lateral, fa-

See map G15

vored along the way with full views of Mt. Whitney's west side. On this path you skirt lush, well-watered Crabtree Meadow, ascend a little canyon beside Whitney Creek, cross the creek, and then recross it to its north side to meet the John Muir Trail (10,640-1.2).

You do not recross the creek, however, if you are seeking campsites with a food locker or the Crabtree Ranger Station. The campsites are scattered among the trees on the southeast side of Whitney Creek, and the station is 0.1 mile northeast along a replaced section of the John Muir Trail. A ranger is available, if not on patrol, from mid-June to mid-October to help with emergencies and to answer questions, but this popular station is not a place to dump off trash. ∎ *The 1982 building near the station houses equipment for the snow pillow, which collects data on the winter snowpack and automatically sends the information via satellite to the California Department of Water Resources. This is important information, since most of California depends on water from the Sierra snowpack.* ∎

With knowledge that the summit can be bitterly cold, and assessing the time and the weather so as not to be caught on the summit or open slopes in an afternoon lightning storm, you proceed northeast on the John Muir Trail north of the creek. After climbing over granite slabs, you amble near the north shore of placid Timberline Lake. ∎ *Once heavily used as a base camp for climbing Whitney, these shores have been closed to all camping and stock grazing since before 1970.* ∎

Above the lake your trail passes the last of the forest on a moderate-to-steep grade away from Whitney Creek. Glacial polish is much in evidence on the granite along this ice-carved canyon of spectacular beauty. The path takes on a pattern of climbing slab staircases up granite benches, then traversing around hollows sometimes holding a tarn or a good-sized lake. After topping a broad, rounded ridge the path approaches Guitar Lake (11,480-2.7), where many hikers camp among the rocks away from the meadow grasses. Above Guitar Lake , the

See maps G15, H1

Foxtail pines and craggy outcrops line the PCT

two tarns at 11,600 feet offer an ideal camp setting as well, and are the last reliable sources of water on this summit quest.

Here the trail levels briefly, allowing you to pause and catch your breath preparing for the high-altitude climb ahead. When the ascent resumes, the Hitchcock Lakes come into view; they were hidden until now in a deep cirque at the foot of 13,184-foot Mt. Hitchcock. ∎ *The rugged appearance of many glacier-carved peaks contrasted with pockets of deep-pink rockfringe flowers instills in some a sense of awe and wonder.* ∎

A few short switchbacks now signal the onset of nine long-legged switchbacks that wind up the rocky slopes on the highest section of the Sierra crest, to a junction (13,560-2.9) with the eastbound Mt. Whitney Trail, which in 8.7 miles meets a road at Whitney Portal. Lines of stashed backpacks at this junction make a colorful collage as they lean against the rocky crags.

You turn left, climb north up a pair of switchbacks, pass Mt. Muir, and labor breathlessly on a long traverse beside a row of gendarmes. ∎ *Between gendarmes, you can look through crestline notches, sometimes called windows, to indigo lakes nestled in polished cirques almost straight down, far below and yet well above the pale Owens Valley. More reassuring are the brilliant blue clusters of fragrant sky pilot that grow in nooks along the path, evoking admiration for these hardy flowers that flourish in such harsh elements.* ∎ Your path makes a final few switchbacks up Mt. Whitney's back, then approaches a stone cabin with its register, and at last attains the summit (14,492-1.8-8.6). ∎ *This mountain was named by members of the Whitney Survey team for Josiah Dwight Whitney (1819-1896), the highly respected chief of the California State Geological Survey.* ∎

∎ *Strictly enforced quotas on the number of hikers allowed to leave Whitney Portal per day have reduced the population problem here, but it is still possible to find a crowd when you arrive—and a line at the outhouse. It is not only the highest toilet in elevation in the country, but it must be the most expensive toilet to maintain, as the "honey pot" has to be flown out regularly by helicopter. Nevertheless, it is a prime necessity.* ∎

See map H1

Smithsonian hut atop Mt. Whitney

❚ *The stone cabin was built in 1909 by the Smithsonian Institute to be used as an observatory. It was added to the National Register of Historic Places in 1978. In 1990 a fatality occurred when a group of hikers thought the hut a safe refuge during a lightning storm—it was not. It still is not, even though fitted with lightning rods.* ❚

❚ *On a clear day you can see almost any of your favorite mountains in the Sierra. Through PCT hikers can note dim, pointed Owens Peak and rounded Mt. Jenkins' tandem silhouette in the southeast, showing the distance they have* *hiked since Walker Pass. They may be able to see the San Bernardino Mountains as well.* ❚

From the summit you backtrack to the junction (10,640-7.4) across the creek from the ranger station. From there you continue on the John Muir Trail, progressing across a sandy flat from lodgepole pines to foxtail pines. A few zigzags and a long westward traverse with lingering views of Whitney lead to a signed junction (10,870-0.9-16.9) where you turn north on the Pacific Crest Trail, which joins the John Muir Trail to begin Section H.

See maps H1, G15

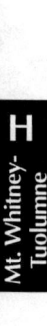

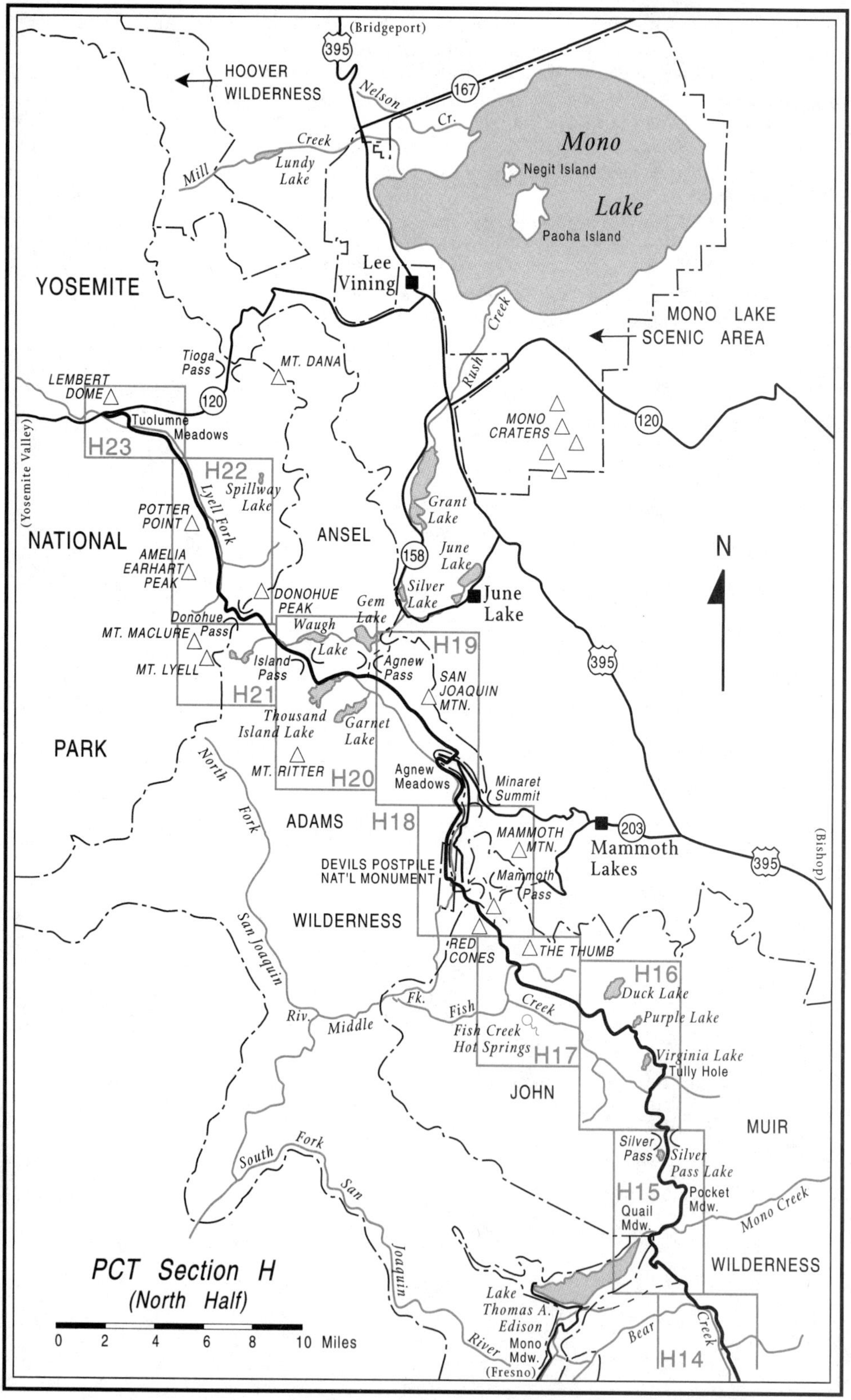

(Bridgeport)
395
167

HOOVER
WILDERNESS

Mono

Lake

Negit Island

Paoha Island

Nelson
Cr.

Mill
Creek
Lundy
Lake

Lee
Vining

MONO LAKE
SCENIC AREA

YOSEMITE

Rush
Creek

Tioga
Pass
120
MT. DANA

LEMBERT
DOME
Tuolumne
Meadows

H23

H22

Spillway
Lake

POTTER
POINT

Lyell Fork

ANSEL

MONO
CRATERS

120

NATIONAL

AMELIA
EARHART
PEAK

DONOHUE
PEAK

Gem
Lake

Grant
Lake

158

June
Lake

Silver
Lake

June
Lake

N

Donohue
Pass

Waugh
Lake

MT. MACLURE

Island
Pass

MT. LYELL

H21

Thousand
Island Lake

Garnet
Lake

Agnew
Pass

SAN
JOAQUIN
MTN.

H19

395

PARK

North
Fork

MT. RITTER

H20

Agnew
Meadows

Minaret
Summit

203

Mammoth
Lakes

395

(Bishop)

ADAMS

H18

San Joaquin

DEVILS POSTPILE
NAT'L MONUMENT

MAMMOTH
MTN.

Mammoth
Pass

WILDERNESS

RED
CONES

THE THUMB

H16

Duck Lake

Purple Lake

Fk.

Riv.   Middle

Fish
Creek

Fish Creek
Hot Springs

H17

Virginia Lake
Tully Hole

South   Fork

San

JOHN

MUIR

Silver
Pass

Silver
Pass Lake
Pocket
Mdw.

Mono Creek

H15
Quail
Mdw.

WILDERNESS

Lake
Thomas A.
Edison
Mono
Mdw.
(Fresno)

Bear

Creek

H14

Joaquin

River

PCT Section H
(North Half)

0   2   4   6   8   10 Miles

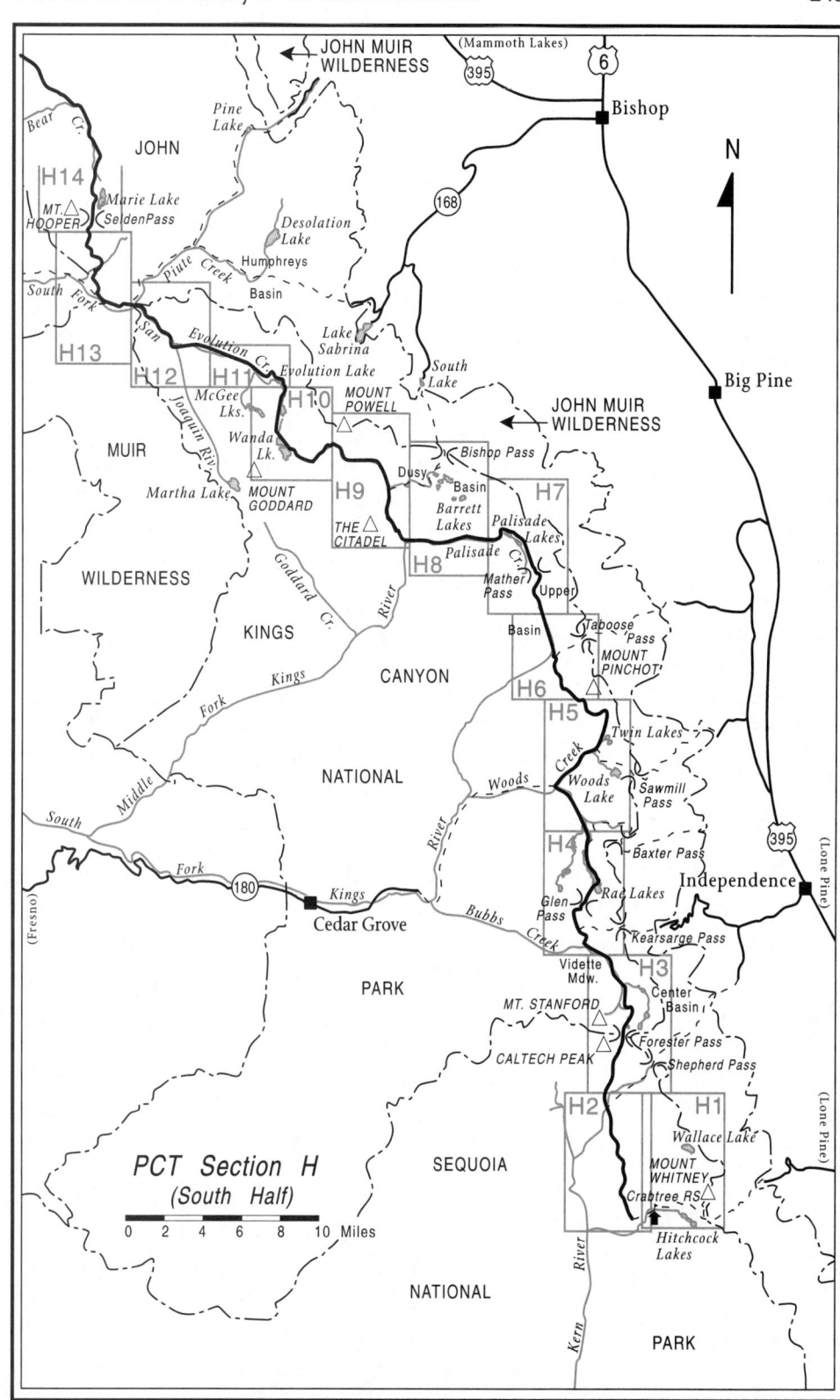

PCT Section H
(South Half)

0 2 4 6 8 10 Miles

Section H
Mt. Whitney to Tuolumne Meadows

Introduction: The Pacific Crest Trail from the Mt. Whitney Trail junction to Tuolumne Meadows passes through what many backpackers agree is the finest mountain scenery in the United States. Some hikers may give first prize to some other place, but none will deny the great attractiveness of the High Sierra.

This is a land of 13,000-foot and 14,000-foot peaks, of soaring granite cliffs, of lakes literally by the thousands, of canyons 5000 feet deep. It is a land where man's trails touch only a tiny part of the total area, so that by leaving the trail you can find utter solitude. It is land uncrossed by road for 150 airline miles from just north of Walker Pass to Tuolumne Meadows. And perhaps best of all, it is a land blessed with the mildest, sunniest climate of any major mountain range in the world. Though rain does fall in the summer—and much snow in the winter—the rain seldom lasts more than an hour or two, and the sun is out and shining most of the hours that it is above the horizon.

Given these attractions, you might expect that quite a few people would want to enjoy them. And it is true that some hikers joke about traffic signs being needed on the John Muir Trail—which the PCT follows for most of this section. But the land is so vast that if you do want to camp by yourself, you can. While following the trail in the summer, you can't avoid passing quite a few people, but you can stop to talk or not, as you choose.

Declination: 14+°E

Points on Route	S→N	Mi. Btwn. Pts.	N→S
John Muir Trail above Crabtree Meadows	0.0		177.2
Wallace Creek	3.3	3.3	173.9
Lake South America Trail	8.6	5.3	168.6
Forester Pass	12.9	4.3	164.3
Bubbs Creek Trail	20.9	8.0	156.3
Kearsarge Pass Trail	23.1	2.2	154.1
Glen Pass	25.4	2.3	151.8
Woods Creek	33.7	8.3	143.5
Pinchot Pass	40.8	7.1	136.4
South Fork Kings River	45.1	4.3	132.1
Mather Pass	50.3	5.2	126.9
Middle Fork Kings River	60.5	10.2	116.7
Bishop Pass Trail	63.8	3.3	113.4
Muir Pass	70.8	7.0	105.0
Evolution Lake Inlet	75.4	4.6	100.7

Evolution Creek in Evolution Meadow 82.8	7.4	93.0
Piute Pass Trail 87.3	4.8	88.2
Florence Lake Trail 89.1	1.8	86.4
Selden Pass 96.7	7.6	78.8
Mono Creek 110.0	13.3	65.5
Silver Pass 117.0	7.0	58.5
Tully Hole 121.8	4.8	53.7
Duck Lake outlet 128.1	6.3	47.4
Reds Meadow 139.6	11.5	35.9
Agnew Meadows Trailhead 147.4	7.8	28.1
Thousand Island Lake outlet 155.2	7.8	20.3
Rush Creek Forks 158.4	3.2	17.1
Donohue Pass 161.8	3.4	13.7
Lyell Base Camp 165.8	4.0	9.7
Highway 120 in Tuolumne Meadows 175.5	9.7	0.0

Supplies: This section does not allow easy resupply. To reach any kind of civilization you must—except at Reds Meadow—walk at least 18 miles round trip. Even then, if you have major needs, you will have to hitchhike many miles farther. At the beginning of this section, you can take the Mt. Whitney Trail 15½ miles to Whitney Portal, where there is a very small store, or hitchhike from the portal 13 miles to Lone Pine, which has almost everything you might want. Twenty-one miles into Section H, at the Bubbs Creek Trail, you can hike 14 miles west to Cedar Grove, with another very small store and a modest cafe plus post office. To hitchhike from there to Fresno would be a major project. About 2 miles farther, at the Kearsarge Pass Trail, you can hike 9 miles east to Onion Valley, and hitchhike from there 15 miles out of the mountains to Independence, which has just one store, albeit a rather large one for such a small town. About 41 miles farther, at the Bishop Pass Trail, you can hike northeast 12 miles to South Lake, which has nothing, and hitchhike 19 miles to Bishop, which has everything. Then, 24 miles farther, at the Piute Pass Trail, you can hike northeast 18 miles to North Lake, which has nothing, and hitchhike 18 miles to Bishop. About 2 miles farther, you can hike north 11 miles along the Florence Lake Trail to the roadend, where there is a tiny store. Then 22 miles farther, from where you bridge Mono Creek, you can walk 6 miles west, mostly beside Lake Edison, to Vermilion Resort, again with a small store plus meals, showers, and a package-holding service. (Write ahead to confirm this service; the address is in Chapter 2, under "Post Offices Along or Near the Route." Enclose an SASE.) Seven miles west by road from there is Mono Hot Springs, with meals, supplies and a post office.

About 29 miles farther, you are at Reds Meadow, with a somewhat-more-than-minimal store and a cafe. Just down the paved road is Reds Meadow Campground, which has a nearby, free public bathhouse fed by a hot spring. If you need more than a few supplies, go to Mammoth Lakes, a recreation-oriented town. From a choice of stops along the Reds Meadow-Agnew Meadow stretch of road, you can take a shuttle bus up over Minaret Summit and down one mile to expansive Mammoth Mountain Inn, opposite the ski area. In 1994 the round-trip fare was $7.00—twice the fare just 6 years earlier, so expect continued increases. For about the same amount you can take a taxi from the inn to central Mammoth Lakes, another 4½ miles farther. The shuttle bus operates from about the weekend before the Fourth of July through the weekend after Labor Day. Note that the charge is for one way only—from the Inn over to the Reds Meadow-Agnew Meadow area. Going the opposite way is a free ride. Out of season, the shortest walk to downtown Mammoth Lakes is an 8-mile route starting from Upper Crater Meadow (bottom of Map H18), and this is described in the trail text. On the other hand, you may be able to hitch a ride in the Reds Meadow-Agnew Meadow area if its road is still in use.

Finally, in the Tuolumne Meadows area, at the end of this section, you can get hot meals and showers at Tuolumne Meadows Lodge, a mile east of the principal meadow, or you can stop at a good store, with a cafe and post office, just southwest of the entrance to Tuolumne Meadows Campground. See the next chapter's Supplies for additional information.

Be aware that the facilities at Whitney Portal, Florence Lake, Lake Edison, Mono Hot Springs, Reds Meadow, and Tuolumne Meadows may close by early or mid-September.

Special Problems:

Snow. For hikers trying to do the whole PCT in one year, the biggest problem in the High Sierra is snow. If you leave Mexico in early April, you will reach the Sierra before the end of May. In most years there will be a lot of snow in the High Sierra in May and June. A few people use snowshoes or skis to travel over the snow, but as the sun cups get deeper, these devices become useless. What you will need for the snowy sections is crampons and an ice ax, and the knowledge of how to use them. You need a tent. You need plenty of warm clothing, including mitts. And you need a basic understanding of avalanches—where they tend to occur, why they tend to occur, what to do if caught in one. *The ABC of Avalanche Safety*, published by The Mountaineers, is a good primer. Finally, where the trail is hidden by snow, you need some skills with map and compass to follow the route. You also need a lot of patience.

Cold. Even in midsummer it may freeze on any given night, so you need appropriate warmth.

Fords. In late spring and early summer, when runoff is at a maximum, a few stream fords can be potentially lethal for careless or inexperienced hikers. Consult Ray Jardine's *PCT Hiker's Handbook*, which devotes a whole chapter to this subject. In short, take the time to find a safe place to cross (perhaps there is a fallen log up- or downstream). If you must ford, doing so in chest-deep slow water is preferable to making one in waist-deep fast water. Never ford just upstream from dangerous fast water. Jardine and the principal author, Schaffer, do have some differing opinions. Jardine prefers using a balancing stick; Schaffer doesn't use one. Jardine recommends unlatching the buckle on the backpack's waist belt. Because a modern backpack will have a quick-release buckle, Schaffer prefers to keep it latched to prevent excessive swaying of a top-heavy backpack, which could cause you to fall. (Jardine travels ultralight and so avoids this problem.) Both are against using a rope.

Bears. In most of this section and adjacent lands, you are in bear territory. The introduction to Section G tells how to save your food from these hungry animals.

Lack of signs. Some hikers are glad to see signs disappear. Others are glad to have signs confirm their notion of where they are. In Sequoia and Kings Canyon National

Parks virtually all place signs have been removed, and there appears to be a trend toward removing or at least not replacing signs at trail junctions too.

To help you cope with some of the difficulties mentioned above, a number of summer rangers are stationed along or near the trail in Sequoia and Kings Canyon National Parks from about July 4th to Labor Day. The trail description below tells where they are. Two points deserve special mention. First, if you go to a summer ranger station to report a friend in trouble and find the ranger out, please realize he might be gone for several days, and so leave a note for him and walk out for help yourself. Second, remember that the ranger has to buy his own food and camping gear, so he, not the government, is the loser if it is taken.

Permits: If you are northbound, you can get a permit for this entire section by writing to Sequoia and Kings Canyon National Parks. If you are southbound, write Yosemite National Park. If you are southbound (or northbound) and are starting in the Mammoth Lakes-Devils Postpile area, write Mammoth Ranger District. (Refer to page 18 for addresses.) Be aware that during the summer season (about late June through mid-September) user quotas are in effect for the three national parks and the wildernesses between them. Popular trailheads do reach their quotas, especially on weekends, so plan accordingly.

Maps: *Mount Whitney*
Mount Kaweah
Mount Brewer
Mount Williamson
Mount Clarence King
Mount Pinchot
Split Mountain
North Palisade
Mount Goddard
Mount Darwin
Mount Henry

Mount Hilgard
Florence Lake
Graveyard Peak
Bloody Mountain
Crystal Crag
Mammoth Mountain
Mount Ritter
Koip Peak
Vogelsang Peak
Tioga Pass

The Great Western Divide rises beyond Bighorn Plateau

H
Mt. Whitney-
Tuolumne

The Route

In this trail section you will be on the John Muir Trail almost all the way to Tuolumne Meadows, 178 miles ahead. Northbound on the combined PCT/John Muir Trail, you skirt what the map calls Sandy Meadow and ascend to a high saddle (10,964–1.7). Beyond it the trail winds among the huge boulders of a glacial moraine on the west shoulder of Mt. Young and brings you to excellent viewpoints for scanning the main peaks of the Kings-Kern Divide and of the Sierra crest from Mt. Barnard (13,990′) north to Junction Peak (13,888′). Soon you descend moderately, making several easy fords, and then switchback down to Wallace Creek and a junction (10,390–1.6) where the High Sierra Trail goes west toward a roadend near Giant Forest and a lateral trail goes east to Wallace Lake. The Wallace Creek ford, just north of the popular campsites, is difficult in early season.

Now your sandy trail climbs up to a forested flat, crosses it, and reaches the good campsite at the ford of Wright Creek (10,790-1.1), also difficult in early season. You then trace a bouldery path across the ground moraines left by the Wright Creek glacier and rise in several stages to Bighorn Plateau. Views from here are indeed panoramic. An unnamed, grass-fringed lake atop the gravelly, lupine-streaked plateau makes for great morning photographs westward over it. Now the PCT descends the talus-clad west slope of Tawny Point past many extraordinarily dramatic foxtail pines. At an unnamed lake beside the trail there are fair campsites and warmish swimming, but hardly any wood. At the foot of this rocky slope a trail departs southwest for the Kern River, and 200 yards past the junction you come to the Shepherd Pass Trail (10,930–3.5) going northeast. Immediately beyond is a formidable ford of Tyndall Creek. On the west side of the creek are many highly used campsites—a good place not to camp.

From these gathering places your trail makes a short climb to the junction with the Lake South America Trail (11,160–0.7), passes some fair campsites, and rises above timberline. As you tackle the ascent to the highest point on the PCT, you wind among the barren basins of high, rockbound—but fishy—lakes to the foot of a great granite wall, then labor up numerous switchbacks, some of which are literally cut into

the rock wall, to Forester Pass (13,180–4.3), on the border between Sequoia and Kings Canyon National Parks. Forester Pass' south side can be dangerous when snow-covered.

Wearing your wind garment, you will enjoy the well-earned, sweeping views from this pass before you start the (net) descent of 9000 feet to Canada. Down the switchbacks you go, unless they are buried under snow, and then stroll high above the west shore of Lake 12248. The trail soon doubles back to ford splashing Bubbs Creek just below that lake, then fords it twice more within a mile. Soon you reach timber, ford Center Basin creek (high in early season), pass the Center Basin trail (10,500–4.5) (bearbox) and then ford more tributaries of Bubbs Creek. Many good campsites are located near some of these fords and along the main creek, but wood is scarce, as it is almost everywhere along the John Muir Trail.

Continuing down the east side of dashing Bubbs Creek, you reach Vidette Meadow (9600–2.8), long a favorite camping spot in these headwaters of South Fork Kings River. High use has made the place less attractive, but its intrinsic beauty has not been lost, and the mighty Kearsarge Pinnacles to the northeast have lost only a few inches of height since Sierra Club founders like Joseph Le Conte camped here at the turn of the century. Camping is limited to one night in one place from here to Woods Creek. A summer ranger may be in Vidette Meadow east of the trail to assist traffic flow. Beyond the meadow, a trail goes west to Cedar Grove and the PCT turns north (9550–0.7) to fiercely attack the wall of Bubbs Creek canyon. You pause for breath at the Bullfrog Lake junction (10,530–1.5) and then finish off the tough climb at a broad, sandy saddle that contains the junction of the Charlotte Lake and Kearsarge Pass trails (10,710–0.7). There is a summer ranger on the east shore of Charlotte Lake. In ¼ mile you pass a shortcut (for southbound hikers) to the Kearsarge Pass Trail, and then you traverse high above emerald Charlotte Lake. As the route veers eastward, it passes another trail to Charlotte Lake, then climbs past a talus-choked pothole and ascends gently to the foot of the wall that is notched by Glen Pass.

It is hard to see where a trail could go up that precipitous blank wall, but one does, and after

See maps H2, H3, H4

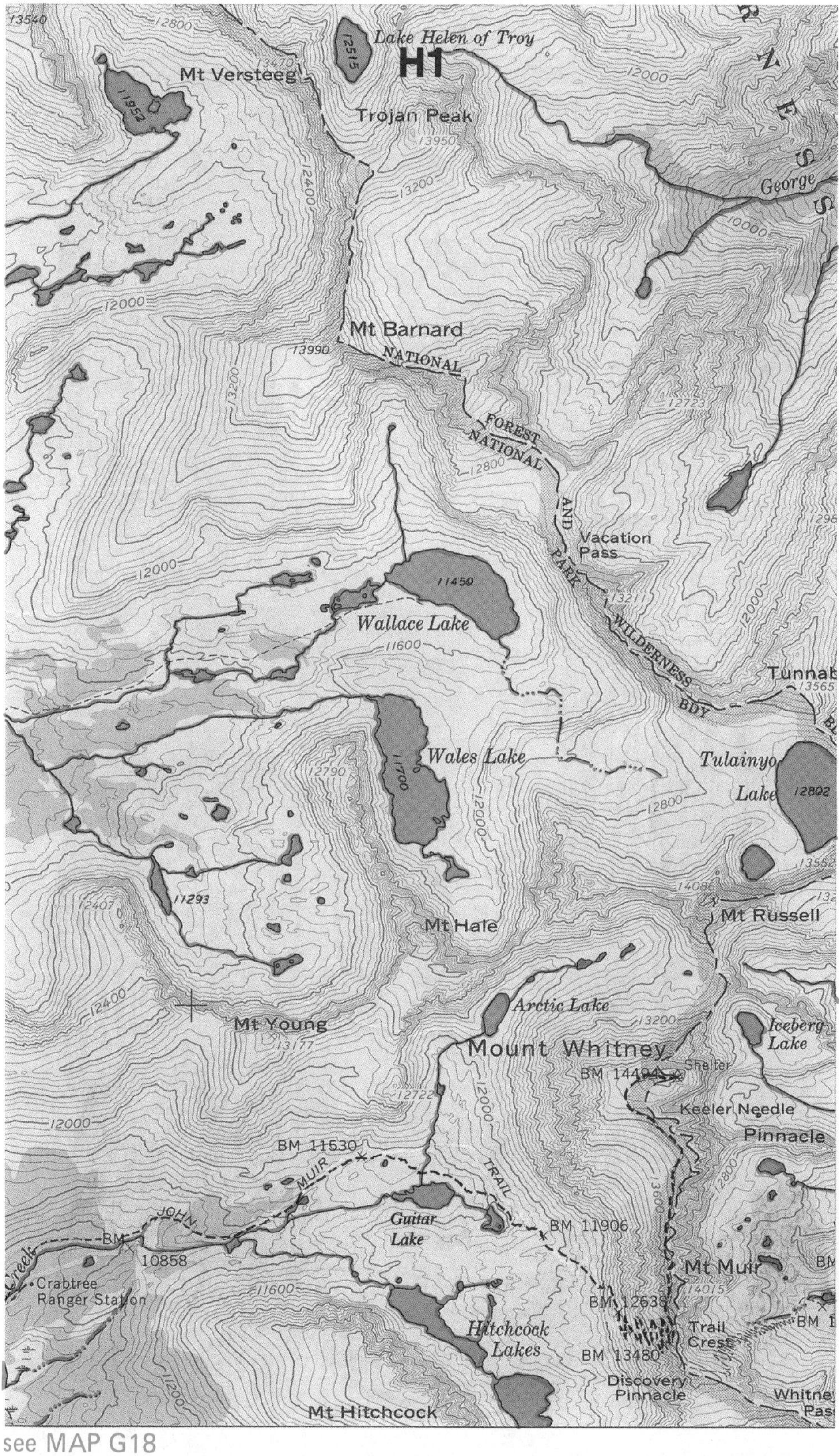
H1
Lake Helen of Troy
12515
Mt Versteeg
13470
11952
13540
12800
Trojan Peak
13950
12000
George
10000
12400
13200
Mt Barnard
13990
NATIONAL
FOREST
NATIONAL
AND
PARK
WILDERNESS
BDY
12723
12800
Vacation Pass
13211
11450
Wallace Lake
11600
Tunnabora
13565
Wales Lake
11700
12790
Tulainyo Lake
12802
11293
12407
Mt Hale
14086
Mt Russell
Arctic Lake
Mt Young
13177
Mount Whitney
BM 14494
Shelter
Iceberg Lake
Keeler Needle
Pinnacle
12722
BM 11530
MUIR
JOHN
TRAIL
Guitar Lake
BM 11906
BM
10858
Creek
Crabtree Ranger Station
Mt Muir
14015
BM 12638
Trail Crest
Hitchcock Lakes
BM 13480
Discovery Pinnacle
Whitney Pass
Mt Hitchcock
11200

see MAP H2

see MAP G18

To LONE PINE

see MAP H3

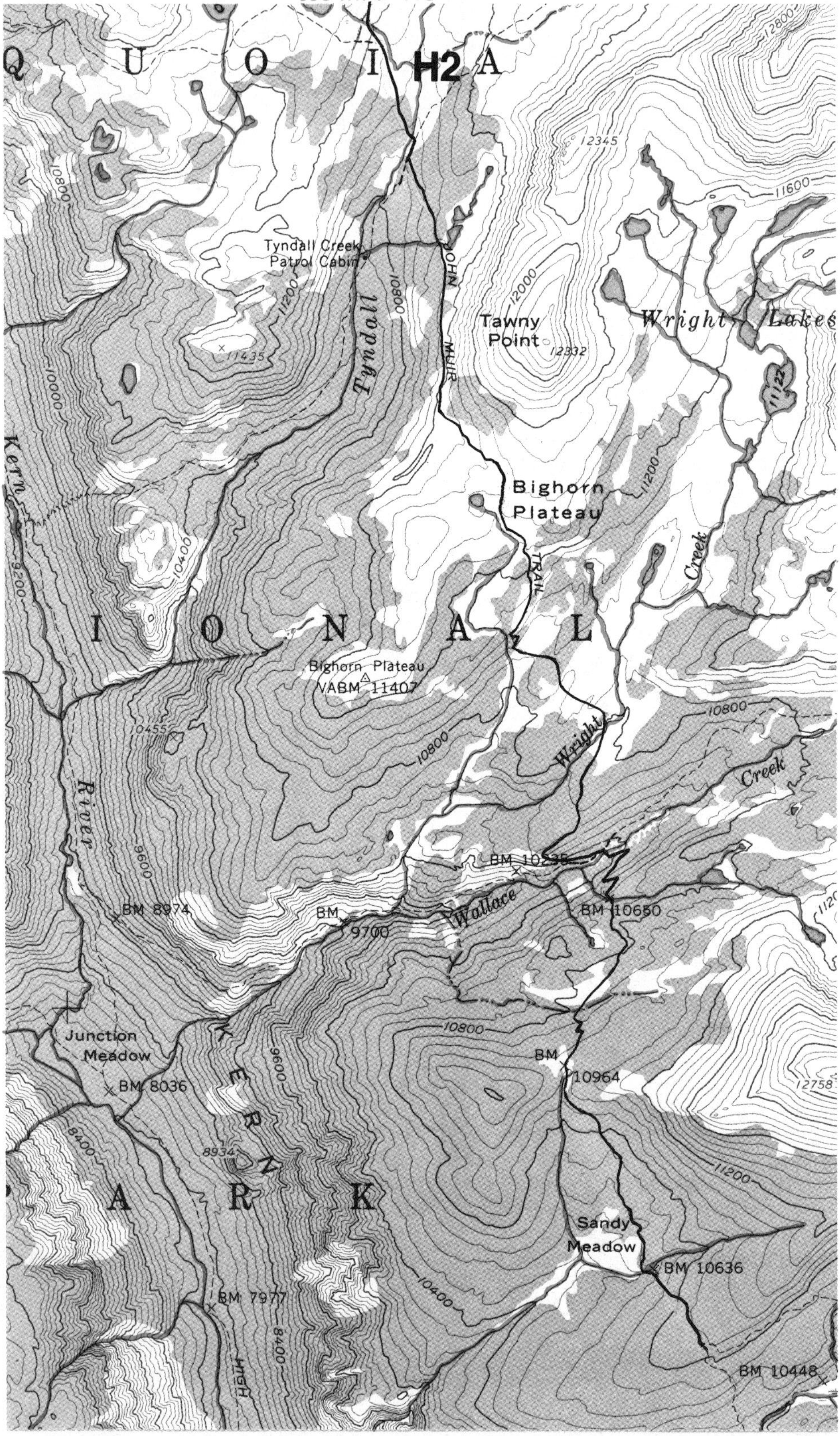

Q U O I A
H2
Tyndall Creek
Patrol Cabin
Tyndall
JOHN
MUIR
TRAIL
Tawny
Point
12332
12345
12800
11600
12000
11200
10800
10000
11435
10400
9200
Wright Lakes
11122
Kern
Bighorn
Plateau
Creek
I O N A L
Bighorn Plateau
VABM 11407
10455
River
Wright
Creek
9600
BM 10235
BM 8974
BM
9700
Wallace
BM 10650
Junction
Meadow
BM 8036
K
E
R
N
BM
10964
12758
8400
8934
A R K
Sandy
Meadow
BM 10636
BM 7977
HIGH
BM 10448

see MAP H1

see MAP G18

see MAP H4

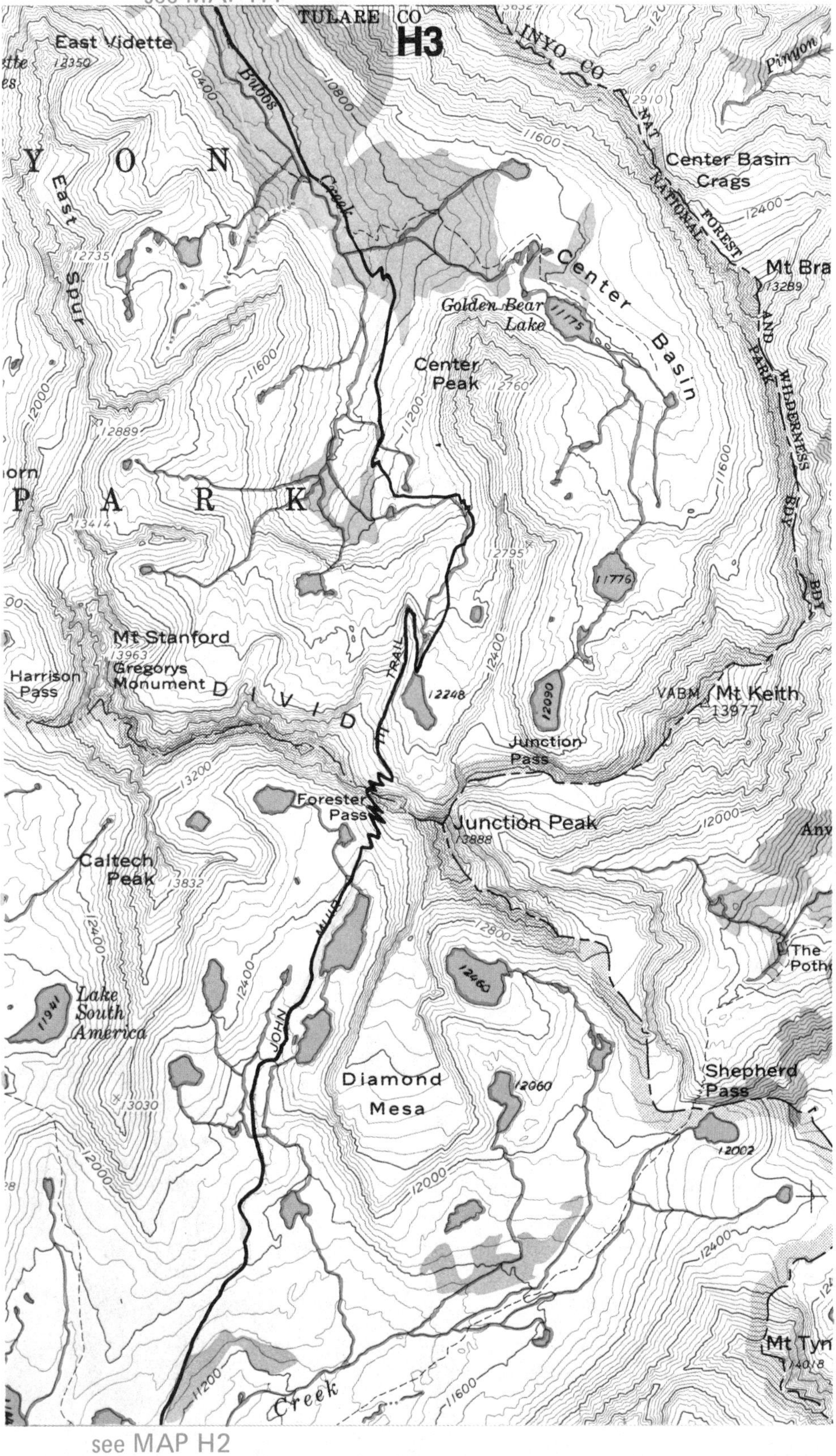

TULARE CO

H3

East Vidette *12350*

INYO CO

Pinyon

Center Basin Crags

3652

12910

11600

NAT

Mt Bra *13289*

East Spur

12735

Center Basin

Golden Bear Lake *11175*

FOREST

12400

CANYON

11600

Center Peak *12760*

AND

PARK

12889

11200

12795

11775

WILDERNESS BDY

13414

12000

11600

BDY

Mt Stanford *13963*
Gregorys Monument

DIVIDE

12248

12090

12000

VABM Mt Keith *13977*

Harrison Pass

TRAIL

Junction Pass

13200

Forester Pass

Junction Peak *13888*

12000

Anv

Caltech Peak *13832*

12400

JOHN

12800

12460

The Poth

Lake South America *11941*

13030

Diamond Mesa

12060

Shepherd Pass

To INDEPENDENCE

12002

12400

12000

11200

11600

Creek

Mt Tyn *1401.8*

H
Mt. Whitney-Tuolumne

see MAP H2

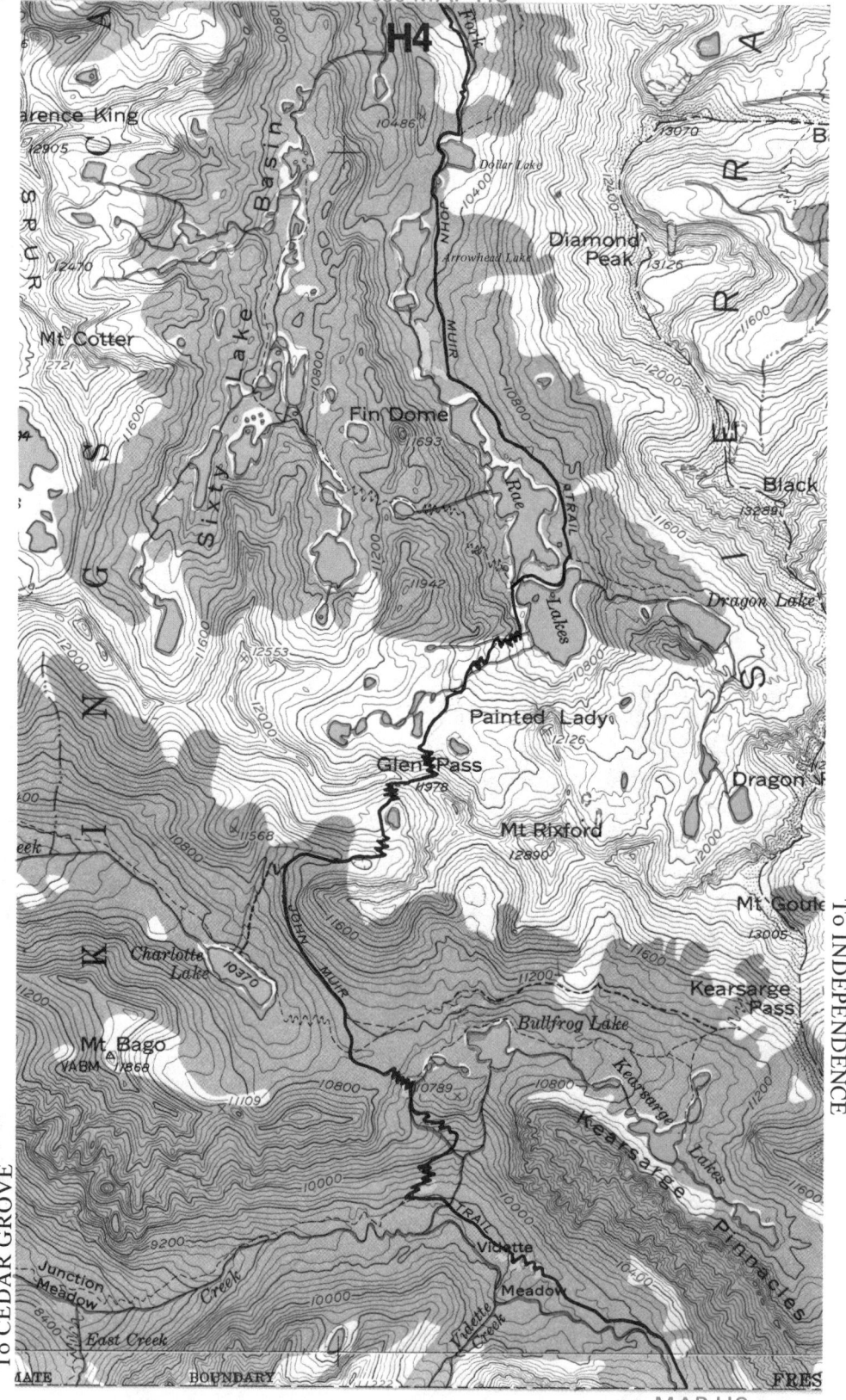

H4

Clarence King
12905

SPUR

12470

Mt Cotter
12721

KINGS

Sixty Lake Basin

10800

10486

Dollar Lake

10400

Arrowhead Lake

Diamond Peak
13126

13070

R

11600

12000

Black
13289

Fin Dome
11693

12000

11942

MUIR TRAIL

JOHN MUIR TRAIL

Rae Lakes

10800

Dragon Lake

12553

12000

Painted Lady
12126

Glen Pass
11978

Mt Rixford
12890

Dragon

11568

10800

JOHN MUIR

11600

Charlotte Lake
10370

11200

Mt Bago
VABM 11868

11109

10800

10000

9200

Junction Meadow

East Creek

Creek

Bullfrog Lake

11200

Kearsarge Pass

Mt Goule
13005

12000

Kearsarge Lakes

11600

Kearsarge Pinnacles

10789

10800

TRAIL

10000

Vidette Meadow

Vidette Creek

To CEDAR GROVE

To INDEPENDENCE

MATE BOUNDARY

FRES

very steep switchbacks you are suddenly at Glen Pass (11,978–2.3). The view north presents a barren, rocky, brown world with precious little green of tree or meadow visible. Yet you know by now that not far down the trail ahead there will be plenty of willows, sedges, wildflowers and, eventually, groves of whitebark, lodgepole and foxtail pines. To be sure you get there, take special care on your descent from Glen Pass as you switchback down to a small lake basin, ford the lakes' outlet and switchback down again.

When you are about 400 vertical feet above Rae Lakes, you will see why Dragon Peak (12,995'), in the southeast, has that name. Where the 60 Lakes Trail turns off to the west (10,550–2.0) your route turns east, then crosses the isthmus (wet in early season) between two of the Rae Lakes and skirts the east shore of the middle lake, passing the Dragon Lake Trail and a summer ranger station. Wood fires are not allowed between Glen Pass and the Baxter Pass Trail, and you may camp only one night at each Rae Lake. Each has a bearbox.

Beyond Rae Lakes your gently descending trail passes above an unnamed lake and drops to the northeast corner of aptly named Arrowhead Lake. Then it fords gurgling South Fork Woods Creek on boulders and reaches scenic, heavily used Dollar Lake. The unsigned Baxter Pass Trail heads northeast from below the outlet of this lake (10,230–2.6). ∎ *The lower slopes just east of Dollar Lake are composed of Paleozoic sediments that were later metamorphosed to biotite schist. Granitic rock separates these metasediments from a higher, north-south band of Triassic-Jurassic lava flows that have been changed into metavolcanic rocks. The metamorphism of all these rock types probably occurred during the Cretaceous period, when bodies of molten granite rising up into them deformed and altered them. As we progress north to Yosemite, we'll see many more examples of similar metamorphosed rocks.* ∎

From the Baxter Pass Trail junction you descend gently down open, lightly forested slopes, crossing several good-sized though unnamed streams, including the creek from Lake 10296. The reward for all this descent is a chance to start climbing again at Woods Creek (8492–3.7), crossed on a wood bridge, where the campsites are good but much used and have

Painted Lady above Rae Lake

bear boxes. Immediately beyond the bridge a trail to Cedar Grove goes south down the creek. As you perspire north from the crossing up the valley of Woods Creek, there is no drinking-water problem, what with the main stream near at hand and many tributaries, some of good size, to ford, jump or boulder-hop. After the junction of the Sawmill Pass Trail (10,370–3.4), the grade abates and you reach the alpine vale where this branch of the Kings River has its headwaters, bounded by glorious peaks on 3½ sides. With one last, long spurt you finally top Pinchot Pass (12,130–3.7), one of those "passes" that are regrettably not at the low point of the divide.

From this pass the PCT swoops down into the lake-laden valley below, runs along the east shore of at-timberline Lake Marjorie, touches its outlet (11,160–1.7), and then passes 4 lakelets, fording several small streams along the way. A summer ranger station is sometimes located beyond the fourth lakelet, just south of

H
Mt. Whitney-
Tuolumne

See maps H4, H5, H6

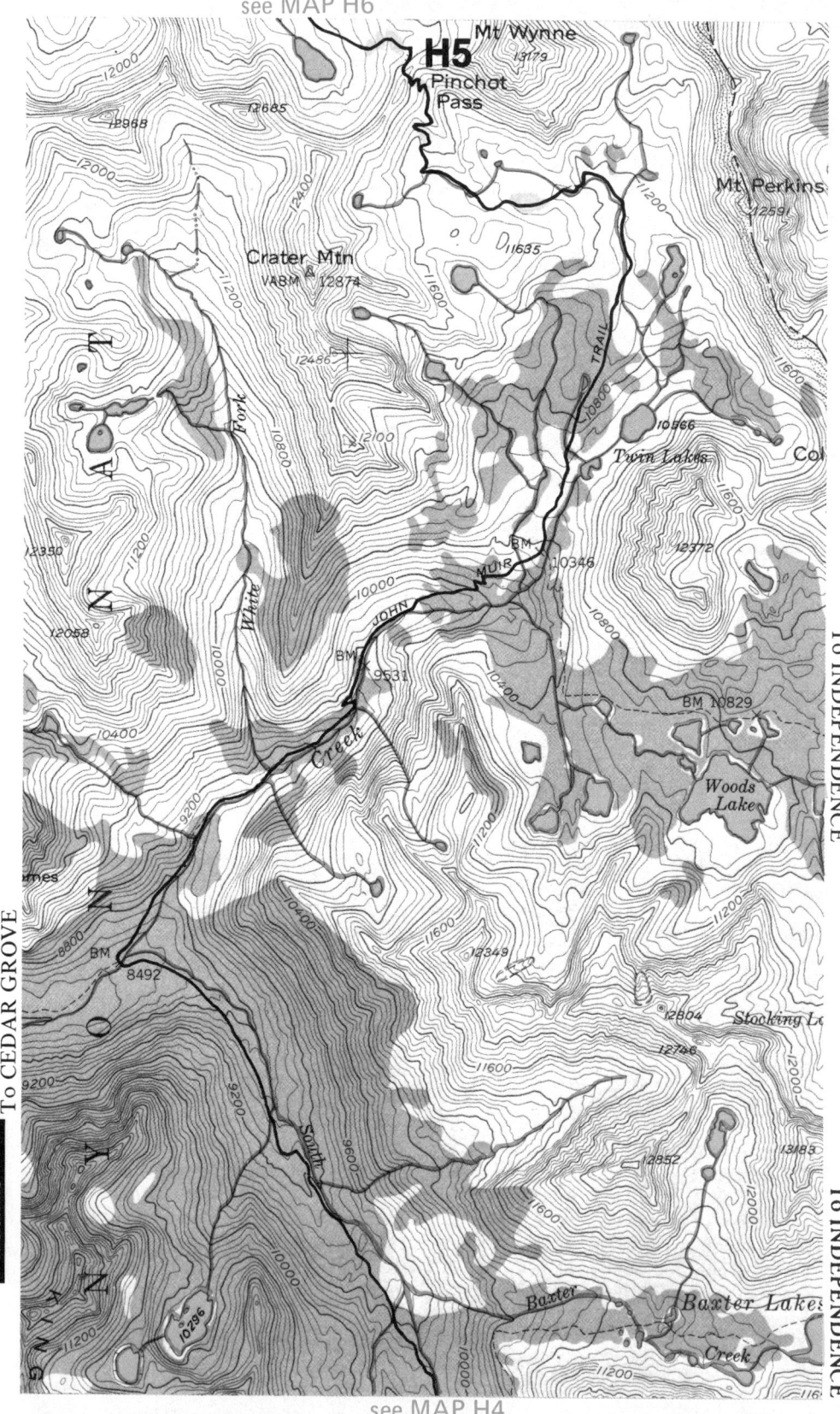

H5

Mt Wynne
13179

Pinchot
Pass

Mt Perkins
12591

Crater Mtn
VABM 12874

Twin Lakes

Col

BM

MUIR 10348

JOHN

BM 9531

White Fork

Creek

BM 10829

Woods Lake

BM 8492

South

Stocking L

Baxter

Baxter Lakes

Creek

To CEDAR GROVE

To INDEPENDENCE

To INDEPENDENCE

Mt. Whitney-Tuolumne

H

see MAP H7

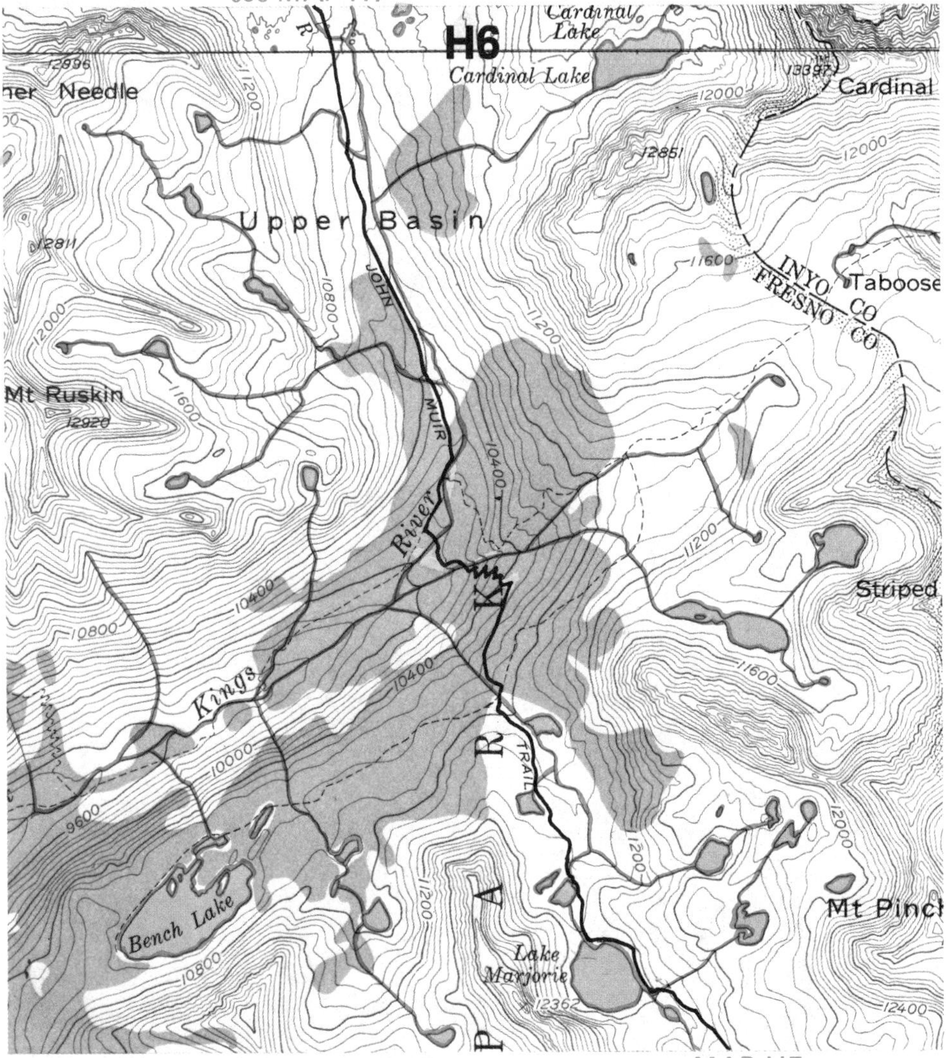
H6
Cardinal Lake
Cardinal Lake
Needle
Cardinal
Upper Basin
JOHN
MUIR
TRAIL
River
Kings
Mt Ruskin
INYO CO
FRESNO CO
Taboose
Striped
Mt Pinch
Bench Lake
Lake Marjorie
12896
12811
12920
13397
12851
12362
11200
10800
12000
11600
10400
10000
9600
12400

see MAP H5

Mt. Clarence King, from Woods Creek Headwaters

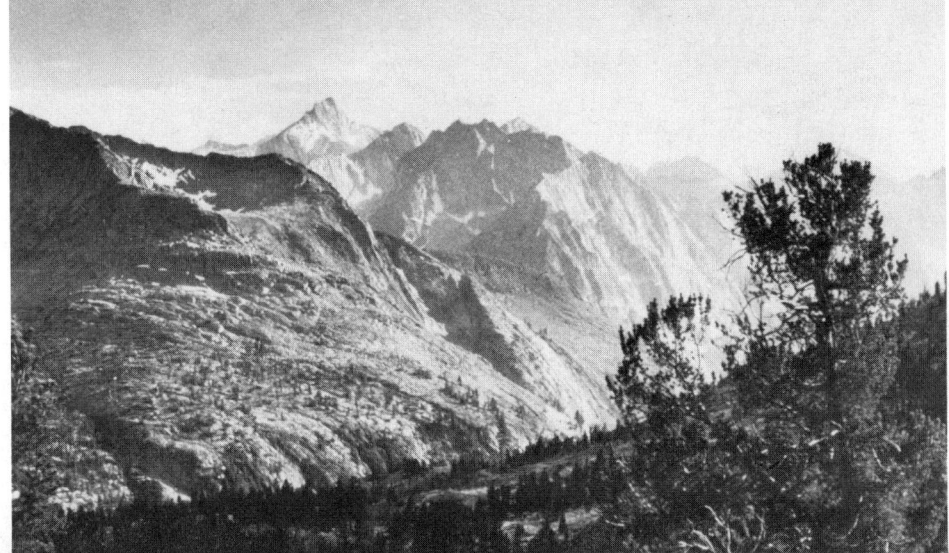

Mt Goode

Bishop Lake

Jigsaw Pass

12622

INYO CO
FRESNO CO

Bishop Pass

1389 Mt Agassiz

Sam Mack Lake

12244

12400

Agassiz Col

Mt Winchell *13768*

Mt Gay

Palisade Glacier

14162

Dusy Basin

11393

Isosceles Pk

Thunderbolt Pk

VABM 14242

North Palisade

Branch

10800

10734

12652

Columbine Peak

Barrett Lakes

Palisade

Rainbow Lakes

10800

11678

Knapsack Pass

11460

Basin

12682

11200

12586

Giraud Pk

12359

A   R   K

11672

12282

12094

Glacier Creek

11200

10800

10000

10027

MUIR

Deer Meadow

9200

TRAIL

Palisade

Creek

8800

9200

Cataract

9204

Doe Lake

10220

11747

11875

12151

Mt Shakspere

11265

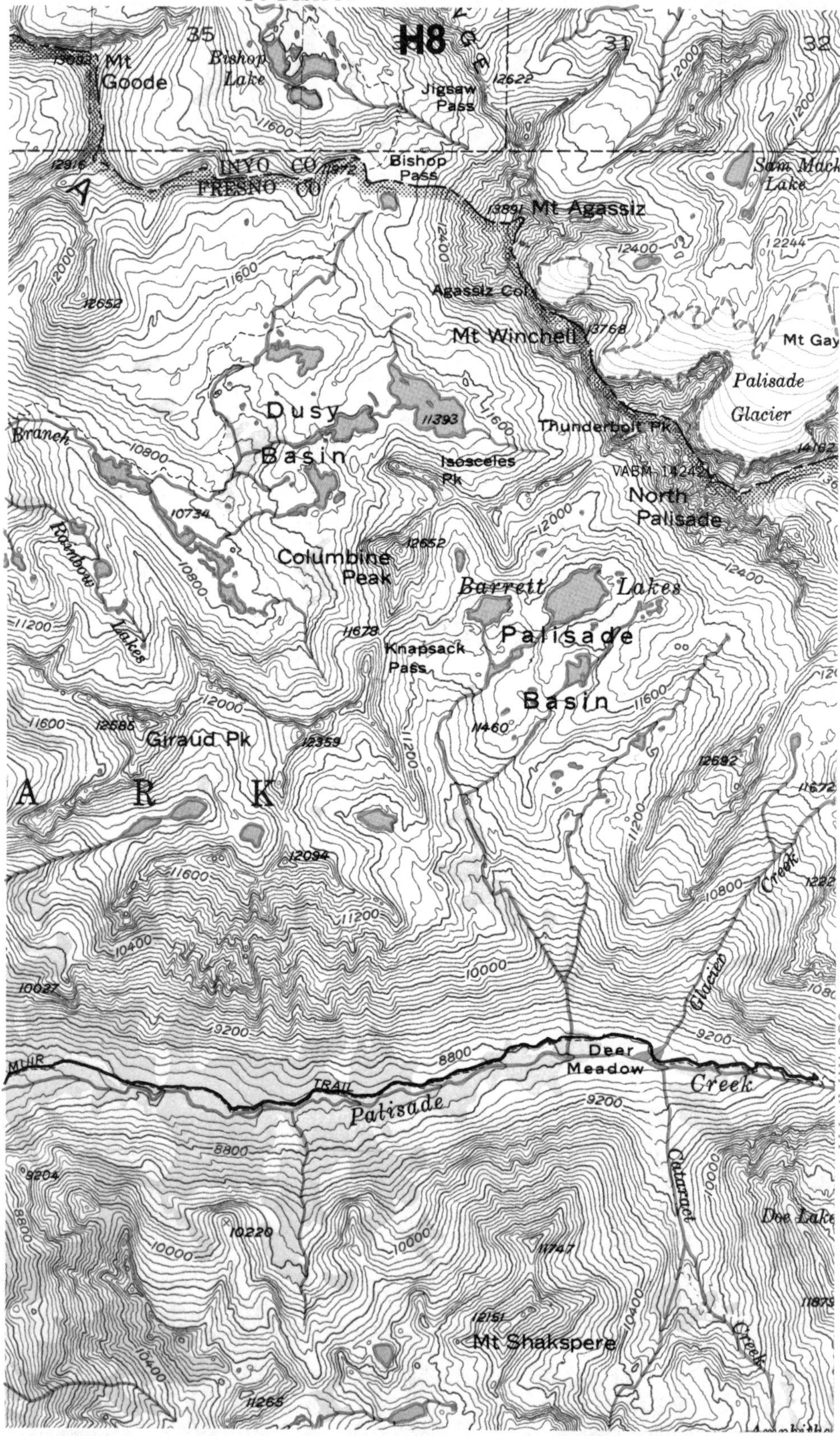

see MAP H9

see MAP H7

Mt. Whitney-
Tuolumne

H

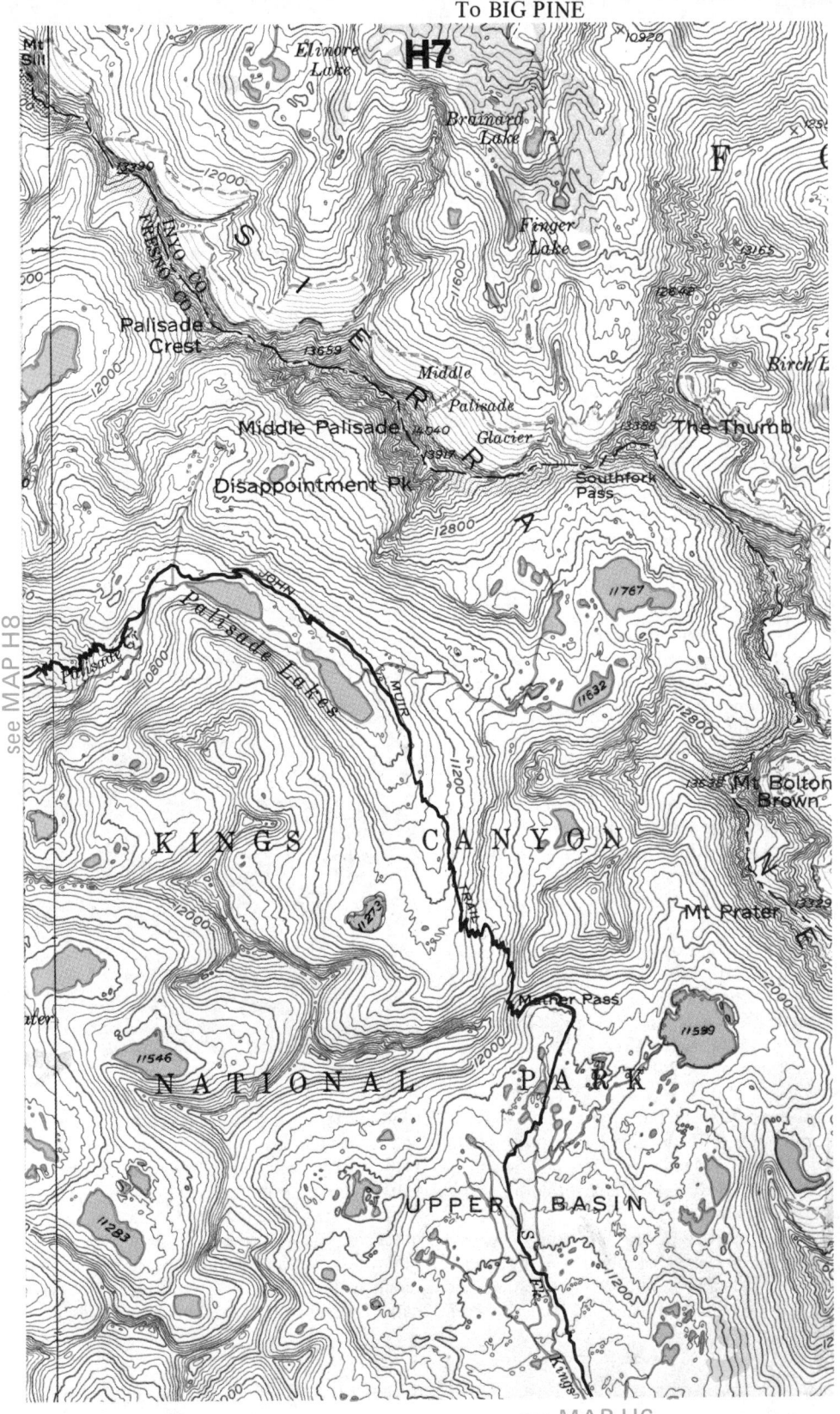

H7

see MAP H8

Mt
Sill

Elinore
Lake

Brainard
Lake

Finger
Lake

10920

Birch L

13165

12646

Palisade
Crest

13559

Middle
Palisade

Middle Palisade
12040

Glacier

13388 The Thumb

Disappointment Pk

13917

Southfork
Pass

12800

11767

Palisade Lakes

JOHN

MUIR

11632

12800

13638 Mt Bolton
Brown

KINGS   CANYON

11273

11200

Mt Prater
13329

Mather Pass

11599

NATIONAL

PARK

11546

UPPER   BASIN

11283

11200

Kings

H
Mt. Whitney-
Tuolumne

the Bench Lake Trail junction. Bench Lake, on a true bench high above South Fork Kings River's canyon, has good campsites that are off the beaten track. Just beyond this junction you ford the outlet of Lake Marjorie and in 200 yards meet the Taboose Pass Trail (10,750–1.3) at the upper edge of a lodgepole forest. Another downhill segment of forested switchbacks brings you to the South Fork, which is best crossed a few yards downstream from the trail. On the far bank the South Fork Trail (10,050–1.3) leads downstream and you turn northeast upstream, passing another trail to Taboose Pass in ⅓ mile.

Climbing steadily, you cross several unnamed tributaries that can slow you down at the height of the melt, and then ford the infant South Fork (10,840–2.2) near some good campsites. ▌*East of the trail, on the Sierra crest, looming Cardinal Mountain (13,397') is named for red but is in fact half white and half dark, in a strange mixture of metamorphosed Paleozoic rocks.* ▌ West of this peak you cross grassy flats and hop over numerous branches of the headwaters of South Fork Kings River. Every camper can have his own lake and lakelet in this high basin—though the campsites are austere.

This ascent finally steepens and zigzags up to rockbound Mather Pass (12,100–3.0), named for Stephen Mather, first head of the National Park Service. The view ahead is dominated by the 14,000-foot peaks of the Palisades group, knifing sharply into the sky. Your trail now makes a knee-shocking descent to the poor campsites ¼ mile southeast of long, blue upper Palisade Lake. The route then contours above the lakes until it drops to the north shore of the lower lake (10,600–3.5), with its poor-to-fair campsites. Knees rested, you descend again, down the "Golden Staircase," built on the cliffs of the gorge of Palisade Creek. This section was the last part of the John Muir Trail to be constructed, and it is easy to see why. In ¾ mile from the bottom of the "staircase" you cross multibranched Glacier Creek and immediately arrive at Deer Meadow (8860–3.0), which is more lodgepole forest than meadow, but pleasant enough anyway.

Beyond the campsites here, the downhill grade continues, less steeply, across the stream draining Palisade Basin and several smaller streams to reach Middle Fork Kings River

(8020–3.7), where a trail takes off downstream for Simpson Meadow. Turning north, you ascend past a series of falls and chutes along the river to Grouse Meadows, a serene expanse of grassland with good campsites in the forest along the east side. Up the canyon from these meadows, you can see repeated evidence of great avalanches that crashed down the immense canyon walls and wiped out stands of trees. The trail climbs gently to turbulent Dusy Branch, crossed on a steel bridge, and immediately encounters the Bishop Pass Trail (8710–3.3) to South Lake. Near this junction is a ranger station occupied in summer.

Grouse Meadows

Our route up-canyon from this junction ascends between highly polished granite walls past lavish displays of a great variety of wildflowers. The trail passes through sagebrushy Little Pete and Big Pete meadows, and swings west to assault the Goddard Divide and search out its breach, Muir Pass. Up and up the rocky trail winds, passing the last tree long before you reach desolate Helen Lake (11,595-5.7)— named, along with Wanda Lake to the west, for

See maps H6, H7, H8, H9, H10

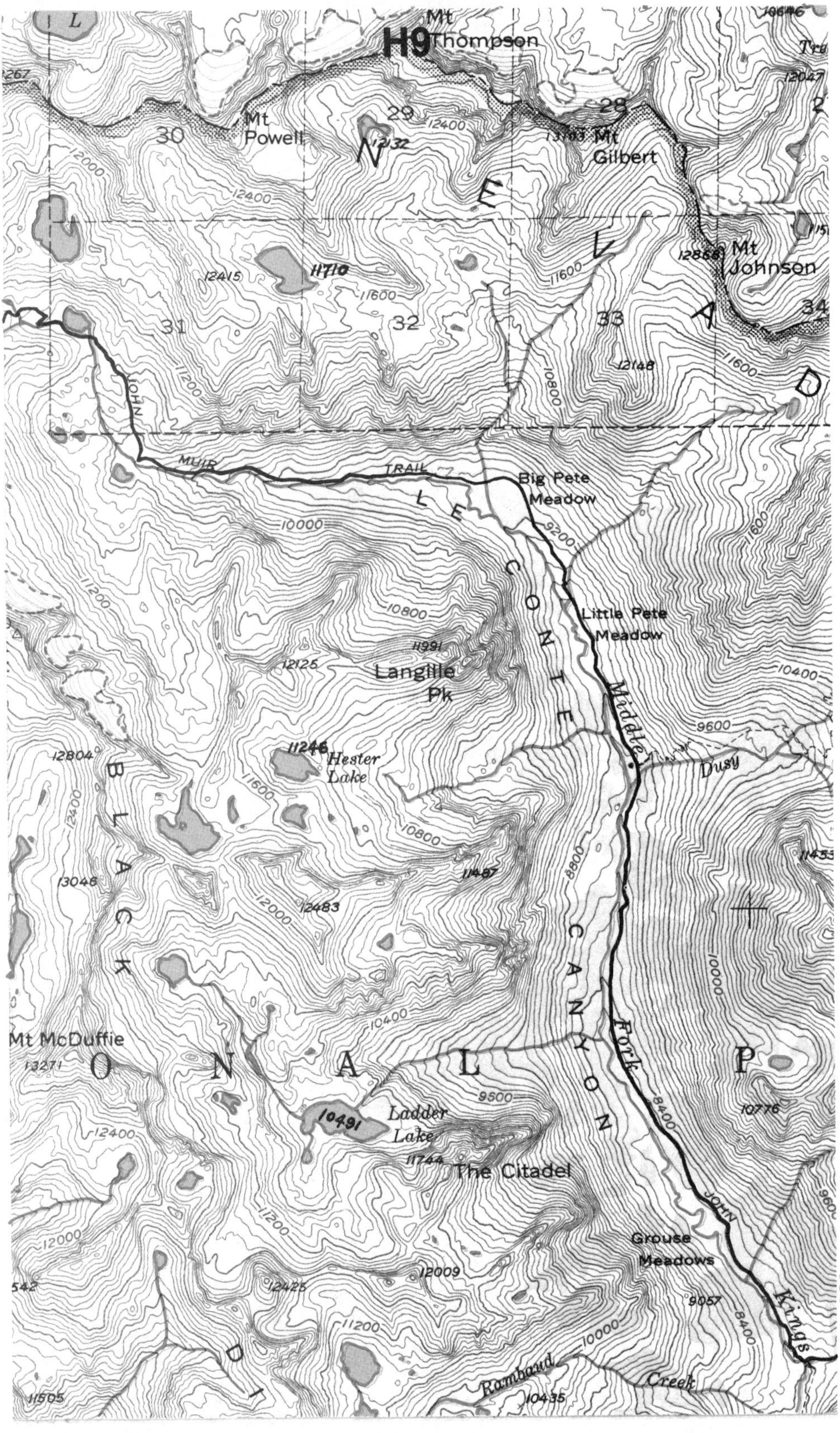

H9
Mt Thompson
Mt Powell
Mt Gilbert
Mt Johnson
N E V A D A
Big Pete Meadow
Little Pete Meadow
JOHN MUIR TRAIL
LE CONTE CANYON
Middle Fork Kings
Dusy
Langille Pk
Hester Lake
Mt McDuffie
BLACK DIVIDE
O N A L P
Ladder Lake
The Citadel
Grouse Meadows
Rambaud Creek
30
29
28
31
32
33
34
13103
12868
12148
11710
12415
12132
11991
12125
11246
12804
13046
12483
11487
13271
10491
11744
10776
12009
12425
9057
11505
10435

see MAP H10

H Mt. Whitney-Tuolumne

see MAP H8

H10

The Hermit

Mt Darwin

Midnight

Mt Spencer

Mt Haeckel

Sapphire Lake

Mt Wallace

I N G S

McGee Lakes

Mt Huxley

Mt Fiske

Mt Goddard

Lake McDermand

Helen L

Muir Pass

Wanda Lake

Basin

C A N Y O N

G O D D A R D

Mt Goddard

Black Giant

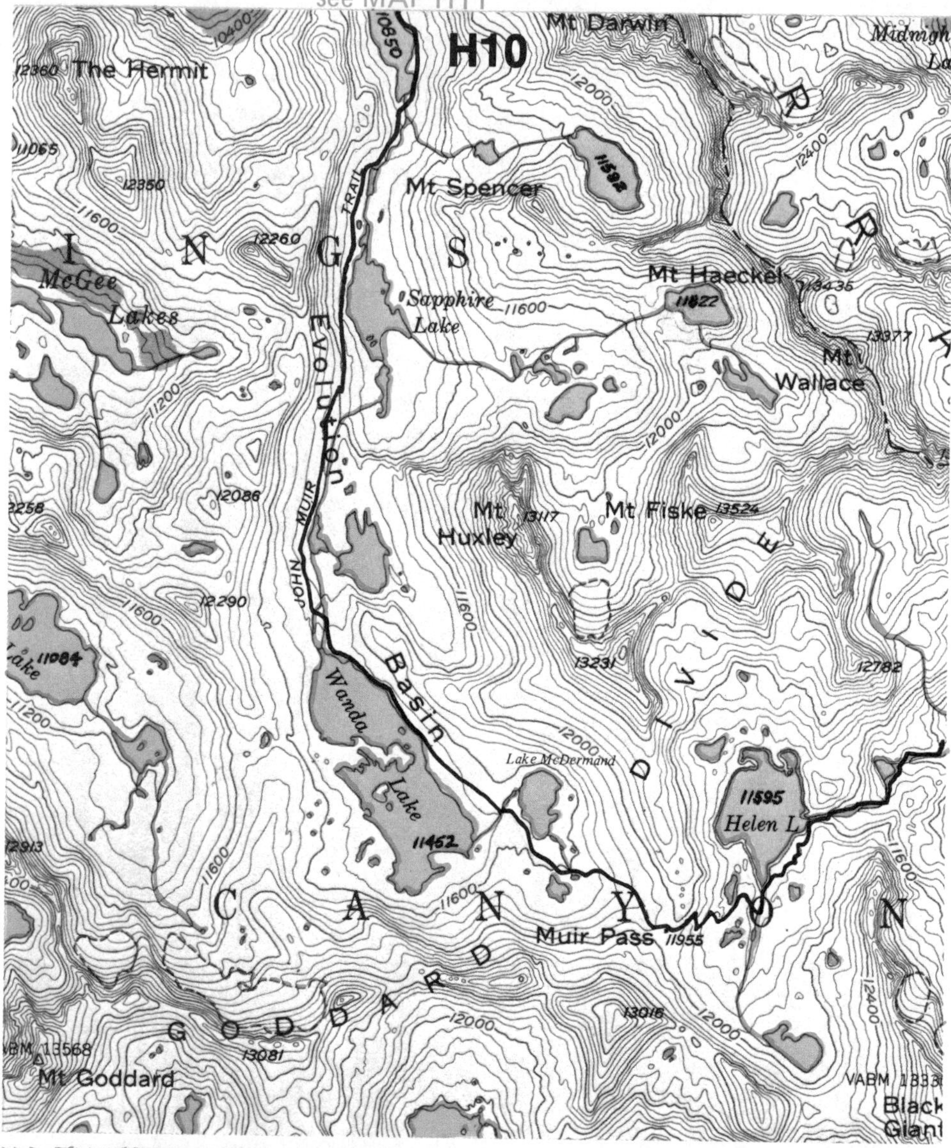

see MAP H9

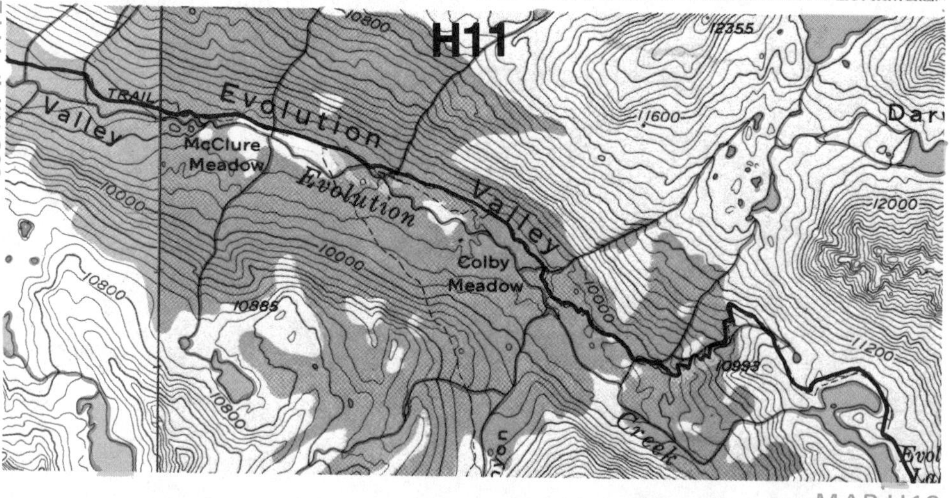

H11

Valley

Evolution

McClure Meadow

Evolution Valley

Colby Meadow

Dari

Creek

Evol

see MAP H12

H

Mt. Whitney-Tuolumne

John Muir's daughters. This east side of the pass is under snow throughout the summer in some years. Finally, after 6 fords of the diminishing stream, you haul up at Muir Pass (11,955–1.3), where a stone hut honoring Muir would shelter you somewhat in a storm. ∎ *The views from here of the solitary peaks and the lonely lake basins are painted in the many hues of the mostly Jurassic-age metamorphic rocks that make up the Goddard Divide.* ∎

From the hut your trail descends gently past Lake McDermand and Wanda Lake, the latter having fair campsites near the outlet. (Wood fires are banned from Muir Pass to Evolution Lake.) You then ford Evolution Creek (11,400–2.2) and descend into the Sapphire Lake basin, where there are fair campsites at the north end of Sapphire Lake. ∎ *The land here is nearly as scoured as when the ice left it about 10,000 years ago, and the aspect all around is one of newborn nakedness. To the east is a series of tremendous peaks named for Charles Darwin and other major thinkers about evolution, and the next lake and the valley below it also bear the name "Evolution."* ∎ The trail fords the stream at the inlet of this lake (10,850–2.4), skirts the lake, which has some campsites in clumps of stunted whitebark pines, and then drops sharply into Evolution Valley. ∎ *The marvelous meadows here are the reason for rerouting the trail through the forest, so the fragile grassland can recover from overtromping by the feet of earlier backpackers and horsepackers.* ∎

At McClure Meadow (9650–4.9) you will find a summer ranger midway down the meadow on the north side of the trail. After several tributary fords, including the creek from Glacier Divide Lake, you wade Evolution Creek (9210–2.5)—difficult during high water; the old crossing 0.3 mile above is probably easier—and soon descend steeply to a bridge across South Fork San Joaquin River (8470–1.3). Past numerous campsites you recross the river on another bridge and roll on down and out of Kings Canyon National Park at the steel-bridge crossing of Piute Creek. Here, where you enter John Muir Wilderness, the Piute Pass Trail (8050–3.5) starts north toward North Lake.

The Pacific Crest Trail continues down the South Fork canyon, away from the river, to a junction with the Florence Lake Trail (7890-1.8).

*   *   *   *

Resupply access: The Florence Lake roadend is 11 miles west down this trail; the Muir Trail Ranch is 1½ miles down it. (The latter is a possible package drop; inquire of the owner by writing Box 176, Lakeshore CA 93634.)

*   *   *   *

Side route: Shortly before the ranch, and just west of signs that indicate the John Muir Trail is 1½ miles away, both to the east and to the north, an unsigned trail goes south ⅓ mile down to riverside campsites. From the campsites on the south side of the river a faint trail goes 150 yards southwest to a natural hot spring—great for soaking off the grime—and a warmish small lake.

*   *   *   *

From the Florence Lake Trail junction, the PCT-John Muir Trail veers right to climb the canyon wall. It rises past a lateral trail down to the Florence Lake trail (8400–1.7), crosses little Senger Creek (9740–2.2) (good campsites), levels off, and below Sally Keyes Lakes meets another trail (10,150–1.6) down to the river valley below. Then your route passes the fair campsites at these lakes, crossing the short stream that joins the two. Leaving the forest below, the trail skirts small Heart Lake and reaches barren Selden Pass (10,900–2.1). At this pass, many-islanded Marie Lake is the central feature of the view northward, and soon you boulder-hop its clear outlet (10,570-0.9), then descend moderately to the green expanses of Rosemarie Meadow (10,010–1.6). From this grassland a trail forks left, soon climbing southwest to Rose Lake, and about ¼ mile beyond another trail departs east for Lou Beverly Lake. Both these lakes provide good, secluded camping. About 200 yards past the last junction you bridge West Fork Bear Creek, and then you make a 1-mile descent in lodgepole forest to a boulder ford of Bear Creek (very difficult in early season).

On the creek's far bank you meet a trail (9530–1.4) that goes up East Fork Bear Creek, but you turn down-canyon and descend gently to the log ford of refreshing Hilgard Creek. Immediately

See maps H10, H11, H12, H13, H14

FLORENCE LAKE 2 MI.

see MAP H12

beyond, the Lake Italy Trail (9300–1.2) climbs to the east, and our trail continues down through the mixed forest cover, always staying near rollicking Bear Creek. You pass campsites near the trail, but for more wood and more solitude it is better to find a place to camp across the creek. Below Hilgard Creek, where the old trail veered west, you begin (9040–2.0) a new trail segment that bypasses the former site of Kip Camp. This new segment gradually veers west as it follows the contour line, then turns north at the foot of a tough series of switchbacks. The south-facing hillside here gets plenty of sun, but it is surprisingly wet even in late season, so that you can

See maps H14, H15

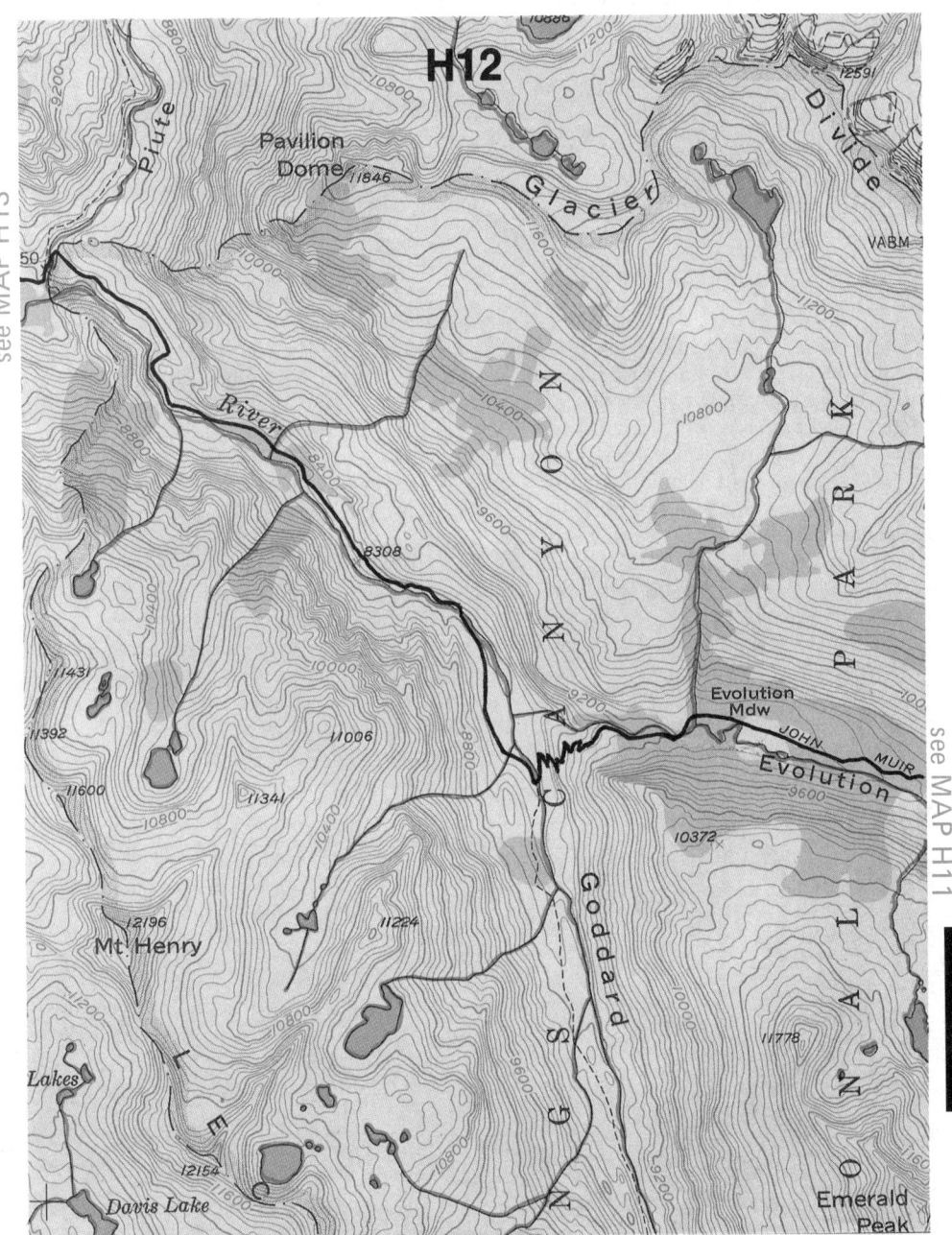

pleasure your eyes with flowers in bloom. Your route then levels off, and at the crest of Bear Ridge passes a trail (9980–1.6) that descends to Mono Hot Springs.

The north side of Bear Ridge is incised with 53 dusty switchbacks, which begin in a pure lodgepole forest but successively penetrate the realms of mountain hemlock, western white pine, red fir, Jeffrey pine, aspen, white fir and, finally, cottonwoods at Mono Creek (7850–4.6). Campsites lie several hundred yards west down the trail after you cross the bridge over the creek.

*   *   *   *

Resupply access: Vermilion Valley Resort is 6 miles away, at the end of this side trail (see "Supplies" above).

*   *   *   *

Beyond the bridge, the PCT turns right, soon crosses North Fork Mono Creek (difficult in early season), and climbs to a junction with the Mono Pass Trail (8270–1.6). Your steep trail levels briefly at lush Pocket Meadow (good campsites), crosses North Fork Mono Creek on rocks (8940–1.4) and then resumes climbing as the route turns up the west canyon wall. The first ford of Silver Pass Creek, on this wall, may be difficult in early season, and it is at the head of a fatally high cascade.

From here to Silver Pass the trail was extensively rerouted and overly constructed in 1980–81. Above a large meadow you reford the creek (9640–1.2) and then rise above treeline. The new trail bypasses Silver Pass Lake and then

ascends past the actual pass (low point) to the sign SILVER PASS (10,900–2.8) at a glorious viewpoint. The descent northward passes Chief Lake and then the Goodale Pass Trail (10,550–1.2), switchbacks northeast down to ford the small outlet of Squaw Lake, and then makes a long, hemlock-lined descent to beautiful Cascade Valley, where there are good campsites near the junction with the Cascade Valley Trail (9130–2.5).

*   *   *   *

Alternate route: Via the PCT, you are now 19.0 miles from the Rainbow Falls trailhead parking lot near Reds Meadow. Via the Cascade Valley-Fish Creek-Rainbow Falls trail, you are 19.4 miles from it. Some backpackers who aren't committed to following the PCT every step of the way prefer this lower, easier, mostly downhill, less-crowded route. Camping opportunities are greater and, if you're experiencing bad weather, you'll find this lower, well-forested route far more hospitable.

*   *   *   *

If you stay on PCT, turn right from the Cascade Valley Trail junction and ascend northeast, soon crossing Fish Creek on a steel bridge. Staying above this good-sized creek, the route ascends gently to the campsites at Tully Hole (9520–1.1), a well-flowered grassland where the McGee Pass Trail departs eastward. Now the PCT climbs steeply north up a band of Mesozoic metavolcanics which sweep east and grade into the Paleozoic metasediments of dominating Red Slate Mountain (13,163'). Be-

See maps H15, H16

Marie Lake, from Selden Pass

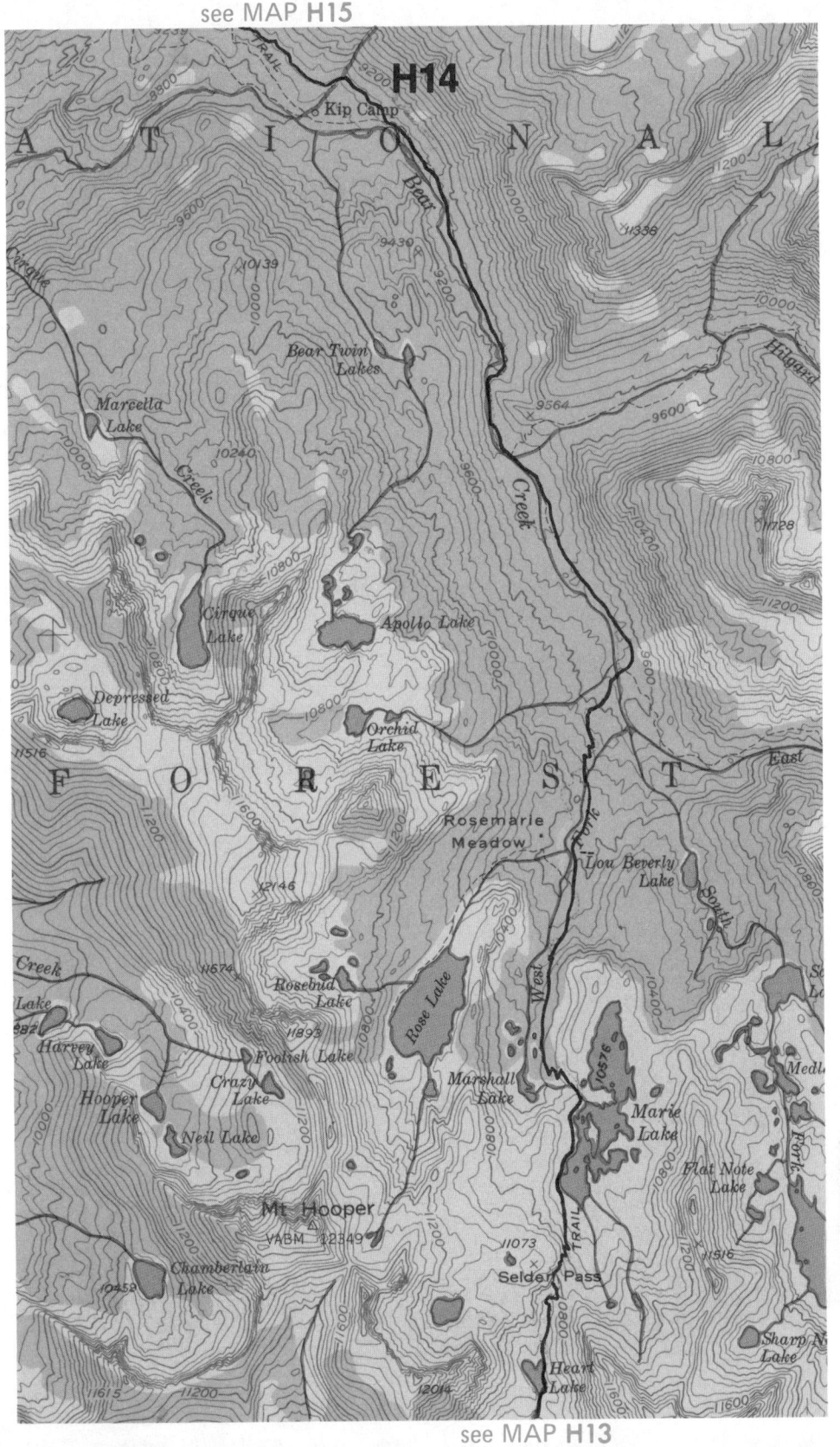

H14

H
Mt. Whitney-
Tuolumne

H15

Chief Lake

Silver Pass

VABM 12221

Goodale Pass

Silver Pass Lake

11428

11363

11512

11259

10831

Silver

Cr

Upper Graveyard Meadow

Feather Lake

10907

North

Pocket Meadow

10276

Shelf Lake

Vermilion Lake

Cliffs

Arrowhead Lake

Vermilion

10279

Graveyard Meadows

Quail Meadows

8079

S I E R

9180

8000

Volcanic

10179

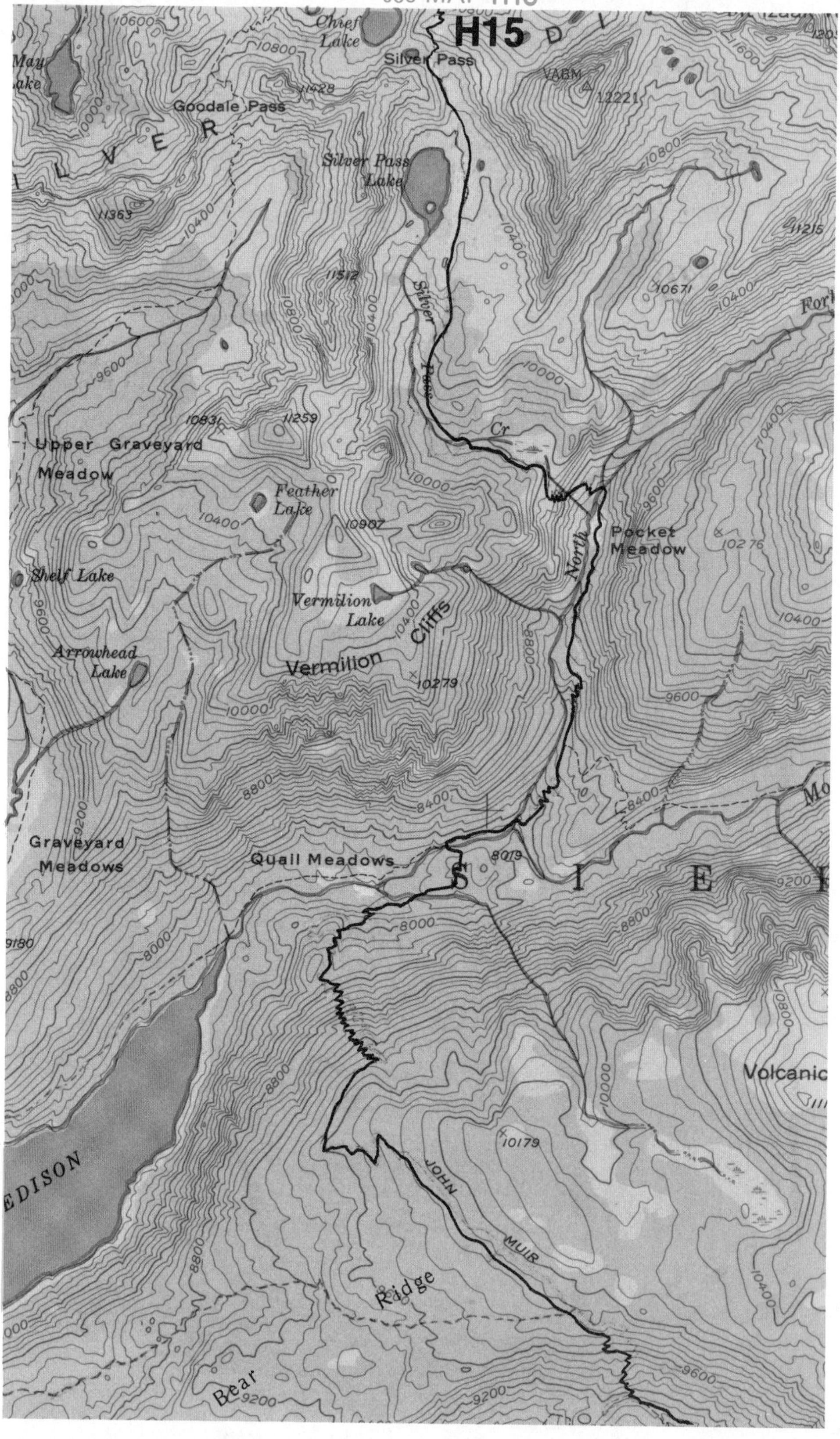

To RESORT

EDISON

JOHN

MUIR

Ridge

Bear

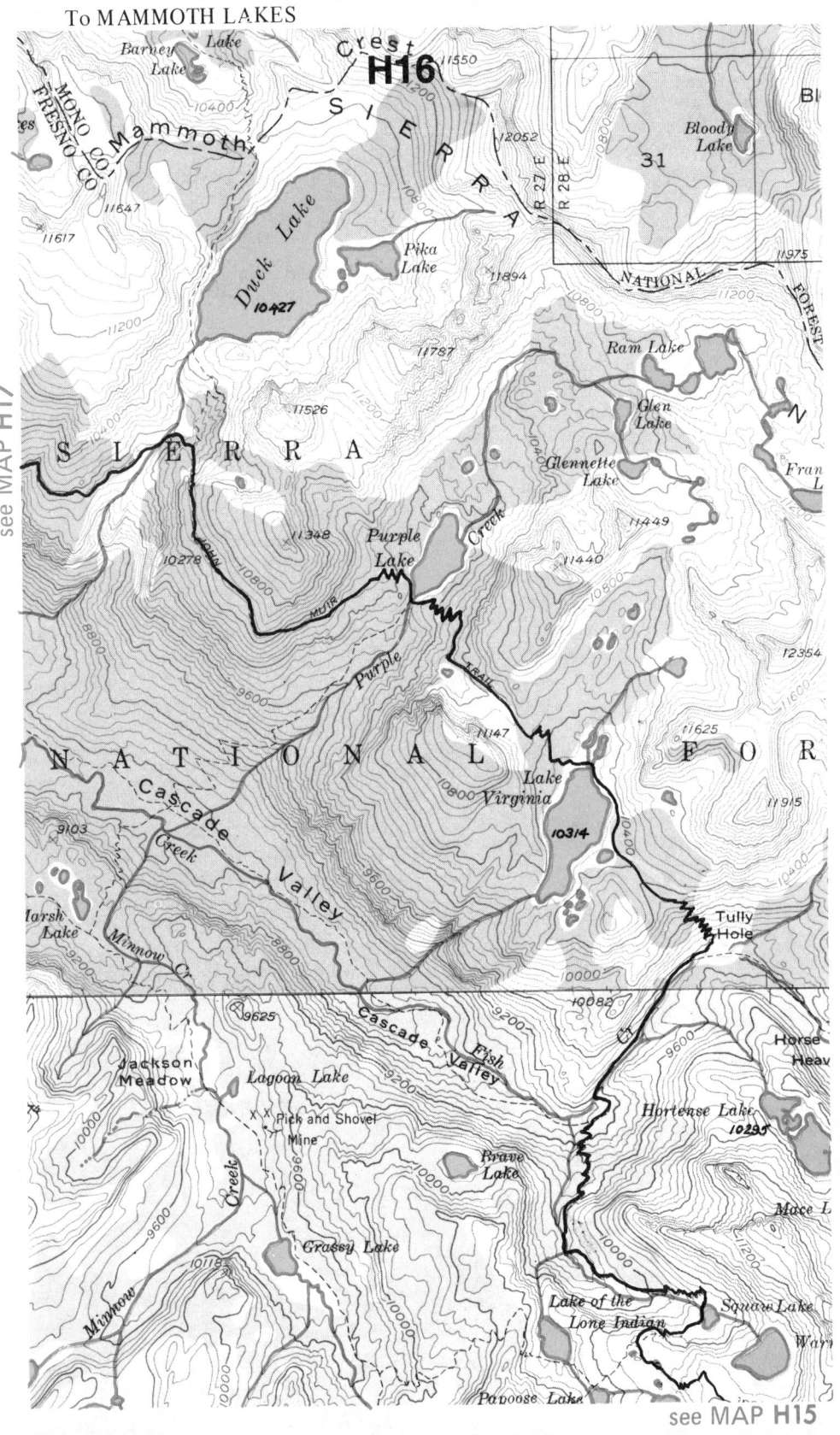

H16

Crest

SIERRA

MONO CO
FRESNO CO

Mammoth

Barney Lake

10400

11550

12052

R 27 E

R 28 E

0800

Bloody Lake

31

Bl

NATIONAL

FOREST

11617

11647

Duck Lake

10427

Pika Lake

11894

10800

11200

11200

11975

see MAP H17

SIERRA

11526

11200

11787

Ram Lake

Glen Lake

Glennette Lake

N

Fran L

10400

11348

Purple Lake

Creek

11449

11440

12354

10278

JOHN

10800

MUIR

Purple

11600

10800

11625

11915

NATIONAL

Cascade

Creek

TRAIL

11147

FOR

9800

9600

Lake Virginia

10314

10400

9103

Valley

10800

9600

Marsh Lake

Minnow Cr

8800

Tully Hole

Horse Heav

9625

10000

10082

Cascade Valley

Fish Valley

9200

Cr

9600

Jackson Meadow

Lagoon Lake

9200

Hortense Lake

10295

X X Pick and Shovel Mine

0096

Brave Lake

10000

Mace L

9600

10118

Grassy Lake

10000

Minnow

10000

Creek

10000

Lake of the Lone Indian

Squaw Lake

Warn

Papoose Lake

see MAP H15

H
Mt. Whitney-
Tuolumne

yond the crest of this ascent you reach deep-blue Lake Virginia (10,314–1.9), with several somewhat exposed campsites. In early season you will have to wade across the head of the lake or detour rather far north. From this boggy crossing your trail climbs to a saddle below the vertical northeast face of Peak 11147 and then switchbacks down to heavily used Purple Lake (9900–2.1), at whose outlet a trail begins its descent into deep Cascade Valley. No camping is allowed within 100 yards of the lake's outlet, so if you want to camp in this vicinity, use the sites by the lake's northwest shore. In late summer and in dry years, you may not have any trailside water until Deer Creek, 7.8 miles ahead, so plan accordingly.

From Purple Lake the rocky trail climbs west and then bends north as it levels out high on the wall of glaciated Cascade Valley. Soon you reach a trail (10,150–2.3) to Duck Lake and beyond, which could be used to escape bad weather or to resupply at Mammoth Lakes.

Just beyond the Duck Lake Trail, you ford Duck Creek near several undistinguished campsites before traversing first southwest and then northwest. If you sharpen your gaze, you will see both red firs and Jeffrey pines above 10,000 feet on this north wall of Cascade Valley, well above their normal range. You also have fine views of the Silver Divide in the south as you slant northwest and descend gradually through mixed conifers. From your last set of excellent views, which are along the south slopes of Peak 10519, the trail begins a westward descent, crossing about a mile of lava-flow rubble before turning north for a rambling drop to Deer Creek (9090–5.5). Here you'll find fair, lodgepole-shaded campsites.

In the next ⅔ mile the trail starts west, climbs briefly over a granitic ridge, and then descends north to a creek crossing in a long, slender meadow. Heading north through it you have views of The Thumb (10,286′), then leave this county-line meadow as you cross a seasonal creeklet. This freshet you parallel for about a mile as you descend a bit to Upper Crater Meadow (8920–2.0).

*   *   *   *

Resupply access: From this junction and one 100 yards later, trails head over to very popular Horseshoe Lake. From it the Lake Mary

See maps H16, H17, H18

Road starts a 4.9-mile descent to a junction with Minaret Summit Road in bustling, recreation-oriented Mammoth Lakes. See Supplies at the start of this section for the seasonal shuttle-bus route to the town. If you would rather hike to it and back, then take the following 7¼-mile route, of which the first 5 miles are on trails and lightly used roads.

You can start from either of the two junctions in Upper Crater meadow. Both trails go about 1½ miles before uniting from where one tread goes about 1 mile northeast to broad Mammoth Pass. Just east beyond it you reach the north shore of McCloud Lake, and beyond it continue ahead (off the map) about ½ mile down to a road on the northwest shore of Horseshoe Lake. Walk over to the north end of the lake, from where you could take the aforementioned Lake Mary Road to town.

A shorter, quieter way, however, is to go but ¼ mile east on the road, take a spur road ¼ mile north past houses to its end and, on a trail, head east, dropping about 300 feet to the west end of Twin Lakes Campground. Continue east through the campground to a road that parallels the east shores of the Twin Lakes. This road you take about ½ mile north to the Lake Mary Road, on which you walk 2¼ miles to town.

*   *   *   *

In about 100 yards, by the north edge of Upper Crater Meadow, you meet the second of the two trails that lead to Mammoth Pass. It also provides an alternate (not recommended) route—the old JMT/PCT—down to the Reds Meadow area. With that goal in mind, you take the newer route down along the creek you've been following, cross it in ½ mile, and then descend to a recrossing with a good campsite (8660–0.8), the last one before Reds Meadow. Here you leave John Muir Wilderness for good

See map H18

Tom and Jason Winnett at Silver Pass

and enter Ansel Adams Wilderness for a short spell.

▮ *This creekside campsite lies between the two Red Cones, products of very recent volcanic eruptions. The northern one is easy to climb and offers a fine view of the Ritter Range and Middle Fork San Joaquin River's deep canyon. You'll also see Mammoth Mountain (11,053')* in the north-northeast, on whose north slopes as many as 20,000 skiers, most of them from southern California, may be found on a busy day. This mountain is a volcano which began to grow about 400,000 years ago. The area around it, including the upper canyon of Middle Fork San Joaquin River, has been volcanically active for over 3 million years, and the last

See map H18

H Mt. Whitney-Tuolumne

Tully Hole

eruption here occurred less than 1000 years ago. It is the Sierra's "hot spot"—ironically, considering that it is also a mecca for skiers due to its large, late-melting snowpack. ∎

Beyond the creekside campsite between the Red Cones the PCT makes lazy switchbacks down to Boundary Creek (7910–2.3). Roughly midway between it and the next junction, you cross a smaller creek, where you exit from an east lobe of Ansel Adams Wilderness. Through a fir forest your well-graded route descends to an abandoned stagecoach road (7700–0.7).

*   *   *   *

Resupply access: Now a broad path, you can walk about 300 yards north on it to Reds Meadow Pack Station. Another 230 yards north along a paved road takes you to Reds Meadow Resort, with a store and cafe, at road's end. The food selection is aimed at campers with ice chests, not at hikers with backpacks. From here and from a number of roadside stops as far north as Agnew Meadows, you can take a shuttle bus to the Mammoth Lakes area (see Supplies at the start of this chapter).

*   *   *   *

Past the abandoned stagecoach road you immediately cross a horse trail that climbs briefly north to the pack station, reaching it at a switchback in the paved road. Just past this horse trail the PCT descends to a crossing of the Rainbow Falls-Fish Valley-Cascade Valley Trail (7600–0.2), on which you'd be ascending if you took the alternate route to here mentioned earlier.

*   *   *   *

Side route: This popular trail starts from the Rainbow Falls trailhead parking lot about 250 yards north of the PCT. If you've got the time, hike 1.0 mile south on this trail for a view of Rainbow Falls. Afternoon is the best time to see and photograph this waterfall, as well as the columns of Devils Postpile just ahead.

*   *   *   *

Beyond the Rainbow Falls trail, you curve southwest over to a low, nearby crest from which an old trail, essentially abandoned, heads north, and then you meander northwest down to a trail junction (7430–0.5) by the east boundary of Devils Postpile National Monument.

See map H18

see MAP H19

H18

see MAP H17

Minaret Summit
BM 9175
9265
MINARET SUMMIT
9043
BM

Upper Soda
Sprs C G

Mammoth Mtn
Ski Area

Ski Lifts

9911

River

BM
7706

Pumice Flat
Campground

R Sta

Pumice Group
Camp

9200

9688

Red's
Lake

S

9200

T

Minaret
Falls

F   O   R   E   S   T

PACIFIC

Reds

Creek

9200

9997

10400

Mammoth
Mtn
VABM
11053

10000

Minaret
Falls
Campground

Devils Postpile
Campground

BM
7559

Sotcher Lake

706

9200

8800

Soda Spr

Devils
Postpile

HORSE

Reds Mdw C G

Reds Meadow
Hot Springs

MAMMOTH   PASS

TRAIL

10458

DEVILS POSTPILE NAT MONUMENT

The Buttresses

JMT PCT

Reds Mdw Resort
Pack Station

Mammoth Pass

Horses
Lake

McCloud
Lake

9600

FOOTPATH

BM 7607

yon

7944

8213

San Joaquin

JMT PCT

7649

Boundary

Creek

Rainbow
Falls

10005

9200

OLD MAMMOTH LAKES-

TRAIL

Mammoth

8000

Lower
Falls

7868

Creek

Reds

Cones

9985

Crater
Meadow

9905

JOHN

S

S

600

86

Upper
Crater

see MAP H17

Ritter Range, from northern Red Cone

H Mt. Whitney-Tuolumne

*   *   *   *   *   *   *   *

Alternate route: Here we recommend you leave the PCT and head ½ mile north to a junction, crossing a creek from Sotcher Lake just before you reach it. From this junction, at the base of a Devils Postpile lava flow, you can head ¼ mile east to the paved road, mentioned earlier, then hike a few yards north on it to the entrance to Reds Meadow Campground. In it you can get a free, luke-warm shower at the bathhouse by the campground's "hot" spring. From the lava-flow junction the alternate route climbs ¼ mile northwest to a ridge, from which you can take a short trail up to the glacially polished top of the Devils Postpile. The main trail skirts along the base of this columnar lava flow, reaching a junction in about ¼ mile, just beyond a junction with a trail from the top of the lava flow. If you were to continue straight ahead from this second junction, you'd reach the monument's small visitor center (with a phone) and its adjacent campground in about ⅓ mile. Instead, to regain the PCT, you turn left at the second junction, descend to a nearby bridge over the San Joaquin River, and in a minute reach a junction. From here, head 0.4 mile north to the PCT.

*   *   *   *

Back at the monument's east boundary, PCT purists immediately cross the San Joaquin River on a sturdy bridge, wind westward past two seasonal ponds, then make a struggling climb north through deep pumice to an intersection with the old, trans-Sierra Mammoth Trail (7710–1.0). This relatively unscenic one-mile slog was built to keep PCT equestrians away from the Postpile. Northbound, the old trail descends ¼ mile to meet the alternate route, while the PCT contours along pumice-laden slopes, soon reaching the end of the alternate route (7660–0.6). Here the John Muir and Pacific Crest trails, which have coincided through most of this hiking section, diverge for a few miles, becoming one tread again near Thousand Island Lake. On their divergence both quickly re-enter Ansel Adams Wilderness, though the PCT briefly leaves it in the Agnew Meadows area.

Alternate route: Briefly, the 12.9-mile JMT segment—the more popular of the two—climbs up to a trail junction near Minaret Creek, quickly crosses the creek (with adjacent campsites) and winds over to another junction by Johnston Meadow (more campsites), 1.4 miles from the PCT junction. The JMT climbs up past knee-deep Trinity Lakes, then later makes a three-stage descent to Shadow Lake, dropping to shallow Gladys and ideal Rosalie lakes along the way (respectively 6.1 and 6.8 miles from the PCT junction). You can camp at either lake but not at Shadow Lake, except near its southwest shore. However, good-to-excellent, popular campsites abound in the ⅔ mile JMT stretch west of the lake, up along Shadow Creek. No campfires are allowed along this stretch, but stoves are okay. From the creek the JMT climbs 1.9 miles up to a high ridge, then drops ¾ mile to the east end of Garnet Lake, which is off-limits to camping. Ruby Lake, about 1⅓ miles farther, offers one campsite, as does Emerald Lake, just beyond it. Emerald, however, is probably the best lake along this 12.9-mile route for swimming. Finally, no camping is allowed near the east end of Thousand Island Lake.

*   *   *   *

Back where the JMT and the PCT split, the pumice-lined PCT winds down to the distributaries of Minaret Creek (7590–0.6), which must be waded except in the late season, just below dramatic Minaret Falls. Still in pumice, the trail bends northeast and almost touches Middle Fork San Joaquin River before climbing north away from it over a lava-flow bench that overlooks Pumice Flat. In a shady forest of lodgepole pines and red firs, you make a brief descent to a bridge across the Middle Fork. From the far side of the bridge (7680–1.4), a trail heads just around the corner to the west end of Upper Soda Springs Campground. Beyond the bridge you head upriver, having many opportunities to drop to nearby eating, drinking and chilly-swimming spots along the dashing Middle Fork. After crossing a permanent stream (7810–1.0), the trail bends from north to northwest

See map H18, H19

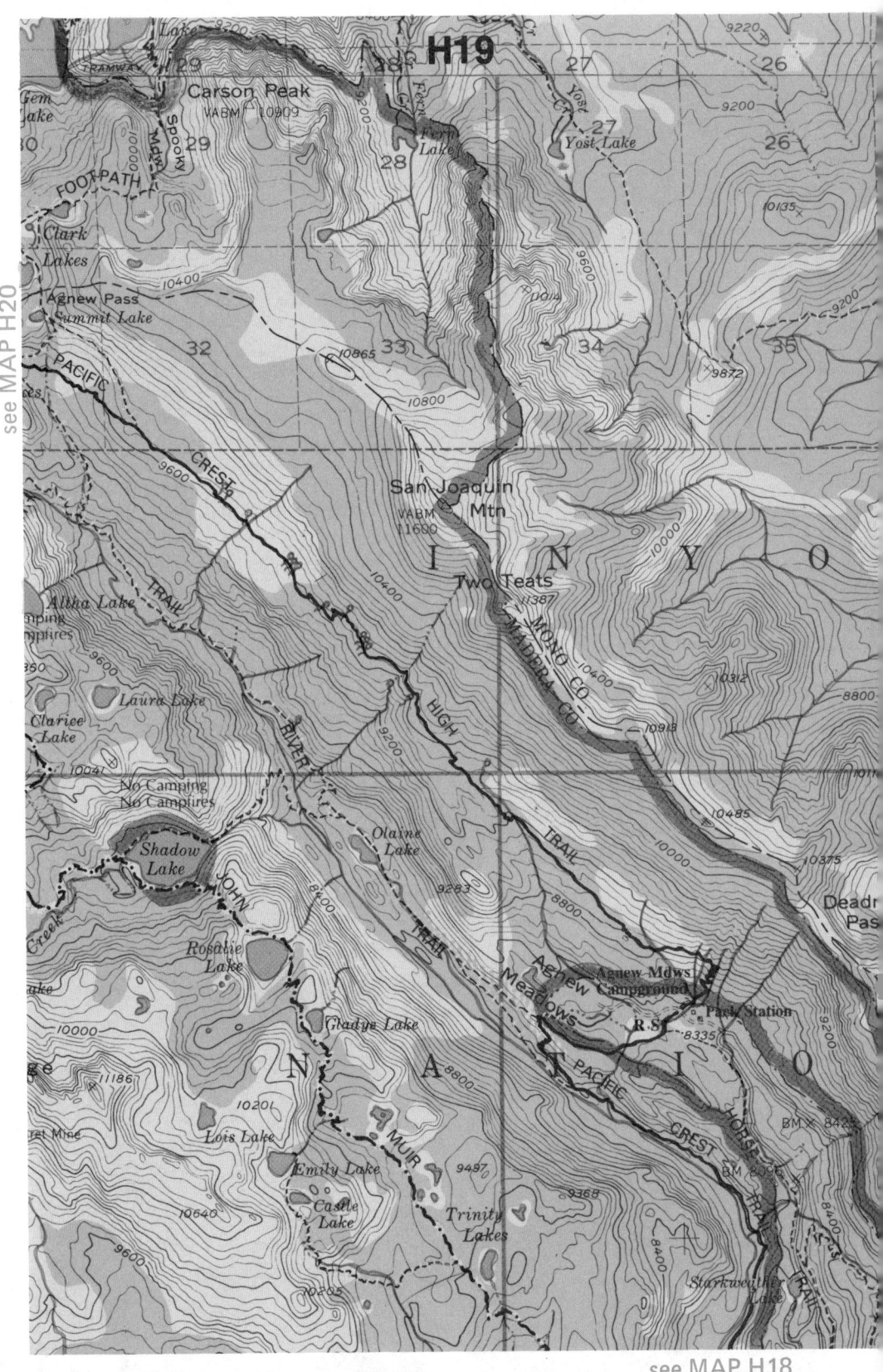

see MAP H20

see MAP H18

Rainbow Falls

and crosses a second stream (7910–1.1). Then, just past a small knoll, it reaches a junction (8000–0.2).

         *   *   *   *

Alternate route: You can continue straight ahead, up river, having many camping oppor-

tunities before rejoining the PCT in 5.9 miles, at a point about ⅓ mile west of the Badger Lakes.

         *   *   *   *

Leaving the river route, the PCT first parallels it northwest, then climbs via short switchbacks to a junction with the River Trail (8280–0.5). You start east up it and in 80 yards meet a fork. The left (east) fork goes 0.4 mile to Agnew Meadows Campground, from which you can walk 0.4 mile east on a winding dirt road, along which you'll find the PCT's resumption by a trailhead parking area. Taking the right (southeast) fork, you hike through a long, narrow trough before curving northeast around a meadow, almost touching the ranger's trailer (with a parking area) before reaching the Agnew Meadows road (8360–0.9), which has water and an outhouse by a trailhead parking area.

         *   *   *   *

Resupply access: The main road to Reds Meadow lies ¼ mile east, and at that junction is the first of 10 stops made by shuttle buses from Mammoth Mountain Inn (see Supplies at start of this chapter).

         *   *   *   *

See map H19

Mt. Ritter, Banner Peak and Shadow Lake, from ridge near the John Muir Trail

From the Agnew Meadows road the PCT route follows the signed High Trail, which switchbacks upward for about 400 vertical feet before climbing northwest. ❚ *Creeks, creeklets and springs abound along the High Trail, for the volcanic-rock formations above us store plenty of water, which they slowly release throughout the summer.* ❚ Views are relatively few until the PCT essentially levels off on a descending ridge (9680-2.8), and then the Ritter Range explodes on the scene, with Shadow Lake and the Minarets, both across the canyon, vying for your attention. Views and water abound over the next 2 miles of alternating brushy and timbered slopes, then your traversing route comes to a junction (9710–2.4) with a trail that climbs easily over Agnew Pass to good camps near the largest of the Clark Lakes, about 1.1 miles distant. Summit Lake, just before the pass, is good for swimming but a bit short on level camping spots. The High Trail, your route, now descends, crossing Summit Lake's seasonal outlet creek before climbing briefly to an intersection of a steep Middle Fork-Clark Lakes Trail (9500–0.8). Westward, your climb abates and you soon reach a de facto trail (9590–0.3), which you'll find just past a lakelet on your left.

*   *   *   *

Side route: This trail goes 0.2 mile southeast to good camps beside the largest of the Badger Lakes, which is the only one that is more than waist-deep. It is one of the best lakes in the entire Ansel Adams Wilderness.

*   *   *   *

Leaving the Badger Lakes area and the last legal campsites on the PCT this side of Rush Creek, you continue westward, passing a third trail to the Clark Lakes in ¼ mile. Soon you make a brief descent to a junction with the River Trail (9560–0.5), then climb moderately northwest before rambling southwest to a reunion with the John Muir Trail near the east end of spreading Thousand Island Lake (9840–1.0). Camping is prohibited within ¼ mile of this lake's outlet, but is legal elsewhere. Particularly look along the lake's southeast shore.

The PCT climbs moderately through a thin-ning forest to two lakelets, reached just before Island Pass (10,200–1.8). The trail then traverses ⅓ mile to a ridge before descending to a sometimes obscure junction (9690–1.0).

*   *   *   *

Side route: From here a trail climbs 0.8 mile south to the tip of lower Davis Lake. Campsites by it are small and quite exposed, but the beauty of this lake and its surroundings makes them a worthy goal.

*   *   *   *

About 250 yards past the Davis Lakes Trail junction you reach the first of several Rush Creek forks. Along the ½-mile trail segment that ensues, the early-season hiker may have three wet fords to make. You may therefore want to keep your boots off until the last ford, just before a junction with the Rush Creek trail (9600–0.4).

*   *   *   *

Side route: This trail descends a lengthy 9.5 miles to popular Silver Lake, on well-traveled State Route 158 (June Lake Loop Road). As such, you will want to take it only for emergency reasons. While you can get supplies in the town of June Lake, the effort is not worth it.

*   *   *   *

In the past the Forks area had many small camps, which now would all be illegal because they are within 100 feet of a creek or a trail. A seasonal ranger, sometimes camped 200 yards southeast of the junction, can give you advice on where to camp in this vicinity.

Leaving the Forks, you quickly engage some short, steep switchbacks that you follow northwest up to a ridge, then cross it and ease up to a junction with the Marie Lakes Trail (10,030–0.8). The lakes' outlet creek, just beyond the junction, is best crossed at an obvious jump-across spot slightly downstream. After the ford the trail winds excessively in an oft-futile attempt to avoid the boulders and bogs of the increasingly alpine environment. Whitebark pines

See maps H19, H20, H21

YOSEMITE

H21

ANSEL

Mt Maclure

TUOLUMNE

Lyell

Glacier

INYO CO

Cathedral Range

NATIONAL

Marie Lakes

Marie Lakes

Mt Lyell

VABM 13114

MADERA CO

MONO CO

NATIONAL

FOREST

ADAMS

Rodgers Lakes

MONO CO

MADERA CO

Rodgers Pk

12978

12037

11627

WILDERNESS

Mt

PARK

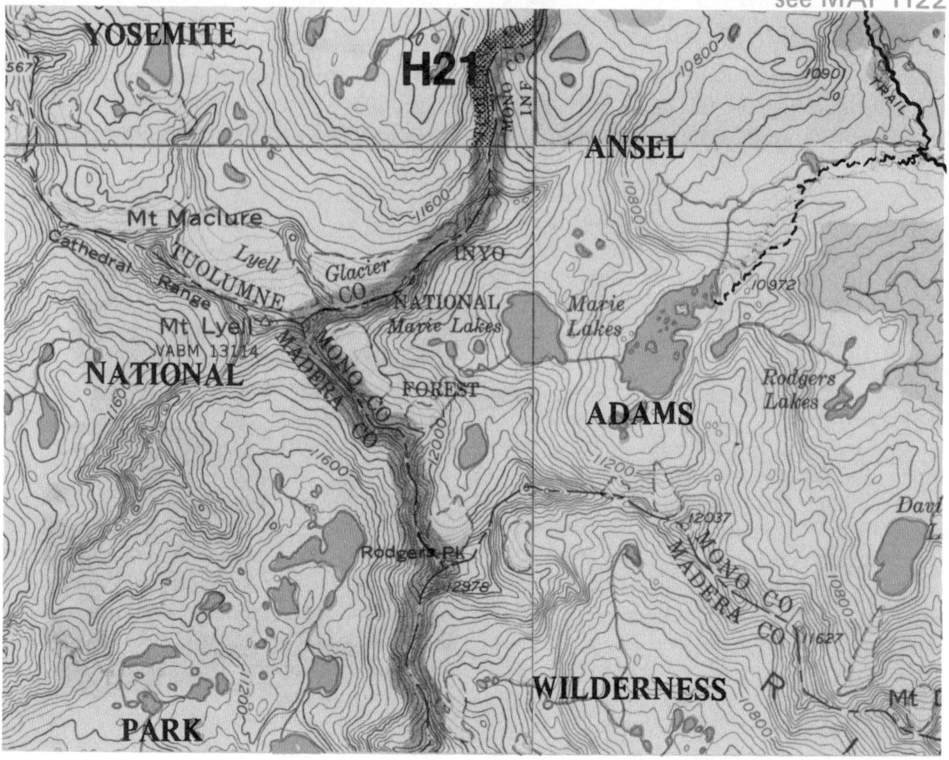

diminish in number and stature as you climb toward a conspicuous saddle—easily mistaken in early season for Donohue Pass. After a wet slog across the tundra-and-stone floor of your alpine basin, you veer southwest toward a prominent peak and ascend a sometimes obscure trail past blocks and over slabs to the real, signed, tarn-blessed Donohue Pass (11,056-2.6), where you leave Ansel Adams Wilderness.

The Yosemite high country unfolds before you as you descend northwest, partly in a long, straight fracture (southbound hikers take note). You then curve west to a sharp bend southeast, a few yards from which you can get a commanding panorama of Mt. Lyell, at 13,114 feet Yosemite's highest peak, and deep Lyell Canyon. Leaving the bend, you now descend southwest ½ mile to the north end of a boulder-dotted tarn that occasionally reflects Lyell and its broad glacier—the largest one you'll see in the

See maps H21, H22

Banner Peak, Mt. Ritter and three unnamed peaks

19

see MAP H21

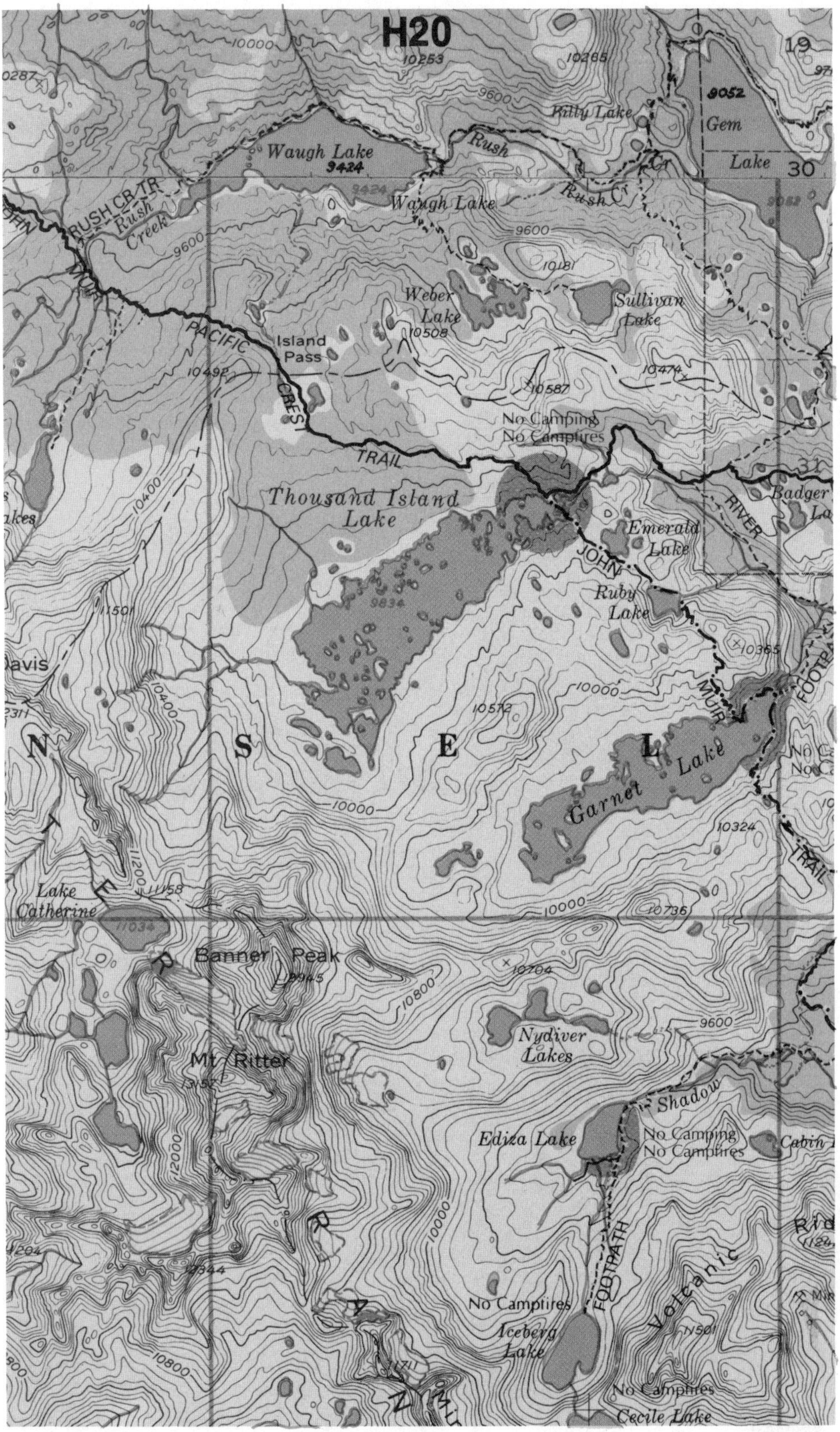

see MAP H19

10000
10253
10265
97
10287

9052

Kitty Lake

Gem

Rush

Waugh Lake
9424

Cr.

Lake

30

9424

Waugh Lake

Rush Cr.

9052

RUSH CR. TR.

Rush

9600

9600

Creek

Weber
Lake
10508

10181

Sullivan
Lake

PACIFIC

Island
Pass

10498

10587

10474

No Camping
No Campfires

CREST

31

10460

TRAIL

Thousand Island
Lake

Emerald
Lake

Badger
La.

RIVER

JOHN

Ruby
Lake

10365

1150?

9834

10512

MUIR

FOOTPA

Davis

N

10400

?311

S

E

10000

L

Garnet
Lake

No Ca
No Ca

10324

Lake
11200
Catherine
11058

10000

10736

10000

TRAIL

11034

Banner   Peak

10800

10704

12945

10800

Nydiver
Lakes

9600

Mt Ritter
13157

R

Shadow

No Camping
No Campfires

Cabin

Ediza Lake

?204

12944

V

10000

FOOTPATH

Volcanic

Ri
(12

No Campfires

Z

?5 MU

900

10800

Iceberg
Lake

N501

No Campfires
Cecile Lake

Sierra. Contour along the tarn's west shore, then briefly climb southwest to a gap in a low ridge. Next, wind north and soon begin a steep northeast descent that ends at the north end of a small meadow, where you cross the Lyell Fork, usually via boulders (10,220–1.8). Immediately above this crossing the creek has widened almost to a narrow lake, and trekkers ascending in the opposite direction may assume (incorrectly) that they have reached the aforementioned tarn. A spacious, well-used camping area exists here among sparse tree cover, the first adequate site since the Rush Creek Forks area. In Yosemite National Park campfires are banned here and everywhere else above 9600 feet.

Large campsites appear on a forested bench by another Lyell Fork crossing (9700–0.8), via a bridge. Now you'll stay on the west bank of the river all the way to Tuolumne Meadows. Beyond the bench you make your last major descent—a steep one—partly across rock-avalanche slopes—down to the Lyell Fork base camp (9000–1.4), at the southern, upper end of Lyell Canyon. This camp, a 3-hour trek from Highway 120, is a popular site with weekend mountaineers. Your hike to the highway is now an easy, level, usually open stroll along meandering Lyell Fork. A major camping area is found at the junction (8880–2.8) with a trail to Vogelsang High Sierra Camp. Past the junction, occasional backward glances at receding Potter Point mark your progress north along trout-inhabited Lyell Fork. With the oft-looming threat of afternoon lightning storms, one wishes the trail would have been routed along the forest's edge, rather than through open meadow. ∎ *Typical of meadowy trails, yours is multitreaded. Numerous treads arise mainly because as the main tread is used, it gets deepened until it penetrates the near-surface water table and becomes soggy. Odds are great that you'll have to leave the tread at least once, thus helping to start a new one.* ∎

Shortly after Potter Point finally disappears from view—and beyond half a dozen campsites—you curve northwest, descend between two bedrock outcrops, and then contour west through alternating soggy meadows and lodgepole forests. Both abound in mosquitoes through late July, as does most of the Tuolumne Meadows area. Two-branched Rafferty Creek soon appears, its second branch being a wet ford in early season. Just beyond it you meet the

Rafferty Creek Trail (8710–4.4), part of the very scenic and very popular High Sierra Loop Trail. You continue west and soon meet another junction (8650–0.7).

*   *   *   *

Side route: From where a trail goes ¾ mile west to a junction immediately east of Tuolumne Meadows Campground. This has 25 sites for backpackers (and other nonmotorized park travelers). From that junction the left branch skirts around the campground's south perimeter while the right branch quickly ends at the campground's main road. This road leads ½ mile west to Highway 120, and just southwest on it you'll find services.

*   *   *   *

Rather than head for the campground, you turn north and soon come to bridges across the Lyell Fork. A photo pause here is well worth it, particularly when clouds are building over Mts. Dana and Gibbs in the northeast. A short, winding climb north followed by an equal descent brings you to a sturdy bridge across the Dana Fork (8690-0.7) of the Tuolumne River, this bridging being only 130 yards past a junction with an east-climbing trail to the Gaylor Lakes. Immediately beyond the bridge you meet a short spur trail to the Tuolumne Meadows Lodge.

*   *   *   *

Resupply access: The lodge offers both showers and meals, but you probably will have to make a dinner reservation early in the day.

*   *   *   *

You parallel the Dana Fork downstream and soon hear the stream as it makes a small drop into a clear pool, almost cut in two by a protruding granite finger. At the base of this finger, about 8–10 feet down, is a hole in it, essentially an underwater arch, which is an extremely rare feature in any kind of rock. Just beyond the pool you approach the Lodge's road (8650–0.3), where a short path climbs a few yards up to it and takes one to the entrance of a large parking lot for backpackers. Now you parallel the paved road westward, passing the Tuolumne Meadows Ranger Station and

See maps H22, H23

see MAP H23

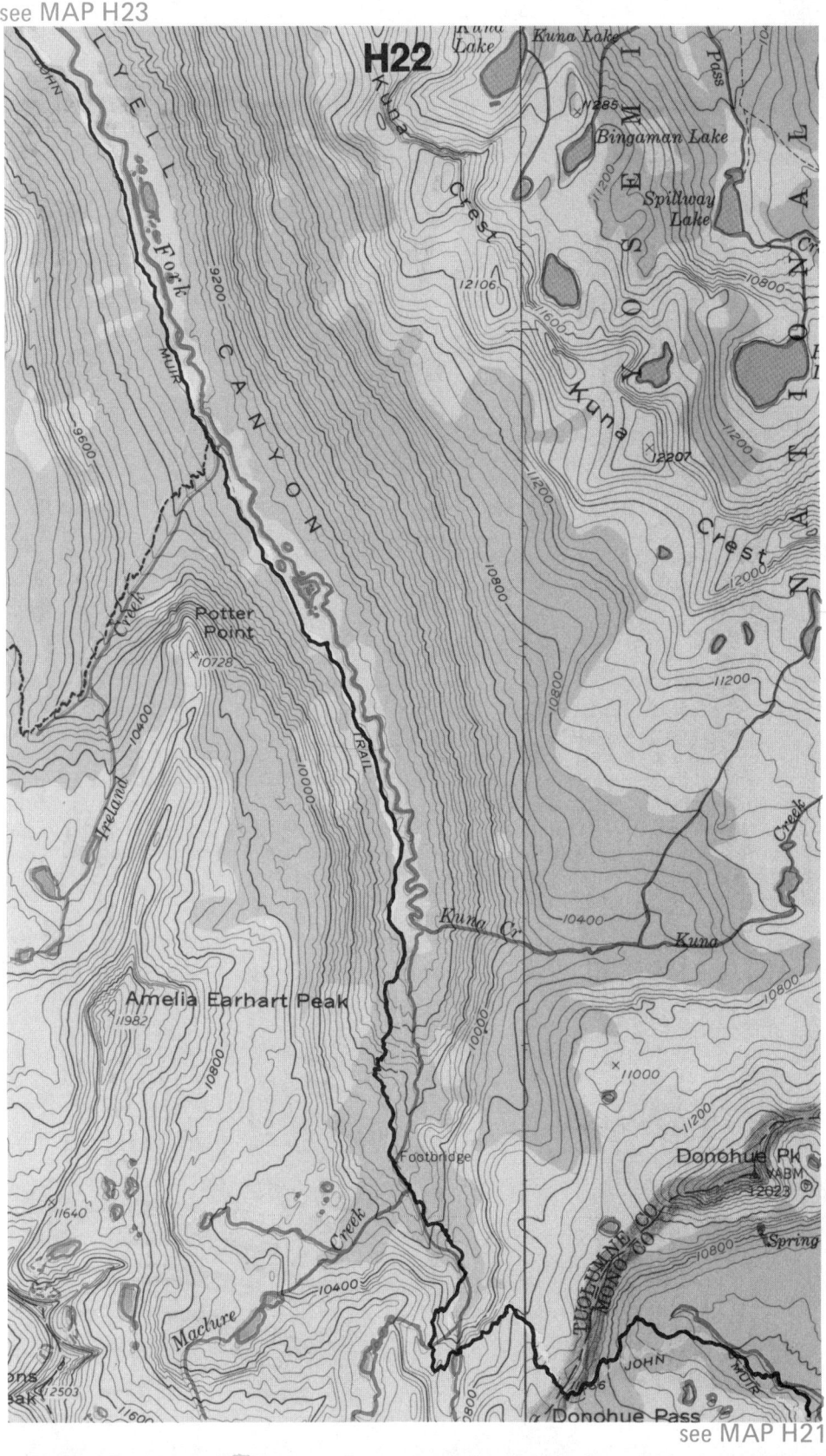

H22

see MAP H21

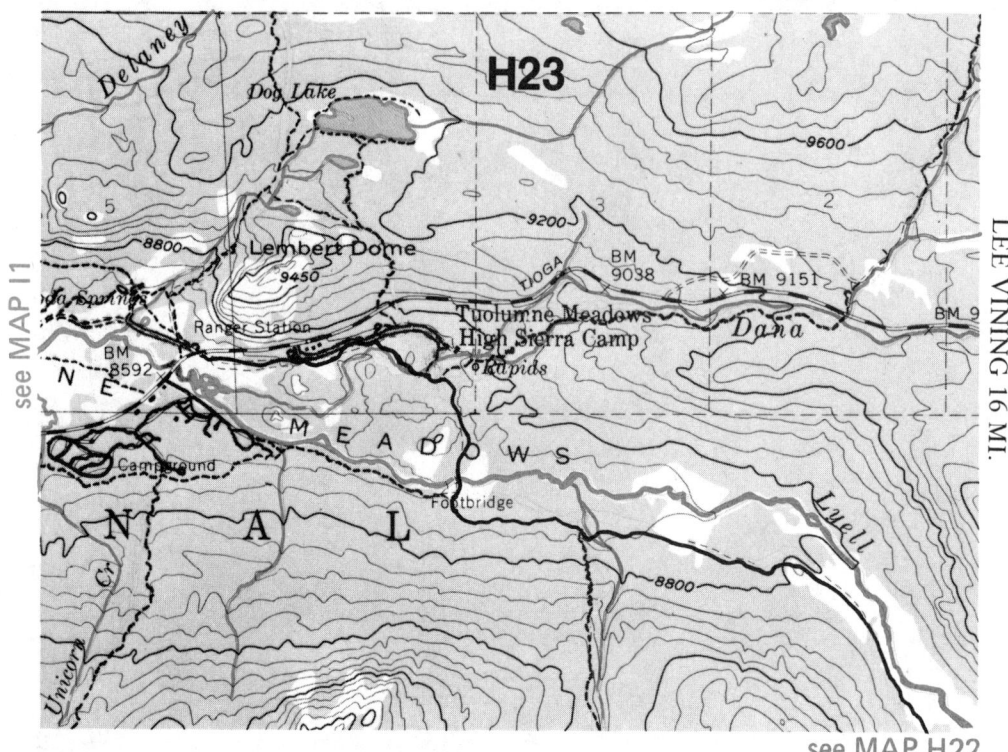

quickly reaching a junction. The main road curves north to the sometimes-noisy highway, but you follow the spur road west, to where it curves into a second large parking lot for backpackers. In its east end you'll find a booth from which a summer ranger dispenses wilderness permits. The road past the lot becomes a closed dirt road and diminishes to a wide trail by the time you arrive at this section's end, Highway 120 (8595–0.8), across from the start of the Soda Springs road. A campground, store and post office lie on Highway 120 just southwest of the Tuolumne River bridge.

See map H23

Banner Peak towers over Thousand Island Lake

282   THE PACIFIC CREST TRAIL

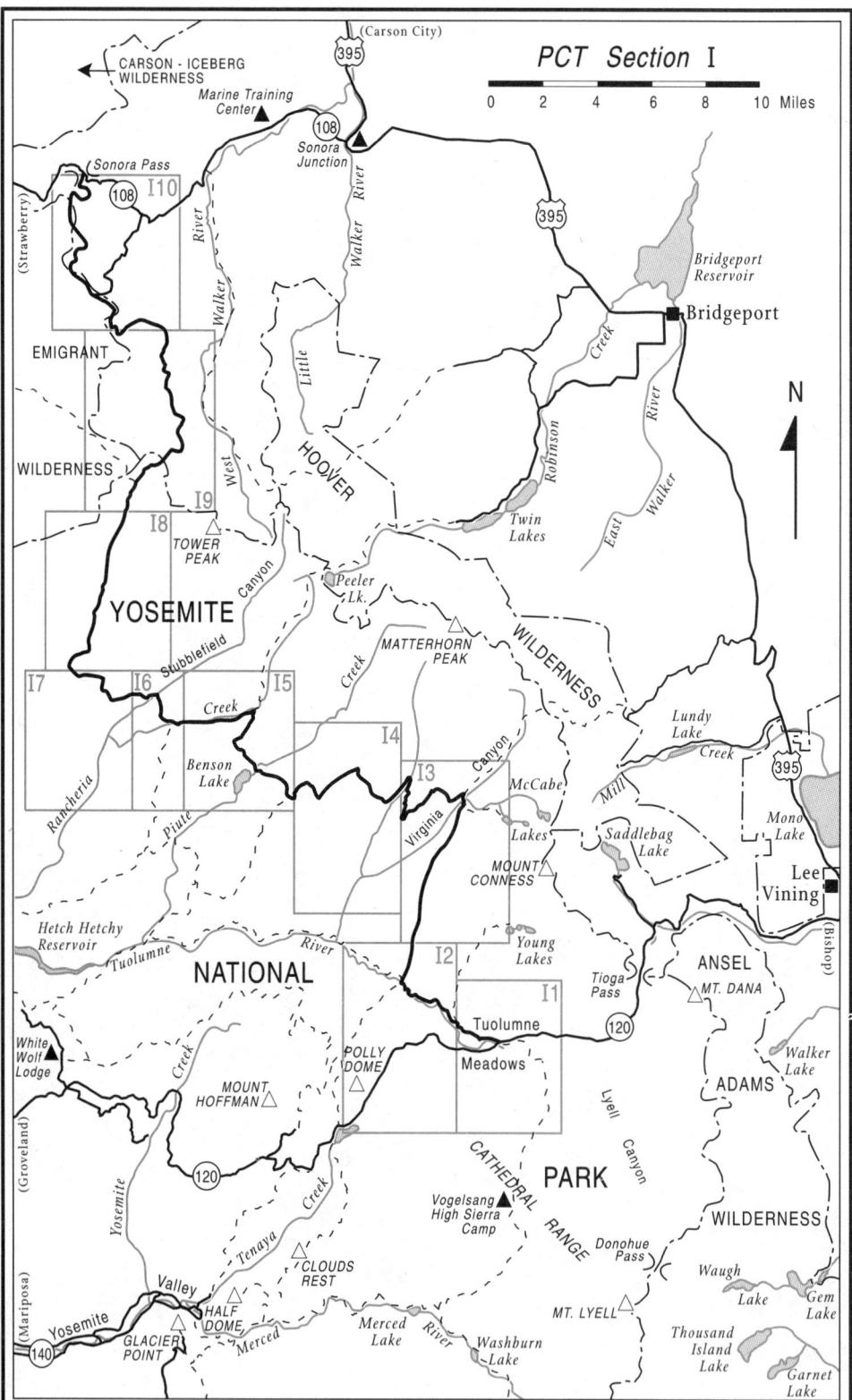

Tuolumne-
Sonora Pass

Section I
Tuolumne Meadows to Sonora Pass

Introduction: Deep, spectacular glaciated canyons, crossed one after another, characterize this section. You sometimes feel you're doing more vertical climbing than horizontal walking. Unlike the previous John Muir Trail section, which also has pass after mountain pass, this section has passes that are all below timberline, and the canyon bottoms can be quite warm and enjoyable—if proper bear-prevention measures are taken (see below). Nearing the north end of this section, you leave the expansive granitic domain behind and enter Vulcan's realm—thick floods of volcanic flows and sediments that buried most of the northern Sierra Nevada, including the Grand Canyon of the Tuolumne River, Hetch Hetchy Valley, and the rest of the lower river's deep canyon.

Declination: 15°E

Points on Route	S→N	Mi. Btwn. Pts.	N→S
Highway 120 in Tuolumne Meadows	0.0		76.4
Glen Aulin	6.0	6.0	70.4
Virginia Canyon Trail	14.0	8.0	62.4
Miller Lake	17.6	3.6	58.8
Matterhorn Canyon Trail	19.8	2.2	56.6
Benson Pass	24.3	4.5	52.1
Smedberg Lake	26.2	1.9	50.2
Benson Lake*	30.8	4.6	45.6
Seavey Pass	33.9	3.1	42.5
Lower Kerrick Canyon	38.3	4.4	38.1
Wilmer Lake	45.7	7.4	30.7
Dorothy Lake Pass	56.2	10.5	20.2
West Fork West Walker River bridge	61.7	5.5	14.7
leave jeep road at switchback	68.3	6.6	8.1
Highway 108 at Sonora Pass	76.4	8.1	0.0

*Although off the official route, Benson Lake is included as part of the PCT since virtually every PCT hiker visits it.

Supplies and Permits: Once you leave Highway 120 at Tuolumne Meadows, you won't encounter an on-route supple point until you reach Echo Lake Resort, north of Highway 50, about 153 miles farther. However, closer, off-route resorts lie on Highways 108, 4 and 88, as mentioned in "Supplies" of the next trail chapter.

Immediate supplies are obtained at the Tuolumne Meadows store, cafe, post office and gas station, which are just west of the Tuolumne Meadows Campground. Don't send any parcels to the post office if you expect to arrive at Tuolumne Meadows before late June or after mid-September, for then all these facilities will be closed. Parcels to be picked up then should be mailed to the Lee Vining Post Office. The town is reached by following Highway 120 east 7 miles up to Tioga Pass (9941'), 12 miles down to High-way 395, and then ½ mile north on it into town. Just one long mile before you reach Highway 395, you'll pass the Lee Vining Ranger Station, where you can obtain wilder-ness permits if you plan to return to the PCT via the Hoover Wilderness. When the facilities at Tuolumne Meadows are open, a shuttle bus operates from Yosemite Valley to the meadows. For a fee, this gives PCT hikers a chance to visit the valley or any spot along the road between these two end points.

In Tuolumne Meadows the Visitor Center, which is located along the Tioga Road 1 mile west of its bridge across the Tuolumne River, dispenses only information, not wil-derness permits. Leave messages there but get your permits from a booth in the parking lot near the west end of the Tuolumne Meadows Lodge spur road. The Park Service realizes that a lot of Yosemite hikers are weekend visitors, so from late June through the Labor Day weekend they keep the booth open 6:30 A.M. to 7:30 P.M. on Saturdays and 7:30 A.M. to 7:30 P.M. the six other days. Reservations for backcountry trips may be made by mail between February 1 and May 31 by writing to: Backcountry Office, P.O. Box 577, Yosemite National Park, California 95389. The reason you should get a reser-vation is that only a certain number of hikers are allowed to backpack in from a given trailhead on each day. Weekends, with their flood of visitors, could be a bad time for you to depart from Tuolumne Meadows if you don't have a permit.

East of the wilderness-permit booth is the Tuolumne Meadows Ranger Station, fol-lowed by another parking lot for backpackers. During the summer, this lot and others up here can be overflowing with vehicles. If you are starting south from Tuolumne Mead-ows, park your car here and, as at any Yosemite location, roll your windows completely up unless you want a bear to rip them out. East of this parking lot, at the end of the spur road, is Tuolumne Meadows Lodge and its parking lot, which is for *guests only*. Meals can be obtained here if you make reservations for them at least a few hours, if not a day, in advance. They are, as you might expect, relatively expensive, since the food has to be shipped in from a long distance. Hot showers, supplied with soap and towels, can be had for a small charge.

Wilderness permits are also required for overnight stays in Emigrant Wilderness, which you encounter near the end of this section. However, the PCT barely enters the wilderness, and since there are no campsites along your 2-mile-high, windswept traverse in it, you won't need a permit.

Special Problems: Bears are quite abundant—see the introduction to section G. Sev-eral stream fords may be dangerous before mid-July—see the introduction to section H.

Maps: *Tioga Pass* *Tiltill Mountain*
Falls Ridge *Tower Peak*
Dunderberg Peak *Pickel Meadow*
Matterhorn Peak *Sonora Pass*
Piute Mountain

─────── **The Route** ───────

Before leaving the parking lot below imposing Lembert Dome, look at the large feldspar crystals in the rock of the dome's base. This rock, called Cathedral Peak granite (granodiorite), solidified as a single unit several miles below the earth's surface about 80 million years ago. The large, blocky crystals make outcrops of this particular gran-ite—a pluton—very easy to identify and they afford rock climbers holds on otherwise slick,

See map I1

Map labels: Dingley, Moraine, see MAP I2, Delaney, Dog Lake, BASE, 9600, 9200, LEE VINNING 17 MI. see MAP H23, Lembert Dome, 9450, 8800, TIOGA, BM 9038, Tuolumne Meadows High Sierra Camp, Parsons Memorial Lodge, Soda Springs, Ranger Station, Rapids, BM 8592, T U O L U M N E, BM 8575, Campground, Footbridge, I O N A L, M E A D O W S, 8800, Unicorn Cr., 8800, 10082, Elizabeth Lake, 10000, Creek, Unicorn Pk, 10400, Johnson Peak, 11070, 9600

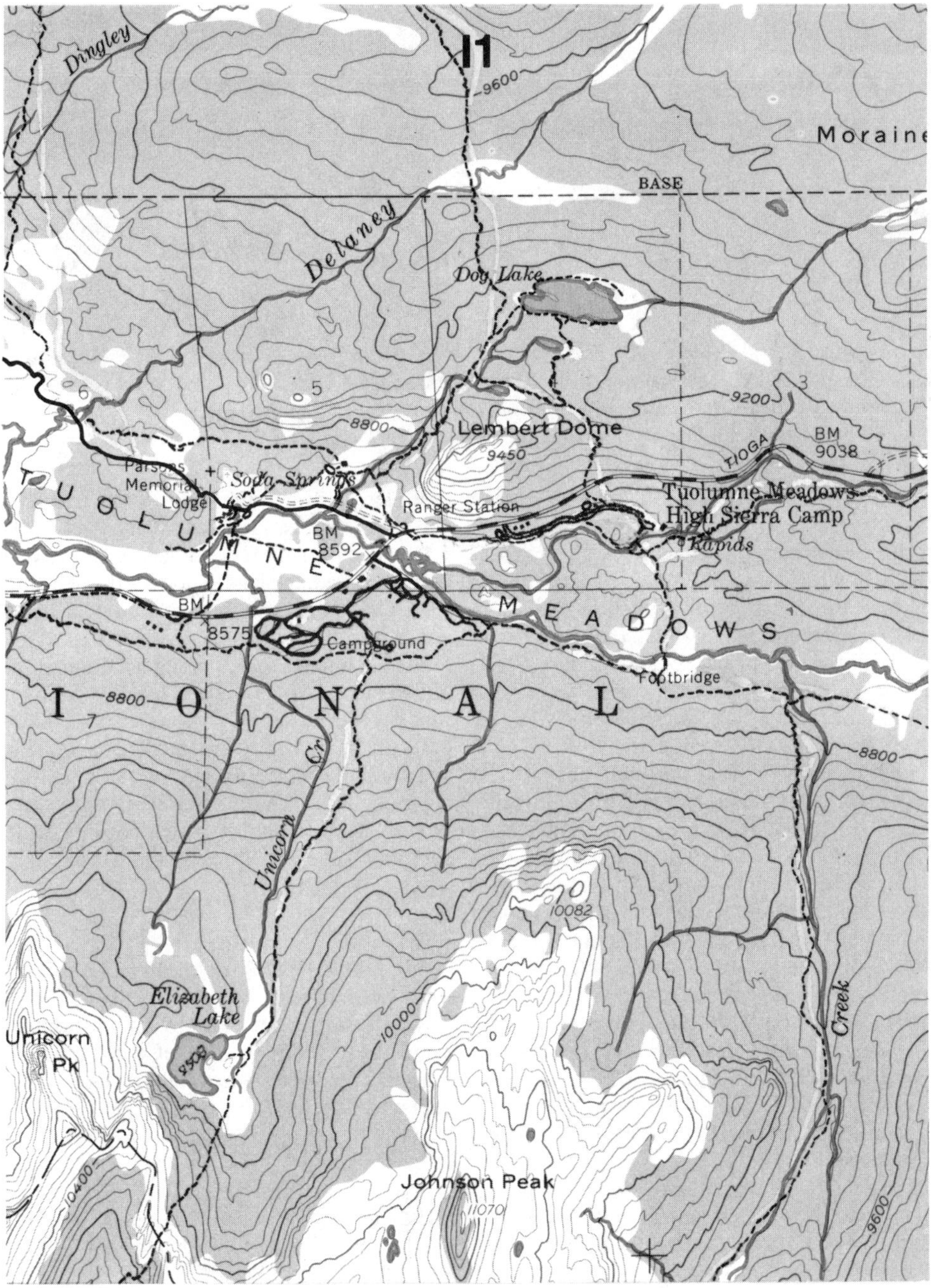

glacier-smoothed rock. ∎

From Tuolumne Meadows north almost to the Park border, the Pacific Crest Trail coincides with the Tahoe-Yosemite Trail. On the Soda Springs road you walk ⅓ mile west and reach a gate where a north fork climbs up to the Tuolumne Meadows Stable. On the closed road you continue west to a fork (8590–0.7) just beyond a minor gap, from where the left branch—the John Muir Trail—traverses south-

See map I1

**Tuolumne Meadows panorama, left to right: Unicorn Peak,
The Cockscomb, Echo Peaks, Cathedral Peak, Fairview Dome**

west to a bridge across the Tuolumne River, bound for Yosemite Valley. At the fork you keep right, climb a few paces, and take a shortcut trail due west to the road again, intersecting it at the Soda Springs area (8600–0.1).

∎ *The effervescent, rust-tainted soda springs are obvious, and if you have some powdered soft drink along, you can stir up a soda pop. Nearby Parsons Lodge, once owned by the Sierra Club, is now Park property.* ∎

From the springs area our well-signed trail starts a rolling traverse northwest from the road. Just 50 yards before you reach multibranched Delaney Creek (8570–0.8), a trail from the stable comes in on the right. No fishing is allowed here or upstream due to a planted population of endangered Piute cutthroat trout. Not far beyond the creek, near two small granite knolls, the Young Lakes Trail (8650-0.4) continues north, straight ahead, but you turn west, then continue northwest. In about a mile your trail approaches the Tuolumne River, and then parallels it, sometimes at a distance, eventually making a short but noticeable climb up granite bedrock.

∎ *In a gorge below, you may see, on the south side of the river, a dark mass, locally known as Little Devils Postpile—a plug of basalt that was forced up through the adjacent granite 9.4 million years ago. Despite repeated attacks by glaciers, this extrusion still remains.* ∎

Now you descend north steeply to a forested flat and traverse southwest to bridge the Tuolumne River (8310–2.7). Continuing northwest, you pass Tuolumne Falls, some minor

cascades, and then the high White Cascade, before your rocky trail meets a junction (7920–1.1) with a trail to McGee Lake. Although it is easily reached, the lake is not worth the effort. The PCT bends north—a direction you'll now pursue for miles—and descends to a bridging of the Tuolumne River. During maximum runoff, you may have to wade to reach the bridge! Just beyond it, the PCT meets a trail (7840–0.2) that immediately bridges Conness Creek to arrive at Glen Aulin High Sierra Camp. Just north of it is the heavily used Glen Aulin campground. Only 15 yards beyond the Glen Aulin spur trail is the Tuolumne Canyon Trail.

*   *   *   *

Side route: About ½ mile down this trail are less-used campsites. When water is high, then it is well worth your effort to continue downcanyon to California Falls, LeConte Falls, and especially to Waterwheel Falls, which is 3.4 miles from the PCT.

*   *   *   *

The PCT climbs north, sometimes alongside Cold Canyon creek, to a forested gap (8800–2.9), then descends ½ mile to the south edge of a large, usually soggy meadow. Midway across it you'll notice a huge boulder, just west. Its overhanging sides have been used as an emergency shelter, but in a lightning storm it is a prime strike target. Beyond it our multitracked route continues north, first for a mile through

See maps I1, I2, I3

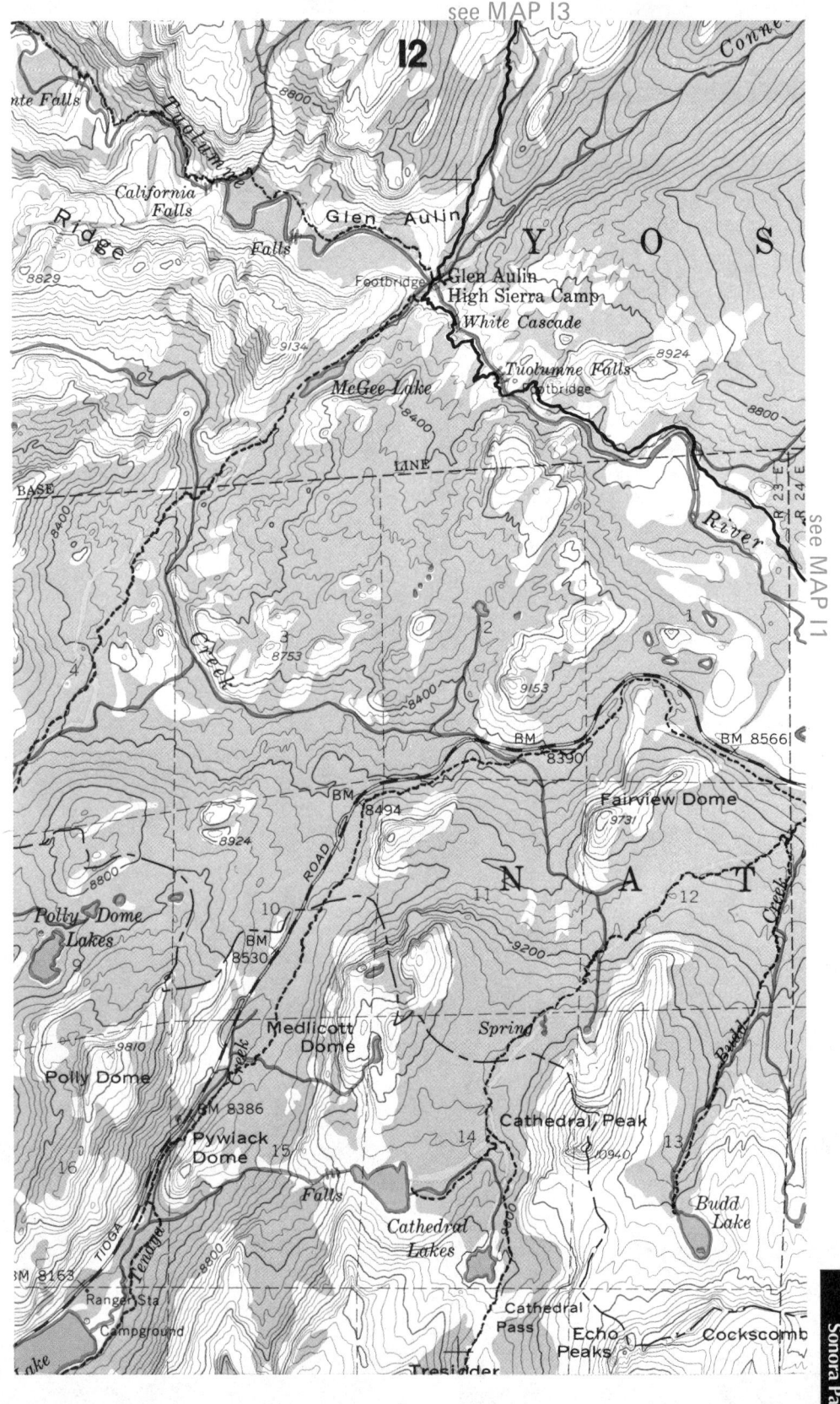

see MAP 11

meadow, then on a gradual ascent through forest to a crest junction with the McCabe Lakes Trail (9080–3.9).

*   *   *   *

Side route: A long-½-mile walk northeast up it will get you to a small campsite just above McCabe Creek; an hour's walk up it will get you to larger, better campsites at scenic lower McCabe Lake.

*   *   *   *

The most popular campsites in this vicinity, however, are along Return Creek and lower McCabe Creek, down in Virginia canyon. You switchback down to this canyon's floor, cross McCabe Creek—a wet ford before July—and quickly come to a junction. A spur trail continues up-canyon past campsites, but you turn left to ford powerful Return Creek, which is usually a wet ford and in early season can be a dangerous ford.

On the west bank you walk but a few steps southwest before your trail veers right and

meets the Virginia Canyon Trail (8540–1.2), which climbs northeast out of Yosemite and into the Hoover Wilderness. On the PCT you start down-canyon, climb west up into Spiller Creek canyon, and then, halfway to a pass, cross the canyon's high-volume creek. Beyond it you soon start up two dozen switchbacks that transport you up to a forested pass (9560–2.2), which offers fair camps when there is enough snow to provide drinking water. Most hikers, however, continue southwest down to shallow Miller Lake (9490–1.4), with good campsites along its forested west shore. From the lake you parallel a meadow north up to a low gap (9680–0.6), then execute over two dozen often steep switchbacks down to a canyon floor and a junction with the Matterhorn Canyon Trail (8510–1.6). On it you descend southwest, reaching this majestic canyon's broad creek in 80 yards. Immediately beyond the often-wet ford lies a large, lodgepole-shaded campsite.

Heading down-canyon for a mile, you pass less obvious, more secluded campsites, then soon leave the glaciated canyon to begin the usual two dozen, short, steep switchbacks—this

See map 13

A rewarding side trip: Lower McCabe Lake

Evening comes to Smedberg Lake

time west into Wilson Creek canyon. You twice ford Wilson Creek, then ford it a last time (9500–3.3) and start a switchbacking climb up to windy, gravelly Benson Pass (10,140–1.2).

As the passes have become steadily higher, so too have the canyons become deeper, and our multistage descent down to and up from Benson Lake is one incredible effort. You begin uneventfully with an easy descent to a large meadow, reaching its peaceful creeklet just before a dropoff. Veering away from the creeklet, you soon begin a switchbacking descent that ends at a south-shore peninsula (9250–1.9) on Smedberg Lake. Most of the campsites, however, lie along the lake's west and north shores.

From the lake's south-shore peninsula—below the steep-walled sentinel, Volunteer Peak—you continue west, passing a spur trail to the west-shore campsites before winding southwest up a poorly defined slab-rock trail to a well-defined gap (9340–0.3). From it the trail switchbacks down joint-controlled granite slabs, only to climb south high up to a meadowy junction (9480–0.7).

*   *   *   *

Side route: From it a trail to Rodgers Lake—an easy half-hour walk south that yields a far

better camping alternative to crowded Smedberg Lake.

*   *   *   *

Starting southwest up from this junction, you soon cross a low moraine and descend northwest to a junction (9390–0.3) with a trail climbing southwest to a broad saddle that harbors shallow, mosquito-haunted Murdock Lake. The next step down to Benson Lake is a typical two-dozen-short-switchback descent to a ford (8720–0.8) of Smedberg Lake's outlet creek. The PCT from that lake to here will be virtually impossible to follow in the snowbound early season. Hikers then will want to make a steep cross-country descent west down to this spot on an almost level canyon floor.

Now on the creek's north bank, you pass a small pond before commencing a steady, moderate, creekside descent to a second ford—a slight problem in early season. Back on the south bank, you make a winding, switchbacking descent over metamorphic rock down to your last, sometimes tricky ford of the creek. The next ⅓ mile sees you climbing up to a brushy saddle just east of a conspicuous knoll, then descending into a shady forest of giant firs before crossing wide Piute Creek and reaching

See maps 13, 14, 15

14

see MAP 15

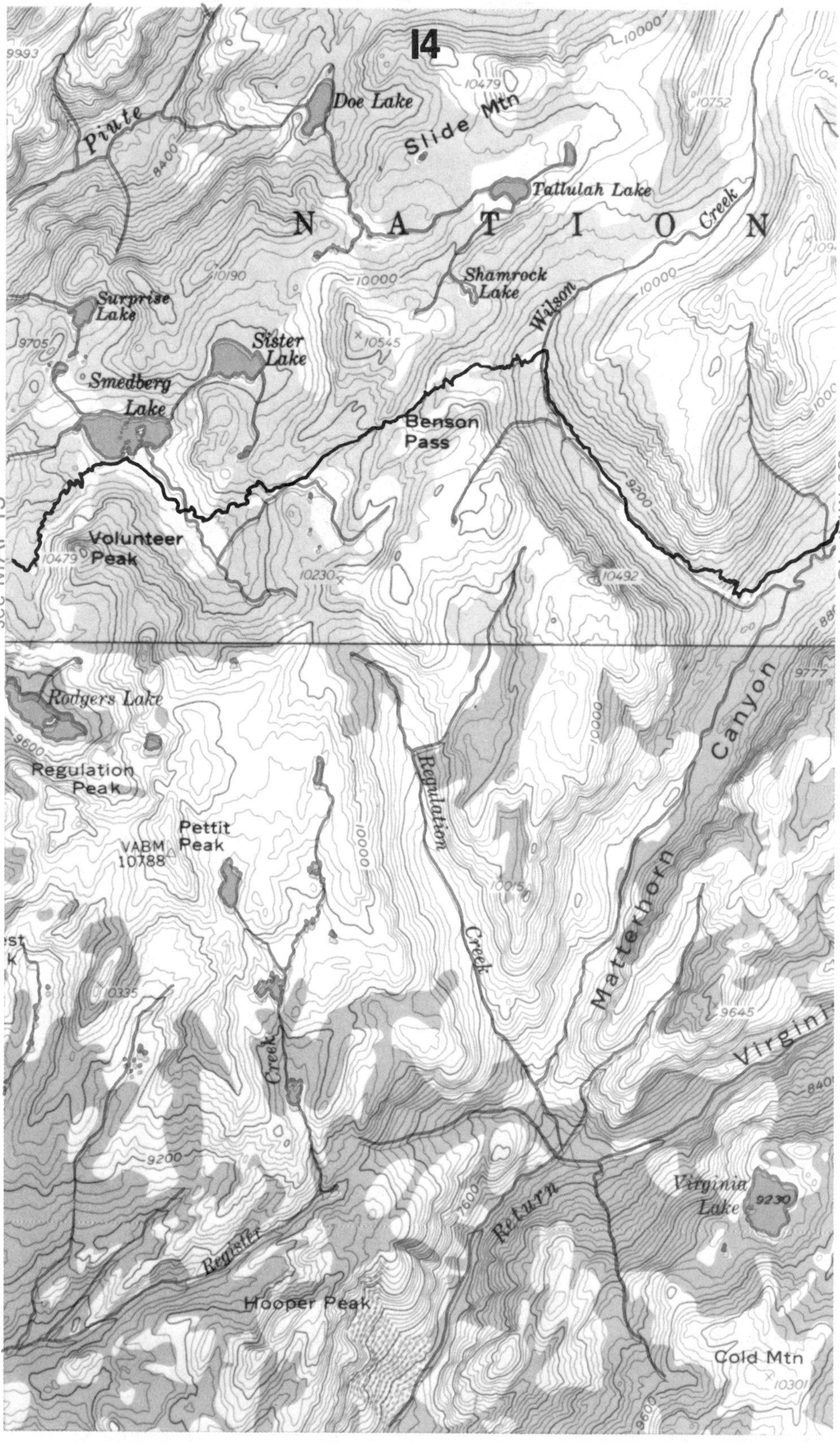

see MAP 13

Piute

Doe Lake

Slide Mtn

10479

10752

Tallulah Lake

N A T I O N

Wilson

Creek

Shamrock
Lake

10000

10000

Surprise
Lake

10190

10000

9705

Sister
Lake

10545

Smedberg
Lake

Benson
Pass

9200

Volunteer
Peak

10479

10230

10492

Canyon

9777

Rodgers Lake

Regulation

9600

Regulation
Peak

Pettit
Peak

10000

Creek

Matterhorn

VABM
10788

10000

9645

Virgini

est
k

10335

9200

Creek

Register

9600

Return

Virginia
Lake

9230

Hooper Peak

Cold Mtn

10301

10278

13

10328

Virginia

Retu

9600

Matt

9600

8800

10085

McCabe

9600

10040

8800

+9836

Miller Lake

8800

9000

Canyon

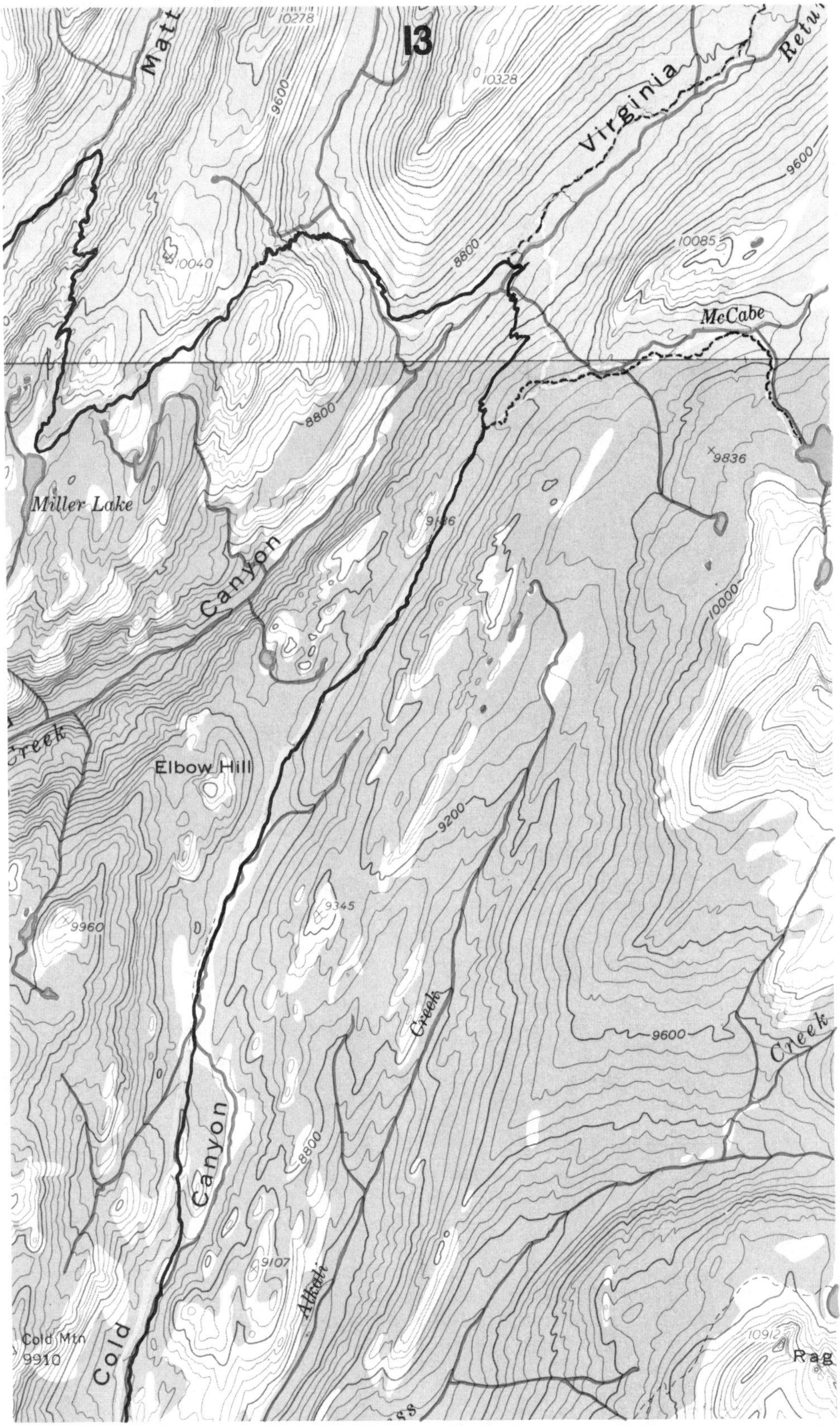

10000

Creek

Elbow Hill

9200

9960

9345

9600

Creek

Creek

8800

Canyon

Atta

9107

Cold

Cold Mtn
9910

10912

Rag

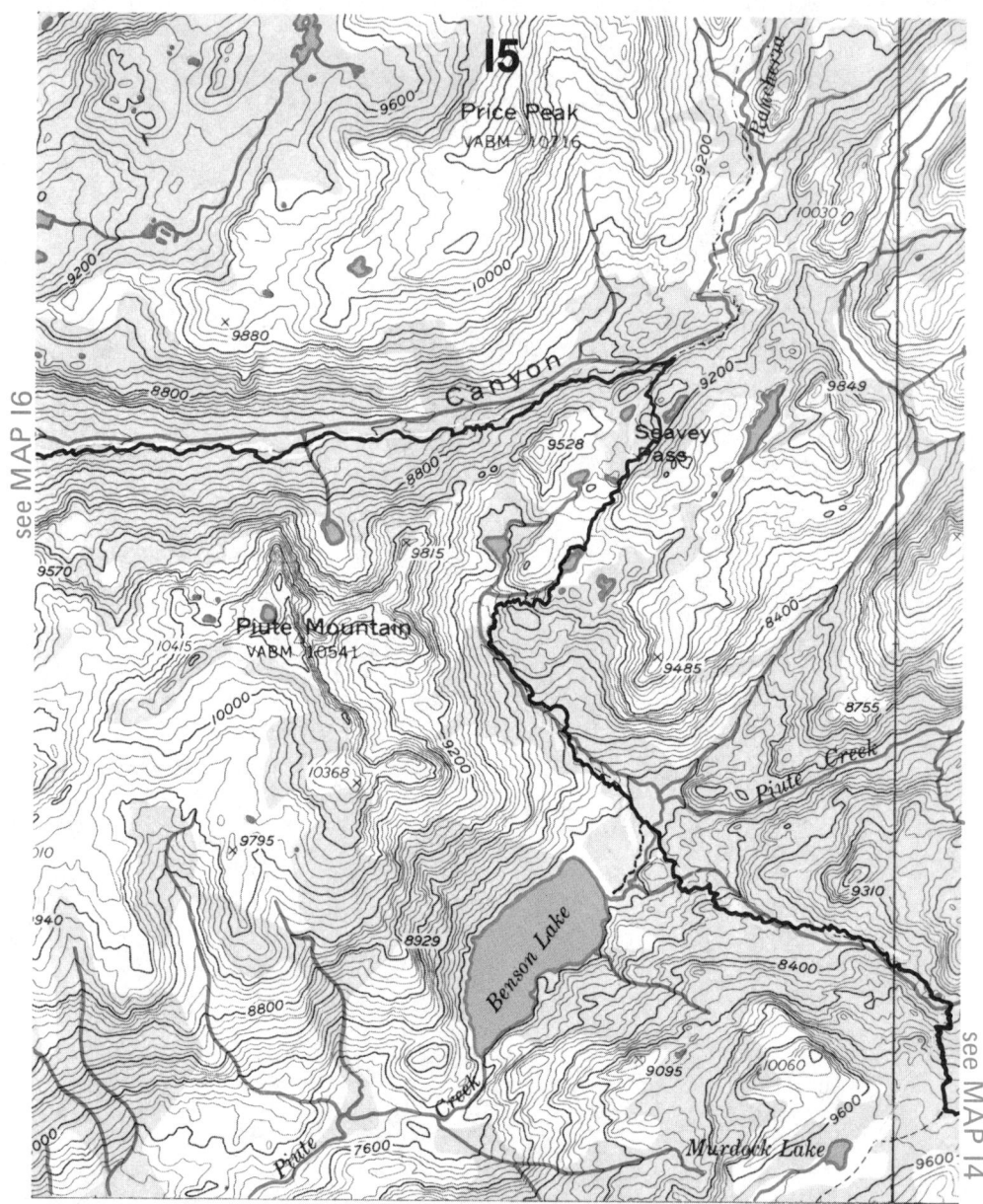

the Benson Lake spur trail (7560–2.1). Piute Creek—almost always a wet ford—can usually be crossed via one or more large, fallen logs.

*   *   *   *

Side route: No one in mid or late season should make this long descent from Benson

Pass without visiting the "Benson Riviera"— the long, sandy beach that forms along the north shore of Benson Lake once the lake's level falls. The spur trail winds southwest along the shady, often damp forest floor to a section of beach (7550–0.4) near Piute Creek's inlet. *Remember this spot,* for otherwise this route back can be hard to locate. Numerous campsites just within the forest's edge testify to the popularity of this broad, sandy beach. Swimming in the lake is brisk at best, but sunning on the beach is superb. However, strong, up-canyon afternoon winds can quell both activities.

*   *   *   *

After your stay, return to the PCT (7560–0.4) and prepare for a grueling climb north to Seavey Pass. At first brushy, the ascent northwest provides views of pointed Volunteer Peak and closer, two-crowned Peak 10060. You cross the creek, continue switchbacking northwest along the base of spectacular Peak 10368, then climb north briefly, only to be confronted with a steep 400-foot climb east. You are eventually funneled through a narrow, steep-walled, minor gap which rewards your climbing efforts with the sight of a relatively wind-free, sparkling pond (8970–2.1). Just past its outlet you'll find a trailside rock from which you can dive into its reasonably warm waters. The PCT parallels the pond's shore, curves east around a miniscule pond, then climbs northeast through wet meadows before switchbacking up to your second gap. At its north base lies a shallow rockbound pond, immediately beyond which you meet gap #3—hopefully signed SEAVEY PASS (9150–0.6). A small meadow separates it from gap #4, beyond which you reach a more noteworthy— the highest—gap (9180–0.2). Now you bend northwest, traverse past the head of a linear lake to gap #6, and switchback quickly down into a southwest-trending trough, spying a shallow pond 200 yards off in that direction. You turn right and immediately top your last gap, from which you descend northeast ¼ mile to a junction (8930–0.5) in Kerrick Canyon.

A cursory glance at the map suggests to the hiker that it is now an easy 3-mile down-canyon walk to the Bear Valley trail junction. Closer scrutiny, however, reveals a longer, winding too-often-ascending route. After 1½ miles of hiking on it, you parallel a moraine, on your right, which dies out in outwash around 8350 feet in elevation. ▮ *The glacier that left this debris retreated up-canyon about 13,000 years ago.* ▮ Below the outwash, the trail passes glacier-polished bedrock, exposed slightly earlier.

A short northward jog of the Kerrick Canyon trail segment ends at the Bear Valley Trail junc-

tion (7960–3.7). Immediately beyond it, you cross voluminous Kerrick Canyon creek, which can be a rough ford through mid-July. On the north bank a spur trail east leads up to popular campsites. The PCT, however, climbs west, affording dramatic cross-canyon views of Bear Valley peak and Piute Mountain. The PCT eventually climbs north to a shallow gap (8720–1.4), and just east of it you'll find a campsite near the west end of a small lakelet. Proceeding north from the gap, you have the usual knee-knocking descent on a multitude of short, steep switchbacks down to the mouth of Thompson Canyon. Here you make a shady, easy descent west to a large camp beside Stubblefield Canyon creek (7740–1.1). The main trail meets the creek just below the camp, and across from it a spur trail up the opposite bank soon meets the main trail. (Southbound hikers may not see this spur trail; rather, they may continue beyond it in a large creekside camp. From here they can rock hop—in late season only—to the north end of *your* large camp.) Cross where you will, locate the main trail near the opposite bank, and start down-canyon. In ¼ mile you leave the shady floor for slabs and slopes, in an hour arriving at a false pass. A short, steep descent west drops you into a corn-lily meadow, from which you wind ¼ mile northwest up to the true Macomb Ridge pass (8910–2.4).

With the deep canyons at last behind you, the 500-foot descent northwest into Tilden Canyon seems like child's play. Just beyond the west bank of Tilden Canyon Creek, you meet the Tilden Lake Trail and follow it 110 yards up-canyon to a signed junction (8390–1.0).

*   *   *   *

Alternate route: A more scenic, slightly longer route is to continue north up to huge, linear Tilden Lake, which has lots of campsites. Head west along it beneath domineering Chittenden Peak and then switchback down alongside Tilden Creek. Backtrack ½ mile south, down-canyon, paralleling Falls Creek at a distance before making a broad, shallow ford that has a good campsite by the west bank, just below the PCT.

*   *   *   *

Faithful PCT adherents, however, turn left at

See maps 15, 16, 17

see MAP 18

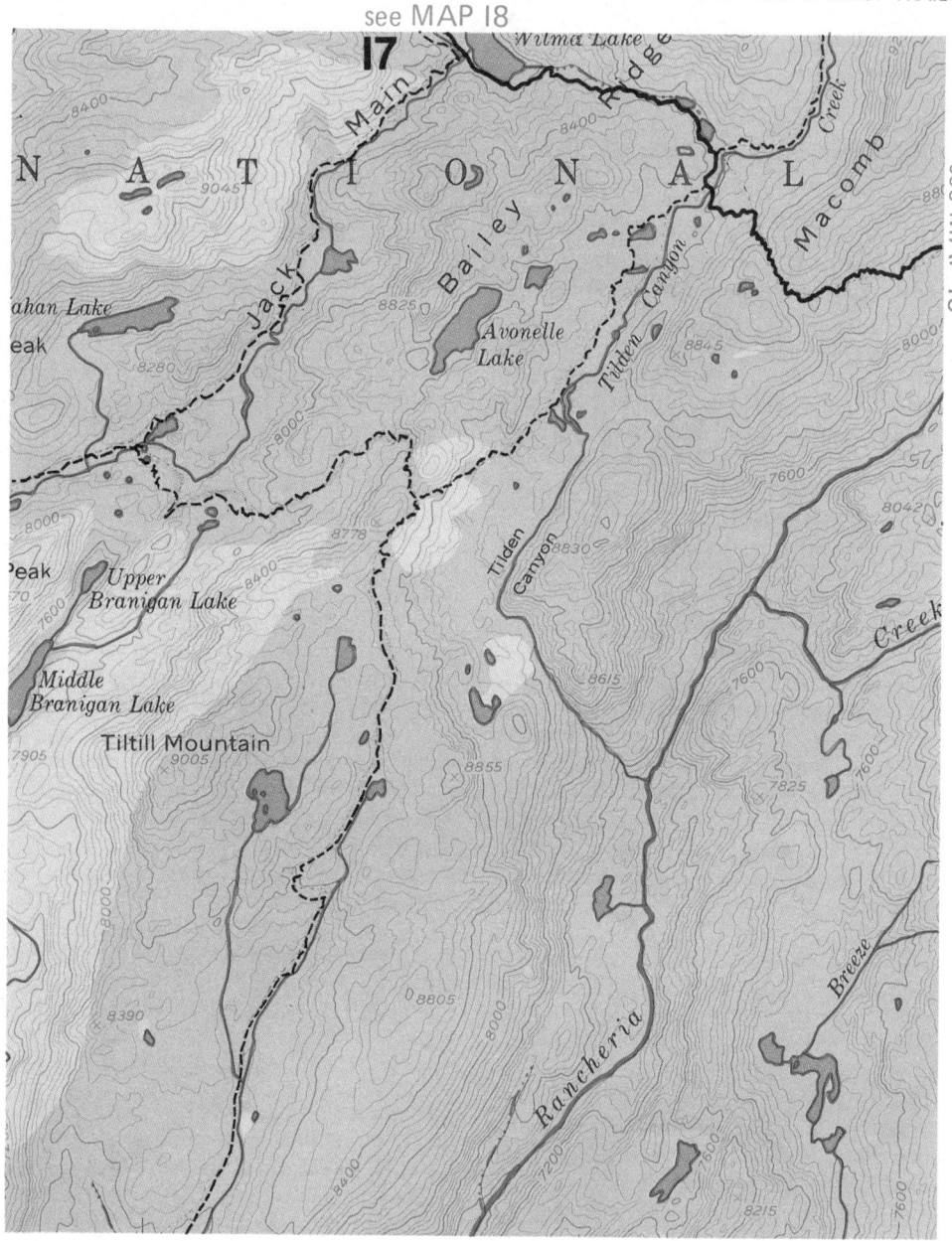

see MAP 16

the junction and wind northwest past several ponds, nestled on a broad gap, before descending west to large, shallow Wilma Lake (7930–1.5). Good campsites are found just beyond it, alongside broad, tantalizing Falls Creek. A few minutes' walk northwest up-canyon takes you to a shallow, broad ford of the creek, then past spacious campsites to a junction (7970–0.3)

with the Jack Main Canyon Trail, near a seasonal ranger's cabin.

From the junction, below the site of a 1986 avalanche, the PCT winds northward up-canyon, touching the east bank of Falls Creek only several times before reaching a junction (8160–1.9) with a trail east to Tilden Lake. At the creek's bank, 80 yards down this trail, is a good

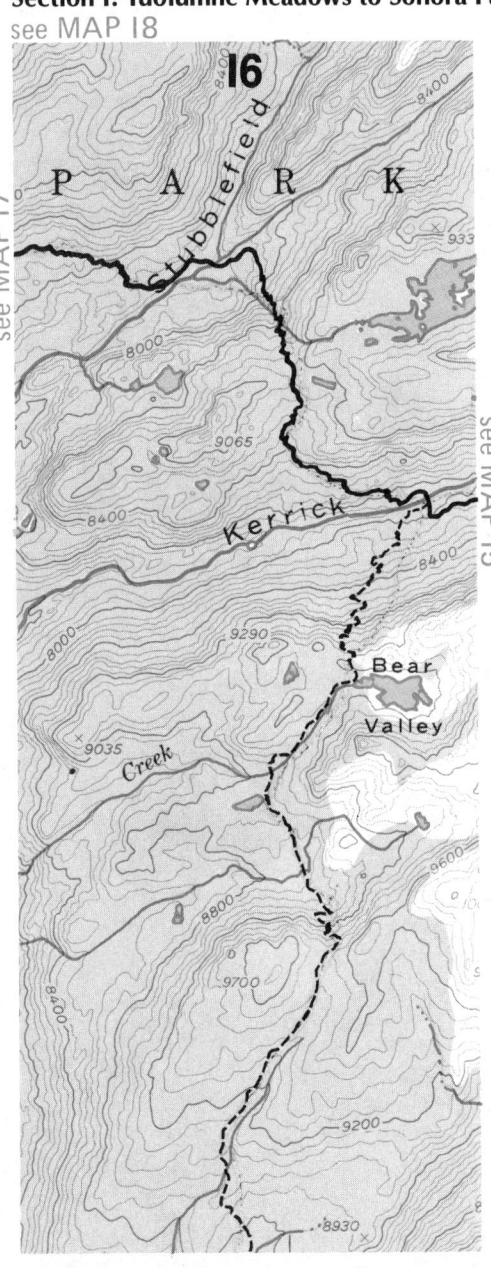

see MAP 18

landmarks. Under lodgepole cover along the meadow's edge you can set up camp. Leaving Grace Meadow, you soon pass through a small meadow before the ever-increasing gradient becomes noticeable. People have camped at small sites along this stretch, perhaps hoping to avoid bears, which are usually found lower down, but, alas, no such luck. Our upward climb meets the first (9280–3.1) of two trails that quickly unite to climb to Bond Pass—the route the Tahoe-Yosemite Trail now takes. Just beyond these junctions, volcanic sediments and exposures are noticed in ever-increasing numbers—a taste of what's to come—before you reach large, exposed Dorothy Lake. Clumps of lodgepoles provide minimal campsite protection from the winds that often rush up-canyon. A short climb above the lake's east end takes you up to Dorothy Lake Pass (9550–1.5), with your last good view of the perennial snowfields that grace the north slopes of Forsyth Peak.

Leaving Yosemite National Park behind, you enter Toiyabe National Forest, pass rocky Stella Lake, approach tempting Bonnie Lake, and then switchback east down to campsites along the west shore of Lake Harriet (9210–1.1). Larger, more-isolated camps are on the east shore. The PCT crosses Cascade Creek just below the lake, and then it makes short switchbacks down confining terrain, reaching a large campsite in about ½ mile. Just 50 yards beyond it, you cross the creek on a footbridge (9040–0.7). Ahead, the way is still winding, but it's nearly level, and you soon reach—just past a pair of ponds— a junction (9000–0.6) with a trail that descends 1.5 miles to the West Walker River Trail. Onward, you start north, then bend west and pass three ponds before winding down to a creek that has a junction (9320-0.9) just past it.

*　　　*　　　*　　　*

campsite. Chittenden Peak and its north satellite serve as impressive reference points as you gauge your progress northward, passing two substantial meadows before arriving at the south end (8630-3.7) of even larger Grace Meadow. The upper canyon explodes into plain view, with—east to west—Forsyth Peak, Dorothy Lake Pass and Bond Pass being your guiding

Alternate route: The original PCT route went west, and it is preferable to the official route. This old route contours 1.0 mile over to Cinko Lake, which has adequate campsites. It then descends to the West Fork West Walker River— a wet ford before mid-July—and arrives at a trail junction that is 0.5 mile past the lake. In 1.5 miles this trail descends to the PCT, fording the river midway along its length.

*　　　*　　　*　　　*

See maps 18, 19

see MAP 19

18

Black Bear Lake

34

MIGRANT
WILDERNESS

Bigelow Peak

10539

T 4 N

9600

Grace Meadow

Creek

Keyes
Peak

10670

9600

9200

× 9980

10390

10000

Tilden

92

10000

Kendrick Peak

10390

8800

9200

8800

ichie Peak

10365

9200

9600

9210

9200

10000

× 10120

9380

8400

Tilden Lake

9200

10380

9600

Y O S E M I T E

9365

Chittenden Pk

9685

Canyon Falls

9335

9200

× 9905

8800

8400

× 9785

Ridge

× 9985

ake

Little Otter Lake

8400

080

8465

Wilmer Lake

see MAP 17   see MAP 16

Bond Pass, Dorothy Lake Pass (center) and Forsyth Peak above Grace Meadow

On the official, lackluster segment, you first parallel the creek you've just crossed, and soon pass several gray outcrops of marble, which differ significantly in color and texture from the other metamorphic rocks you've been passing. Beyond them you curve left into a small bowl, with lots of snow in early season, then make a short, steep climb through a granitic notch before dropping west to a seasonal creeklet. After winding briefly northwest from it, your trail turns northward, taking almost ½ mile to descend to the West Fork West Walker River Trail (8670–2.0). On it you descend to a nearby junction (8610–0.2) by paltry, sedge-choked Lower Long Lake. Here you take a steel bridge across a small gorge that confines the West Fork West Walker River, and you find a large, lodgepole-shaded campsite immediately past it.

█ *Most of your California trek, particularly in the High Sierra, has been across granitic landscapes. That is now about to change, for quickly you'll enter one of many volcanic landscapes, and these will dominate your trek for about the next 500 miles, ending just before Interstate 5 near Castle Crags State Park.* █

*　　　*　　　*　　　*

Alternate route: The original PCT route stays closer to the river, but usually is lost among cow paths where it crosses meadows. After 2.0 miles north, it turns west and ascends Kennedy Canyon, staying close to the north bank of its creek. In 1.6 miles it reaches a junc-

tion (9060) with the official PCT. This west-climbing part of the alternate route might be used for two reasons. First, in years of heavy snowfall there may be considerable avalanche damage to the official trail. Second, also in those years, and in early season of normal years, the north-side trail will be more snow-free.

*　　　*　　　*　　　*

From near the steel-bridge crossing you meander ⅓ mile west to an ephemeral stream bed, then bend north and walk past one of the Walker Meadows to a seasonal creek laden with volcanic sediments. About a half mile past it you approach another creek (8610–1.6) with more staying power, and its two-step waterfall invites you to pause for a break. Below is another Walker Meadow, and you'll find more campsites (and often cows) both north and south of it. The trail briefly reverts to a granitic tread as you enter avalanche-prone Kennedy Canyon, up which you hike west to a ford of its creek (9060-1.9), where you may see the old, original tread heading down-canyon. This spot is one of your last chances to make an adequate camp this side of Sonora Pass. An exposed, alpine traverse lies ahead. Now you face a 1500-foot climb, first curving southwest up to a closed jeep road (9670–1.2), reaching it about 0.2 mile north of the saddle above Kennedy Canyon. Up this road one switchbacks above timberline, leaving virtually all the whitebark pines behind and obtaining fantastic panoramic

See maps I9, I10

see MAP J1

see MAP I9

views just before leaving the road at a switchback (10,580–1.9). Here you're just inside Emigrant Wilderness, whose boundary runs along the crest. You'll weave in and out of the wilderness until you finally leave it where you start a 1200+ foot drop to Sonora Pass.

*   *   *   *

Alternate route: Before mid-July, short parts of the remaining stretch to Sonora Pass can be potentially dangerous. If you've been encountering lots of snow, you might consider taking the following alternate route.

Continue up the road to a gate on a saddle (10,640–0.2), then take the main jeep road down to the outlet creek of Leavitt Lake (9556-1.5). Here you can find campsites among small stands of whitebark pines. You may find more-protected sites along the closed road descending from the lake to Highway 108 (8440–2.9). The alternate route turns left, climbing northwest to a junction with Road 062 (9100-2.4), by which you could camp, and then continue west up to Sonora Pass (9628–1.3). You could also camp near the pass, obtaining water from the headwaters of either Sardine or Deadman creek.

*   *   *   *

Back on trail again, you have a stark, yet stunning, often-windblown traverse along a 2-mile-high volcanic ridge. Heading northwest, you pass several crest saddles before your trail turns north and finally crosses the Sierra crest (10,640–2.3). Should you want to "bag" Leavitt Peak, ¾ mile to the northwest, you can start up the crest or else hike ¼ mile farther along the trail and, in a bowl, start west up a talus slope. About ½ mile beyond the bowl you cross a ridge (10,880–0.7), which is the PCT's highest point since the previous section's Donohue Pass area. Latopie Lake lies well below you, and is difficult to reach because of steep slopes. In early season this short stretch of trail across steep slopes is snowbound and dangerous.

Ahead, beyond a nearby gully, you traverse along the base of an overly steep wall that is avalanche-prone in early season. You head through a notch in this wall (10,780–0.7) and bid farewell to the last of your excellent views of the Yosemite hinterlands. The route drops ¼

See map I10

Northernmost view of Tower Peak (far left) and the Yosemite hinterlands

mile north, then angles northwest, passing two very youthful glacial moraines before climbing to another crest crossing (10,780-0.8). Because volcanic rock is so porous, no lake ponds up behind the moraines. From the crest crossing, your route north hovers around timberline, passing dense, isolated clumps of prostrate whitebark pines before you once again cross the crest (10,870–1.2). You now tackle a 1200+ foot drop to Sonora Pass. In early summer the first ¼ mile of this descent—across steep slopes—is snowbound and potentially lethal if you fall. Near the end of your descent you cross some closely spaced gullies, with one usually containing water (9820–1.7)—the first creek since Kennedy Canyon. Now in open lodgepole forest you meander slightly up to the Sierra crest, then wind down it to cross Highway 108 (9620–0.7) immediately north of signed Sonora Pass. From the pass a jeep road climbs northeast up the crest to a nearby, fairly level area, which serves as an emergency, if windblown, dry campsite, should you not be able to reach an acceptable campsite farther on by dark. Less windy sites lie ¼–½ mile down either side of the pass beside the road.

See map I10

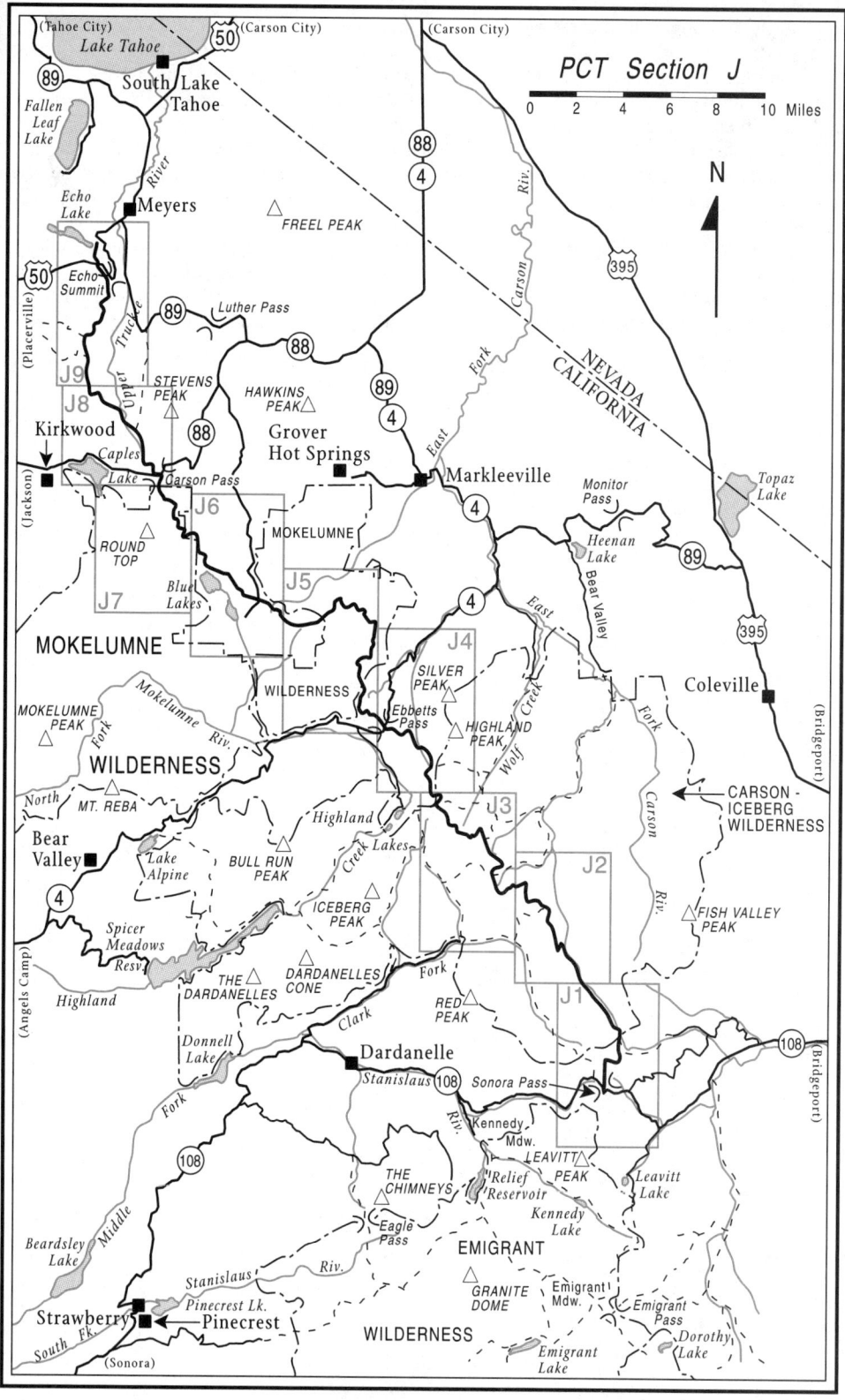

Section J
Sonora Pass to Echo Lake Resort

Introduction: By the time you reach Sonora Pass, you'll notice that the Sierra crest has taken on a new character. Virtually all the peaks you'll now see in this section are volcanic in origin—either plugs of pre-glacial volcanoes or remnants of volcanic flows. The erosion of these flows and their associated volcanic sediments has created an impressive, even sometimes surrealistic, landscape, particularly between Ebbetts Pass and the Blue Lakes Road. As in the High Sierra to the south, glaciers flowed down virtually every canyon along this crest route. However, unlike the High Sierra, this landscape is lake-deficient, and the reason for this character lies in its volcanic rocks. The High Sierra is composed mostly of granite rocks, which can be almost 100% resistant to glacier action if they are free of *joints*—a geologist's term for cracks. The joint pattern varies so that in any given area you might see, as you hiked down-canyon, an abundance of joints followed by a paucity of joints. Glaciers cut into the abundant-joint sections but then rode over the relatively joint-free sections, which served as effective dams for the basins. In contrast, volcanic flows and sediments lack the joint patterns of granitic rocks, and they are also intrinsically less resistant to glacier attack. In this volcanic landscape, then, a glacier usually advances smoothly down-canyon without carving any basins. The few lakes that do form tend to be small. If you were to explore the expansive landscape between Sonora Pass and Echo Summit, you would find that most of its lakes lie in glacier-carved granite basins that are situated below the younger, overlying volcanic ridge-and-crest sediments.

Declination: 15¼°E

Points on Route	S→N	Mi. Btwn. Pts.	N→S
Highway 108 at Sonora Pass	0.0		76.2
Wolf Creek Lake saddle	4.1	4.1	72.1
East Carson River Trail	9.3	5.2	66.9
Paradise Valley/Golden Canyon trails	17.5	8.2	58.7
Wolf Creek Pass	24.4	6.9	51.8
Noble Lake	27.8	3.4	48.4
Highway 4 near Ebbetts Pass	31.6	3.8	44.6
Eagle Creek	36.7	5.1	39.5
Raymond Lake Trail	41.1	4.4	35.1
Blue Lakes Road	49.3	8.2	26.9
Lost Lakes spur road	53.5	4.2	22.7
rejoin the Tahoe-Yosemite Trail near Frog Lake	59.2	5.7	17.0
Highway 88 at Carson Pass	60.4	1.2	15.8
east shore of Showers Lake	65.7	5.3	10.5
Highway 50 near Little Norway site	74.7	9.0	1.5
Echo Lake Resort	76.2	1.5	0.0

Supplies: At Sonora Pass you are a long way from any town. From the pass Highway 108 descends 11 miles east to the U.S. Marines Mountain Warfare Training Center (emergency help; in the opposite direction, Kennedy Meadows Resort, with minimal supplies, is about the same distance). Highway 108 then goes 5¼ miles farther east to Highway 395. This takes you 17 miles south to Bridgeport, which should have any kind of food and equipment that you might need. On the far side of town is the Bridgeport Ranger Station.

After 31½ miles of PCT hiking north from Sonora Pass, you'll cross Highway 4 almost at Ebbetts Pass. The closest supplies are at Lake Alpine Lodge, open during the summer, which lies 14 miles southwest down the highway. However, we recommend you go 18 miles northeast down the highway to Markleeville, a peaceful little town with a few eating establishments, a post office and the Forest Service Markleeville Guard Station. If you want to have an enjoyable layover day, hike 4 miles west up Alpine County Road E1 to Grover Hot Springs State Park, where, for a small charge, you can get a hot bath or a warm swim.

From Ebbetts Pass the PCT continues 28¾ miles to Highway 88 at Carson Pass. Like every pass along Section J, this one lacks on-route supplies. Caples Lake Resort, about 4 miles west down the highway, is your closest point for aid and minimal supplies.

It is a relatively easy hiking day—16 miles along the PCT—from Highway 88 at Carson Pass to Echo Lake Resort, which has a post office. Because Echo Lake Resort caters to a large backpacker population, it keeps its store well stocked with trail food. However, if you need new boots or other major equipment, or if you are hiking out of season, you then will have to descend to Meyers or go beyond it to South Lake Tahoe— a city that has everything (except gambling, which is just across the border). This chapter offers a relatively traffic-free, direct route to Meyers, from which you can hitch a ride to South Lake Tahoe. (Hitching a ride along Highway 50 is difficult in the Echo Summit area.)

Permits: Unfortunately (unless you have a through-permit), to enter Carson-Iceberg Wilderness, just north of Sonora Pass, you'll have to get a permit at the Summit Ranger District office, along Highway 108 at the Pinecrest Lake road junction, which is about 36 miles west of Sonora Pass. Their address is No. 1 Pinecrest Lake Road, Pinecrest, CA 95364; their phone is (209) 965-3434.

In Mokelumne Wilderness, as in Carson-Iceberg Wilderness, permits aren't required for day hikers. If you start your hike from Highway 4 near the south boundary of Mokelumne Wilderness, you will be in the Carson Ranger District, which has the user-friendly policy of self-service permits at the trailheads—no need to write, phone, or go out of your way. Unfortunately if you are starting a hike south from Highway 88's Carson Pass near the north boundary, you'll be in the Amador Ranger District, whose office is at 26820 Silver Drive & Highway 88, Star Route 3, Pioneer, CA 95666; their phone is (209) 295-4251. This office is an inconvenient hour's drive southwest from the trailhead. The staff prefers that you pick up your permit in person. Because this office is out of the way for those *not* driving northeast up Highway 88, the Forest Service operates, seven days a week during the summer season, a tiny station at the south end of the Carson Pass parking lot.

Maps: *Sonora Pass*   *Pacific Valley*
            Pickel Meadow   *Carson Pass*
            Disaster Peak   *Caples Lake*
            Dardanelles Cone   *Echo Lake*
            Ebbetts Pass

---------------------------------- **The Route** ----------------------------------

From Sonora Pass (9620') the PCT starts north, paralleling westbound Highway 108, and it quickly crosses a trailhead-parking spur road (9610–0.2) at a point about 70 yards from the highway (no camping allowed at trailhead). On a generally northward course, it then winds in and out of more than a dozen gullies before reaching a switchback (10,080–1.7). Ahead, the eastern traverse can be made impassable in early season by steep snowbanks. Also, in some years, the tread virtually disappears in one steep-sloped spot just before a crest saddle. So if you encounter intimidating problems, backtrack and take a cross-country route around them.

*   *   *   *

Alternate route: To do this, start from the switchback and take the path of least resistance down a bit to where you can contour west to a highly visible old jeep road. Follow it north, the road soon giving way to a trail that you take for a short, steep climb to St. Marys Pass. From it you climb northeast up a ridge to a nearly flat bench just below the west slope of Sonora Peak. You could climb straight up the slope to the summit, and then descend northeast, staying just east of a county-line ridge. This route provides spectacular views, but it requires a lot of effort even with just a day pack. Therefore, head about ½ mile north along the bench to a conspicuous saddle and then head northeast down a cirque to the PCT, about 1200 feet below. In early season, this 25%-gradient descent can be an enjoyable snow slide.

*   *   *   *

If the trail is passable, then from the switchback you make an ascending traverse east to a county-line ridge (10,420–0.7), recognized by a group of prominent pinnacles. The sweeping panorama achieved from the nearest summit is well worth the short scramble to it. Dark, volcanic Leavitt Peak dominates the southern skyline, while more-distant, mostly granitic Tower Peak pierces the sky in the south-southeast. Leaving the pinnacles on a gently-climbing trail, you wind in and out of stark gullies, then top the Sierra crest at a saddle (10,500–0.3).

Now you traverse across steep slopes well above the floor of Wolf Creek canyon. Iced-over snow patches can be a real hazard in at least one spot, so be prepared if you're passing through before late July. In about ¼ mile these slopes give way to gentler ones, across which you make a safer, more-relaxing traverse that has whitebark pines reduced to shrub height by

See map J1

Wolf Creek Lake and the West Walker River canyon

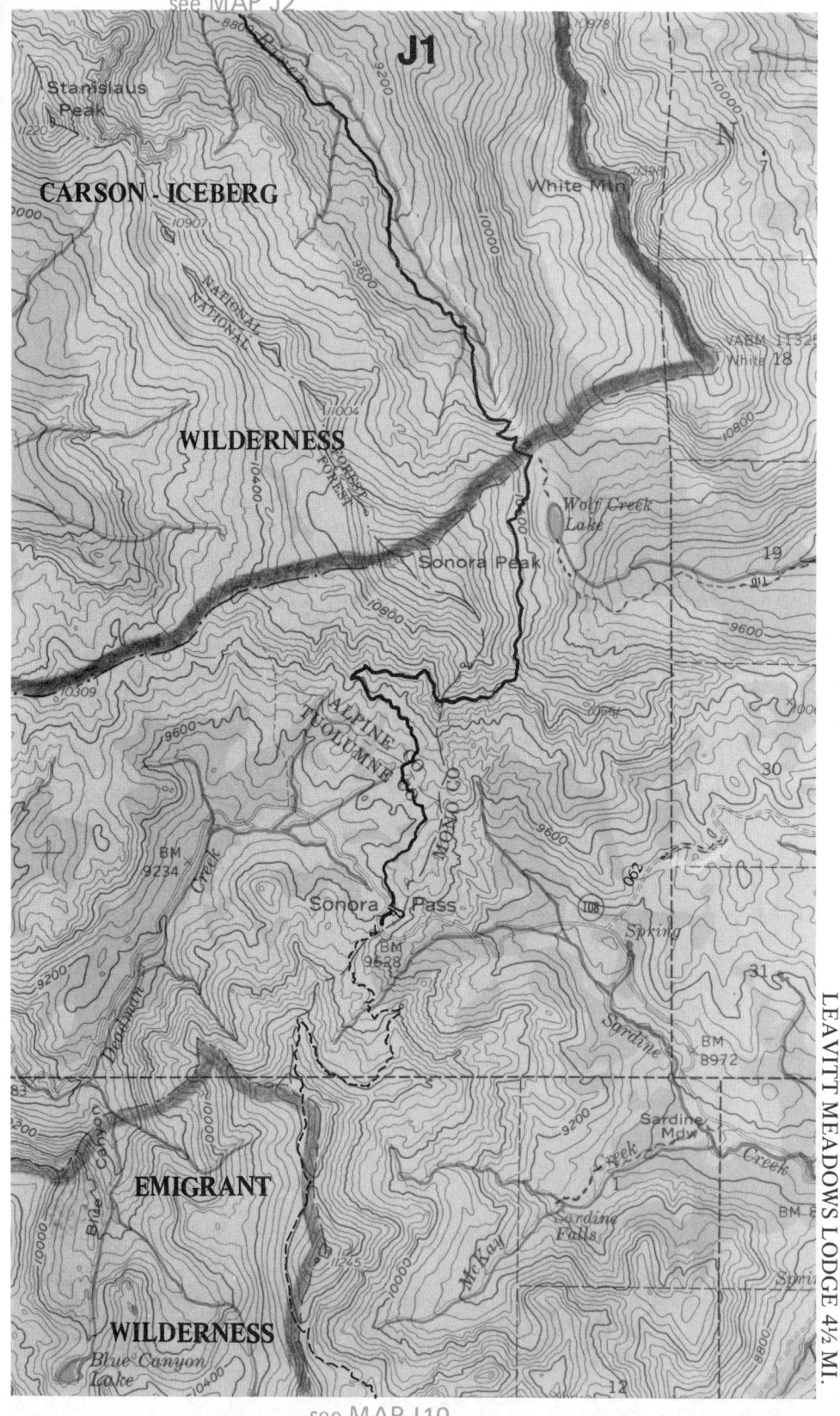

see MAP J2

J1

Stanislaus Peak

CARSON - ICEBERG

White Mtn

WILDERNESS

VABM
White 18

Wolf Creek Lake

Sonora Peak

ALPINE CO.
TUOLUMNE

MONO CO.

BM 9234

Creek

30

9600

Sonora   Pass

BM 9628

Spring

Deadman

Creek

Sardine

BM 8972

Sardine Mdw

EMIGRANT

Creek

Creek

BM

Blue

Canyon

McKay

Sardine Falls

Spring

WILDERNESS

Blue Canyon Lake

12

see MAP I10

winter's freezing winds. As little as 16,000 years ago there would have been no vegetation at all, just a thick river of ice slowly flowing east down Wolf Creek canyon.

Your trail continues to traverse north along the bleak, volcanic lower slopes of Sonora Peak, and below you you soon see Wolf Creek Lake, with the first campsites since Kennedy Canyon, south of Sonora Pass. Well into August this part of the PCT can be obscured by snow, hiding the spot where your trail bends right and quickly reaches a granitic ramp. This bend is located near two creeklets found immediately beyond a cluster of wind-cropped willows. Hikers who want to climb easily accessible Sonora Peak can leave the trail here. The rest head down the steep, usually snowbound ramp, which is bordered by a granitic cliff on its west side. At its base you exit onto a field of fractured granitic blocks, then snake among them to a junction (10,250-1.2) atop a windblown saddle.

*   *   *   *

Side route: From here one or more use paths descend ⅓ mile south to campsites at the west edge of the sedge meadow that contains shal-

low Wolf Creek Lake.

*   *   *   *

The PCT enters Carson-Iceberg Wilderness as it leaves the saddle, and then it switchbacks steeply down past sharp, ice-shattered boulders, lingering snow patches and windswept whitebark pines. You quickly drop below the 10,000-foot level, never again to reach it on your trek north to Canada. The trail's gradient then eases considerably before you ford a permanent stream, along which those taking the alternate cross-country route will descend. Continuing down the East Fork Carson River canyon, you pass exposures of glaciated, granitic rock that contain large feldspar crystals, as did the Cathedral Peak granodiorite of Yosemite. Beyond these exposures you cross several avalanche tracks. After a couple hours' descent from the saddle, you reach a small flat (8100–5.2), with fair camping, on which the unmaintained East Carson Trail forks right, and in about 150 yards cross to the east bank of East Fork Carson River.

You veer left, immediately cross two adjacent creeks, and then embark on a steep though well-planned tread up the canyon's west wall. Your

See maps J1, J2

Stanislaus Peak, from the East Fork Carson River canyon

see MAP J3

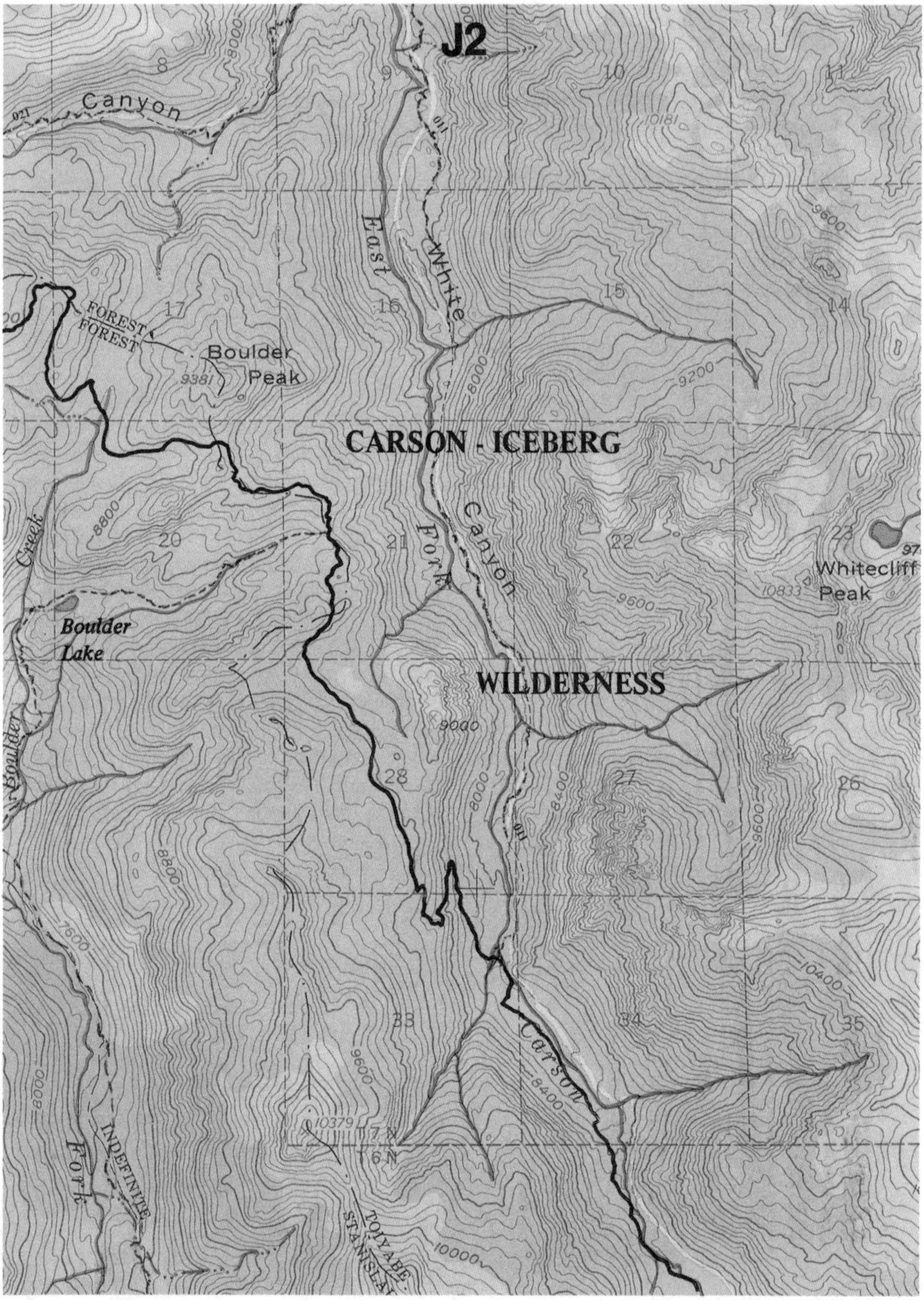

J2

Canyon

East White

FOREST
FOREST
Boulder
Peak
9381

CARSON - ICEBERG

Canyon

Fork

Boulder
Lake

WILDERNESS

9000

Whitecliff
Peak

Creek

Boulder

INDEFINITE

Carson

STANISL

TOIYABE

see MAP J1

gradient soon levels, contours to a shallow
bowl, and then drops to a larger, forested one.
A moderate ascent northeast out of it brings
you to the canyon's crest, from which you make
a short, increasingly steep descent north to a
small flat with an east-end pond. A low knob
separates this flat from a prominent crest saddle

¼ mile north of you (8590–3.1).

*   *   *   *

Side route: From it a trail descends 1.5 miles
through a scenic side canyon to Boulder Lake
(a recommended site for a layover day), and

See map J2

then it continues 4.2 miles out to the end of the Clark Fork Road. If you need help, head out to it; you'll certainly encounter people along it, since it parallels Clark Fork Stanislaus River, a fishermen's mecca.

$$* \qquad * \qquad * \qquad *$$

From this saddle you switchback steeply north, soon following an easier gradient west up the crest and then north to a saddle just south of Boulder Peak. A straight, joint-controlled canyon lies below you, which you descend west, and then you curve north around Boulder Peak's lower flank to step-across Boulder Creek (8600–1.6). From it our path climbs northwest briefly, then quickly jogs southwest—an easily missed switchback for southbound hikers. You soon climb northwest again, quickly spying shady campsites, then continue north back up to the crest. This you promptly leave for a curving traverse around volcanic Peak 9500, staying above the soggy cow meadow at the peak's southwest base. A traverse around the meadow's north end is followed by a climb southwest up to a granite summit, from which you descend an easy ¼ mile to a saddle (9170–2.3). Here an abandoned trail starts southeast, but you make a brief walk northwest to camps just east of a willow-fringed lakelet, Golden Lake, which usually dries up by late summer. You curve northwest, crossing its outlet creek, which can be buried under early-season snow. Now you contour in and out of gullies to Golden Canyon creek, a large campsite and, shortly beyond it, a trail intersection (9170–1.2). From this spot, the Paradise Valley Trail climbs initially, and *invisibly*, northwest to a descending ridge, on which tread appears and climbs steeply southwest up to a well-defined saddle. Also from the spot, the Golden Canyon Trail starts a 3.8-mile descent to the East Carson Trail.

The PCT climbs northeast across sagebrush slopes and past old paths before topping a saddle (9340–0.7), with a view toward conspicuous Peak 9500 and beyond to dominating Stanislaus Peak. The buff-colored outcrop you see on this saddle is composed of rhyolite, a volcanic rock that is common east of Yosemite but rare here. An ensuing minor descent northwest winds past several campsites near the headwaters of Murray Canyon. It then climbs

up to another saddle (9080-1.5) immediately south of a highly fractured, steep-sided volcanic butte. You descend northwest merely 80 yards to meet Trail 015 forking north to round the butte, bound for the Murray Canyon Trail. Staying northwest, you pass a conspicuous spring in 0.4 mile, and then soon turn north and descend a ridge to a small flat. You head west across it, then traverse south, having fine views of Arnot Peak and the Wolf Creek drainage. You then switchback twice and wind down to the slightly cloudy east fork of Wolf Creek (8320–2.0), with a small camp above the west bank, just below the trail. A northwest traverse takes you past caves and pinnacles to the wide, blocky middle fork (8310-0.4). Harmless, nearly microscopic volcanic particles make this fork quite cloudy. Here you'll find some small campsites on a narrow floodplain below the trail. More traversing brings one to the multi-branched west fork (8400–0.5), which also has potential camping. Check especially by the north edge of a meadow that is just above the trail and is just east of the branch where the trail turns from west to northwest.

Onward, you climb briefly north, then west, and finally curve north around a ridge up to a very poorly defined crossing of the Sierra Nevada "crest" (8800–0.8). Now having a leisurely descent, you first curve north down to a flat saddle with an ephemeral pond and here turn abruptly west. The PCT next descends a small gully and stays close to the crest as it heads northwest down past a large lobe of cow-dotted Lower Gardner Meadow. The meadow's creek heads through a small gorge, and you can camp hereabouts. Then in about 300 yards you reach an intersection with a trail on Wolf Creek Pass (8410–1.0).

$$* \qquad * \qquad * \qquad *$$

Side route: A 1.7-mile hike west on it will get you to a trailhead near the Highland Lakes, which has a popular campground between the two lakes—a worthy layover spot.

$$* \qquad * \qquad * \qquad *$$

From the minor pass the PCT starts northwest, climbs north, and then by a gully reaches a junction (8480–0.3).

See maps J2, J3

*   *   *   *

Side route: From here a trail climbs north steeply up a gully to Asa Lake. If you plan to visit it, take this trail, although from the crossing of the outlet creek of Asa Lake (8520–0.3), a brief northeast climb ahead, you could also reach the lake. This cold, overfished spring-fed lake is sometimes home to beavers as well as to campers.

*   *   *   *

From the gully the PCT climbs briefly northeast to Asa Lake's outlet creek (8520–0.2). Next it arcs west above the lake's spacious north-shore campsites, then soon curves north into a shady bowl, before resuming a steady climb north across sagebrush slopes to a saddle (9330–1.7). Along this ascent you'll have numerous views of the Highland Lakes area, to the southwest. Now the PCT meanders northeast down past whitebark pines to a junction (9110–0.6) with the Noble Canyon Trail, which climbs east over a saddle and down into Bull Canyon.

The PCT descends ⅓ mile north to a narrow stringer at the head of large meadow. In early season, when snow may still obscure the route, you're likely to continue ¼ mile north across a bench and arrive at a lakelet with acceptable camping. The PCT, however, crosses the soggy stringer and follows the meadow's edge, first southwest and then north, but soon descends to the lakelet's outlet creek (8900-0.6), which you encounter just above the north end of Noble Lake. Here you'll find marginal campsites crammed between the trail and the lake's outlet. Expect cattle or their droppings.

The trail continues north, then soon switchbacks down juniper-dotted slopes to cross the lake's outlet creek. About ¼ mile beyond it you reach a junction (8360–0.9) with the northern part of the Noble Canyon Trail. You then immediately curve west across a ridge and descend to a nearby ford of boulder-choked Noble Creek, which is carving a dramatic landscape out of volcanic sediments. The PCT now climbs northwest, passing five seasonal creeklets before reaching a granitic knob, which it rounds counterclockwise. Then it passes a second knob, just southwest, via a clockwise

Canal flowing into Asa Lake

curve. With a granitic canyon below you and spectacular eroded cliffs above, you follow your cow-trodden path west, shift gears north up to a spur ridge, and then briefly descend west to a junction. From here a spur trail descends ¼ mile north to a PCT trailhead parking lot, but you wind ⅓ mile, first southwest and then northwest, to Highway 4 (8700–2.9), at a road bend only 200 yards northeast of Ebbetts Pass.

With a surrealistic volcanic landscape awaiting you, you eagerly push northward from Highway 4, crossing an old spur road before climbing quickly northeast to an overlook of the Ebbetts Pass area. With ⅓ mile behind you, you strike northwest to a notch just west of a crest pond, and descend steeply west to a pond and a lakelet (8760-0.6), the latter, known as Sherrold Lake, providing an adequate campsite. Your often faint tread gradually snakes northwest from the lakelet, ducking in and around obstacles of this granite landscape, then traverses west between a shallow pond and a granite knob just north of it. Following the path of least resistance, you traverse granite benches and then curve northwest to a forested ridge just above and 150 yards south of upper Kinney Lake—an oversized pond in late season when this reservoir is low. Nev-

See maps J3, J4, J5

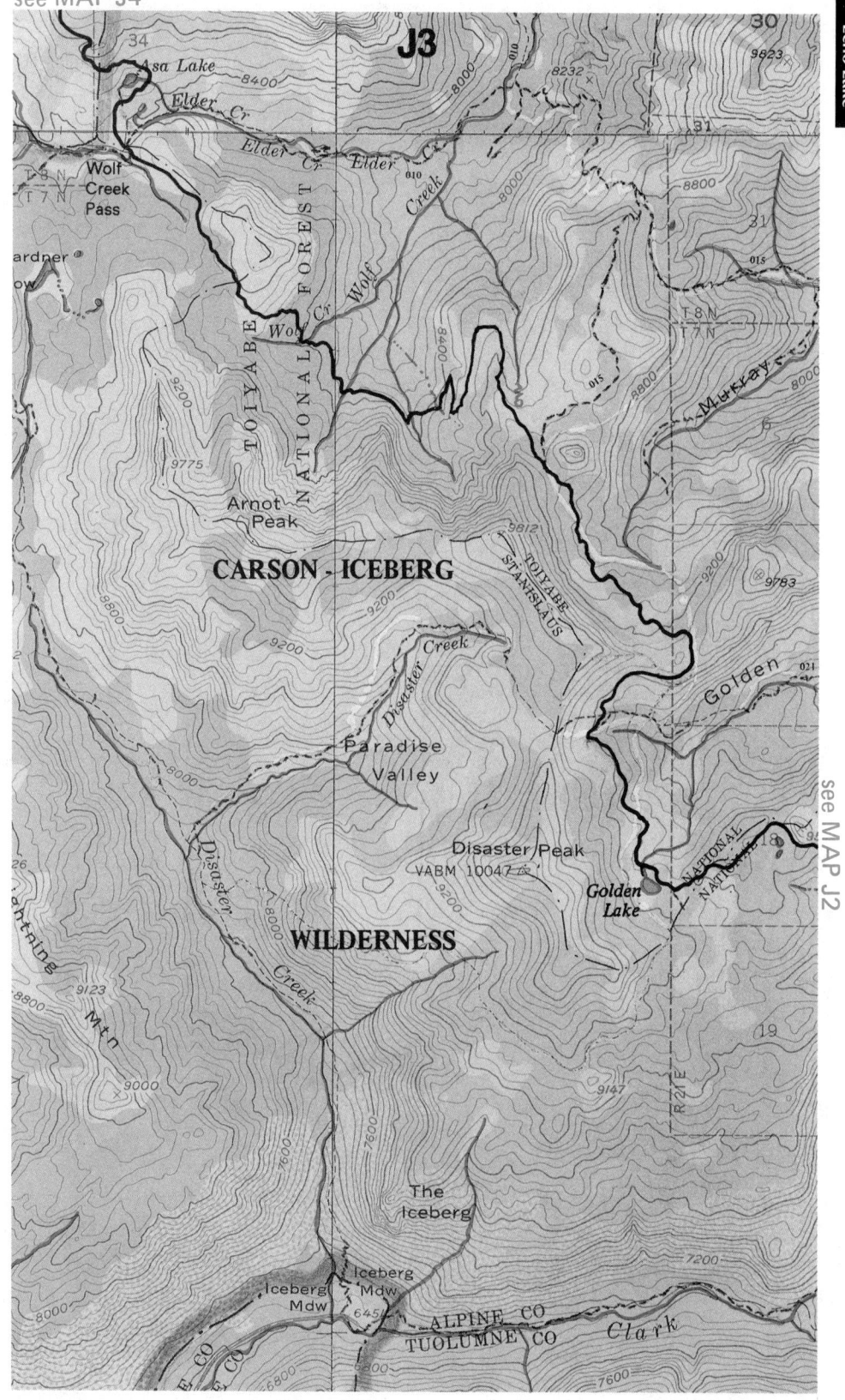

see MAP J2

see MAP J5

see MAP J3

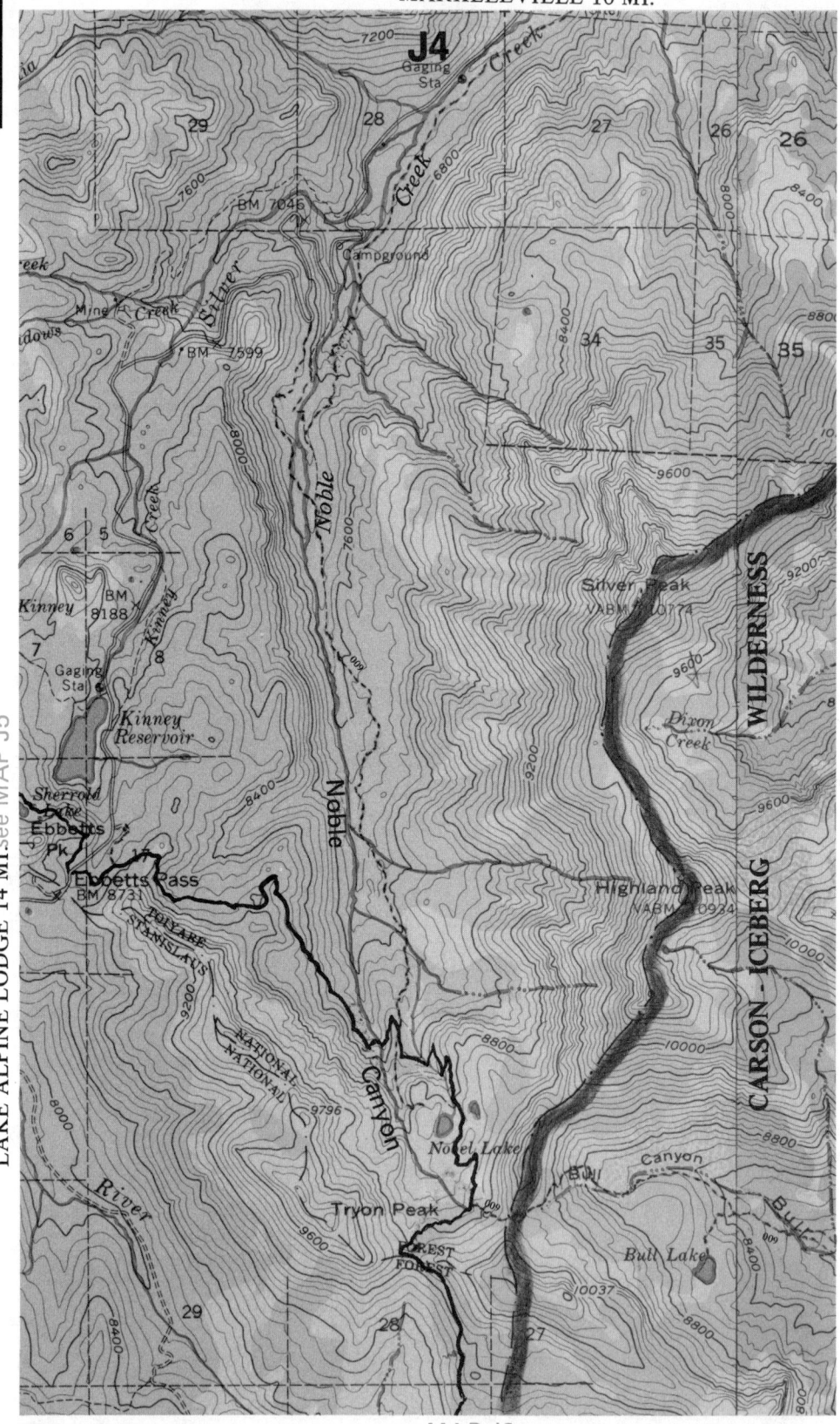

LAKE ALPINE LODGE 14 MI.

ertheless, you can camp by it. A westward ¼-mile traverse through a shady forest of lodge-pole pines, western white pines and mountain hemlocks brings you to a small broad-crest pond, beyond which your trail curves north, and over the next 1½ miles skirts along the boundary of Mokelumne Wilderness before entering it in the Raymond Meadows area.

The distance from here to the Indian Valley area could be cut by two-thirds if your route were to go northwest to it. Instead, your trail bends northeast up to a broad ridge to begin an incredible route past one of the most bizarre, yet beautiful, landscapes to be seen along the PCT. You descend to a sloping meadow, cross its lower end, and start a sagebrush traverse north past colorful pinnacles and clefts in the flank of Peak 9540. Two more broad spur ridges are crossed before you descend west to the headwaters of Raymond Meadows Creek (8640–3.4), below the rugged, serrated Sierra crest. Since the creek dries up by early August, you continue north to another spur ridge, engage a northwest-ascending jeep road at the crest, and parallel the road north to where it begins a steep descent northeast.

Before following the trail west, one may be overwhelmed by the symmetry and beauty of a huge dome looming before you. Surpassing any manmade dome in stature, it, together with towering, cathedral-like Peak 9700, on the far skyline, can be a very humbling sight, particularly when they are glowing in the warm rays of early evening. Onward, you descend west to barely

flowing Eagle Creek (8460–1.1) and a campsite just beyond its step-across ford. Late-season hikers will find water flowing just downstream, where a tributary joins this creek.

You cross this tributary and, engulfed by forest, cross many more as you traverse northeast along the lower slope of the largely unseen dome. This dome sits atop the west end of a ridge, which, eastward, takes on a new appearance. Crowned by high Point 8850, this section of ridge displays an incredible army of sentinels—pinnacles that challenge the rock climber to try them. The temptation lingers all the way to a deep crest saddle (8510–1.3), from which you switchback through forest down to always flowing Pennsylvania Creek (8140–0.6). Here a small camp could be established just before the jump-across ford. Your odyssey continues with a diagonal climb north to a wind-cropped sagebrush saddle (8660–1.0), followed by an easy descent to seasonally numerous tributaries of highly gullied Raymond Canyon. Your rollercoaster route winds in and out of these before climbing to a broad east-west crest. Here our faint tread strikes west into a forest that is thriving on the long, north-descending spur from Raymond Peak. You begin to descend northwest across this spur, then meet a trail (8640–1.5).

*   *   *   *

Side route: This climbs 0.7 mile south up to tightly confined Raymond Lake. Camping on

See map J5

View northwest across upper Noble Canyon

J5

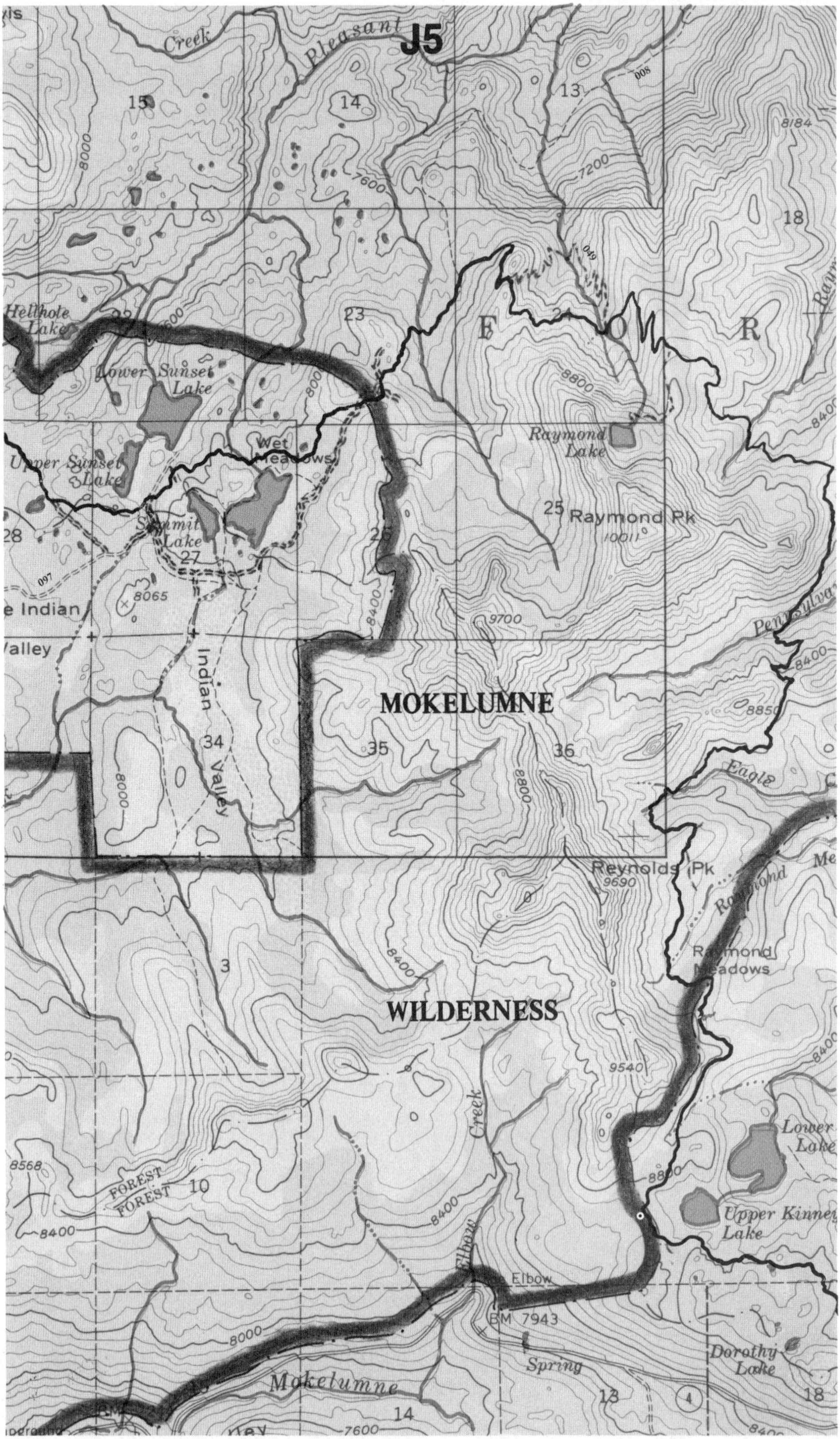

see MAP J6

see MAP J4

Hellhole Lake

Lower Sunset Lake

Upper Sunset Lake

Wet Meadows

Summit Lake

Indian Valley

Indian Valley

Raymond Lake

Raymond Pk

MOKELUMNE

Reynolds Pk

Raymond Meadows

Eagle

Penn

WILDERNESS

Lower Lake

Upper Kinney Lake

Elbow

BM 7943

Dorothy Lake

Spring

Mokelumne

FOREST

FOREST 10

Creek

Pleasant

Creek

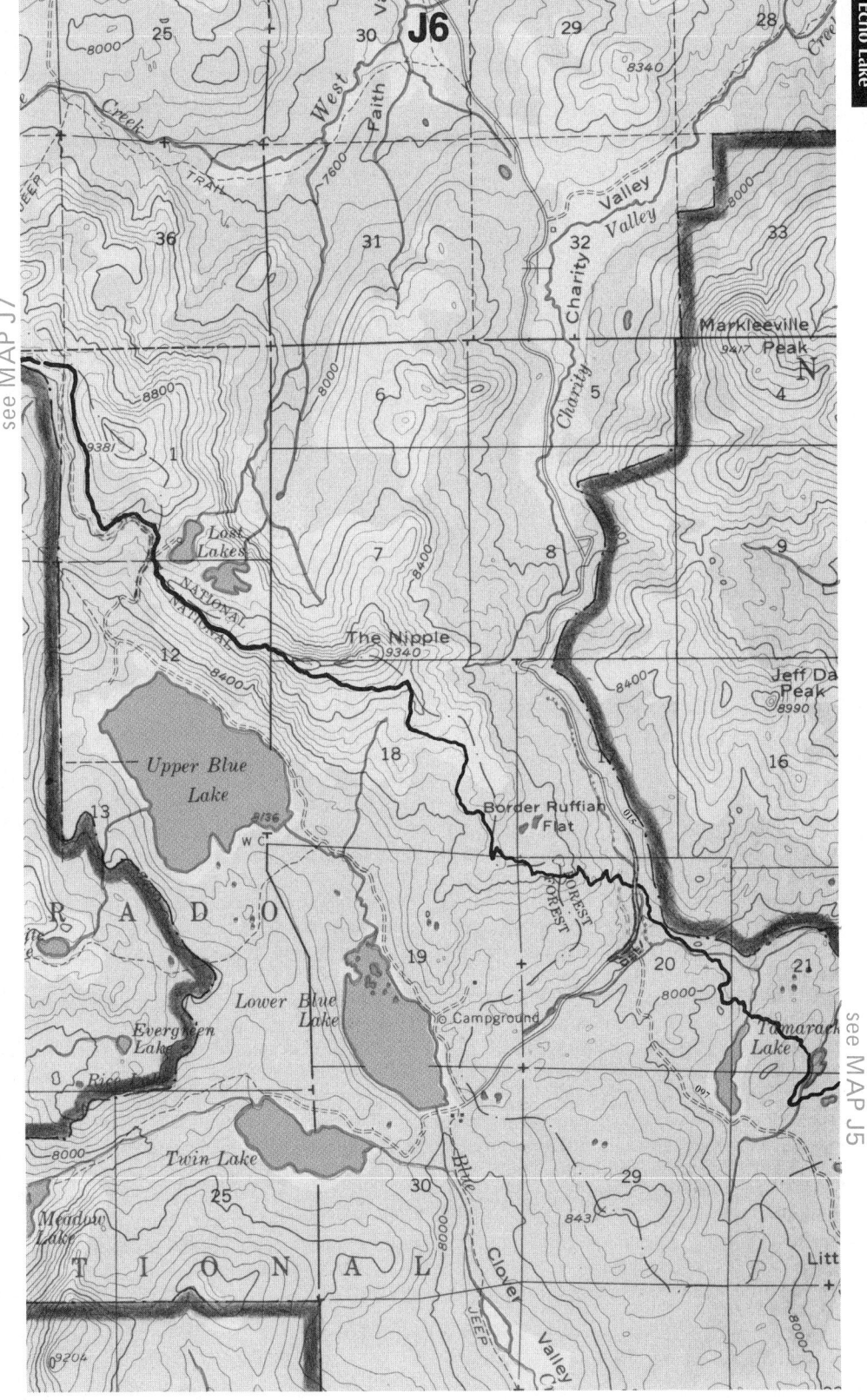

see MAP J7

see MAP J5

J6

Lost
Lakes

Upper Blue
Lake

The Nipple

Border Ruffian
Flat

Evergreen
Lake

Lower Blue
Lake

Campground

Tamarack
Lake

Twin Lake

Meadow
Lake

Markleeville
Peak

Jeff Da
Peak

West Va

Faith

Charity

Valley
Valley

NATIONAL

FOREST

RAD O

T I O N A L

Blue

Clover Valley Cr

JEEP

The Blue Lakes, from slopes west of The Nipple

its shoreline by whitebark pines is fair at best, though the lack of level ground is partly compensated for by the next morning's sunrise, which once again fires up this Vulcan landscape.

*   *   *   *

From the junction a switchbacking descent, with far-ranging vistas, guides you down to a ford of refreshing Raymond Lake creek (8150–1.0), immediately followed by fords of two smaller creeks. Now you traverse across open, eroded slopes to a saddle, noting along the way the old PCT route below you, Trail 049, which once switchbacked 500 feet down before switchbacking up to a junction only 30 yards before you reach the conspicuous saddle (8230–0.8). On west-facing slopes you switchback down to a junction with Pleasant Valley Trail 008 (7820- 0.6), enter cow country, and climb gradually southwest to a campsite near a tributary (7860–0.4) of Pleasant Valley Creek. On its west bank you start northwest, then angle southwest in and out of gullies up to a crest jeep road, which you follow south 70 yards to a saddle (8200- 0.5), where you leave the eastern part of Mokelumne Wilderness. You swing

southwest to parallel a road, just above you, cross it in a few minutes, and soon reach a large trailside juniper. The trail now curves south, levels, and passes the east shore of a pond in the aptly named Wet Meadows area. Early-season hikers, trying to follow a snowbound trail, will be frustrated as their compass rebels to give false readings that are influenced by a close-lying magnetic body. Not until you cross the Blue Lakes Road will your compass *begin* to behave.

From the pond the trail curves west at the north edge of a small meadow, beyond which lies a large lake with fair campsites. The westward traverse—looking easy on the map—is actually complicated by numerous ups and downs that lie well hidden between the contours. You bend southwest where you cross a narrow road that climbs from a nearby road going to visible Lower Sunset Lake. In a couple of minutes you reach that road (7900–1.6) at a point 200 yards north of a junction with a southeast-climbing road. This road is the same saddle road you briefly paralleled and then crossed before reaching the juniper. It is recommended as an alternate route if you've been having route-finding problems due to lingering snow patches.

See map J5

Bearing generally west, the PCT crosses the road, avoids the damp soils around Upper Sunset Lake, flirts with an ill-defined Sierra crest, then descends to a spur road, which it follows a few yards west to the road's terminus, a car-camping site (7860–0.6). Immediately beyond it lies a serene lakelet, Lily Pad Lake, whose northeast corner the PCT passes before winding northwest through viewless forest. Midway to the Blue Lakes Road you climb north above the west shore of a shallow lake, with possible camping, then continue northwest, dropping to cross the outlet creek of unseen Tamarack Lake. Soon the forest briefly opens, and almost due north of you stands defiant, steep-sided Jeff Davis Peak—your best beacon to guide you through Blue Lakes country. In the next ½ mile you twice cross the headwaters of Pleasant Valley Creek, the second time immediately before a junction with a short spur trail to an oversized PCT parking lot. An even larger lot, for horsemen, is on the south side of the road. A creeklet, usually lasting through July, bisects the short spur trail, and it provides water of questionable purity to those who might want to camp at the parking lot. The PCT turns north and winds ¼ mile up to the Blue Lakes Road (8090–2.7), crossing it at a bridge over the creeklet. This road gets a lot of use during summer, so if you have to hitch out for help or supplies, here's a good spot to do it. From the creeklet's west bank you meander 140 yards northwest to the *old* Blue Lakes Road, along which you stroll 60 yards north before leaving it at a bend. You could camp in this vicinity. Back on trail, you make a convoluted climb westward, your trail weaving around a myriad of granitic bedrock outcrops.

▮ *On this disorienting climb, one can glance east at monolithic Jeff Davis Peak. Listed at 8990 feet on your topo, this volcanic peak is listed at 9065 feet on a newer topo. Either the peak is growing at 4 feet per year or one of the maps is wrong—undoubtedly the latter. The contour lines on any given map are the expression of the cartographer's best effort or guess. Therefore if you try to do precise field work using a topo as a base, you often run into problems. Mapping the PCT in detail is much more difficult than one would guess!* ▮

The trail skirts between two stagnant ponds, then soon heads north up a definable crest, quickly leaving it for a mile-long climb toward The Nipple. From the saddle at its southeast base (8830–2.4), you see distant Freel Peak in the northeast, this granitic massif standing sentinel above the south shore of unseen Lake Tahoe. Soon, views of the Ebbetts Pass landscape give way to those of the Blue Lakes, which serve to mark your progress to the Sierra crest west of The Nipple. Along the crest you descend one mile to a closed jeep road, then go 100 yards past it to the Lost Lakes spur road (8660–1.8). Here, by the western lake are

See maps J5, J6

Round Top, Elephants Back and the Blue Lakes road

see MAP J8

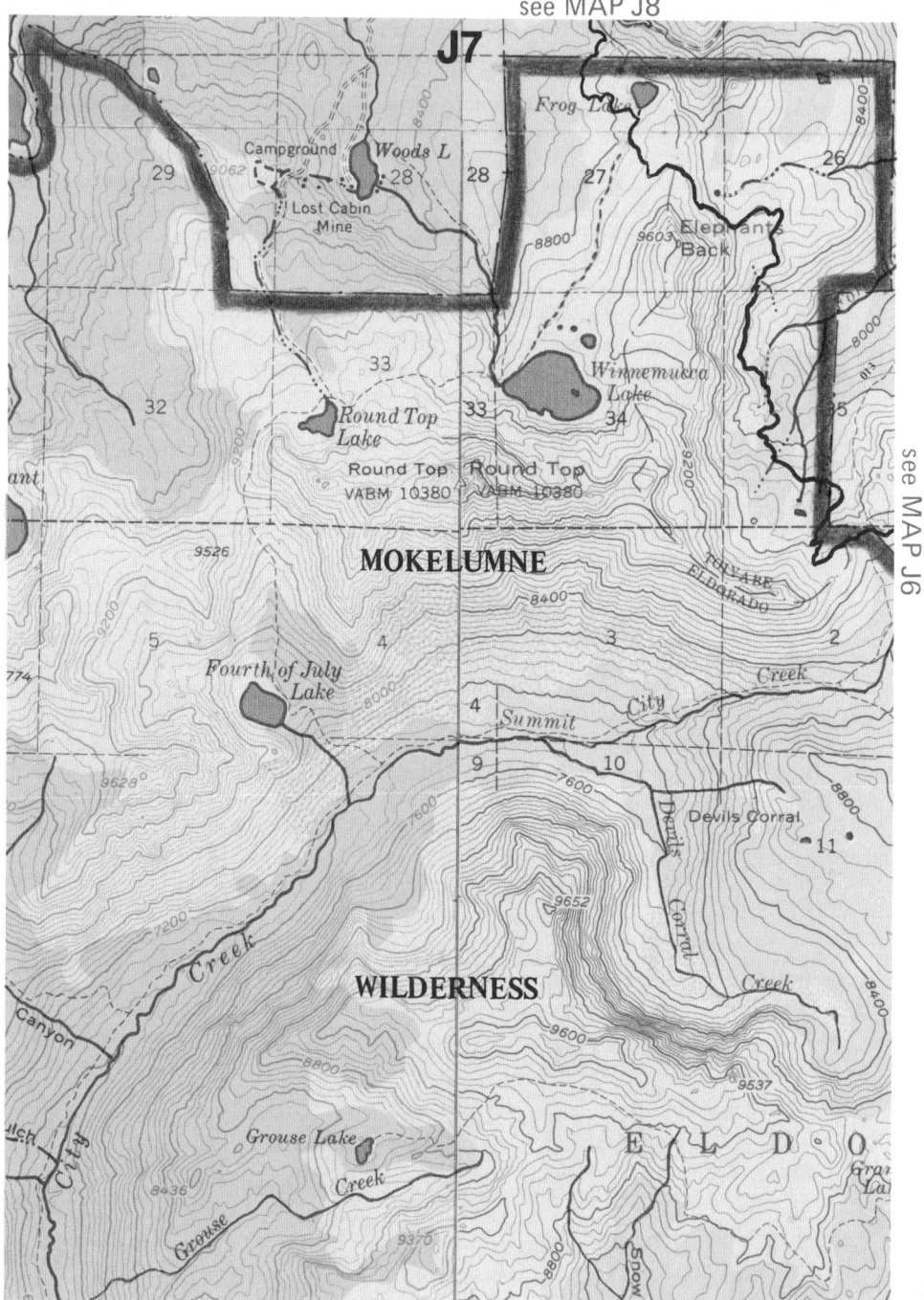

see MAP J6

your best campsites this side of Carson Pass, though the lake's snags and the presence of car campers do little for wilderness ambience.

Now your famous trail parallels the Blue Lakes Road along the slopes of Peak 9381, which at first are forested, but then open. The open slopes give you views down severely glaciated Summit City Creek canyon and up at hulking Round Top, the highest summit between Ebbetts Pass and Echo Summit. The trail

See map J6

almost reaches the Sierra crest, but instead veers west, soon crossing Blue Lakes Road and reaching, in about 200 yards, a muddy pond (8830–1.6). You can camp here, though better possibilities lie ahead. Just past the pond you cross a closed jeep road and, momentarily, cross Summit City Canyon Trail 18E07 (8880-0.2). Immediately past it you top Forestdale Divide and put the popular Blue Lakes country behind you. You now re-enter Mokelumne Wilderness, and generally will stay within it until just south of Carson Pass. Botanists will appreciate the wonderful wildflower assemblage along the switchbacks down toward several lakelets. Camping is best near the largest one, which is about 200 yards from the trail. The PCT approaches a second one, only knee-deep, then

circles a third (8630-0.8), a tiny pond. Immediately past it you spy a fourth, equally small, then cross a creek coming from the fifth, which is unseen. Your trail crosses two more creeklets before it initiates a winding climb among granitic outcrops. At last you mount a flat, brushy ridge, from whose west end you make a generally moderate climb northwest to the Sierra crest, crossing it just north of dome-shaped Elephants Back. After descending for a few minutes, you reach a junction (8860–3.1) with a trail that leads south to large, windy Winnemucca Lake and beyond.

Now reunited with the Tahoe-Yosemite Trail, which you left below Bond Pass in northern Yosemite National Park, you quickly reach a junction (8870–0.1) immediately south of Frog

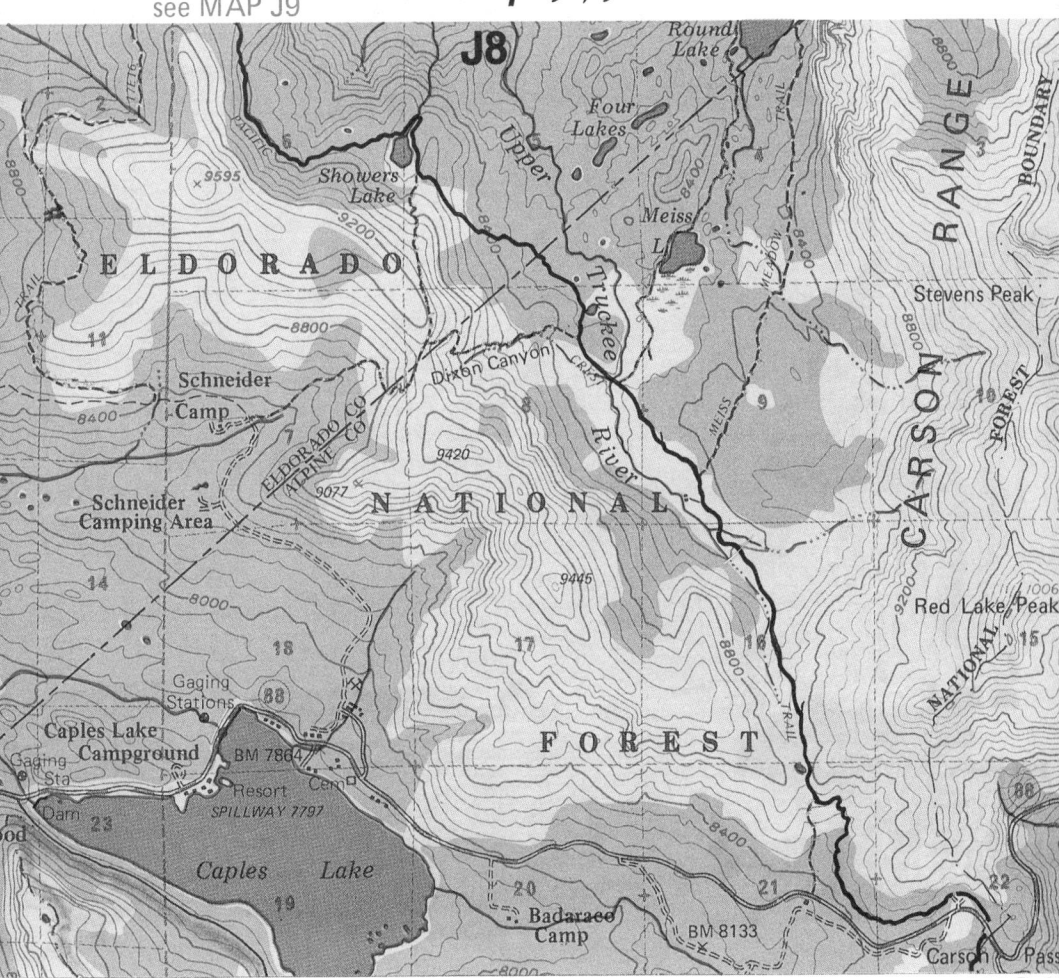

See maps J6, J7

see MAP J9

see MAP J7

Dayhikers on the PCT in the Upper Truckee River canyon

Lake. An older PCT route used to continue north past the lake and then steeply down to a closed stretch of the old Highway 88. You veer left for a snaking traverse northward to the south end (8580–1.1) of a long parking lot with two historic markers at Carson Pass. From the lot's north end you cross the sometimes busy highway and parallel it on an abandoned road to a flat parking area—the trailhead for north-bound hikers (8550–0.2).

From the northwest corner of the parking area trekkers first climb southwest and then round a ridge to make an undulating traverse north-west past junipers and occasional aspens to a gullied bowl. After winding in and out of several gullies, you follow short switchbacks north, then traverse west to a junction with a steep trail that descends south to the highway. In 110 yards your north-climbing trail tops a pond-blessed saddle (8800–1.4). In early season its water is quite fresh, but with time, horses and cattle muddy the situation. Your route follows jeep tracks ⅓ mile north to a junction, where you turn left and descend tracks to a campsite (8460–0.8) by the infant Upper Truckee River. You now make an easy descent northwest, cross the river, and on level terrain pass a trail branching left to two cabins only 200 yards before

you meet another one branching right (8380–0.7).

*　　*　　*　　*

Side route: Starting as jeep tracks, this trail, the Meiss Meadow Trail, traverses 2.3 miles to the northeast corner of Round Lake. You can follow this trail over a low, broad ridge to reach a lodgepole-fringed meadow in 0.5 mile. From it you can then leave the trail and head cross-country 0.6 mile northwest down gentle slopes to the southeast shore of shallow, warm Meiss Lake.

*　　*　　*　　*

The PCT continues northwest from the Meiss Meadow Trail junction, passing another set of northbound tracks in ¼ mile—these to the meadow south of Meiss Lake. Just before you meet a major ford of Upper Truckee River (8310–0.6), you see that lake.

*　　*　　*　　*

Side route: Immediately before the ford a faint trail provides the hiker with an easy half-

See maps J7, J8

mile meadow traverse to Meiss Lake. The cow-dotted meadow, however, is often damp, if not downright boggy, particularly near the south end of the lake, and until early August this wet environment nurses a multitude of mosquitoes. Before mid-August take the cross-country route to Meiss Lake. From mid-August through mid-September this chest-deep lake is ideal for swimming or just plain relaxing.

*   *   *   *

After jumping across the Upper Truckee River for the last time, you continue northwest along a meadow's edge and, just before crossing a shallow gap, see a faint trail, on your left, which comes 2.1 miles from Schneider Camp. Just beyond the gap you descend north to a pond and resume your lodgepole-and-meadow traverse. Your jeep tracks soon curve left up an increasingly steep slope on which they narrow to a trail. Nearing a crest, this trail is joined by

an abortive set of jeep tracks. You then cross the broad crest and, as you start a descent to nearby Showers Lake, you see a second trail (8650–1.5) from Schneider Camp. Momentarily you reach the east shore of granite-bound Showers Lake (8620–0.1). An old trail may still be seen traversing northwest across willowy slopes west of the lake, but the time you save by taking this shortcut route will be negated by the mud you'll collect on your boots and socks.

Leaving the lake's campsites, sheltered under western white pines, mountain hemlocks and lodgepole pines, you make a steep descent to the lake's outlet creek, only to make an equally steep ascent up its opposite bank. This, unfortunately, is necessary because a linear wall of granite on the lake's north shore prevents an easier alternative. Behind the linear wall you climb easily west to a junction with the old trail—kept alive by equestrians—then continue onward, passing just beneath an impressive, overhanging volcanic point. Gradually curving

See maps J8

Meiss Lake and volcanic hill

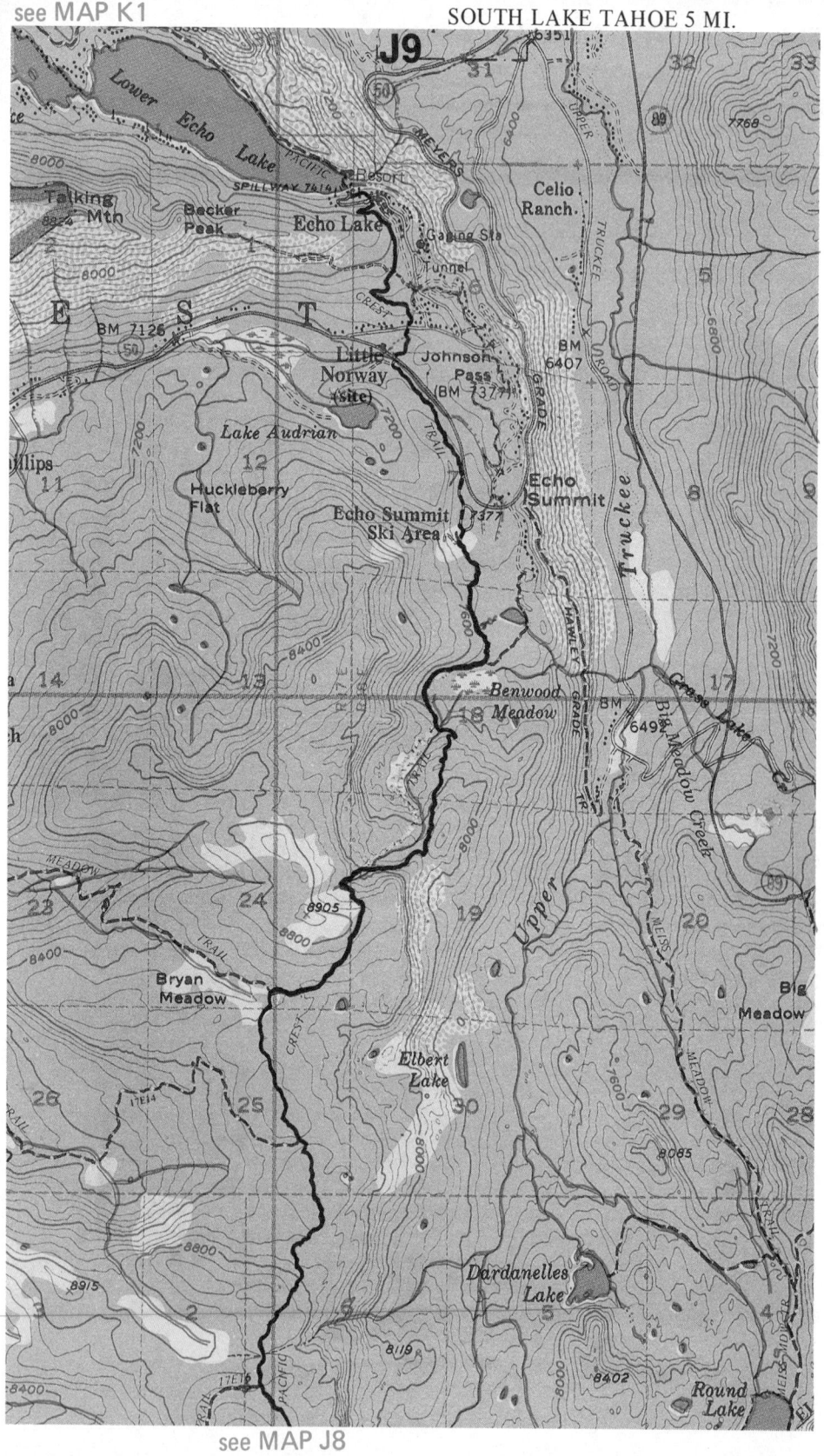

Talking
Mtn

Lower Echo Lake

PACIFIC
SPILLWAY 7414 Resort
Becker
Peak
Echo Lake

CREST

Gaging Sta
Tunnel

MEYERS

Celio
Ranch.

E S T

BM 7126
50

Little
Norway
(site)

TRAIL

Johnson
Pass
(BM 7377)

BM
6407

GRADE

Phillips
11

Lake Audrian

12

Huckleberry
Flat

Echo
Summit

Echo Summit
Ski Area

7377

14

13

Benwood
Meadow

18

BM
6492

Truckee

Cross Lake

17

Big Meadow Creek

23

MEADOW

24

8905

8800

TRAIL

19

Upper

20

Bryan
Meadow

CREST

Big
Meadow

26

17E14

25

TRAIL

Elbert
Lake

30

29

28

8065

Dardanelles
Lake

8915

2

8800

3

5

4

8119

Round
Lake

8400

17E16

PACIFIC

TRAIL

8402

see MAP J8

northward, you stay just above a granite bench as you cross numerous creeklets. Leaving the bench, you climb steeply north for a moment to a broad, gently sloping area, which you must cross on a mucky traverse northwest through a soggy, deteriorating meadow to a junction (8960–1.9) with Trail 17E16, which eventually descends to Schneider Camp.

Your forested crest route north now quickly descends to a shallow gap (8890–0.2), from which a faint, discontinuous path strikes east 250 yards down a linear meadow to a camp with a fine view, just beyond the meadow's far end. To the west, a similar tread descends 330 yards to the upper edge of a large meadow, then angles at 330° for 130 yards to a cow camp among a cluster of lodgepoles. Both camps usually have water nearby through July.

From the shallow gap the PCT climbs briefly, and then descends a rocky way to a soggy creek crossing in a small meadow. A short climb from it soon turns into a gradually increasing descent to a saddle junction (8630–1.4) with Sayles Canyon Trail 17E14, starting west. Another easy crestline ascent and descent take you to a trail junction in the upper end of Bryan Meadow (8540–0.9). An old trail once cut straight down the meadow, and you can follow it 50 yards west to a small, poor campsite in a cluster of lodgepoles. The new trail starts north before curving west. The PCT climbs 200 yards east to a saddle, crosses it, briefly descends, and then makes a generally viewless climb northeast to the east spur of Peak 8905.

Now begins a fairly continuous descent to Benwood Meadow. First you drop northwest into a lovely cove, cross its refreshing creek, and then in 0.2 mile recross it (8340–1.1). On a small flat just above the east bank is camping room for six. The trail descends northeast along the base of some intimidating cliffs to reach, in ⅓ mile, a saddle with a view south and east of the Upper Truckee River country. It then descends moderately northward, snaking considerably in its lower part before recrossing the creek. Shortly thereafter, the trail arcs clockwise around Benwood Meadow, staying high enough to avoid the meadow's boggy soil. After the trail traverses along the meadow's north edge, it comes to a junction (7475–1.8).

* * * *

The current, official PCT route goes through the Echo Summit Ski Area, but besides being unattractive, it can be hard to follow. Therefore, some folks still prefer taking a 1.3-mile alternate route. From the junction this initially heads east, then traverses northeast to cross the outlet creek of a lily-pad pond.

▌ *This rests behind the crest of a huge west-side lateral moraine of the Upper Truckee River canyon and appears to be dammed by it. Actually, the pond exists because it sits in a shallow hollow on a granitic bench. Furthermore, the lateral moraine, resting on the bench about 1000 feet the floor of the canyon, is a poor gauge for the thickness of the glacier when it was at its maximum about 20,000 years ago. Back then, the ice surface here would have been some 600 feet higher, giving a maximum thickness of about 1600 feet, possibly more. The lat-*

See maps J8, J9

Showers Lake

eral moraine came into existence only during the waning days of the glacier, when its surface had melted down to the level of the bench. It was then that the glacier dropped its sediments along the edge of this bench. Unfortunately in this century geologists failed to realize this, and consequently in the Sierra Nevada west of the crest, many if not most glacial deposits have been improperly identified with respect to both age and thickness of the glaciers. The greatest errors have been made in Yosemite Valley, which has led to serious errors around the world in the field of glacial geomorphology. ∎

Past the pond the trail winds north up past large boulders to reach a trailhead, ⅔ mile from the junction, on the crest of the moraine. The last 100 yards can be hard to follow, but the crest road and its attendant cottages are obvious. This narrow, paved road goes ⅓ mile north to Highway 50 at Echo Summit, from which one then walks 0.3 mile northwest, passing a highway-maintenance station, before reaching the ski area's entrance.

*   *   *   *

Beyond the Benwood Meadow junction, the newer PCT route meanders north, passing a spring in 0.2 mile, then soon reaching a ski run. This it crosses and then descends about ¼ mile north to the base of another ski run. In past years, the tread has been hard to follow, so to play it safe, you can just descend the first ski run, which narrows to a road, and then take that road down to the ski area's lodge. From its adjacent parking loop, head ¼ mile north along the paved entrance road (Road 1N03) to a resumption of PCT (7390-1.0), this spot being only a few yards before you reach the highway. Note that just 100 yards before this highway, you'll pass a trailhead parking area, with room for about a dozen vehicles.

The PCT winds northwest, staying near the highway and eventually paralleling an alderlined creek down to a road that bridges it. From the other side of the creek the trail resumes for a few yards up to busy Highway 50 (7220–0.7), just southeast of the former resupply site of Little Norway, which closed after a fire.

∎ *About 70 yards northwest along the road is an artificial creek that drains the Echo Lakes away from the Lake Tahoe Basin. Water that originally ended up at Pyramid Lake, on Early American (Indian) land, for decades has flowed west to Euro-American (Anglo) settlements.* ∎

From Highway 50 the PCT crosses Johnson Pass Road in 0.2 mile, the artificial creek in 0.1 mile, and a two-road junction in 0.5 mile, then skirts above Echo Lakes summer homes before making a switchback down to the east end of a backpackers' parking lot above Echo Lake Resort (7525–1.3). Cross Echo Lakes road and follow a tread of sorts down to the resort and its boat dock at Lower Echo Lake (7414-0.2).

*   *   *   *

Resupply access: Should you be traveling on the PCT out of season, when Echo Lake Resort is closed, then you will have to resupply at the Meyers Post Office, along Highway 50, or even go several miles farther to South Lake Tahoe. One could hike down Highway 50, but this is dangerous. An alternative route exists, which we describe from where the PCT crosses Johnson Pass Road (the former Highway 50).

Take this east just beyond the Sierra Nevada crest to where it angles north (7350–0.5) and switchbacks down to the new Highway 50 (7110–0.5). Carefully cross it to resume your northern descent (now called Meyers Road). This ends at Upper Truckee Road (6351–1.5), which you take briefly north to Highway 50 (6347–0.2). The highway here has a broad shoulder. Take it northeast across the Truckee River to the Highway 89 junction (6340–0.4). Continue briefly northeast to the post office (6340–0.1–3.2), which is on the north side of Highway 50.

See map J9

Scenic Round Lake, off the PCT, makes an attractive layover-day site

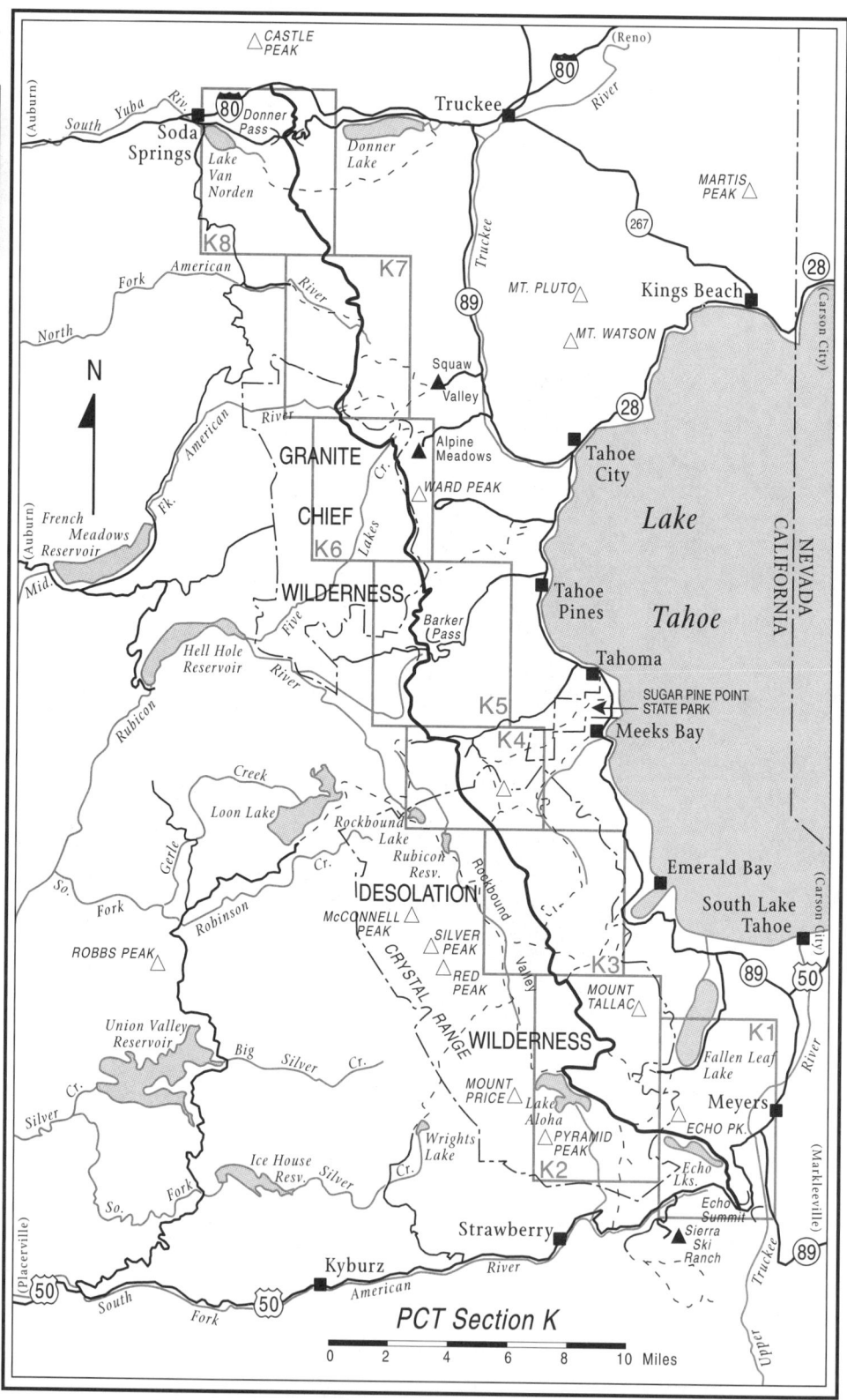

PCT Section K

0   2   4   6   8   10 Miles

Section K
Echo Lake Resort to Interstate 80

Introduction: Of all the roadless areas in California, compact Desolation Wilderness probably ranks number one in popularity—at least, it has a greater density of hikers per square mile than any other roadless area. The reason for its popularity is simple: it is a beautiful area and it is incredibly easy to reach, lying north of busy Highway 50 and just west above sprawling, urban South Lake Tahoe. It also competes for the number-one spot in density of mountain lakes. From Echo Lake north to Middle Velma Lake you're never more than a few minutes away from a lakeshore or a lake view. The glaciers that scoured out these lake basins, lasting until about 13,000 years ago, also removed the pre-existing soils and loose rocks. Hence in some areas, particularly Desolation Valley, the landscape has a pronounced lack of trees—whence the name *Desolation*. Desolation Valley has been made even more desolate by large Lake Aloha, a Sacramento City reservoir, which floods it. A stand of lodgepoles once greened the south end of this flat-floored valley, but today you'll see only gray snags rising out of the shallow lake, a stark complement to the valley's gray granite walls.

North of Middle Velma Lake, you hike a few miles through viewless forest on a wandering, non-crest trail that certainly deserves replacement by a high-standard crest route. Better tread appears before you leave Desolation Wilderness, and not far north of it you reach Richardson Lake, which offers lakeshore camping and a nice swim. Onward, you enter Granite Chief Wilderness and can make a short diversion to the popular Five Lakes basin or, a few miles farther, make a 20-minute diversion to lightly used Little Needle Lake. Beyond, you climb to a saddle, and if you're not too exhausted, you can climb to nearby Granite Chief for panoramic views of the Tahoe area. After a considerable drop, you climb up to the base of Tinker Knob, which also offers a 360° panorama of the Tahoe area. Good crest views continue as the northbound PCT stays on or close to the volcanic, windswept crest for about 5 miles, then another group of views—of the Donner Pass area—urge the hiker onward for a 2-mile drop to Old Highway 40. You conclude the section with a 2-hour, rambling hike over to bustling Interstate 80, one of the nation's busiest arteries.

Declination: 15½°E

Points on Route	S→N	Mi. Btwn. Pts.	N→S
Echo Lake Resort	0.0		63.7
reach Lake Aloha	6.1	6.1	57.6
Dicks Pass	13.3	7.2	50.4
jct. above s. shore of Middle Velma Lake	17.1	3.8	46.6
Richardson Lake's northwest corner	26.1	9.0	37.6

McKinney-Rubicon Springs Road	28.0	1.9	35.7
Forest Route 3 near Barker Pass	32.3	4.3	31.4
North Fork Blackwood Creek campsites	34.7	2.4	29.0
Five Lakes Trail	43.7	9.0	20.0
Granite Chief Trail to Squaw Valley	49.6	5.9	14.1
Tinker Knob saddle	53.3	3.7	10.4
Old Highway 40 near Donner Pass	60.7	7.4	3.0
trailhead-parking lateral near I-80	63.7	3.0	0.0

Permits and Supplies: You'll need a wilderness permit to enter Desolation Wilderness but won't need one to enter Granite Chief Wilderness. For the former, write the Forest Service within 90 days of the date you expect to enter the wilderness. Write the Lake Tahoe Basin Management Unit at 870 Emerald Bay Road, Suite 1, South Lake Tahoe, CA 96150, or phone (916) 573-2600. They are located in the Plaza 89 center in South Lake Tahoe. (Emerald Bay Road is also Highway 89.) You'll find *Plaza 89* on the southwest side of the highway, 0.3 mile northwest of the South Lake Tahoe **Y**, at which Highway 50 branches northeast. If you are driving up Highway 50 from the west, get your permit at Eldorado National Forest Information Center, 3070 Camino Heights Drive, Camino, CA 95709, or phone (916) 644-6048. Watch for the signed exit a few miles east of Placerville.

This section starts at Echo Lake Resort, which has a store well stocked with trail food and miscellaneous supplies. It also has a post office that is open only a few hours a day. Major supplies are obtained in South Lake Tahoe, 9 miles northeast down Highway 50 from Echo Summit. Ahead, you won't find any on-route supply points in Section K. However, virtually every trail and road east from the PCT will eventually take you, in less than a day's hike, to Highway 89, the Lake Tahoe shoreline, and some nearby highway settlement. Two communities are recommended for emergencies only; under ordinary circumstances they aren't worth the effort. The first is reached by detour after 28 miles. Follow the dusty McKinney-Rubicon Springs Road 8 miles east to Tahoma. The second is Squaw Valley, which can be reached by three routes of nearly equal length, starting from the vicinities of 1) Five Lakes, 2) Emigrant Pass, and 3) Mountain Meadow Lake. Due to esthetics and to private-property constraints, only the last route, Granite Chief Trail 15E23, is recommended.

When you reach Old Highway 40 near Donner Pass, 3 miles before this section's end, you can head 3.2 miles west to the Donner Trail Grocery, a relatively complete store that is adjacent to the Soda Springs Post Office. These are about 0.4 mile west of a junction with Soda Springs Road, at which you'll find a laundromat.

Maps: *Echo Lake*   *Wentworth Springs*
        Pyramid Peak   *Granite Chief*
        Rockbound Valley   *Tahoe City*
        Emerald Bay   *Norden*
        Homewood

——————————————————— **The Route** ———————————————————

Over half the distance to and from the Ralston Peak basin lakes area can be eliminated by taking the Echo Lakes water taxi.

Since the Pacific Gas and Electric Company owns the top 12 feet of the lake (because they dammed it that high), they have the right to

See map K1

lower the water by that amount, and by mid-September they usually have done so. Then the lake reverts to its natural, upper-lower pair of lakes, and the taxi service stops.

The Pacific Crest Trail coincides with the Tahoe-Yosemite Trail (17E01) through most of Desolation Wilderness, the two splitting just north of Middle Velma Lake. You begin this PCT section by crossing Lower Echo Lake's dam. Then you make an initial climb south before heading west on your sparsely treed, rollercoaster trail. The trail traverses below some prominent granodiorite cliffs, and then switchbacks twice and climbs high above lakeshore summer homes. Scattered Jeffrey pines give way to thick groves of lodgepoles as you descend toward the lake's north shore. Then you traverse to a rusty, granitic knoll, round it to forested slopes above Upper Echo Lake, and continue westward. The tree cover is thick enough to blot out any possible view of the public pier at which the water taxis land, and several short trails down to the lake add to the confusion. (The proper one is usually signed.) One can follow any of them down to the shore, then follow a shoreline trail to the obvious pier on the lake's north corner. If you've taken the taxi, you'll know which trail to take to get back on the PCT.

Beyond the lake you climb a rocky tread up open slopes and quickly reach a cryptic junc-

tion (7700–3.1) with a lateral trail north to a saddle and Triangle Lake. At the Triangle Lake lateral, your trail enters Desolation Wilderness and then it rounds a bend and reaches another trail junction (7865–0.5). From here a ducked trail descends south over barren bedrock to Tamarack Lake, largest of the Ralston Peak basin lakes. Camping is prohibited at all of them. You continue west up the Tahoe-Yosemite Trail to a tiny creek in a gully. Rather than shortcut up the gully, you follow two switchbacks up to a bench, from where you see a lateral trail (8250–0.7) traversing east across a slope to the saddle above Triangle Lake. Just ⅓ mile past this lateral, your trail brings you to the east fringe of Haypress Meadows, rich in wildflowers.

*　　　*　　　*　　　*

Side routes: You'll find good camping at Lake of the Woods, Lake Margery and Lake Lucille, and along the east shore of Lake Aloha. Lake of the Woods can be reached by three trails, two starting in the Haypress Meadows area and the third starting opposite the first of two trails down to lakes Margery and Lucille. Between those two trails is one west down to the southeast corner of Lake Aloha. Just before it reaches that corner, it meets a third trail to Lake of the Woods—one that southbound

See maps K1, K2

Ralston Peak reflected in Ralston Lake; pond lilies invading Cagwin Lake

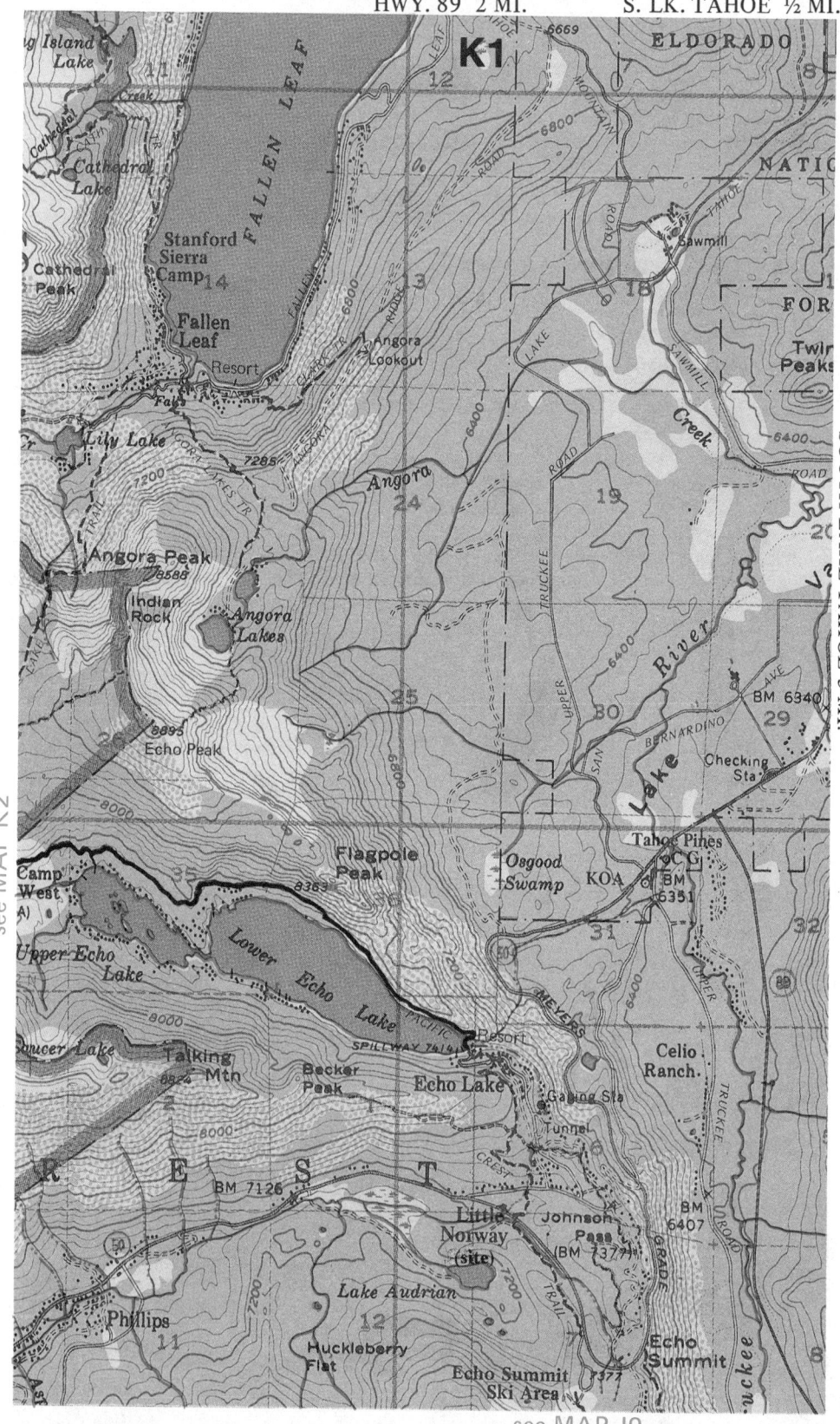

K1

ELDORADO

NATIO

FOR

Twin
Peaks

g Island
Lake

Cathedral
Lake

Cathedral
Peak

Stanford
Sierra
Camp 14

Fallen
Leaf

Resort

FALLEN   LEAF

Angora
Lookout

Sawmill

18

Creek

Lily Lake

7285

Angora
24

19

Angora Peak
9588

Indian
Rock

Angora
Lakes

35

6809

Lake   Truckee   River

San   Bernardino

BM 6340

Checking
Sta.

29

30

9895
Echo Peak

8000

Flagpole
Peak
8363

Osgood
Swamp

Tahoe Pines
CG
BM
6351

KOA

Camp
West
(A)

Upper Echo
Lake

Lower   Echo   Lake

31

32

89

see MAP K2

Saucer Lake

Talking
Mtn
6824

Becker
Peak

SPILLWAY 7414

PACIFIC

Resort

Echo Lake

Gaging Sta.

Tunnel

Celio
Ranch.

BM 7126

CREST

Johnson
Pass
(BM 7377)

BM
6407

R   E   S   T

Little
Norway
(site)

Lake Audrian
12

TRAIL   GRADE   TRUCKEE

Phillips
11

Huckleberry
Flat

Echo Summit
Ski Area

Echo
Summit

7377

see MAP J9

View southeast across Lake Aloha

PCT trekkers would use if they wanted to camp at that lake. At small lakes in the heart of Desolation Valley (between Lake Aloha and Lake of the Woods), there are relatively isolated camps.

*   *   *   *

At the east fringe of Haypress Meadows is a trail that forks southwest, going ⅔ mile to justifiably popular Lake of the Woods. After an easy stroll northwest, you reach a north-facing-slope junction (8350–0.5) with a second trail to Lake of the Woods. From this junction you contour only 150 yards before you come to yet another trail, this one veering right and winding ⅓ mile north down to Lake Lucille. In the opposite direction, another trail crests the nearby divide and drops steeply to Lake of the Woods. After a pleasant traverse above Lake Margery—except for snowbound early-season hikers—you pass a trail (8340–0.5) that leaves

See map K2

Pyramid Peak above Lake of the Woods

see MAP K3

K2

Lake

Snow Lake

L   D   O   R   5   A   D   O

Kalmia
Lake

Tallac
Lake

Dicks Lake

VABM Mt Tallac
9735

Dicks
Pass

9579

9376

Floath

Dicks Peak
9374

7

8

9

Half Moon
Lake

Gilmore
Lake

17E06

Alta Morris
Lake

Jacks Peak
9856

18

17

16

1

Susie Lake
7928

Campground

Mosquito
Pass   16E05

19

20

Heather Lake

Grass
Lake

Glen Alpine
Springs

Lake
Le Conte

8782   Cracked Crag

17E01

Jabu
Lake

Lake Lucille

Triangle
Lake

SPILLWAY
8116

American
Lake

Lake
Margery

8646   Kelths
Dome

Lost
Lake

LAKE ALOHA

Waca Lake

Desolation

29

28

Heypress
Meadows

Pyramid
Lake

Channel
Lake

Valley

Lake of
the Woods

Tamarack
Lake

17E01

BM Pyramid Pk
9983

Desolation
Lake
Gaging Sta

32

Frata
Lake

33

34
Harvey

Gefo
Lake

Toem
L

Ralston
Lake

Cagwin
Lake

Ropi Lake

Osma L

Pilt Lake

Ralston
Peak
9235

6

Avalanche Lake

Horsetail
Falls

9155   3

Cup Lake

see MAP K1

your crest and descends to the southeast corner of Lake Aloha. You descend the amorphous crest northwest to an indistinct saddle, where, by the westernmost of three ankle-deep ponds, you meet a trail (8310–0.2) going first east to Lake Margery then northeast down to Lake Lucille. Now you enter a thick forest and soon descend on a broad trail down to a junction (8140–0.6) above Lake Aloha. You join the lake's shoreline trail and parallel the lake's unsightly northeast edge.

▌ *This part has hundreds of dead lodgepole snags that once grew in this basin, Desolation Valley, before the city officials of Sacramento decided it had to be flooded to supply water for their growing population.* ▌

As you traverse northwest along the lake's shore, you can glance across the lake and see ragged, domineering Pyramid Peak, crowning the south end of the snow-mantled Crystal Range. Soon your trail takes you alongside a fairly clear, chest-deep, large pond, which like Aloha is good for swimming. Walking 150 yards beyond it, you reach a gully (8190–0.5) up which your trail may seem to head. A snowbank, lasting through July, obscures the cor-

rect route, which makes a brief climb southwest before traversing northwest again. Had you gone straight ahead, you would have reached chilly, rockbound Lake LeConte—very scenic, but lacking campsites. Continuing northwest just above Lake Aloha, you now traverse along a nicer, snag-free section, and then reach its northeast corner, which has a 2-foot-high retaining wall to prevent the lake from spilling over into Heather Lake, below you to the east. Don't take the abandoned trail at the east end of this wall; rather, climb a few yards west beyond the wall to a junction (8120–0.9) with the Rubicon River Trail, which climbs west over Mosquito Pass.

The PCT leaves this junction and descends east, giving you views of the Freel Peak massif to the east. A switchback takes you to a delicate 20-foot-high waterfall just above deep Heather Lake's northwest shore (7900–0.7). Near a large red fir and the fall's creek is an adequate campsite. The trail leaves Heather Lake at its low dam, climbs a low, barren ridge, and descends to a cove on the southwest shore of heather-ringed Susie Lake. On a weekend several dozen backpackers may be seen camped

See map K2

Rusty, metamorphic Jacks Peak looms over Susie Lake

at poor, tiny campsites along this easily accessible, dark-shored lake below the towering,
rusty, metamorphic shoulder of Jacks Peak. You
cross the outlet creek (7790–1.1), follow the
rocky trail over a low ridge, pass two stagnant
ponds, and descend to a flowery, swampy
meadow, where the trail forks (7680–0.6).

*   *   *   *

Resupply access: From here a well-used trail
to popular Fallen Leaf Resort branches southeast across the meadow. This resort, at the lake's
south shore 4½ miles away, has a store and other
amenities.

*   *   *   *

The PCT, now all uphill to Dicks Pass, first
switchbacks northeast up to an intersection
(7940–0.5) with a second trail southeast down
to the Fallen Leaf Lake area. This trail (17E06)
also continues northwest to Half Moon and Alta
Morris lakes. Beyond this intersection the PCT
switchbacks up to a junction (8290–0.6) with
Trail 17E09.

*   *   *   *

Side route: This trail leads ¼ mile to good
campsites above the south and east shores of
orbicular Gilmore Lake. This lateral then continues 1¾ miles up to Mt. Tallac's summit,
which gives you perhaps the best view of Lake
Tahoe you'll ever see—strongly consider a
summit ascent.

*   *   *   *

As you start west up toward Dicks Pass, you
get a peek through the lodgepole forest at
Gilmore Lake, and then you ascend steadily
northwest, climbing high above the pale brown
metavolcanic-rock basin that holds Half Moon
and Alta Morris lakes. Lodgepoles, mountain
hemlocks and western white pines are soon
joined by whitebark pines, the harbinger of timberline, as you approach a saddle east of Dicks
Peak. From it, a faint but popular unofficial trail
leads up a ridge to the rusty peak's summit.
Rather than descend north from the saddle,
the trail climbs ¼ mile east up alongside the

ridgecrest in order to bypass the steep slopes
and long-lasting snowfields that lie north of the
saddle. The trail reaches Dicks Pass (9380–2.3),
an almost level area on the ridge where clusters of dwarfed, wind-trimmed conifers serve
as windbreaks or shelters for those who want
to camp overnight here to experience the glorious sunrise falling upon the richly hued metamorphic massif to the west. Lingering
snowpatches usually provide campers with a
water source. Here, on the highest pass in Desolation Wilderness—and also the highest pass
on the PCT north of Sonora Peak's Wolf Creek
Lake saddle—you get far-ranging views both
north and south.
Ducks guide you across Dicks Pass, the
boundary between metamorphic rocks to the
south and granitic rocks to the north, and then
you descend on hemlock-lined switchbacks,
rich in thick gravel from the deeply weathered
bedrock. After descending northwest to a rocky
saddle, you reach a junction (8500–1.7).

*   *   *   *

Resupply access: From here one can descend
north to another trail junction, traverse northeast over to the Emerald Bay Trail, and take it
down to the Eagle Falls Picnic Area, along
Highway 89 (right edge of Map K3). From your
junction, the route is 4.0 miles long. There are
no settlements for miles around, but if you
needed help, you could hitchhike along the busy
highway either north to several small Lake
Tahoe settlements or south to metropolitan
South Lake Tahoe.

*   *   *   *

You descend south from the rocky saddle and
quickly reach a spur trail (8450–0.2). This in
turn descends 100 yards to a shoreline trail that
leads you to campsites along the north shore
and east peninsula of Dicks Lake. From the
spur-trail junction, you follow the PCT northwest down to a large tarn with a good campsite. Soon you descend a gully to a small cove
on Fontanillis Lake's east shore and parallel this
shore northwest to the outlet creek. Campsites
are fair to poor around this lake but, like most
of the Desolation Wilderness lakes, it is stocked
with trout.

See maps K2, K3

see MAP K2

To leave this rockbound lake, you cross its outlet creek, make a brief climb north to a shady lateral moraine, and then descend part way along its crest before curving left, jumping an intermorainal creek and descending a slightly older lateral moraine to a trail junction (7965–1.9) above the south shore of Middle Velma Lake.

*   *   *   *

Resupply access: From this junction you could also head out to Highway 89, mentioned above, but the first part of that hike—east—is uphill, and the overall route is 4.4 miles long.

*   *   *   *

See map K3

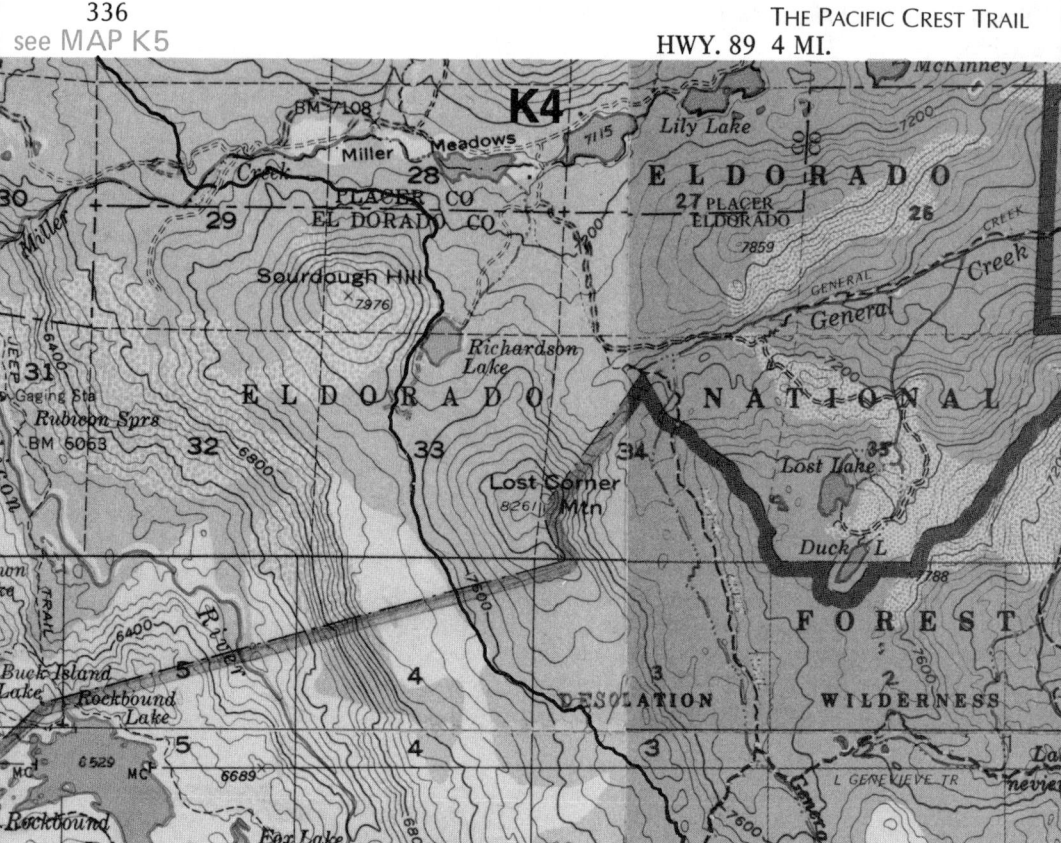

see MAP K3

From the junction you reach, in only 70 yards, a good view of Middle Velma Lake, and here you'll probably want to descend to campsites by the lake's shore, which are about the best you'll find in Section K. On weekends this lakeshore is crowded, since it is readily accessible from Emerald Bay and it has inviting water that tempts hikers to swim out to and dive from or sunbathe on the lake's rock-slab islands. Westward, the PCT reaches, only 35 yards beyond a sluggish creek, a trail (7940–0.3) that descends west to Camper Flat.

* * * *

Alternate route: If you're hiking the PCT in early season, you may find the PCT over Dicks Pass too snowy. Then, you should consider an alternate route to Middle Velma Lake. From the northeast corner of Lake Aloha, head 3/4 mile west over to low Mosquito Pass, drop 6½ miles

north to Camper Flat, then climb 2¼ miles east to your junction near the southwest arm of Middle Velma Lake.)

* * * *

The PCT makes a brief descent north to the lake's southwest arm, then it negotiates a muddy traverse across the lake's swampy outlet before it heads north again to an abrupt change in gradient. An old trail used to continue ahead, but now the route first climbs east and then curves northwest to a junction with the old one, from which you climb ⅓ mile north to an important junction (8090–1.1). Here, the Tahoe-Yosemite Trail, which has often coincided with the Pacific Crest Trail since its start in Tuolumne Meadows, forks northeast and climbs 2.7 miles, via lazy switchbacks, to Phipps Pass before descending 9.1 miles on a lake-blessed route to Lake Tahoe's Meeks Bay.

See map K3

Leaving the TYT for good, the PCT forks northwest, briefly ascends a shallow gully to an almost imperceptible spur ridge, and then makes a long descent to seasonal Phipps Creek (7620–1.5). On glacier-polished granodiorite slabs just north of the sluggish creek you can find campsites that are relatively mosquito-free. Beyond the creek you climb moderately to better water, which flows down a rock slab into a small pool. You cross its outlet, make a gentle climb to a forested spur-ridge saddle, and descend a shallow gully along the edge of a narrow meadow that runs down it. Your trail passes northeast of a 50-yard-long pond, crosses a boggy meadow beyond it, and then commences a 200-foot climb almost to the top of Peak 8235. From your trail's high point (8120–2.0) one can take a 40-yard spur trail southwest to some rocks from which you see Rubicon, Rockbound and Buck Island reservoirs in the deep canyon to the west.

From this spur-trail junction the PCT descends to a level, northwest-trending ridge, on which you go ½ mile through an open forest to a junction (7880–0.9). From here the Lake Genevieve Trail forks right and plunges via short switchbacks down to General Creek. You fork left, and in about ½ mile have a good view before you drop into a shallow basin. You then descend a shallow gully, and after the trail levels off, one can leave it at any point for an easy, short descent west to a very open bedrock bench that provides usually dry, relatively mosquito-free camping. Along this level PCT stretch you leave Desolation Wilderness and then, about 0.7 mile later, you reach a snowdepth indicator in a small meadow. From it you climb about 200 yards to a jeep road junction atop a forested saddle (7570–2.7). The eastbound jeep road drops to shallow Richardson Lake, as does the more-direct, better graded PCT. Along the lake's west shore both nearly touch, and then they diverge at the lake's northwest corner (7400-0.5). Ample space for camping lies along the north shore. Be aware that campsites here are legally accessible for ORVs. Indeed, ORV enthusiasts seem to visit this site more than do PCT trekkers.

Beyond the lake, the forest is usually so dense that you are unaware you are circling Sourdough Hill. In about 3/4 mile, where the trail turns from north to west, you come to within 250 yards of unseen Miller Meadows lake.

*　　　*　　　*　　　*

Water access: When the trail was constructed through here in the 1970s, the lakes in this area were on private land, and perhaps for that reason the trail was route away from them. The land later was acquired by the Forest Service, and so you can visit them, either by going cross-country or by later heading east on a road. Although large-looking on the map, they are not pristine, alpine lakes, but rather shallow, murky, oversized lily ponds. Still the water is drinkable after treatment, and there is ample flat space for camping. As at more pristine Richardson Lake, these lakes also are visited by ORVs.

*　　　*　　　*　　　*

After ½ mile of westward traverse you approach the westernmost Miller Meadow and then, in another ½ mile, cross a lightly used road (7020–1.7). In 100 yards you cross Miller Creek and can camp nearby. Past the usually flowing creek the trail quickly reaches the McKinney-Rubicon Springs Road (7000–0.2).

*　　　*　　　*　　　*

Resupply access: This road goes about 8 miles east to Tahoma, on Lake Tahoe's shore. This town is not suitable for resupplying, but the road to it is a rather direct, easy way out to civilization in an emergency. From just south of Tahoma, in Sugar Pine Point State Park, public-transit (TART) buses run north 8 miles to Tahoe City which, like South Lake Tahoe, has everything you might need.

*　　　*　　　*　　　*

The PCT continues its traverse through viewless forest, crossing Bear Lake's reliable outlet creek about ⅓ mile before slanting across Bear lake road (7120–1.9). For almost ½ mile the PCT parallels this road northwest, keeping within a stone's throw of it. Where the trail curves away from the road, you can drop to it and follow it about 200 yards over to Barker Creek, with abundant camping space fre-

See maps K3, K4, K5

quented by car campers. About ¼ mile past the road the PCT crosses a sloping meadow whose north edge is demarcated by a spring-fed creek. You pass a trickling spring midway to a second sloping meadow, which is about ⅓ mile past the first one. After a couple of minutes' walk beyond that one, you see an old logging road just below the trail, and it parallels your route northeast for about ½ mile. Along this trail stretch at least three springs flow through mid-summer, and you could get water at one and then descend to the nearby road and make a *de*

See map K5

facto camp. Past the last spring, which is near a deadend logging spur, the trail climbs ⅓ mile to cross Road 15N03—Forest Route 3 (7650–2.4) near Barker Pass.

* * * *

Resupply access: This well-used road climbs ½ mile south along the crest, then descends 7 miles east to Kaspian Picnic Ground, on the west shore of Tahoe. Tahoe Pines is about ½ mile south on Highway 89; Tahoe City, with major supplies, is about 4½ miles north.

* * * *

Immediately beyond wide Road 15N03, you cross a jeep road, which vaults Barker Pass proper. If you've got enough water, you can make a dry camp at this turf-and-forest pass. Leaving camp lands behind, you climb west, having views of past and present logging operations in and around the Barker Creek basin, below you. In a short while you top a ridge and view Lake Tahoe to the east and two small volcanic buttes to the north. Your trail switchbacks into a spring-fed gully, then traverses ½ mile over to a saddle (8240–1.6) by the southwestern butte. Here you see, among other sights, conical Barker Peak in the foreground, with Dicks Peak, 14 miles away, on the skyline just above it.

Beyond the buttes the PCT swings past seasonal springs along its drop to a nearly level camping area along the headwaters of North Fork Blackwood Creek (7960–0.8). The possible sites here are the most isolated trailside camps along the PCT in Section K. Onward, you descend north for ½ mile, contour northeast for another ½ mile, then climb switchback legs of differing gradients almost to the Sierra crest, which you reach after rounding minor Peak 8434. Here you enter Granite Chief Wilderness. About 100 yards later, on the north side of a low knoll (8370–2.4), you have excellent views in almost all directions. Of course, those from Twin Peaks, about ½ mile to the northeast, are even better.

* * * *

Side route: To reach Twin Peaks, start here, where the PCT traverses north from the crest, and climb northeast up the peaks' south ridge. The gradient increases as you approach the base of a lava knoll, and you leave the ridge, veering left (north) and climbing steeply up behind it. You then see the easy, obvious route up to the west summit of Twin Peaks. The east summit can be tackled by a number of routes, all requiring extensive use of hands. Do note that all routes up to this summit require caution, since all are fairly steep and loose rocks abound.

* * * *

See map K5

PCT heading southeast toward Twin Peaks

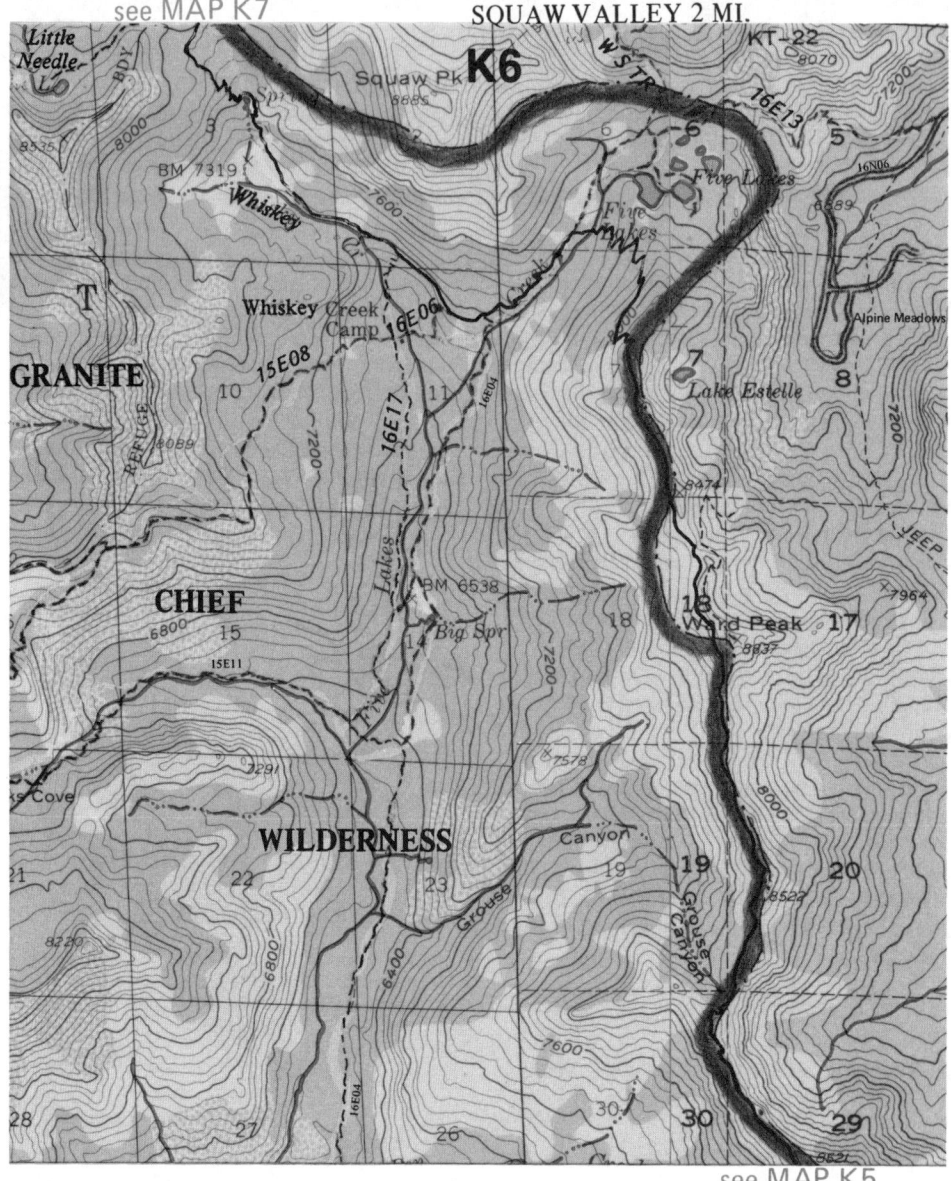

see MAP K5

The PCT contours past Twin Peaks back to the crest, then stays on or very close to it for the next 4 miles. Classic crest-views prevail.

▮ *Early on this crest traverse you see massive, columnar lava flows on the flanks of Powderhorn and Little Powderhorn canyons, to the southwest. These flows dwarf the one seen at Devils Postpile, south of Yosemite National Park. Beyond Peak 8522, a remnant of a lava flow perched high above Grouse Canyon, you pass beautiful, trailside hexagonal columns like those at Devils Postpile. As you head north to-*ward *Ward Peak, note how the lava flows dip away from deep Ward Creek canyon, to the east. Evidently, there was once a volcano situated there and today all you see are parts of its western flank.* **▮**

The PCT nearly tops Ward Peak, and just northwest of it the trail closely approaches the peak's maintenance road (8470–3.5).

*　　　*　　　*　　　*

Resupply access: On this road you can de-

See maps K5, K6

scend to Alpine Meadows Ski Area (which you'll see ⅓ mile farther along the PCT), then head 3½ miles out to Highway 89. Tahoe City is 4 miles southeast up it.

*   *   *   *

Past the view of Alpine Meadows, the trail, which has been mostly across volcanic rocks since Barker Pass, completes its crest traverse on older rocks, first metamorphic and then granitic. Beyond the last crest knoll the trail switchbacks 16 times as it descends to Five Lakes Creek. If you want to reach the largest and westernmost of the Five Lakes, leave the trail at its ninth switchback, traverse on a slight descent north for a minute or two, and you should find yourself on a crest about 100 feet above the lake. Continue down the crest to this warm, shallow lake. Due to overuse, camping is now prohibited at all of the lakes. If you stay on the PCT, you'll cross Five Lakes Creek with a bathtub-size pool, about 130 yards before you meet Trail 16E04 (7430- 3.1).

*   *   *   *

Resupply access: Here's another opportunity to head over to Lake Tahoe to resupply. First, climb 0.6 mile northeast to a junction with the unmaintained W S (Western States) Trail, and then in a minute or two pass a spur trail south to the nearby Five Lakes. Continue eastward on Five Lakes Trail 16E13 1.9 miles down to Alpine Meadows Road, the trailhead located just opposite the road's junction with the upper end of Deer Park Drive. Take Alpine Meadows Road 2.1 miles down to Highway 89, and follow this busy highway just under 4 miles up along the Truckee River to bustling Tahoe City.

*   *   *   *

Continuing along the PCT, you parallel Five Lakes Creek down-canyon as you cross generally brushy, flowery slopes. As you're about to curve west through a forest, you come to a junction. Here an old trail starts south, bound for Diamond Crossing. On the PCT you make a forested 250-yard traverse west to a junction with Whiskey Creek Trail 16E06 (7170–1.0).

*   *   *   *

Side route: This trail makes a 0.4-mile descent to Whiskey Creek, above whose west bank one finds Whiskey Creek Camp. The spacious camp, with bunkhouse, storage shed and a roofed stove, was popular with equestrians. The structures are now in poor shape, and camping within 250 feet of them is prohibited. Head west or north 100-200 yards and find legal sites.

*   *   *   *

Beyond the Whiskey Creek Trail junction, you soon start a ½-mile traverse across steep, brushy slopes, which ends just before your trail reaches the floor of a hanging valley. Here you can walk a few paces over to Whiskey Creek and get water before the creek plunges over the valley's brink. Anywhere over the next ⅓ mile you can leave the PCT and make a camp near this creek, which usually flows through midsummer. The trail then climbs, moderately to steeply, above a 50-acre field of mule ears to a spring among some alders. Short switchbacks follow, giving way to a meadowy climb that in turn yields to a brief, rocky traverse to a forested saddle. On slopes immediately north below it you meet the Tevis Cup Trail (7915–2.1).

*   *   *   *

Side route: For isolated camping, you can head 100 yards northwest down this trail to where, by the edge of a meadow, you find a faint, unmarked trail climbing west-southwest upslope. This ¾-mile-long trail becomes more prominent higher up, then dies out past a campsite above the northwest shore of Little Needle Lake.

*   *   *   *

Northward, the PCT doubles as the route of Tevis Cup Trail 16E09, and you cross and recross the headwaters of Middle Fork American River before the two routes split (8140–0.6).

*   *   *   *

Resupply access: The Tevis Cup Trail climbs rather steeply 0.6 mile east to Emigrant Pass,

K

Echo Lake-
I-80

See maps K6, K7

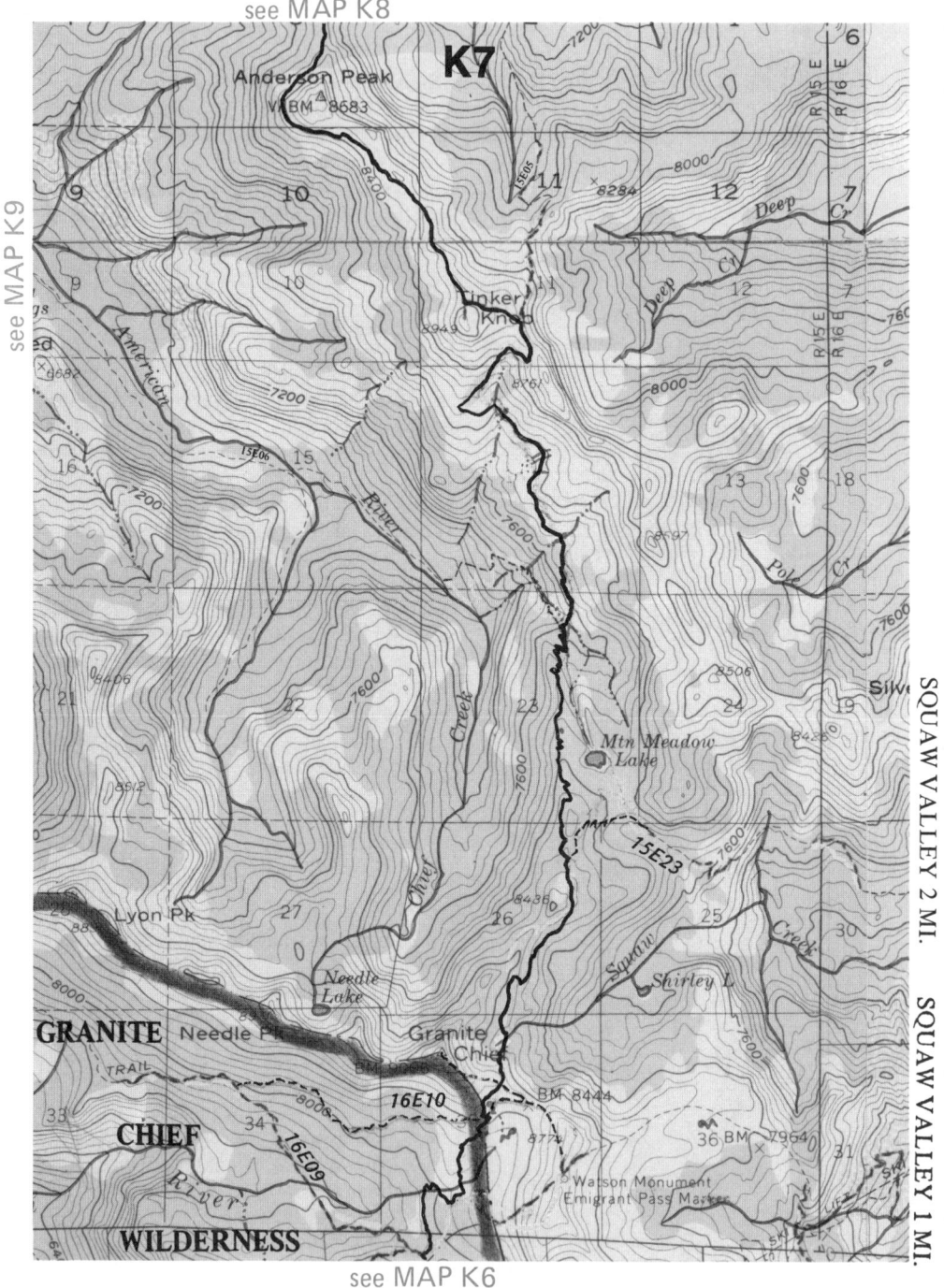

see MAP K8

see MAP K9

see MAP K6

from which one could descend a road about a mile to the top end of an aerial tramway. Both the road and the tramway descend to Squaw Valley. In summer, the tramway receives quite a bit of use by day hikers bound for the summit of Granite Chief.

See map K7

*   *   *   *   *   *   *   *

Leaving the junction, you cross the miniscule headwaters of Middle Fork American River in 100 yards. Northward, you make a switchbacking climb to an intersection of Western States Trail 16E10.

*   *   *   *

Resupply access and side routes: Eastward this trail contours 0.2 mile over to a trail junction on a Sierra-crest saddle before climbing southeast to Emigrant Pass. From that saddle, a trail (used by Squaw Valley tram riders bound for Granite Chief) parallels the crest west-northwest, and you intersect it about two minutes past a spring and only a few heartbeats before the PCT crosses the Sierra crest. This trail climbs steeply 0.4 mile to the summit of Granite Chief—a worthy side trip, for it is the highest point (barely) for miles around.

*   *   *   *

The PCT crosses the Sierra crest at a minor gap (8550–0.7) immediately beyond this trail, which lies just outside Granite Chief Wilderness. The wilderness setting is disrupted here by the presence of a ski tower just above the trail. You have a hemlock-filtered view of Mt. Rose, which rises above the north shore of Lake Tahoe, but it disappears as you descend short, steep switchbacks—snow-covered in early summer—down to a fragile, subalpine meadow. At its east end you cross the headwaters of Squaw Creek (8270–0.4), and 200 yards northwest of it encounter a small gravel flat, which makes an adequate campsite. The PCT makes a short traverse north before crossing beneath granite cliffs and then later descending to an important junction with Granite Chief Trail 15E23 (8170–1.1).

*   *   *   *

Resupply access: This trail winds 3.8 miles down to the north side of a fire station, along Squaw Valley's main road. For supplies, follow the road a short way down-valley to a small shopping center, where you'll also find the Olympic Valley Post Office.

Continuing, the PCT first crosses a minor saddle, then it follows a descending ridge north, offering views south toward Granite Chief, southwest toward Needle and Lyon peaks, northwest down the North Fork American River canyon, and north across the canyon toward your next main goal, Tinker Knob. The views actually improve as you get lower, and then you leave the crest and switchback down to a junction with Painted Rock Trail 15E06 (7550–1.5). Along the last part of this stretch you may see signs of an old trail that once went to Mountain Meadow Lake. This lake lies on private land and is part of an ecological study area that is closed to public entry.

From the junction the PCT descends a few yards to cross the North Fork's headwaters, then it climbs around and over granitic outcrops, reaching a bowl with water and a campsite in ⅔ mile. About ⅓ mile past this bowl, the trail enters a larger one, with more-spacious camping on a waterless flat below the trail. Beyond the bowl you contour past two usually flowing springs and then, in ¼ mile, switchback for a sustained 0.6-mile climb to Tinker Knob saddle (8590–2.2). Sharp-crested Peak 8761, just south of you, divides the impressive panorama you have to the south and east.

*   *   *   *

Side route: For a 360° panorama of the Lake Tahoe Basin/Donner Pass area, head ⅓ mile northwest on the PCT, to where it starts to drop along the Sierra crest. Leave the trail and climb south carefully up to the highly fractured summit of Tinker Knob, reached in 5 to 10 minutes.

❚ *Inspecting the terrain seen from today's summit, you view a volcanic landscape that has undergone severe erosion, partly due to glaciers, and this erosion has exposed the underlying granitic and metamorphic bedrock. Among the more prominent landmarks is Mt. Rose (10,776'), which stands high above Lake Tahoe's north shore. To the south stands aptly named Granite Chief, devoid of volcanic rock, and in the distant south shines the snowy, granitic Crystal Range, which forms the backbone of Desolation Wilderness.* ❚

See map K7

Tinker Knob saddle and Peak 8761

*   *   *   *

On the PCT head north along the open, wind-swept crest, with drought-resistant wildflowers.

▌ *As you drop west around Anderson Peak, note how its massive lava flow dips to the southeast, indicating its source was a volcano standing in the northwest.* ▌

The PCT momentarily returns to the crest at a saddle just north of Anderson Peak, and here it passes below the Sierra Club's Benson Hut. It then rounds Peak 8374 to a shallower saddle (8170–2.6), from which you have excellent views of the Truckee basin, to the east.

Backward glances toward Anderson Peak mark your progress northward, and after a while you have your first views of Donner Lake, seen as you approach a broad saddle in Section 33. In this section, most of the land west of the crest is private property. You enter USFS land where the PCT leaves the crest for an arc north across steep, gullied slopes of Mt. Lincoln. Past the mountain you enter a sheltering pine-and-fir forest as you descend easily to another broad saddle, Roller Pass (7900–2.8).

*   *   *   *

Side route: From here, one can take a recommended USFS loop-trail route 0.4 mile northeast up to the summit of Mt. Judah for your last and best view of Donner Lake. This summit also provides the best view of the Donner Pass environs.

▌ *As you can see, this area is quite rugged, and it hampered the westward progress of early emigrants. Roller Pass was one of three localities where they breached the Sierran divide. The more (in)famous locality is Donner Pass, site of the 1846 Donner Party tragedy.* ▌

*   *   *   *

On leaving Roller Pass you have your first view northwest down into a popular skiers' playland: Soda Springs, on Old Highway 40, just beyond Lake Van Norden. At first the PCT contours around Mt. Judah, but after ¼ mile it begins to drop, rather moderately, and it crosses a one-lane road (7520–0.8). Soon the forest is replaced by open slopes covered with dense huckleberry-oak scrub. The trail then reaches a rocky bench above a talus slope, From a switchback, the trail makes a short, steep descent west—a stretch that can be snowbound well into July. The descent ends at a road junc-

See map K7, K8

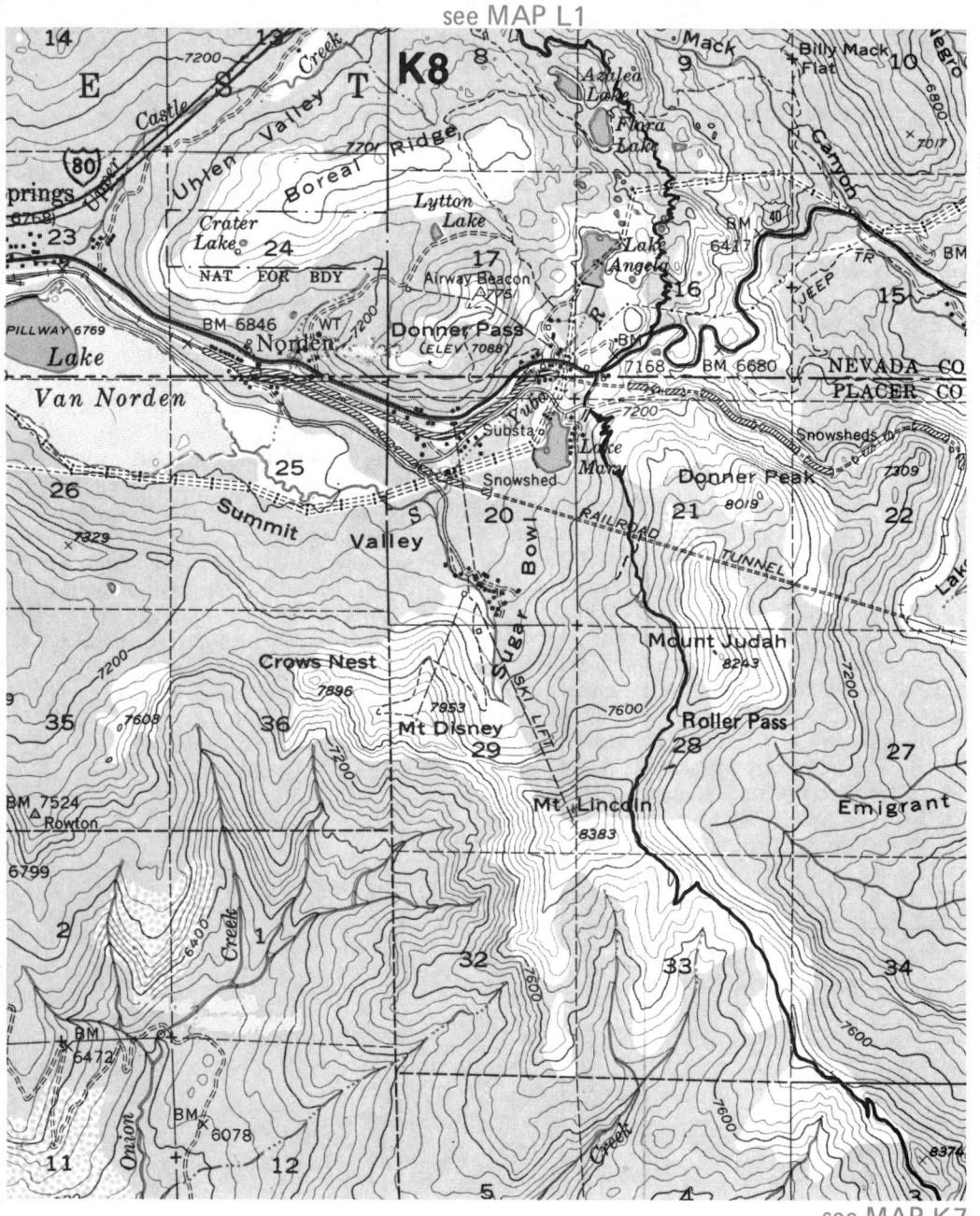

see MAP K7

tion (7060-1.0), from where a private road to some Lake Mary homesites branches southwest from an eastbound road. Pace 40 yards northwest on this road to a better road, turn right, and walk north up to nearby Old Highway 40 (7090–0.2).

*   *   *   *

Resupply access: See the last paragraph of this section's "Permits and Supplies" for PCT services available west along this road.

*   *   *   *

Across the highway, PCT tread resumes by first traversing northeast, part of this short

See map K8

stretch blasted out of bedrock cliffs. It then turns north and soon passes other cliffs popular with rock climbers. Next it winds north through a bowl and then, with a plethora of switchbacks, climbs to a divide that is about ¼ mile due east of Lake Angela's northeast corner. You then descend north to a Section 16 pond, cross under powerlines, and arrive at a Section 9 pond. About 0.2 mile past this pond you cross the brush-lined creek draining Flora Lake. The trail then climbs to the base of some prominent cliffs, heads north past them through a shallow saddle, and then turns west. After about ¼ mile, the trail abruptly turns north and almost tops a higher, shallow saddle. On the other side of the saddle is a shallow basin that holds Azalea and Flora lakes. Be aware that both lakes are on private land and are sources of domestic water supply. The PCT was routed around them so that the water supply wouldn't be contaminated.

From the higher shallow saddle, you begin a ¼-mile descent, which momentarily enters a shady forest. This can have snow through mid-July and hordes of mosquitoes through mid-August. The PCT levels off at the edge of a meadow, where there is a junction (7190–3.0). Here, ¼ mile south of Interstate 80, is where we've chosen to end Section K's PCT, since where the trail crosses *under* the busy highway, there is no legal parking.

*   *   *   *

Side route: To reach I-80's trailhead parking lot, branch 200 yards west along a trail to a junction just above a shallow, murky lakelet. Here you join the 0.6-mile-long Glacier Meadow Loop Trail 15E32, a nature trail with signs. Northwest, it goes 250 yards to eastbound Interstate 80's Donner Summit Safety Roadside Rest Area, which receives heavy use by motorists. Continue west, then southwest on the nature trail. It then turns north, and you immediately reach another junction, ¼ mile from the last. Here you leave the nature trail, which continues 230 yards north to the safety roadside rest area. You take a westward-meandering trail for 300 yards over to the east end of the trailhead parking lot.

To reach this lot by vehicle, take the Interstate 80 exit signed for Castle Peak and Boreal Ridge. This is the first exit west of the interstate's two safety roadside rest areas, and it is the first exit east of the Soda Springs exit. Immediately south of the eastbound lanes' onramp and offramp, you'll reach an obvious road which you follow 0.3 mile east to its end at the trailhead parking lot.

*   *   *   *

See maps K8, L1

In Desolation Wilderness, the PCT skirts Dicks Peak and drops to Middle Velma Lake; view is from the Tahoe-Yosemite Trail

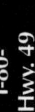

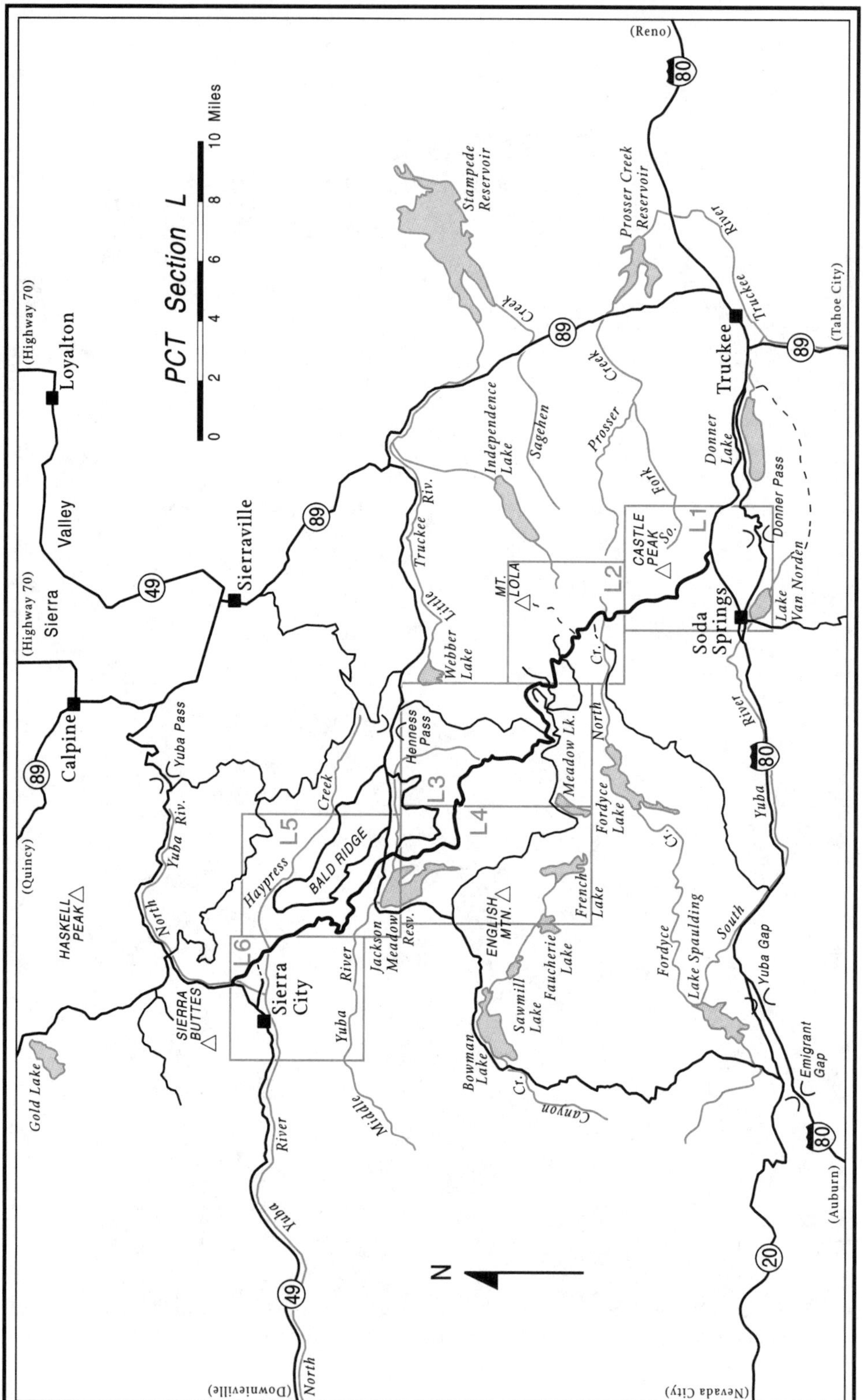

PCT Section L

10 Miles

0   2   4   6   8   10

(Reno)

80

(Highway 70)

Loyalton

Stampede
Reservoir

Prosser Creek
Reservoir

Truckee River

89

Truckee

(Tahoe City)

Sierra
Valley

89

Independence
Lake

Sagehen   Creek

Prosser   Creek

Creek

Donner
Lake

89

Sierraville

49

Creek

Truckee Riv.

North   Fork

Donner Pass

Soda
Springs

L1

Donner Pass

Lake
Van Norden

(Highway 70)

(Quincy)

Calpine

89

Little   Truckee Riv.

Webber
Lake

MT.
LOLA

CASTLE
PEAK

L2

80

Yuba River

Yuba Pass

Henness
Pass

L3

Meadow Lk.

North   Cr.

Yuba   River

L5

BALD RIDGE

Haypress   Creek

L4

Fordyce
Lake

Yuba

HASKELL
PEAK

North

ENGLISH
MTN.

French
Lake

Fordyce   Cr.

Lake Spaulding

South

L6

SIERRA
BUTTES

Sierra
City

Jackson
Meadow
Resv.

Bowman
Lake

Sawmill
Lake

Faucherie
Lake

Fordyce   Cr.

Yuba Gap

Gold Lake

Middle   Yuba   River

Cr.

Canyon

Emigrant
Gap

80

(Auburn)

N

49

20

(Downieville)   North

(Nevada City)

Section L
Interstate 80 to Highway 49

Introduction: Only 38.4 miles long, this section is easily the shortest one in this guide. It is actually short enough for strong day hikers to complete it in one long day. Heavily laden tri-state backpackers can do it in two. The first two-thirds of the distance is mostly on or close to a sinuous crest of volcanic rocks, and you have abundant views of Sierra crest terrain from Tinker Knob northwest to the Sierra Buttes. But then you drop toward Jackson Meadow Reservoir, hiking generally on metamorphic rocks, and views are few. The stretch descending along Milton Creek is about as far from the crest as one can get, but after going miles between reliable water sources, this chorusing creek is music to one's ears as well as relief for one's dry throat.

Declination: 15¾°E

Points on Route	S→N	Mi. Btwn. Pts.	N→S
trailhead parking lateral near I-80	0.0		38.4
Peter Grubb Hut	4.2	4.2	34.2
Magonigal Camp jeep road	8.3	4.1	30.1
Meadow Lake Road 19N11	15.9	7.6	22.5
Road 07 near Jackson Meadow Reservoir	27.5	11.6	10.9
first (southern) Milton Creek crossing	33.8	6.3	4.6
closed road to Wild Plum Campground	35.8	2.0	2.6
Highway 49 near Sierra City	38.4	2.6	0.0

Supplies: There are no post offices along the route at which to pick up your parcels. See the last paragraph of the previous section's "supplies" for services available along Old Highway 40, about 3 trail miles south of the start of Section L. Near the section's north end you can head over to Highway 49 and follow it down to nearby Sierra City, which has a post office, motels, restaurants and stores.

Maps: *Norden* *English Mountain*
Soda Springs *Haypress Valley*
Webber Peak

The Route

You begin this section just south of Interstate 80. If you're starting your trek in this vicinity, consult the last paragraph of the previous section for driving directions to the trailhead parking lot. Then follow in reverse the next-to-the-last paragraph for trail directions to the PCT. Basically, you go 300 yards east to a nature trail, ¼ mile up it, then 200 yards east to the PCT (elev. 7190). Here is where Section L's mileage begins.

From the junction the northbound PCT skirts the west edge of a wet, willowy meadow and

See map L1

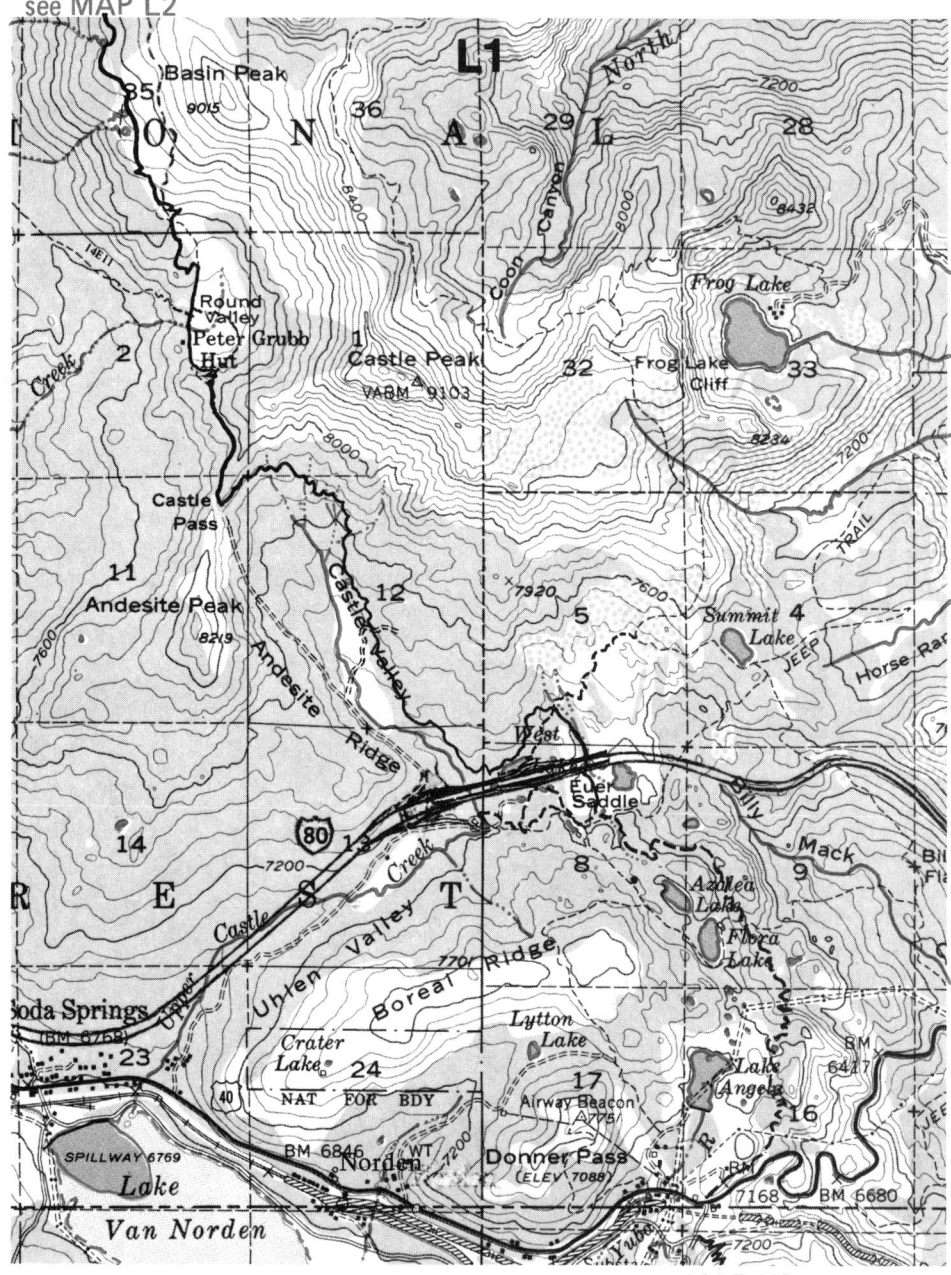

see MAP K8

in ¼ mile reaches Interstate 80. A horse-and-hiker tunnel had been constructed under both the westbound and eastbound lanes—a decided plus for equestrians. However, a stream also goes beneath the lanes, and at times of high runoff, it backs up and overflows through the horse tunnel. Under these circumstances, hikers may opt for a dash across I-80. The PCT then heads 0.2 mile upstream before intersecting Summit Lake Trail 15E09. This descends about 400 yards southwest to the east side of a building at westbound I-80's Donner Summit Safety Roadside Rest Area. The PCT makes a brief climb west, then turns southwest to descend, like the Summit Lake Trail, to the grounds of the rest area. Just northwest of the

See map L1

building, the PCT joins a loop trail that circles a lakelet lying immediately west of the building. Walk about 150 yards along this trail to a junction (7230–0.9), by the lake's west shore, where the loop trail turns south.

Now you leave the confusing array of trails of the I-80 rest areas by starting a climb west-southwest across glaciated granitic slabs, then soon turning northwest and paralleling a major fracture in the bedrock. Beyond it the PCT veers west toward Castle Valley and, staying within tree cover, follows the valley's meadow northwest to a road (7440–1.0). Onward, the early-season hiker is likely to encounter at least a dozen seasonal streams, some of them quite impressive. And before mid-July you just might get wet feet—and find much of the trail under snow. From the last seasonal stream the PCT curves southwest up to a junction with an abandoned jeep road where it crosses Castle Pass (7910–1.4).

*   *   *   *

Alternate route: This road descends 1.9 miles to the on- and offramps of westbound I-80, and in former days it was a temporary part of the PCT route. Today it provides the most direct way down to the Interstate 80 trailhead.

*   *   *   *

From Castle Pass the PCT stays just above the old jeep road for ¼ mile, coincides with it for 100 yards, then stays just below it. Soon both drop into Round Valley, the PCT switchbacking down to Peter Grubb Hut (7820–0.9), which is one of several Sierra Club cabins in the Sierra Nevada. It is open for public use, but please treat it properly. A minute past the hut you jump across Lower Castle Creek, and a minute later you reach westbound Sand Ridge Lake Trail 14E11. Soon you start to climb again, shortly reaching the back side of a glacier-smoothed-and-striated granitic outcrop, from which one has westward views of the Sand Ridge environs. Your climb continues, first up along a persisting creeklet, and then you cross and recross the old jeep road. The PCT then takes an undulating course north, and along it the trail reaches its highest elevation in this section, about 8350 feet. Eventually the PCT

crosses the old jeep road (8270–2.2). Before late July, you can expect hordes of mosquitoes just ahead in North Creek canyon.

At first your trail descends alongside the road, but then you switchback down through a forest dominated by mountain hemlocks, which can be snowbound well into July. Later you leap across North Creek, and quickly pass mosquito ponds for a short traverse to the Magonigal Camp jeep road (7580–1.9).

*   *   *   *

Side route: This crossing is immediately west of a large, boggy meadow—something to look for if you plan to head east 1.1 miles up to Paradise Lake and then back again. Formerly most of the lake was on private land, but now it (and the route to it) is entirely on Forest Service land. Still, one has to contend at times with ORVs, which use the jeep road, and with the seasonally abundant mosquitoes. However, the rocky east shore, reached by a cross-country traverse around the south tip, does merit a layover day. Just before the south tip you'll hit some bedrock cliffs, but these are quite safely negotiated with a bit of prudent route finding.

*   *   *   *

From the jeep road crossing, you first head north past a stagnant pond, then make a climbing effort northwest, emerging from forest shade to soon reach a knoll (8120–1.1), where a rest is in order. Next you round a nearby ridge and then switchback down steep slopes cloaked with a dense, snow-harboring forest. The gradient abates, and soon you reach White Rock Creek (7630–1.2), which is likely a wet crossing for all but late-season hikers.

*   *   *   *

Side route: Just before this crossing is the start of a 1990s trail that heads northeast over past the south shore of relatively close White Rock Lake (camping opportunities) before starting an arduous climb to the top of Mt. Lola. At 9143 feet, it is the highest summit between several Desolation Wilderness peaks, about 40 miles to the south, and Lassen Peak, about 95 miles to the northwest. On a clear day you

See map L1, L2

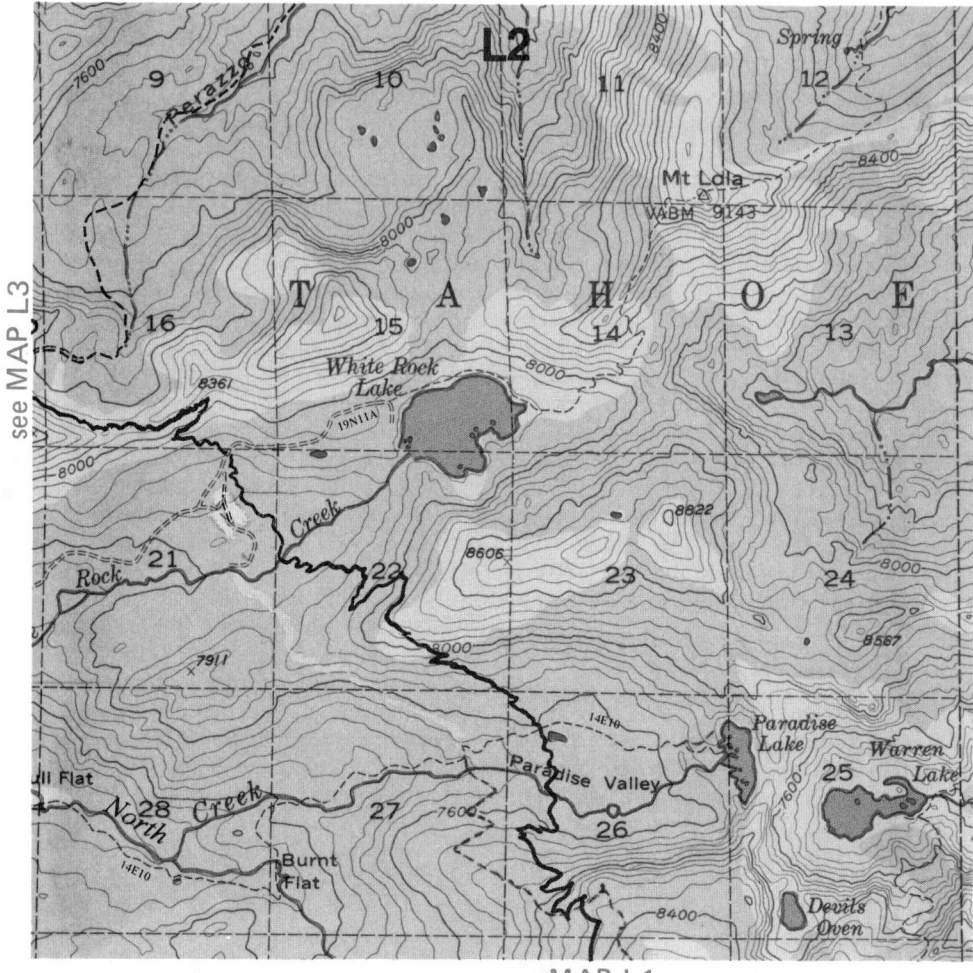

see MAP L3

see MAP L1

should see these summits, but most hikers will not find the climb worth the effort.

*   *   *   *

Due to the presence of jeep tracks and cow tracks and to a dearth of trees suitable for blazes, the stretch ahead can be hard to follow, particularly for those southbound. In essence you go about 120 yards north-northwest to a meadow, slog through a boggy stretch near its lower end, then soon parallel the northeast edge of a larger meadow, on your left, as you climb northwest. A road climbs north from this meadow, and you almost touch it as your trail snakes briefly north up to a bend in Road 19N11A (7760–0.7). This bend is 100 yards north of Road 19N11A's junction with the meadow's road.

With the meadowy mess behind you, you climb generally west, ducking in and out of many gullies cleft in steep volcanic slopes. The soil is rich in clay, and when wet the route can be quite slippery—something to watch for over the stretch to Jackson Meadow Reservoir. Without too much effort you cross a saddle (8140–0.8), and have your first of many views to the north. You continue west on slopes below Peak 8450, first past meadows with springs, and then through a forest of mountain hemlocks, which in years of heavy snowfall can retain snow patches into September. The trail then curves to descend a north-trending ridge, and you quickly reach its low point, where you cross a road on a viewless saddle (8060–0.7).

You climb north-northeast for a few minutes to reach an 8086-foot knobby, precarious viewpoint, the top of an autobrecciated lava flow. This offers superb views to the north and north-

See maps L2, L3

east of the extensively glaciated, volcanic landscape. You descend briefly southwest from the viewpoint, almost touch the road you just crossed, and then head north to another ridge saddle (7830–1.0), this one at the head of Bear Valley. Now both ridge and trail turn west, and you have some views as you head over toward point 7942 on a volcanic ridge. For views as far northwest as the Sierra Buttes, make a brief climb north to that point. Ahead, the ridge turns southwest, as does the trail, which soon starts a 1¼-mile descent. You drop into a selectively logged forest of red firs and western white pines, and eventually turn northwest for a short traverse over to Tahoe N.F. Road 86 (7530–2.1). This spot is immediately past a usually flowing creek, which drains a meadow you'll see beginning just south up the road. One could camp hereabouts, though mosquitoes can be fierce through early August.

North, this road goes 6½ miles to Tahoe N.F. Road 07, the same road that skirts the north shore of Jackson Meadow Reservoir. You, however, go a few yards south to find the PCT beginning southwest from the road. Past a small meadow the trail soon turns north and climbs to a ridge (8000–1.1). This it ascends, giving you views of Fordyce and Meadow lakes plus views of the peaks along the PCT north and south of Donner Pass. The trail then curves west, reaching a local high point just beneath Peak 8214 (which provides a 360° panorama of most of the Section L area). Just west of the summit area the PCT offers trekkers their first view of Webber Lake. About ¾ mile past the local high point, the trail starts a descent along a lower, north-trending ridge, leaving views behind as it heads over to a logging road (7640–2.1).

A switchbacking climb ensues, with views improving once again as you strive for, but do not attain, the summit of Peak 8166. Now the route is essentially downhill all the way to Jackson Meadow Reservoir. Views along your descending, volcanic crest are plentiful and interesting, though not on a par with those near Peak 8214. After a descent west past knobs of autobrecciated lava, the PCT heads north, descending 0.2 mile almost to a creek (7330–3.6) that flows through most of the summer. You switchback almost to it a second time, then descend to a major road that crosses a minor saddle (7135–0.4). You could camp in this vicinity and get water from the seasonal creek, reached by walking about 0.2 mile north down the road.

Westward, you climb just a bit before skirting past autobrecciated lava buttes on Peak 7348. As your descending route curves north down a ridge, you enter an area of selective logging, cross a good road, and in ⅓ mile cross another good road (6740-2.3). Now hiking on slopes of metamorphic rocks, you leave the ridge, parallel the west edge of an old road for 0.4 mile, then drop ever closer to the northeast shore of spreading Jackson Meadow Reservoir.

See maps L3, L4

View south toward Jackson Meadow Reservoir and English Mountain

Meadow Lake Hill separates Fordyce Lake (left) from Meadow Lake (right)

Heading northwest toward Jackson Meadow Reservoir and the Sierra Buttes

Nearing the reservoir, the PCT almost touches a south-climbing road.

* * * *

Water access: If you plan to visit East Meadow Campground and the adjacent reservoir, then head 0.1 mile down this road to the paved campground road.

* * * *

The PCT curves northeast away from the campground, then quickly reaches its paved road (6170–1.7) only a few yards west of a junction with southeast-climbing Pass Creek Loop Road.

* * * *

Water access: East Meadow Campground lies ⅓ mile west along the paved road, and it is perched just above the welcome, fairly warm waters of Jackson Meadow Reservoir, a boaters' mecca. On the paved road walk north across nearby Pass Creek to the north bank of its tributary, from which the trail resumes, curving northwest ¼ mile over to paved Tahoe N.F. Road 07 (6200–0.4).

* * * *

Water access: If you head ¼ mile west along this road, you'll reach the entrance to Pass Creek Campground, which is situated above the northeast corner of the reservoir.

* * * *

From Road 07 the trail continues northwest, passing by springs emerging from volcanic soils as it climbs through an old logging area to a minor saddle (6450–0.8). The Sierra Buttes loom dead ahead as you descend through a linear minicanyon. A series of short, descending switchbacks take you out of the minicanyon, and then you cross its usually dry creek. Water here may flow underground, for rocks on the southwest wall appear to be marble (the stuff caves are formed from).

Next you contour across slopes above miniature Bear Valley. Today, "Cow Valley" would be a more accurate name, and besides, you al-

ready passed another Bear Valley about a day's hike ago and don't need the confusing name duplication. Beyond a ridge west of and above Bear Valley you traverse northwest, reaching in ½ mile a view of the canyon you'll soon drop into. After another ½ mile you circle a knee-deep lily-pad pond. Then in ¼ mile you breach the canyon's rim and start down an intricate route with over two dozen switchbacks in it. If you're heavily laden and heading south up the PCT, you'll appreciate the trail's easy gradient; northbound hikers are typically unappreciative. At last you cross Milton Creek (5240–5.5), and just past it spy a small campsite.

❚ *You're now entering a lower forest, one dominated, to be sure, by white firs, which you've often seen before. However, now some of its low-elevation associates appear, notably incense-cedar, sugar pine, ponderosa pine, Douglas-fir and black oak, all of which have been infrequent along the PCT.* ❚ After a descent north, you make a short jog southwest to bridge Milton Creek (4990–0.8). Now on the creek's west bank, you pass several spots with creekside camping as you leisurely stroll northward down to a road (4810–1.2).

* * * *

Resupply access: Eastward, the road immediately bridges Milton Creek, and on a large, flat stream terrace near the confluence of Milton and Haypress creeks there is room for dozens of trekkers. Consider staying here rather than down at Wild Plum Campground, which at times can get quite rowdy.

Since 1980 the permanent PCT has existed over to Highway 49. Nevertheless, many PCT hikers still take the "supply" route to Sierra City, descending 0.9 mile along the closed road to the east end of Wild Plum Campground, hiking 0.3 mile through it to Milton Creek, and traversing 1.4 miles west to Highway 49. "Downtown" Sierra City is 0.5 mile southwest down the highway; the PCT is 1.0 mile northeast up it.

* * * *

Those hikers adhering strictly to the PCT follow the closed road only 40 yards west, branching northwest from it down a sometimes

See map L4, L5, L6

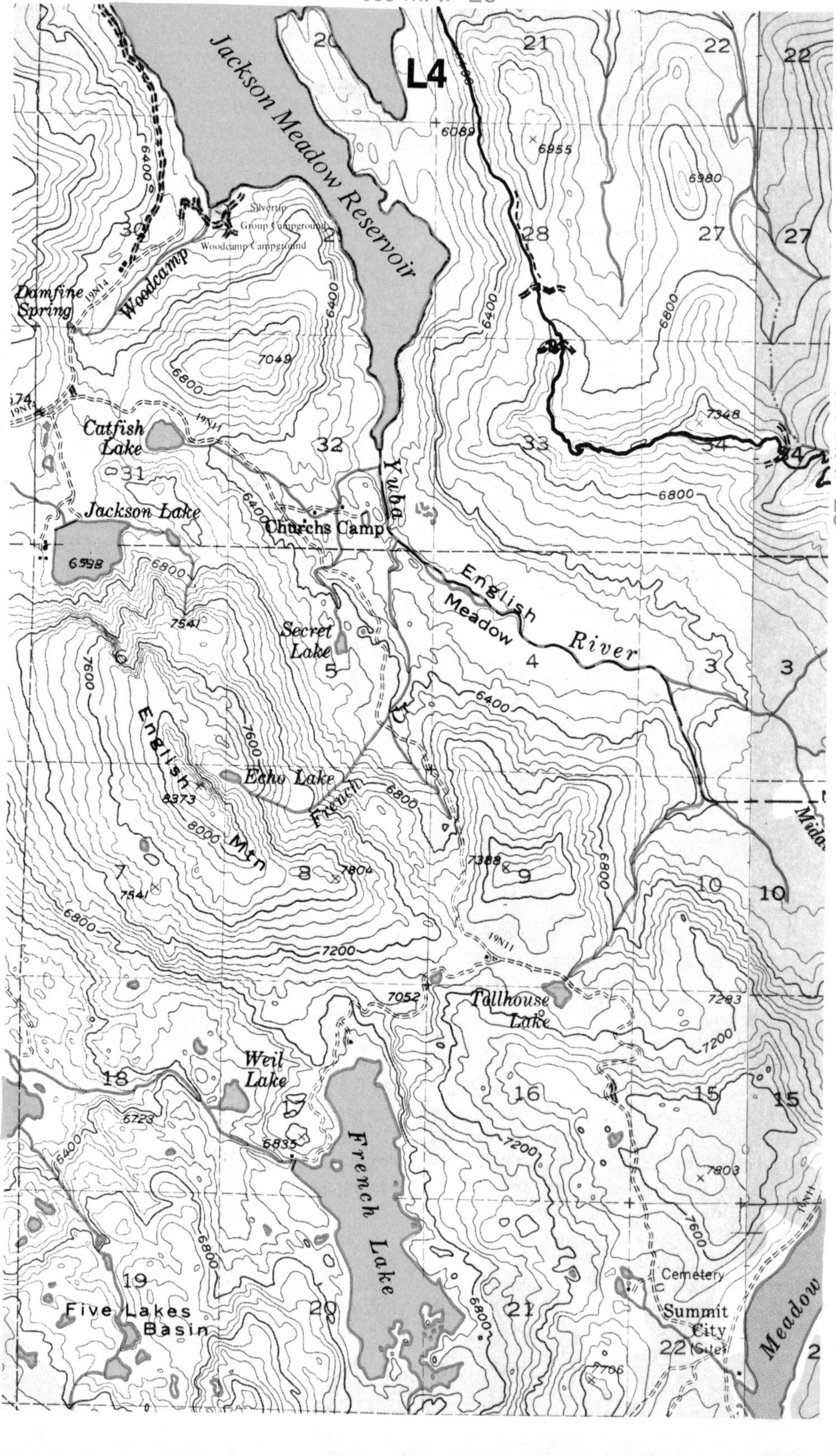

L4

Jackson Meadow Reservoir

Silvertip
Group Campground
Woodcamp Campground

Woodcamp

Damfine
Spring

Catfish
Lake

Jackson Lake

Churchs Camp

Yuba

English Meadow River

Secret
Lake

English Mtn

Echo Lake

French Ct

Midas

Tollhouse
Lake

Weil
Lake

French Lake

Five Lakes
Basin

Cemetery

Summit
City
(Site)

Meadow

see MAP L4

see MAP L2

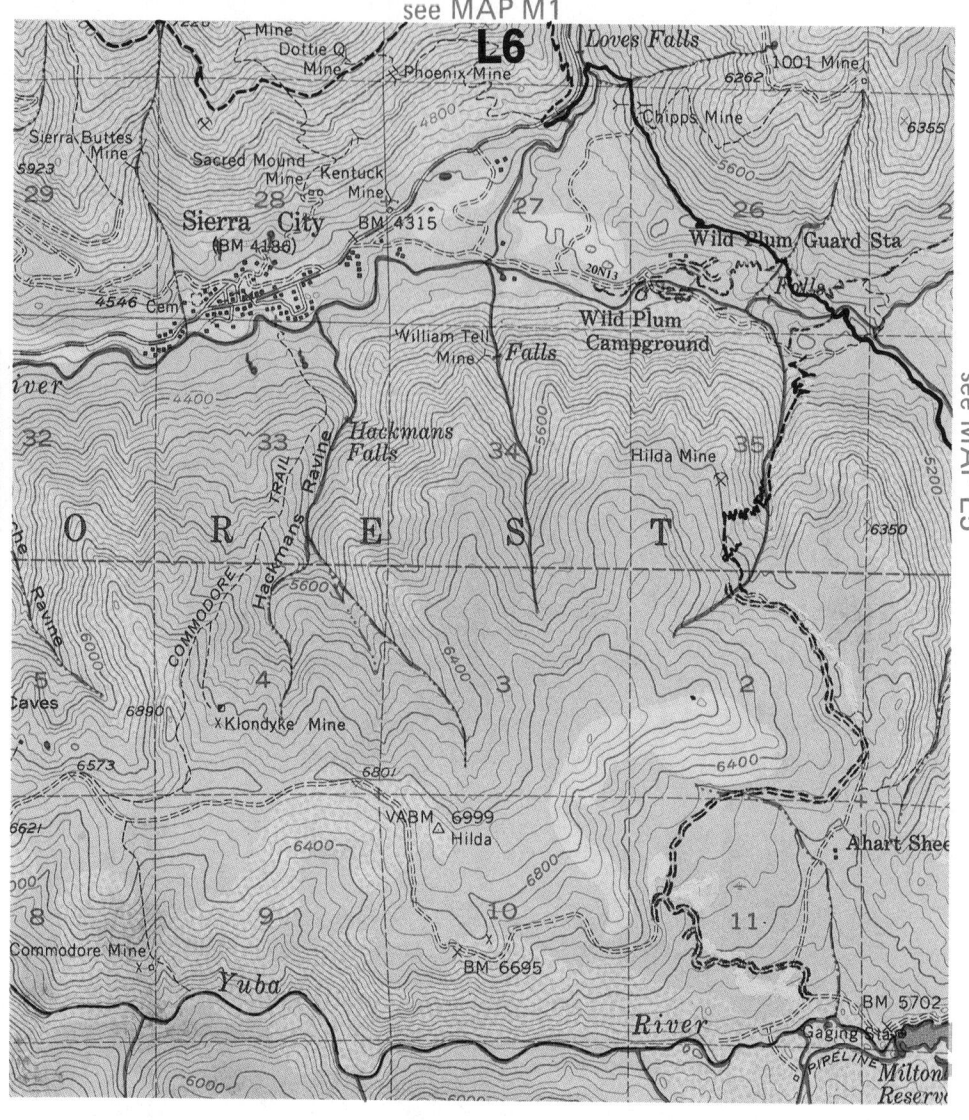

see MAP L5

I-80-
Hwy. 49

L

indistinct tread. Heading toward the Sierra Buttes, you quickly reach a bridge (4720–0.3), which spans Haypress Creek about ¼ mile above its low but roaring falls. A westbound trail at the bridge's south end gives hikers a second chance to head out to Wild Plum Campground. Nearing the end of this section's short hike, you traverse across dry slopes that are often hot and fly-ridden in summer.

*   *   *   *

Side route: The PCT runs along or close to a trail that begins from a trailhead parking area

about 0.2 mile west of the entrance to Wild Plum Campground.

*   *   *   *

After leaving this trail just beyond a gully with a seasonal creeklet, you contour over to a bedrock ridge, cross over it, and traverse past live oaks and their seemingly omnipresent flies to an old jeep road. From it the PCT descends to a seasonal creek, then drops, with the aid of short switchbacks, to a prominent bridge (4600-1.9) that vaults the North Yuba River. Here the river has cut a minigorge through the resistant

See map L6

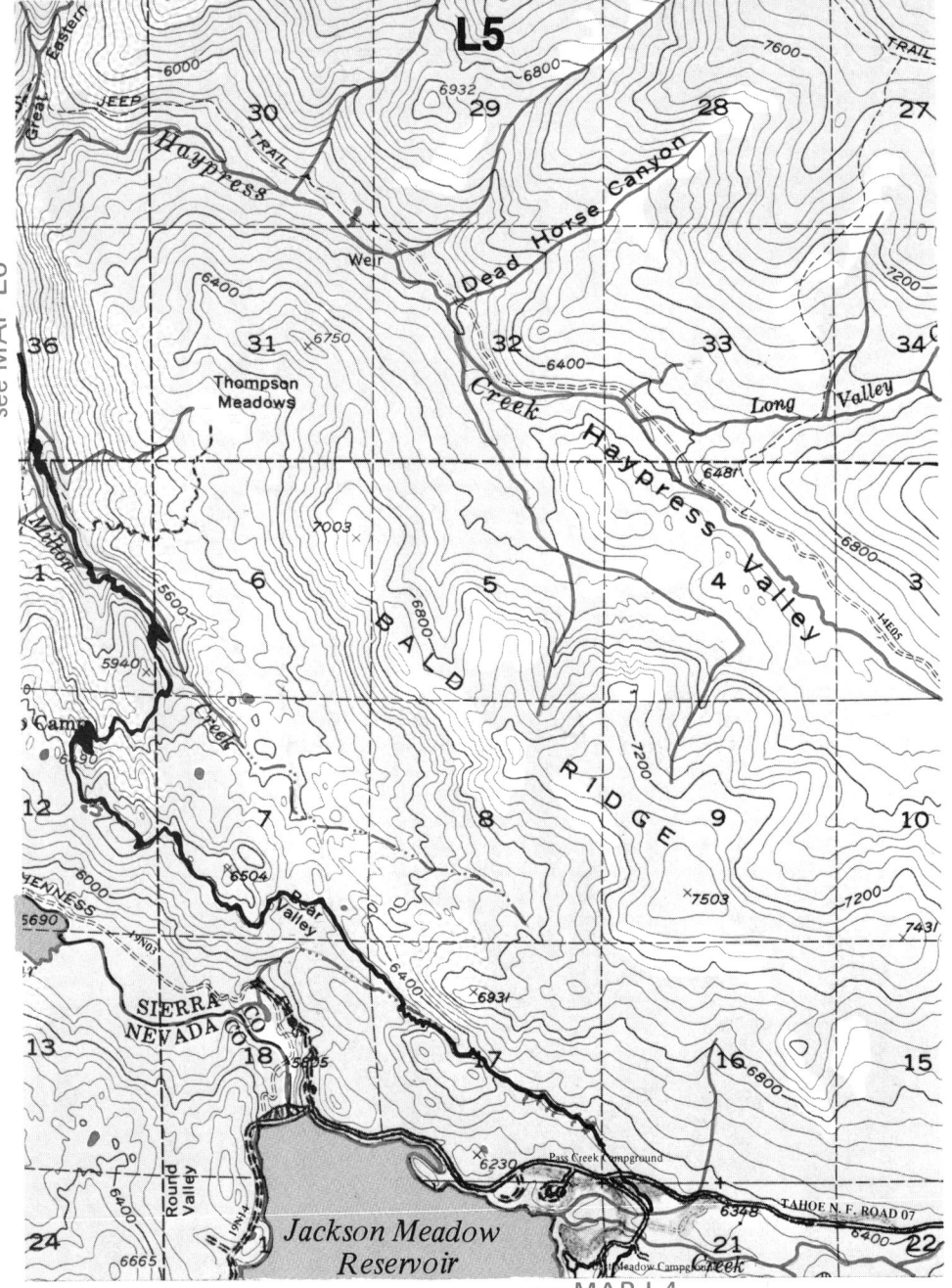

see MAP L6

see MAP L4

Mesozoic-age metavolcanic rocks. By late summer the river's volume diminishes sufficiently to allow safe swimming in its inviting, though nippy, pools. The trick is descending safely to them. If you are low on water, get some from the spring you pass between the bridge and Highway 49 (4570–0.4). Your route ahead is usually dry in summer until you reach some springs about 7½ miles ahead, just past the PCT's crossing of the Sierra Buttes jeep trail.

See map L6

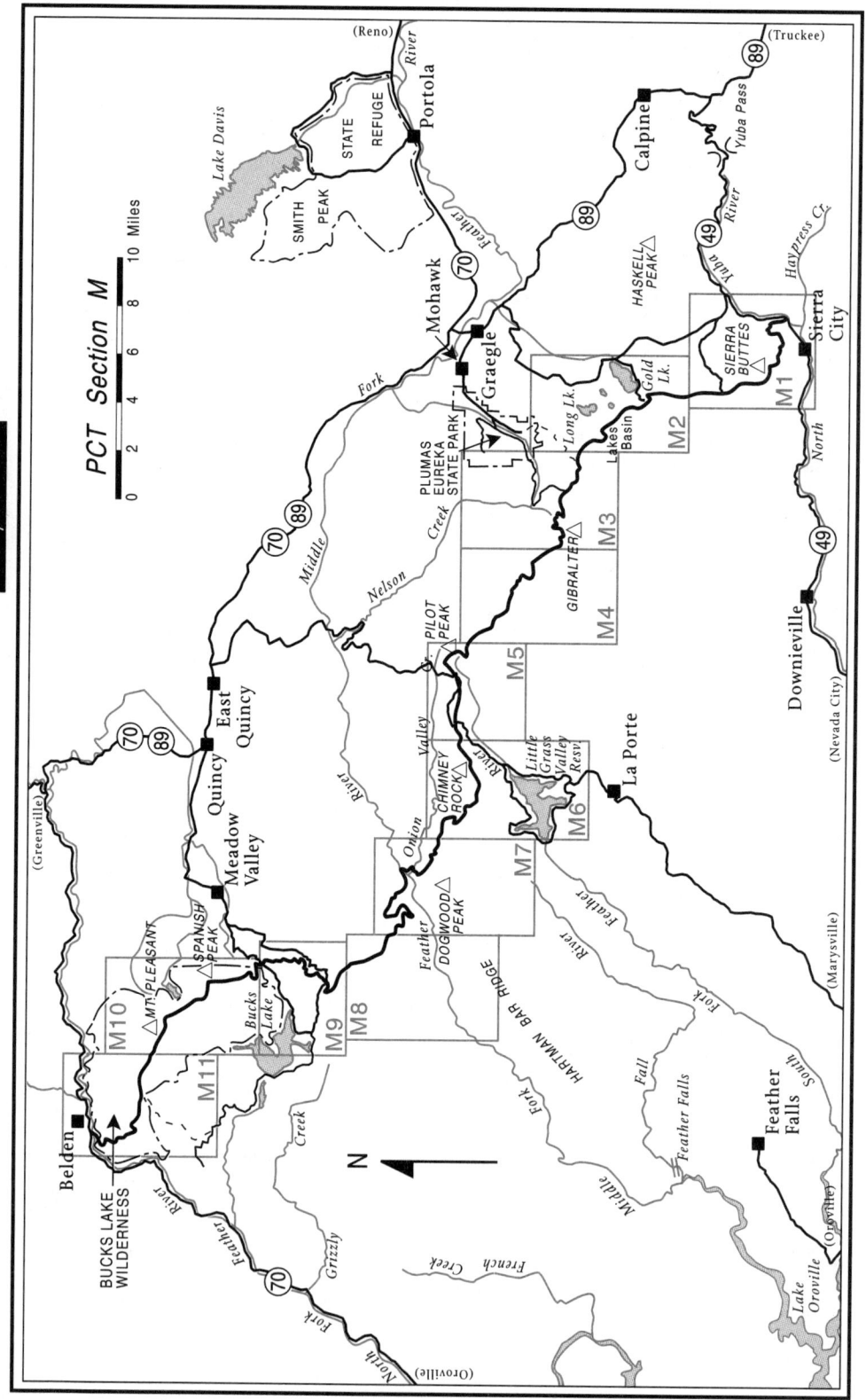

Section M
Highway 49 to Highway 70

Introduction: Great diversity characterizes this rather long section. Glaciated lake-basin environments contrast strongly with those of Feather River's deep Middle and North fork canyons. Red firs, mountain hemlocks and western white pines give way at lower elevations to other trees, which in turn give way to others until finally, along the forks of the Feather River, Douglas-firs, California nutmegs and ponderosa pines—among others—are seen. Cool snow patches yield to hot canyon bottoms, and mosquitoes are replaced by flies. Many types of rocks abound, ranging in age from late Paleozoic ocean sediments to volcanic flows that are only a few million years old. These flows generally make up most of the crests and ridges along the PCT, but they have been largely eroded away in the highly glaciated Sierra Buttes-Lakes Basin area, where underlying metavolcanic rocks have been exposed. These metavolcanics in turn give way northward to granitic rocks of the Bucks Lake-Three Lakes area. Between these two areas the PCT route is mostly along relatively youthful volcanic sediments when it is near the crest, and along ancient, usually metamorphosed marine sediments when it traverses the Middle Fork Feather River canyon.

Most of Section M's lakes are passed along the first quarter of the trail. The trail, however, stays high on the crest, avoiding all but Summit Lake, which is more of a pond than a lake. Lakes Basin—a miniature Desolation Wilderness—is barely seen, and when it is, you see it from along a portion of crest with such steep slopes that descent into the basin is dangerous and impractical. The basin is day-use only, so the Forest Service routed the PCT well away from it, to prevent PCT hikers from camping in it. This may be unfortunate for you, but it is fortunate for the basin, which now receives much less human impact than it would if camping were allowed, as it was in the past.

Declination: 16°E

Points on Route	S→N	Mi. Btwn. Pts.	N→S
Highway 49 near Sierra City	0.0		91.7
		7.2	
Sierra Buttes jeep trail	7.2		84.5
		2.6	
Packer Lake Saddle	9.8		81.9
		4.4	
Summit Lake road	14.2		77.5
		4.5	
saddle with a diminutive pond	18.7		73.0
		3.6	
A Tree saddle	22.3		69.4
		7.6	
Johnsville-Gibsonville Road	29.9		61.8
		4.5	
unnamed lake below Bunker Hill Ridge	34.4		57.3
		3.6	
Quincy-LaPorte Road	38.0		53.7
		7.3	
Black Rock Creek Road 22N56	45.3		46.4
		1.2	

leave PCT for Fowler Lake 46.5		45.2
	7.4	
Middle Fork Feather River 53.9		37.8
	3.5	
Bear Creek 57.4		34.3
	6.8	
Lookout Rock 64.2		27.5
	3.6	
Big Creek Road 33N56 .... 67.8		23.9
	4.8	
Bucks Summit 72.6		19.1
	5.6	
trail down to Gold Lake Trail 78.2		13.5
	4.4	
Clear Creek 82.6		9.1
	9.1	
Highway 70 at Belden Town bridge 91.7		0.0

Supplies: Sierra City, 1½ miles southwest along Highway 49 from the start of this section, is a small town with post office, motels, restaurants and adequate, though not trail-oriented, supplies. At the opposite end of this section is Belden, which is little more than a pleasant resort. However, it does have, besides scant supplies, a post office. Between these two settlements you'll find no on-route supply points. However, a supply route many hikers take is our alternate route along the shore of sizable Bucks Lake. Along this route you can get lodging, meals or foodstuffs at Bucks Lake Lodge and at Lakeshore Resort. At the start of this alternate route you could also take Big Creek Road 6.9 miles down to Bucks Lake Road, then follow that road 2.2 miles down to the Meadow Valley Post Office. (If you need major supplies or boot repairs, continue east on this busy road 7.2 miles to Quincy, your last sizable near-route town until Chester, in Section N). From Meadow Valley, return to the Big Creek Road junction and continue 3.4 miles past it up Bucks Lake Road to the PCT at Bucks Summit.

Rattlesnakes: These are common at lower elevations, generally below 5000 feet, so watch where you step when you descend and ascend the Middle Fork canyon, and when you descend the North Fork canyon to Belden. At these lower elevations, however, you are more likely to pick up ticks or get poison-oak rashes than meet rattlesnakes.

Maps: *Haypress*   *Dogwood Peak*
        Valley   *American House*
        Sierra City   *Haskins Valley*
        Gold Lake   *Meadow Valley*
        Mount Filmore   *Bucks Lake*
        Blue Nose Mountain   *Storrie*
        Onion Valley   *Belden*

The Route

This section begins on Highway 49, about 1½ miles northeast of Sierra City and 1.0 mile northeast of a road branching east to Wild Plum Campground. During the summer, your first reliable water is 7½ miles away, at a spring about ¼ mile beyond the Sierra Buttes jeep trail. The climb around Sierra Buttes is mostly sunny, so try to get an early start so that you won't be guzzling water. If you need some immediately, cross Highway 49 and follow the southbound trail about two minutes to a creeklet that origi-

nates at a spring just below the highway. If by chance that is dry, then continue ¼ mile farther to the North Yuba River.

■ *The first part of this trail section is on a narrow, abandoned road through a forest of black oak, ponderosa pine and incense-cedar. Mountain misery, a low, sticky shrub, permeates the air with a subtle fragrance as the day's temperature rises.* ■ After the PCT bends north onto cooler east-facing slopes, you meet Douglas-firs and their associated vegetation. About

See map M1

M

Hwy. 49-
Hwy. 70

a mile from the start, your sporadically switchbacking trail leaves noisy Highway 49 and switchbacks relentlessly upward to a flume (5720–2.7) that today is bone-dry. About ¼-½ mile north lie smooth, bushy ridges, a smaller set within a larger one. These are lateral moraines left by glaciers that descended east from the Sierra Buttes. The earlier glacier left the outer ridges; the later, smaller glacier left the inner ones.

Your well-graded ascent has mostly been a forested one, but you leave all the trees behind just before the switchbacking ascent tops off on a ridge (6070–0.7). From it you have views both up and down the North Yuba River canyon and views up at the east buttress of the Sierra Buttes. ▌ *Now shrubs line the trail, mainly huckleberry oak, greenleaf manzanita, tobacco brush and bitter cherry, but also a dab here and there of snow bush and squaw carpet.* ▌ The shadeless route west is an easy one, which is fortunate, for if the climb were steep, it would be miserable on a hot summer day. After weaving around several ridges and gullies and getting saturated with views, you finally arrive at a saddle and the Sierra Buttes jeep trail (7150–3.8).

Stairway up to the Sierra Buttes fire lookout

*   *   *   *

Side route: The Sierra Buttes Fire Lookout stands over 1400 feet above this junction, and normally we wouldn't recommend such a strenuous side trip. However, the Sierra Buttes rise so far above other local summits that one has nonpareil views which extend, on clear days, from the Tahoe area north to Lassen Peak. And nowhere along the tri-state PCT route will you find such a narrowly perched (though safe) lookout. We recommend you leave your heavy pack behind at the junction and travel as lightly as possible to the lookout.

Start up the steep jeep trail, partly shaded by red firs and western white pines, then after ¾ mile reach a junction at 7910 feet in elevation. From here you could follow a winding trail northwest down a ridge to the PCT, but only if you've carried your backpack up to this spot. If you're traveling lightly, continue ¾ mile up the switchbacking jeep trail to the base of the lookout, and after soaking up the views, return the way you came. By the time you reach the

base, you'll have left trees behind and will have some alpine wildflowers for companions. The lookout sits atop a Sierra Buttes crest pinnacle, and you'll have to climb about 176 steps to reach it, most of the steps on steep, airy ladders—no place for the faint-hearted.

The pinnacle's summit is so small that the lookout actually projects out into space, and through the iron-grating view deck you stand on, you can look straight down the 600-foot nearly vertical northeast escarpment. The deeply glaciated Sardine Lakes canyon to the northeast contrasts strongly with the barely eroded slopes up which your jeep trail climbed. To the south lie slopes of intermediate erosion, cut by tributaries of the North Yuba River. The views are far-ranging. On the distant northwest horizon stands snowy Lassen Peak, about a two-week backpack trip away. Numerous high peaks dot the Lake Tahoe environs to the southeast. With compass in hand you can identify Mt. Rose (10,776'), 114°; Mt. Lola (9143'),

See map M1

see MAP L6

126°; and the light-gray Crystal Range of Desolation Wilderness (9983' maximum), about 155°. Many lower summits and ridges, both near and far, are seen in every direction.

*   *   *   *

Back at the Sierra Buttes jeep trail junction, the PCT traverses ¼ mile over to a spring, then in about two minutes you pass another one, both lying just below the trail. About ½ mile farther you start a traverse northeast across a bowl that can be snowbound into early summer, and then

See map M1

you quickly arrive at a ridgecrest trail junction (7350–1.1). South, a trail soon curves southeast as it climbs almost one mile up to the 7910-foot junction mentioned in the side trip to Sierra Buttes Fire Lookout. North, the PCT traverses along the ridgecrest. Before describing it, we'll first mention a lake-blessed alternate route.

*   *   *   *

Alternate route: The PCT, unfortunately, too often has a "look but don't touch" character to it: you'll see a number of lakes, but they'll be too far away for easy access. This is unfortunate, in terms of both esthetics and campsites. Therefore you might consider this well-watered alternate route.

It begins as a steep trail that makes an initial jog southeast from the crest. Then it switchbacks and continues steeply ¼ mile north down to an old logging road that climbs northwest back to the PCT. Straight ahead, you now descend moderately on a closed jeep road, passing just west of and above upper Tamarack Lake. You'll spy a jeep road that leads over to it. Just past this spur, you come alongside lower Tamarack Lake, which has a very shallow west half, but a swimmable, fishable east half. Camping is discouraged due to the area's heavy use.

Just past the lower lake you reach a junction (6700–1.0), from which a closed jeep road heads over to the Sardine Lakes. Keep descending north on your closed jeep road, whose tread splits and then rejoins before passing an east-

ward, gated road only ¼ mile before you reach paved Forest Route 93. From here you could head 1½ miles up the road to Packer Lake Saddle and the PCT. Rather, follow it about 250 yards north down to the Packer Lake Picnic Area (6230–1.0). Here you'll find the entrance road to Packer Lake Lodge. The lodge serves good meals and PCT trekkers are welcome. After a refreshing swim in warm, fairly shallow Packer Lake, continue down Road 93 to Packsaddle Camping Area, on your right. Just 70 yards beyond it, you leave the road at the start of Deer Lake Trail 12E02 (6130–0.3).

The trail traverses northwest past four unequal-sized creeks that drain Packer Lake and the slopes north of it. Departing from the lush, streamside vegetation, you begin to climb upward, mount two well-graded switchbacks, and swing past a two-stage lateral moraine—an indication of two separate glacier advances. Your comfortable trail underfooting becomes rocky as you curve over to the first Grass Lake's outlet creek, and it remains so almost to the lateral to the second Grass Lake. The first Grass Lake turnoff is about ¼ mile up the trail from the outlet creek.

*   *   *   *

Side route: Where you encounter a ridge jutting 10–15 feet above the trail's west side, you can climb up it, and from it an easy, 100-yard, cross-country descent to the east shore will become immediately apparent. There are four

M

*Hwy. 49-
Hwy. 70*

See map M1

Sierra Buttes peeking through trees by shore of Deer Lake

Grass Lakes in this part of the Sierra, and this one is the smallest, diminished by invading grass. Two small flats provide adequate campsites. One is above the lake's east side, the other just southwest of its outlet creek.

* * * *

From the trailside ridge, you confront a steady, bush-lined ascent. Eventually your trail levels off at an open-forested flat (6830–1.5), on which you may see a sign to the second Grass Lake.

* * * *

Side route: If you wish to hike ¼ mile to it, start northeast, cross a seasonal creek in 30 yards, then follow a faint, ducked trail that crosses a gentle ridge and gradually descends its north slope to the willow-lined lake, which provides warm midsummer swimming. Larger and deeper than the first Grass Lake, this chest-deep, grass-bottomed lake also differs in that its water is not crystal clear. Should you decide to camp near this somewhat-hard-to-find lake, obtain fresh water from audible Sawmill Creek, which is 300 yards from the lake's north shore.

* * * *

Only 60 yards north of the Grass Lake route junction you can bear west-northwest across a small flat toward a conspicuous gully.

* * * *

Side route: From its bottom a rocky path, ducked and blazed, goes ½ mile northwest to Deer Lake. Small campsites can be found along the west, south and east shores, and diving and swimming are best on the east.

* * * *

Past the lateral you climb northeast briefly up to a low ridge, then veer northwest over a ford of Sawmill Creek just below its small pond. Continuing northwest, you quickly reach a saddle (7100-0.6) and a trail to Salmon Lake. A second trail to Deer Lake starts just before this junction. It is essentially a use trail that bears west-southwest, ending near the lake's northeast shore. Leaving the Salmon Lake Trail only 15 yards north of the saddle, your trail continues by first starting west up a shallow gully. The trail then climbs and descends a slab into a larger gully, follows it to its head, and bends southwest across a slope to a jeep road. Downslope, you can take it ¼ mile to Deer Lake, but you take it ¼ mile up to the PCT (7440–0.7–5.1).

* * * *

From the 7350-foot trail junction high above the Tamarack Lakes, the PCT traverses ⅓ mile along a ridgecrest, then trail tread ends at a rough road where it cuts southeast through the

See maps M1, M2

Mt. Elwell, Long Lake and Silver Lake

M

ridgecrest. This is the logging road mentioned early in the above alternate route. The road is now part of the permanent PCT route, and on it you wind northward down to a gap (7010–0.9), where you meet a good road, which curves west. You take it 0.2 mile north along the ridge up to paved Forest Service Road 93—also part of the permanent PCT—and you follow it down to a second ridge gap, Packer Lake Saddle (7020–0.6). Here you have a second chance to drop to Packer Lake.

Now back on PCT trail tread, you climb north along the ridge, staying just east of a crest road. Past a jeep road to the Wallis Mine, the trail curves northeast, switchbacks twice, and then climbs northwest to the edge of a clearcut. A two-minute walk north through it to a hemlock-adorned crest saddle saves you ¼ mile of walking. PCT purists head east to a point, are rewarded with excellent views, then head west to the crest saddle. The PCT stays immediately west of the crest for ¾ mile, then runs more or less along it, giving you views of alluring Deer Lake. After ⅓ mile you reach a jeep road (7430–2.6) that drops 300 feet in ⅓ mile to west-shore campsites. After the snow melts away in early or mid-July, you can expect to see 4WDs driving down to these sites.

Over the next ¼ mile the PCT crosses and recrosses an abandoned jeep road, then crosses a west-climbing jeep road, the one you'd be ascending if you had taken the alternate route past Packer, Grass and Deer lakes. Red firs at first obscure your views, but they soon reappear and are particularly good near Peak 7503, where you can see the Sierra Buttes, the Salmon Lakes and giant Gold Lake. Forest cover returns north of the peak, though you end your descent in a clearcut that extends down to Summit Lake road (7050–1.8). This road tops out at a jeep-road junction about 150 yards to the southeast. Small, shallow Summit Lake is immediately south of that junction, and camping space is plentiful in this vicinity.

North of the Summit Lake road the PCT parallels the jeep road, first at a distance, then alongside it. Near the north end of a fairly level ridge, a jeep road cuts northeast across the crest (7290–1.3), and you have two alternate route choices.

*   *   *   *

Alternate routes: First, you can head a few paces west to the jeep road you've been paralleling and take it 0.3 mile northwest down to Oakland Pond, which is like Summit Lake in water purity and camping potential. About 200 yards past the pond, where the road turns west, a trail climbs moderately north 0.3 mile back to the PCT. Second, one can follow the northeast-heading jeep road. The PCT route does this for a few yards before leaving it, but you can continue onward and drop to Round Lake. The road soon narrows to a trail and the route down to the lake isn't very obvious. Make sure you pass a nearby pond on its west side. Furthermore, 300 yards below the pond, be sure you curve northwest to a 5-foot deep gap rather than descend a gully northeast toward the broad saddle above Gold Lake. Camping is *not* allowed in Lakes Basin, but you might take a layover day, staying at Lakes Basin Campground, then later rejoining the PCT at a saddle in Section 11 (in the west part of Map M2).

*   *   *   *

The lakeless PCT route leaves the northeast-bound jeep road in a few paces, then climbs almost to Peak 7550, switchbacking needlessly several times just south of it. From the switchbacks you get excellent views of the western Sierra, particularly of the closer terrain that includes Snake Lake, Little Deer Lake and Oakland Pond. North of Peak 7550 you have views down into well-named Lakes Basin, which has been severely glaciated. ∎ *Glaciation in the entire Sierra Buttes-Lakes Basin area was quite extensive. From the Sierra Buttes, glaciers descended first northeast to the North Yuba River canyon, and then down it to the 4300-foot level, just east of Sierra City. From the Lakes Basin and the canyons both east and west of it, glaciers extended north down to Mohawk Valley (4400') and may have dammed the upstream part of the Middle Fork Feather River, which may have led to the creation of a 200-square-mile lake.* ∎

∎ *Steep slopes of granitelike rock prevent you from dropping into the sparkling Lakes Basin. The bedrock here, as along most of your section's hike so far, is metamorphosed volcanic rocks that were erupted perhaps 300–400 million years ago, roughly 100 times earlier than the eruptions of the volcanic rocks you traversed in the previous chapter's hike.* ∎ At a

M

Hwy. 49–
Hwy. 70

See maps M1, M2

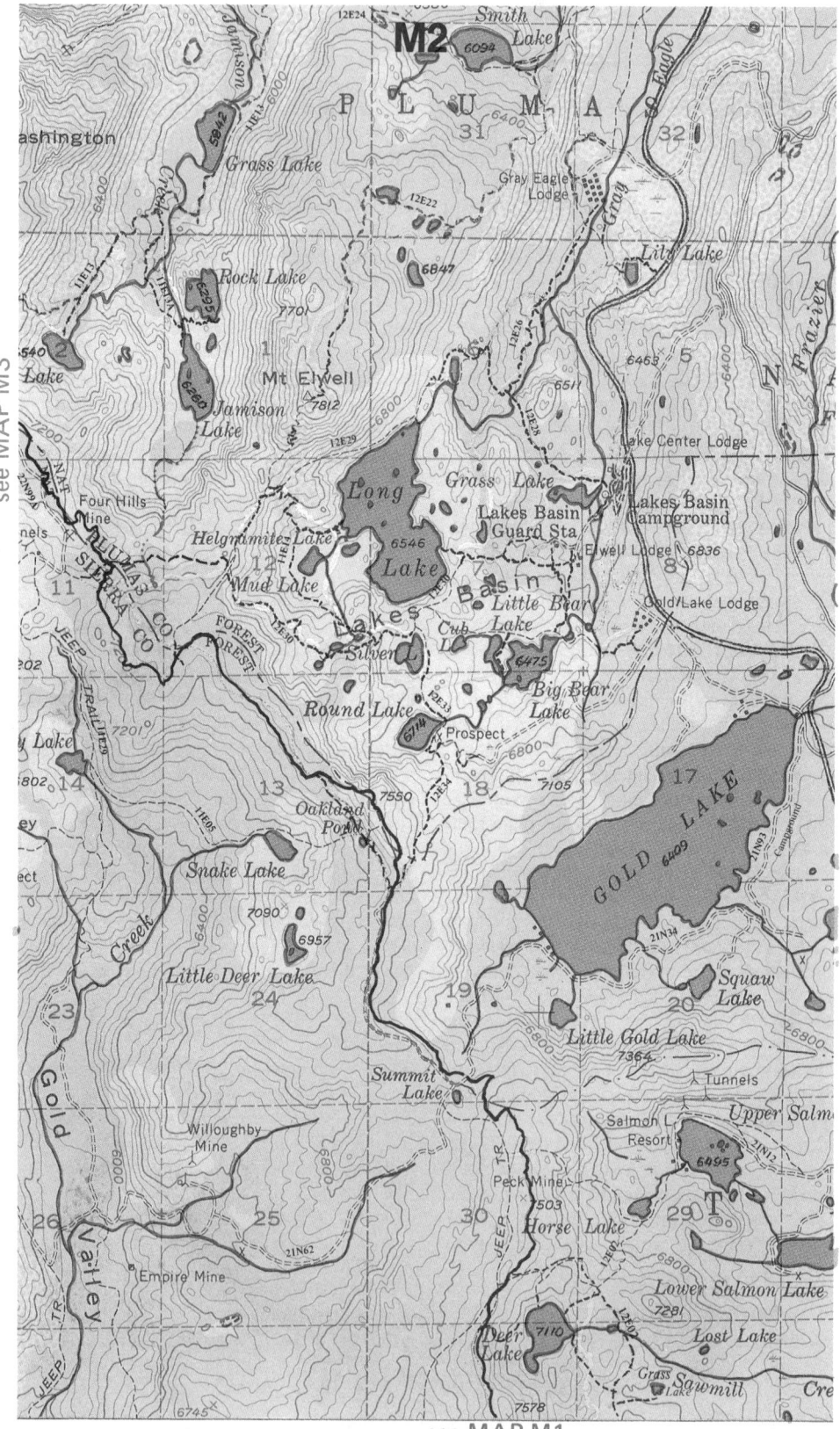

see MAP M3

nearby saddle, your views of the Lakes Basin disappear, and you drop back into forest cover and reach a junction (7355–0.9). Had you taken the Oakland Pond route, you'd be climbing northwest to meet the PCT here.

The PCT heads briefly west to a ridge that provides views to the south and west, then enters viewless forest for a traverse almost a mile long. Next, it curves southwest through a shady forest growing on a flat, ill-defined crest that can harbor snow patches into July. Momentarily you cross a jeep road that heads north to a ridge above the west edge of Lakes Basin. The PCT curves south to a ridge, then curves west to an excellent viewpoint above Hawley Lake. You re-enter forest again and descend ⅔ mile to a jeep-road crossing at a county-line crest saddle (7050–2.3). Those who made excursions through Lakes Basin rejoin you here. Immediately west of the saddle is a diminutive pond that nevertheless has enough staying power to hold water through most, if not all, of the summer. You could camp here, but get water at a spring-fed creek, reached by following the jeep road about 200 yards east.

The trail briefly parallels the road west, then swings north, taking a tortuous course that has to be hiked to be believed. (More such diversions lie ahead between here and the Middle Fork Feather River.) Twice you almost touch the jeep road, only to veer away, but you finally cross it (7330–1.3) near a high point on the Sierra crest. A moderate descent, just over ⅓ mile, brings you back to the road, and then you leave it for an increasingly easy descent across open slopes that provide views of Spencer Lakes, too far below the trail to be of any use to you. After heading west for a spell, your trail hits an old jeep road that descends to the lakes. You, however, contour northwest ¼ mile along it, leave it, and then parallel it through forest down to a saddle (6630–1.8), where you almost touch the jeep road. You then curve around the south and west slopes of Peak 6822 down to a second saddle, the A Tree (6550–0.5), a focal point for five roads. By starting southwest down a jeep road, you should quickly find a spring, the first *fresh* trailside water since the two springs on the west flank of the Sierra Buttes, about 19¼ miles back.

*　　*　　*　　*

Resupply access: Here is your last chance for a while for a rather short exit to "civilization." You can take the main road, 22N99, first north and then northwest 2.3 miles out to a junction with the Johnsville-Gibsonville Road. Just before this junction is a popular car-camping area centered on Jamison Creek. Emergency aid can be obtained at bustling Plumas Eureka State Park, about 5 miles east down the road.

*　　*　　*　　*

∎ *The stretch of PCT northward to the Johnsville-Gibsonville Road was the last part of California PCT north of southern California to be completed—in September 1985—although there have been some reroutings since then, especially in Hat Creek Valley.* ∎ From the A Tree saddle the PCT at first parallels the Cowell Mine road west, but soon diverges from it to rise to a saddle (6920–1.1). Just beyond it you have some brushy terrain, which gives you open views southeast to the Sierra Buttes, to the right of the much closer Spencer Lakes. To the south lies Lavezzola Creek canyon, largely ravaged of its forest cloak. ∎ *Ahead, the trail should have contoured across Gibralter's relatively gentle south-facing slopes. Indeed, most of the stretch from the Johnsville-Gibsonville Road southeast to the A Tree had been built, only to be aborted by the refusal of right-of-way by a local landowner with property east of the Cowell Mine.* ∎

A less practical new route had to be built, and you could find it quite snowbound before early July. This route starts out uneventfully enough by climbing moderately to the county-line crest, proceeding west up it to a jeep road, and then paralleling it 280 yards northwest over to a saddle (7380–0.8) at the south end of McRae Ridge. Now the "fun" begins. Leaving the road, you descend southwest across steep slopes to a switchback, from where you have a superb view of Gibralter's foreboding, pock-marked face. Several more switchbacks lead you down to the base of a towering trailside pinnacle, from which you make a gentle descent south toward Gibralter's massive face—a cliff composed of layer upon layer of volcanic mudflows. You turn west and skirt just below this cliff, crossing several gullies, none of them with a reliable creek. From a switchback the aborted PCT segment once began a climb south-southeast to a county-line saddle.

Your route next descends to gentler slopes, and you cross one usually flowing creeklet just

See maps M2, M3

M4

PLUMAS CO.
SIERRA CO.

BM 6065

Blue Nose Mtn

Blue Nose Ridge

Blue Nose Rav.

Black Diamond Ridge

East Br

Staffords Mtn

Mt. Etna

Bunker Hill Cr

Plumas Co.
Sierra Co.

Ridge

Sawmill Ridge

Bunker Hill

Bunker Hill Mine

Hopkins

Turkeytown Diggings

Beartrap Mtn

North Fork

East Fork

South Fork

Gibralter Mine

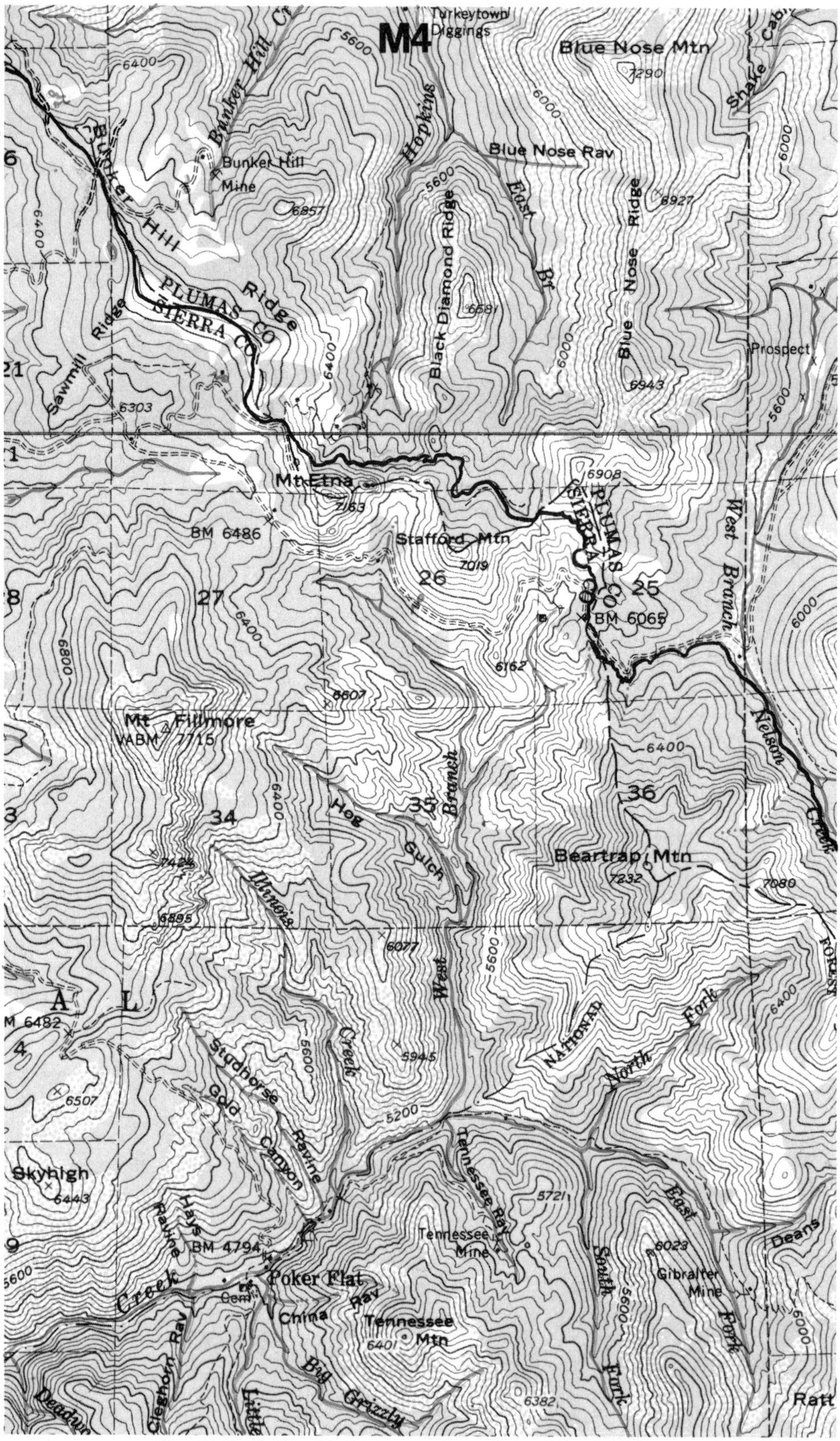

Tennessee Rav.

Tennessee Mine

Tennessee Mtn

Big Grizzly

Little Grizzly

Poker Flat

China Rav.

Deadwood

Gleehorn Rav.

Skylign

West Branch

Branch

West

Hog Gulch

Illinois

Creek

Studhorse Canyon

Gold Ravine

Hays Ravine

Mt. Fillmore
BM 7715

BM 6486

Nelson Creek

FOREST

BM 6482

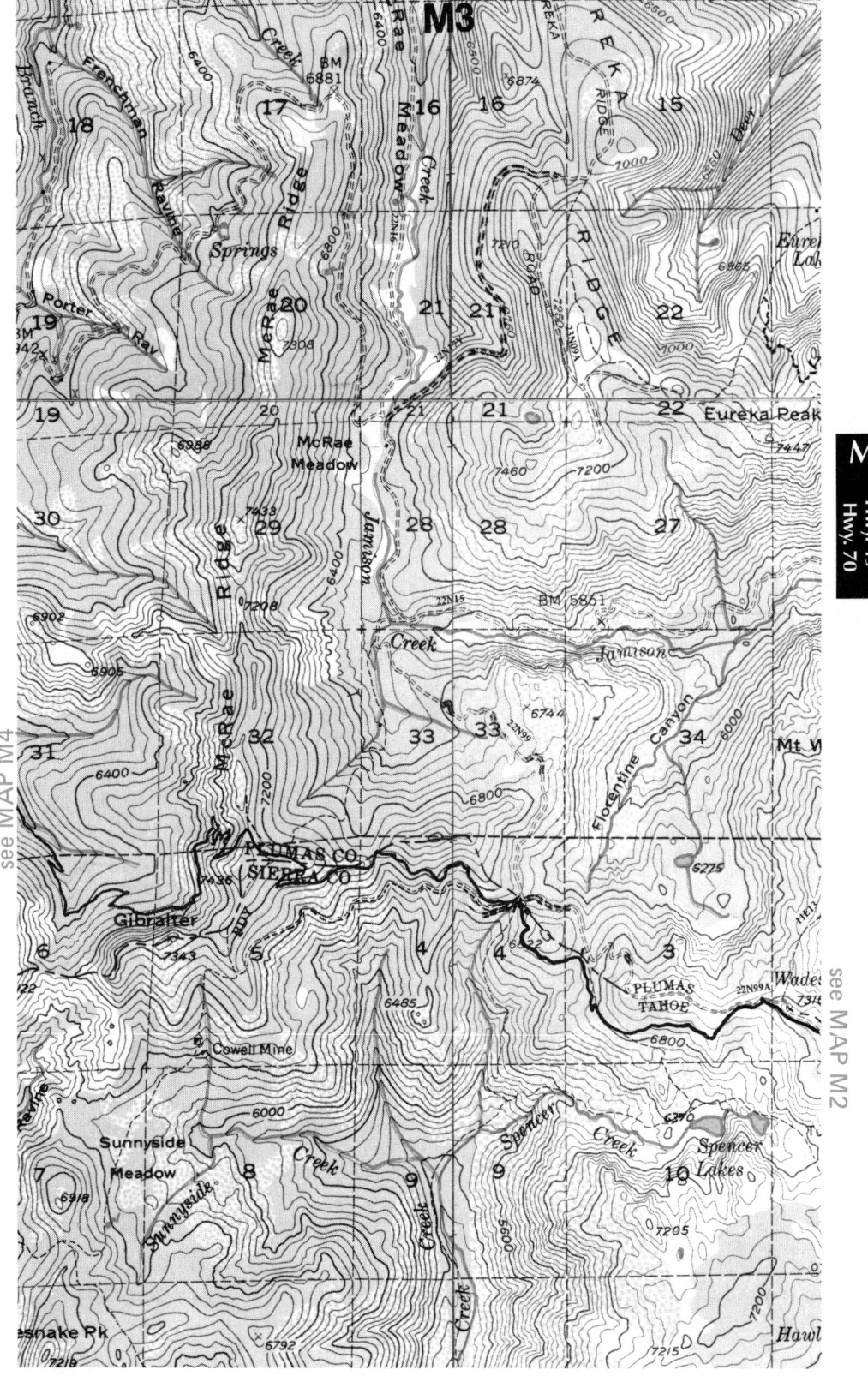

see MAP M4

see MAP M2

a few minutes before reaching a gully in which your route turns northward. Soon you make a short switchback and almost touch the headwaters of West Branch Nelson Creek. You then turn northward and descend 300 yards to a spot (6150–3.2) from which you can meander a few yards northeast to the first possible campsite in some time. From this spot, about 100 yards north of Section 31's south edge, you follow the creek down-canyon, always keeping well above it, due to the rather steep-sided gorge the creek has cut. From about the middle of Section 31 onward for ⅓ mile, you'll be able to reach any of about a half-dozen campsites by scrambling down to the creekside. You'll see a road paralleling the creek's far side, and at the road's upper end (near the east edge of Map M4) there is a fine campsite with lots of level spots. In the past, it has been complete with table and shelves.

You barely enter Section 30, and where you leave it (5790-1.3), you also leave West Branch Nelson Creek. Be sure you have plenty of water, for after midsummer the route ahead will usually be waterless for 24 miles, until just before Middle Fork Feather River. However, there are places along the way where you can find water by detouring ½ mile or less. Beyond Section 30 your descent ends, and soon you traverse west in and out of gullies, then make a moderate climb from the last one up to a crossing of the Johnsville-Gibsonville Road (6065–1.2) at a minor county-line saddle.

Mt. Etna is about 1¼ miles away, but you'll take twice that distance to reach it, for you're faced with another intricate trail route. Weaving in and out of gullies and microgullies, the trail takes almost a mile to reach a saddle that is barely ½ mile away from the previous one. Skirting the back side of Stafford Mountain, you have pleasant views even though part of the area has been logged. After nearly one more mile you crest another saddle, which is just over ½ air mile from the previous one. You pass gully after gully as you traverse west beneath the crest, and some of them provide snowmelt water through early July. On your traverse you skirt below volcanic pinnacles and then, below Mt. Etna proper, beneath volcanic cliffs.

■ *Mt. Etna and Stafford Mountain appear to be two resistant plugs that were once part of a large volcano. Much of the layers of volcanic rocks you see in this vicinity probably came*

from this source. You won't pass any more sizeable volcanoes, active or extinct, until the Lassen Park area. ■

You finally gain the Sierra crest and cross a jeep road at the south end of Bunker Hill Ridge (6750–3.0). The route ahead is now direct, and once atop Bunker Hill Ridge proper you can enjoy leisurely walking and panoramic views (see title-page spread). Pilot Peak, Blue Nose Mountain, Stafford Mountain and Mts. Etna and Fillmore are readily identified. As your crest route descends into a red-fir forest, you view a small, unnamed lake on a bench just below and west of the trail (6810–1.5), and the bench has adequate camping. On a saddle just over ⅓ mile north of the lake you cross two intersecting roads, then you contour an equal distance to a second saddle (6700-0.7). If you start north on a road crossing this saddle, you should locate, in a minute or two, seasonal springs just below you.

Rather than head directly over to Pilot Peak, the trail soon veers left off the crest, traverses needlessly west to the north end of Gibsonville Ridge, and then heads back to the crest proper. The Pilot Peak Fire Lookout provides far-ranging views, but since the jeep road to its summit is on the other side of the mountain, you just angle northwest and descend its lower, forested slopes to a road (6680-1.9), which you come to immediately before a crest saddle.

*　　　*　　　*　　　*

Water access: If you are low on water, then you should take a 1¼-mile alternate route. Head southwest down the road to the Quincy-LaPorte Road, follow it 100 yards east to the headwaters of the South Fork Feather River, backtrack to the junction, and continue ¼ mile past it to a PCT saddle.

*　　　*　　　*　　　*

Those with an adequate supply of water stay on the PCT, descending it to a trailhead, then heading 0.1 mile west on a level spur road out to the aforementioned saddle (6474–1.0).

*　　　*　　　*　　　*

Resupply access: The Quincy-LaPorte Road, crossing the saddle, heads north to Quincy, a

See maps M3, M4, M5

long day's walk away, should you have to get out. However, you could probably hitchhike out. To the south, the road goes 11½ miles to LaPorte, a hamlet with minimal supplies and a post office. It is too far away to be a practical supply access.

*   *   *   *

From the Quincy-LaPorte Road westward down toward the Middle Fork Feather River, you may encounter ongoing logging or evidence of recent logging, and the associated roads. Leaving the saddle, you head southwest 0.1 mile on paved Kenzie Ravine Road 22N60, then branch right, back onto trail again. In a minute you hit the Fowler Peak Trail, a closed, crest-running jeep road that you'll follow most of the way to Fowler Peak. On this jeep road you cross Road 22N60 at a saddle (6510–0.9), then ½ mile past it, you drop northwest off the crest on a mile of trail tread. In a logged-over area near the bottom of your descent, you regain the jeep road and follow it almost ½ mile west down to a recrossing of Road 22N60 at another saddle (5900–1.9).

Your Fowler Peak Trail climbs ⅓ mile almost to a volcanic crest summit (6045'), traverses over to a second one (5948'), then drops to a saddle crossed by Bear Wallow Trail, a jeep road (5755-1.4). You should be able to find water by dropping about ½ mile south along it. The Fowler Peak Trail continues southwest along the crest, and a fragment of PCT tread parallels this jeep road's north side, crossing the road just as it starts a short, steep climb. Your path takes an easier, albeit longer, route, looping around summit 6031 before rejoining the jeep road immediately west of the summit. Eastbound hikers may miss this brushy junction and continue along the jeep road, which is fine. Views of distant Lassen Peak and of massive, not so distant clearcuts reappear, as they have in many places along your westward traverse. After about a ¼-mile descent, you reach Chimney Rock (6000–1.0), at a bend in the road. PCT tread branches left a few paces before this bend, only to end at the road where its gradient slackens. ∎ *Steep-sided, blocky, easily climbed Chimney Rock is a remnant of a lava flow that once rumbled down a valley floor. Today it sits atop a ridge, an example of reversed topography. Ancient streams cut along*

Chimney Rock

the sides of the resistant flow, and in several million years cut through loose volcanic sediments to resurrect the buried Onion Valley canyon to the north and the buried South Fork canyon to the south. ∎

From where the PCT rejoins the Fowler Peak Trail below Chimney Rock, you have an easing ⅓-mile descent to a saddle. From it you can head ¼ mile south, down to the headwaters of Black Rock Creek, for water. On the jeep road you climb for a minute or two to a crest high point, then have a pleasant, occasionally shaded one-mile descent to the base of a minor ridge point. The road angles northwest over the point while the PCT tread branches south and goes ⅓ mile, mostly through forest, down to a recrossing of the jeep road immediately east of an important saddle (5460–2.1). From here Black Rock Creek Road 22N56 descends south, and about ¼ mile down it you should be able to find water. A major logging road contours west, giving rise to a newer Black Rock Creek Road in about a mile. Both of these descending roads take you close to a north arm of Little Grass Valley Reservoir. Head along its west shore if you have to go out for aid. The PCT heads northwest across the saddle and briefly goes along the Butte Bar Trail, an old jeep road now closed to motor vehicles. This it leaves at the northeast base of Fowler Peak, and you have a relaxing, increasingly shaded descent west.

See maps M5, M6

see MAP M7

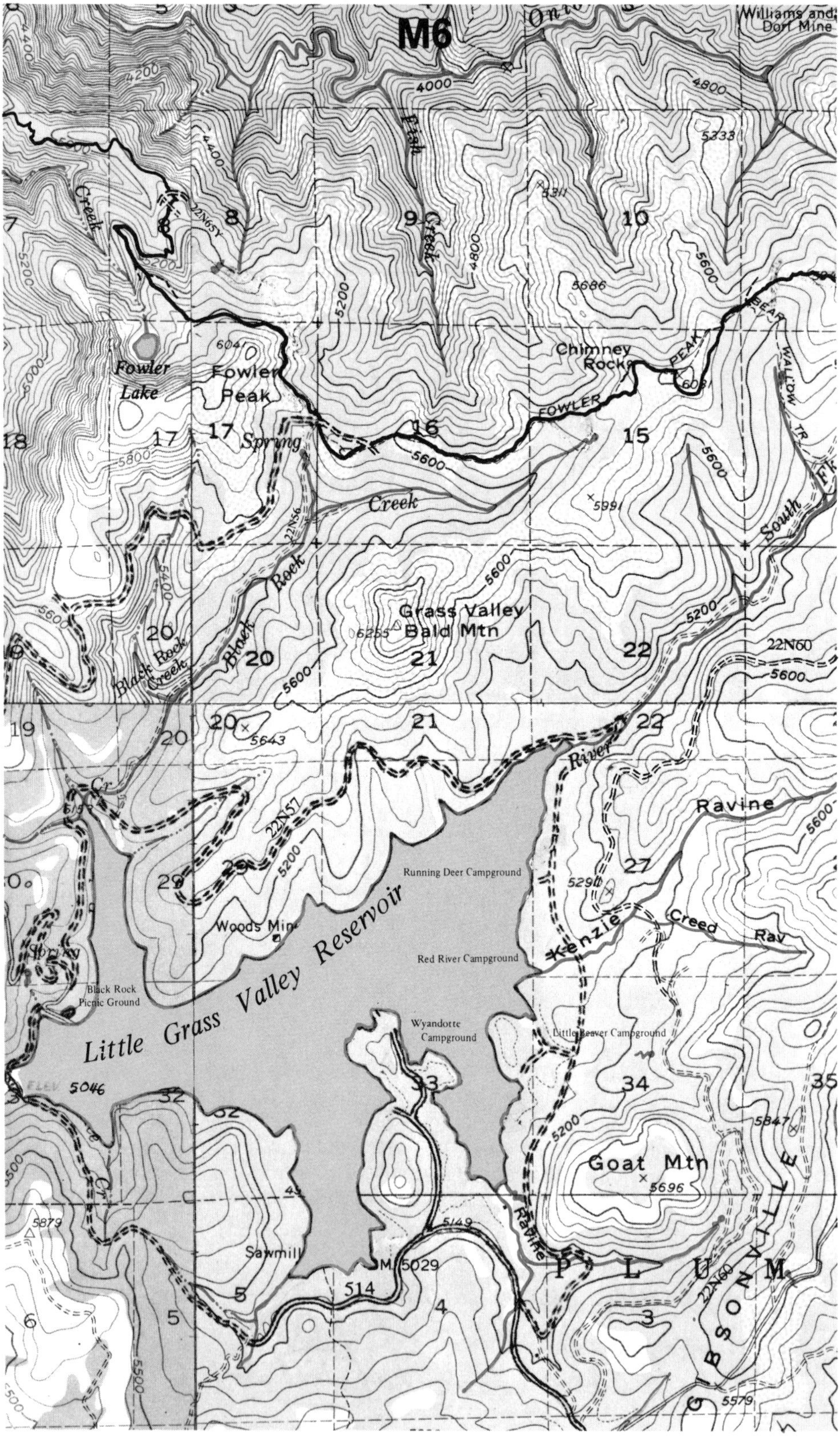

see MAP M5

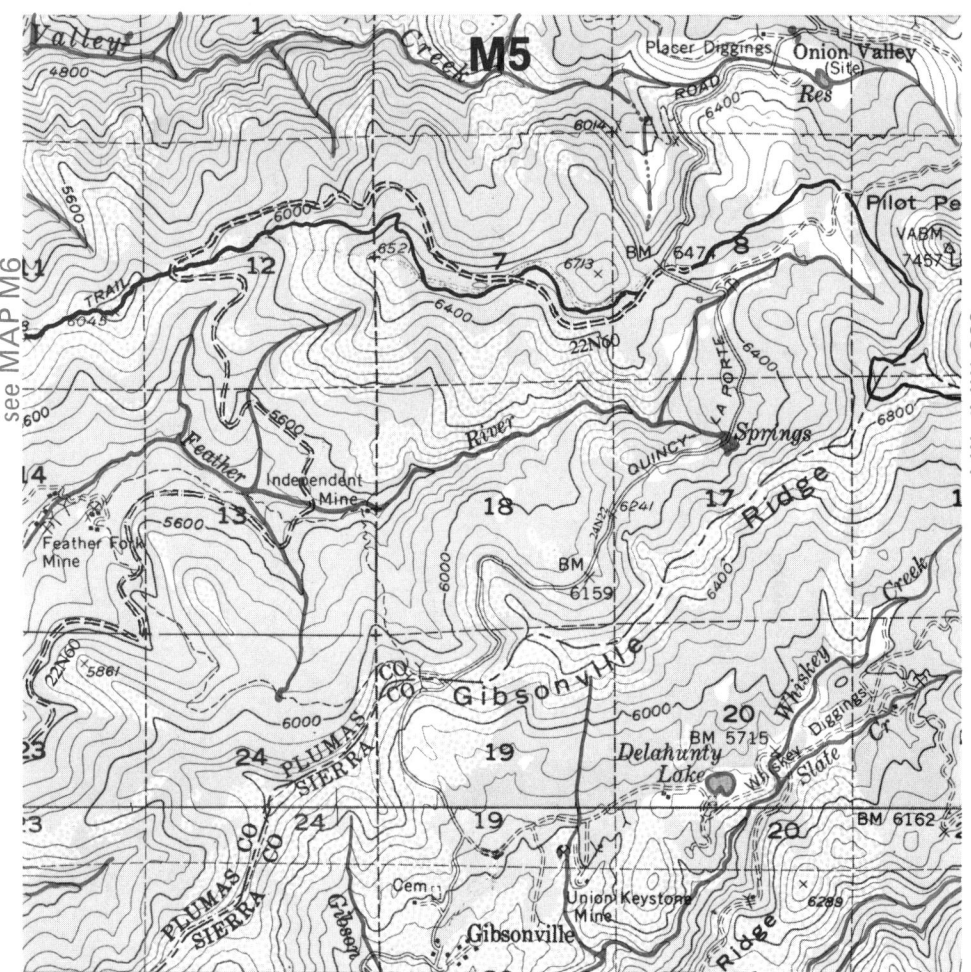

see MAP M6

see MAP M4

*   *   *   *

Alternate route: From where the trail bends northwest in dense forest to descend along the east side of a minor ridge, you can leave the trail (5500–1.2) and head ¼ mile down to Fowler Lake, crossing a second ridge halfway to it. Shallow and adorned with water lilies, it nevertheless offers the best campsites between the earlier nameless lake and the Middle Fork Feather River, 7½ miles ahead. To rejoin the PCT, follow the lake's outlet creek down to a road and hike north briefly down it to a ridge junction with another road, the PCT route.

*   *   *   *

If you don't visit Fowler Lake, you descend northwest along the minor ridge. ∎ *This happens to be a glacial moraine, and within the last 200,000 years, perhaps several glaciers developed in the cirque containing the lake. The youngest barely flowed past the lake, an older one advanced ¼ mile beyond it, and yet another one (or perhaps an earlier stage of the older one) advanced almost a mile past the lake. What is remarkable about these glaciers is that they originated in a cirque whose headwall was below 6000 feet in elevation.* ∎

The trail's tread ends about ¼ mile down the glacial moraine, and then you make a fairly steep descent about 150 yards northwest along a narrow, abandoned road to a crest junction

See map M6

see MAP M8

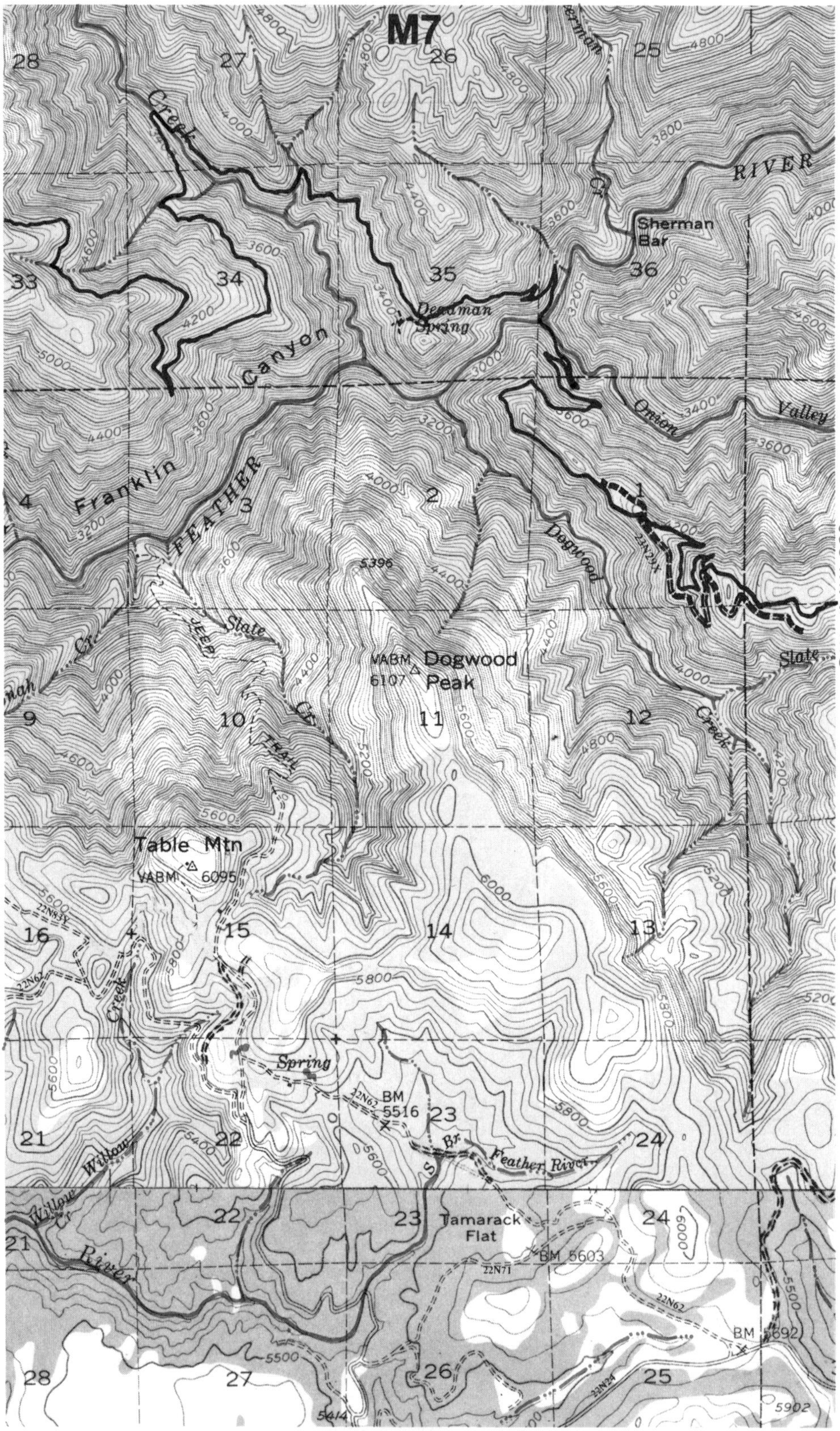

see MAP M6

Hwy. 49–
Hwy. 70

M

28   27   26   25

33   34   35   36

Sherman
Bar

RIVER

Creek

Deadman
Spring

Onion   Valley

4   3   2   1

Franklin

FEATHER

Canyon

Dogwood

Slate

5396

WABM   Dogwood
6107   Peak

Slate

9   10   11   12

Creek

Jeep

Trail

Table Mtn
VABM   6095

16   15   14   13

Creek

Spring

Willow   22   23   24

12N63
BM
5516

S   Br   Feather River

21

Willow   Cr

River

21   22   23   24

Tamarack
Flat

BM 5603

22N71

22N62

BM 5592

28   27   26   25

5414   5902

with a second road (5280–0.3). Slate Creek usually flows through most of July, and you can reach this lake-fed creek by heading a bit south up the road to it.

From the junction you continue on a lesser gradient down the closed road, leaving it in 0.2 mile for an unnecessarily long traverse east. On a major crest, which you'll be descending to the Feather River, you cross broad Sawmill Tom Creek Road 23N65Y (5060–1.0), then make an uneventful 0.4-mile traverse along the northwest side of the crest. The crest bends west and, being logged, is not a beautiful sight. Therefore the trail runs immediately below and south of the crest, crossing an incredible array of gullies that drive PCT *mappers* crazy. You only have to *hike* along this convoluted route, though you could take the road you see below you. You almost touch the road at a saddle (4910–1.8), then almost touch it again ¼ mile later. After switchbacking down the ridge, you finally cross this road, known as Dogwood Creek Road, Butte Road and Road 23N29X (4240-1.6). Here the road crosses to the northeast side of the ridge while the PCT crosses to its southwest side, thereby avoiding—temporarily—an unsightly logged-over area.

After a mile of easy descent northwest, your trail abruptly bends east and you can gaze down at the churning Middle Fork Feather River, about 850 feet below you. Only ½ mile to the northwest lies Deadman Spring saddle; the trail

will take 3.0 miles to reach it. Shortly, your trail bends again and you descend southeast along the lower part of a ravaged, clearcut area. You then switchback three times under forest cover, the last time at a delicious spring (3180-2.3). Southbound hikers should tank up here, for their climb out of the canyon is waterless and summer afternoon temperatures can soar into the 90s. Northbound hikers draw even closer to the tempting waters of Onion Valley Creek. Among Douglas-firs, maples and dogwoods that line it, you'll find a lovely campsite. The long descent ends near Middle Fork Feather River (2900–0.4), which you cross via a massive arch bridge, the largest equestrian bridge on the entire PCT.

❚ *Down in the lower part of the river canyon, you are in the Middle Fork's National Wild and Scenic River Area. It lives up to its designation. Immediately beyond the bridge is one of the river's many fantastic pools, and a small outcrop of water-polished granite provides smooth, warm slabs for sunbathing. Metamorphosed, Paleozoic-age marine sediments prevail elsewhere throughout this part of the river gorge. From late July through mid-August, when summer temperatures are at their maximum, the pool warms to 70°F or more by midafternoon. In early or late summer or early in the morning, the temperature can be 60°F or less. To reach this pool, leave the PCT just before it climbs up to the bridge.* ❚

See maps M6, M7

Middle Fork Feather River bridge

Campsites abound along the river's north bank, but the river's slightly cloudy water makes these sites less attractive than the one on Onion Valley Creek. The well-graded trail climbs up-canyon past the sites, then switchbacks for a climb west to Deadman Spring saddle (3590–1.4). The spring is unreliable and furthermore is on private, sometimes-patrolled land. Onward, you contour along the forested east wall of Bear Creek canyon, swatting flies that are so prevalent below 4000 feet in elevation. You cross a refreshing tributary in a deep gully, then continue over to Bear Creek (3240–2.1), which you cross on a large steel bridge. Look for a camp about 1/8 mile northwest of this bridge.

You now confront a 2700-foot, 7-mile climb to Lookout Rock. Fortunately, the trail is well-graded and generally well-shaded, and there's water along the route. The trail heads briefly up-canyon, then climbs about ½ mile south to a permanent creek before heading southeast to a prominent east ridge. From it you climb southwest to a switchback on another ridge (4250–2.5), and leave behind most of the river views, poison oak and fly-harboring live oaks. Conifers prevail by the time you recross the east ridge, and you're shaded by Douglas-firs, ponderosa pines and sugar pines. You climb west, cross a large, often-dry gully, round a smaller ridge, and in ½ mile arrive at a seasonal spring (5350–2.3), flowing among dogwoods, alders and moss. In normal-rainfall years, you can count on it through early or mid-August. If you don't mind dry camping, you can fill up here and then, about 0.9 mile later, set up camp on a broad, white-fir forested ridgecrest that the trail almost tops.

An outcrop of granitic rock now lies just below you as you climb northwest across dusty volcanic rock to a sunny crest saddle (5750–1.4). Bending north, you continue upward and in ⅓ mile meet a willow-lined spring with staying power through midsummer. Southbound hikers can get water here and dry-camp on the sunny saddle. Treading the contact between volcanic rocks above and granitic ones below, the trail climbs ⅓ mile to Lookout Rock (5955–0.6), a resistant outcrop of tonalite. For southbound hikers, it provides the first good views of your descent ahead. For northbound hikers, it shows you Spanish Peak, the eastern

point of a flat-topped highland rising northeast above unseen Bucks Lake. A small flat in this vicinity makes an adequate dry camp.

Leaving Lookout Rock, the route descends to a nearby crest gap, goes about ¼ mile north on the Lookout Rock jeep road, and then parallels its east side down to a saddle crossed by Road 23N19 (5870–0.7). Northbound, this road drops 1¾ miles to Road 33N56. Keeping just northeast of the crest, you parallel old, crest-hugging Road 23N74Y northwest, and after you descend to a saddle, you quickly arrive at a road branching north (5880–1.3). This shortcut road switchbacks 0.7 mile down to the PCT and paved Road 33N56, but your tread takes a much longer route, heading northwest for tempting views of Bucks Lake before circling east for a forested descent to Road 33N56 (5505–1.6). You should get water at either of two near-road, spring-fed creeklets, the eastern one located where the trail crosses the road. By the road's north shoulder you'll find a 40-foot wide pond, fed by the creeklet. You can camp nearby.

*   *   *   *

Alternate route: Many hikers prefer to head west down to Bucks Lake either for supplies or for a lazy day at the lake. Should you wish to take this 6.8-mile alternate route, first walk west along paved Big Creek Road. After 2.5 miles you meet the Bucks Lake Road, also paved, and head 0.2 mile north to Haskins Valley Campground, operated by Pacific Gas and Electric. The utility company uses Bucks Lake water to power one of their generating plants on North Fork Feather River, about 2000 feet below you. By late summer they've released quite a bit of water from Bucks Lake, and then it loses its attractiveness.

Just 0.3 mile up the road past the campground you reach Bucks Lake Lodge, which has a market, restaurant, RV campground, cabins and marina. Bend northeast along the lake 0.7 mile to Lakeshore Resort, which has the same facilities. Continue east past private summer cabins, and perhaps drop to the lake's east tip for a swim. In 1.0 mile from the resort you bridge Bucks Creek, then amble 0.5 mile over to Whitehorse Campground's entrance. Since this USFS Campground is your last source of reli-

See maps M7, M8, M9

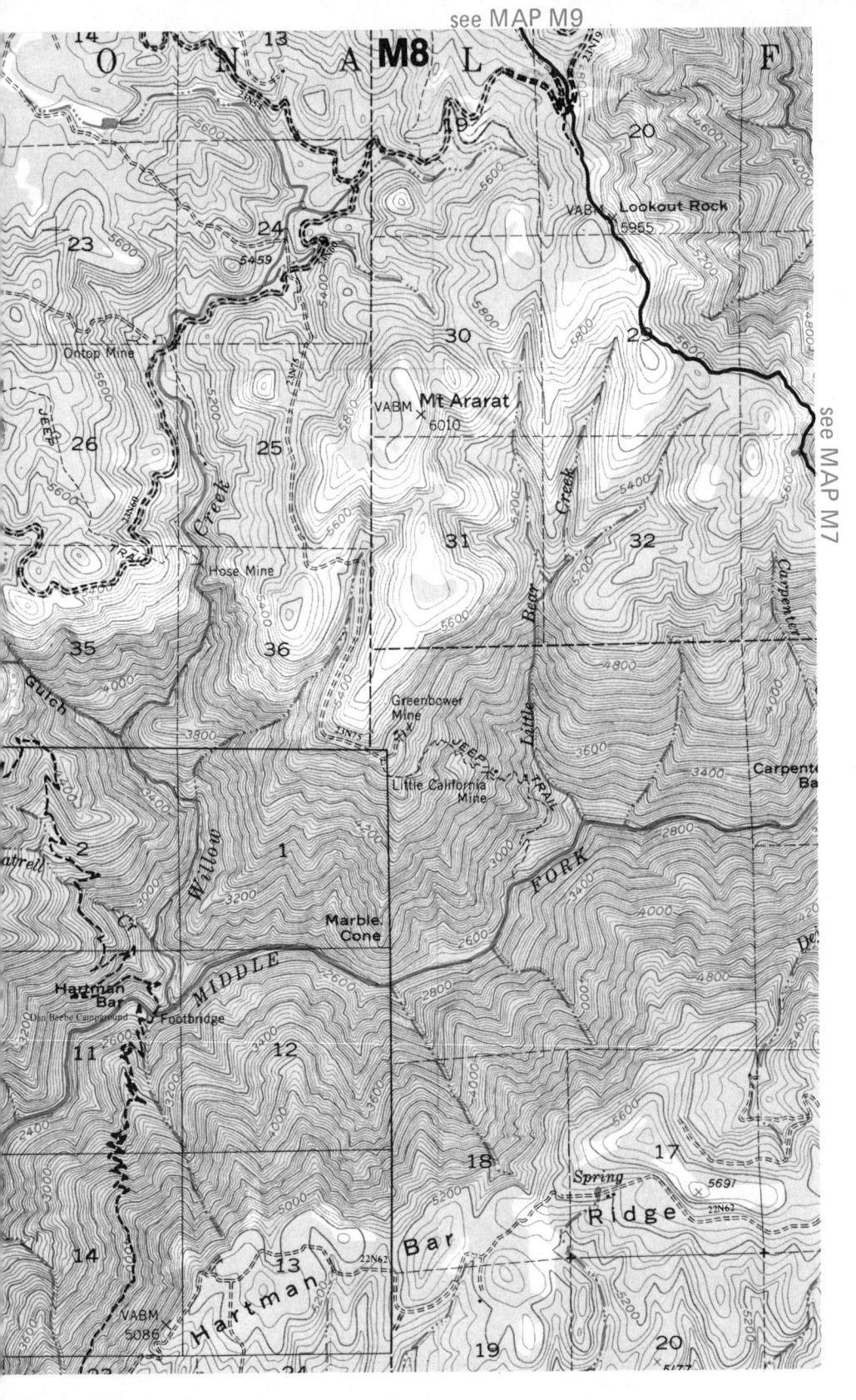

see MAP M7

M8

O N A L F

14   13   19   20

23   24   Lookout Rock
VABM
5955

Ontop Mine   30   29

VABM Mt Ararat
6010

26   25   31   32

Creek   Bear Creek   Carpenter

Hose Mine   Carpenter

35   36   Greenbower
Mine
Little California
Mine   FORK   Carpenter
Bar

Gulch   JEEP TRAIL

2   1   Marble
Cone
MIDDLE

Hartman
Bar   Footbridge

11   12   18   17
Spring   5691
22N62

Ridge

14   13   22N62   Bar   19   20

VABM
5086   Hartman

Aspens along east shore of Bucks Lake

see MAP M10

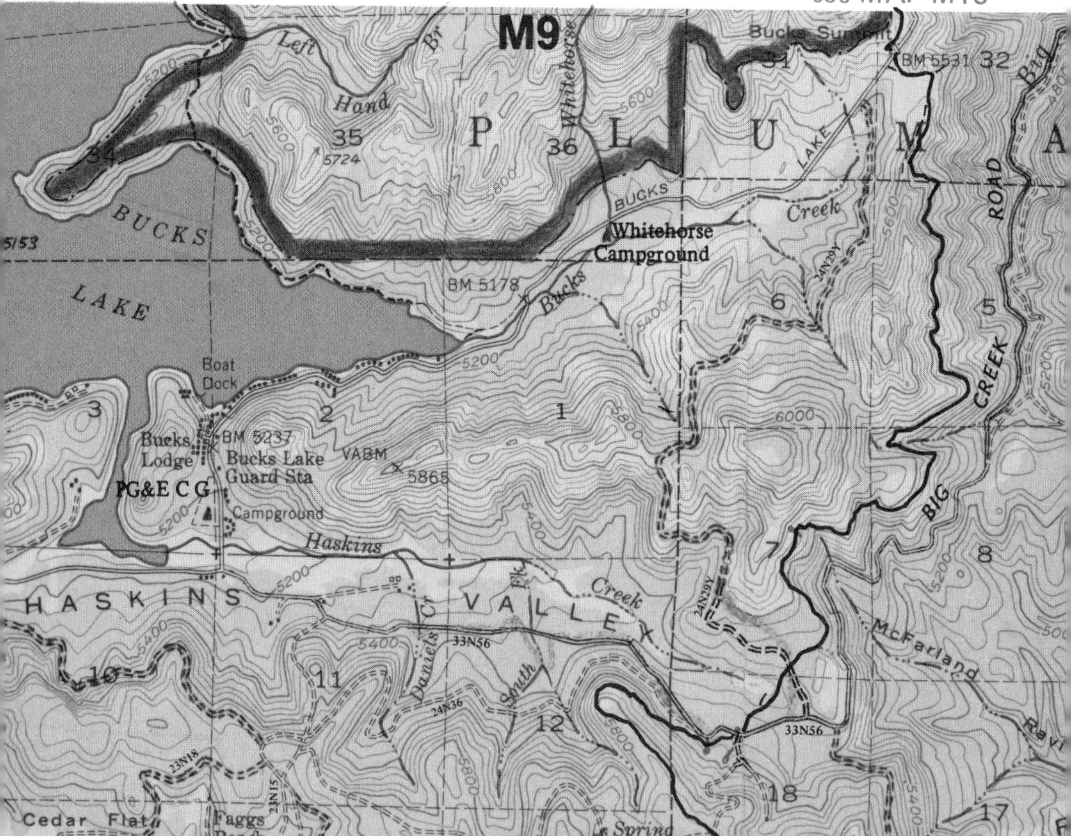

see MAP M8

able water until Clear Creek, 11.6 miles away, you ought to spend the night here or at least tank up. To regain the PCT, hike 1.6 miles up Bucks Lake Road to Bucks Summit.

*   *   *   *

If you're in a hurry, be aware that the PCT route from Big Creek Road north to Bucks Summit is 2.0 miles shorter than the supply route. A few paces east of the 40-foot pond, you'll hit the bottom end of the shortcut road, mentioned earlier. From this junction, you descend 200 yards northeast on a closed road toward a meadow, then fork right on trail tread. This path skirts around the meadow's east end, staying just within the forest. In ¼ mile it slants across Road 24N29Y, the old temporary PCT route before this section of trail was completed. The road ends at Bucks Lake Road only 0.2 mile southwest of Bucks Summit, and the temporary route may be a better route than the trail when there's lots of snow.

Just beyond the road the path curves east to a creeklet, crosses it, then climbs about ½ mile north to several seasonal springs. About ⅓ mile farther, in a gully past a definable ridge, you have two more springs, then ¾ mile farther, after you jog west down into a deep gully, you reach your final water supply, a creeklet (5520–2.4). Midway between Haskins Valley and Bucks Lake roads, you now face 12.4 miles to Clear Creek, your next reliable source. The mile-high trail contours northward in and out of gullies,

eventually merges with an old logging road, and follows it 200 yards north down a ridge before turning sharply west. You stay on this old road as it traverses a rejuvenating logged-out flat, then fork right for a 150-yard climb northwest to Bucks Summit (5531–2.4), which presents you with a good view to the east.

Across Bucks Lake Road you start up the closed Spanish Peak road and enter Bucks Lake Wilderness. This narrow, rutted road switchbacks up slopes covered with shallow, granitic soils. ▮ *Once forested, these slopes were logged over before 1950, and for three decades they supported a thick, mature mantle of chaparral. Jeffrey pines are finally establishing themselves, and perhaps by the turn of the century there will be sufficient shade along this once shadeless route.* ▮ It's still a good idea to ascend this moderately graded climb quite early in the morning. Switchbacking upward, you twice cross the often-flowing headwaters of Bucks Creek, then climb to another switchback, from where you get a view northeast down into Meadow Valley, a once rural setting that is increasingly becoming a retirement community— sort of a western extension of Quincy. From it your western route jogs north after ½ mile, enters the forest's fringe, keeps right at a fork, and soon arrives at a path (6550–2.6) on a shady flat where the road turns sharply counterclockwise from northwest to south, and you take the path.

The path begins by skirting along the base of the north-trending volcanic ridge, staying just

See maps M9, M10

Lassen Peak, from Spanish Peak environs

27

26

25

30

Fales

Creek

Creek

JEEP

31

5471

34

35

Creek

6

BM
6667

3

2

VABM
6924

Mt Pleasant

Silver Lake

7

10
6341

6750

11

BUCKS

18
Gold Lake

15

14

VABM
6850

JEEP

13

TRAIL

Lookout

Spanish Pk

19

LAKE

Mill

22

23

24

30

WILDERNESS

27

26

25

VABM
6637

VABM
6412

Spring

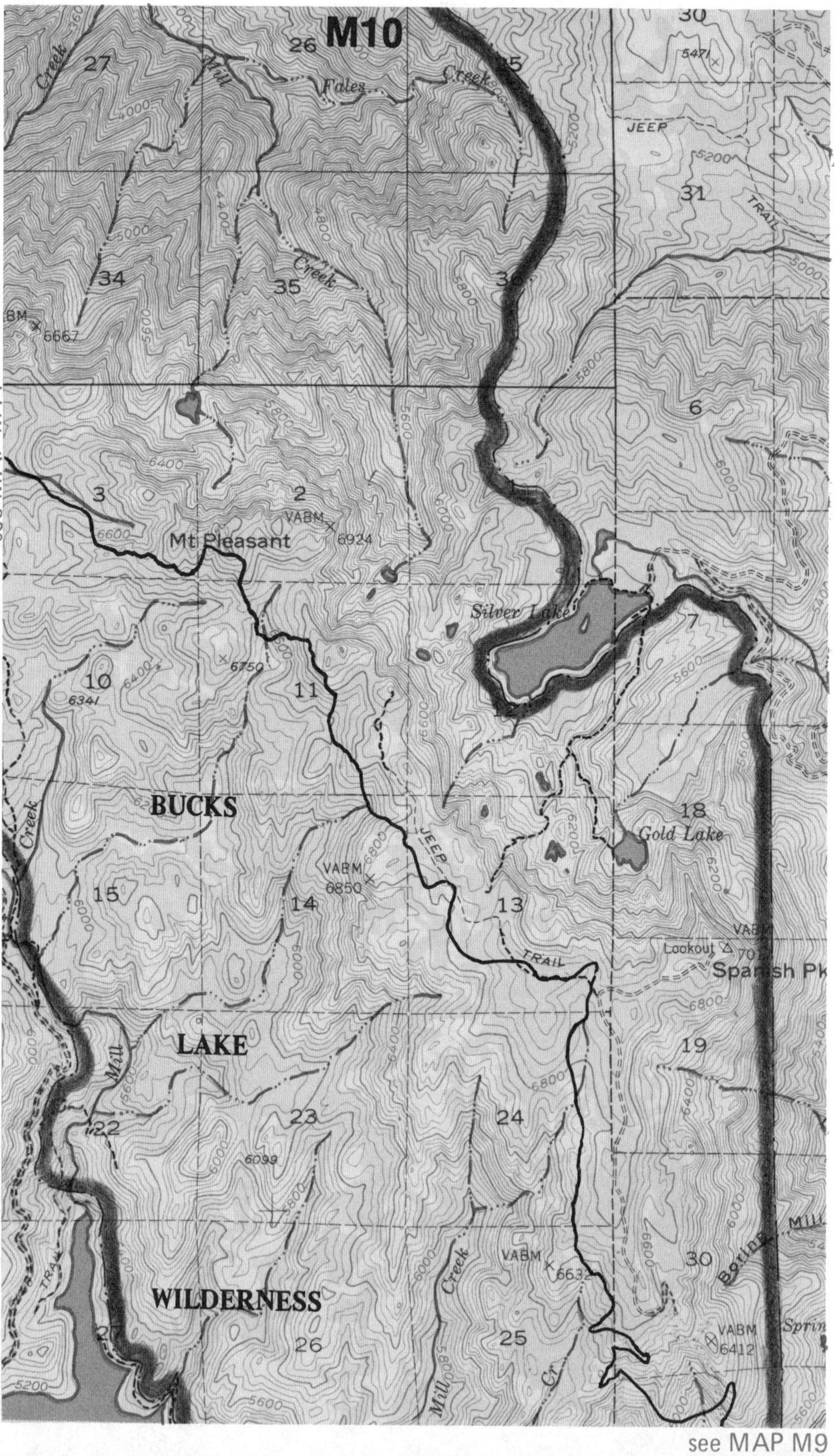

see MAP M9

high enough above meadows to keep one's feet dry. Snow doesn't finally melt in this vicinity until mid-July, and until at least then you'll encounter two large, shallow ponds that give rise to thousands of croaking tree frogs. ∎ *Even before snow melts from the ponds' edges, corn lilies sprout and begin to grow skyward through the freezing water.* ∎ Your gradual climb north soon leaves the meadows behind, passes through a dense forest, and emerges high on fairly open slopes garnished with clusters of magnificent red firs. Your route traverses above a conspicuous granitic bench, whose low, brushy cover permits you to look east 3000 feet down on serene Meadow Valley.

Beyond the bench, the trail gradually becomes a faint, old road, which passes a cluster of water-loving shrubs and trees that tap a near-surface water table. Your road comes to an open gully, and beside it you see a collapsed log shelter. ∎ *Above it, you enter a pure stand of mature red firs, whose tall, straight trunks are embellished with a chartreuse cloak of staghorn lichen. Note that the lower 10–15 feet of each tree is devoid of lichens, for this part of the trunk is annually buried by snow.* ∎ A brief stroll up your road along the shady, forested, gentle slope brings you to a shallow saddle (6920-1.6), on which you again meet the Spanish Peak road.

*   *   *   *

Side route: The ⅓-mile hike east to its end provides rewarding views. The shallow saddle approximately marks the boundary between ridgecrest volcanic mudflows and much older granitic rocks on which the flows were deposited.

*   *   *   *

From the saddle you take a path initially north, then make a relaxing traverse along the crest above usually unseen Gold Lake. As you curve northwest along the rim of a cirque wall, you can see large, shallow Silver Lake in the distance below. ∎ *Partly obscuring it is a smooth, rounded, brushy moraine that the conspicuous Gold Lake Trail traverses. This lateral moraine buries a bedrock ridge that separated the Silver Lake glacier from the Gold Lake glacier. Abundant red firs, together with some western white pines and a few Jeffrey pines, filter this view.* ∎

The rim trail gradually curves north, then turns to descend west to a trail junction (6870–1.4) on the west side of the head of a steep gully. The faint, steep trail descends to the popular, highly visible Gold Lake Trail, starting from the north end of Silver Lake. Your scenic rim route continues northwest through open forest, ascending and descending increasingly larger ridge knolls. The first is barely noticeable; the second you breath a little heavily to top; on the third you begin to wonder why your trail doesn't contour around them. On the third you cross a jeep road (6880–1.2), which climbs up to its bouldery summit. This road has more-or-less paralleled your path ever since you began it. This area's snow pack lasts well into July, and before then you may want to follow the road, although much of it too is then snow covered. You climb the fourth and last knoll almost to its very top, only to start on a 250-foot descent to a forested saddle (6710–1.0). Now below the east end of Mt. Pleasant—the high point of your ridge—you traverse west across its slopes, cross its low west spur ridge, and descend northwest to cross the headwaters of Clear Creek.

See map M10

Three Lakes' rocky, brushy middle lake

see MAP N1

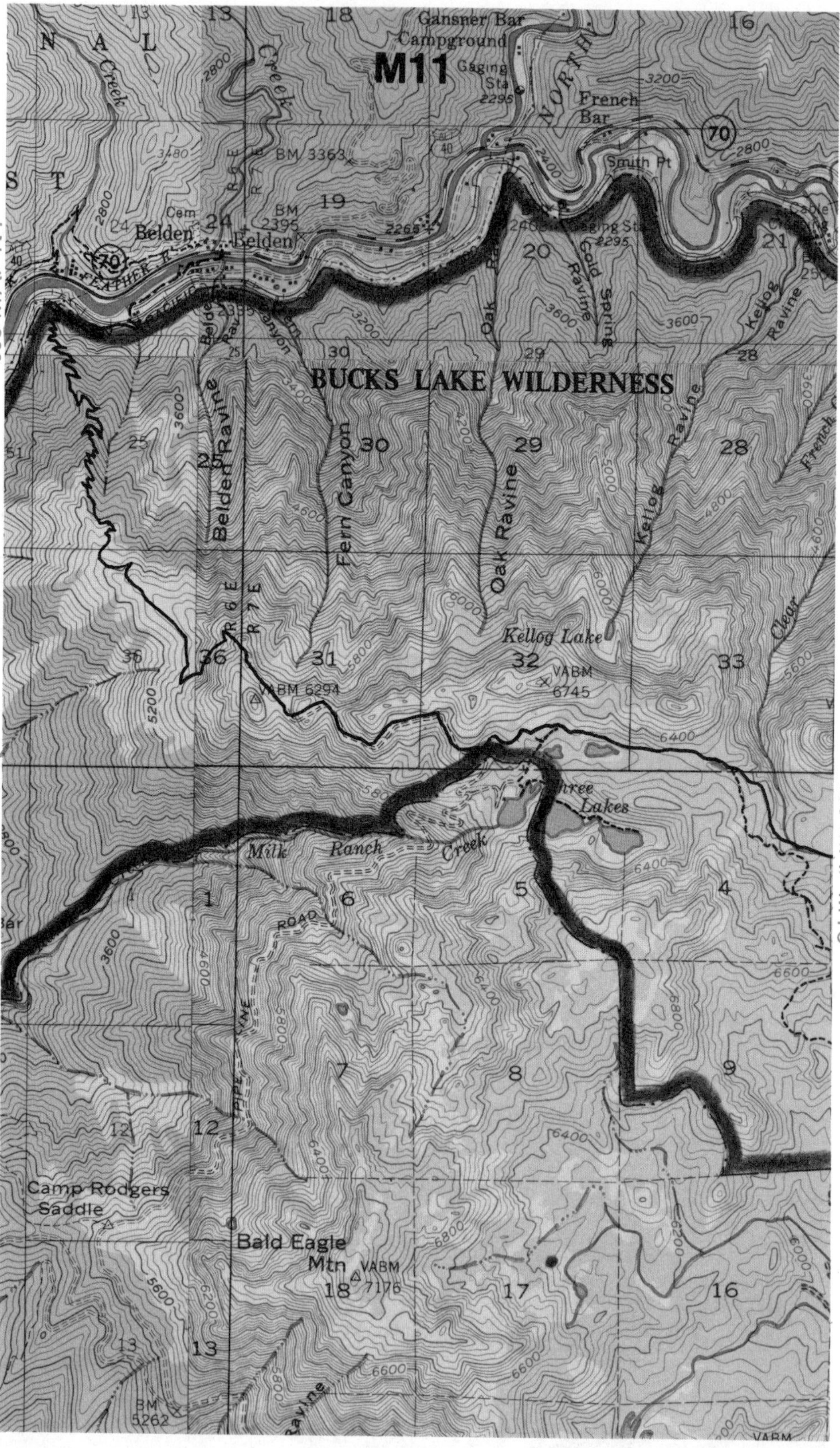

see MAP M10

M

Hwy. 49-
Hwy. 70

Gansner Bar
Campground

Gaging
Sta
2295

French
Bar

70

Smith Pt

NORTH

BM 3363

BM
2395

Belden

Belden

Cem

BM
2265

Gaging Sta
2295

Gold
Spring

Oak
Ravine

Kellog
Ravine

Kellog
Ravine

French

FEATHER

Belden
Canyon

Belden Ravine

BUCKS LAKE WILDERNESS

Fern Canyon

Oak Ravine

Kellog Ravine

Clear

Kellog Lake

VABM
6745

VABM 6294

Three
Lakes

Milk Ranch Creek

ROAD

Camp Rodgers
Saddle

Bald Eagle
Mtn
VABM
7176

BM
5262

13 13 18

16

19

20

21

30 29 28

30 29 28

31 32 33

1   6   5   4

7   8   9

12 12

18 17 16

13 13

70

40

40

24 24

25

25

The route west—faint at times—descends to within sight or hearing of this cattle-visited creek, almost levels off, and crosses an unsigned north-south trail. Not far beyond this intersection, the trail crosses Clear Creek (6190–2.2) where it turns north to flow down through a deep gap. Before leaving this creek you might consider establishing camp on the nearly level ground east of it. Campsites in this area are about as isolated as one can expect to find in California.

You head west across Clear Creek, then climb northwest up to its junction with the old California Riding and Hiking Trail (6240-0.5). Just west of this junction you pass a shallow pond choked with grasses and pond lilies. Your gently undulating trail then skirts the base of a granitic ridge and along your traverse you pass a second, larger but shallow pond. Late-summer hikers will see only a wet meadow. Beyond it your fir-lined trail passes a more distant pond, but white and red firs hamper your efforts to see it. Then you come to a trail junction (6270–1.0), from which a newer segment of the PCT climbs right but the older CRHT descends left.

*   *   *   *

Side route: If you want to descend to Three Lakes, head down the CRHT. This recommended side trip starts a southwest descent, quickly encounters a short lateral trail that climbs northwest back up to the PCT, then makes a fairly steep, fern-lined descent past large boulders before dead-ending at a curve in a road. To get to nearby Three Lakes from the end of the CRHT segment, turn left and follow the road southeast to the north arm of the lower lake. This lower lake, when full, extends all the way up to the middle lake, but in late season its level falls at least 15 feet, turning it into an unattractive mudhole. From the north arm a muddy, rutted road curves east over to the northwest shore of the more scenic middle lake, which has trout—ranging up to at least 16 inches—jumping from its warm waters. Like the lower lake, this one drops considerably, but not drastically, in late season. Unlike the lower lake, this one is not dammed, and the Bucks Lake Wilderness boundary runs between the two. Your road traverses to the lake's east end, from where a trail starts up the north side of the refreshing outlet creek from the upper lake.

Starting on a terrace at a point about 12 yards north of this creek, this trail climbs up a brushy slope of huckleberry oak, tobacco brush, manzanita and chinquapin. Nearing the upper lake, you pass scattered specimens of sugar pine and white fir, then encounter more luxuriant growth in the form of mountain ash, dogwood and bracken fern. The upper lake is a pleasant surprise in that it is natural and its level stays high. In late summer, however, its fairly warm water becomes slightly cloudy. Finding a good campsite is another matter. Because this lake is so hemmed in, there is very little level ground. Nevertheless, small sites can be found just above the lake's north, east and southwest shores.

*   *   *   *

Back where the PCT and CRHT fork, you follow the PCT right and make a brief climb, then come to another junction, from which a lateral trail descends back to the CRHT. This spur is for the convenience of southbound PCT trekkers who want to camp in the Three Lakes area. From the junction you have an easy ⅓-mile traverse to a shady bend on an old fire road (6260–0.4). If you descended to Three Lakes, you can rejoin the route at this bend by following Three Lakes Road ("Pipe Line Road" on Map M11) ¼ mile down-canyon from the lowest lake, then veering west up a closed, brush-lined jeep road, which quickly switchbacks northeast up to the bend. (If you encounter a fair number of people at Three Lakes, it's likely because the people have driven to them via the Three Lakes Road, which became a popular RV route in the '80s.) From the shady bend you climb west out onto sunny slopes which are clothed with manzanita and chinquapin, and lesser amounts of wild cherry and aromatic tobacco brush. Looking south across the canyon, you see Three Lakes Road winding a tortuous route toward unseen Bucks Lake's dam.

Your sunny, curving road descends northwest toward a crest saddle, and, approaching it, you see snowy Lassen Peak (10,457') on the horizon ahead of you. Leaving the saddle, you pass some low, granitic blocks and pinnacles that cover the broad crest and tempt rock climbers

M

Hwy. 49-
Hwy. 70

See maps M10, M11

to boulder a while. A second northwest descent takes you to another saddle and another view of Lassen. Seen in the north-northeast is a fire lookout atop well-named Red Hill (6330'), whose rusty color is derived from an iron-rich belt of ultramafic rocks—the same fault-bounded belt that underlies Meadow Valley. The road continues beyond the saddle, descends the north slopes of Peak 6294, then crosses its west ridge just before a secondary summit and dead-ends in 200 yards (5900–1.8). From the road's left side, the Belden Trail segment of the PCT begins.

A long switchback leg starts south on a moderate-to-steep descent, then quickly bends southwest and maintains its gradient across brushy slopes. You pass a trickling spring before reaching a ridge and switchbacking north past a few scattered pines. The descent ahead of you is perfectly clear, and you soon pass a second trickling spring before your trail curves northwest and descends toward Chips Creek canyon, which is a prominent cleft in the opposite wall of the Feather River canyon.

Your rapidly descending section of the PCT reaches a prominent ridgetop, briefly curves northeast across it, and then quickly rejoins it. The ridgetop descent is only momentary, for you soon leave brush behind and switchback under verdant forest cover north down toward the Feather River. ∎ *Note the succession of vegetation zones as you descend on the PCT. Mt. Pleasant's slopes of red fir and western white pine gave way to the Three Lakes area's cover of white fir and sugar pine. Brushy, deforested slopes along the Belden jeep road interrupted the sequence, but now, as you descend some* *36 switchbacks, you enter the realm of Douglas-fir, ponderosa pine, black oak and incense-cedar. Growing along moist gullies traversed by your winding trail are dogwood, big-leaf maple, thimbleberry and bracken fern. Found in this zone are the usual hazards of poison oak, ticks and rattlesnakes. These aren't problems if you watch your step and what you brush against. Unrelated to this change in vegetation is a change from diorite to phyllite and metachert—metamorphosed sediments of the Calaveras formation.* ∎

As your trail approaches the river, bay trees and live oaks appear. Nearing the end of your route, you traverse eastward and cross an ephemeral creeklet. Not far beyond, you leave Bucks Lake Wilderness and your trail reaches a trailhead beside Western Pacific's two railroad tracks (2310–4.7). Sometimes a freight train stops for about ½ hour on one track to let another train pass. If so, cross with caution or wait for the parked train to move. About 0.1 mile down a paved road from the tracks you'll pass a trailhead parking area on your left, made especially for equestrians. Then 0.2 mile farther you'll pass the entrance road to former Belden Campground, which was eradicated by a 1986 flood. Still, PCT hikers and equestrians camp there beside the Feather River. Not much farther on you reach Belden Town (2310–0.6), which has a small store, a saloon, a motel, RV sites, a laundry, a PCT register, and most important, a post office (ZIP 95915). This section of PCT ends as you follow the road across North Fork Feather River, with excellent swimming, to adjacent Highway 70 (2330–0.1).

See map M11

M

Hwy. 49-
Hwy. 70

M

Sierra Buttes Fire Lookout

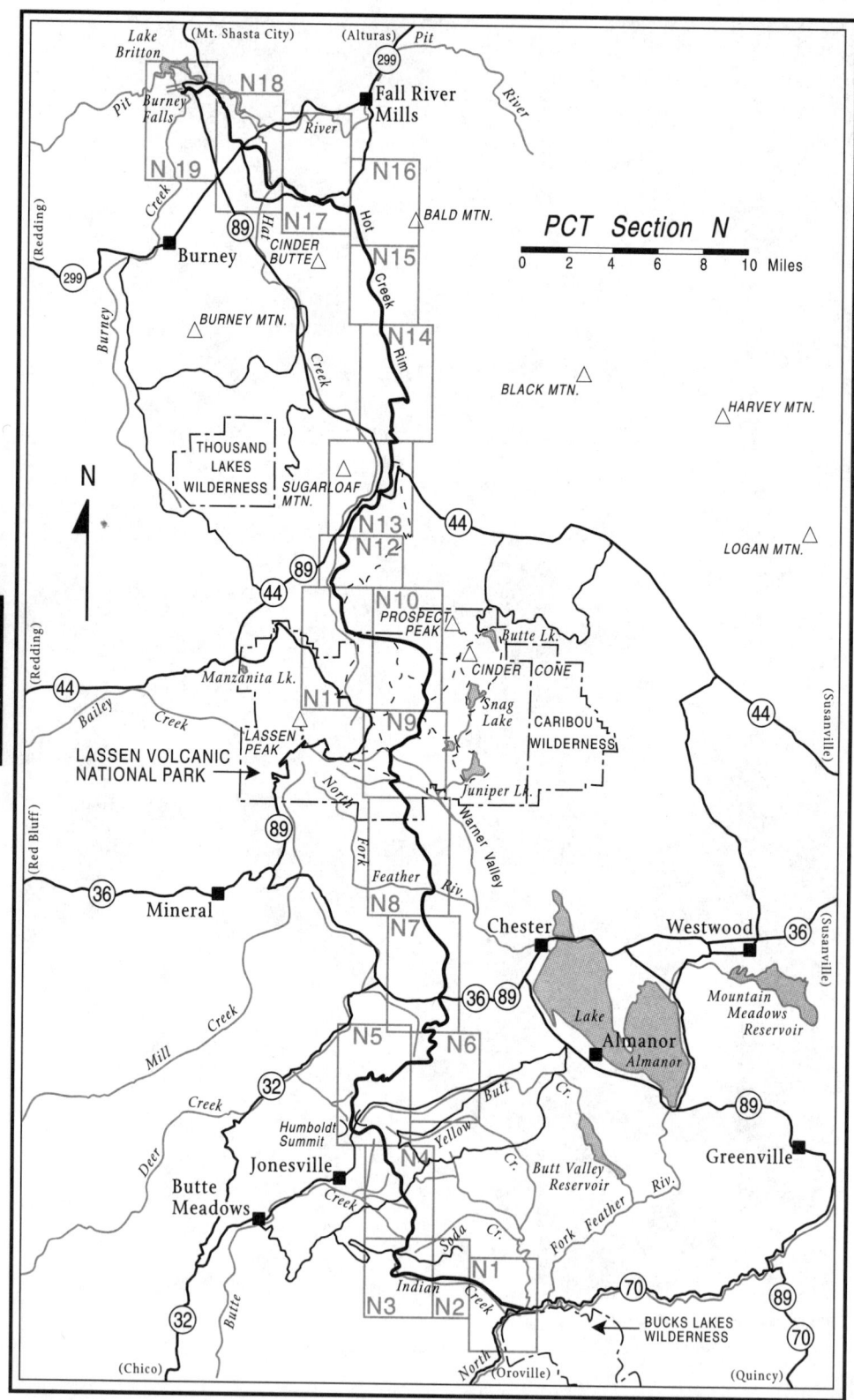

Section N
Highway 70 to Burney Falls

Introduction: After only a few hours' walk on this section, you leave a few scattered outcrops of granitic rocks behind and then belatedly say goodbye to the 400-mile-long Sierra Nevada. The PCT route through it was about twice as long. Challenging you ahead are the snow-blessed slopes of the Cascade Range and the dry slopes and escarpments of the Modoc Plateau. The overall geologic character is unquestionably volcanic, but the plant life is quite diverse. Not only do you see differences due to elevation change, as you did in the previous section, you also see longitudinal changes: the landscape is progressively drier to the east. The best example of this is Hat Creek Valley. Its west rim is cool, lake-bound and forested—the ideal terrain for the Pacific Crest Trail. The *trail*, however, has been built on the east rim, a faulted escarpment, which is hot, virtually waterless, and offers only token shade under its open, woodland cover. Lassen Peak, the southernmost volcano of the Cascade Range, is the highlight of this section, and you may want to spend some extra time exploring the thermal wonders of Lassen Volcanic National Park.

Declination: 16½°E

Points on Route	S→N	Mi. Btwn. Pts.	N→S
Highway 70 at Belden Town bridge	0.0		134.3
		6.2	
Williams Cabin flat	6.2		128.1
		6.8	
Poison Spring	13.0		121.3
		6.3	
Humbug Road at Cold Springs	19.3		115.0
		6.8	
Humboldt Road at Humboldt Summit	26.1		108.2
		6.2	
saddle south of Carter Meadow	32.3		102.0
		10.5	
Soldier Creek springs	42.8		91.5
		3.7	
Highway 36	46.5		87.8
		3.2	
Stover Camp	49.7		84.6
		6.7	
Chester-Childs Meadows road	56.4		77.9
		8.5	
Warner Valley Campground	64.9		69.4
		7.6	
Lower Twin Lake, north end	72.5		61.8
		5.6	
Badger Flat, east end	78.1		56.2
		7.0	
Road 32N12	85.1		49.2
		3.3	
road to Hat Creek Resort	88.4		45.9
		4.1	
Highway 44 near Subway Cave	92.5		41.8
		2.9	
Highway 44's trailhead parking area	95.4		38.9
		11.1	
Hat Creek Rim Fire Lookout site	106.5		27.8
		2.8	
Road 22	109.3		25.0
		8.8	
Cassel-Fall River Mills Road	118.1		16.2
		4.3	
PG&E road south to Cassel	122.4		11.9
		4.2	
Highway 299	126.6		7.7
		7.7	
Burney Falls	134.3		0.0

Supplies and Permits: Although this section is the second longest one presented in this two-volume guidebook, its topography is gentle, and therefore most backpackers can do it in 8 days or less. This is fortunate, since there are no supply points along the route. Where you cross Highway 36, about 46½ miles along your way, you can head 8 miles northeast into Chester, where you can get virtually any trail item you might need. North of Lassen Volcanic National Park, many hikers leave the PCT at about mile 88.4 and head over to nearby Hat Creek Resort and the Old Station Post Office. The resort's store is camper- and fisherman-oriented, so don't expect much in the way of supplies. If you're heading past Burney Falls, your last near-route post office before Interstate 5 will be in Cassel, about one mile south of Baum Lake. From the lake you can leave the PCT and head south up a road, passing a good campground only minutes before reaching the Cassel Post Office and a small store. Later, when you reach Highway 299, you can take it 2½ miles southwest to its Highway 89 intersection, 2 miles farther to Johnson Park, with a store and a couple of cafes, and then 3 miles more to Burney, which has virtually all the supplies you'll likely need. However, the best supply access in the northern part of Section N is the concessionaire's store in McArthur-Burney Falls Memorial State Park, which will hold mailed parcels free of charge. Mail them to: Burney Falls Camper Services. McArthur-Burney Falls State Park, Route 1, Box 1240, Burney, CA 96013. The store is well stocked and the nearby campground has free hot showers. The state park is now a better place to resupply than is the Cassel Post Office and furthermore it is a great place for a layover day.

You'll need a wilderness permit to camp overnight in the backcountry of Lassen Volcanic National Park. Write for one several weeks in advance. However, note that if you camp overnight only at the park's Warner Valley Campground and not in its backcountry, you won't need a permit. Equestrians are *not* allowed overnight in the backcountry, so if you plan to have horses overnight, you'll have to make advance reservations with the park service. You have only three choices, and the Juniper Lake corral is too far off the PCT to consider. The other two corrals are at Summit Lake, about 4½ miles west of the PCT from Lower Twin Lake, and Butte Lake, about 4½ miles east of the PCT along the Nobles Trail.

Rattlesnakes: These may be encountered at a number of stretches along this route, particularly in lower Chips Creek canyon and on the Hat Creek Rim escarpment. However, they'll stay out of your way if you'll stay out of theirs. Ticks are likely in the same areas. For summer hikers, stickers will be more of a problem. Schaffer wore gaiters when he mapped this stretch. Ray Jardine makes a more economical suggestion: use duct tape on your pants, socks and shoes.

Water: Although this section is in northern California, it can be quite dry by mid-summer and pose drought problems similar to those of southern California sections. North of Cold Springs you have to walk 23½ miles before you reach Soldier Creek springs. Between the two, your route is dry once the snowmelt creeks and seeps disappear, usually by late July. However, about halfway along this dry stretch you can head north on the Carter Meadow Trail and find water (and campsites) in ½ mile or so.

A more serious problem is lack of water along the Hat Creek Rim escarpment. The Forest Service spent thousands of dollars trying to provide fresh water to this often hot, usually shadeless stretch. At Baker Lake and Porcupine Reservoir they drilled exploratory wells hundreds of feet deep—to no avail. A few years later, they developed a campsite near Baker Spring, but the spring proved to be unreliable. Then in 1987 a major fire torched much of the rim, which exacerbated the water-shortage problems and also obliterated miles of PCT. Fortunately the southern part of the Hat Creek Rim PCT route has been abandoned in favor of a 1992 water-blessed route that goes along the floor of upper Hat Creek Valley. You still have one long dry stretch, from near the Highways 44/89 junction up to the Hat Creek Rim and then along it and down to Rock Spring creek, a distance of about 30 miles.

Maps: *Belden*
Jonesville
Humboldt Peak
Humbug Valley
Stover Mountain
Mount Harkness
Reading Peak
Prospect Peak

West Prospect Peak
Old Station
Murken Bench
Hogback Ridge
Cassel
Dana
Burney Falls

The Route

This section starts on Highway 70 at the Belden Town bridge, by the PG&E Belden Power House, which empties into Yellow Creek. Immediately west of the creek you come to the Belden Rest Area, and from its west end, by the Ely Stamp Mill, you start west on PCT tread. The trail parallels the highway and some powerlines for about ½ mile, then swings northwest for a traverse to a bridge over Indian Creek (2370–1.1). Shaded by Douglas-fir, big-leaf maple, black oak, live oak and bay tree, you traverse out of the creek's canyon, meeting a trail (2400–0.3) immediately after turning west to parallel the busy highway. Should you want to take a last swim in the Feather River—here an inviting reservoir—take this trail ¼ mile down to the highway. You now face a shadeless, rocky traverse above Highway 70 as you cross nearly vertical beds of the Calaveras formation. Beneath the buzzing of giant powerlines, you cross a low ridgecrest, quickly spot Chips Creek below you, and once again enter shady forest. After a pleasant traverse through the forest, you reach a junction (2470–0.6).

*　　　*　　　*　　　*

Side route: From here a trail descends briefly northwest to a short, nearly level segment of an old road. Get water—and perhaps a brisk, refreshing bath—from Chips Creek, not too far below the road. If you were to wade or boulder-hop a few minutes downstream, you'd see the site where the road once bridged the creek. Today only a fine swimming hole—a worthy goal—remains.

*　　　*　　　*　　　*

From the trail down to the old road, your Chips Creek Trail continues its shady traverse, begins to climb, and then executes four switchbacks to get you high above the creek. ∎ *Beyond the last switchback, your ascent northwest is a moderate one, across metamorphic rocks that were metamorphosed in part when a granitic pluton—partly seen across the canyon—intruded them. In several places along your trail, you cross small bedrock exposures of this granitic pluton, and these mark the northern boundary of the granitic Sierra Nevada. From the headwaters of Chips Creek, volcanic rocks extend northward in a continuous mantle to central Washington, where granitic rocks once again appear.* ∎

After a protracted, moderate ascent, your trail levels off, then even descends, crossing two welcome seasonal creeks. Several more are crossed on a traverse west, and then you arrive at a small cabin on a white-fir-shaded flat (3700–4.2). This level area, only 100 yards north of bounding, noisy Chips Creek, makes a spacious campsite, and Rex and Conrad Williams allow PCT hikers to use their cabin. They only ask you to observe a few rules: Build fires only in the stove or in the fire pits. Make sure

See map N1

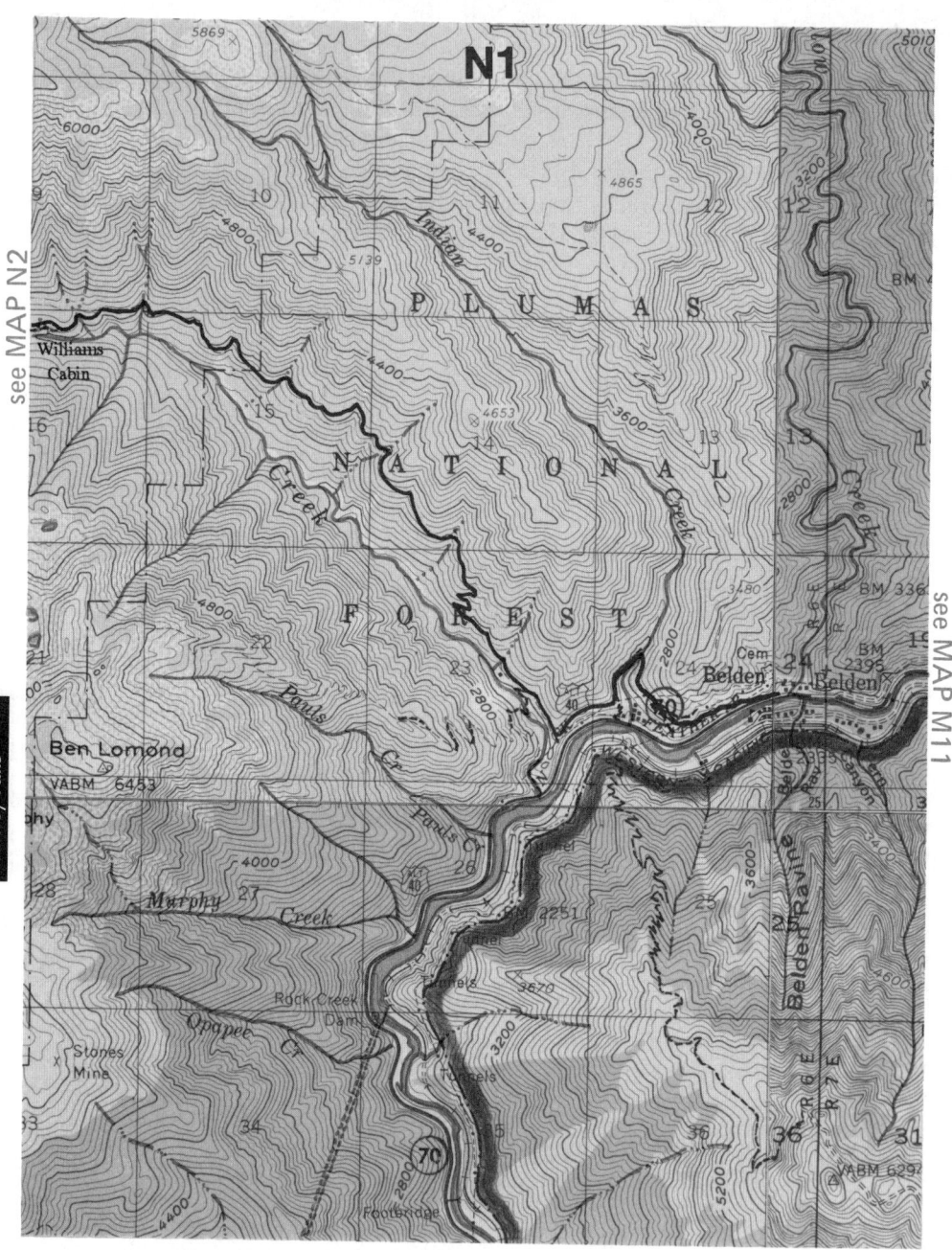

all fires are completely out before leaving. Make sure the cabin door is closed and latched. You can use anything in the camp, but please replace any wood you use, and if you use their pots, pans and dishes, please wash them. Unfortunately, their open hospitality has been countered at times with vandalism. Obtain wa-

ter from a nearby creeklet when it is flowing. Otherwise make a very steep, potentially hazardous descent to Chips Creek proper.

The west-climbing PCT crosses the flat's creeklet (slippery boulders in early season), then soon climbs to Myrtle Flat Camp (4180-0.9). Like at the previous flat, this one has a

See maps N1, N2

steep, narrow water-access trail, which descends west to a small, cold, invigorating pool on Chips Creek. As you make a protracted climb west, passing ephemeral creeklets on the way, ponderosa pines yield to sugar pines and white firs. You may find one or two flat spots to camp at before reaching the canyon's headwall, which you switchback up, crossing and recrossing an old jeep road, to a ford of a creek from Poison Spring (5650–3.8) just above a series of small waterfalls. Hikers have camped on the old road just beyond the crossing. You start up it, then follow a switchbacking trail up to the lip of a glaciated bowl, in which your trail ends at a junction with the old road (5920–0.4).

On this gently climbing road you hike west, passing an aspen-bordered campsite where a seasonal creek curves north toward Poison Spring. As you approach the headwall of Chips Creek canyon, you leave the old road, forking right on trail tread (6100–0.5) and then climbing up to the vicinity of Poison Spring (6680–1.2). The spring flows into a nearby pond, which lies about 60 yards below the trail. ∎ *If you descend to this pond and its adjacent road and campsite, you'll become acquainted with stickseeds, at least from midsummer onward. These plants produce barbed seeds that tenaciously cling to your socks. The few plants here are nothing compared to the numbers you'll meet on the Hat Creek Rim.* ∎

Beyond the spring you climb north to a wide lumber road (6900-0.4), from which your trail continues northeast. Now you climb ¼ mile up to a crest, follow it east ½ mile, and then switchback down its north-facing slopes, passing a spring before curving north across a lower spur ridge to a roadend (6620–2.5). On this closed road you amble north for about 10 minutes to another PCT trail segment (6610–0.7), on your left, beginning just after your road curves right and starts a noticeable descent. From this junction the PCT makes a somewhat confusing descent north gently down through a partly logged-over area, then around a forested slope to two crossings of an old jeep road. Only 150 yards north of the second crossing, the trail segment ends on the road's east side, and you walk 50 yards north-northeast on it to a junction where the east-west trending Road 26N02 (6380–1.0) intersects the north-south trending Humbug Ridge Road.

From the northwest corner of the intersection you follow a signed trail segment 0.3 mile northwest to an old road and walk northwest on it less than 100 yards, to where it starts to curve northeast. Here a short trail segment bears northwest to the south end of a long, mule-eared meadow. Rather than taking an obvious, but erroneous, short trail north, you follow PCT diamonds west across the south edge of the meadow, and, 30 yards into a lodgepole forest on an old westward logging road, you reach yet another trail segment. Following it north,

See maps N2, N3, N4

Butt Mountain and distant Lassen Peak

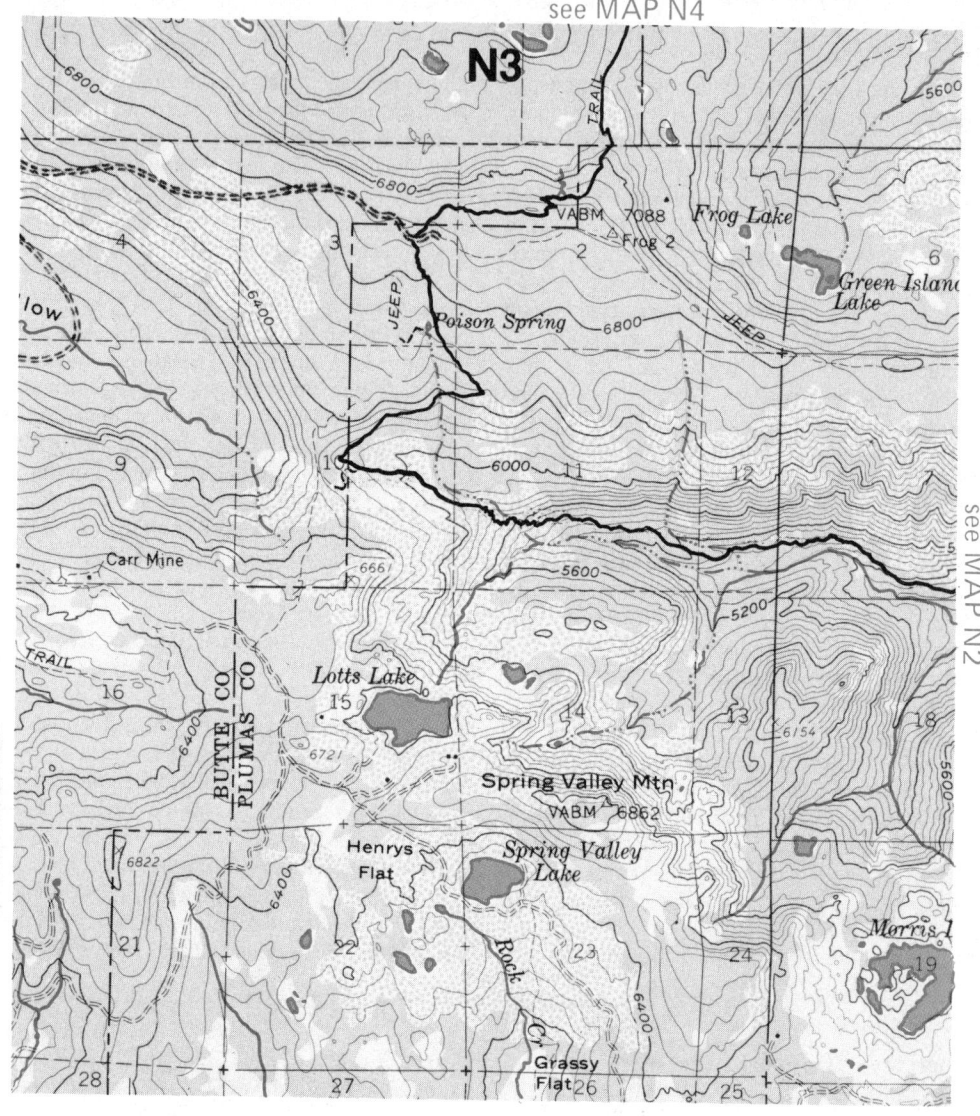

see MAP N2

you parallel at a distance the long meadow's west edge. Your trail ends at another old logging road, and on this you hike north, still parallelling the meadow, then leave it on another trail segment that climbs above the meadow's northwest corner, switchbacks west and reaches, on a low ridge, yet another old logging road.

This you follow ¼ mile northwest to an intersection of Humbug Road 27N01 (6450–1.7). You walk a few paces west and find Cold Springs, from which the trail angles right. Among conifers just below the springs you'll find a car-camping area. You are 23½ miles from

your next reliable trailside water, Soldier Creek springs, and about 30½ miles from your first decent campsite with water, Stover Camp. The latter destination is quite a far day's hike away. Fortunately, you can get water and make camp in the Carter Meadow area, about ½ mile from the PCT after you hike 13 more miles.

From Cold Springs the PCT climbs past two roads, the second one (6710–0.7) heading southeast across a clearcut to nearby Humbug Summit. Continuing north, you attain a minor ridge that is a drainage divide between east- and west-flowing creeks. Up it you wind northwest, largely under the shade of mature red firs,

See map N4

p. 51, col. 1, par. 2, line 4: The road around Lake Morena's campground perimeter is now paved.

p. 51, col. 2, line 1: PCT Association volunteers have installed new signs leading north around Lake Morena, so now the route is more certain. Ignore intersecting paths made by local homeowners which cross the PCT for lake access. Stay essentially level, and don't head away from the shore line until PCT emblems mark the way .

p. 53, col. 2, par. 1, line 5: Boulder Oaks Store management has resolved their differences with the USFS—the store and campground will remain open.

p. 56-57: Maps A7 & A8: The 35,080 acre-Sawtooth Mountains Wilderness was designated in 1994. It lies east of and below the PCT as the trail courses around Stephenson Peak, Monument Peak and Garnet Peak.

p. 57, col. 2, par. 2, last line: The ex-Air Force installation on Stephenson Peak is now a Federal Aviation Administration navigation control site.

p. 58, col. 2, par. 1, line 3: Laguna Campground is now named Laguna/El Prado Campground.

p. 58, col. 2, last line: GATR Road: This intersection is now a trail, and marks an important detour to water: Just beyond a pipe swing-gate, there is now an unmarked trail junction, where the roadbed used to be. Continuing straight ahead, northwest, a recently constructed spur trail curves gently down and west, then momentarily south, to reach Sunrise Highway S1 in less than 0.1 mile. Here, a monument to the Penny Pines reforestation program stands beside a busy trailhead parking area. Directly across 2-lane Highway S1 is the start of Noble Canyon Trail 5E04, which strikes west-southwest only 50 yards to find a permanent water supply. Here lie a green faucet and a galvanized horse trough, in an open stand of black oaks. This level flat is quite hospitable, but, unfortunately, no camping is allowed in this vicinity. A moment farther on is found a junction with the southbound Big Laguna Trail, which heads back to Mount Laguna.

p. 59, col. 2, line 9: Water at Pioneer Mail Trailhead Picnic Area: Getting water here is now more convenient: a 4-foot diameter con-crete water trough is now fed by the tank. It is alongside the trail, just past the large trailhead information sign.

p. 61, col. 2, par. 1, lines 4-8: Emergency water. If the spigot is locked, look 10 feet uphill, in a grove of Coulter pines: the large cistern has an unlocked metal access plate. But don't count on it!

p. 69, col. 2, line 6: Thanks to the efforts of PCT Association volunteers, trail tread is now much better defined near San Ysidro Creek.

p. 74, Supplies: Warner Springs. The Warner Springs Golf Grill is a delightful place to cool off and dine. It is located just south of the gas station, which, in turn, is next to the post office. Pay phones are available. The gas station has limited snack foods.

The Valley Store, in Terwilliger, has now closed. Instead, use Kamp Anza Kampground, as described on page 83, column 2. They will hold packages for through-hikers. Send them to:

> c/o Your Name
> Kamp Anza Kampground
> 41560 Terwilliger Road
> Space 19
> Anza CA 92539
> Phone: (909) 763-4819

p. 78, col. 1, par. 3, line 5: Lost Valley Spring. The spring has been rehabilitated, and has continued to flow during recent summers. Check it out.

p. 88, col. 2, par. 4, line 9: Fobes Saddle: PCT Association volunteers rerouted about ¼ mile of the PCT just south of the saddle. The spur path west down to the spring was also brushed-out.

p. 91, col. 1, par. 2, last line: Mount San Jacinto State Park personnel have expressed concern that some PCT hikers do not fully understand specific restrictions within that park. Please note that all camping must be in designated sites only. Along the PCT, there is only one approved camp site: at Strawberry Junction Trail Camp. USFS Wilderness Permits are NOT valid for camping in the State Park. You must get a separate camping permit for a specific date, to use State Park campsites. No dogs or fires are ever allowed within the State Park. PCT travelers are welcome at the

The Pacific Crest Trail Volume 1: California
1998 UPDATE

Acknowledgments page. Photo credits of some photographers should read: Lyn Haber 238; J.C. Jenkins 230, 234; Ruby Johnson Jenkins 186, 189, 198, 205, 212, 220, 221, 239, 240. Add to acknowledgments, with many thanks from the authors for updating input: Tony deBellis, Bruce Gilbert, Terry Astle, Chris Landa, Karl Duff and Rob Langsdorf.

p. 5: First person to hike the PCT, CDT, and AT. This may be Jim Podlesny, who did the AT in '73, the PCT in '75, and the CDT in '79.

p. 8: PCTA. New phone numbers: (888) PCTRAIL and (916) 349-2109.

p. 8: PCTA services. For members they provide a free wilderness permit for travel in excess of 500 miles on the PCT.

p. 9, list of registers: There is one at the Tehachapi post office.

p. 9: ALDHA. The Jardines are no longer associated with ALDHA.

p. 15: A new National Forest Adventure Pass system for Angeles, Cleveland, Los Padres and San Bernardino National Forests is required for all vehicles, if parking along roads in those forests. It is not required for PCT travelers, per se. Cost is $5 per visit to one forest, or $30 per year (good for all four forests). Plans are to return 85% of collected monies to the individual forest for human-use enhancing projects. Passes can be purchased from the USFS, southern California outdoor shops, and multiple vendors near or in the forests.

p. 16, line 22: If you are planning to climb Mt. Whitney, you will need a special permit. Ask for it at the same place that you obtain your wilderness permit. If you have questions about this, call Mt. Whitney Ranger Station, (760) 876-6200.

p. 18, col. 1: Sequoia National Forest headquarters were not moved; they are still at 900 W. Grand Ave., Porterville.

p. 18: Rogue River Nat. For. New phone number is (541) 858-2200.

p. 27, last line: The word after "latitude" should be "is".

p. 39, par. 2, line 14: add 15°, getting 90°. This statement is correct if you use a true-reading compass, such as a Brunton. However, most people use a reverse-reading compass, such as a Silva or a Suunto, which are much cheaper, and they need to *subtract* 15°. To use these you need to purchase *Be Expert With Map & Compass* by Bjorn Kjellstrom. The book, over 100 pages long, is testimony to the difficulty of backsighting. A Brunton is so simple that it does not require a book. Unfortunately, it is expensive, about $200.

p. 46, Supplies: Campo now also has a ranch supply store, with most equestrian needs. A PCT Association trail register is kept at the post office. Cameron Corners, one mile north of Campo on Highway 94, has a hot dog stand, a convenience store and a branch of Wells Fargo Bank.

p. 47, par. 6, last line: make enough noise. Rattlesnakes are deaf, so they won't hear you. However, the statement above—they are sensitive to vibrations—is true.

p. 48, col. 1, line 17: Fifty feet south of the border monument, another dirt road has been bulldozed, parallel to the border. Its southern verge, the border itself, is protected from the Mexican hordes by a 4-to-6-foot-high fence of metal runway repair panels, painted olive-green. Hikers, however, should be aware of increased illegal activity in the vicinity of the PCT.

p. 48, col. 2, par. 2, line 10: A 2000-acre fire that started near Tecate in November 1995 burned eastward across the PCT's route from near the border, and north past Castle Rock Ranch. Trail tread is still easily visible.

p. 50, col. 2, line 9: The park is now called, "John Lyons-Lake Morena Regional Park". A trailhead parking area with informational sign has been constructed, but no primitive camping area has yet been established.

Park's "Hike and Bike" campsite in Idyllwild, near the ranger station. Phone (909) 659-2607.

p. 91, col. 1, Second side route: "Marion Ridge Trail" should be named "Deer Springs Trail".

p. 93, col. 2, par. 3, line 17: Snow Canyon Road. There is now a 3-foot-tall concrete water fountain at the trail junction. The defunct dead-end trail that continued across the road is no longer evident.

p. 102, col. 2, par. 2, line 20: narrow pass. This is now the approximate southern boundary of the expanded San Gorgonio Wilderness Area, which the PCT will climb through, to the head of North Fork Mission Creek.

p. 103, col. 1, par. 2, line 9: Whitewater Canyon. Hikers have been consistently unwelcome at the Whitewater Trout Farm, in a beckoning oasis of trees and lush grass, just across the Whitewater River to the east. Please avoid this private property.

p. 104, col. 1, par. 2, line 4: Forks Springs. A delightful detour to Randy Testman's "PCT Wilderness Hostel" can be made here. Reconstructed trail leads up the South Fork Mission Creek canyon (maps C3 & C4) 1.7 miles to a streamside grove of cool cedar trees. Here, at 5880', the hostel offers free camping, filtered water and solar showers to all. Small fees are charged for laundry, meals, snack items and a hot tub. Horse feed, corral and picket-line are available for equestrians. First-aid supplies and a radiotelephone are also present. Helicopter evacuation of injured hikers has even been arranged, in the past! Call (760) 567-8709 for voice mail information. Hikers can continue west, up the South Fork Mission Creek canyon from the Wilderness Hostel, on rough foot trail. (The path is impassable to horses). It leads a further 4.2 miles to dirt Road 1N93, where the official PCT route is rejoined, at Mission Creek Trail Camp, at the head of North Fork Mission Creek.

p. 112, par. 1: Water may not have been restored at Doble Trail Camp.

p. 116, col. 2, par. 2: It should begin, "Just 300 yards after Holcomb Camp, the rerouted PCT climbs southwest on tread coincident with the Crab Flats Trail. In about another 300 yards, steel pipes mark the junction where the PCT leaves the Crab Flats Trail. From there, the PCT traverses west on fairly level tread while the Crab Flats Trail continues its climb to the southwest. Gently ascending, your way alternates in forest and high chaparral."

p. 118, col. 1, line 2: The 40 yards of trail that were washed out have been corrected by the placement of a wooden bridge and the rebuilding of the trail. It is now safe for equestrian traffic—no detour is required.

p. 118, Map C13: The Deep Creek Campground shown in Section 18 no longer exists. Also, the road shown arcing east from Section 13 to Section 18 along the top of the Mojave River Forks Reservoir is not open to motorists.

p. 118, last par. to p. 119, line 23: Substitute: "Upon reaching the spillway, walk southwest across the broken-glass-strewn flat top of the spillway toward a paved ramp that leads north to the top of the dam. Walk steeply up to the top of the ramp, where you will see a PCT marker. Turn left here and stroll along the broad top of the dam 0.4 mile to where a wide, rutted dirt road goes steeply downhill, southeast. Walk down this road adjacent to signs which, every few yards, proclaim the water elevation behind the dam (there is almost never any water at all.) At the bottom, turn right, west, and walk over the top of a cement structure, below which a small amount of water is being released through the bottom of the dam. Continue west down a steep grade on the other side of the cement structure. Then, angle left, south, to cross the broad, usually dry West Fork Mojave River channel. Scramble up the south bank and resume trail tread by turning right, west, and proceed on an abandoned, torn up road at the base of a cliff (3010-1.1)."

p. 119, col. 2, first full sentence: the path never comes to a jeep road.

p. 120, col. 1, line 3 from bottom: Substitute: "About half way to Silverwood Lake you come to a flat area where an ascending jeep road from Highway 173 seems to terminate upon reaching the PCT (3480-2.6)."

p. 123, map C16: The black trail line was printed about one twelfth of an inch too low.

p. 129, Supplies: Line 4: Agua Dulce. As of January 1998, postal services for PCT travelers through Agua Dulce are located at:

Century 21 Realty
33358 Agua Dulce Canyon Rd.

Agua Dulce, CA 91350
(805) 268-0121

The realty is open 7 days a week. Note that this is not a complete post office (the closest is in Acton), but they attempt to be of any service.

Agua Dulce also has a veterinarian's office.

p. 132, col. 1, par. 2: Substitute: "Soon the trail crosses the newer Southern Pacific Railroad tracks (3020-0.8) and swings to the right along a dirt access road for 30 yards, before bending southwest to wind....alluvium. At one point you amble south along a jeep road (keeping to the right where the road forks) for 100 yards, before trail tread resumes on the right side of the road."

p. 132, col. 1, last par: Insert a second sentence: "Upon reaching the second powerline road, ascend south up the road for 150 yards before resuming trail tread on the right side of the road."

p. 136, col. 2, line 3: The Narrows Fire, a 9,437-acre wildfire, burned a large portion of the headwaters of East Fork of San Gabriel River canyon hereabouts during August, 1997. It was started by a hiker who was conscientiously, but unwisely, burning toilet paper. Suppression of the blaze required 1,700 firefighters from 18 agencies, 10 air tankers, 21 helicopters, 7 bulldozers and 12 water tenders. The cost: an estimated $8 million. We will encounter burned terrain off-and-on, all along upper Blue Ridge, to Grassy Hollow Visitor Center.

p. 138, col. 1: The Grassy Hollow Family Campground has been closed.

p. 145, last line: The next certain water is at North Fork Ranger Station, in 5.5 miles. Water is variably found in early spring just before the PCT crosses Moody Canyon Road—1.4 miles from Messenger Flats Campground.

p. 149, par. 1, line 24: Mattox Canyon creek. There may be no water in the stream bed where the PCT crosses. However, there may be a very nice flow a short way up-canyon.

p. 150, col. 1, par. 2: This section, which changes with every spring's floods, is often confusing. The overall directions, however, are constant: Having emerged from your sometimes-wet ford of the river, the trail climbs a few feet as it swings around to the right. The indistinct path empties you onto a flat alluvial maze of dirt roads, debris piles, and other assorted rubble. Don't dismay if you lose the route; simply head north toward the far valley wall. Find a dirt road adjacent to a barbed wire fence, then follow the road a short distance right, east, to where you come to a break in the fence marked with PCT emblems. These usher you left, north... (continue on p. 151).

p. 151, col. 1, par. 2, line 16: The gap near the head of Bobcat Canyon is at an elevation of 2780, not 2980.

p. 151, col. 2, last par., line 4: After the first two sentences, substitute this description of new alignment: "Looking north, one sees the old PCT leading steeply up a hillside. However, the PCT continues to head downstream, crossing the creek six more times until finally turning west and heading up and over the southwest end of a ridge. After about 200 yards your trail drifts downhill a bit and comes to a four-way junction. An equestrian trail takes off to the left, but you follow the PCT to the right, heading northeast up a very steep section of trail that deposits you on a little-used dirt road on the north rim of Escondido Canyon. Once on the rim you start a very gentle...junction (2535-0.9), by a yellow pipe post. Head left down this dirt road for a short distance to another PCT marker. Turn right at this marker and follow a new section of PCT as it loops around north of a large grassy area. The path then rounds north of the two most spectacular rock outcroppings (made famous by dozens of cowboy movies and TV ads). The trail eventually passes within 50 feet of a trailhead parking area and continues around half a dozen clifflets to strike paved Escondido Canyon Road (2510-0.9).

p. 152, col. 2, line 1: Camping is now allowed at Vasquez Rocks County Park.

p. 156: Section E Mileage Summary: North-to-South mileages do not add up on the chart. The mileages in the last column should be: 108.8, 107.0, 100.7, 98.5, 92.4, 86.1, 78.5, 71.5, 65.5, 61.2, 54.4, 47.7, 45.9, 42.4, 31.3, 24.7, 20.8, 8.6.

p. 157: Water: Be aware that, as of Spring 1998, all campground water in the Saugus District of Angeles National Forest (north of Agua Dulce) has been turned off, because of uncertain contamination of the water supplies with giardia and cryptosporidia. This should not inconvenience PCT travelers overly, since the (untreated) streams and springs that supply the campgrounds are still as accessible as ever. Purification of all water sources must be considered.

p. 160, col. 1, Par. 2: The first sentence should finish: "...then ascends moderately again, staying left at the first fork in the road, but going steeply uphill (next to a chain link fence) at the second fork in the road, to trail tread some 50 yards past a large steel electrical tower."

p. 160, col. 1, last par: Substitute this beginning: "Leaving the saddle, one sees the old Big Tree Trail heading steeply up the spine of the ridge. The PCT, however, starts a traverse to the left of the ridge, gaining elevation gradually at first, and then more rapidly as it drifts off to the northwest. Eventually, you switchback steeply up almost to the ridge, where you switchback again, back to the north. The climb moderates...on Sierra Pelona Ridge Road 6N07 (4500 2.7)."

p. 160, col. 2, line 7: Bear Spring is about 35 feet uphill from the trail, not the metal trough below the trail.

p. 160-61, Mileages: The last mileage on page 160 should be, " ... a junction (3785-0.6)", and the first on page 161 should be, "... Bouquet Canyon Road 6N05 (3340-0.9)."

p. 161, col. 2, line 2: A fire in September 1996 burned the hillside on the north slope of Bouquet Canyon. The PCT is still passable.

p. 164, col. 1, Par. 2, line 17: Green Valley Ranger Station: San Francisquito Picnic Area is closed, but picnic facilities and water are still available in front of the fire station. San Francisquito Campground no longer exists, but there is a trail camp near the ranger station. A restaurant is now found at the junction of San Francisquito Canyon Road and Spunky Canyon Road, 1.7 miles southwest of the ranger station.

p. 165, col. 1, Resupply Access: There is now a small convenience store at the intersection of Elizabeth Lake Canyon Road and Newvale Drive.

p. 167, col. 1, par. 2, line 6: Upper Shake Campground: Water here is turned off, indefinitely, due to the protozoal scare. Go to the creek for seasonal water, which flows well into summer of most years.

P. 171, col. 2, par. 1, Line 7: 270th Street West: This is now signed as, "269th Street West".

p. 171, col. 2, par. 2, 2nd to last line: "The Country Store" is about 1.3 miles west on Hwy 138. Use it as a resupply point, if needed, instead of going to Tehachapi or Lancaster. Seven days a week, you'll find water, cold drinks and snacks, minimal groceries, medical items and a phone. Also available are horse feed, a corral, and even a PCT Association trail register. The Country Store will accept PCT traveler's resupply boxes and hold them for no charge. Send them to:

> c/o Your Name
> The Country Store
> Star Route 138 (mail)
> 28105 Hwy 138 (UPS direct)
> Lancaster, CA 93536-9207
> Phone (805) 724-9097

p. 171, col. 2, par. 3, line 3: Although the signs and gates still exist, the trail tread between Highway 138 and Old Lancaster Road has fallen into disuse. Walk the quiet shoulder of 269th Street West, instead.

p. 171, col. 2, par. 3, 4th from bottom: The first road of this pair, 260th Street West, is now paved. Much of the route north from here has been re-marked by (hopefully) indestructible 3-foot-tall brown-painted iron posts, each emblazoned with a large white PCT emblem.

p. 177, col. 1, par. 3, line 9: There is probably water in Gamble Spring Canyon in springtime, but it cannot be relied upon.

p. 181, col. 2, Resupply Access: Add to last line: To walk into Tehachapi, avoid Highway 58. Instead, turn left, west, along the aforementioned railroad tracks. Walk the roadbed that parallels the railroad, keeping well away from the heavily used tracks. Cross under Highway 58 in 1.5 miles, and then at the first opportunity, walk north over to paved Tehachapi Road, which parallels the tracks and the freeway. You should be able to hitch a ride here. Continue west on that road 7.5 miles more to town. You pass a Travelodge with a gas station, a restaurant, a bar and a minimart at the Steuber Road intersection, 2.0 miles en route. To reach the post office from the town, turn right (north) on Green Street, left on H Street, right on N. Mill, which becomes Capital Hill and crosses over Highway 58, left on Voyager Drive to the large, tan stucco building with blue trim, 1.1 miles north of town.

p. 183, Supplies: Tehachapi is now recommended for package pickups.

p. 184, Water, line 4: There is now a series of springs in Sections F and G that has been upgraded in the 1990s to remove cattle contaminants from them: Golden Oaks (p. 189), Robin Bird (p. 192), Willow (p. 196), upper Yellow Jacket (p. 201), Joshua Tree (p. 213) and Fox Mill (p. 217). All have above-ground pipes for easy water collection, but all still need treating before drinking.

p. 184, Rattlesnakes, line 7: The size should read 16-64 inches.

p. 185, The Route, par. 1: There is often litter and a strong stench on the north side of Cameron Overpass. Hikers have been blamed, but it is the truckers who use the summit of Cameron on ramp as a nature break. Hurry past. Authorities have been made aware of the problem.

p. 187, col. 2, par. 2, line 10: It should read, "Soon the PCT parallels the jeep road, crosses it again..."

p. 189, col. 1, line 7: ...Enron's Sky River project...

p. 196, Water access: The BLM has upgraded Willow Spring and installed a special pump-action faucet for people. Next water is at upper Yellow Jacket Spring 0.7 mile up the side canyon.

p. 201, col. 1, 7 lines from bottom: The mileage figure should be $\frac{1}{3}$.

p. 201, col. 2, Water access: The Forest Service has installed a new spring box and piping to the old trough at upper Yellow Jacket Spring. The other two springs nearby remain unimproved.

p. 202, bottom of page: It should say, "See maps F11, F12, F13."

p. 211, par. 3, line 4: Numbers for the campsite should be (6190-2.1).

p. 213, col. 1, Side Route: This road in Cow Canyon has been closed to vehicles since becoming part of Owens Peak Wilderness.

p. 234, Photo: It was inadvertently flopped, left to right.

p. 244: The mileages in the last column should be 175.8, 172.5, 167.2, 163.9, 155.9, 152.7, 150.4, 142.1, 135.0, 130.7, 125.5, 115.3, 112.0, 105.0, 100.4.

p. 258-261. Campsites: Except for the spartan campsites at Wanda Lake, there are virtually no campsites between the 10,700-foot level on the east side of Muir Pass and those in the stunted whitebarks at the north end of Evolution Lake.

p. 261, col. 1, par. 3: Evolution Valley. The stream crossing below Evolution Meadow is dangerous, as deep holes have formed around large rocks there. The ranger directs hikers to a crossing near the head of Evolution Meadow.

p. 261, col. 2, par. 3, line 4: Lateral trail to the Florence Lake Trail. There is no longer any evidence of this trail.

p. 261, col. 2, par. 3, 11th line from end: Lou Beverly Lake junction. It's now signed *Three Island Lake.*

p. 261, col. 2, par. 3, 9th line from end: You bridge West Fork Bear Creek. It's no longer bridged.

p. 264, Resupply access: Vermilion Valley Resort. The owner, Butch Wiggs, and his family are very nice (even some freebies) to PCT hikers, and their resort is considered by many hikers to be the best rest-resupply stop along the entire trail. To get in touch: P.O. Box 258, Lakeshore, CA 93634; (209) 259-4000 (seasonal at resort—cell phone).

p. 264, col. 1, par. 4: Between Pocket Meadow and the meadow above the cascade on Silver Pass Creek the trail is exposed, loose, and rocky (very poor footing), and involves two hair-raising stream crossings.

p. 272, col. 2, par. 1: No camping at Shadow Lake or between the trail and Shadow Creek where they are parallel.

p. 276, col. 2, line 3: *southeast* should be *southwest.*

p. 309, col. 2, lines 12-14: east fork of Wolf Creek & small camp. A major flood eroded away part of the west bank, including the camp. In 1997 the bank escarpment was virtually impassable for stock. The trail crossing may have to be rerouted downstream.

p. 310, col. 2, line 5: The fraction is $\frac{1}{4}$.

p. 323, col. 2, par. 2, line 2: Echo Summit Ski Area. Now the Echo Summit Sno-Park.

p. 324, col. 1, par. 3: Beyond the Benwood Meadow junction. The route has been slightly changed, and it is more obvious than in the past. The PCT tread ends at the south edge of the Sno-Park's flat parking area, and you head north through it to the PCT's trailhead parking area, where the PCT tread resumes.

p. 328, Mileage: The mileage between the Five Lakes Trail and the Granite Chief Trail is 6.3, not 5.9; so Section K's total mileage is 64.1.

p. 328, Permits and Supplies: In 1997 the Forest Service began charging a $5 fee to camp during summer in Desolation Wilderness. However, this fee is only for those entering the wilderness and camping in it. If you are hiking the PCT *entirely* through the wilderness, you are exempt from the fee, even if you camp in it one or more days. Those hiking only *part way* through on the PCT need to make reservations through the Eldorado Nat. For. Info. Center (listed on p. 18), open 7 days a week.

p. 337, col. 2, Resupply access: 8-mile road to Tahoma. The road goes about 6.8 miles to Chambers Lodge, just south of Tahoma. In Tahoma, you can take a TART bus, which goes 9 miles, not 8, north to Tahoe City.

p. 337, col. 2, 6th line from bottom: lake road should be Lake road.

p. 341, col. 1, last line: (7170-1.0). The correct mileage is 1.4.

p. 344, col. 1, par. 3: 2.6 miles from saddle east of Tinker Knob to saddle northwest of Peak 8374. The miles can be divided into 0.3 to Tinker Knob side route, 1.8 to saddle just north of Anderson Peak, and 0.5 to saddle northwest of Peak 8374. From the saddle just north of Anderson Peak, a 250-yard trail climbs steeply south up the ridge to Benson Hut, which is available as an *emergency* shelter (no water).

p. 344, col. 1, bottom, Roller Pass, col. 2, Side route: From Roller Pass a 90-yard-long spur trail heads east to a sign about the Donner Emigrant Trail. Then 120 yards beyond the pass the PCT reaches a junction with the 2.3-mile-long Mt. Judah Loop Trail. On the PCT you reach its north junction in only 0.9 mile. Should you walk the extra 1.4 miles? If you have the time and energy, yes, for it is very scenic, which is why it is so popular. From the south it switchbacks ¾ mile up to Mt. Judah, then descends northward to a saddle at the southwest base of Donner Peak. (The peak's rewarding, if somewhat acrophobic, summit area is reached in a 0.2 mile scramble.) The loop trail then heads west to a minor saddle, from which a use trail heads briefly north to a granitic outcrop with more fine views. Then the loop trail descends 0.3 mile southwest to the PCT.

p. 350, Map L1: Trails crisscrossing the PCT between old Highway 40 and I-80 are abandoned and do not exist.

p. 351, col. 1, lines 2 and 4: lakelet/lake's. Should be lakelet/lakelet's.

p. 351, col. 1, par. 2, last 2 lines: Castle Pass. Actually, the PCT reaches the abandoned jeep road (a popular trail) 110 yards below the pass. At the pass is a conspicuous use trail—also popular—which climbs directly up a ridge, first north then east, to the three summits of Castle Peak.

p. 351, col. 2, par. 2: leap across North Creek. It now has a 1996-vintage horse bridge.

p. 351, col. 2, bottom, Side route: The Mt. Lola Trail begins about 0.1 mile before White Rock Creek, which now has a 1996-vintage horse bridge. The trail climbs ⅔ mile to the dam of White Rock Lake, then skirts along the south shore before climbing northeastward above the southeast shore, bound for Mt. Lola. You can find small campsites on its bedrock peninsula. More-spacious sites are along the northeast shore, and these are best reached by the jeep road to the lake. If you want a layover day at the lake, you might plan to climb Mt. Lola, doing so from the jeep road, not its excessively oscillating namesake trail. From the lake's east shore, the jeep road climbs gently 0.3 mile east to a south fork, then continues 0.2 to where it becomes extremely steep. The summit is only 1.3 miles from here, and other than the extremely steep initial stretch, the route is a good one.

p. 353, col. 2, 5th line from bottom: another good road (6740-2.3). From this junction an equestrian trail meanders ⅓ mile north along the crest and then descends ½ mile northeast to Little Lasier Meadow Horse Camp, sandwiched between Pass Creek Loop Road (Forest Route 70) and a north-flowing creek. In June 1997, the start of this trail was cryptic, and parts of it were in terrible shape. Therefore, if you want to descend to this horse camp, don't take the trail if it still looks unmaintained. Rather, take the good road 0.4 mile east down to the loop road, then 0.7 mile north above the creek's west bank to the horse camp (in northeastern Section 28 and east of Peak 6955). From it the road's west part continues 1.3 miles, first north, then west, to end at the entrance to East Meadow Campground.

p. 355, col. 2, Resupply access, par. 2: 0.3 mile through it to Milton Creek. Should be Haypress Creek.

pp. 363-87: The running head should have Highway 49 instead of Highway 40.

p. 363, Side route, par. 2, line 3: junction at 7910 feet in elevation. OHVs are allowed to drive up to a small parking area at this junction. Above, mountain bikers take the jeep trail to the lookout, while hikers can take a new trail 0.3 mile up to a rejoining of the jeep trail at about 8200 feet.

p. 365, Alternate route, last sentence: The first Grass Lake turnoff is about ¼ mile up the trail from the outlet creek. Due to a reroute, the trail now crosses the creek higher up, just 90 yards below the lake. The following Side route (p. 365-66) is out. Just above this lake is another trail reroute.

p. 366, col. 2, Side route: The trail northwest to Deer Lake has been abandoned.

p. 366, col. 2, par. 2, line 7: a use trail. This now is the official trail to Deer Lake.

p. 366, col. 2, par. 2, line 14: bend southwest across a slope to a jeep road. The jeep road is thoroughly abandoned, and the trail now is rerouted northwest, reaching the PCT at a junction 2.7 miles from the start of the Deer Lake Trail, just 25 yards before the PCT reaches a minor knoll with the first excellent view of the Salmon Lakes. This junction is 0.3 mile north of a conspicuous jeep road descending to Deer Lake—see next entry.

p. 367, col. 1, par. 2 & 3: After ⅓ mile you reach a jeep road...next ¼ mile...west-climbing jeep road. The first jeep road is abandoned. In just under 0.2 mile you cross and then recross the ridgecrest jeep road, and at a saddle, can take a jeep road that descends steeply east to

good camping along the west shore of Deer Lake. Just north of the saddle, the "west-climbing jeep road" is unnoticed and abandoned, as mentioned in the previous entry.

p. 368: "Helgramite Lake" label is at the wrong lake. This small lake is between two trails, just below the "a" in "Lakes Basin."

p. 382, Map M10: The trail line was printed about one centimeter to the left of where it should be.

p. 413, captions: The upper photo: A churning Hat Creek cascade; the lower photo: Subway Cave.

p. 424: PCT Section P map should be on p. 446.

p. 444, col. 2, last full par., substitute: "Upon reaching the upside-down 'T' junction of the two roads, go left and immediately cross Soda Creek. Then, after two minutes you bridge the fairly wide Sacramento River, followed quickly by the Southern Pacific's railroad tracks."

p. 446: PCT Section O map should be on p. 424.

p. 479, Mileage table: The mileage from Buckhorn Spring to Grider Creek Trail at Road 46N72 is 6.7 miles (not 7.7). Just delete the mileage and elevation reference (4820-1.0)— p. 492, 10th line from bottom—and everything else remains correct. The total length of section Q is, of course, one mile shorter.

p. 480, col. 1, line 13: Although a wilderness permit used to be required for the Marble Mountain Wilderness, it no longer is. Thus, delete the references regarding same on p. 480, lines 12-13, and on p. 448 in the "Permits" section.

p. 484: Map Q3. There should be two ponds drawn on a bench above the north shore of Man Eaten Lake, roughly where the north-south line between Sections 8 and 9 crosses the bench.

p. 493. The Grider Creek footbridges are washed out.

p. 496: PCT Section R map needs to show creeks, rivers, and lakes in blue, not black.

Back cover: The mileage should read 2665 miles.

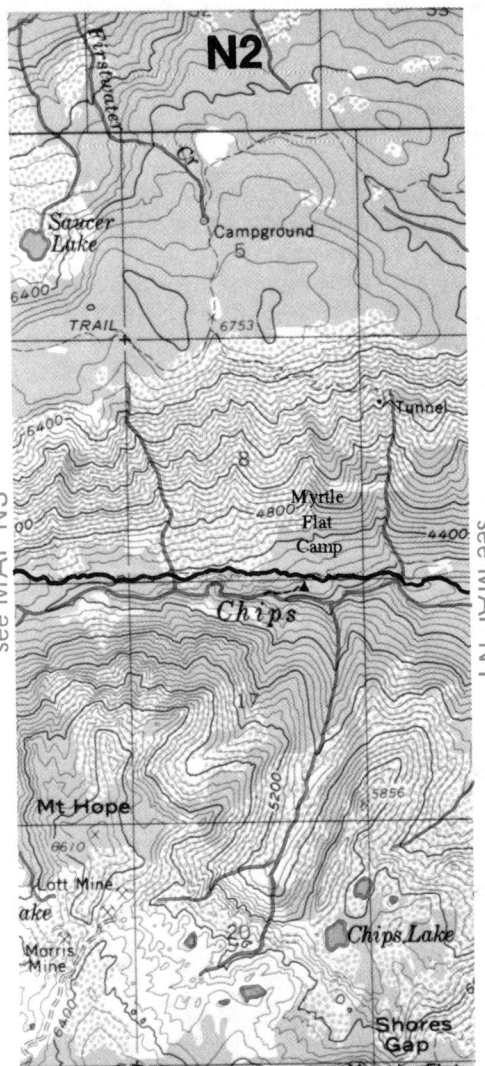

see MAP N3

see MAP N1

until just before your crest route starts to curve west. You now have views, with the dark, prominent Eagle Rocks (7063') looming ½ mile to the northeast. You can scan the Cascade crest that rims the upper Butt Creek basin. A prominent gap on the north rim is the saddle south of unseen Carter Meadow. The gap is 2¾ air miles away, but the PCT will take 7½ miles to get to it. As you progress west, you pass two volcanic pinnacles, just to the north, then pass smaller trailside pinnacles and blocks. You leave the crest and your panoramic views disappear as you enter a forest on the northwest steep slope of Humboldt Peak (7087'). Snowbound at least until early July, this stretch first drops, then climbs to the Humboldt Road at Humboldt Summit (6610–3.6).

▮ *In the winter of 1993–94 the once stately red firs in this area suffered considerable blowdown—enough to cause a temporary rerouting of the PCT through this area. (Note that here and elsewhere in the Sierra Nevada the damaging windstorms are from the northeast while the snowstorms are from the west.) The ambience here has not always been delightful in the past, for the de-facto car-camping area formerly here occasionally attracted drunken and/or gun-crazed campers. If such types are absent, then you should find a suitable, pleasant campsite. Lingering snow patches may provide you with water through early July, but after that you may have to descend 1½–3 miles north from Humboldt Summit to find water flowing in Butt Creek.* ▮

West of the summit the PCT makes a traverse and slight descent to a spur ridge before switchbacking down to a saddle on the county-line crest. Leaving the logging scar of this area, your well-graded trail stays close to the crest without any unnecessary climbing or descending. Shady forest cover alternates with shrubby slopes that provide views of Lassen Peak and, on clear days, the Sacramento Valley. One-half mile beyond a crossing of a set of old jeep tracks, you descend to the lowest of several saddles (6155–3.9). Your climbing trail now turns gradually eastward, passes an interesting outcrop of volcanic rocks, and veers north to cross a long spur ridge before descending southeast to the Carter Meadow Trail junction, on a saddle (6600–2.3). The trail goes only about a mile north to a logging road. Along it, you

then traverse north across an open flat. A pond lies just west of the trail (7100–1.6) but it usually evaporates by mid or late July. From the flat's north end you traverse northwest on an old jeep road and have your first views of the Lake Almanor area and the Lassen Peak environs. The closed road then switchbacks down to a narrow ridge and your views disappear. Near the north end (7000–0.9), a blocked-off jeep road forks right and drops about 500 feet as it descends to the Lost Lake environs. Your jeep road ends in 0.1 mile and you fork left down a bush-lined trail.

You quickly re-enter forest and stay within it

See maps N4, N5

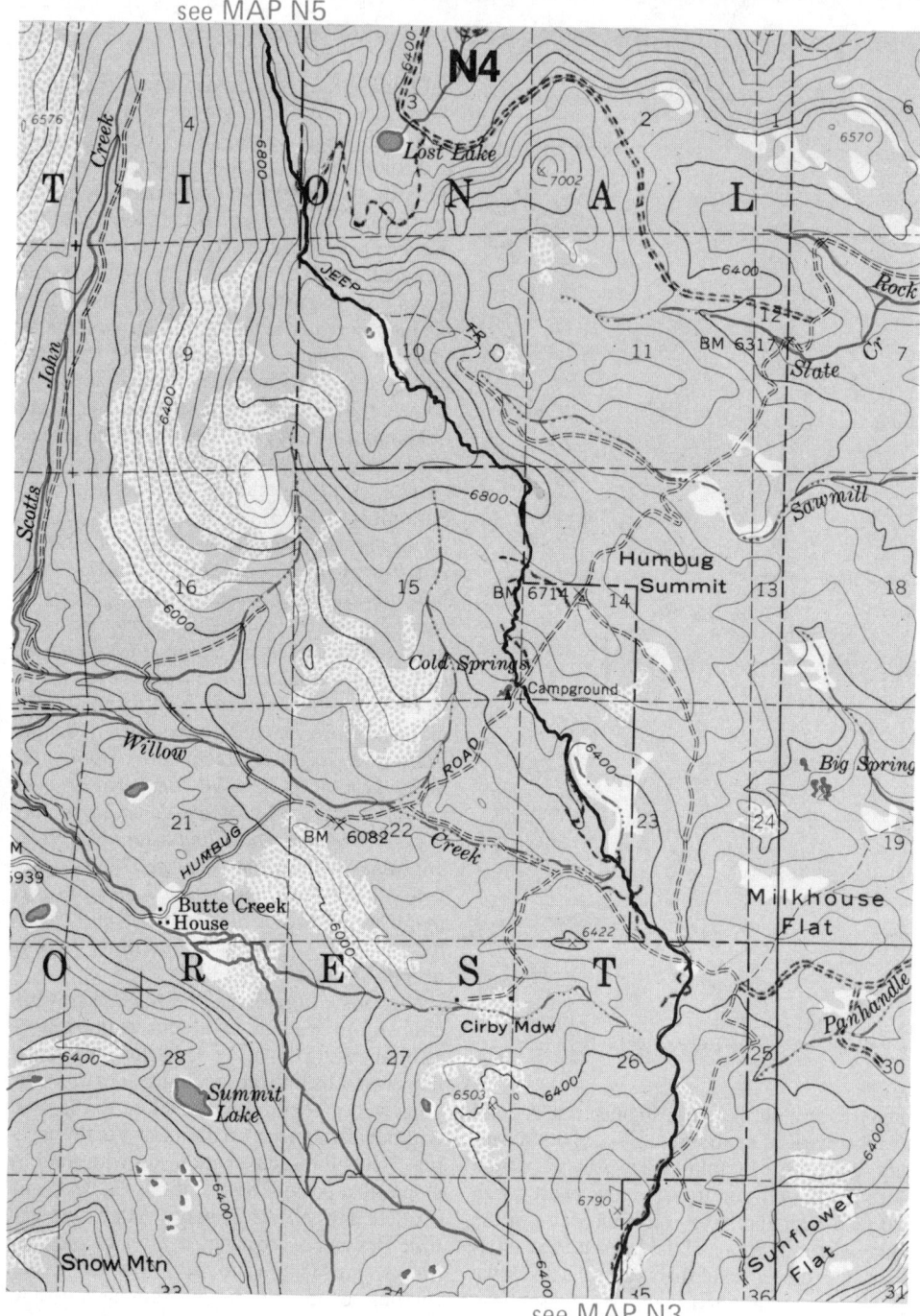

see MAP N3

should only have to go about ½ mile to find water and campsites. If you need to get out of the mountains, follow the road 7½ miles down to Highway 32. Lots of logging roads complicate this exit, but generally head north down to Deer Creek Meadows, then 2 miles west out to the busy highway.

The PCT climbs east up the divide to some interesting rim volcanics, then switchbacks across forested slopes to climb above rugged cliffs. About 1½ miles from the saddle your route starts climbing northeast on a moderate

See map N5

grade, and then it descends a bit through brush to a long, nearly level crest. Along it you have views south of logged-over Ruffa Ridge and views north of Lassen Peak, which stands in the distance above the glaciated canyon lying below you. From the northeast end of the crest you make a moderate climb of ½ mile and then skirt the south end of Butt Mountain, along which you meet a junction (7590–3.7).

* * * *

Side route: Although there are great views just ahead, you can get a 360° panorama by taking the Butt Mountain Trail north about 0.7 mile to its summit.

* * * *

From the junction you quickly reach the west end of another long, nearly level crest. ∎ *Along it you see not only Lassen Peak, but also Brokeoff Mountain, west of it. Brokeoff Mountain (9235'), second only to Lassen in height, is the southwest remnant of a now-eroded stratovolcano that may have stood 11,000 feet high about 500,000 years ago. Lassen Peak, at 10,457 feet, is considerably smaller than the older, spreading stratovolcano. Lassen, a huge dome of pasty lava, is also considerably younger, having been squeezed onto the surface roughly 18,000 years ago.* ∎

Leaving the east end of your crest, you descend almost a mile east across brushy slopes that give you ample opportunities to survey the south end of Lake Almanor to the east, and past and present logging operations to the south. Your route enters a red-fir forest as it begins to curve north, and then it descends ½ mile to a secondary ridge, which it rounds before descending ½ mile northwest to a shallow gully (6920–2.6). Before mid-July you may find water in this gully, but it quickly disappears after the snow melts. You start east down the gully, but soon veer away and, on a southeast-facing slope, see your first sugar pine on this descent. White firs clothe the slopes as you continue your descent, though ¼ mile before your second major gully you have an opening with your first good view of giant Lake Almanor. Beyond the second gully you descend ¾ mile northeast to a ridge, then more than a mile west to the seasonal headwaters of Soldier Creek. You cross its gully and

then descend, in just under a mile, to its recrossing (5480–4.2). The creek is flowing here, for your ford lies just below permanent Soldier Creek springs. Unfortunately, topography limits camping space to just one tent site. Don't expect any decent camping until Stover Camp, still 6.9 miles away.

Ponderosa pines and incense-cedars are now commonplace among the white firs as you traverse east and drop into private property just before crossing an old road (5150–1.5). You continue ¼ mile east to a newer road, then switchback and parallel it ¼ mile northwest before crossing it. On nearly flat ground you head north to a grassy trough (4870–0.7), which becomes Soldier Creek only during flooding. ∎ *The grass grows on porous, scoriaceous basalt, so the creek along this stretch is largely subterranean. Lodgepole pines, taking advantage of this underground source, line the trough. This stand of water-loving conifers is near its lower-elevation limit; you see few lodgepoles below 5000 feet. Along the northeast side of the grassy trough runs a dirt-bike path, which is a remnant of the Lassen Trail. Danish immigrant Peter Lassen pioneered it back in 1847, providing settlers with the first route into northern California. The route, however, was not efficient, and it fell into disuse after William H. Nobles pioneered a shorter, better route in 1851. You'll hike several miles of his route in the northern part of Lassen Volcanic National Park.* ∎

Terminal Geyser

See maps N5, N6, N7

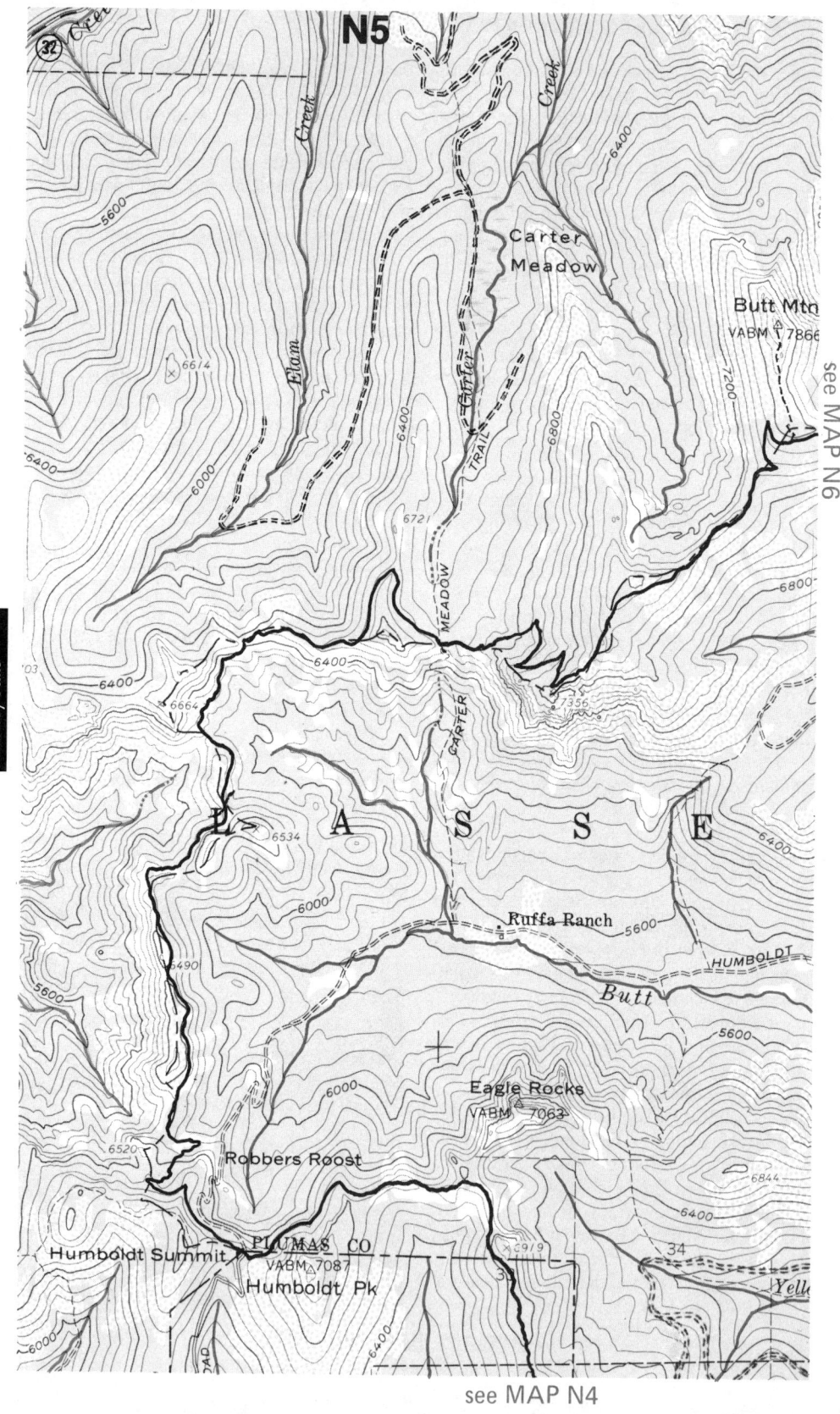

see MAP N6

Creek

Carter
Meadow

Butt Mtn
VABM 7866

Elam

Creek

Carter

TRAIL

MEADOW

CARTER

6614

6721

7356

L A S S E

6664

6534

Ruffa Ranch

HUMBOLDT

Butt

6490

Eagle Rocks
VABM 7063

6844

6520

Robbers Roost

Humboldt Summit
VABM 7087
Humboldt Pk

PLUMAS CO

34

Yello

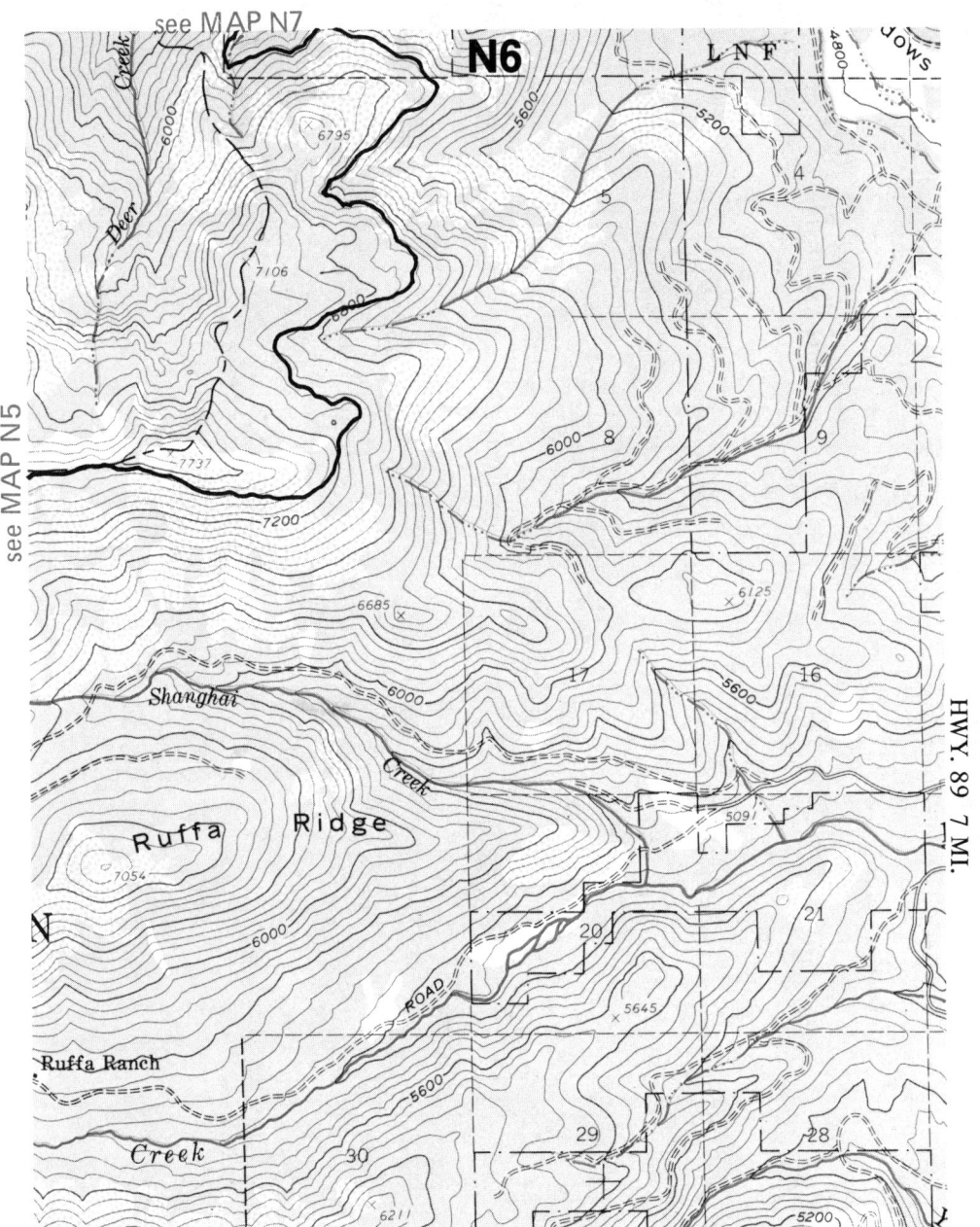

Leaving the grassy trough and the lodgepole pines which tap the near-surface water, you climb just a bit into a dry, open forest of Jeffrey pines. The soil derived from the geologically young basalt is extremely dusty, and your boots and socks get covered with it by the time you reach a minor road. Immediately past it you cross a heavily used logging road, then climb ½ mile across less dusty terrain to Highway 36 (4990–1.5). The highway lacks parking, which is unfortunate for those wanting to do just the enjoyable Highway 36-Highway 44 stretch. The St. Bernard Lodge lies 1.5 miles west along Highway 36 and the Black Forest Lodge, with the menu preferred by Schaffer and Schifrin, lies 0.2 mile past it. Chester, a "full-service" community, lies 8 miles to the northeast.

North from Highway 36 you cross three roads

See map N7

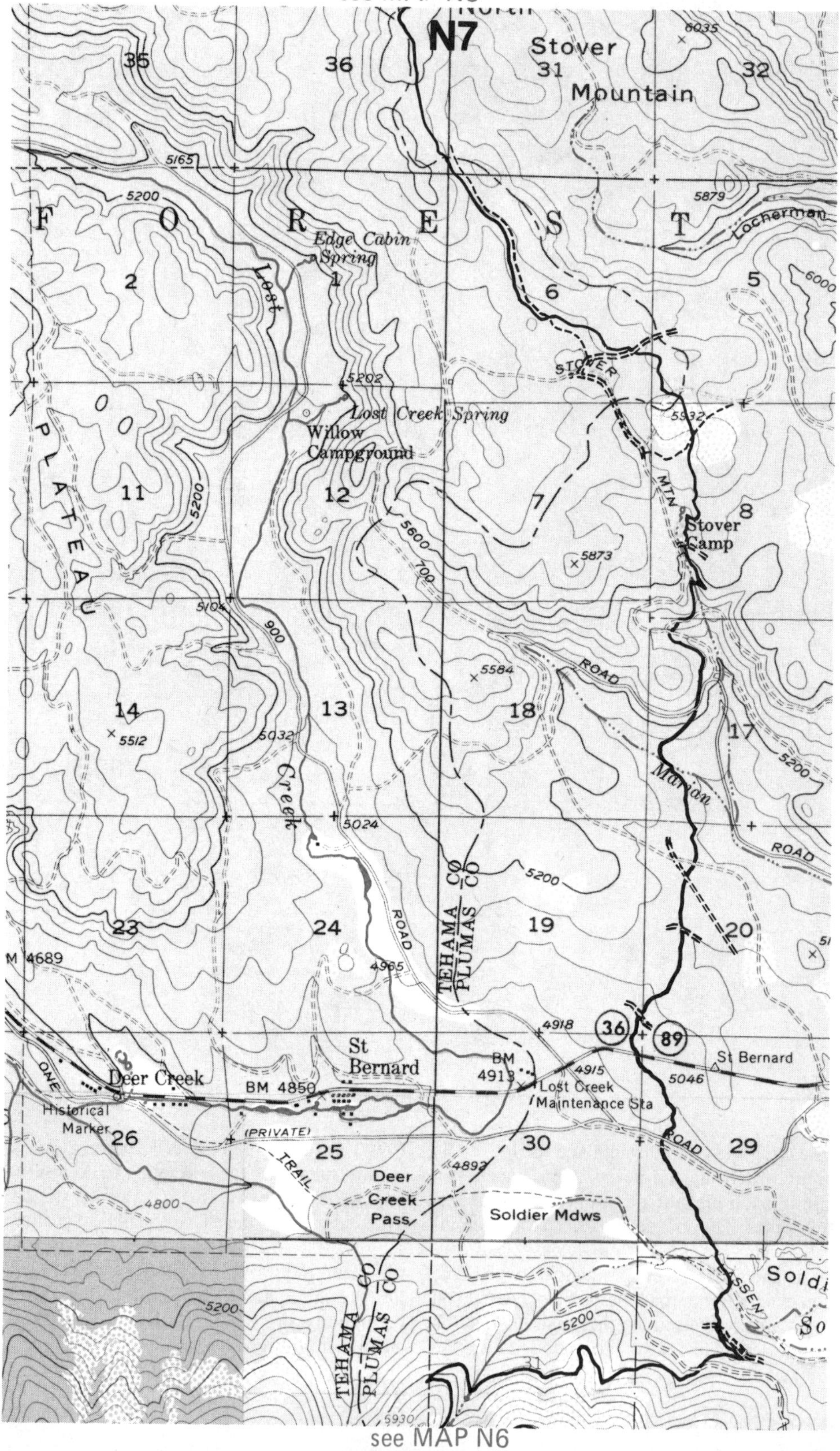

N7

North
Stover
Mountain

FOREST

PLATEAU

Edge Cabin
Spring

Lost Creek Spring

Willow
Campground

Stover
Camp

Locherman

STOVER MTN

ROAD

Marion

ROAD

TEHAMA CO
PLUMAS CO

Deer Creek

St
Bernard

BM 4850

Historical
Marker

(PRIVATE)

TRAIL

Deer
Creek
Pass

Soldier Mdws

Lost Creek
Maintenance Sta

St Bernard

ROAD

LASSEN

Soldi

So

TEHAMA CO
PLUMAS CO

in one mile, the third one a major road. Just 130 yards past it you cross a fourth, then weave ½ mile over to Marian Creek (5060–1.6), which is usually dry during most of the summer. You then climb 0.4 mile to another major road, cross it, circle counterclockwise ½ mile to a similar road, cross it and in 110 yards cross yet another one. Quickly you start a climb up the west side of a gully, cross it midway up, then continue your climb to Stover Camp (5660–1.6). With spring water, this undeveloped Forest Service campground, halfway between Highway 36 and North Stover Mountain, can be one of the section's nicer camps—if it hasn't been recently trashed when you pass through. Also, the water which gushes in spring, can dwindle to a seep by mid-summer.

You leave the camp by a short climb east, then resume your northward ascent, crossing an abandoned road in ½ mile. An old clearcut lies between it and a low divide, a county boundary. After ⅓ mile of traverse, you cross a major road (5810–1.1) just west of the county-line crest. You parallel it briefly west, then traverse across logged lands to an abandoned road, which you cross ½ mile past the major road. This you parallel almost a mile northwest back up to the county-line crest (5920–1.4), the last 125 yards being on private logging land in the southwest corner of Section 31. A gentle climb ensues, taking you north-northwest through a logged area to flat, viewless North Stover Mountain (6050–0.7), clothed in firs and sugar pines. A well graded, shady descent follows, and it provides you with several views of Lassen Peak before you cross a major logging road (5400–1.6) on a ridge.

From the ridge your trail first descends to a

large bridge over North Fork Feather River (5020–1.0), making an unnecessary climb along the way. From the bridge's north end the trail jogs a few paces west before climbing east out of the small gorge. You'll find good campsites just upstream from the jog in the trail. Out of the gorge, you have a level route north and cross a long, narrow clearcut a minute before crossing a major logging road. About two minutes past it you meet a minor road.

* * * *

Side route: If you want to visit Domingo Spring Campground, follow this road northeast to a quick junction with a major road going 0.3 mile east to the campground. The water there is definitely more dependable than at Stover Camp.

* * * *

After another two-minute walk on the PCT, you cross the major road, Chester-Childs Meadows road (5110–0.9).

* * * *

Resupply access: This road goes 8.0 miles west, ending at Highway 36 as Wilson Lake Road. It also goes 8.8 miles east to Chester, ending at Highway 36 as Feather River Drive.

* * * *

The PCT north of this road begins along a short, abandoned road spur, which makes a convenient trailhead parking area. Staying quite

See maps N7, N8

Marshy Little Willow Lake

level, the trail traverses along the base of a volcanic-rubble slope, then climbs briefly onto a closed road. Up it you count off 110 yards before the trail resumes. It switchbacks once across this steeply ascending road, then joins it where the road's gradient reduces to moderate. You now follow the road for 0.4 mile to where it ends at a 1986 clearcut, which was planted in 1989. Judge for yourself how fast the forest is regenerating. At least you do get a view of Stump Ranch meadow and, in the distance beyond it, Butt Mountain. Just after you pass it, you cross a second, smaller clearcut of similar vintage, this one extending downslope from a shallow saddle. Just above it the PCT crosses and immediately recrosses the crest, then crosses it about ½ mile later. It soon arrives at the brink of an east-west trending secondary ridge, from which you can see Willow Lake northeast below you and Lassen Peak northwest above you. From this viewpoint you can't see the conspicuous lakelet about ¼ mile to the east. Neither it nor the pond west of it is worth a visit.

Beyond the viewpoint the trail contours west, descends to a saddle on the main ridge, crosses it, and traverses northwest across the west slope. Up the canyon to the west, a private road climbs to a broad saddle, where your now-descending trail almost touches it, then finally diagonals across it after a 0.1-mile paralleling descent northwest (5960–4.1). Here you'll see an abandoned road branching left, and you walk along it but 45 yards to where trail tread resumes, along the road's left (south) side. The trail quickly curves north, soon reaches Little Willow Lake's outlet creek, and then climbs steeply up this seasonal creek to a junction along the east fringe of swampy Little Willow Lake (6100–0.7). Since its basin is your first potential camping area in Lassen Park, you should remember that in the park no camping is allowed in meadows or within 100 feet of a lake or creek. You'll also need a wilderness permit to camp outside the park's campgrounds. Since the Little Willow Lake marsh is prime mosquito land, at least before August, you'll probably want to push on to Warner Valley Campground, your first real camping opportunity. Like trails of old, the next stretch of northbound PCT climbs over a ridge and drops to a junction rather than contours over to it (6030–1.0).

* * * *

Side route: From here you can make a short side trip, descending ¼ mile to a road going briefly north to Terminal Geyser. Midway along this descent you'll meet a spur trail that goes east to a nearby overlook of the Terminal Geyser bowl, but the geyser is better viewed from below. Therefore, follow the road north 180 yards to the roaring geyser, at road's end. Continually churning out steam, it is technically a fumarole, not a geyser. Observe it with caution. On the broad area at road's end you'll see a capped well, drilled in 1978 by Phillips Petroleum Company, which was doing geothermal exploration.

* * * *

Back at the PCT junction, your trail splits in just 25 yards. If you are on horseback, you have to take the right trail, which goes 1.6 miles to a junction just north of Boiling Springs Lake. If you are on foot, take the more scenic left trail which in 1⅓ miles climbs over a divide and drops to a junction by a ravine just above Boiling Springs Lake. Again here, you can go either right or left, though the official, more scenic PCT route goes left. On the park's Boiling Springs Lake Nature Trail, you head northwest past the scalding-hot lake's fumaroles, mudpots and rotten fumes. Just beyond the lake you cross its short-season outlet creek and by its east bank meet the end of the counterclockwise nature trail around the lake. Then, in about 0.2 mile, you meet the horse trail (5800–1.8). Your well-traveled route descends ¼ mile to a trail climbing west to Drake Lake, then a few paces later passes a trail northwest over to nearby Drakesbad Guest Ranch. You start east and immediately see this resort's tempting pool, heated by hot springs. The pool, unfortunately, is for guests only, and the resort is usually booked several years in advance. However, you can get a meal at the lodge if you give them sufficient warning; their supplies are limited.

Beyond a couple of hot springs the trail descends to a bridge across Hot Springs Creek. Despite its name, the creek is very, very cold. Between creek and meadow, you walk a few minutes east to a picnic area, head over to the nearby Drakesbad road, then make a short walk

See maps N8, N9

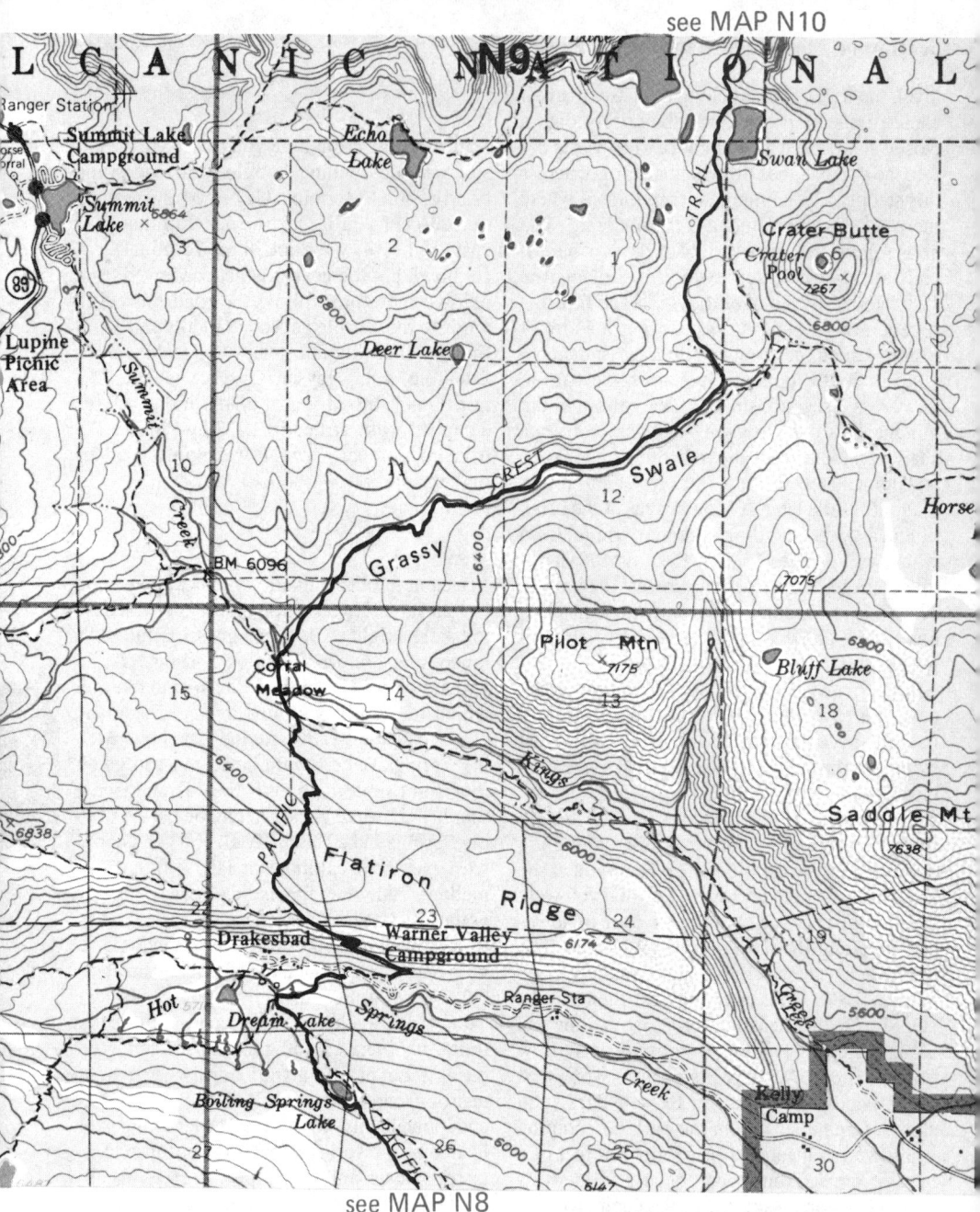

see MAP N10

see MAP N8

east on it to a fork. You branch left, climbing past a few campsites to the east end of Warner Valley Campground (5670–0.9), where PCT tread resumes near a spring-fed creeklet. If you camp here and not in the park's backcountry, you won't need a wilderness permit.

From the campground, the trail crosses the creeklet in less than 40 yards, then soon switchbacks twice. It makes a very well-graded ascent northwest on glaciated lava flows, one thick flow forming a prominent band of nearly vertical cliffs. ▌*You started in a forest of white firs, Jeffrey pines, incense-cedars and sugar pines, and when you re-enter forest higher up,*

See map N9

Drakesbad Guest Ranch, Lower Twin Lake and West Prospect Peak, Silver Lake

the last two species are no longer with you. Until that re-entry, you have some fair views of the Drakesbad area, and you pass some drought-resistant wildflowers and ferns. ▮ You gradually leave the cliff escarpment and ease into a fir forest, shortly arriving at a junction (6180–1.0). The trail branching left leads to others climbing to Bench Lake, Sifford Lake, Kings Creek Falls and the Lassen Park Road.

As you continue upward, white firs disappear, red firs become dominant, and western white pines join them. Your trail crosses the western part of Flatiron Ridge, which is composed of relatively flat layers of lava flows topped with glacial sediments. ▮ *The flows are among the park's older volcanic rocks, probably being on the order of 1–1½ million years old.* ▮ From the crest of a glacial moraine you wander down the gullied north slopes of Flatiron Ridge and arrive at a trail junction at the outskirts of Corral Meadow. Here, a trail takes off down Kings Creek. This infrequently used trail offers hikers some pretty impressive views of the Kings Creek gorge. The PCT quickly crosses two seasonal creeks, the second one the more persistent of the two, and ¼ mile past the previous junction reaches another junction amidst campsites (5990–1.4).

*   *   *   *

Side route: Summit Lake and the heavily used Lassen Park Road (open from about mid-June through September) are about 2⅓ miles away along the trail climbing left from the junction. There is a campground above both the north and south shores of the lake. Just northwest of the lake is a horse corral and a ranger station.

*   *   *   *

From the spacious west-bank campsites the trail crosses to the east bank of Kings Creek—definitely a wet ford. However, you might find a log bridge just upstream, providing a dry crossing. From the log you then head back down to the trail's resumption, although a misleading *de facto* trail continues upstream, leading hikers astray. The trail goes a bit over 100 yards to the confluence where Grassy Swale and Summit creeks become Kings Creek. You

can find an additional campsite in this vicinity. Immediately above the confluence, Grassy Swale creek noisily cascades 30 feet down into a small, shallow pool, which in turn spills into a deeper one—this one a cozy, if chilly, swimming hole.

Before August the stretch of trail from Corral Meadow northeast through Grassy Swale abounds with mosquitoes. The trail makes an initial climb, then wanders through a variable red-fir forest, arriving after one mile at a small, wet meadow, which is an excellent place to look for diminutive wildflowers, including the rather uncommon round-leaved sundew. You loop around the meadow's south border and then, about ⅓ mile beyond it, you log-cross or boulder-hop Grassy Swale creek. For the next ⅓ mile, you stay close to the creek, yet just far enough above its bank to be on dry, gravelly soil. You then return to mosquitoland, a marshy meadow lined with western blueberrries, which extends for several hundred yards. Almost ½ mile past the marshy Grassy Swale creek meadow, you come to a junction (6470–2.5) with a trail to pleasant, but out-of-the-way Horseshoe Lake. The trail continues ⅓ mile up the northwest bank of Grassy Swale creek before leaving it for a moderate one-mile climb to meet a second trail (6710–1.3) that joins the first to go to Horseshoe lake.

*   *   *   *

Side route: Should you want to climb a small volcano with a lake in its crater, then climb nearby Crater Butte, rising 500 feet above you to the southeast. This "cinder cone" is—like its northern neighbor, Fairfield Peak—more lava flow than cinders, and both probably originated during the last episode of glaciation.

*   *   *   *

About 250 yards past the junction the PCT crests a low divide and leaves behind the headwaters of the North Fork Feather River. Entering the headwaters of the Pit River, you'll quickly note Swan Lake, a short distance below you. If you plan to camp at this typical backcountry lake, leave the trail here and look for a site above its south shore or ones on its east-shore bench. Your trail almost touches the

See map N9

lake at its northwest corner, then immediately crosses its barely discernible outlet creek (6620–0.5) before dropping ½ mile to a junction on the southeast shore of lodgepole-fringed Lower Twin Lake.

*   *   *   *

Side route: Westward, a 4¼-mile route skirts along the lake's south shore, then climbs past Upper Twin and Echo lakes to Summit Lake's north-shore campground.

*   *   *   *

On a ¼ mile stretch, the PCT starts east, immediately passing a campsite before curving north to an east-shore junction with a trail that first climbs ⅔ mile to Rainbow Lake, and then continues 3 miles down to the park's famous Cinder Cone, beside the Nobles Trail. After several more minutes of east-shore walking on the PCT, you reach Lower Twin Lake's north shore and a trail (6545–0.9) that skirts along it. You may see a cabin here, which is sometimes occupied by a seasonal backcountry ranger. Just a short hike past this junction, your route, now a closed road, gives rise to a trail descending left (6520–0.4).

*   *   *   *

Alternate route: The Pacific Crest Trail takes a 5¼-mile waterless route along old, gravelly roads to the east end of Badger Flat. If you'd rather take a lake-blessed route, then follow the

4⅔-mile trail that branches left here. Be fore-warned, however, that before August mosquitoes can be quite fierce along it. In ¼ mile the trail crosses Twin Lakes creek and then it traverses nearly ½ mile over to a pond, which is chest-deep, just like the one you meet a few minutes later. Feather Lake lies immediately beyond it, and is perhaps the nicest of all the Cluster Lakes. A triangular lake 200 yards north of it is pleasant too, for though it is shallow, it probably has the fewest mosquitoes of any of the Cluster Lakes—an important consideration before August. By early August all the Cluster Lakes, like the Twin Lakes, drop about a foot or so, and then a narrow yellow ring of tiny primrose monkey flowers circles each lake. A low divide separates Feather Lake from Silver Lake, and ¼ mile past that lake you come to a junction with a trail that climbs 4¼ miles to Summit Lake's north-shore campground. Continuing northwest, you skirt past Cluster Lake, with a couple of campsites near its north end, then circle around an unnamed lake that severely shrinks in volume by late summer. You next descend along the seasonal Cluster Lakes creek, cross it where it bends east, vault a low divide, and descend 1⅓ miles to a reunion with the PCT at the east end of Badger Flat.

*   *   *   *

If you're adhering to the official PCT, then descend along the lodgepole-pine-lined road, heading toward Prospect Peak, a late-Ice Age shield volcano. About 1¾ miles beyond the beginning of the alternate route, you cross grav-

N
Hwy. 70–
Burney Falls

See maps N9, N10

Cinder Cone, lying 3½ miles northeast of Lower Twin Lake, is a very rewarding trip

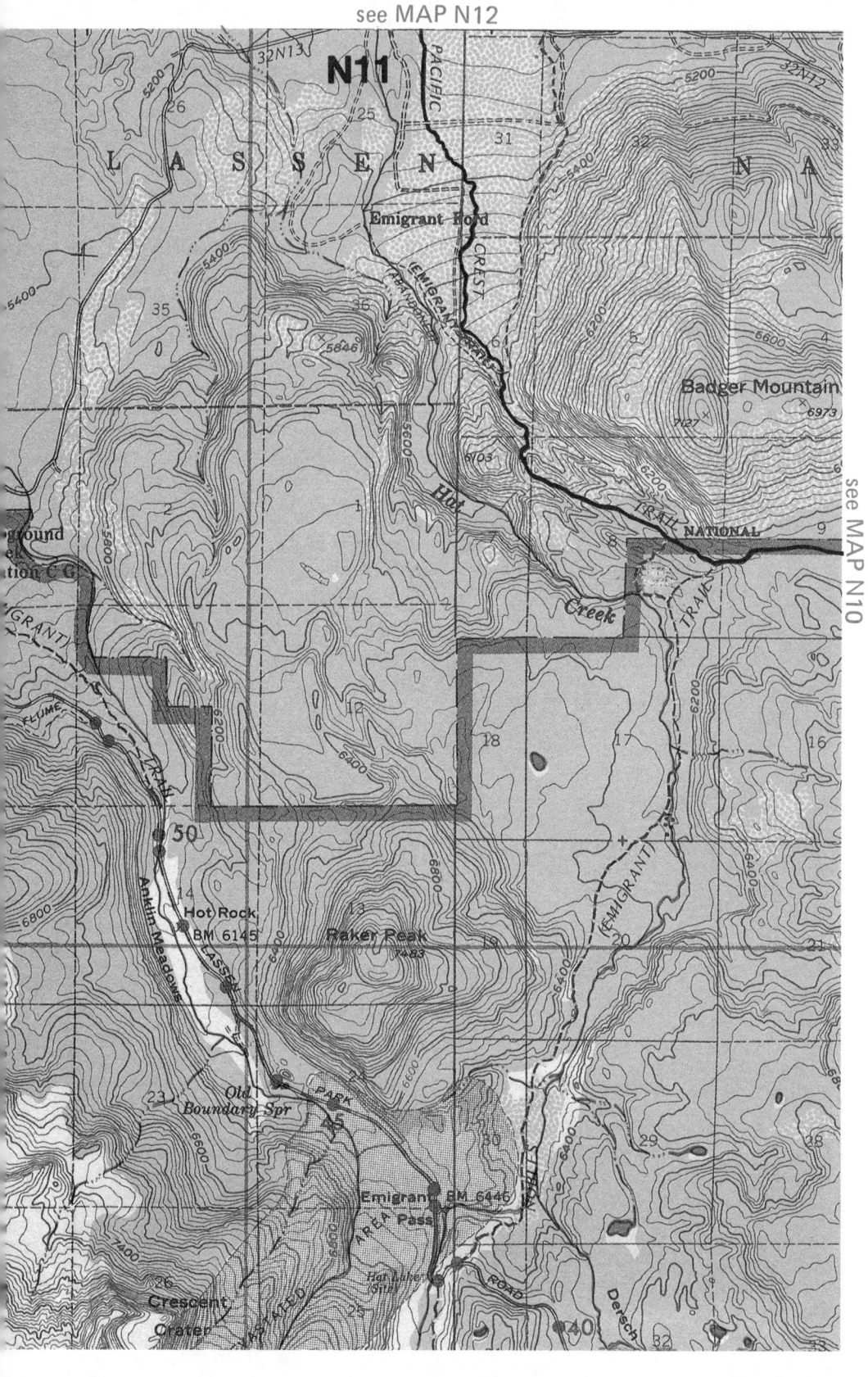

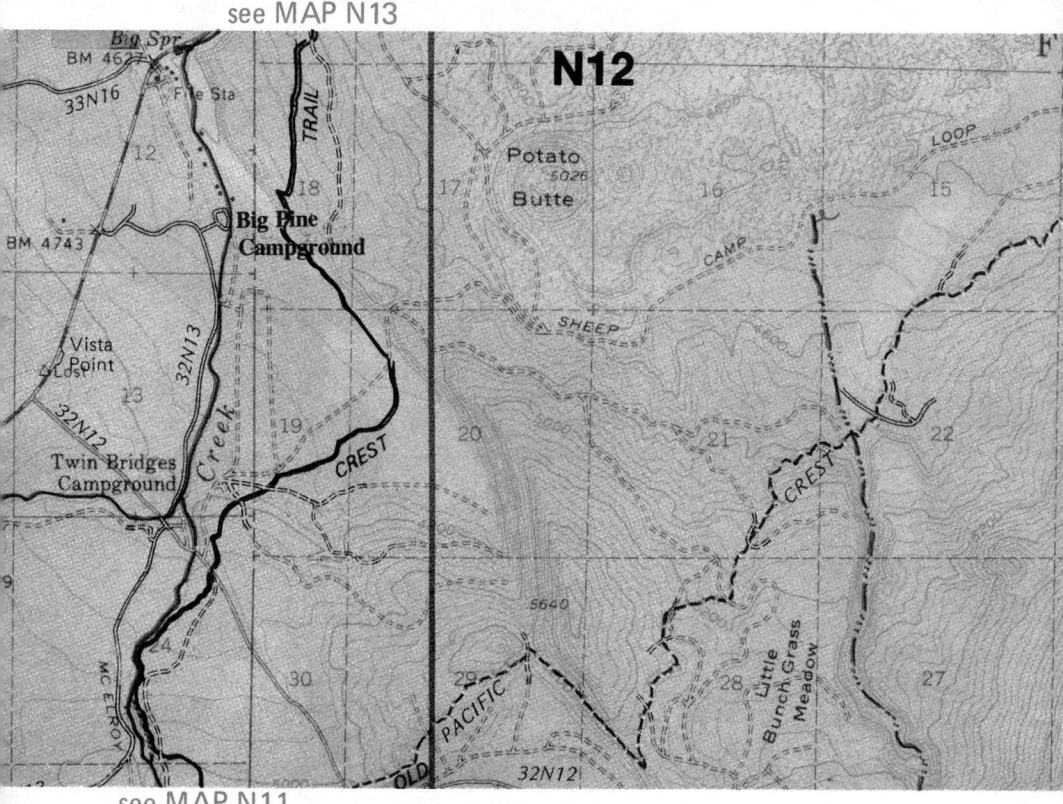

elly Twin Lakes outlet creek, which often dries up before the Fourth of July. The road, almost level, climbs near its end to a junction with the Nobles Trail (6354–2.6), which has come about 2½ miles west from the Cinder Cone. Now on the route pioneered by William H. Nobles in 1851, you climb briefly northwest to a minor divide, then traverse through viewless terrain until you reach an opening (6320–1.0), from which you see shallow Soap Lake just to the south. Being rather low in elevation, this lake provides acceptably warm swimming even in early July, when most of Lassen Park's lakes still have snow nearby.

A forested, viewless traverse continues all the way to the east end of Badger Flat, where the alternate route rejoins the PCT (6270–1.6). A creek draining this meadow usually flows through mid-July, and if it's flowing, you might want to camp nearby. As you follow your climbing road west, you'll note evidence of a 1984 fire. After about ½ mile from the junction, you cross a low ridge and then descend briefly to a shallow pond, on the right. If it's dry, so too will be the springs in the upper west end of

Badger Flat, so don't waste your time looking for them. Your mainly viewless route traverses westward until just before the old emigrant road begins a moderate drop. On a flat, you branch northwest on trail tread, then in ¼ mile reach a trail junction by the park's north boundary (6200–2.1).

* * * *

Side route: From here a trail winds 0.4 mile southwest across glacial moraines to a former horse camp. Located beside Hat Creek, it is still a fine site for backpackers, certainly one of the best in water-and-camp-deficient Section N.

* * * *

From the park boundary, the PCT descends the crest of a glacial moraine. After about ½ mile of crest descent, with views south of Lassen Peak above a dry gorge below, the man-zanita-and-tobacco-brush-bordered PCT descends ¼ mile through a gully, then continues a similar distance on an easier gradient to a

See maps N10, N11

section of the Plantation Loop Road (5560–1.5). Formerly the PCT route turned right and headed north down this road, which skirts the base of fault-cleft Badger Mountain, eventually to climb to the essentially waterless Hat Creek Rim. Since July 1992 it has taken an anti-crest route, hugging the floor of the upper part of Hat Creek Valley.

From the Plantation Loop Road the newer, descending segment parallels the western arm of the road northward through a plantation of Jeffrey pines, eventually crossing an east-west road (5090–1.7), and then curving west to cross the western arm of the Plantation Loop Road (4980–0.7). The route then winds northward, trapped between the road on the east and Hat Creek on the west. You could camp anywhere in this vicinity, but especially between ¼-½ mile beyond the road crossing. The trail gradually veers away from the creek to closely parallel the loop road to its junction with northwest-heading Road 32N12 (4830–1.0). By hiking in that direction, you'll immediately pass a car-camping area on your right as you go 0.1 mile to a bridge over Hat Creek.

From Road 32N12 the PCT initially parallels a road north, soon climbs to the top of a low lava flat, then curves northeast to descend across two roads in rather quick succession. Paralleling the initial, unseen road at a distance, your trail continues a meandering course northeast over to the western edge of a sagebrush flat—a downfaulted depression—from which it heads 0.2 mile north to cross the initial road (4690–1.4). Now it heads northwest for 0.6 mile before crossing a linear, dry creekbed to climb to a switchback atop a faulted escarpment (4720–0.9). After an initial jog east, the PCT angles north and makes a gentle descent, soon paralleling the east side of a one-lane road before curving northeast for a quick drop to a crossing of a north-trending road (4590–0.8). This you parallel north to a gate across the road (4580–0.2).

*   *   *   *

Resupply access: This road goes ⅓ mile north to Highway 89, passing by the back side of Hat Creek Resort in the process. There you'll find the Old Station Post Office.

*   *   *   *

From the gate the PCT follows a fence as it soon curves northeast around a lava-block ridge and past the back side of the resort. At a distance it parallels Road 32N89 northeast over to a crossing of northwest-trending Road 32N20 (4545–0.5), which has a cattle guard. You quickly pass through a gate to almost touch Road 32N91, then wind northward to cross a one-lane road just 80 yards before crossing Road 32N91. After paralleling its west side for 270 yards, you recross it and then head 380 yards over to a crossing of Road 32N99 (4480–0.7), which loops around a hill. The trail climbs north to a shallow notch just south of the main summit, then descends northeast to a quick crossing of Road 32N99 (4540–0.3). Onward, the trail winds gently northeast down to a crossing of the Spatter Cone Nature Trail immediately west of where that trail forks (4500–0.4).

*   *   *   *

Side route: A 370-yard descent northwest down the nature trail gets you to the trailhead (with a water faucet), and a dump station for the spreading Hat Creek Campground, whose entrance is on the west side of Highway 89. You might consider camping there.

*   *   *   *

From the nature trail (which is worth taking), the PCT first continues ⅓ mile northeast to the end of a northwest trending road and then traverses east across forested slopes, providing you with views of the Old Station settlement and the linear Hat Creek Rim. Eventually the trail drops rather steeply to cross a north-trending, little used road, then after 260 easy yards north, it crosses Road 33N22 (4590–1.3).

*   *   *   *

Resupply access: If you walk 150 yards west on it, it then becomes a paved road that heads north to Highway 89, with a gas station/mini-mart nearby.

*   *   *   *

Onward, the PCT makes a highly winding arc northward across a lava flow, and eventually

N
Hwy. 70-
Burney Falls

See maps N11, N12, N13

passes between two collapsed sections of a lava cave. You can easily descend into the western one, if you are in an exploratory mood. In 350 yards the PCT crosses Highway 44 at a point (4365–0.9) that is about ¼ mile east of the Highways 44–89 junction—your last opportunity to get *safe* water until you descend from the Hat Creek Rim.

*   *   *   *

Water access: A trail heads 0.2 mile north-northwest over to the Subway Cave loop trail, along which you can head about 250 yards

See map N13

northwest to a parking loop, which has a water faucet at its north end. You can also follow the road west to Highway 44, where you'll find the entrance to the popular Cave Campground— your last opportunity for "civilized" camping. From the campground the distance to the first safe water at Rock Spring creek is about 30 miles, and then you have an additional 1¼ miles to PG&E's Cassel Campground. This is quite a long day hike, although most of the route is either level or downhill. Still, you might consider filling up your water bottles at Subway Cave and then in the late afternoon and evening hours do 5–10 miles of hiking and spend the night on Hat Creek Rim.

*   *   *   *

From the junction, which is by a 12-foot-high lava pressure ridge, the PCT is routed on an abandoned road (5E27), which meanders eastward before curving northeastward, its meandering tread governed by the numerous pressure ridges. The road eventually meets the former Highway 44 (4360–1.4), which heads arrow-straight west-northwest to Highway 89. Up it you wind northward for 0.7 mile, to where it is blocked off, and from there take a winding trail up along the Hat Creek Rim, having splendid views up and down Hat Creek Valley from Lassen Peak to Mt. Shasta. Soon the PCT curves east and descends to the nearby Highway 44 trailhead (4870–1.5), located on the west side of a road that lies immediately west of usually dry Mud Lake.

From the spur trail south to the trailhead parking area, the PCT starts north and reaches Hat Creek Rim after ½ mile. You follow it almost ¾ mile before reaching the southern edge of a

See map N13

N
Hwy. 70-
Burney Falls

Z

Hwy. 70-
Burney Falls

18 MI. TO HWY. 299

PACIFIC CREST TRAIL

RIM

FOR

4465

4488

4222

4928

34N63

Lookout
5142

35N14

34N36

34N34

34N94

34N34

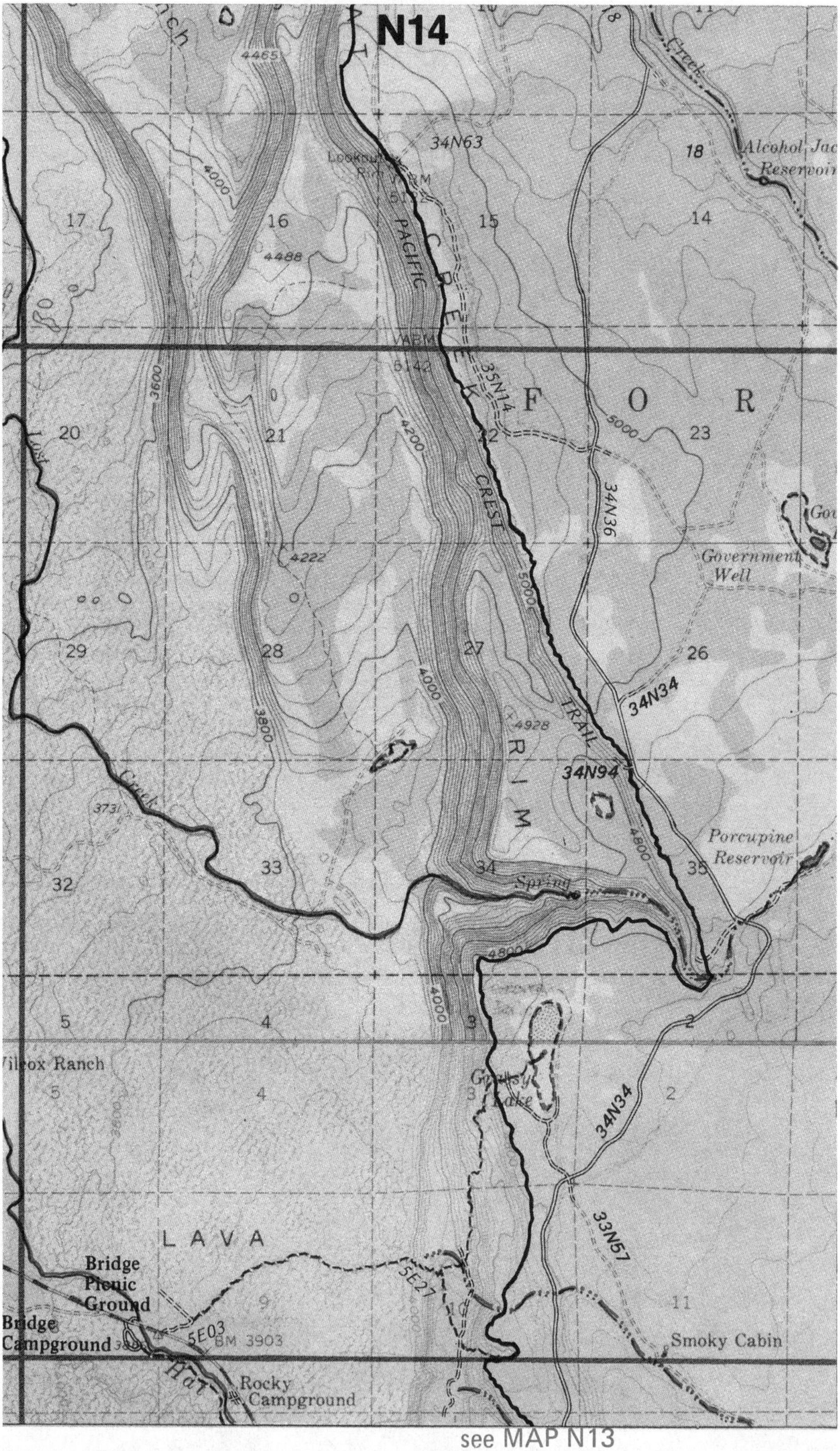

33N67

5E27

5E03
BM 3903

3731

3800

3600

4000

4200

4000

3800

4000

4800

5000

5000

4800

18 Alcohol Jac
Reservoir

17   16   15   14

20   21   22   23

29   28   27   26

32   33   34   35

5   4   3   2

Government
Well

Porcupine
Reservoir

Spring

Wilcox Ranch

Goose
Lake

LAVA

Bridge
Picnic
Ground

Bridge
Campground

Rocky
Campground

Hat

9   10   11

Smoky Cabin

1987 burn. In addition to being dry, the rim lands were only sparsely forested, and hence there was little shade. Since the burn, shade is essentially nonexistent, so you'll find no protection from the piercing sun of summer afternoons. The burn extended north until about a mile beyond the Hat Creek Rim fire lookout, which was engulfed in the fire.

In ¼ mile you veer east into a sizable gully and soon cross its usually dry creek (4640–1.8). Northward, the PCT climbs a few yards up from the creek, then descends northwest to the rim, only to veer immediately east into another dry-creek gully (4600–0.9).

*   *   *   *

Side route: Near the head of the gully, a side trail begins a plunge west 0.3 mile to a dirt road, on which you could walk 115 yards north to the trail's resumption. You could then drop 0.3 mile north to a trail junction. A westward descent would take you to Highway 89 near Bridge Campground.

*   *   *   *

The PCT briefly returns to the rim again, leaves it, and climbs to a higher rim which, like the first, is the result of uplift along a north-south-trending fault. A ½-mile winding traverse on the rim ensues, soon bringing you to a shallow depression (4820–1.6). A faint trail (essentially cross-country) strikes northeast ¼ mile to usually dry Grassy Lake, and in its center is a cattle watering hole. Avoid this seasonal mudhole.

The PCT goes to the rim again and winds along it to the brink of Lost Creek canyon, and you may hear a spring-fed creek flowing down its lower section. Rather than descend to it, however, your trail stays high and follows this canyon's rim 1½ miles east to a usually dry crossing of the upper canyon, now just a gully (4810–2.1). ∎ *In 1982 the Forest Service was going to build a spur trail west down to the spring, but lack of funds stopped the project. All too often those of us working in the mountains heard similar fates of other very worthwhile projects. Lost Creek spring would have been the only freshwater source for the entire Hat Creek Rim.* ∎

Northwest, the PCT quickly climbs onto another fault-formed rim, almost touching Road 33N21 where the trail crosses a spur road that heads west down to Little Lake—almost always dry. With one more mile behind you, you continue your dry-rim traverse, fervently believing that distant Mt. Shasta *is* getting noticeably closer while Lassen Peak *is* fading away. After several more miles of winding to and from rim views, you eventually spy and reach the site of Hat Creek Rim Fire Lookout (5122–4.7). The wooden lookout cabin atop the tower burned

N

Hwy. 70-
Burney Falls

See maps N13, N14

Burney Mountain, from PCT just north of small reservoir

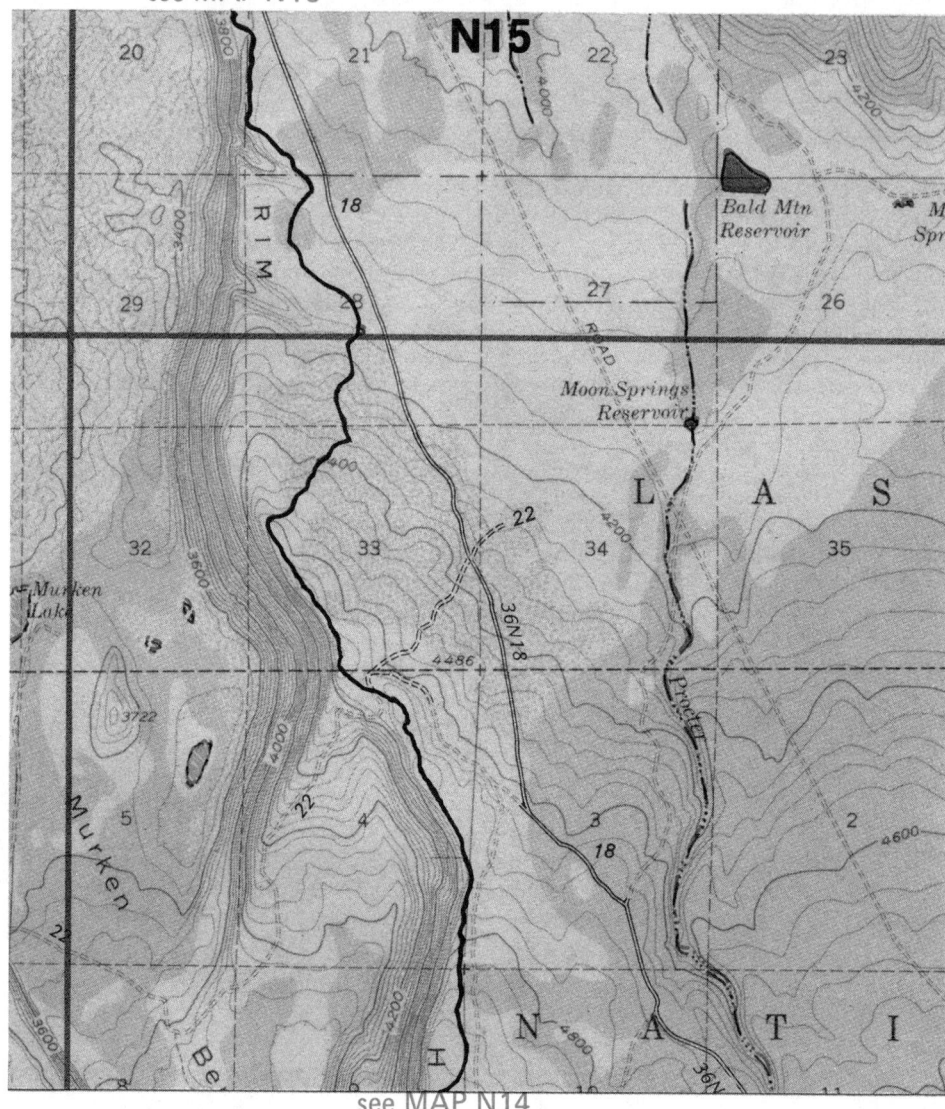

see MAP N14

in the 1987 fire, and in 1992 this site was converted to a microwave repeater station.

Northward, your sometimes weedy tread provides you with an almost continual line of views, for it never veers far from the rim. Every escarpment you see around you is due to faulting, which in this area goes hand in hand with volcanism. Cinder Butte, a sparsely vegetated conical hill to the northwest is, like Sugarloaf Peak to the south, a young volcano. You leave the scorched lands of the 1987 fire in about ½ mile, and about there the trail begins a serious, lengthy descent before making a shorter traverse to an intersection of Road 22

(4660–2.8) about 100 yards west of a low pass. Ahead, the PCT climbs northwest to a knoll on the rim that evidently has been used as a take-off spot for hang gliders. ❚ *And why not, for here the escarpment rises a full 1100 feet above Murken Bench. This is the highest unbroken escarpment along the entire rim, an inducement to glider pilots.* ❚ From the knoll the trail makes a drop of its own, nearly 600 feet down to a small reservoir (4140–1.9), which is just 200 yards west of Hat Creek Rim Road 36N18. As at other rim reservoirs, the quality of its water is questionable at best.

Ahead, the trail wanders for almost 1.2 miles

See maps N14, N15

before breaking through to the rim at a spectacular viewpoint. ∎ *The wildflower gardens along the way to it can be fantastic in May, but by late June the flowers turn just plain sticky.* ∎ After a lengthy rim traverse you come to a closed gate (4030–3.1), which is just 80 yards below Road 36N18. The trail now leaves the rim and descends to an abandoned jeep road, which you briefly follow before switchbacking just beyond a powerline. On a south tack you descend to quickly recross the powerline, then after 40 yards you switchback northwest. The route quickly turns southwest for a 250-yard winding descent across youthful lava to semilevel ground, then arcs northwest to an intersection of a north-climbing road. If you were to hike north on this road, you'd reach an old powerline road in 200 yards. The PCT reaches this road in 250 yards, 1.0 mile from the switchback 40 yards beyond the powerline. You parallel the powerline about 20 yards west, then angle northwest on a faint road that soon narrows to a trail. After 0.8 mile you almost reach Cassel-Fall River Mills Road, then parallel it 1.4 miles westward before crossing it (3480–3.8). If you've mailed yourself supplies to the Cassel Post Office, you could reach it directly by hiking 3.3 miles west down this paved road. However, you recommend a longer, less direct route to it.

Like others, you take the PCT, starting north from Cassel-Fall River Mills Road. The trail quickly veers west and meanders across a youthful lava flow with caves before crossing and recrossing the same powerline you met south of the road. About 0.6 mile past the recrossing you exit from Section 3. If you must camp before Highway 299, do so before you leave this section, the last of Lassen National Forest land. Private lands now lie ahead and camping is prohibited. The trail heads northwest through a dry, open woodland of juniper, gray pine, mountain mahogany and oak, and you have views of Mt. Shasta until you enter a ponderosa-pine forest where you cross Conrad Ranch road (3270–2.1).

Under welcome shade, you climb ⅓ mile northwest to a low gap, drop ¼ mile west to a gully, then wind southwest to a road (3025–1.7) that is just above Rock Spring creek. This is the first fresh water you've had since the Subway Cave area, just north of Highway 44 and about 30 miles back. Descend the road, which crosses the creek in 100 yards. Your route crosses the creek about 10 yards sooner, though you'll want to walk a few paces upstream and cross it where you can keep your boots dry. The trail then leads northwest, passing between a horse corral on the east and a residence on the west. Immediately beyond them you walk along the east side of a PG&E powerhouse, then cross the adjacent bridge which spans Rising River/Hat Creek. Next you parallel the main road briefly northwest, staying just above it and having oak-filtered views across it toward Crystal Lake State Fish Hatchery (visitors welcome). The trail momentarily curves southwest and you reach a PG&E road (2990–0.5) only a stone's throw from where it reaches the paved Crystal Lake State Fish Hatchery road.

* * * *

Resupply access: You head south up this road, climbing moderately for ½ mile, and then soon reaching PG&E's Cassel Campground, located on both sides of the road. You might stay there for the night after first walking a

See maps N15, N16, N17, N18

Bald Mountain and a small reservoir near Road 36N18

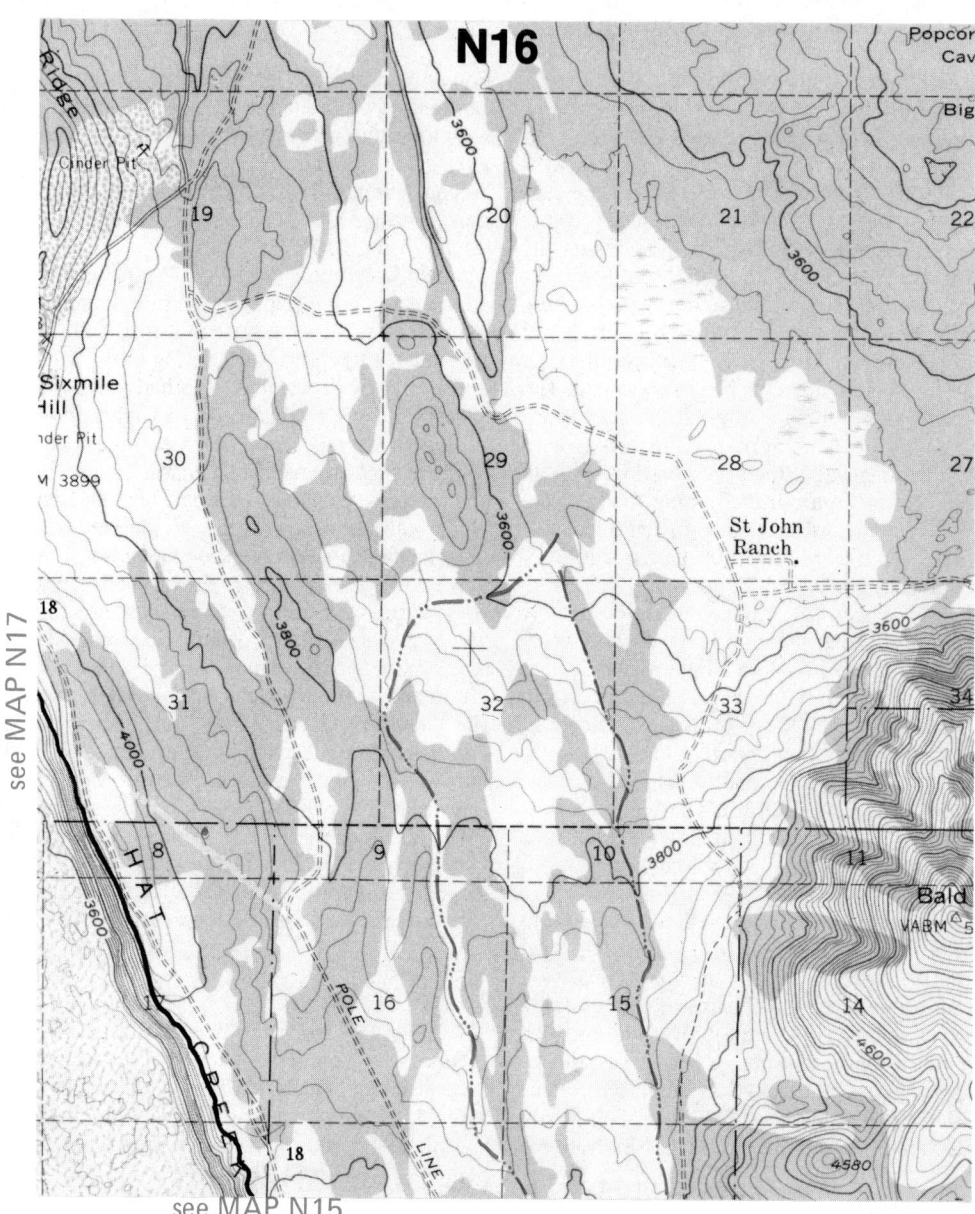

couple of minutes farther to the road's south end, at the Cassel-Fall River Mills Road. By this junction, 1.0 mile from the PCT, you'll find the Cassel Post Office and a small general store.

*   *   *   *

On the PCT you follow it briefly northwest to a crossing of the Crystal Lake State Fish Hatchery road (3000–0.1). Now the PCT heads through poison oak, skirts along the west side of a long fishery tank, then reaches, just beyond it, a short trail east over to a picnic area. No camping is allowed here along the shore of Baum Lake, at Crystal Lake, or essentially anywhere between here and Highway 299. Crystal Lake drops a few feet down to Baum Lake and you bridge this spillway, then walk 0.9 mile along the west shore of Baum Lake, leaving most of the fishermen behind. The trail then switchbacks southwest over to a small gully, ascends it, rounds a ridge, and then, in a sec-

See map N18

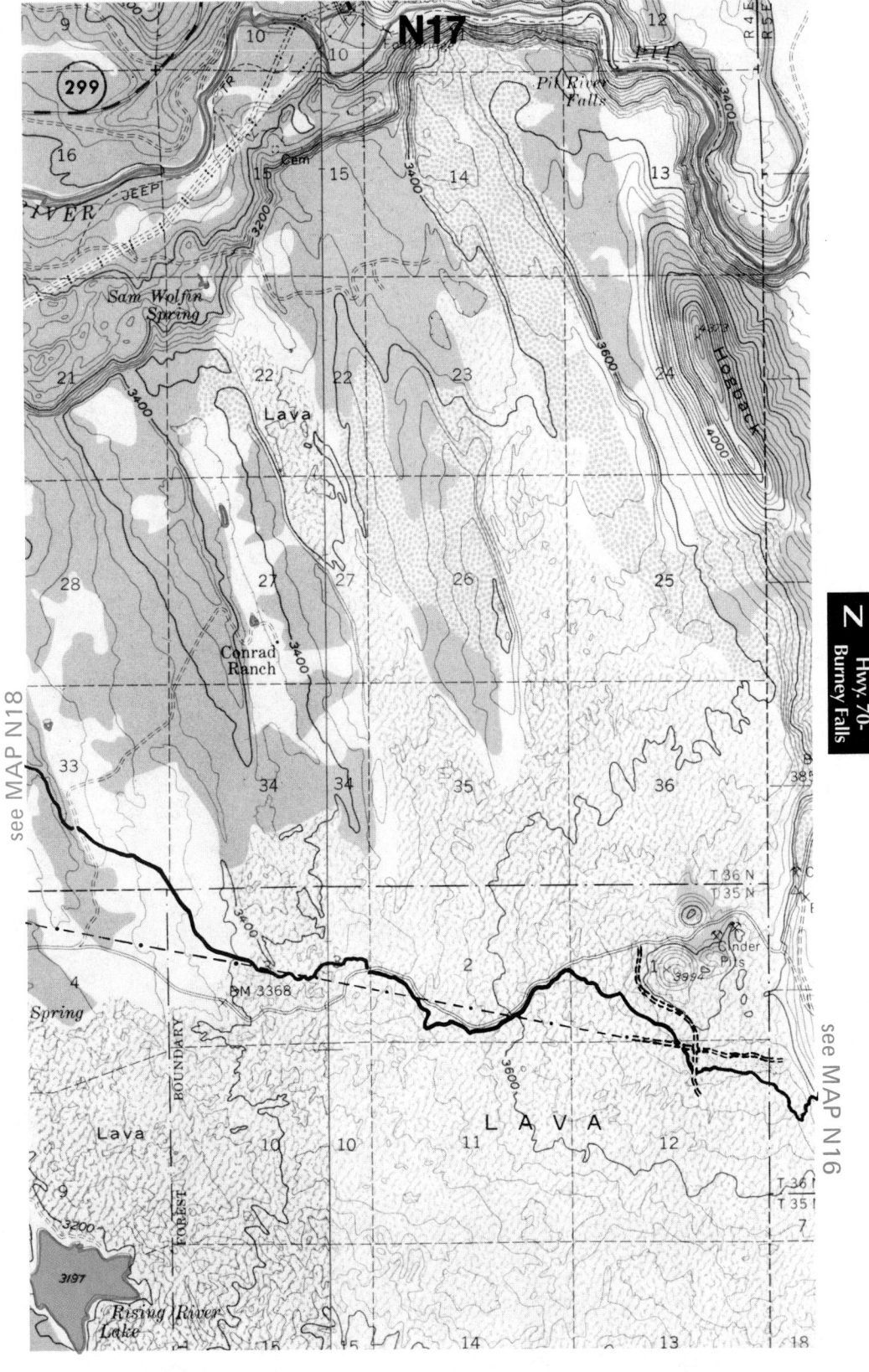

299

Pit River Falls

N17

Sam Wolfin Spring

Lava

Conrad Ranch

see MAP N18

Hogback

see MAP N16

T 36 N
T 35 N

Cinder Pits

BM 3368

Spring

4

BOUNDARY

FOREST

Lava

L A V A

T 36 N
T 35 N

3197

Rising River Lake

R3E
31
32

36
R3E
R4E
31
0
31
32

Arkright
11
12
Lake
Britton
3574×
2910

Chalk
Reservoir

7
8
3000

Sand Pits

Sand Pits
Hat
PIT

14
13
Sand Pit
18
17

2800
2900

Braden
Sand Pit

299
BM 3137
20

23
24
19
No. 2 Powerhouse

3103
3120

O R E S T
3330
Creek
JEEP
TRAIL

26
25
30
29
3200

BM 3203

Hidden Valley
Ranch
Baum
Lake

35
36
31
32
Fish Hatchery

Crystal Lake
No. 1 Powerhouse

TRAIL
JEEP

Brush Mtn
3612
3600
3200
H
A
T

89
1
6
Cassel C G
Cassel
BM 3182

2
PO
BM 3199
Rock

LASSEN

NATIONAL

FOREST

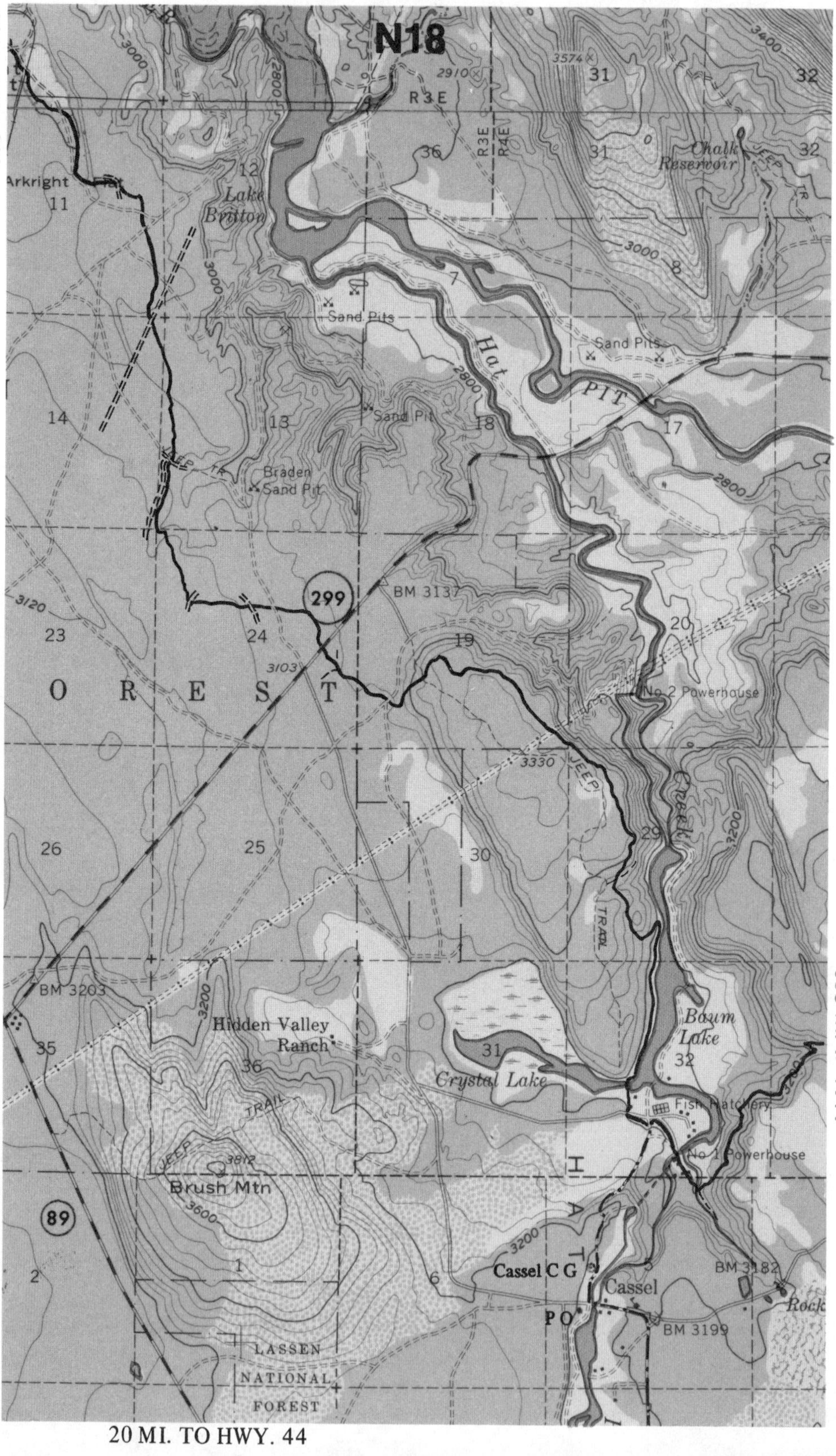

BURNEY 5 MI.

20 MI. TO HWY. 44

ond gully, crosses a jeep road (3150–1.5). You now stay close to the east rim of a lava plateau and have several oak-and-pine-framed views east toward the Pit River. Midway along your northwest traverse you diagonal under some major powerlines, then at the north end of the plateau make a short descent to another jeep road (3240–1.8). ▌ *You may note that the plateau's west edge is quite linear, for it has been uplifted along a north-northwest-trending fault.* ▌ You quickly cross this fault where your trail angles northwest, then in a minute cross a good road. The trail continues along a northwest course, partly following bits of abandoned jeep tracks. Other tracks may lead you astray, so watch for trail markers along this short stretch out to Highway 299 (3110–0.8).

*   *   *   *

Resupply access: The town of Burney lies about 7 miles southwest.

*   *   *   *

From the highway the trail starts north through Shasta-Trinity National Forest land and quickly turns west to avoid private land. You cross two roads and then, at a third, 0.8 mile past the highway, resume a northward course. You loop around the head of a trough and then parallel a road, just above you, 0.4 mile to a crossing of a road that has been upgraded from "jeep trail" status. With occasional views back toward

Burney Mountain and ahead toward Mt. Shasta, you stroll ¾ mile along fairly level, oak-dominated terrain and slant across a major, straight road (3070–2.3). You cross four more roads in the next mile, then descend for a few minutes to a road crossing that is at the south edge of Arkright Flat (2995–1.3). Since the route ahead is largely across private land, dry camp, if you must, before you reach Arkright Flat. ▌ *The flat is a fault-formed basin and the cliff on its east side is a fault scarp.* ▌

On private land, the trail heads along the west side of the flat, crosses some railroad tracks, then crosses a nearby road (3005-0.4). Paralleling this road, you quickly cross a minor road striking east, and from it you have a walk northwest along the rim of the Pit River canyon. ▌ *Douglas-firs, climbing up the canyon's cooler slopes, offer you shade along with Oregon oaks, ponderosa pines and occasional incense-cedars.* ▌ In 0.4 mile you cross two roads where they join a third, then continue along the rim about 0.6 mile farther before turning south and crossing nearby Rim of Lake Road (3010–1.2). The PCT then winds southwest across rolling, logged terrain before turning west and heading over to Highway 89 (2995–1.5), which you cross by the east side of a closed road. Actually, the trail dies out 40 yards before the highway, to hide it from motorcyclists who might take it east onto private land. If you happen to be southbound toward Lassen Park, then from the highway head due north, and you'll quickly find the trail. In the other direction, the trail is very obvious.

See maps N18, N19

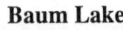

Baum Lake

see MAP O1

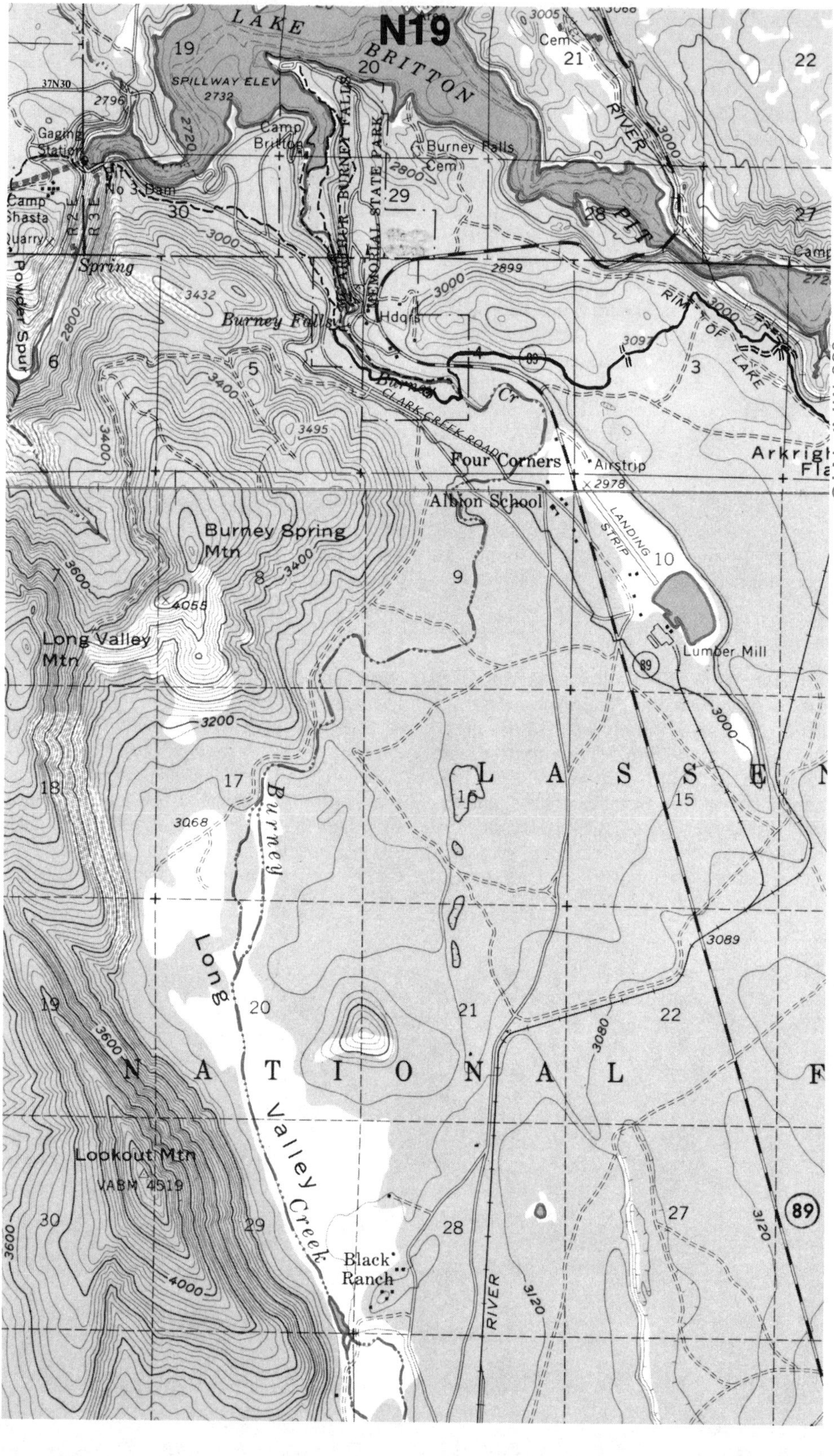

see MAP N18

Hwy. 70-
Burney Falls

N

LAKE BRITTON

PIT RIVER

SPILLWAY ELEV 2732

Camp Britton

Burney Falls Cem

Gaging Station

Camp Shasta Quarry

No 3 Dam

Spring

RIM OF LAKE

MCARTHUR-BURNEY FALLS MEMORIAL STATE PARK

Burney Falls

Hdqrs

Burney Cr

CLARK CREEK ROAD

Four Corners

Airstrip

Arkright Flat

Albion School

Burney Spring Mtn

Long Valley Mtn

LANDING STRIP

Lumber Mill

L A S S E N

Burney

Long Valley Creek

N A T I O N A L   F

Lookout Mtn
VABM 4519

Black Ranch

RIVER

Powder Spur

*   *   *   *

Resupply access: You are now inside McArthur-Burney Falls Memorial State Park, and you can shortcut by heading nearly ½ mile west along the highway over to the park's entrance road. You'll find a store just past its entrance station and a sprawling campground just beyond that.

*   *   *   *

You can conclude Section N in either of two other ways. Both cross Highway 89 and follow the PCT 220 yards to a trail junction above Burney Creek.

*   *   *   *

Alternate route: This route leaves the PCT here, taking a trail downstream. The trail starts northwest along usually dry Burney Creek, but in 90 yards, the first springs appear, and in another 90 yards, where the trail and the creek bend west, additional springs have given rise to a sizable creek. Continuing ⅔ mile west along the trail, you'll see Burney Creek metamorphose from a creek to a raging torrent. The trail ends by the east side of a 40-yard-long bridge that is just upstream from Burney Falls. To view the falls, head right 35 yards up to a parking area, then take a broad, 160-yard-long trail along the west side of the parking lot's road almost to the park's entrance station. Continue

50 yards farther, paralleling the park's main road, to where you'll meet a crosswalk. From it a path goes over to the park's nearby store, which caters mainly to the car campers in the campground just north of the store. You go another 27 yards alongside the main road to the start of a paved trail, on your left. Just 10 yards down it, you'll reach the park's best view of thundering Burney Falls.

*   *   *   *

The PCT goes 35 yards to a sturdy bridge that spans Burney Creek. Although the creek is dry when most hikers cross it, it can be a raging torrent in heavy rains. The trail briefly climbs to flat land above the creek's south bank and then heads about 300 yards to one of the largest backpackers' camps you're ever likely to see (2970-0.4). It is also used by sometimes-large groups of equestrians or bicyclists. Onward, the PCT winds first west, then northwest, usually staying within sound of Burney Creek, but not within sight of it. You then intersect a broad path (2950–0.6) west, which takes you in a minute to a small parking area on paved Clark Creek Road. East, it goes almost 60 yards to Burney Falls Nature Trail, a 1.0-mile loop trail. To reach the entrance station, store and falls' viewpoint mentioned in the previous paragraph, turn right and head just 27 yards over to the aforementioned, obvious, 40-yard-long bridge.

See map N19

Arkright Flat

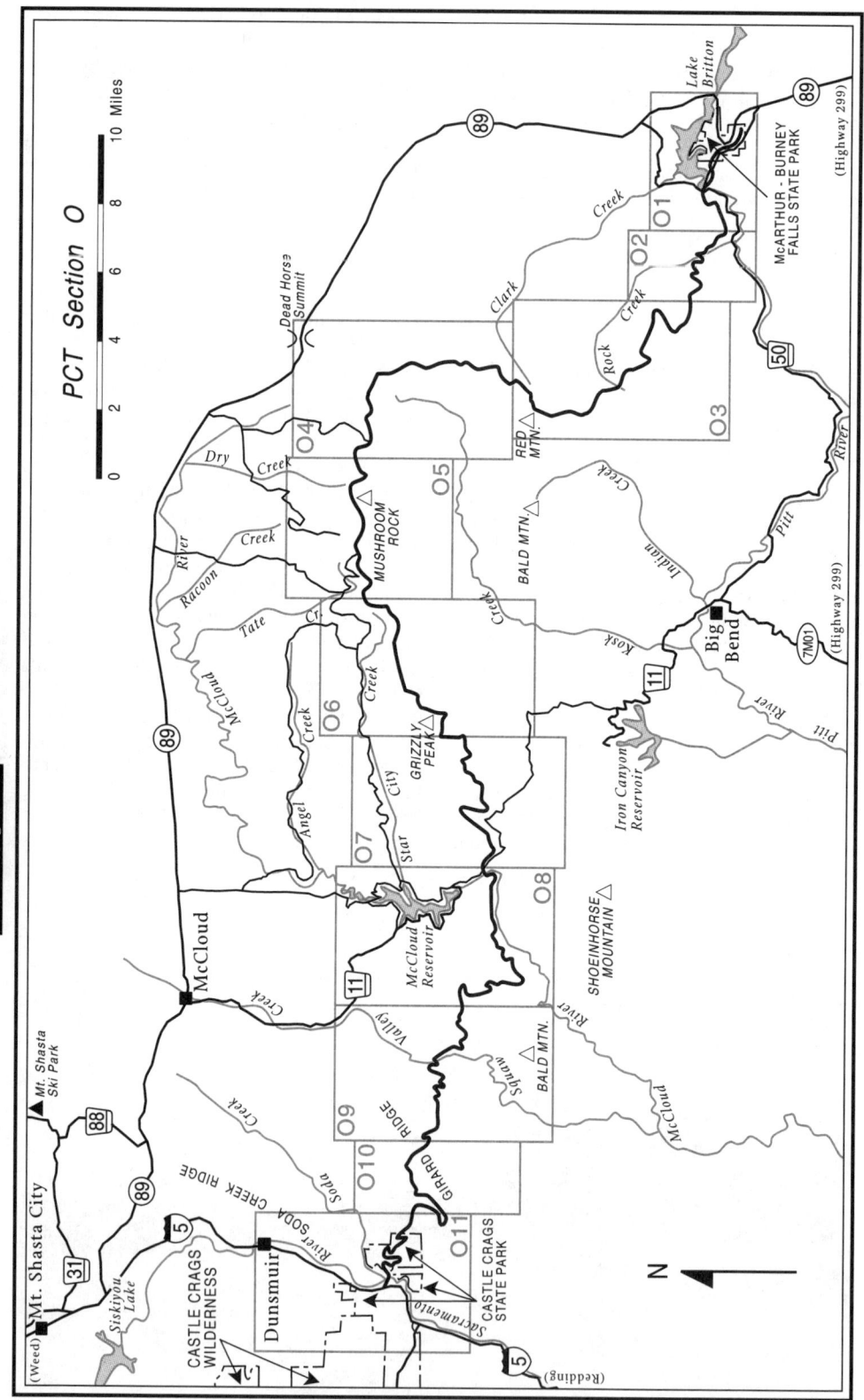

Section O
Burney Falls to Castle Crags

Introduction: Those who hiked through the San Bernardino Mountains of southern California (Section C) may be reminded of that mountain scenery while hiking through Section O. Glaciation was minimal in each, so natural lakes are a rarity. In Section O, glaciation was restricted to the north slopes of Mushroom Rock and of Grizzly Peak. Man-made lakes occur in both sections, although Section O's are milky blue-green in color. During the summer, water—or lack thereof—can be a problem in both sections, even though Section O receives twice the precipitation. This extra precipitation has created denser forests and consequently this low mountain country is prime logging country. Therefore, you may not escape the sounds of civilization, for most of the route lies within earshot of motor vehicles.

Section O makes a long arc, from north to west, connecting the scenic but hot and dry Hat Creek-Burney Falls area with the equally scenic, often hot Castle Crags area. As the route arcs westward, it leaves behind the younger volcanic rocks of the Modoc Plateau and gradually crosses older and older rock units until you are walking across rocks that are as old as 400 million years. No other trail section along the entire PCT displays such a succession of rock strata. Along this arc the Shasta red fir replaces the common red fir you saw throughout the Sierra Nevada, and you'll see this new fir time and again all the way into southern Oregon.

Declination: 16¾°E

Points on Route	S→N	Mi. Btwn. Pts.	N→S
Burney Falls	0.0		82.9
		5.4	
Rock Creek	5.4		77.5
		8.7	
Peavine Creek	14.1		68.8
		2.8	
road junction at south base of Red Mountain	16.9		66.0
		4.6	
saddle west of Harlow Flat Road	21.5		61.4
		4.6	
road southeast down to pond	26.1		56.8
		3.3	
springs at Moosehead Creek's headwaters	29.4		53.5
		4.8	
Tate Creek road	34.2		48.7
		2.6	
Alder Creek Trail	36.8		46.1
		2.1	
Grizzly Peak Road before Pigeon Hill	38.9		44.0
		3.2	
Grizzly Peak Lookout road	42.1		40.8
		2.1	
Deer Creek	44.2		38.7
		8.0	
McCloud-Big Bend Road	52.2		30.7
		2.7	
Ah-Di-Na Campground road	54.9		28.0
		11.1	
Squaw Valley Creek	66.0		16.9
		5.7	
Girard Ridge Road	71.7		11.2
		4.9	
Fall Creek	76.6		6.3
		6.3	
Interstate 5 near Castle Crags State Park	82.9		0.0

Supplies: No on-route supplies exist along this section. If you are hiking north, use the Burney Falls Camper Services, mentioned in the previous section. If you are hiking south, use the Castella Post Office, mentioned in the next section. Ammirati's Market is next to the Castella Post Office, and its fairly large inventory caters to both Castle Crags State Park visitors and local residents.

Rattlesnakes: These can be found in all but the highest elevations in this section, but you probably won't see any. Ticks can be a problem at the lower elevations, though flies will probably pester you more than anything else.

Trail Condition: Section O's PCT steadily degenerated in the 1980s to the point that some of it was little better than cross-country hiking. You can expect one or more ongoing logging operations to confuse you, though the main problem is that brush reclaims sections of the trail. Forest Service maintenance has been virtually zero, and Section O's area is so sparsely populated that there aren't enough volunteers to do the job. Many of the residents work for lumber companies and couldn't care less about the trail. Furthermore, who can blame them for wanting to get out of the mountains when the weekends come. We hope the Forest Service once again gets funds to maintain the trail, but until it does, anticipate some really nasty stretches.

Maps: *Burney Falls*   *Lake McCloud*
      Skunk Ridge   *Shoeinhorse Mountain*
      Dead Horse Summit   *Girard Ridge*
      Grizzly Peak   *Dunsmuir*

─────────────────────────────── **The Route** ───────────────────────────────

Roughly 130 feet high, Burney Falls is no match in height for Yosemite Valley's towering waterfalls. But in volume, Burney Falls exceeds most of them, and it rivals Vernal and Nevada falls, both along the Merced River just above the valley. That river's discharge averages, for the year, about 225 million gallons a day, whereas Burney Falls averages about 200 million. However, the Merced River, being largely fed by snowmelt streams, is very seasonal, with high discharge from mid-April to mid-August. For the remaining eight months of the year, Burney Falls ranks as California's most voluminous waterfall, producing enough water to cover one square mile of land one foot deep in water every day. Because Burney Falls is fed by a huge, underground reservoir, its volume and its temperature (about 42°F) are very constant from day to day. ∎

If you've just finished hiking Section N, you'll know where to find the Pacific Crest Trail. If you're just starting your hike north in Section O, then head over to the McArthur-Burney Falls Memorial State Park's entrance station. The main road goes past a nearby store to a large parking lot and the start of the Burney Falls Nature Trail. You branch left at the entrance station and go down to a small parking area just west of the station. The nature trail ends here, and on it you immediately cross a bridge. Before you can say "McArthur-Burney Falls Memorial State Park," you reach a junction and climb a few yards west over to an intersection with the broad Pacific Crest Trail. A westbound trail from here goes 140 yards over to a small parking area on Clark Creek Road. If you're driving northwest along this road, look for this parking area 1.8 miles after you leave Highway 89.

Because the Pacific Crest Trail is for equestrians as well as for hikers, it was built away from Burney Creek and Burney Falls. Hence, you only hear these features, not see them. Your hike begins by paralleling Clark Creek Road, which you cross in almost a mile and then continue above the road, finally switchbacking down to it at the east end of Lake Britton's dam. Walk across the dam and find the trail's resumption in about 35 yards (2760–1.9). Before starting up the trail, you might take a swim in Lake

See map O1

Britton.

The PCT switchbacks 210 yards up almost to a junction of two roads. On the paved road, walk 30 yards to the junction with a graded road and then a few yards past it to the PCT's resumption. Parallel the graded road ¼ mile up to another road. Here the trail turns southwest for a while before crossing two more roads just as it starts to climb. You climb into a shady gully, then up to a ridge, from which you have views down into 600-foot deep Pit River canyon, with its inviting river. Along the lower parts of Section O's route, such as on this stretch, midafternoon summer temperatures are typically in the 90s. ∎ *Ponderosa pines are the primary shade trees, although on wetter, cooler slopes you'll find Douglas-firs predominating. Incense-cedars and Oregon white oaks do better on the drier slopes, but you'll leave these behind not long after crossing Rock Creek.* ∎

With that destination in mind, you follow the PCT as it winds northwest, descending into Rock Creek canyon to a small bench above an inner gorge. Here you cross an abandoned, south-heading road. Then, 0.2 mile later and a bit higher, you meet a jeep road (2930–2.9), which drops 200 precipitous yards to Rock Creek. You'll find more camping space down there than on creekside gravel where the PCT bridges Rock Creek (2980–0.6). This latter site is more esthetic, however, for it is perched just above two-tiered Rock Creek falls. A somewhat chilly swimming hole lies at the base, and it can be reached by descending *loose, steep* slopes on the west side of the creek. Be extremely careful if you make this descent.

From the bridge the PCT switchbacks out of the canyon and up to paved Road 37N02 (3100–0.4). On it you can head ⅓ mile up-canyon to Rock Creek Campground, a primitive car-camping area. During most of the summer you won't find a potential campsite with adequate water until you reach the Peavine Creek area, 8.3 miles past Road 37N02.

Beyond this paved road the PCT climbs 0.2 mile northwest to a graded road and a saddle, from which it starts southwest. After 150 yards it hits an abandoned road on which you walk 35 yards south to the trail's resumption. The trail continues southwest to a minor ridge, then climbs up it, first ¼ mile north, then ¼ mile west. Then, starting south, you face a long as-

Rock Creek falls

cent across slopes up to Peavine Creek. The first part of your ascent is dry, rather open, and partly logged, so you have views of lofty Burney Mountain, standing in the south-southeast, 16 miles away. ∎ *By the time you cross the 4000-foot contour, ponderosa pine, Douglas-fir and incense-cedar have largely replaced oaks.* ∎ Soon you enter a small bowl and cross its abandoned, southwest-descending road. You climb into a second bowl, then curve clockwise up shady slopes to a west ridge, almost topping it as you cross a road (4480–4.3). Your trail now climbs northeast, crossing a good road in 0.7 mile and then, a bit past it, turning west and traversing over to the southeast edge of an old clearcut (4660-1.4). Here, early-season hikers will find seeping water of questionable quality, the first water since Rock Creek, 6.1 miles back.

In ⅓ mile you cross a major logging road, then traverse over to a gully and climb south to a closed jeep road. This route north is being narrowed to a trail by encroaching shrubs. ∎ *Tobacco brush and snow bush have replaced deer brush, which is another Ceanothus you've seen, and perhaps smelled, lower down. All three are*

See maps O1, O2, O3

very aromatic when in bloom. Greenleaf manzanita and chinquapin are also present, and they will be common trailside companions in many places as you make a 1½-day fir-forest crest loop around a large basin. ∎

Your abandoned road crosses another abandoned road, then in 100 yards crosses an active road and parallels it down to a road junction located immediately before Peavine Creek (4760–2.6). You can camp by this creek, pause to refresh yourself in its small pond, or head north over to an adjacent road and follow it 120 yards west to better campsites along Peavine Creek. Your next trailside water won't be until springs at Moosehead Creek's headwaters, 15⅓ miles ahead. Closer sources, however, lie just off the route. In late summer, Peavine Creek may dry up, but you can always head north on the road down Peavine Creek, tank up at Rock Creek, and take the Rock Creek road north up to the PCT near Red Mountain.

Over the next 22.7 miles you cross, recross and often parallel Summit Lake Road 38N10. If you are hiking in June or in October, you may have some snow problems and therefore may want to take the road instead of the PCT. From the road junction immediately north of Peavine Creek, the PCT winds northwest through a forest of white firs and sugar pines, crossing one road and then Road 38N10 before breaking out to views near a set of giant, crackling powerlines (5200–1.6). Bald Mountain, a Miocene-age volcano standing just above you 3 miles to the northwest, serves as a reference point to mark your progress as you traverse north. Grizzly Peak, which you'll reach in a day or two, stands above and right of Bald Mountain. Beyond the powerlines traverse a while and then duck into forest cover for a short spell just before turning northeast and reaching a road junction at the south base of Red Mountain (5380–1.2).

*   *   *   *

Side route: If you want to get a 360° panorama of Section O's terrain, follow an old jeep road ½ mile north up to the mountain's summit. ∎ *From it you can see part of Lake Britton, about 10 miles to the southeast, Grizzly Peak, about 10 miles to the west-northwest, and of course Mt. Shasta and Burney Mountain, volcanoes which you've seen many times before.*

See map O3

You scan about 200 million years of geology. The volcanoes are certainly less than one million years old, and the flat lands around Lake Britton may be that young or slightly older. The volcanic rocks get older toward your viewpoint, perhaps 5–10 million years on lower, eastern slopes and 10–20 million years along your north-trending rim. About 2 miles to the north and northwest lies Kosk Creek, and the rocks extending north from it almost up to Bartle Gap and Mushroom Rock are continental sediments about 40–50 million years old. The rocks of the western half of the basin are much older, deposited on an ocean floor roughly 200–225 million years ago. West beyond Grizzly Peak the rocks get increasingly older. ∎ To get back to the PCT, either retrace your steps or continue north ⅓ mile down to a saddle and then east on a logging road to Road 38N10. Walk

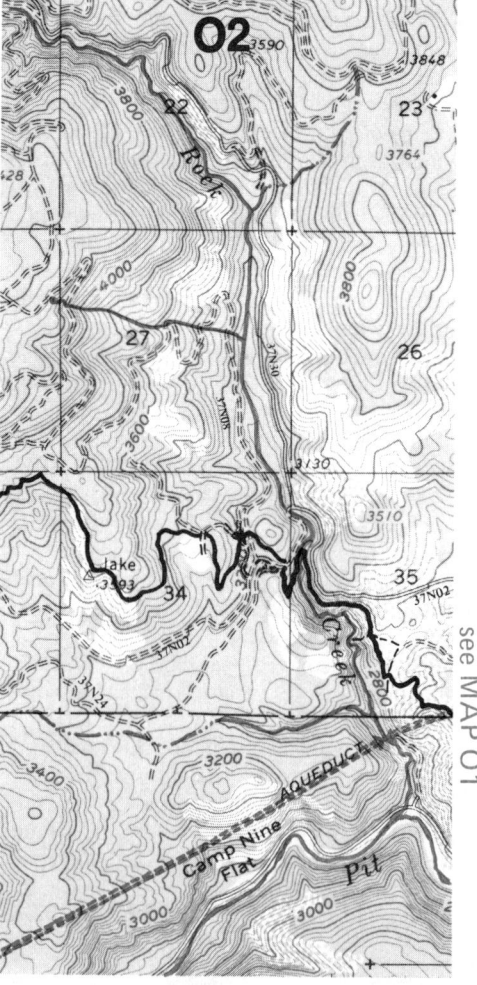

see MAP O3

see MAP O1

Burney Falls-Castle Crags

O

several yards south on it and then go 80 yards southeast on another road to the PCT.

* * * *

From the south base of Red Mountain, the PCT heads north-northeast, traversing in and out of gullies before it drops to cross Road 38N10 (5410–0.8). In 60 yards you cross the southeast-dropping road just mentioned, and then you traverse a small, seasonal bog, round a low ridge, and finally drop to another spur road (5290–0.7). You wind for one mile down to a third and in 340 yards arrive at a fourth. Up it you pace 20 yards to the trail's resumption then more or less parallel Road 38N10 over a broad ridge and down to a crossing of two roads by their junction (5060–2.1). The first road quickly ends, but the older one, a few yards north of the first, heads east down to Deadman Creek.

* * * *

Water access: In early summer, you can usually find water by hiking ½ mile or less down the road. In late summer, you may have to hike a mile or more.

* * * *

From these roads your trail climbs up to a crossing of Road 38N10 (5140–0.2).

* * * *

Side route: If you have to exit to civilization, go one mile along this road, first north up to a saddle, then east down to a fork. Branch right and take Harlow Flat Road 8 miles down to Highway 89 and hitch a ride south to Burney or north to McCloud or Mt. Shasta City.

* * * *

Your crest trail loops around a broad, fir-forested ridge and in ¾ mile almost reaches a saddle and Road 38N10. Your shady route then climbs north but soon starts descending to a major logging road (5150–1.4), which you cross at the north base of Peak 5537.

See maps O3, O4

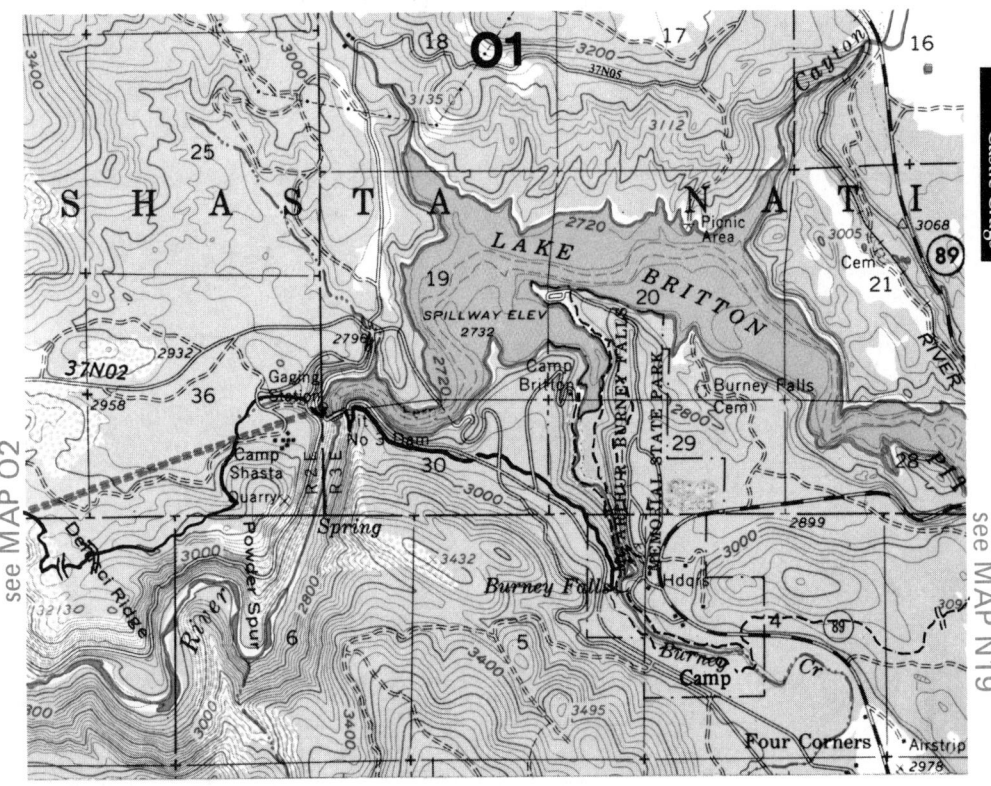

O3

SNF

North
Red Mtn

36

30

29

28

5200

5200

SNF

Red Mtn
VABM 5571

N   Fk
Rock   Creek

5000

1

37N11

5200

31

Squaw
Flat

32

4800

33

N Fork Cr.

5200

5455

5455

SUMMIT   LAKE

12

7

8

9

4400

4400

4400

Creek

Rock   Creek

18

17

16

3N10

37N30

13

Peavine   Creek

19

4800

4400

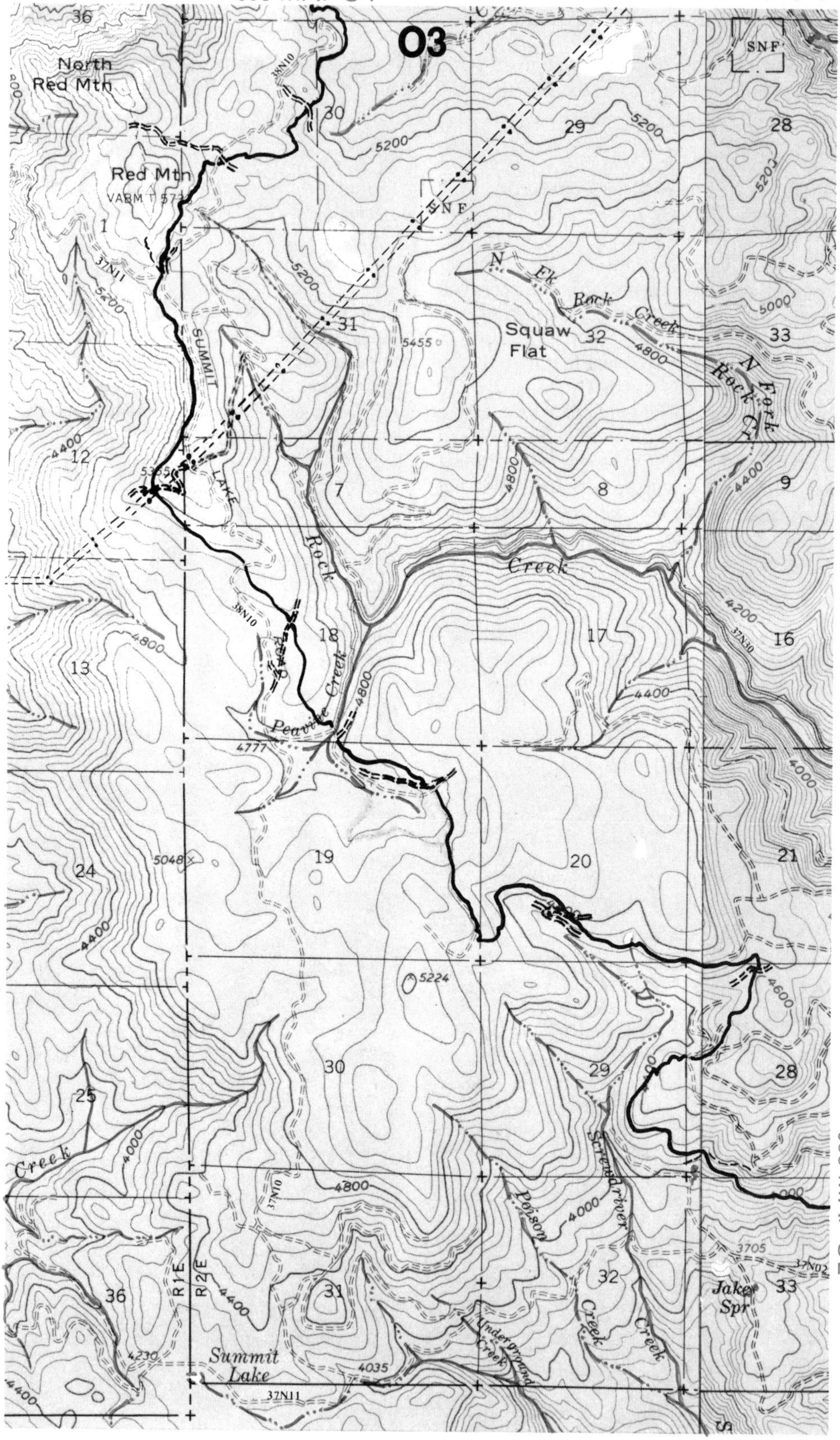

4800

4777

4600

20

21

4400

24

5048

4400

5224

25

30

29

28

4600

Creek

4000

37N10

4800

4000

Poison   Creek

Spencer River

Burney Falls-
Castle Crags

O

36

R1E R2E

31

32

Underground Creek

Jakes
Spr

33

4239

Summit
Lake

4035

32N11

4400

37N02

3705

*　　*　　*　　*

Side route: By heading down this and other roads, you can reach Highway 89 in about 6 miles, should the need arise.

*　　*　　*　　*

Over the next ⅔ mile, Road 38N10 is your constant rim companion; then it veers east to tackle slopes while the PCT winds northward. After a brushy ascent, you cross Peak 5432 in a shady gap just east of the summit and descend about 150 yards to a spot (5390-1.8) from where you can walk a few paces west to gain a panoramic view of coarse volcanic sediments that are deeply gullied and sparsely vegetated.

Road 38N10 encroaches upon you again, almost forcing the trail off the sometimes narrow rim. In just over one mile, the first half of it very scenic, the PCT splits northwest and the road splits northeast. In less than ¼ mile from this fork your route crosses an outcrop of unstable volcanic rock, which tends to slide occasionally, wiping out the tread. This is no major problem for hikers but it can be one for equestrians. In ¼ mile you round a small alcove and in another ¼ mile round a second. This one has a seasonal spring about 50 yards below the trail. In one more ¼ mile you cross a descending road (5110–2.2).

*　　*　　*　　*

Water access: You can take this ½ mile southeast to a small roadside pond, a suitable campsite.

*　　*　　*　　*

Your trail, now westbound, presents you with a last view south down into the spreading basin before touching Road 38N10 just after it crosses over to the north-facing slopes of the basin's rim. Across these slopes you make a gentle descent through a cool fir forest back to Road 38N10 (5070–1.6), crossing it just below Bartle Gap.

*　　*　　*　　*

Water access: Here, another camping opportunity presents itself, for if you descend 270

Road 38N10 forces PCT onto narrow rim

yards north along the road, you'll reach a spring-fed creeklet that usually lasts through July. Northward, the creeklet is longer lasting, and the road goes about 5 miles out to Highway 89.

*　　*　　*　　*

The PCT climbs to the creeklet's usually dry headwaters gully, crosses it, and then crosses nearby Road 39N90 (5190–0.4). Now you traverse north to a ridge, bend southwest, and climb back into National Forest land. Since the powerlines, you've been hiking mostly on private land. After climbing gently about ½ mile southwest, you'll come to within 200 yards of Moosehead Creek, which is visible just below you. You might plan to camp in this general vicinity, since the next spacious campsite with water is at Ash Camp, on the McCloud River, a lengthy (though easy in this direction) 23½

O
Burney Falls-
Castle Crags

See maps O4, O5

miles away. Several other off-route camping possibilities exist between these two camps.

The trail continues about ¼ mile up your mildly glaciated canyon, then arcs northwest over to some nearby springs at Moosehead Creek's headwaters (5440–1.3). For late summer hikers, these springs will be your last source of permanent water until you cross Deer Creek, 14.8 miles ahead. There is limited space near the springs for one or two persons. Many trekkers will find snowpatches burying sections of trail along north-facing slopes, especially if they hike the trail before early-July.

The PCT switchbacks above the springs, climbs ½ mile northwest to a crest, and then continues ½ mile west up to a higher one. Views up at Mt. Shasta and down into Dry Creek canyon briefly appear, then disappear as you arc

See map O5

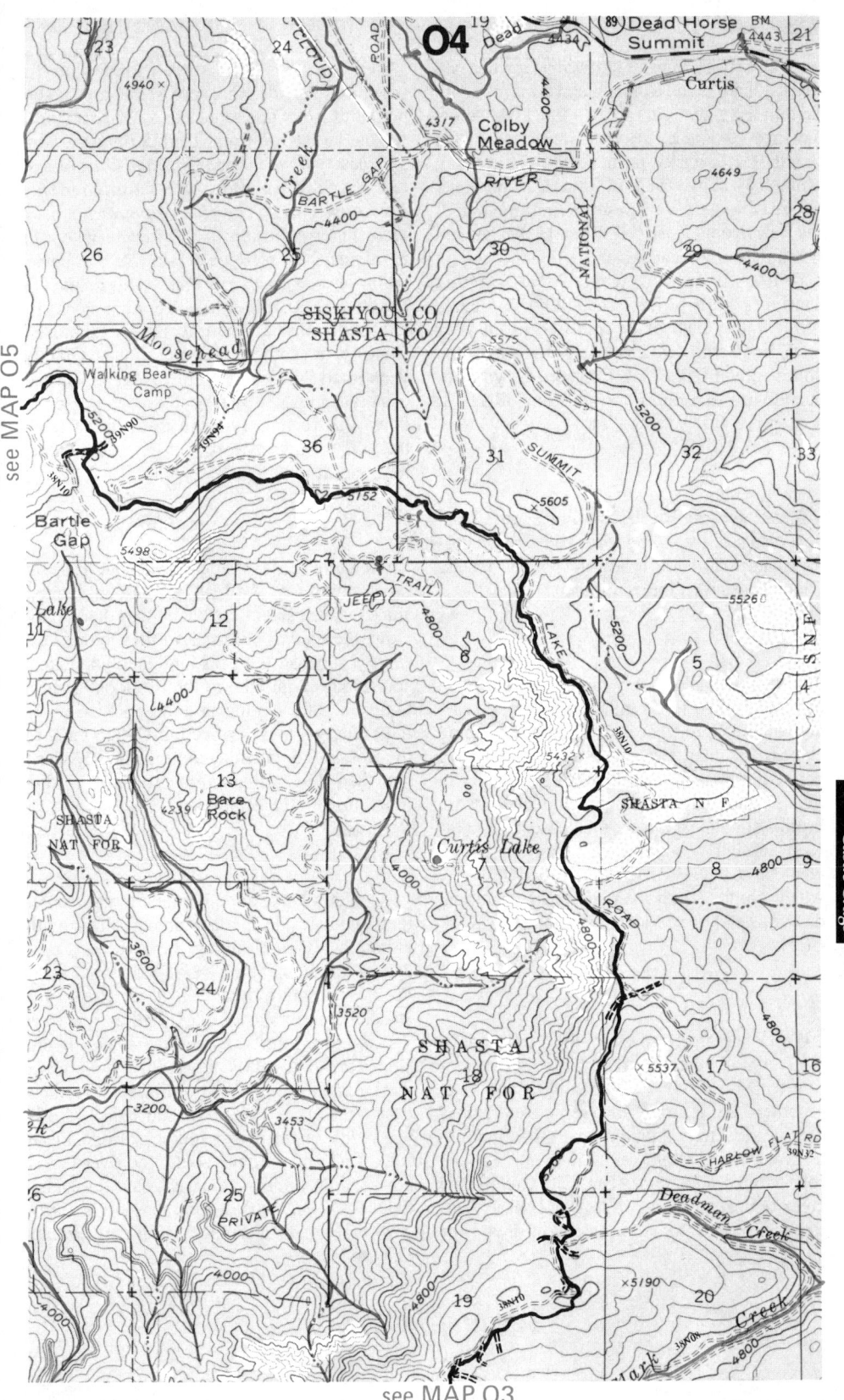

see MAP O5

see MAP O3

O4

O Burney Falls-
Castle Crags

through a shady forest. They reappear when you reach a sharp ridge, from which you climb south up into the glaciated, forested bowl just below Mushroom Rock. You can take a viewful breather at a rocky point (6080–2.3), rising ominously above the trail, or at a second one, about a minute's walk past the first. Beyond it, the trail rejoins Road 38N10 and stays just beneath it as both head west.

Your trail crosses Road 38N10 at this section's high point (6120–1.4), which is immediately east of Peak 6213. From your bush-lined trail you have ample views to the south, down Live Oak Canyon, as you descend west to a reunion with Road 38N10 at a road junction (5580-1.1).

*   *   *   *

Water access: By descending ½ mile from here on a north-trending road, you'll reach possible campsites at the headwaters of Tate Creek, which flows well into summer.

*   *   *   *

Westward, the PCT stays along the south side of Road 38N10 for ⅓ mile, crosses it, takes a convoluted course across gullied north-facing slopes, and then twice approaches that road before recrossing it again (5610–1.5). Your rim trail parallels the road—largely hidden by dense brush—for almost ½ mile, then descends southwest another ½ mile, leveling off in an old clearcut at the Alder Creek Trail (5440–1.1), which climbs south over the nearby rim and descends to lower Alder Creek and the Kosk Creek road.

*   *   *   *

Water access: Northward, this "trail" (definitely a road) goes ⅓ mile over to an intersection with Road 38N10. You could camp here, as others have done, and get water from a nearby, seasonal pond, though you'll find better water if you continue 0.2 mile north on the road to the headwaters of Star City Creek. This creek typically dries up in August or early September, even in the Stouts Meadow area.

*   *   *   *

Your rim route west stays within white-fir cover for ½ mile, then crosses a repeatedly burned stand of knobcone pines, the first you'll see on the Pacific Crest Trail. ▌*Between here and the dry slopes above Cook and Green Pass, near the Oregon border, you'll see this tree only a few times. Here, the pines are growing near their upper elevation limit. They survive well in frequently burned areas because fires cause their cones to open, and their seeds do well in freshly burned soil.* ▌You see more stands of knobcone pines as you traverse across brushy slopes to a saddle and a crossing of Grizzly Peak Road (5540–2.1). Before August, you can usually find water by descending ½ mile or so down this road. Staying just above the road, the PCT follows it west over to a saddle, then recrosses it (5420–0.6).

*   *   *   *

Alternate route: If you've got your heart set on climbing Grizzly Peak, which you've seen since the east rim of the basin, then start south along the road. It climbs 1.9 miles to the west ridge just below the peak, and then you take a spur road 0.2 mile up to the fire lookout atop the peak. After taking in a sweeping view of the scenery—most of Section O—go back to the west-ridge junction, continue briefly west, and then descend southeast to a south-ridge junction with the PCT.

*   *   *   *

If you don't take the 2.9-mile alternate route, then you face a PCT route almost as long with almost as much climbing, *sans* views. Logically, the trail should have climbed to Grizzly Peak or started a descent to Deer Creek. Instead, it contours for about 1.2 miles, and then you round a ridge and face the steep, barren slopes of Grizzly Peak. Confronted with these, the builders dropped the trail almost to their base, then made it climb for more than ½ mile to a saddle on the peak's southeast ridge. From it the trail should have contoured over to another saddle, ¼ mile to the west, then descended to Deer Creek. Instead, it climbs ½ mile northwest to a road on the south ridge of Grizzly Peak (5640–2.6).

Reunited with the alternate route, you now

See maps O5, O6

Burney Falls-
Castle Crags
O

The PCT route southwest toward Grizzly Peak

face a 10-mile descent, which—fortunately—is very well graded, making the climb in the opposite direction a relatively easy, if lengthy, task. Your trail starts west, crosses the usually dry headwaters of Deer Creek, switchbacks and quickly diagonals southeast across a road and an adjacent major powerline to recross the headwaters. It then descends southward through a shady forest of white firs and Douglas-firs. After weaving in and out of several dry gullies, the trail switchbacks north and quickly brings you to delightful Deer Creek (4700–2.1). Southbound hikers, be aware that this is your last reliable water along the trail until you reach the springs at Moosehead Creek's headwaters, 14.8 trail miles to the east.

Since camping space is nil, you push on, at first following the creek, though at a distance, downstream, then veering into a side canyon with a refreshing creek (4360–1.4). ∎ *Umbrella plants, which you'll recognize by their large leaves, line this creek's banks and those of others you'll see on your westward trek through Section O.* ∎ Again, camp space is nonexistent, so you trek onward, in and out of gullies, and watch Deer Creek drop farther and farther below you. At last you cross a ridge and descend gently north for more than a mile to broad Butcherknife Creek (3300–3.2), also without

sites. Now you have the pleasure of weaving in and out of gullies (some with seasonal water) as you parallel the creek and watch it gradually drop away from you. After 1.6 miles you cross a narrow ridge, descend into a nearby gully, and then circle over to usually dry Doodlebug Gulch (3000–2.1). Now on lower, south-facing slopes, you're pestered by flies as you traverse to a second ridge and make a gullied descent northwest past marble outcrops to Centipede Creek. This you cross at the McCloud-Big Bend Road (2404–1.3).

*   *   *   *

Resupply access: If you have to get out to civilization, hitchhike north out to McCloud, about 14½ miles away. This settlement has few services, and so you would have to continue about 12 miles west on Highway 89 to Mt. Shasta City.

*   *   *   *

You can camp along the road, but it's better to continue west on the PCT and descend to nearby Ash Camp (2390–0.2) along the McCloud River. This small camp is not as pleasant as Ah-Di-Na Campground, ahead, but

See maps O6, O7, O8

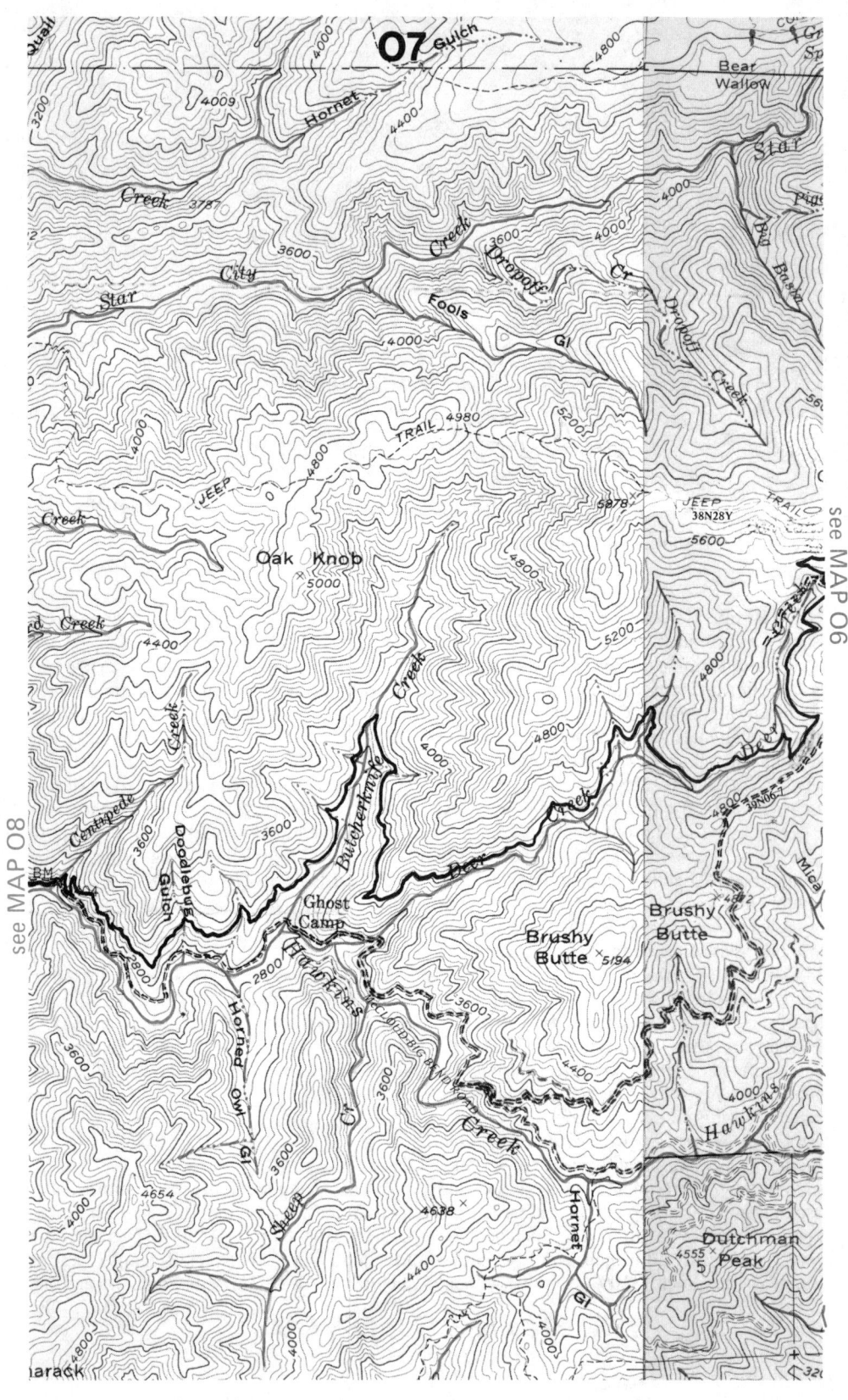

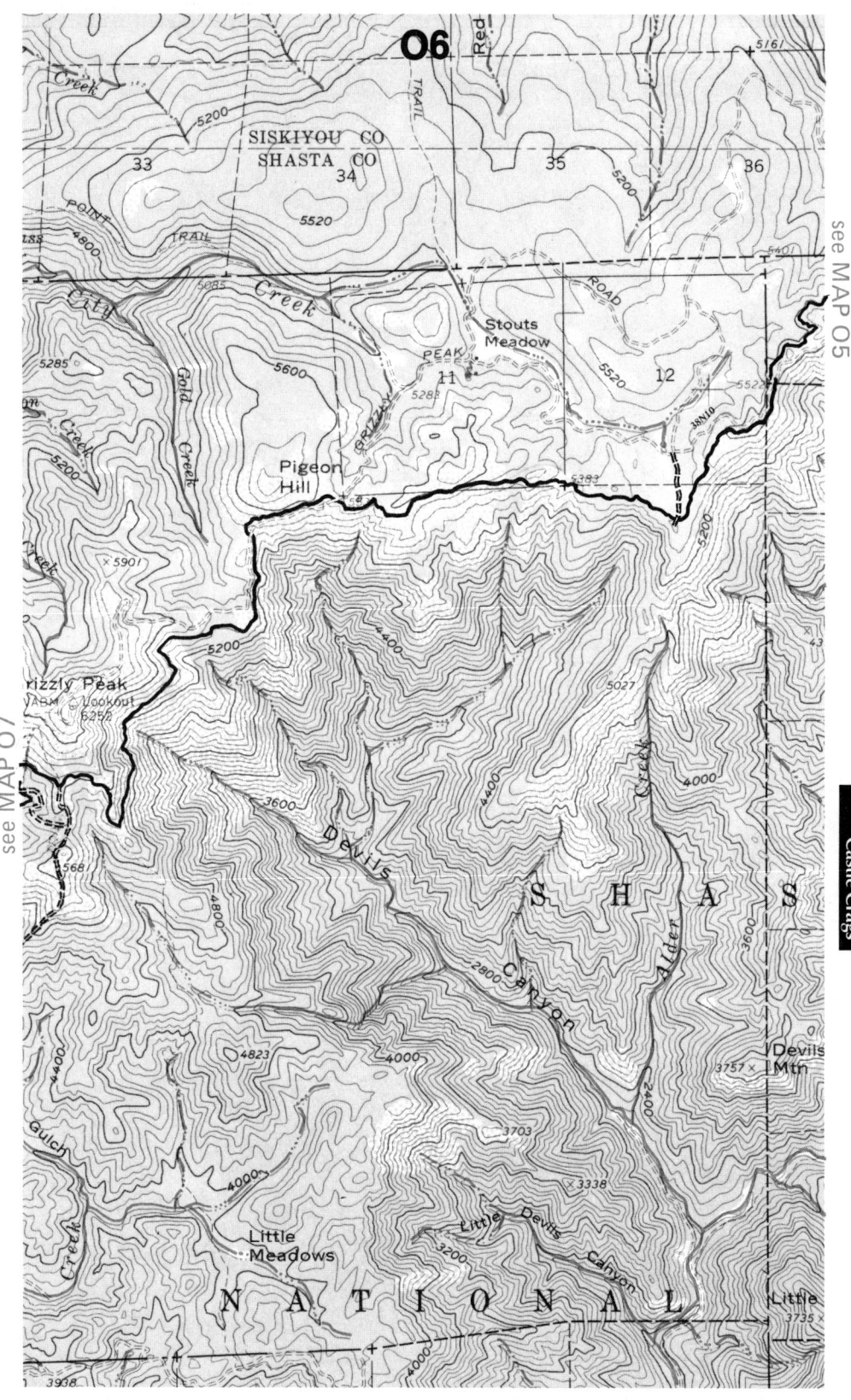

see MAP O5

see MAP O7

SISKIYOU CO
SHASTA CO

33   34   35   36

Stouts
Meadow

PEAK
11   12

Pigeon
Hill

Grizzly Peak
Lookout

Devils

Canyon

S   H   A   S

Alder Creek

Devils
Mtn

Gulch

Little
Meadows

Little Devils
Canyon

N A T I O N A L

Little

O
Burney Falls–
Castle Crags

O9

O8

see MAP 09

see MAP 07

Bridge over Squaw Valley Creek

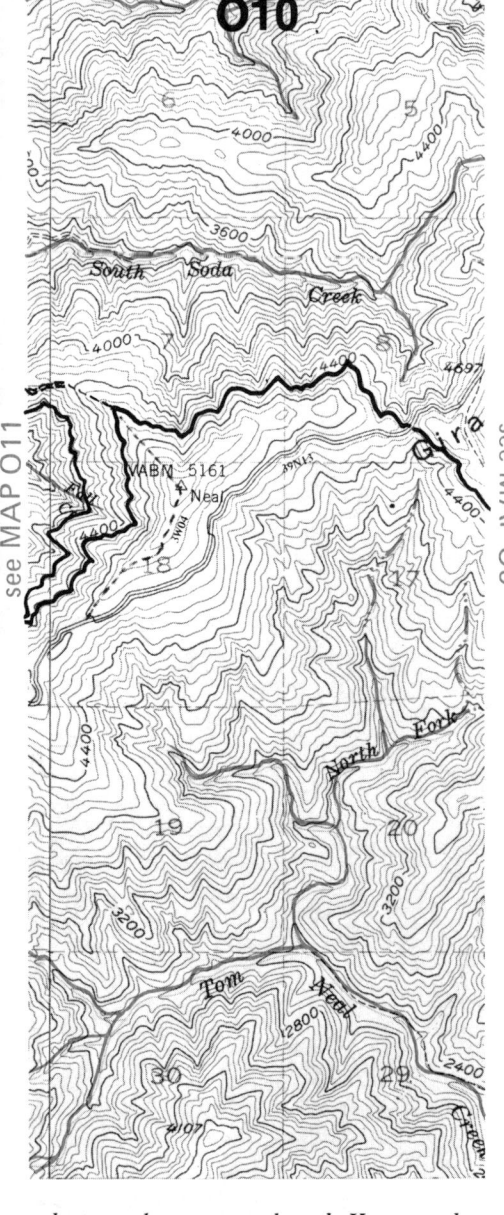

neither is it ⅔ mile out of the way.

Leaving the campground, you follow the trail 0.1 mile up the McCloud River, then span it on a 50-yard-long bridge. Rather than parallel the river, the trail climbs ¼ mile south to a minor gap, then contours west for 1¼ miles, staying disappointingly high above the McCloud River and its alluring pools. ∎ *However, there is method to the trail planners' madness: they have purposely kept the trail high to discourage you from reaching the river since it periodically floods when the gates on the McCloud Reservoir dam are opened.* ∎ Finally your hot route starts to descend, then turns north onto an abandoned road, on which you could camp. You head briefly up Fitzhugh Gulch and come to its creek (2320–2.1), which usually flows through early August. This will be your last trailside water until Trough Creek, 3.0 air miles away. You, however, will walk 8.3 miles to reach it. ∎ *Most of the rocks you've seen over the last few miles are, like those ahead, volcanic rocks that erupted on the earth's surface about 200–250 million years ago and then were*

subsequently metamorphosed. However, beyond Bald Mountain Road, to which you're now going to climb, these metavolcanics give way to metasediments, rocks that were originally deposited on a shallow ocean floor. These rocks are older, roughly 300-350 million years old. By the time you approach the Sacramento River, the rocks will be twice as old as those you've

See map O8

just traversed. ∎ From the creek in Fitzhugh Gulch you follow a short trail segment over to a dry gulch and climb up to nearby Road 38N53 (2400-0.4).

*　　*　　*　　*

Side route: This descends 0.6 mile to the entrance to pleasing Ah-Di-Na Campground, which is located on the site of an old resort. Here is a good place for a layover day, particularly if you're an angler. Fishing is also supposed to be good at Squaw Valley Creek, your next major goal. Halfway down Road 38N53 you'll find a flowing creek, though the creek is usually dry where the PCT crosses it, about 400 feet higher.

*　　*　　*　　*

Just ½ mile past Road 38N53 the PCT crosses this creek, and then it makes a steady, gentle ascent into ravines and out to ridges, presenting you views through live oaks, incense-cedars and Douglas-firs. Flies can be terrible along this stretch, swarming to such an extent that you're likely to inhale a few. They particularly love you if you're sweaty, so try and hike this stretch in the morning. You'll have lots more fly problems in the remainder of Section O, particularly when you are hiking across dry, oak-covered terrain. Finally, you cross Bald Mountain Road (3380–3.1), parallel it southwest for a bit, and then turn north and gently climb to another road (3520-0.8), which you meet at a road bend on a ridge (southbound hikers take note). Ahead, the road is closed to motor vehicles, and you take it around the bend, into two gullies, around another bend, and then into two more gullies. ∎ *This stretch of road is being overgrown by deer brush, and in early summer these wild lilacs bloom and permeate the air with their sweet fragrance.* ∎ The road dies out among brush and you follow a trail segment that first climbs northwest up a dry gully, then south around a ridge. The route then climbs ¾ mile north, veering in and out of minor gullies before topping out on a ridge saddle (3880–1.9). In another ¾ mile you descend to the head of a beautiful, linear canyon. ∎ *About the only time you'll see water flowing down it, however, is during a heavy*

rainstorm, for the canyon is lined in marble and the drainage is subterranean. ∎ After a mile of hiking through this cool, verdant canyon, you swing over to nearby Trough Creek (3030–2.1), whose water provides a welcome sight.

Beyond it, your shady route contours 0.4 mile west over to a seasonal creek fed by an equally seasonal lake, and then it contours ⅔ mile over to a ridge. Douglas-firs and ponderosa pines begin to thin out by the time you contour over to another ridge, ½ mile away. Then black oaks, live oaks and flies take over as you descend to Squaw Valley Creek (2580–3.2). By late afternoon the creek warms sufficiently to provide an enjoyable swim in the alluring pool by the route's arch bridge.

*　　*　　*　　*

Side route: In this minigorge, a westbank trail runs upstream to nearby Cabin Creek. You'll find several campsites along this trail, and you should plan to camp at one of them, since in the remaining 16.4 miles of Section O there are no more campsites with water. Until you reach the Sacramento River, near this section's end, your only other reliable water source will be spring-fed Fall Creek, 10.6 miles away.

Like the McCloud River, Squaw Valley Creek was flowing even before these mountains started to rise millions of years ago. Hence it cuts across the mountain range and its headwaters originate on the southeast slopes of Mt. Shasta. Before that volcano developed and blocked south-flowing streams, Squaw Valley Creek might have drained a larger area, which would explain how it could have cut such a deep canyon.

*　　*　　*　　*

You climb out of the canyon, ending your ascent on an abandoned road that climbs southwest to a deep saddle (3059–0.9). From here roads head in all directions, but the one you want starts from the base of a large cut on the west side of the saddle. You head 190 yards north-northwest on an abandoned road, then spot the PCT and start south on a switchbacking ascent, which takes you to the top of a west-climbing ridge. You follow it momentarily, and then head over to Douglas-fir-shaded north

See maps O8, O9

O11

see MAP P1

see MAP O10

slopes that provide you with occasional views of Mt. Shasta. After about 2 miles, the trail regains the ridge, follows it briefly west, and then switchbacks up south slopes to recross the ridge higher up. Again you traverse shady north slopes, barely climbing to a descending, abandoned road, but then climbing with effort back to a last crossing of the ridge. You conclude your climb by traversing ¾ mile northwest gently up to a saddle crossing of Girard Ridge Road (4600–4.8).

▌ *Mt. Shasta now reveals itself for full inspection, a magnificent sight when it is snowy white in early summer or early fall. West of it stands conical Black Butte, a smaller, younger volcano that lies midway between the towns of Weed and Mt. Shasta. Like Section N's Lassen Peak, Black Butte is a plug dome, and it erupted over perhaps a year or two roughly 9500 years ago. Shasta, on the other hand, is a stratovolcano, and it has been building up over tens of thousands of years. Just in the last 2000 years, it has erupted six times.* ▌

The PCT contours across brushy, logged-over slopes to a ridge, from which you get your first view of Castle Crags. ▌ *These are the first granitic rocks you've seen since climbing up Chips Creek canyon back at the start of Section N. You'll see lots of them in Section P. The granodiorite rock comprising Castle Crags solidified in the earth's crust roughly 140 million years ago, then tens of millions of years elapsed before the overlying rock was eroded away. In contrast, most of the rocks along the first part of your descent from Girard Ridge originated as sediments laid down on an ocean floor roughly 300–400 million years ago.* ▌

Views continue as you contour west to a northwest-descending ridge (4640–1.8). The original, temporary PCT route once plunged across private property down this ridge, allowing hikers to reach the Sacramento River in about an hour. Southbound hikers, however, faced quite a struggle up this steep, sometimes hot ridge. The permanent PCT is too gentle and far too long, but this is partly due to the necessity of routing it around private logging lands. From the northwest-dropping ridge you make a largely open, barely perceptible descent past marble outcrops to a switchback on a prominent ridge (4330–1.8). You then contour ½ mile east before dropping into a gulch containing Fall Creek (4050–1.3). Level ground, unfortunately, is absent, and no camping is allowed on the private land and the state park land ahead.

From the creek, the trail actually climbs a bit, and then descends ever so gently, passing through a logged area before reaching the northwest-descending ridge where a road crosses it (3770–1.5). Here you enter Castle Crags State Park and make a protracted, switchbacking descent in and out of dry, fly-infested gullies. ▌ *Vegetation ranges from shady Douglas-fir on north slopes to live oak on southwest slopes.* ▌ As you approach the Sacramento River, whose flowing water sounds are drowned out by trucks on nearby Interstate 5, you eventually reach a closed road (2420–3.2). The former PCT route once descended it, but now PCT tread crosses it, parallels it briefly up a gully, and then makes a gently graded, winding descent in and out of additional gullies before intersecting a trail that heads south up to the nearby, more-direct road you crossed. A minute's walk farther gets you to a crossing of paved Riverside Road (2180–0.9).

*   *   *   *

Resupply access: The official PCT does not go past the Castella Post Office, so Schaffer proposes a route that does: starting along Riverside Road, it winds, climbs and dips, but it is shady and lightly driven, and provides access to the Sacramento River.

From the PCT crossing head southeast up the road, then wind south for about ½ mile to a bridge across Fall Creek and an immediate junction with southeast-climbing Road 38N23. From this vicinity you could head over to Castle Crags State Park's nearby River Trail, which provides an alternate route. From the road junction Riverside Road turns southwest to immediately enter the park, and in about 250 yards it reaches a small turnout. From it a short trail goes 70 yards northwest to an environmental campsite, located in the southwest side of the trail. Unfortunately, it is not for trekkers. Immediately beyond it the trail deadends at the River Trail, which now has a westward course. For the next mile Riverside Road follows its namesake at a distance and then reaches the entrance to a combined campground/picnic area.

See maps O9, O10, O11

From its east end a spur trail heads briefly upriver to a junction with the River Trail. From that point the River Trail bridges the Sacramento River and then continues west for about ¼ mile, being sandwiched between Southern Pacific's railroad tracks and Frontage Road, crossing the latter to tunnel under Interstate 5. The 2.2-mile-long River Trail quickly ends at a turnaround loop of the park's main campground. You can head north up it to find PCT campsite 25. Taking this described route, while pleasant, is not recommended. If your goal is to reach campsite 25, then you might as well stick with the official PCT route. Furthermore, it does not get you to a post office or store.

Therefore, from the campground/picnic area continue about 280 yards west on Riverside Road to a junction from which your road angles north to quickly cross the Sacramento River, pass a small laundromat, and reach adjacent railroad tracks immediately before ending at Frontage Road. Since the latter parallels Interstate 5, it is not a desirable route to this junction.

You take Frontage Road 0.2 mile to Castle Creek Road, turn right, and on it quickly pass under Interstate 5 to immediately arrive at the Castella Post Office and adjacent Ammirati's Market, both on the left. The store is well stocked with junk food and beer—the salvation of many a hot, weary trekker. From these facilities continue about ¼ mile up Castle Creek Road to the main entrance to Castle Crags State

Park, this spot being 2.0 miles since the start of this access route. The start of the trail description in the next chapter begins from this spot.

*   *   *   *

From where the PCT crosses Riverside Road, it initially parallels the road southeast before switchbacking and paralleling it southwest, ending in 230 yards, at the road's junction with northeast heading Soda Creek Road.

❙ *In the roadcut immediately above the start of Riverside Road is a light-brown volcanic tuff that originated in a sizable Mt. Shasta eruption. Beneath it appears to be a volcanic mudflow from the same volcano. The towns along the flanks of Shasta and down the Sacramento River canyon could be eradicated should a significant future eruption occur.* ❙

From the junction of the two roads, the PCT route goes westward along paved Soda Creek Road, and after a few minutes of passing private-property signs you bridge the fairly wide Sacramento River and then reach nearby Southern Pacific's railroad tracks.

*   *   *   *

Resupply access: Unfortunately, no road connects your road to Dunsmuir—a town that has just about everything, including boot repair. So if you need services there, you may have to hike

See map O11

Mt. Shasta and Black Butte, from Girard Ridge

north along these patrolled tracks. After about 1.2 miles you can branch onto a spur road and then take 3 miles of roads to central Dunsmuir.

*   *   *   *

Just past the railroad tracks you curve over to Frontage Road, then cross under nearby Interstate 5, just beyond which Section O ends at a locked gate (2130–0.7) along the eastern boundary of the west half of Castle Crags State Park.

See map O11

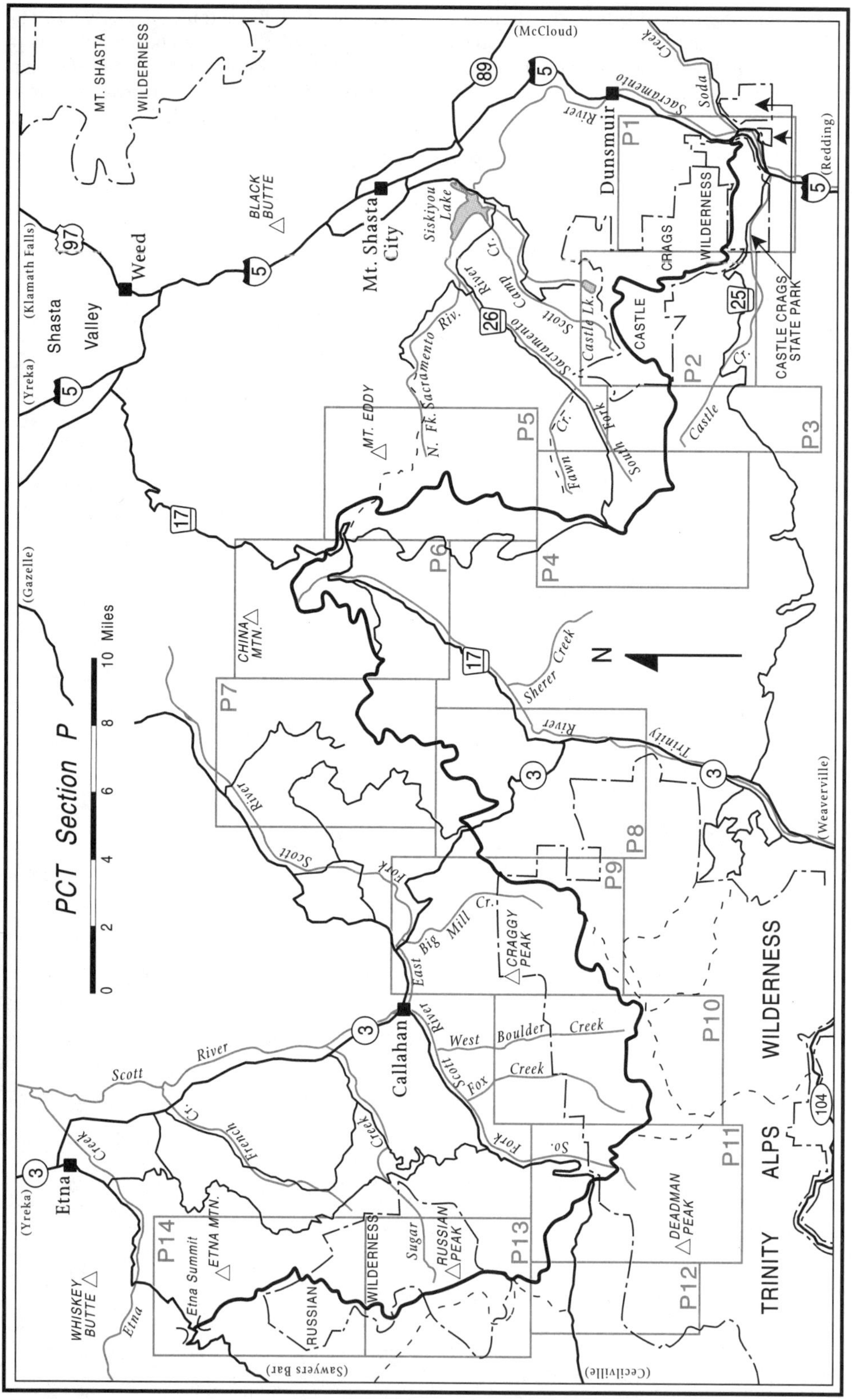

(Yreka) 3

Etna

WHISKEY
BUTTE △

Etna   Creek

Scott

P14

Etna Summit
△ ETNA MTN.

French

Cr.

River

Creek

RUSSIAN

(Sawyers Bar)

WILDERNESS

Sugar

RUSSIAN
△ PEAK

P13

Scott

Fork

River

West

Fork

Boulder

So.   Fork

Creek

Creek

East Big Mill Cr.

△ CRAGGY
PEAK

P9

P8

P12

DEADMAN
△ PEAK

(Cecilville)

P10

P11

TRINITY   ALPS   WILDERNESS

104

(Weaverville)

PCT Section P

0   2   4   6   8   10 Miles

(Gazelle)

(Yreka)   (Klamath Falls)

5   Shasta
Valley   97

Weed   MT. SHASTA

17   WILDERNESS

5   BLACK
△ BUTTE

P7

CHINA
MTN. △

Scott   River

Callahan

3

17

3

Sherer Creek

River

Trinity

3

N

P6

△ MT. EDDY

N. Fk. Sacramento Riv.

MT. SHASTA
CITY

Siskiyou
Lake

26   Scott Camp   Cr.

River

P5

Sacramento

Fawn   Cr.

South   Fork

Castle Lk.

P4

Dunsmuir

89

(McCloud)

5

River

P1

CASTLE

CRAGS

WILDERNESS

Soda

Castle

Cr.

25

P2

CASTLE CRAGS
STATE PARK

P3

5   (Redding)

Section P
Castle Crags to Etna Summit

Introduction: Like the Sierra Nevada, this area we are about to hike has been heavily glaciated. Therefore, lakes abound, although the trail skirts only three: the two Deadfall Lakes and Paynes Lake. Nevertheless, about three dozen lakes lie within a half-hour's walk (or less) from the PCT. The reason the PCT doesn't visit more lakes is that most lie in deep basins that don't become snow-free until mid-July or later. The PCT, routed along many south- and west-facing slopes, becomes mostly snow-free by late June.

Like the area's lakes, its rocks may remind you of the Sierra Nevada. Like that range, much of Section P—an eastern part of the Klamath Mountains—is granitic. Still, about half of the miles we walk will be across ultramafic terrain and a few will be across mafic terrain. Ultramafic and mafic rocks, like granitic rocks, are intrusive rocks, all solidifying within the earth's crust. Granites are light gray, mafics are intermediate, and ultramafics are dark gray—when fresh. This last type, rich in iron and manganese, weathers to a rusty color, as you'll see just north of Toad Lake. This color makes them easy to identify, and you'll see them time and again on your way to Oregon.

As in the previous section, Shasta red firs dominate at the higher elevations, and if you're going to have any early-season snow problems, they will be in these forests and in stands of mountain hemlocks. Loggers are harvesting these firs as well as white firs and Douglas-firs lower down. Though you'll see some clearcuts that are real eyesores, the trail generally avoids such areas and the feeling of wilderness often prevails. Still, loggers and logging roads abound, which are convenient if you have to exit down to civilization.

Declination: 17°E

Points on Route	S→N	Mi. Btwn. Pts.	N→S
Interstate 5 near Castle Crags State Park	0.0		99.8
		6.6	
Sulphur Creek	6.6		93.2
		3.4	
Section 31 tributary of North Fk. Castle Creek	10.0		89.8
		5.7	
crest saddle 5983	15.7		84.1
		6.7	
Trinity Divide	22.4		77.4
		2.3	
Road 40N30	24.7		75.1
		5.6	
Porcupine Lake spur trail	30.3		69.5
		5.4	
upper Deadfall Lake	35.7		64.1
		3.3	

Parks Creek Road 42N17 .... 39.0	8.4	60.8
Bull Lake saddle... 47.4	7.9	52.4
Masterson Meadow saddle 55.3	4.4	44.5
Highway 3 at Scott Mountain Summit....................... 59.7	8.1	40.1
E. Boulder Lake/Marshy Lakes saddle 67.8	6.0	32.0
Trail 8W07 near Section Line Lake 73.8	5.8	26.0
Forest Highway 93 at Carter Meadows Summit 79.6	6.2	20.2
s.e. rim of South Russian Creek canyon 85.8	4.8	14.0
slopes below Statue Lake 90.6	3.3	9.2
Paynes Lake 93.9	4.2	5.9
Upper Ruffey Lake saddle 98.1	1.7	1.7
Somes Bar-Etna Road at Etna Summit 99.8		0.0

Supplies: Dunsmuir lies a few miles north of this section's starting point. It should have just about any kind of food and equipment you might need. Food and minor supplies can be bought at Ammirati's Market, which lies just east of the main entrance to Castle Crags State Park. The Castella Post Office is next to the store, and you should mail your parcels to it. Plan to make your "CARE" package last all the way to Seiad Valley, at the end of Section Q, for there are no nearby towns, post offices or resorts anywhere between. Rather than mail your supplies to the Seiad Valley post office, which like others is closed weekends and holidays, mail them to the adjacent Mid River R. V. Park, which holds them for free. Their address is: P.O. Box 707, Seiad Valley, CA 96086. Unless you are a strong backpacker, count on 10+ days to do both sections.

If you have to go out for supplies, you can leave the PCT at Scott Mountain Summit. Follow Highway 3 for 8½ miles to Callahan, with post office, store and ranger station, then climb southwest 12 miles back to the PCT at Carter Meadows Summit. Unfortunately, the 20 miles of PCT you would thus bypass are among this section's best. Later, at Etna Summit, where Section P ends and Section Q begins, you can descend northeast 10½ miles to Etna. Sawyers Bar, 15 miles west from the summit, is too distant to consider.

Permits: There are three wildernesses in Section P: Castle Crags, Trinity Alps and Russian. You'll need a wilderness permit only for Trinity Alps Wilderness. In Section Q, you'll need a wilderness permit for Marble Mountain Wilderness. You hike through Trinity Alps Wilderness in Section P's stretch between Highway 3 and Forest Highway 93, and through Marble Mountain Wilderness in most of Section Q. If you're driving through this general area, pick up a permit for both areas at the Callahan Ranger Station in Callahan or at the Scott River Ranger Station in Fort Jones. As usual, it's best to write in advance. See Chapter 1 for addresses.

Water shortage: After mid-August in normal years and before that in drier years, water may be absent in this section's first 22 miles. If you are hiking this stretch in late summer or early fall, be sure you carry enough water to last until Upper Seven Lake.

Hazards: Particularly watch for rattlesnakes along the first 11 miles. They are usually less common westward, higher up, though they have been relatively common from Cooper Meadow south to Scott Mountain. Ticks and poison oak may be a problem below 4000 feet, but flies will pester you the most. Up by the crest, mosquitoes can be locally abundant before late July.

Castle Crags

Maps: *Dunsmuir*
    Seven Lakes Basin
    Mumbo Basin
    South China Mountain
    Mount Eddy
    Scott Mountain

Tangle Blue Lake
Billys Peak
Deadman Peak
Eaton Peak
Etna

--- **The Route** ---

Resupply access: The last chapter's supply-access route ended at the main entrance (mile 0.0) to Castle Crags State Park, which is about ¼ mile west of the Castella Post Office. To conclude this route, head past the park's entrance station to meet a service road branching left. You start along the main road, which curves right. If you are heading for the park's PCT backpackers' campsite (no equestrian campsite in the park), then continue east about ¾ mile to the center of the campground. You'll find campsite 25 immediately west of the campground's campfire center. However, if you want to regain the northbound PCT, then you will almost immediately leave the main road to branch left on a north-climbing trail.

This trail was built to bypass employee residences located along the lower part of the service road. This trail climbs about ¼ mile up almost to the service road, then parallels it about 250 yards east to a tight bend in the road (2260–0.5). Here you'll meet the Milt Kenney Trail, which makes a very winding 0.9-mile traverse eastward to PCT campsite 25. Northbound trekkers from that site will take this trail west to join us at this junction.

From the trail junction you start up the service road and in 40 yards meet a fire road which, after 1.2 miles of winding eastward traverse, ends at the park's main road. You continue northwest up the rather steep service road, and after about 0.4 mile, at a switchback by a ridge,

See map P1

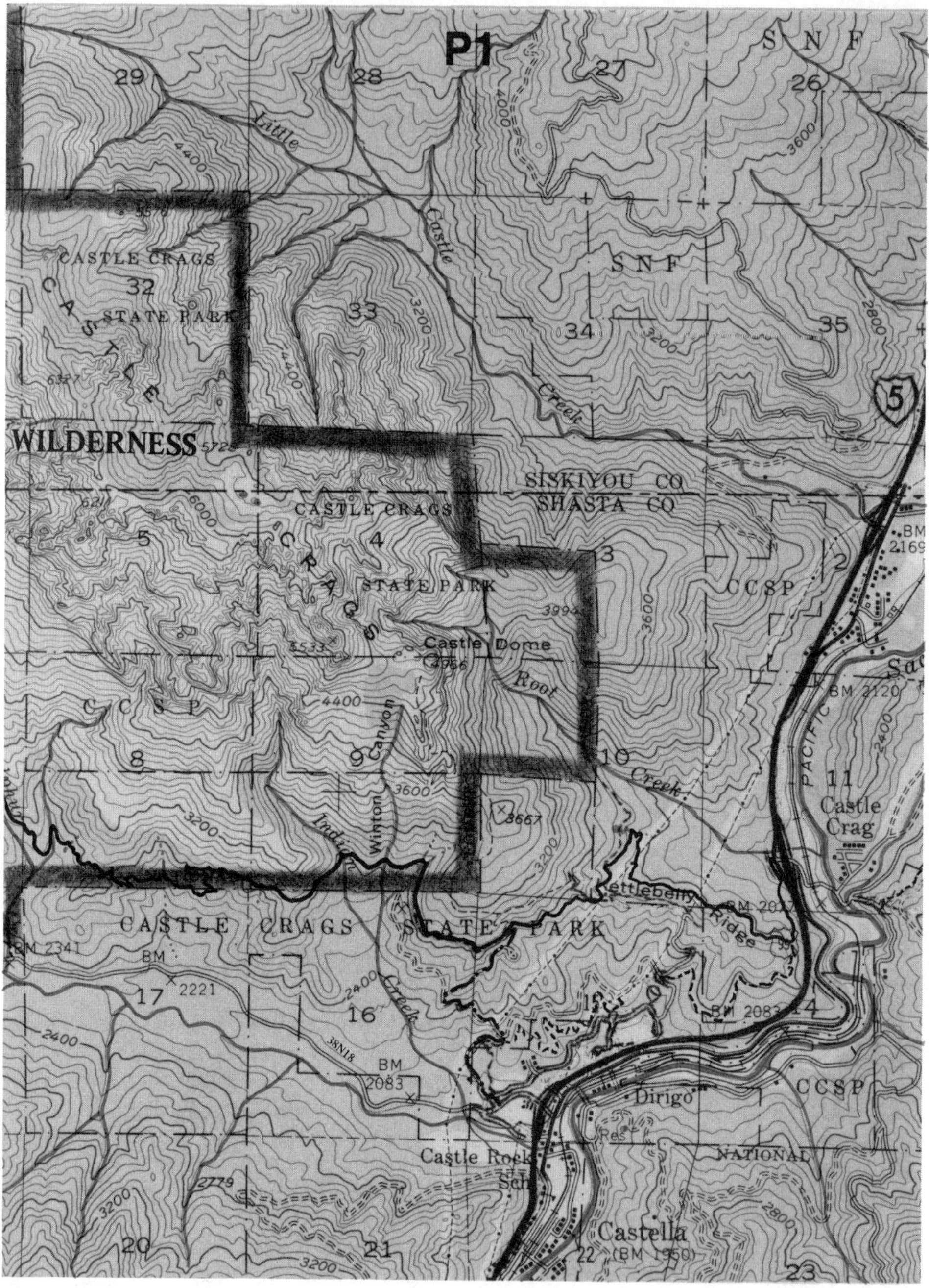

see MAP P2

see MAP O11

meet another traversing fire road, heading northwest. From the switchback you now climb about 0.4 mile northeast to a turnaround loop atop a minor ridge. Walk briefly along the Bobs Hat Trail to a quick intersection of the PCT (2820–1.0–1.5).

*　　　*　　　*　　　*

Section P arbitrarily begins at the west side of an Interstate 5 onramp-offramp, the next one north of the Castle Crags State Park onramp-offramp. Here, by a locked gate, you enter the park and immediately turn left (south) on an old road. North, it goes 80 yards to refreshing Root Creek. You follow this narrowing road,

See map P1

hiking under the pleasant shade of Douglas-firs, ponderosa pines, incense-cedars, black oaks and big-leaf maples. Although sheltered from the sun, your low-elevation route can get up into the 90s on hot summer afternoons. Characteristic of this environment is a profusion of poison oak, which in Section P grows up to about 3500 feet in elevation. From the start of this section's PCT, you go about ⅓ mile south up a narrow, closed road to a fair viewpoint, then angle west for a 160-yard stroll to a junction (2420–0.5) with the Kettlebelly Trail.

* * * *

Alternate route: The state park has set aside campsite 25 for PCT hikers—camping outside the campground is prohibited. While there is no direct route to the campsite, the route beginning here involves the least amount of effort. It begins south on the Kettlebelly Trail, which is a winding, though fairly level, route composed of alternating short stretches of trails and abandoned roads. This circuitous trail ends at the park's paved main road (2270–1.2), which climbs north toward Kettlebelly Ridge. About ⅓ mile before reaching that road you'll meet the Vișta Point Trail, which climbs northward up a spur ridge to the main ridge.

On the main road you go but a few paces west along it to the obvious start of a fire road. Branching from a switchback of the main road, this closed road heads northwest to a gully, then southwest from it to a ridge (2210–0.3). Ahead, the fire road continues 0.9 mile to the park's service road. Instead you take a short, steep trail that switchbacks down to the park's campfire center (3080–0.1), which is immediately east of campsite 25. To regain the PCT, take the Milt Kenney Trail, which starts from the campsite and winds excessively over to the park's service road (2260–0.9). This road is mentioned in the resupply-access route at the beginning of this chapter, and you follow its last paragraph, which directs you back up to the PCT. You meet it where it intersects the Bobs Hat Trail (2820–1.0–3.5).

* * * *

From the junction with the north end of the Kettlebelly Trail, the PCT snakes westward on an amazingly level course in and out of gullies along the lower north slopes of Kettlebelly Ridge. Midway along this traverse you pass beneath a set of powerlines. At the end of the traverse you then veer north for ¼ mile, crossing under a larger set of powerlines, then briefly switchback up, almost touching a spring-fed seasonal creeklet before you climb ¼ mile south to the Root Creek Trail (2590–1.3).

* * * *

Water access: On it one could hike ¼ mile north to the often-flowing spring or to trail's end at Root Creek, about 0.4 mile farther.

* * * *

▮ *The Pacific Crest Trail was built around the southwest base of Castle Crags, not up over the crest of the crags. In a way, this is unfortunate, since the crest, studded with pinnacles, blocks and domes, is a far more exciting route. But the park people rightly felt that a trail blasted along the crags' crest would ruin its wilderness character. However, experienced mountaineers can traverse the Castle Crags high country. In 1972, Schaffer and another mountaineer, Bob Ng, made such a traverse, starting up Root Creek and ending on the saddle in the northwest quarter of Section 30. Traveling very light, they didn't have to use ropes. Don't attempt such a route with a heavy, awkward pack. One can avoid the initial cross-country climb up Root Creek by starting cross country from Castle Dome, at the end of the Crags trail. Again: for experienced mountaineers only; others can expect real trouble.* ▮

For a short distance south the PCT coincides with the Root Creek Trail as it immediately crosses a gully and, midway south to a next one, leaves that trail (2590–0.1), which continues 0.4 mile east to a parking lot at the end of the park's main road. Now the PCT goes up to a nearby powerline saddle (2650–0.1), on which it crosses the Crags Trail. Eastward, this quickly reaches the Root Creek Trail; westward, it climbs to Castle Dome, mentioned above. Leaving Kettlebelly Ridge, you traverse west across gullies to meet the Bobs Hat Trail (2820–0.5), where the supply access route, mentioned in the first paragraph, ends at the PCT. In about 27 yards the Bobs Hat Trail branches right and climbs steeply up to the Crags Trail.

The PCT now swings clockwise over to two

See map P1

adjacent creeklets, entering Castle Crags Wilderness. Just 0.2 mile past them you bridge Winton Canyon creek (2875–1.0) and then in ¼ mile cross Indian Creek. Over the next hour you cross two spur ridges, leaving Castle Crags State Park ¼ mile beyond the first one. Before the second one, you cross many gullies and have lots of views up at the Crags, and then the trail drops to the shady east fork of Sulphur Creek. Next it loops around another spur ridge and climbs northwest to Sulphur Creek (2750–3.1). Like all the creeks mentioned so far, this one is usually reliable through early- or mid-August. Knobcone pines briefly join ponderosa pines, Douglas-firs, incense-cedars and manzanitas as you climb southwest up to a spur ridge. Just 120 yards after you round it, you meet the Dog Trail (3040–0.6).

*   *   *   *

Side route: This trail descends ½ mile to North Fork Castle Creek and Whalen Road 38N18. Since the road and creek are on Forest Service land, you could camp by them—the first real camping opportunity since the park's campground. The Dog Trail is for the dogs—literally. Dogs aren't allowed in the park, so northbound hikers with dogs have to hike west up Whalen Road to the creek and then rejoin the PCT via the Dog Trail. Southbound PCT hikers with dogs must exit on the Dog Trail. Now if you have a cat. . . .

*   *   *   *

The PCT climbs north from the Dog Trail junction, then contours in and out of about a dozen gullies, some with early-season freshets, before switchbacking briefly down to two converging branches of a North Fork tributary (3110–1.8). During most of the summer, these are either seeping or dry. You then switchback up one of the branches, twice crossing it before winding around a ridge and descending to a seasonally flowing tributary of North Fork Castle Creek (3370–1.0). After mid-July, this could be dry. This creek, when flowing, is the last near trail water you'll have access to until you leave the trail for either the Seven Lakes, about 12 miles ahead, or for Upper Gumboot Lake, about 14½ miles ahead.

The real climbing now begins—about 2500 feet of it—up to a crest saddle. In one mile you

climb about 500 feet, first away from the creek, then almost back to it. You then climb southwest to a south-dropping ridge, finally leaving the live oaks and their hordes of flies behind you. Ponderosa pines, sugar pines and Douglas-firs offer some shade as you switchback up the ridge, but the vegetation is predominantly brush, especially huckleberry oak. The brush, however, lets you have many views, and these improve as you climb. To the east rise massive granodiorite faces, most of them with the same orientation, for this pluton is being slowly eroded along major fracture planes. To the west lie denuded slopes, the first of many logging scars you'll see in Section P.

After crossing the ridge several times, you climb about ½ mile north to a west-dropping ridge, from which you see miles of PCT tread heading westward and see a cascading creek, to the north, that drops well below you. After ⅓ mile of moderate ascent you reach a flat-topped bedrock outcrop, from which the inaccessible cascades are even more tempting. A final ⅔ mile haul, mostly through a fir forest, brings you to a forested saddle (5620–3.6) just beyond the northernmost boundary of Castle Crags State Park. Trees prevent a view of Mt. Shasta, to the northeast, but they don't restrict views to the

California pitcher plants

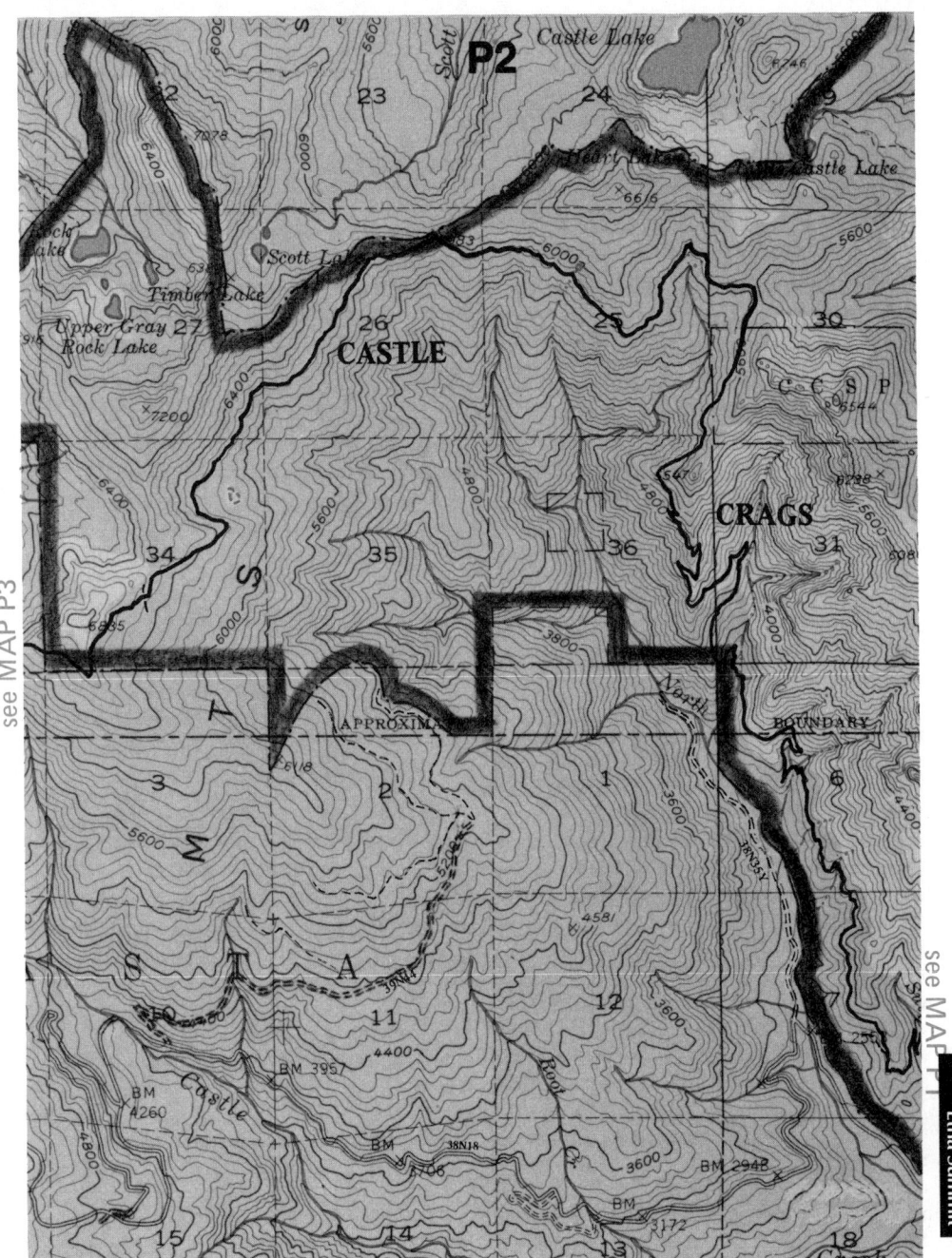

west. If you've brought along enough water or are willing to descend west to get some, you can camp here. Before August you can also obtain water about 10 minutes up the trail at the headwaters of the cascading creek (5750–0.4). Most of the creek's springs, unfortunately, lie below the trail in extremely dense brush.

Beyond the brush-covered springs and the audible, cascading creek, you contour around a ridge and reach a seasonal, densely vegetated creeklet (5840–1.0). ❚ *Among other plants you'll see is the California pitcher plant, a cobra-shaped plant that derives part of its nourishment from insects. Flies and other insects,*

See map P2

tempted by the alluring odor, venture down its hollow, tubular stem, only to find that downward-pointing hairs prevent their retreat. Other organisms, including bacteria and small invertebrates, digest the hapless insects and the plant absorbs the juices. This bog plant welcomes you to the Klamath Mountains, the only area where it is likely to be seen, though it is occasionally found in a few places outside these mountains. The Klamath Mountains are a collection of smaller mountain ranges that include, among others, the Trinity Alps and the Scott, Salmon, Marble and Siskiyou mountains. This mountain province differs from all other North American ranges in that it has an abundance of ultramafic rocks. In Section P, half of the PCT's length is across such rocks. Ultramafic rocks are related to granitic rocks in that both are igneous in origin and intrusive in nature. That is, both began as molten material within the earth's crust or mantle and solidified there, rather than on the surface. Ultramafic rocks, unlike their granitic relatives, are rich in iron and manganese, and hence heavy. The commonest ultramafic rock in the Klamath Mountains is peridodite, which geologists believe is the kind of rock that makes up the lower part of giant oceanic plates. If so, what you see, up here in the Klamath Mountains, are remnants of rock that once lay beneath an ocean floor. Oceanic plates, colliding with plates carrying continents, buckled and injected huge slabs of their ultramafic rocks into the continental masses. During this process of intense, low-temperature, high-pressure deformation, most of these rocks were altered, with the addition of water, to serpentinite. These rocks weather to serpentine soils which, when boggy, prove to be very popular grounds for pitcher plants. ∎

On such rocks and soils you contour west over to a saddle (5983-0.7), shaded by white firs, red firs and mountain hemlocks. Through the trees you have your first view of Mt. Shasta, which you last saw on Section O's descent west from Girard Ridge. The peak will now appear quite regularly time and time again all the way into southern Oregon.

* * * *

Water access: By descending northwest cross country across north-facing slopes, you can reach Scott Camp Creek in less than 10 minutes. The nearly level terrain by it provides sites for small camps.

* * * *

Beyond the saddle your trail traverses 1¾ miles southwest, providing you with ever-changing perspectives of Castle Crags. Some of the best views are from a scrubby ridge (6320–2.0), which you reach just after circling a basin with a usually dry lakelet. Just beyond the ridge you enter forest cover and climb gently southwest to an intersection of the Soapstone Trail (6500–0.5), which descends south to a maze of logging roads that lead down to Whalen Road. Your southwest climbing ends atop Peak 6835's south ridge (6670–0.5), on which you briefly enter and then leave Section 3. ∎ *Like so many privately owned sections you see along the PCT, this one belongs to the Southern Pacific Company, California's largest private-land owner. With close to 4000 square miles in its domain, this company manages an area about the size of Los Angeles County, about twice the size of the San Francisco Bay Area.* ∎ Starting northwest, you leave Section 34 in a few minutes, and doing so, leave Castle Crags Wilderness.

Westward to Trinity Divide and beyond, you will now walk across a glaciated terrain of mafic intrusive rocks. ∎ *These are intermediate between the light-gray granitic rocks of Castle Crags and the dark-gray ultramafic rocks you've just traversed. The latter, due to their high iron and manganese content, weather to a rusty color, which is very conspicuous where the vegetation is thin. Mafic rocks, like granites, intruded older, continental rocks. Ultramafic rocks, in contrast, first formed beneath the ocean floor and only later intruded continental rocks; they are usually older than the rocks they've intruded.* ∎

Your westward path skirts across several crest saddles, giving you views to the north down into the glaciated South Fork Sacramento River canyon and beyond it to Mt. Shasta. Most of your traverse is brushy, so you have almost continual views to the south, where the appropriately named Grey Rocks at first hold your attention. This mass of ancient metamorphosed volcanic rock yields to steep-sided Boulder Peak and Echo Lake. After more than 3 miles of westward traverse, your trail bends southwest and Upper Seven Lake, 550 feet below,

See maps P2, P3, P4

P

Castle Crags-Etna Summit

gets your attention, particularly if your route so far has been dry. However, huckleberry oak, cream bush, greenleaf manzanita, chinquapin and tobacco brush grow in such a dense stand that access to the lake is nearly impossible. To reach Upper or Lower Seven Lake, continue a bit farther to a major crest cleft, Trinity Divide (6780-3.7).

* * * *

Water access: From this saddle descend cross-country to an obvious jeep road that heads down to the lakes and a selection of campsites. Also leaving this saddle is Trail 6W12, in poor condition, which goes to jeep roads leading down to Lake Helen.

* * * *

At Trinity Divide you exchange Sacramento River drainage for Trinity River drainage. ∎ *It's interesting to note that water draining down the two sides of the divide will enter the Pacific Ocean at two points that are 280 miles apart.* ∎ On a curving traverse from north to northwest, you have ample opportunities to survey a part of the Trinity River basin, one so large that most hikers will take three or four days to circle its headwaters. The shallow Mumbo Lakes, in a glacial cirque below you, serve as reference points to mark your progress. As you continue to descend northwest, your trail vacillates along the crest, providing you with views down into both the Trinity and Sac-

ramento river drainages. Just ¼ mile beyond a notable crest saddle above Upper Gumboot Lake, you come to a second one, which is breached by Road 40N30 (6460–2.3).

* * * *

Side route: To reach the lake, about 250 feet below the saddle, head cross country straight down to it. Gumboot Lake, about ⅓ mile below it, has a primitive USFS campground. The campground's road descends ⅔ mile to Road 40N30, which in turn descends about 11 miles along South Fork Sacramento River to Lake Siskiyou, then continues about 4 miles beyond it up to Mt. Shasta city.

* * * *

From the Road 40N30 saddle, the PCT switchbacks up to a higher one crossed by Road 40N45 (6550–0.8). Your next stretch of PCT starts out on an old jeep road, and you have views west down upon shallow Picayune Lake and its swampy satellite. After ¾ mile, your road narrows to a trail as it contours the forested slopes west of Bear Ridge. It then dallies along the crest for ½ mile before contouring across cow-infested slopes to a major saddle (6770–2.1), crossed by the Little Picayune Trail. About 0.4 mile north of it, as you traverse the slopes west of White Ridge, you meet three springs, one of them with considerable staying power. Twenty-eight miles into Section P, this is your *first* really reliable *trailside* water.

See map P4

Mumbo Lakes in Mumbo Basin

see MAP P3

P

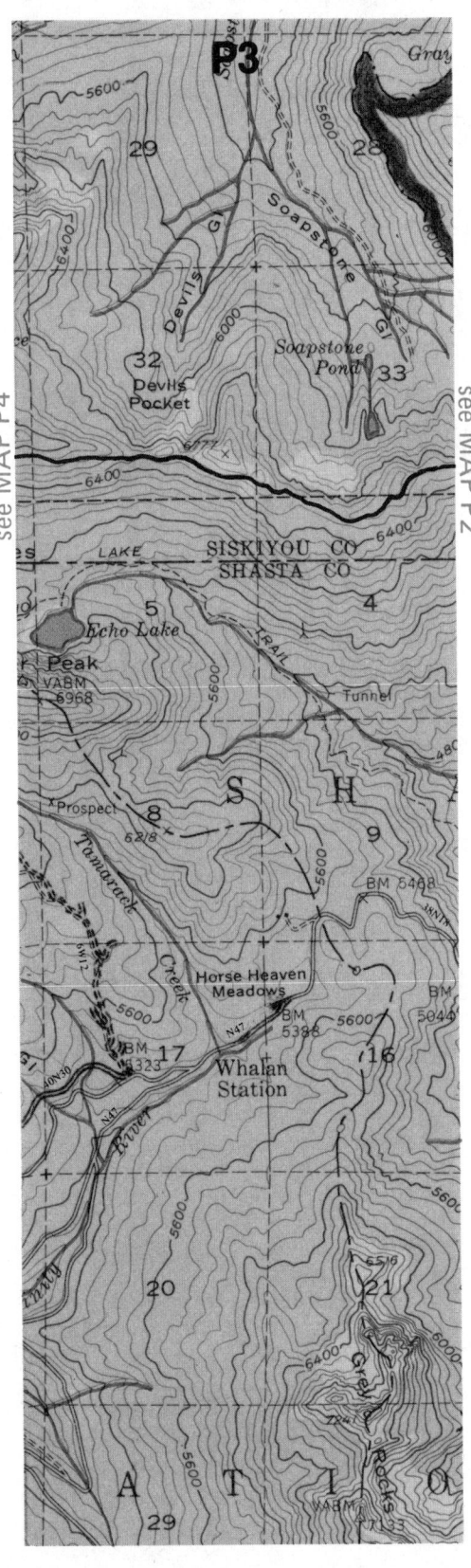

In about 300 yards you cross the crest at a minor saddle, then pass above a small meadow after a few minutes, and in ⅓ mile come to a small spring, immediately below the trail. ▮ *Typical of such seeps in ultramafic terrain, this spring has its colony of pitcher plants.* ▮ Your traverse through a shady red-fir/western-white-pine forest continues, and after ⅔ mile you pass another spring, this one seasonal. From it your trail traverses ⅓ mile east-northeast to an east-dropping ridge (7130–2.2), which gives you an excellent view of Lake Siskiyou, Mt. Shasta city, and its namesake, Mt. Shasta. Now on mafic igneous rocks such as diorite or gabbro, you contour along a blasted tread, first across a brushy rock field, then through a bouldery forest before arriving at a spur trail junction (7220–0.5).

*   *   *   *

Side route: Up this trail, you have scarcely a five-minute walk to beautiful Porcupine Lake, which is one of Section P's most desirable gems. However, the west-shore area, with level ground, can handle only a few backpacking parties. From the moraine at the lake's outlet you see Castle Crags and Lassen Peak—a rare view indeed.

*   *   *   *

Beyond the Porcupine Lake spur trail, the PCT climbs briefly to a crest (7300–0.3).

*   *   *   *

Side route: From here a steep trail descends 350 feet over a half-mile stretch to the west shore of Toad Lake. Lying at the bottom of an 800-foot-deep cirque, this glacial lake can be fed by melting snow till mid-July or later. Nevertheless, swimming can be quite agreeable in the lake's shallow east waters. A campground once ringed the lake, but the jeep road to it was closed, and not too many campers or fishermen walk the steep half-mile route up to it. If you plan to spend a layover day at a lake, consider doing it at Toad Lake.

*   *   *   *

From the crest above Toad Lake, the PCT traverses clockwise around the basin, intersect-

P

**Castle Crags-
Etna Summit**

See map P5

Mt. Shasta peeks over ridge above Toad Lake

ing Trail 6W06 (7420–0.9) on the basin's north slopes. Gently climbing, your trail leaves red firs for western white pines, then those for open, view-packed slopes as you climb to a minor gap on the east ridge (7620–0.9). ∎ *Standing here on Section P's highest point, you can compare the rusty ultramafic rock of Mt. Eddy, 2 miles to the north, with the drab-colored mafic rocks of the ridge just south of you. Light-gray granitic rocks show up on White Ridge, about 3 miles to the southeast, and on Castle Crags, beyond the ridge.* ∎

∎ *The geology lesson over, you cross the gap and traverse west for a climatology lesson. Here you'll note samples of whitebark pine and then mountain hemlock. The former you haven't seen since the Dicks Pass vicinity in Lake Tahoe's Desolation Wilderness. Its characteristic habit is one at high elevation where winter winds are extreme. The hemlock, on the other hand, requires some protection from the wind and typically grows where snow accumulation is deep and long-lasting. You can deduce, therefore, that this area is a very inhospitable place to spend a winter.* ∎

Your trail circles a small bowl that once spawned glaciers, then descends ⅔ mile north, usually on a gentle gradient, to a trail intersection on a windy saddle (7440–1.2).

*   *   *   *

Alternate route: To avoid inclement weather, you can make a moderate one-mile descent

northwest on this trail to a trail junction, then head 0.1 mile north to a roadend. This road descends almost one mile to Road 40N45, which you crossed earlier. On it you go 1¼ miles north to Deadfall Creek, which has many campsites on both sides of the creek just upstream from the road's bridge across it. In 260 yards you'll reach a junction with Road 42N17, which takes you 2 miles up to a saddle and the PCT.

*   *   *   *

The PCT leaves the saddle separating Bear Creek from North Fork Sacramento River and contours northwest through an essentially viewless fir forest to a crest. ∎ *Watch for a notable change from ultramafic rocks to granitic ones along this traverse.* ∎ You then traverse ½ mile southeast across steep, blocky slopes, passing above disappointing lower Deadfall Lake before coming to an 80-yard spur trail (7250–2.1) that goes over to shallow, enjoyable upper Deadfall Lake. Several campsites exist along the northwest shore's granitic rocks; more-secluded ones lie among the shadier southeast shore's ultramafic rocks. Upper Deadfall Lake is Section P's only essentially trailside lake that merits an overnight stay.

Your trail heads north above the east shore of lower Deadfall Lake, which by late summer can lose most of its volume. Just past this view you cross the Deadfall Lakes Trail (7230–0.3), which ascends southeast from the switchback on Road 42N17.

See map P5

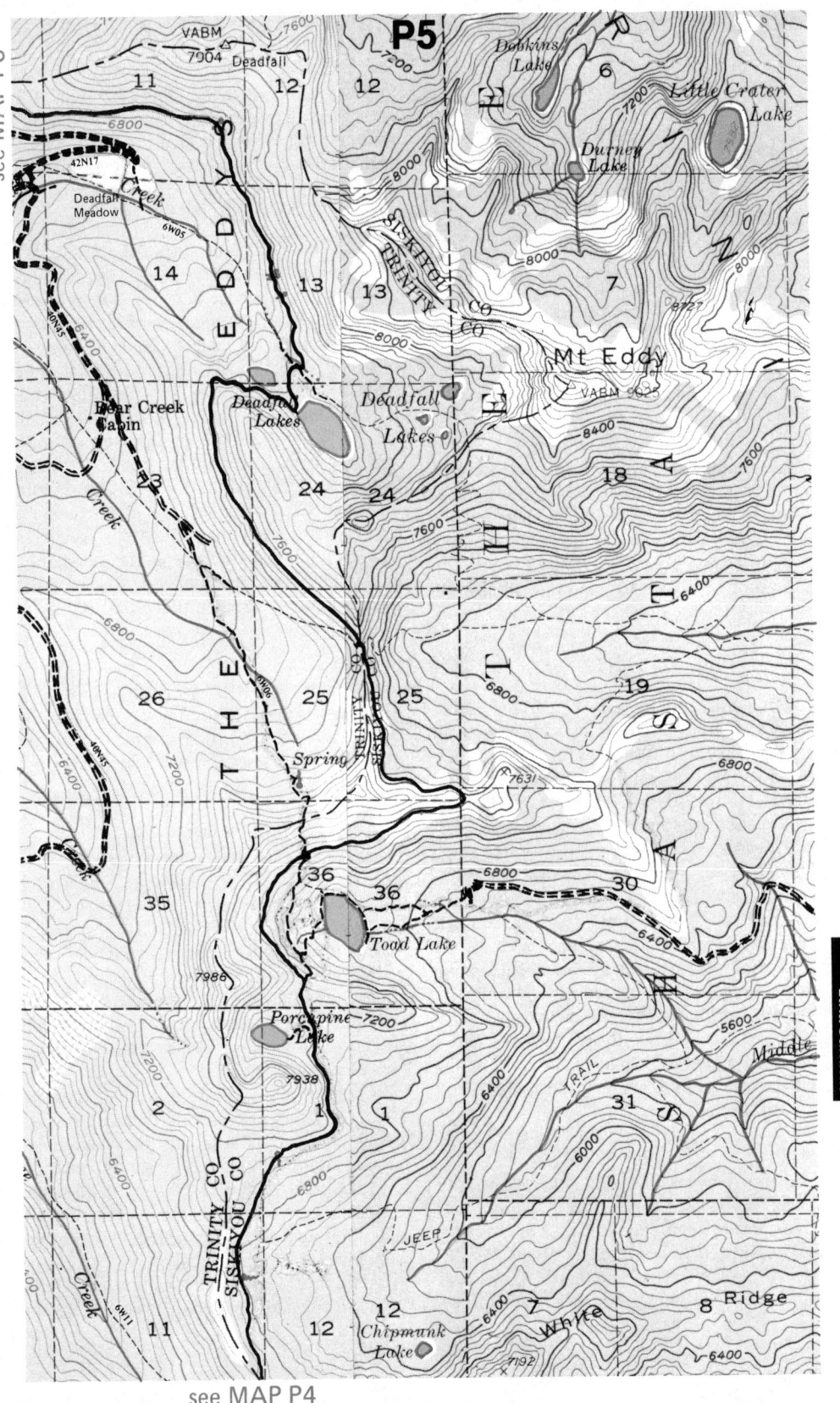

see MAP P6

see MAP P4

Upper Deadfall Lake

*   *   *   *

Side route: This trail curves eastward, climbing a mile to a shallow gap on the watershed divide. Along it you can labor a short mile up to the top of Mt. Eddy, which at 9025 feet elevation tops Trinity Alps Wilderness' Mt. Thompson by 23 feet to claim title of the highest summit in the Klamath Mountains.

*   *   *   *

Your well-graded PCT then immediately crosses infant Deadfall Creek and starts an almost imperceptible descent north past springs, views and wildflowers. At a gully with a permanent spring (7080–1.4), granitic rocks yield to ultramafic ones and the trail bends west. Midsummer hikers may not find water until Chilcoot Creek, about 8 miles away. Late-summer hikers will have to travel even farther, going out of their way to drop to Bull Lake, about 1¾ miles beyond Chilcoot Creek.

The PCT continues its almost imperceptible descent, gradually losing red firs and white firs while gaining manzanitas and Jeffrey pines. Finally the trail curves north and, hemmed in by a jeep road on the right and Road 42N17 on the left, it reaches a shallow crest saddle (6830–1.6).

*   *   *   *

Resupply access: Northward Road 42N17 descends about 14 miles, mostly along Parks Creek, to a road junction just west of Interstate 5's Edgewood exit, which is about 3 miles northwest of Weed (full supplies). At its lower end Road 42N17 is signed as Stewart Springs

Road. South from the PCT, Road 42N17 switchbacks down to the Trinity River and follows it all the way to Highway 3. You won't find emergency help in that direction, except perhaps down at the de facto campground.

*   *   *   *

Ahead, the PCT starts along the east side of a jeep road, quickly crosses it, and then contours 0.4 mile out to a ridge that is ¾ mile due east of Cement Bluff. Your circular route will take 4.2 miles to reach a shallow saddle just west of that bluff. The trail stays almost level, circling around a logged forest in the basin below you. Halfway around the basin, just past a snowmelt creeklet, the trail passes through a small meadow before crossing an old trail by the meadow's edge (6770–3.0). Heading south now, the northbound PCT crosses two more ephemeral creeklets, beyond which it crosses two dry gullies. It turns east in the second one and more or less contours over toward Bluff Lake, situated on Southern Pacific land.

*   *   *   *

Side route: The lake has inviting campsites, which are sometimes used by car campers. If you plan to visit the lake, leave the trail before it climbs above steep, loose bouldery slopes.

*   *   *   *

Above these, the trail tops out on an adjacent ridge (6650–1.6). ■ *The ridge, like Cement Bluff immediately east, is part of an old, eroded glacial moraine. This moraine is indeed cemented, for calcium, weathered from ultramafic rocks above the moraine, has combined with carbonate to form calcite, a strong cementing agent. Large boulders clinging to the overhanging north wall of Cement Bluff attest to the binding power of calcite.* ■

Your route gently climbs just over ½ mile to usually dry Salt Lick Creek, then finishes its ascent, ⅓ mile later, on another glacial moraine. Now, in almost a mile, the trail gently descends to Chilcoot Creek (6650–1.7) and in 80 yards reaches a spring-fed creeklet. The creek typically dries up by late July, the creeklet by early September.

Past the creeklet, you contour just over ⅓ mile to another glacial moraine that is composed of

See maps P5, P6

large, cemented boulders just like those at Cement Bluff. ∎ *In colder times, glaciers developed in all the canyons you've traversed, including Bull Creek canyon, just to the south. They all flowed down their canyons and converged to form an ice pack in the upper Trinity River basin. However, unlike Sierran glaciers, they didn't flow very far down-canyon, for they were too low in elevation to produce enough ice to do so. Beyond Bull Creek canyon you'll see dozens of canyons that held short, thick glaciers during the last major glacial advance.* ∎

From the bouldery moraine's crest the PCT climbs gently southwest up the north slopes of Bull Creek canyon. If you plan to camp at Bull Lake, which is one of the most accessible along your route, then leave the trail as soon as you see the lake. By the time you climb moderately to a poor, ¼-mile spur trail down to it, you've climbed too high. About ¼ mile past this trail and 10 yards below a crest saddle, you meet the old Sisson-Callahan Trail. Eastward, this trail descends to Bull Lake in about ¼ mile. From the saddle (7100–2.1) the old trail descends past three shallow lakelets before turning north and dying out in Robbers Meadow, which is good for camping. ∎ *This old trail, like so many others in the Klamath Mountains, was meant for stock animals. It goes past lakes and meadows, unlike the modern, freeway-like*

PCT. Equestrians will find the lack of pasturage very annoying. ∎

Leaving a postcard view of Mt. Shasta over Bull Lake, you start a contour northwest, then gently descend west, staying well above the three lakelets. The middle one, larger in historic times, is now no more than a pond. You round a ridge, enter a glacial bowl and soon cross its seasonal creek. Beyond it, the trail circles the bowl, eventually dropping to a saddle (6770–1.6) on a secondary crest. You contour from it and meet a seasonal spring in about two minutes. From it, as well as northwest of it on the trail, you have a view of miles of PCT as it threads along the upper west slopes of logged-over Little Trinity River canyon—Section P's most unsightly stretch. The tall, granitic mountain rising above the canyon is Craggy Peak, 8098 feet high and 9¾ miles away. The tiny settlement of Callahan lies at its north base, 5000 feet below the summit. Your trail, contouring at first, changes to a gentle descent, then later, as you enter a logged-over area, shifts into a moderate descent as if to speed you through it. The descent momentarily ends on a broad saddle, where you meet two trail junctions (6480–0.9).

*   *   *   *

Side routes: Here, at Section P's mid-way

See maps P6, P7

Bull Lake, Mt. Eddy and distant Mt. Shasta

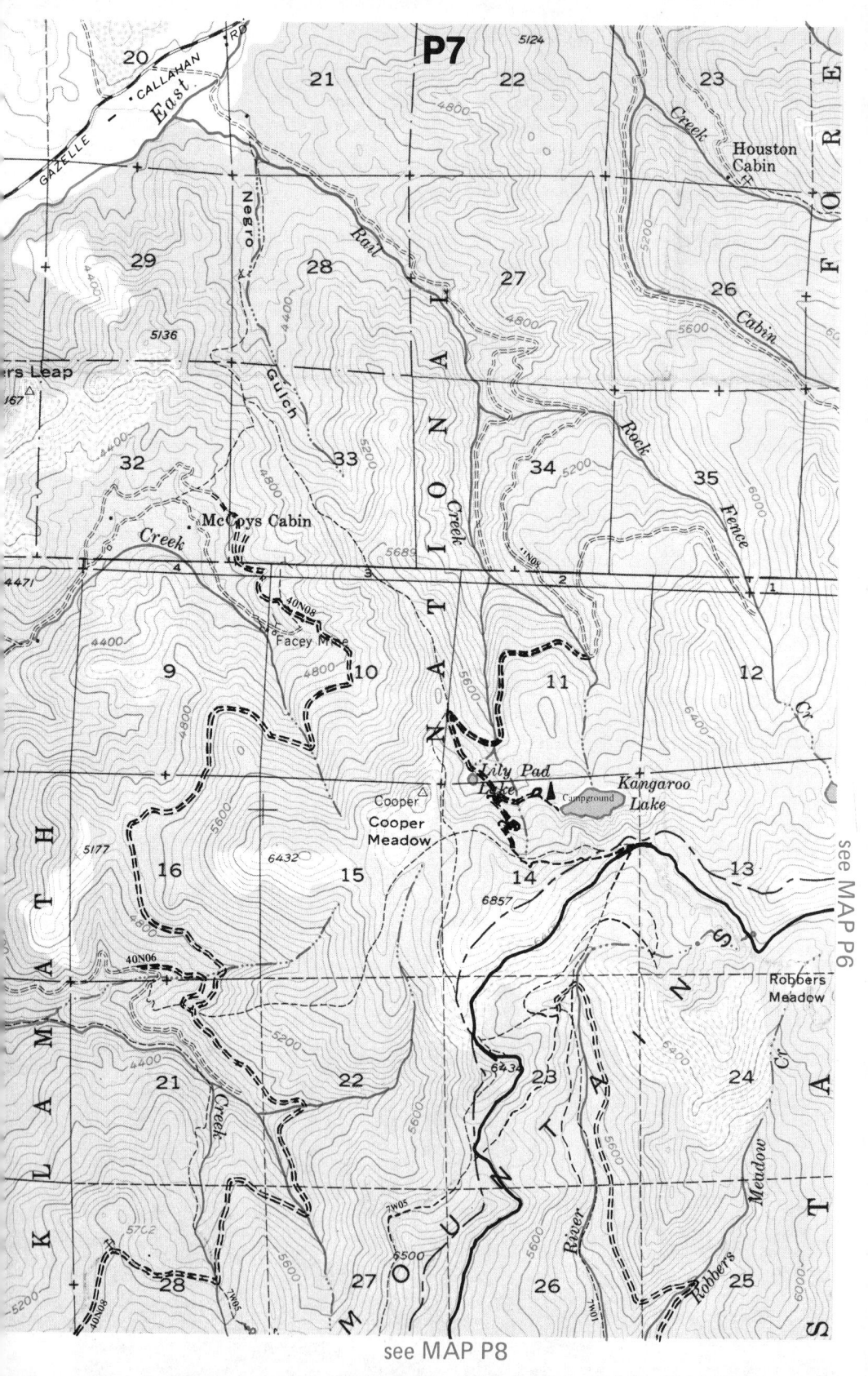

see MAP P6

see MAP P8

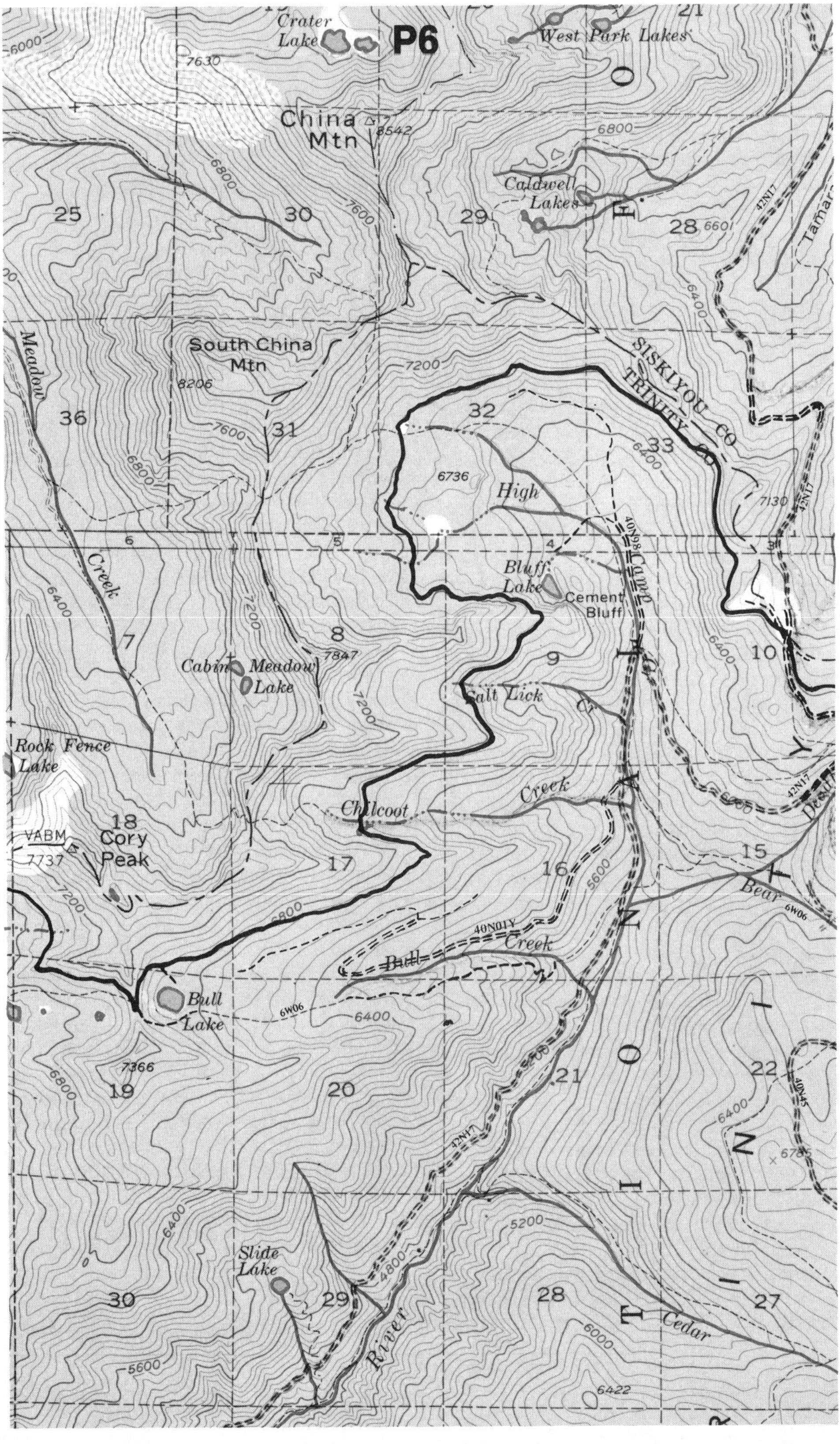

see MAP P5
see MAP P7

point, you first meet Little Trinity River Trail 7W01, which drops to relatively close logging roads. The second, in 20 yards, is the Sisson Trail, which first climbs west and then descends to a road that leads down to Kangaroo Lake Road 41N08. Unseen Kangaroo Lake is scarcely ¼ mile north of your junction. Play it safe and use the trail and road down to the lake's campground, if you go there. Alternatively, at the PCT's broad saddle you could make a waterless camp among some wind-sheltered spots.

*   *   *   *

On the PCT a long, gentle descent, hot on most summer afternoons, takes you southwest across brushy slopes of granitic Peak 6857 to the next saddle (6160–1.3). In ¼ mile you pass the faint Cooper Meadow Trail 7W05, which climbs up Peak 6434, then descends into logging debris. You're treated to more views of grand-scale logging as you round the peak, passing outcrops of peridotite and serpentinite before descending to an abandoned logging road on another saddle (6030–0.9). Past it you contour ⅓ mile southeast to a ridge, from which you can look up-canyon and see 2 miles of constant-angle PCT tread. Here you encounter a few Douglas-firs and incense-cedars, which are near their upper-elevation limit. You now contour through an open forest, largely of white firs and western white pines, and through it view logging roads and logging scars. Just after crossing a conspicuous, rusty-boulder field, you meet two springs (6080–1.3), the second one lying among azaleas, ferns and pitcher plants. This one usually lasts through mid-August, several weeks longer than its companion. The PCT quickly rounds a blocky ridge, then contours through a forest punctuated by two boulder fields of ultramafic rocks. Just past the second one, which provides a view of Lost Lake 0.4 mile below you, you cross a secondary ridge (6100–1.1). Now you contour northwest through a shady fir forest to lasting springs at the upper edge of a meadow (6110–0.7). Here, the Masterson Meadow Trail begins a descent south along your meadow and the Cooper Meadow Trail begins a traverse northeast toward Peak 6434.

Immediately past the spring-fed meadow, you enter private land and cross a wide, densely forested saddle. You could camp on it. From its west end (6130–0.2), the Grouse Creek Trail descends one mile northwest to Road 40N08, a major logging road that winds southwest to your next major destination, Scott Mountain Summit. The PCT angles southwest and climbs ¼ mile up to a shallow gap in the crest.

*   *   *   *

Side route: From this spot you could go cross country, contouring ⅓ mile west to shallow Grouse Creek Lake. For camping, it certainly beats slimy bottomed, knee-deep Masterson Meadow Lake, ahead.

*   *   *   *

Starting through a willow grove, you traverse southwest across partly logged slopes, entering a swale in about ⅔ mile. Just below you, in a small meadow, is a spring, and this is a visual clue for those who want to visit Masterson Meadow Lake, which lies 100 yards south, over a low moraine. In a logging mess the trail crosses the lake's seasonal creek (6180–1.1). The lake is a 100-yard walk away, up boulders and logging debris. Fortunately, the lake's shore and the slopes above it are unscathed.

You now make a momentary climb to a minor ridge, then start a contour across Scott Mountain's southeast slopes. Trees give way to brush, and you see Mt. Shasta towering above rusty Mt. Eddy. To the south-southwest you see a sawtooth ridge, in Trinity Alps Wilderness, standing high above unseen Tangle Blue Creek. The PCT contours through an open forest to a rocky knoll on a ridge (6170–1.3), then starts a well-graded descent northwest. About ½ mile past the end of an old logging road, the trail switchbacks (5790–1.3), and then it descends 0.4 mile at a moderate grade to a narrow old road. On it you go 50 yards, then branch right, and in 75 more yards recross it. Immediately west, this road ends at newer, wider Road 40N08, which traverses northeast to Big Carmen Lake, Grouse Creek and beyond. On an abandoned road you parallel Road 40N08 south for 250 yards, then west for 75 yards. With Scott Mountain Summit in sight, you walk 90 yards west on Road 40N08 to Highway 3 (5401–0.6).

*   *   *   *

Water access: Just south of the summit you'll

The northbound hiker's first good view of the Trinity Alps

meet the entrance to Scott Mountain Campground, a good if sometimes noisy place to spend the night. Sometimes the camp's water system works; at other times you have to head ¼ mile south to the cow-pied headwaters of Scott Mountain Creek. For better quality water, head ½–1 mile south on Highway 3 before dipping into the creek.

*   *   *   *

From Highway 3 at Scott Mountain Summit, eastbound hikers face a 700-foot climb. Westbound, you face a 1200-foot climb, but at least it is on shadier slopes. You walk 50 yards west on a wide road, which forks, with Road 40N63 starting north. You continue west on PCT tread, cross a good road in 300 yards, and shift to a moderate upward grade. Now the PCT switchbacks one mile up brushy slopes to a crest saddle, shaded by red firs, then switchbacks up another mile, past firs and brush, to a second shady saddle. You stay on the crest barely ¼ mile before climbing west across a small, logged slope, then turning south to immediately enter the Trinity Alps Wilderness (6370–2.8). With the bulk of your ascent completed you now have an easy stroll south through a shady fir forest. Road 40N63, which you left by Scott Mountain Summit, gradually climbs to meet you, and you touch it on a shallow crest gap (6630–1.1). Mountain scenery opens up here, but after you walk a minute much more scenery explodes into view as you turn a minor ridge. A sawtooth range rises 3–4 miles to the south, and from each of the range's deep cirques a pair of fresh-looking glacial moraines stream either north down to Tangle Blue Creek, 2000 feet below you, or east down toward the Trinity River. Looking east-southeast, you see several waves of increasingly higher ridges, the highest one capped by the unmistakable Grey Rocks (7241′ and 7133′).

You now parallel Road 40N63, keeping below it to minimize its presence. In a few minutes Mt. Shasta comes into view as you continue across bushy slopes on a descending route. About ¾ mile past your crest crossing, you meet a seasonal spring, then about ¼ mile later cross a small meadow with two springs, a creeklet and cows. From it you angle south, crossing a final spring in about 100 yards. You can usually expect all these springs to dry up between late-July and mid-August.

With the road only a stone's throw above the trail, you parallel it southwest, mostly through dense brush. You'll see evidence of a landslide on the opposite side of the canyon before your trail curves west and crosses Road 40N63 (6210–2.0). If you have an emergency, you could follow Road 40N63 east to a nearby road junction and then take the westbound road ¾ mile up to Mosquito Lake. There lies a summer camp with leaders who take youths on rigorous backpack trips in this eastern part of the wilderness. From the lake, a use trail climbs

See maps P8, P9

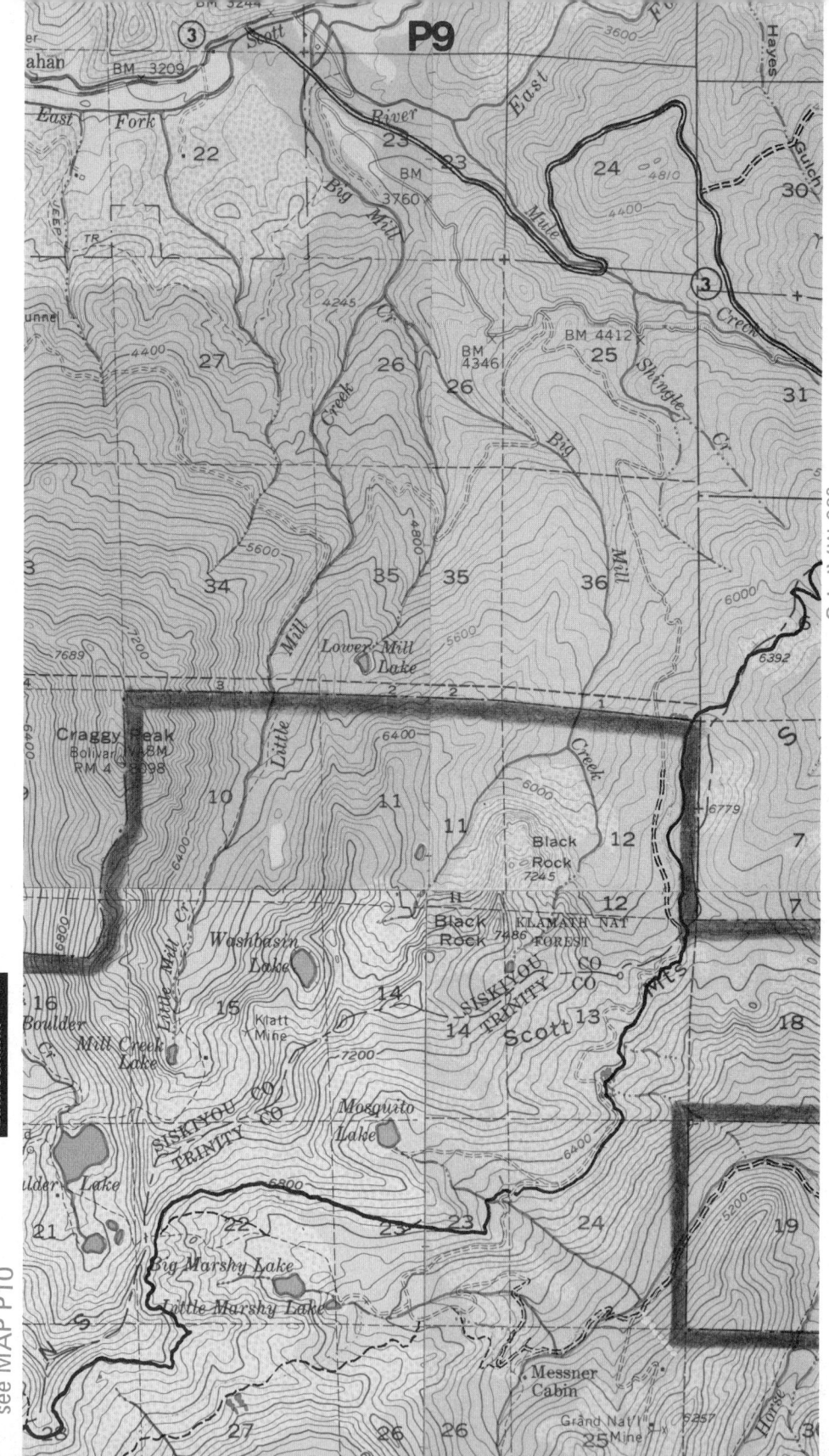

see MAP P8

see MAP P10

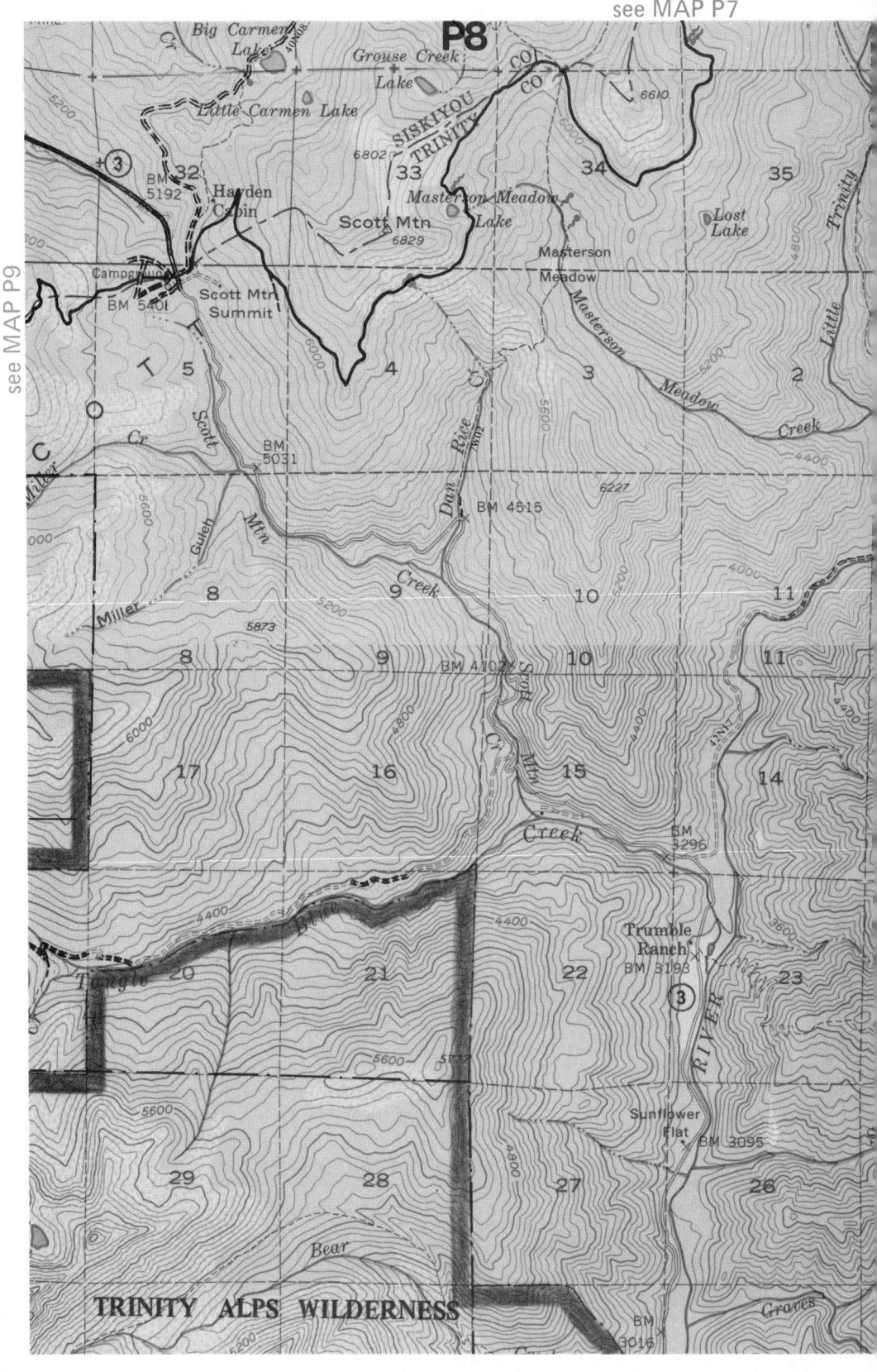

see MAP P9

Big Carmen Lake

Grouse Creek Lake

Little Carmen Lake

6610

③

BM 5192

32

SISKIYOU CO.
TRINITY CO.

6802

33

34

35

Hayden Cabin

Masterson Meadow Lake

Scott Mtn 5829

Lost Lake

Masterson Meadow

Campground

BM 5401

Scott Mtn Summit

T 5

4

Masterson

3

Meadow

Creek

2

C O

Cr

Scott

BM 5031

Dan Rice Cr.

5600

6227

Gulch

Mtn

Miller

BM 4515

Creek

8

9

10

11

5873

8

9

BM 410?

10

11

6000

17

16

Scott Mtn

15

14

Cr

Creek

BM 3296

42N

Blue

4400

Trumble Ranch
BM 3193

Tangle

20

21

22

③

23

RIVER

5600

5600

Sunflower Flat
BM 3095

29

28

27

26

Bear

TRINITY ALPS WILDERNESS

BM 3016

Graves

southeast over a ridge and then descends southwest to the PCT.

From the road crossing you start toward that trail junction and in 90 yards cross a cow-frequented creeklet. Two minutes later you cross Mosquito Lake creek (6240–0.2), which bears the dubious distinction of being the first truly permanent stream the PCT has crossed since the Sacramento River, about 66 trail miles to the east. Your trail climbs ¼ mile south to a ridge, then turns west and climbs moderately up drier slopes of Jeffrey pine, incense-cedar and brush. Soon you meet the summer camp's primitive trail (6460–0.5), which crosses the PCT and continues southwest toward inviting Big Marshy Lake. The PCT continues its moderate climb west through an open forest, which becomes dominated by western white pines before the trail starts to curve southwest up to a junction (7020–1.5). Here, a trail climbing from the Marshy Lakes basin crosses your route and pops over a crest saddle, about 70 feet above you.

*   *   *   *

Side route: A small campsite exists by this junction. However, better ones lie off route. If you don't mind a half-mile-long, 400-foot drop, then take this trail down to East Boulder Lake, the largest lake close to Section P's PCT. Hikers with less energy can take this scenic drop halfway and choose a camp near one of three smaller lakes.

*   *   *   *

From the junction you embark south on an exceedingly curvy, exceptionally scenic stretch of PCT. ∎ *At 7100 feet here, you're not at Section P's actual highest point, but you're at the place of highest elevation plants. Here you'll see rockfringe and other species that grow around 10,000–11,000 feet in the High Sierra.* ∎ Before mid-July, snow often buries part of this route. After ¾ mile of winding, you crest an east-trending ridge. A rocky ridge knoll, just east of the trail, provides a very impressive panorama of the Tangle Blue Creek and Eagle Creek canyons. From this ridge you climb ¼ mile southwest across warmer slopes to a notch in a ridge, then climb west a few minutes to the edge of a talus slope (7240–1.3).

*   *   *   *

Side route: From here, in a small trough, you could head south cross country down to a knee-deep pond, 130 feet below the PCT, and camp near it.

*   *   *   *

Now the PCT climbs southwest, first across a talus slope of large, black boulders which, being ultramafic, will weather to a rust color. However, before that happens, more boulders are likely to break loose from the unstable bedrock above the trail. Your trail continues to climb, heading through a forest of red fir, western white pine and mountain hemlock as it tops out at 7400 feet of elevation. You then descend a bit to a nearby ridge, on which you'll see weeping spruce. ∎ *This subalpine tree, never common, is found only in the Klamath Mountains, and you can easily recognize it by its long, hanging branches that have hanging cones up to 6 inches long—considerably longer than those of mountain hemlocks.* ∎ Westward, the PCT contours ¼ mile over to the east end of a windswept crest (7400–0.9), at which you enter an extensive granitic realm.

*   *   *   *

Side route: From this east end a trail drops north into a glacial bowl that contains two shallow tarns, both quite exposed, though adequate for nearby camping when good weather prevails. With an average grade of 20%, the steep trail continues ½ mile farther down to sheltered campsites at Middle Boulder Lake, which is not worth the effort unless bad weather forces you off the crest.

*   *   *   *

Protected by wind-sheltering trees, your high route stays just below the crest then soon angles southwest and passes above a small meadow. Beyond it you see the sawtooth range above Tangle Blue Creek and the distant Grey Rocks. In ¼ mile you arrive at another meadow (7260–0.4), this one with a spring-fed creeklet that usually persists through early August. You can camp near it. A ⅔-mile-long trail to Telephone

P

Castle Crags–Etna Summit

See maps P9, P10

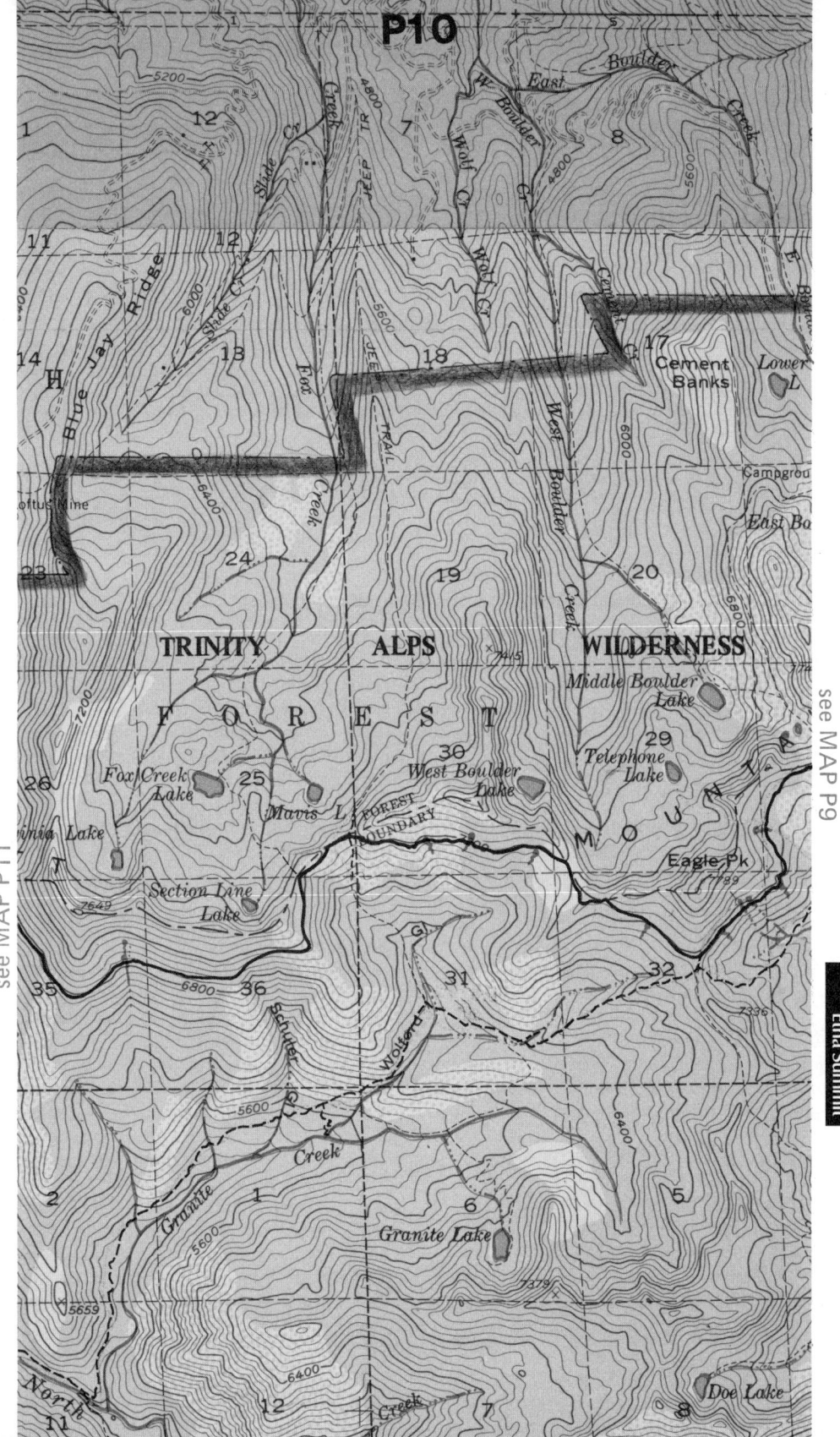

TRINITY ALPS WILDERNESS

FOREST

see MAP P11

see MAP P9

P Castle Crags-
Etna Summit

Blue Jay Ridge

Shade Cr

Shade Cr

JEEP TR

JEEP TRAIL

Fox Creek

Creek

W. Boulder Cr

Wolf Cr

Wolf Cr

East Boulder Creek

West Boulder Creek

Cement Banks

Lower L

Campground

East Bo

Loftus Mine

Middle Boulder Lake

Telephone Lake

West Boulder Lake

Fox Creek Lake

Mavis L

Virginia Lake

Section Line Lake

FOREST BOUNDARY

Eagle Pk

MOUNTAIN

Schute Cr

Wolford

Granite

Creek

Granite Lake

Doe Lake

North

View north down West Boulder Creek Canyon:
Craggy Peak, Cement Bluffs below it and distant Scott River Valley

Lake once headed west over the nearby crest saddle, but now the route is partly cross country. The PCT next circles Eagle Peak, passing four springs that usually last through midsummer before reaching a junction above the north end of a crest saddle (7160–0.9). Bloody Run Trail 8W04 starts south down the crest, intersecting Eagle Creek Trail 7W05 in 130 yards. From this crest your trail climbs gently northwest, and midway along this ascent, the forest opens to give you your first good view of the Trinity Alps. ∎ *The tallest peak, 19 miles to the southwest, is 9002-foot Thompson Peak, the Trinity Alps' ermine-robed monarch. It is the only peak in the entire mountain system to support glaciers—two incipient ones exist.* ∎

On a crest at the end of your gentle climb (7300–0.6) you have a view north down West Boulder Creek canyon. The view is quite revealing, for you see all the way down to irrigated fields in the Scott River Valley, over 4000 feet below. Dry, brown hills line the valley and, closer by, Craggy Peak dominates your canyon's east flank. However, you can't help but notice the barren Cement Bluffs below the peak, whose origin is similar to the Cement Bluff you crossed more than 28 miles ago.

Your trail next descends to a windswept, sagebrush-covered crest saddle (7190–0.4), then it contours west, first passing above a spring-fed alder thicket, and then just below two others. At the east end of a long crest saddle, you come to a trail junction (7170–1.2). Trail 8W05 descends one mile south to a trail junction by Wolford Cabin Snow Survey Shelter while Trail 8W10 descends 3 miles north to Road 40N17— neither a desirable goal. You traverse the saddle, then climb southwest to a higher point on the crest (7230–0.3).

*   *   *   *

Side routes: From here Trail 8W07 starts a ⅔ mile descent to Fox Creek Lake. If you don't mind cross-country travel, aim for Section Line Lake, ¼ mile to the southwest and only 130 feet below the trail junction.

*   *   *   *

Now you begin a long, erratic descent to Carter Meadows Summit. First you descend south to a dry ridge sporting greenleaf manzanitas and huckleberry oaks, then descend west through a forest of red and white firs. A swath of alders (6850–1.4) breaks the forest cover and in it you cross several freshets that provide water through most of the summer.

See map P10

Back in forest cover, you descend past an outcrop of car-size granitic boulders, then round a ridge that supports aromatic tobacco brush. Now you contour northwest past firs and brush, meeting a seasonal spring in an alder patch ¼ mile before you reach a crest saddle (6780–1.2), which generates Trail 9W01, dropping steeply south to Saloon Creek. From the saddle's west end (6780–0.1), another branch of Trail 9W01 drops south, an abandoned trail starts south, and a misleading, tempting trail contours southwest.

Leaving Shasta-Trinity National Forest and entering Klamath National Forest, you head ¼ mile northwest down an old jeep road, leave it in a shallow gully, and follow a poor, winding tread up to a gap in a narrow crest (6660–0.5). From it your poor segment descends too steeply to a switchback, then heads south at a moderate gradient down into a glaciated bowl. You can camp near its alder-lined creeklet. ∎ *The last glacier to occupy this bowl left conspicuous morainal ridges on both sides of the bowl, and you can estimate by their lengths that the glacier was roughly ½ mile long. Earlier glaciers were longer and joined with others from adjacent canyons to flow north down the upper part of South Fork Scott River canyon.* ∎

On poor tread—one of the worst sections of "new standard" PCT—you descend north along the canyon's west slopes, then head west to a rocky point before descending southwest to a junction with South Fork Lakes Trail 9W13 (5810–1.5). This trail climbs to South Fork Lakes through a giant, hanging jungle of alders. The exhausting push up through them certainly negates any advantages found at the lakes. These lakes lie in a deep, narrow cirque that shelters long-lasting snow patches which make the alder jungle possible. From the junction the PCT descends to cross 10-foot wide South Fork Scott River (5780–0.2), crossing it near the base of the jungle. Early-season hikers can expect a wet ford. Now your poor tread climbs gently northwest to a shallow gully with an alder-lined creeklet (5880–0.5), this one lasting through most of the summer. From the gully you make an annoyingly steep climb north to a ridge, where you take leave of Trinity Alps Wilderness. Just ahead lies Forest Highway 93,

which was blasted through Carter Meadows Summit (6160–0.4).

*   *   *   *

Side routes: From this paved road, a spur road—the old highway—climbs 100 yards southeast to a small flat with room enough for four cars or several hiking parties. If you dry-camp here, get water by descending ½ mile west on the highway to a road that branches southwest over to the adjacent headwaters of East Fork of South Fork Salmon River. Don't take the trail starting southwest from the summit, for it goes up to Hidden Lake, not down to the river. During mid and late summer, your route ahead can be waterless all the way to Bingham Lake's outlet creek, 7.1 miles ahead.

*   *   *   *

∎ *The first few miles of ascent westward are mostly across metamorphosed volcanic rocks that originally formed about 450–500 million years ago. They may have been part of an island chain, like Japan today, which later was crunched against sediments as a major oceanic plate slid beneath a continental one. Your last trail stretch north from South Fork Scott River climbed up a wedge of such sediments.* ∎

Climbing northwest, the PCT quickly crosses a road, which it later meets as another road branches southwest from it on a crest saddle (6660–1.1). The views back into deep South Fork Lakes canyon now lie behind you, and as you progress northwest, you can peer first into Long Gulch, then into Trail Gulch and Dark Gulch—all deeply cut by glaciers. In several places your trail almost tops the crest, and short walks to it presents the inquisitive hiker with views northeast across a variegated landscape. As your trail curves west under a crest saddle (6910–1.7), it starts a traverse past a row of ragged outcrops of ancient, metasedimentary rock known as phyllite. The metavolcanic rocks you've just seen are blocky and rather drab whereas the sparkling phyllite is composed of thin, beautiful bands of light and dark crystals. After ¾ mile of traverse below the phyllite outcrops, your trail peaks out at 7150 feet and starts a descent northwest. Your new views are not too pleasant, for the upper slopes across Trail

See maps P10, P11, P12

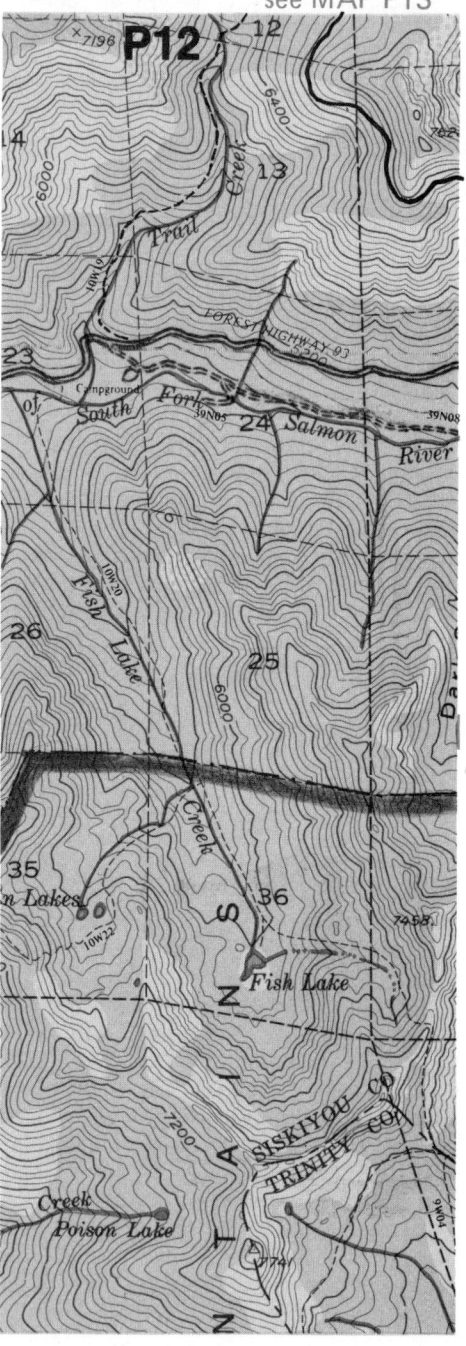

Creek canyon were ravaged by a fire. The slopes were then cleared and later terraced to reduce erosion and promote new plant growth.

Beyond more phyllite outcrops your trail levels off and contours northeast. In an old, selectively logged forest, the trail starts a short climb to a jeep trail (6940–2.3). The PCT then climbs northwest through open grazing land to another jeep trail (7030–0.2), passing some seasonal springs along its way.

*　　*　　*　　*

Water access: If these are dry, you can take the jeep trail west ¾ mile gently up to camping possibilities at Siphon Lake.

*　　*　　*　　*

From the jeep trail the PCT switchbacks almost to the granitic summit of Peak 7383, but at the last moment chooses to skirt past mountain hemlocks on its steep east slope.

*　　*　　*　　*

Side route: Consider climbing 150 bushy, bouldery yards to the peak's summit, for three major streams are born on the peak's three slopes. To the north lies the deep canyon of South Russian Creek, which drains into North Fork Salmon River. You'll soon start a 4⅓-mile traverse high along this granitic canyon's east wall. Above the canyon, the southeast limb of the Salmon Mountains, in Marble Mountain Wilderness, stands in the hazy distance. To the east you'll see large, deep Jackson Lake, on private land, 1200 feet below you. Fed by your peak's snowfields, the lake spills down to Jackson Creek, which empties into South Fork Scott River. Bits of Highway 3 and the Scott River lie below, about 10 miles away, and to the northeast your view extends about 50 miles to the high peaks of the Cascade Range. You also see Craggy Peak, 9 miles due east, but far-ranging views to the southeast are blocked by the high ridge the PCT has been following. However, you have views south and southwest down into the sprawling canyon of East Fork of South Fork Salmon River.

*　　*　　*　　*

After taking in the views, go back to the trail and traverse the peak's steep east slope and a

north-trending ridge. This stretch may be snowbound in early summer. At a saddle you enter Russian Wilderness, then switchback southwest, and then resume your northward course, a trail blasted across cliffs. The cliffs give way to large boulders, and you hike through a fir forest interspersed chiefly with chinquapin, huckleberry oak and greenleaf manzanita. Af-

See maps P12, P13

P11

see MAP P12

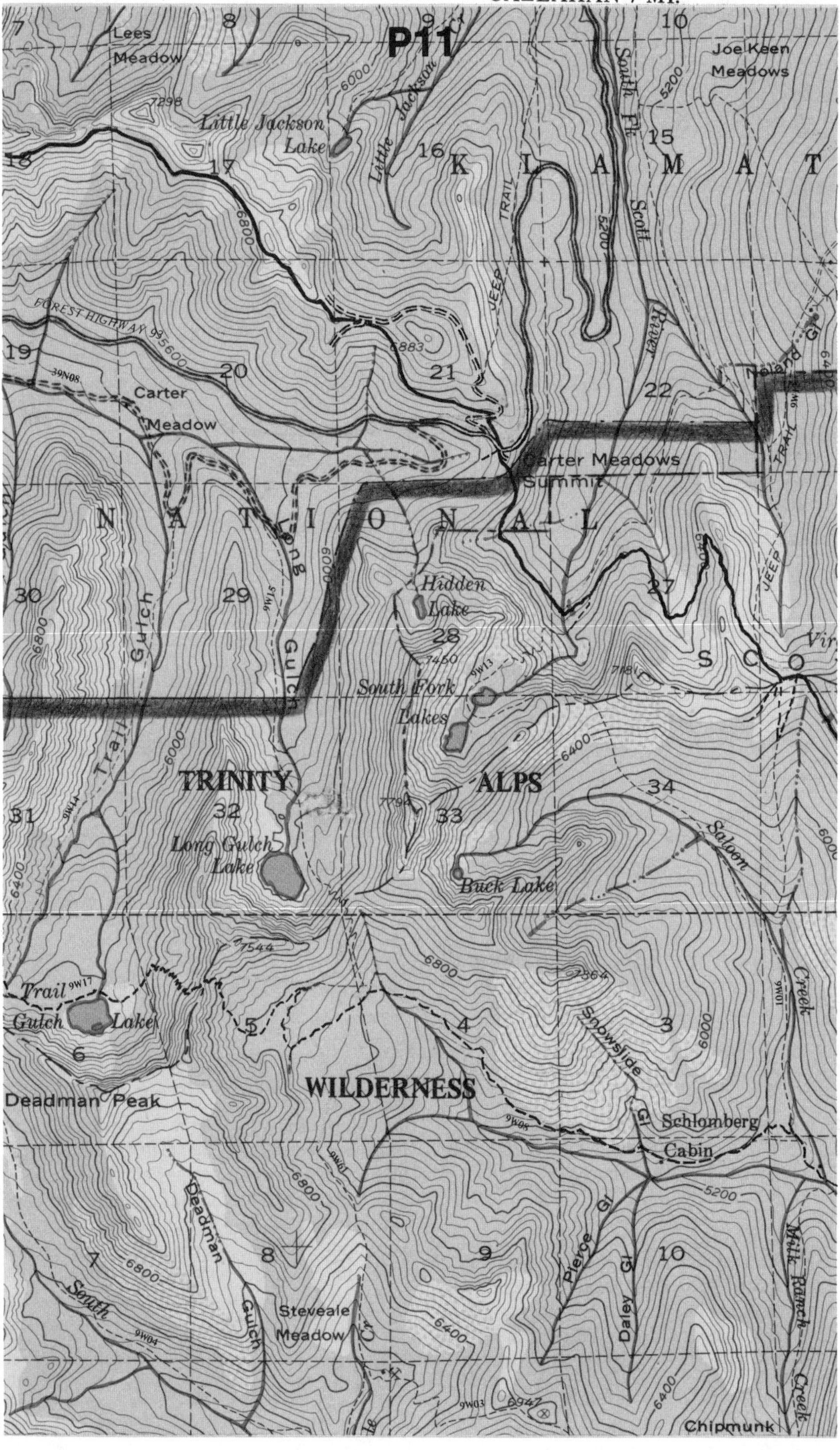

see MAP P10

Lees Meadow

Joe Keen Meadows

Little Jackson Lake

7298

K L A M A T

FOREST HIGHWAY 93

39N08

Carter Meadow

6883

Roland G.

Carter Meadows Summit

N A T I O N A L

Hidden Lake

28

7450

South Fork Lakes

S C O

Vir

TRINITY

Long Gulch Lake

7894

ALPS

34

Saloon

Buck Lake

7544

6800

7864

Creek

9W01

Trail
Gulch   Lake

9W17

5

4

3

6

Snowslide G.

Deadman Peak

WILDERNESS

Schlomberg Cabin

Pierce G.

Daley G.

Milk Ranch   Creek

7

South

6800

Deadman Gulch

8

Steveale Meadow

9

10

6400

9W04

9W03   6947

Chipmunk

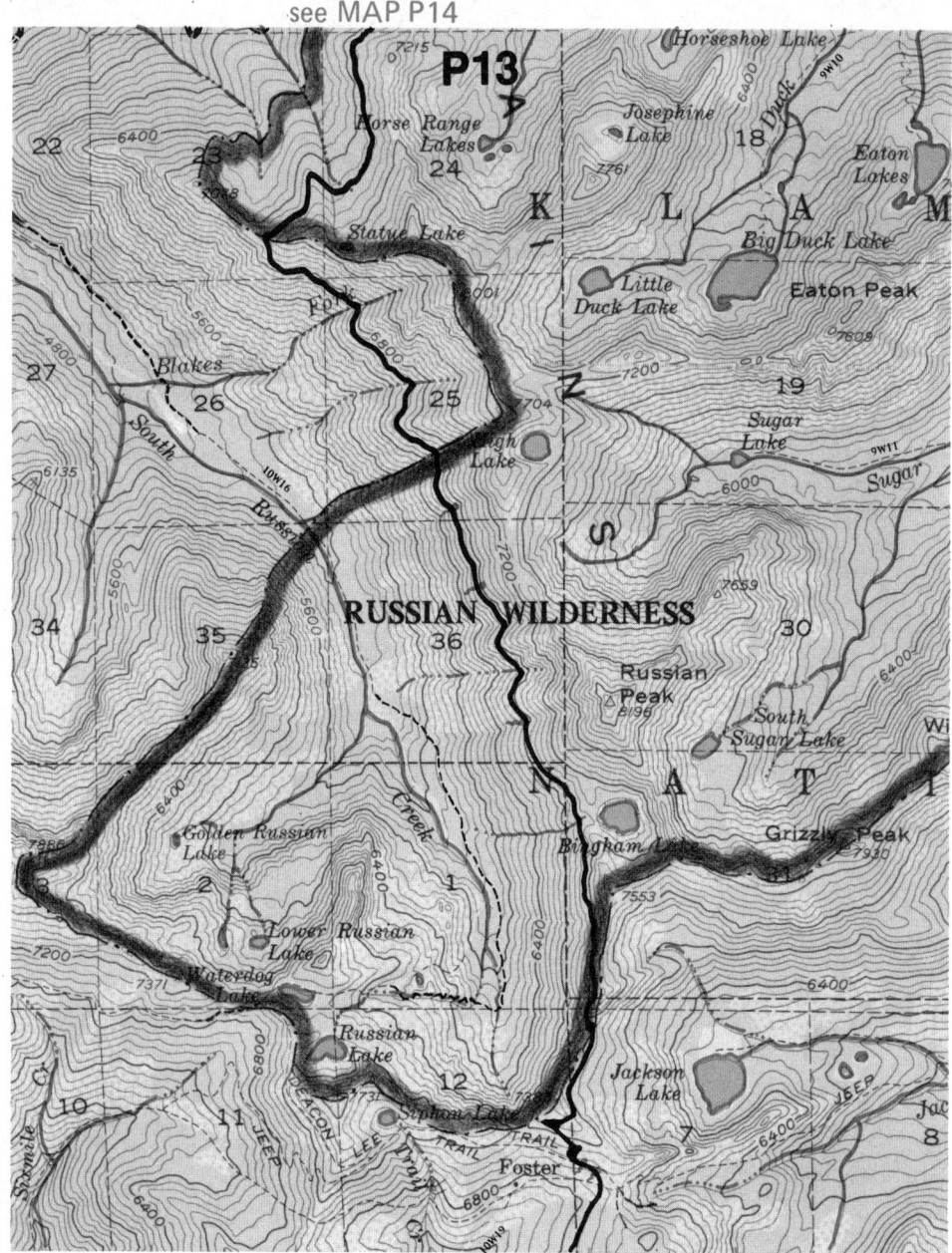

see MAP P12

ter almost a mile of traverse you reach Bingham Lake's outlet creek (6940–1.8), which mostly flows beneath large boulders.

*   *   *   *

Side route: Although the Section P PCT passes close to dozens of lakes, it touches only three: Paynes Lake, ahead, and the two Deadfall Lakes, way to the east. The Forest Service could have easily routed the PCT past Bingham Lake, but instead they chose to drop it 120 feet below the bouldery moraine damming the lake. Normally, a 120-foot climb would be an easy side trip but, as you'll find out, this climb is very bouldery, very steep, and very overgrown with almost impenetrable brush. If you're determined to visit this hidden lake, start your climb among the trees south of the lake's creek.

*   *   *   *

See map P13

Northward, your trail is more brush-lined than tree-shaded, and you pass several creeks and springs of variable persistence. After nearly 2 miles of very gentle descent, you cross a distinctive bedrock water chute that is often dry. Just ¼ mile past it you round a ridge and are hit with a powerful view of a massive wall of granitic rock, and you may feel that you are again back in the High Sierra. This South Russian Creek canyon certainly appears to be a transplant from that mountain range. ∎ *In a way, it is a transplant. An extensive belt of granitic plutons was intruded along much of the western edge of Mesozoic-age North America, but later this belt was broken up. One section was transplanted hundreds of miles northwest to the San Francisco Bay area via lateral movement along the San Andreas Fault System. The South Russian Creek pluton was transplanted tens of miles to the west. Originally it formed over by the Cascade Range, just north and east of Mt. Shasta.* ∎

In another ¼ mile you meet a boulder-strewn, alder-choked creek that usually flows through most of the summer, and then your trail makes a generally gentle ascent, reaching Blakes Fork (6700–2.8) in ½ mile. Like an earlier creek, this one slides down a bedrock chute, and hence runs dry well before the alder-choked creek. You are now below the massive, granodiorite wall. Near its northwest crest stands a conspicuous pinnacle, The Statue. Unseen Statue Lake is just 100 yards north and 200 feet below it. After a gentle climb for about 15 minutes, you break through a notch in a granitic ridge. Instantly your views disappear, and the dense huckleberry-oak/greenleaf-manzanita brush is replaced by a red-fir/mountain-hemlock forest. Over the next, shady, viewless 1¾ miles, early-season hikers can anticipate snow problems. Your trail gently descends ⅓ mile to a minor ridge, then contours several hundred yards southeast to a point where it starts to curve northeast (6930–1.1).

* * * *

Side route: If you want to visit Statue Lake, ¼ mile away and 250 feet above the trail, leave the PCT here. If you pass a seasonal spring, you've gone too far. Despite its tiny size, Statue Lake once had great fishing. However, now that the PCT has been built close to it, the lake is likely to be overfished.

* * * *

Beyond a seasonal trailside spring you traverse a viewless mile to a saddle breached by Trail 9W09 (6710–1.1).

* * * *

Resupply access: West, this goes ½ mile to Road 40N54, which then descends about 9 miles to the Somes Bar-Etna Road, meeting it just east of the entrance to Idlewild Campground. The town of Sawyers Bar lies 5½ miles west down that road. East, Trail 9W09 goes about a mile to roads leading down to a section of Highway 3 between Callahan and Etna.

* * * *

From the saddle you have a glimpse of Mt. Shasta, and then you have a few views west as you climb about ½ mile to a crest. You then traverse the headwall of a cirque, passing bedrock and tobacco brush, then descend northeast, staying high above Lipstick Lake and its eastern twin. Neither is worth visiting. With Paynes Lake next on your agenda, you turn a ridge, dip across a lakeless, glaciated bowl, then continue northeast down toward another ridge. ∎ *Nearing it, you have a "top of the world" feeling, for you have excellent views east down into agricultural Scott River Valley. Low, dry mountains rise to its east, and far beyond them rises your old acquaintance, snowy Mt. Shasta. More such views will appear—and improve— until you leave the Smith Lake environs.* ∎

You duck around the upcoming ridge and in ⅓ mile reach Paynes Lake Creek, with a descending, north-bank trail (6460–2.2). Paynes Lake is just a few heartbeats up the trail. Hemmed in by steep slopes, the lake is fairly scenic, but it is also deficient in campsites. You might set up camp on the lake's moraine, just south of the trail junction. Better camping lies ahead, so follow the PCT ½ mile northeast to a ridge, from which it parallels an old logging road, immediately below, west to the headwaters in a glacial bowl (6620–0.7). You could establish camp either on the old road or near

P
Castle Crags-
Etna Summit

See maps P13, P14

P14

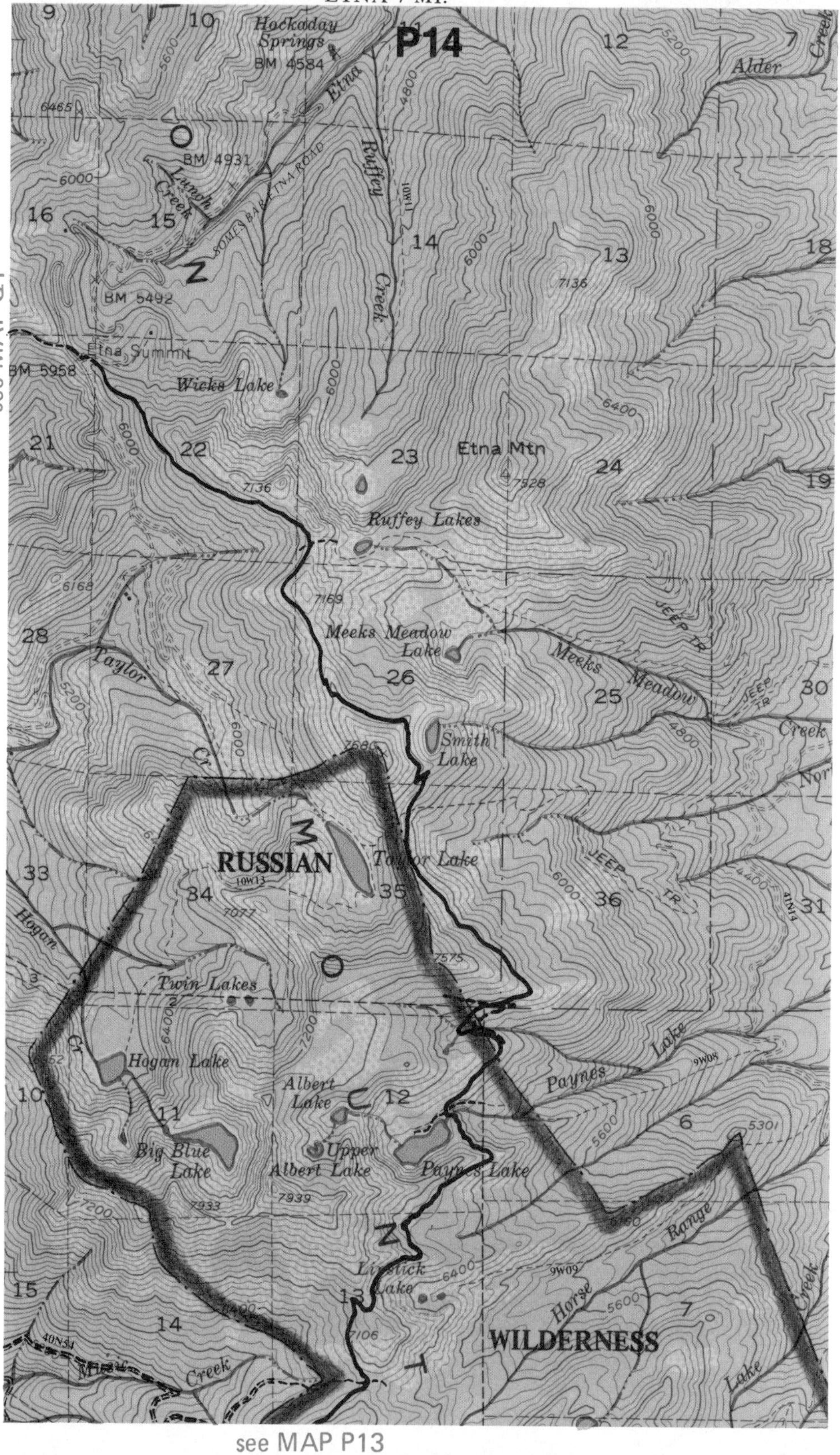

see MAP Q1

Hockaday
Springs
BM 4584

BM 4931

Lamb Creek

BM 5492

Etna Summit
BM 5958

Wicks Lake

Ruffey Creek

Etna Mtn
7528

Ruffey Lakes

7169

Meeks Meadow
Lake

Meeks Meadow

Smith
Lake

Taylor Cr.

RUSSIAN

10W13

7077

Taylor Lake

7575

Twin Lakes

Hogan

Hogan Lake

Albert
Lake

Big Blue
Lake

Upper
Albert Lake

7939

7933

Paynes

Paynes Lake

Lipstick
Lake

Russian Range

7106

Horse Range

WILDERNESS

see MAP P13

the trail just before it crosses a permanent creek. For northbound hikers in dry years this creek is the last reliable water until Shelly Lake's outlet creek, about 15.9 miles away. Past the permanent creek you go 70 yards north to a seasonal one, which some trekkers claim has better-tasting water. You then make a short, moderate climb to an abandoned logging road that steeply descends to the one you've just paralleled. The road continues to climb, as does your trail, out to a ridge. ▌ *Here, if you look south, you'll see pairs of glacial moraines descending east from Paynes Lake canyon and the canyons south of it. The glaciers that left these lateral moraines averaged about 2–3 miles long and they descended to about the 4000-foot level. Though short, they were quite massive, becoming up to 400–500 feet thick.* ▌ You now head northwest across selectively logged slopes, ending your traverse at a trail junction (6970–1.5) by a notch in a knife-edge ridge.

* * * *

Side route: The trail crossing the notch makes a steep 550-foot descent to large Taylor Lake. You might brave this knee-knocking descent, for the lake has ample flat ground at its north and south ends. Just north of the Taylor Lake Trail is Trail 9W08, starting east toward Road 41N14. Given that you can reach more-travelled Somes Bar-Etna Road in 1–1½ hours, Trail 9W08 is not a good route out to civilization.

* * * *

Over the last 2 miles, the PCT has flirted with the Russian Wilderness boundary, but now the trail leaves the Wilderness for good as it climbs just over ¼ mile—rising above a tree farm—to a switchback near the crest of a descending ridge.

* * * *

Side route: If you want to visit Smith Lake, seen from the nearby crest, leave the trail here and descend the brushy, bouldery ridge.

* * * *

In ⅓ mile the PCT climbs to a spectacular viewpoint above the lake, and one can see that its steep, bouldery shoreline makes camping likely only at the forested notch above its northeast shore. Your views east to Mt. Shasta and northeast to southern Oregon's Siskiyou Mountains end as your trail turns west to contour through a mountain-hemlock forest. Westward views appear as you cross a granitic crest, and among sagebrush and mountain mahogany you descend ⅓ mile to a level stretch of crest. You then round the west ridge of a crest summit before descending to a jeep-road junction (6910–2.0) immediately beyond a logged area.

* * * *

Side route: East, this road immediately tops a saddle, then descends ¼ mile to the small, cow-habited basin of Upper Ruffey Lake. ▌ *Although the glacier that scoured this lake basin flowed mostly north, today the lake drains east below the south slopes of Etna Mountain. Standing at the brink of the lake's north shore, you'll also note that the former cirque glacier spilled north into another cirque (Lower Ruffey Lake), which in turn spilled north into a third cirque—an interesting arrangement.* ▌ Given that the next decent camping area with water is in the Shelly Meadows area, 12½ miles away, you should seriously consider camping at Upper Ruffey Lake.

* * * *

Leaving the nearby saddle and its jeep road, the PCT also leaves the granitic landscape as it descends northwest moderately down toward Etna Summit. ▌ *The first half is through a shady forest growing in soil derived from mafic intrusive rocks. The second half is through an open forest growing in soil derived from metavolcanic rocks, which you'll tread most of the way to Shelly Meadows.* ▌ At the southeast edge of Etna Summit, you cross the summit's older road. Immediately beyond it you cross a trailside parking area that can hold a dozen cars, then take a brief trail segment over to the wide, paved Somes Bar-Etna Road, which you cross at the northwest edge of Etna Summit (5960–1.7).

See map P14

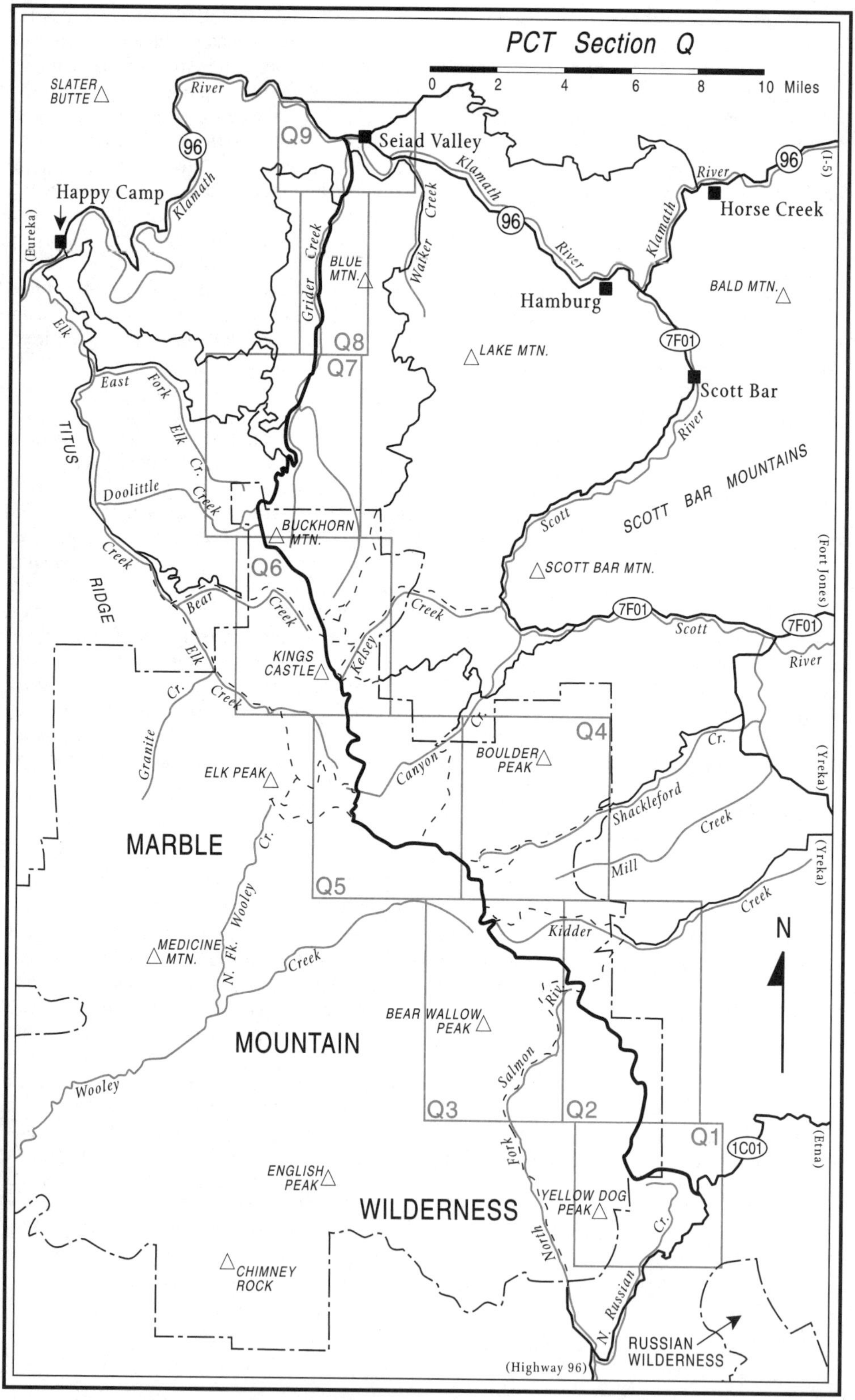

Etna Summit-Seiad Valley Q

Section Q
Etna Summit to Seiad Valley

Introduction: Although this stretch is one of the shortest sections in this California PCT guide, its features are still quite diverse. Little more than half the length of the previous section, it nevertheless has more rock units, each with its own characteristic hue and texture. And with more rock units comes greater diversity of wildflowers and other vegetation. Over the first two thirds of the route, the trail stays high, generally traversing from the head of one glaciated canyon to the head of another. Midway through your journey you pass the crown jewels of the Marble Mountain Wilderness: Black Mountain, Kings Castle and, of course, Marble Mountain itself. With about a half-hour's walk you can make a side trip up to the top of Marble Mountain and survey much of northwestern California. The last third of the route is mostly a long descent through a deep canyon that nurtures a Douglas-fir forest. The walk through it is a refreshing change from your typical crest hiking, which all too often can be deficient in water. If you're hiking this section only, you'll want to end (or start) at Grider Creek Campground rather than at Seiad Valley, for the 6½ miles at the north end are along roads. Then your route is a comfortable 50-mile backpack hike.

Declination: 17¼°E

Points on Route	S→N	Mi. Btwn. Pts.	N→S
Somes Bar-Etna Road at Etna Summit 0.0		11.2	56.8
Shelly Fork trail/Shelly Meadows trail 11.2		4.4	45.6
older PCT route to Kidder Lake trail 15.6		5.2	41.2
Red Rock Valley Trail/west Cold Spring Trail 20.8		3.3	36.0
Marble Valley G. S./Canyon Creek Trail 24.1		5.3	32.7
Paradise Lake 29.4		1.6	27.4
Bear Lake-Turk Lake trails 31.0		4.0	25.8
Buckhorn Spring 35.0		7.7	21.8
Grider Creek Trail at Road 46N72 .... 42.7		7.6	14.1
Grider Creek Trail at Grider Creek Campground 50.3		6.5	6.5
Highway 96 at Seiad Valley 56.8			0.0

Supplies and Permits: See "Supplies" and "Permits" in Section P.

Potential Problems: Until mid-July, snow may obscure parts of the route, as in the Sierra Nevada. Also you may see an occasional bear, so the Forest Service recommends that you bearbag your food (see the introductory material at the start of Section G).

Maps: *Etna*
       Yellow Dog Peak
       Boulder Peak
       Marble Mountain

       Grider Valley
       Huckleberry Mountain
       Seiad Valley

The Route

From the northwest edge of Etna Summit, the PCT leaves the Somes Bar-Etna Road and makes a usually gentle climb, first west, then north to a crest saddle. After climbing briefly, the trail bends westward down to a longer saddle, from which it contours across a brushy, south-facing slope. South, you'll see snowy Thompson Peak, which at 9002 feet is the paramount peak in the Trinity Alps and the only one to sport glaciers—two miniscule ones. You rejoin the crest and in 200 yards enter Marble Mountain Wilderness (wilderness permits required). Staying close to the crest, you have views north down into deeply glaciated Mill Creek canyon and views south into less glaciated North Russian Creek canyon. Your trail exits from but soon re-enters the wilderness, doing so as it heads northwest toward a saddle. You cross the crest and for just over ½ mile you have views down into Big Creek canyon before you hit your sixth saddle, a notch at the southeast end of Razor Ridge (6690–3.7).

Here, at the head of Pointers Gulch, you start a forested descent northeast, quickly passing a seasonal seep that drips from a massive, mossy outcrop above the trail. Later, after you traverse open, rocky slopes, you cross an ephemeral creeklet, bend east into a bouldery gulch and cross a more persistent creeklet (6450–1.0). North, your route usually descends almost imperceptibly, rounding two bowls before veering west out to a ridge and north past it to another creek (6170–2.0), the best one so far. Beyond the next ridge, you contour more-open slopes, passing a seasonal creek, then in ⅓ mile rejoining the crest at the head of Babs Fork Kidder Creek (6290–0.9). The trail skims a long crest saddle, which divides metavolcanic rocks to the southeast from metasedimentary ones to the northwest, then climbs gently west and then gently north, coming close to the summit of Peak 6667 before plunging to the saddle just north of it (6430-1.4).

*   *   *   *

Water access: From here you can drop east into the head of a deep canyon and reach one of several springs that give birth to Glendenning Fork Kidder Creek. Be forewarned that none of the springs and creeklets between Etna Summit and Kidder Lake are reliable in drought years.

*   *   *   *

On the PCT you climb ⅓ mile north, almost to the top of another crest saddle, this one dividing metasedimentary rocks to the southeast from younger granitic rocks to the northwest. Starting a descent west, you come upon a short trail that drops to nearby Shotgun Spring, in a meadow immediately below the trail. Continuing on a usually gentle grade, you soon turn northwest and descend brushy slopes that permit you to survey half a dozen major gulches that feed into the canyon of Right Hand Fork of North Fork Salmon River. After crossing a lateral moraine left by a former glacier, you momentarily come to Shelly Lake's outlet creek (6150–1.7), your first usually reliable trailside creek. You could camp nearby or, better yet, just ahead, near the site of Wilson Cabin, which is immediately past the north tip of southern Shelly Meadow. In a fir-and-hemlock forest, you quickly reach a junction (6220- 0.3), from where a lateral trail descends ⅓ mile northwest, meeting the Shelly Meadows Trail in northern Shelly Meadow. You can find more water and a possible campsite in this vicinity. Curving north, you make a brief struggle up the PCT to a crest junction with the Shelly Fork Trail (6340–0.2), which descends steeply northeast. All the trails you meet in the wilderness that descend east or northeast go to roads that take you ultimately down to paved Scott River Road, on which you can hitch a ride east to the small but growing town of Fort Jones. In a minute's time you meet the Shelly Meadows Trail.

Immediately beyond the trail your PCT route turns west to start a contour around Peak 7085 to a saddle, then west below Peak 7109 to another saddle (6410–2.2), this one at the head of Timothy Gulch. After a short descent you switchback down to a creeklet (6190-0.3), with campsites, then continue on to more sites by

See maps Q1, Q2, Q3

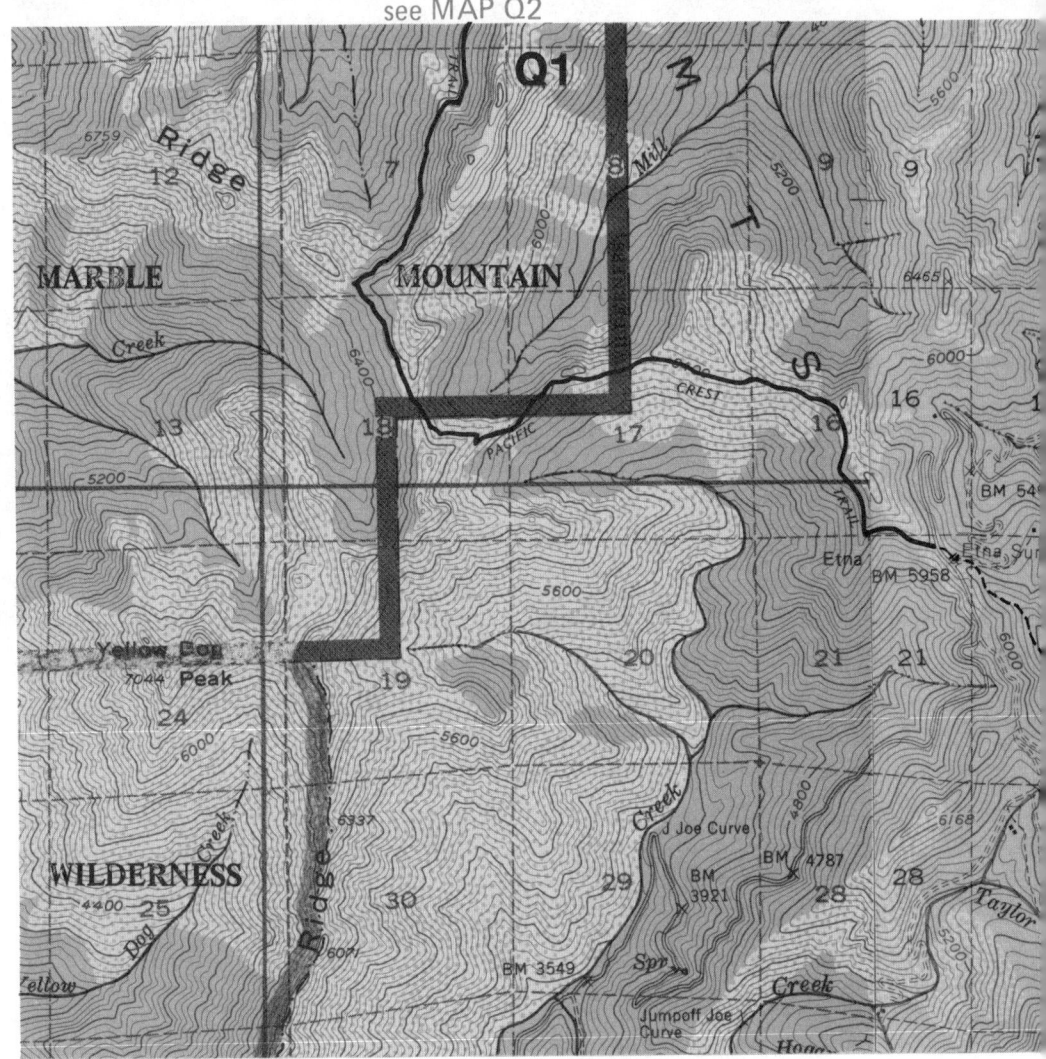

Fisher Lake (6220–0.4). Climbing up open, metavolcanic bedrock, you soon reach smaller Marten Lake (6360–0.3), with no real campsites, though it provides a swim, as Fisher Lake does, after the snow melts in mid-July. Taking advantage of various bedrock ledges, your trail undulates northwest, passing a pond on a bench. Just beneath it the trail crosses a usually trickling creek and then climbs 90 yards to a junction (6560–1.2).

*   *   *   *

Alternate route: Until 1991, when the Forest Service constructed the newer stretch of PCT, you took this dramatic stretch. This older segment is a bit shorter, and it has less eleva-tion gain and loss. On the down side, it lacks any nearby camping, and it can be more snow-bound.

From the junction, the older PCT climbs northeast to a ridge junction with the Kidder Lake Trail (6640–0.4), which in 1.1 miles makes a net drop of 750 feet (too much for most trekkers) down to the lake and its popular campsites.

You now face an overly steep climb (by modern PCT standards), one that switchbacks up to a crest above Cliff Lake. ▌ *This gem-shaped cirque lake, seen from the crest, is 175 feet deep—the deepest lake in this wilderness. In the past, glaciers as thick as 800 feet developed in this cirque and flowed 6 miles down Shackleford Creek canyon.* ▌

See map Q3

Q Etna Summit-Seiad Valley

Deep Cliff Lake and shallow Campbell Lake

Until late summer the hiker usually faces a traverse west across a steep snowfield, *which presents an impassable barrier for stock* (hence the reroute). Once beyond it you see Campbell Lake, resting below Cliff Lake, and then you traverse past mountain hemlocks up to a shallow gap in a serrated crest (7230–0.9). Formerly this was Section Q's high point. From it you make a short descent southwest to a junction (7180–0.1–1.4) with the north end of the newer PCT segment.

*   *   *   *

From the junction with the older PCT segment, the newer one switchbacks southwestward up to a conspicuous saddle (6870–0.5). From it the PCT switchbacks several times and then makes an open, descending traverse above stark Man Eaten Lake.

*   *   *   *

Water access: To minimize climbing effort you can camp near two semistagnant ponds on a bedrock bench high above the lake's northeast shore, and descend to the lake only to get fresh water or to swim. To reach the ponds leave the trail just after it enters forest cover and then drop about 200 feet in elevation directly downslope.

*   *   *   *

Soon after entering forest cover the PCT starts an ascending traverse. This part is across *active* talus slopes, and so parts of the trail can be buried if a recent trail crew hasn't worked this stretch. The trail switchbacks several times, and then soon curves over to a junction (7180–1.1) with the older PCT segment. This is the new high point for Section Q.

The two segments now united, the PCT route descends ¼ mile to a saddle on a narrow ridge. Leaving that, you soon lose your spectacular lake views and make a traverse to another crest saddle, this one cloaked with Shasta red fir, mountain hemlock and western white pine. Advancing toward the next saddle, you climb northwest, cross an open field of ankle-high eriogonum, wind through a near-crest forest, and momentarily descend to the first of two scenic switchbacks. Don't get too close to the precipitous edge, for the landslide debris you

See maps Q3, Q4

see scattered around Summit Lake, way below you, came from the area you're standing on. A large landslide scar on the canyon's opposite wall gives further testimony to the instability of this glaciated canyon's overly steep walls.

You now switchback steeply down the crest to its saddle (6590-1.7), from where the Shackleford Creek Trail descends 0.4 mile to a bowl 300 yards below Jewel Lake, then switchbacks ½ mile down to Summit Lake. From the junction you engage a northwest traverse through a thinning forest that gradually is replaced with abundant brush and a smattering of Jeffrey pines. The forest cover returns again as you regain the crest and get your first views of the Marble Mountain area, dominated by Black Mountain, named for its dark gray-brown cap of metamorphosed sediments. ∎ *Closer to you are the burnt-red slopes above Red Rock Valley. These rocks are ultramafic intrusives, and if you were to break open a fresh sample, you would see that it is blackish-green, for it is partly composed of the green mineral olivine. This mineral and its associates, being rich in iron, weather to produce the rust-colored landscape.* ∎

A two-minute walk down the crest brings you to an important trail junction (6310-1.6).

*   *   *   *

Side routes: From this level spot a steep trail winds about 100 yards north, dying out on a ridge just a few feet away from the Red Rock Valley Trail, which is a good route out to civilization. To the south, another trail weaves ¼ mile south moderately down to a trail junction just

above Cold Spring bench. With at least three springs and ample camping space, the bench is a welcome goal for weary PCT trekkers.

*   *   *   *

On the shady crest the PCT continues a traverse to a second set of trails (6370-0.3).

*   *   *   *

Side routes: The Red Rock Valley Trail drops 1/4 mile east to the ridge that the north-winding trail died out on, then continues 1/4 mile north down this glacial moraine before curving northwest and giving rise to a spur over to a vegetated lakelet. Camping here is definitely inferior to camping by Cold Spring. Southbound trekkers reach the spring by leaving the crest junction and descending 0.3 mile to the previously mentioned junction just above the Cold Spring bench.

*   *   *   *

Your crest route now climbs a bit west to the east end of the Shadow Lake Trail (6480-0.3).

*   *   *   *

Side Route: This trail, sometimes hard to follow, goes ½ mile northwest over to the lake, which is perched on the brink of a cliff above Sky High Lakes. You'd be hard pressed to find a more dramatic campsite.

*   *   *   *

See maps Q4, Q5

Light Marble Mountain and dark Black Mountain

Q3

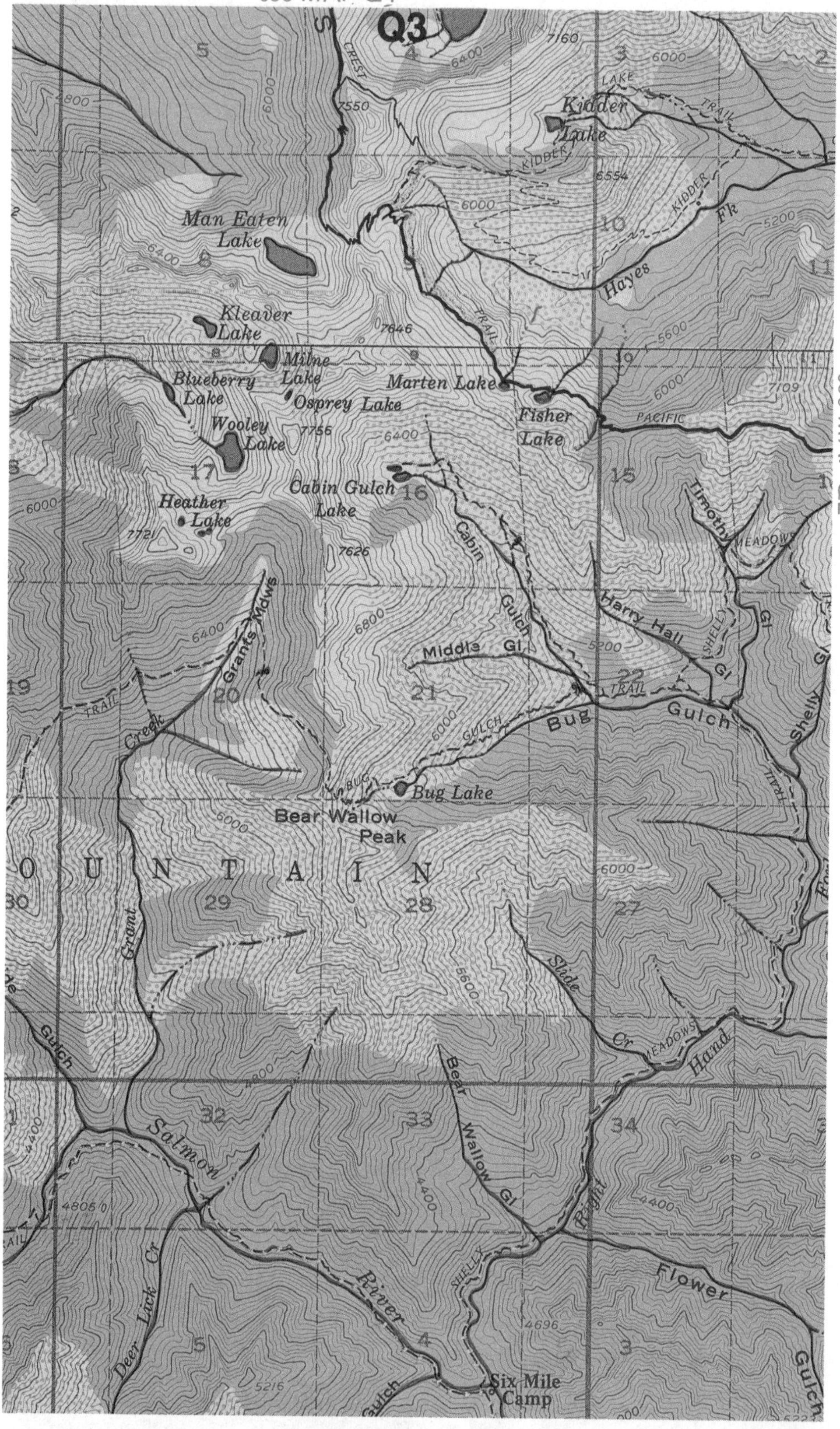

see MAP Q2

Kidder Lake

Man Eaten Lake

Kleaver Lake

Milne Lake

Blueberry Lake

Osprey Lake

Marten Lake

Fisher Lake

Wooley Lake

Heather Lake

Cabin Gulch Lake

Grants Mdws

Middle Gl

Harry Hall

Bug Gulch

Bug Lake

Bear Wallow Peak

MOUNTAIN

Salmon

Deer Lick Cr

Bear Wallow Gl

Six Mile Camp

Flower

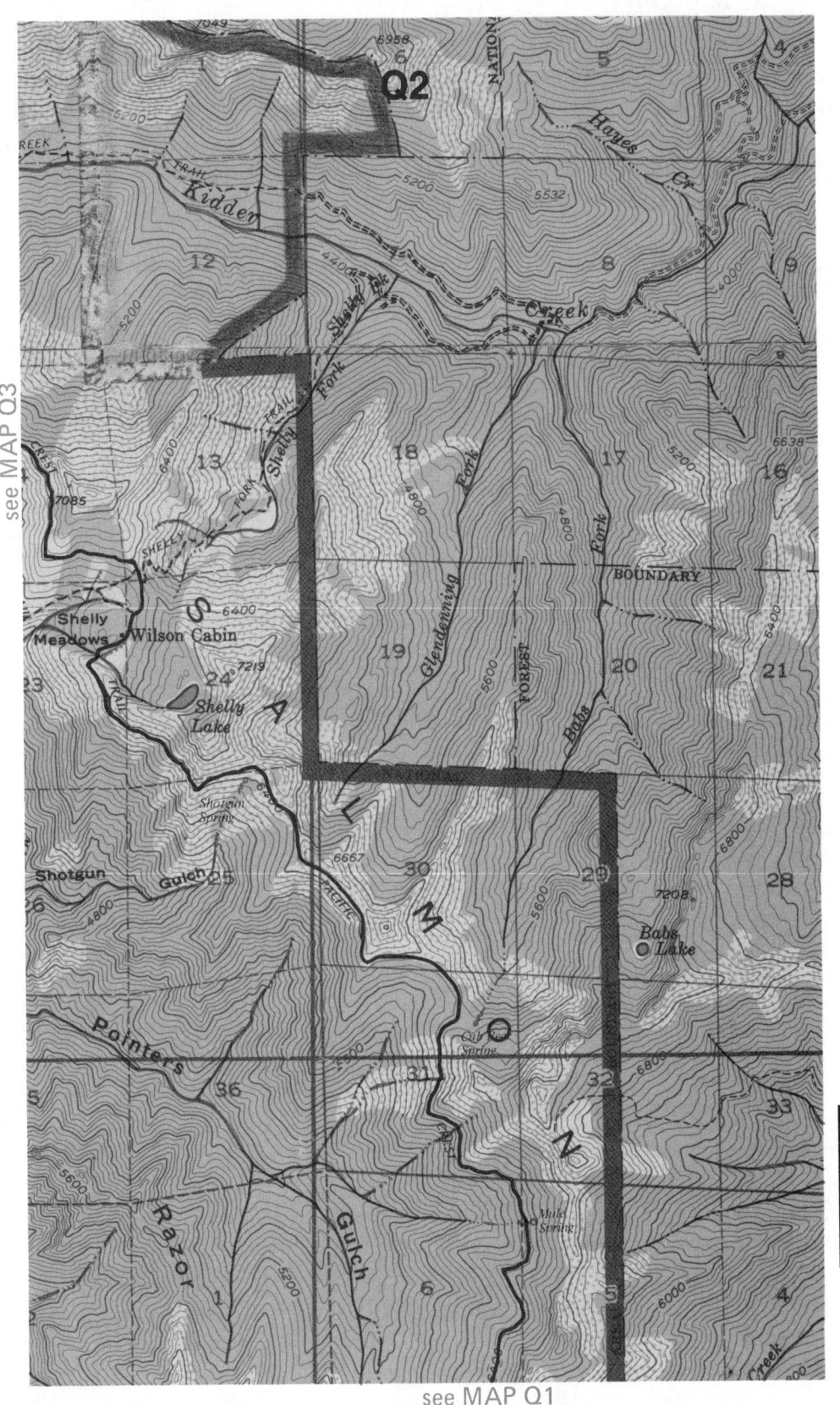

see MAP Q3

Q Etna Summit-
Seiad Valley

Westbound, the PCT traverses the southeast slope of Peak 6817, then on its southwest slope encounters a short, sometimes hidden trail traversing over to nearby Soft Water Spring. The PCT passes just a few yards above this seeping spring (6580–0.6).

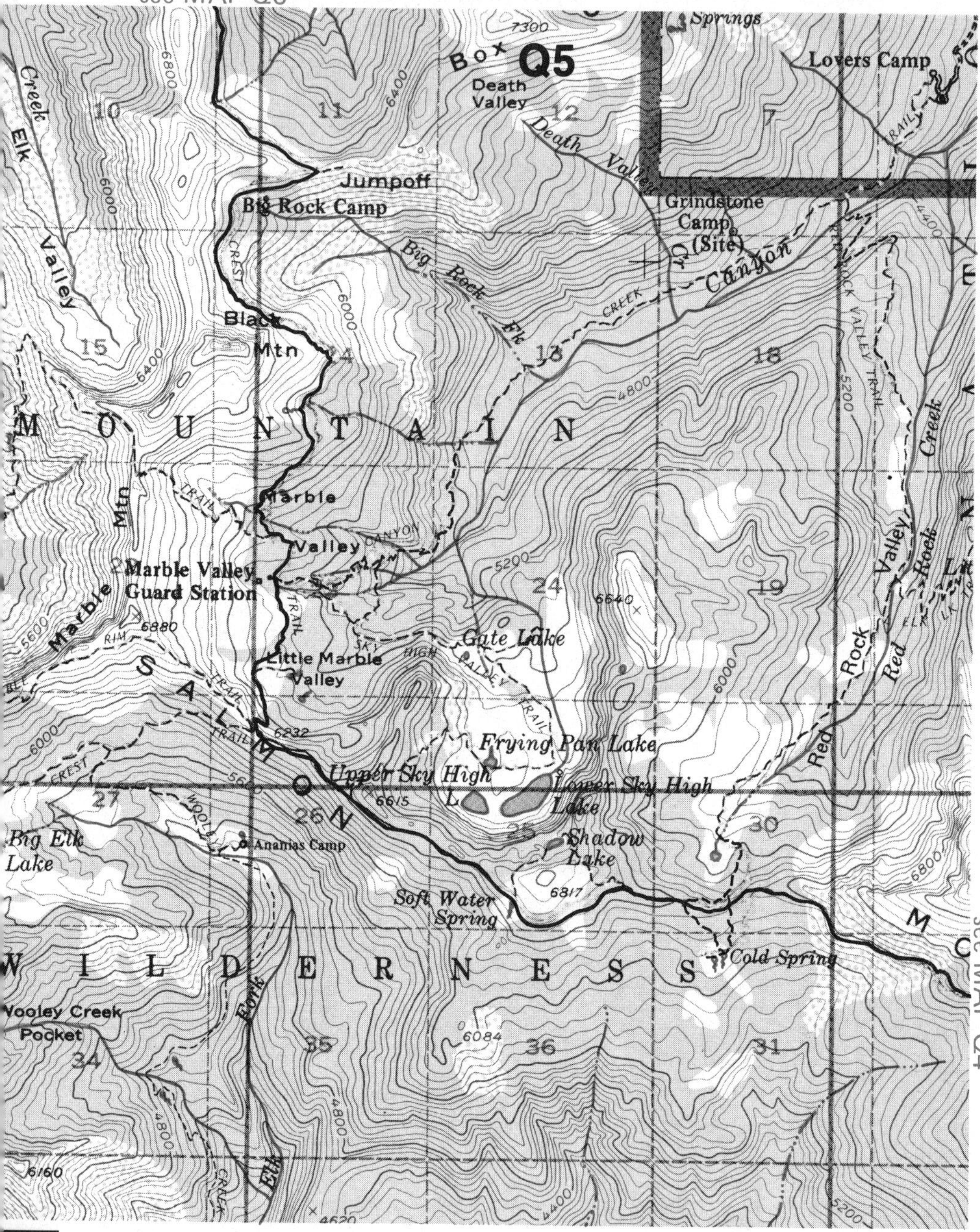

*   *   *   *

Side Route: From this spot the west end of the Shadow Lake Trail takes off over the adjacent crest, then drops ¼ mile northeast to that lake.

*   *   *   *

See map Q5

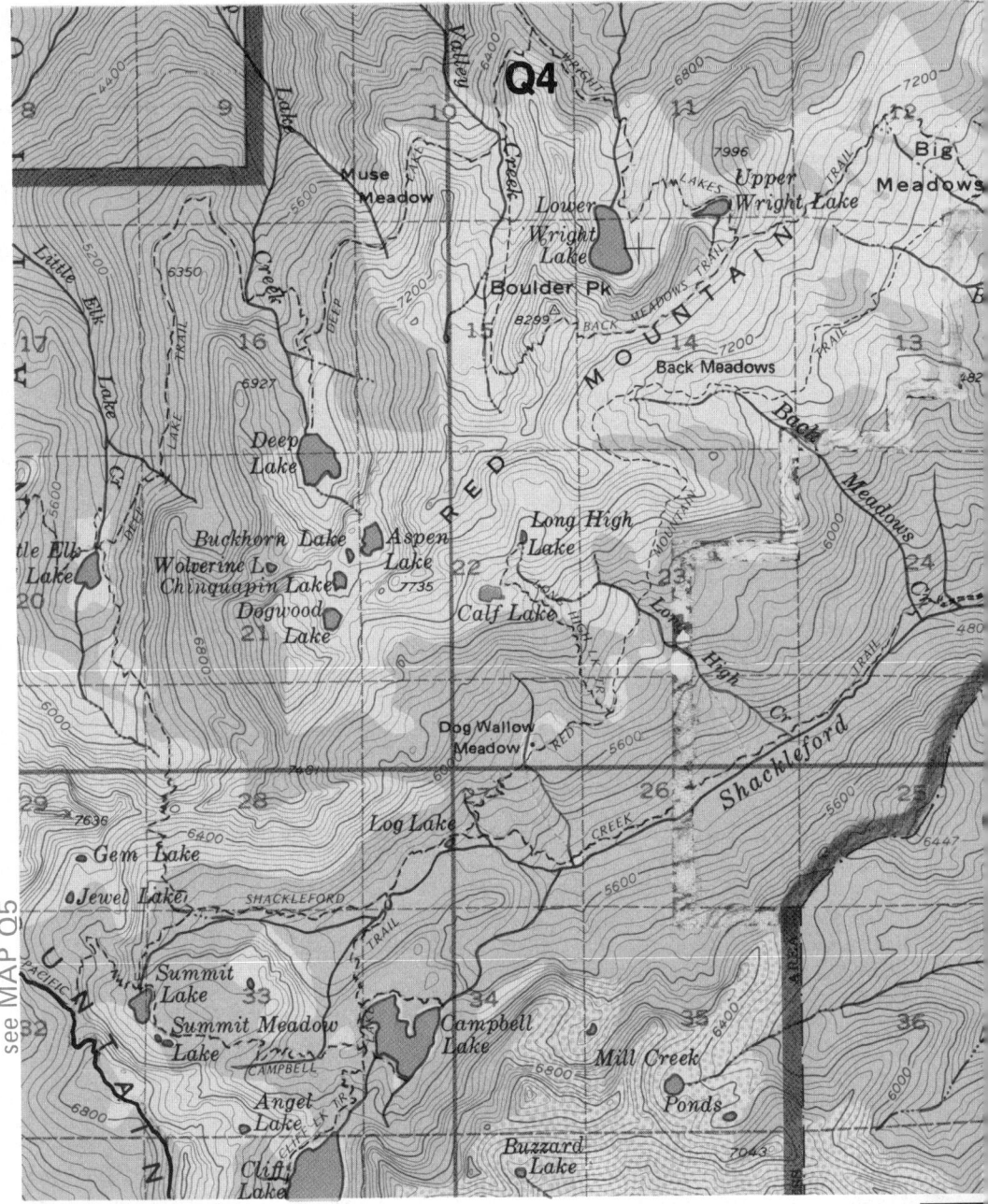

see MAP Q5

see MAP Q3

You now make an easy ¼ mile descent to a crest saddle above the Sky High Lakes, then stick close to the crest as you contour northwest to the first of two Sky High Valley trail junctions (6400-0.9). The first path climbs 60 yards to the crest, where it joins the second, which originates from your trail in 120 yards. Past it you follow the crest down to a saddle with a trail intersection (6232-0.5). From here a wide trail to Big Elk Lake descends west, the Marble Rim Trail—a footpath—continues ahead along the crest, and the PCT drops north

See map Q5

into deep Little Marble Valley.

*   *   *   *

Side route: For perhaps the best view in all of Marble Mountain Wilderness, hike ⅔ mile northwest on the Marble Rim Trail, then climb cross country up to the nearby summit of 6880-foot high Marble Mountain. From it, most of the wilderness spreads below you. You can distinguish the different kinds of rocks: medium-gray marble, light gray granodiorite, brownish metavolcanics and rusty ultramafics. Red Mountain, the huge ultramafic mass to the east, is capped by 8299-foot Boulder Peak, which is the highest mountain in the wilderness and one of the highest in the Klamath Mountains.

On the PCT, you drop into Little Marble Valley, and in about ⅓ mile your trail levels just before it starts a northeast descent. From that level area an old tread—essentially cross-country—descends 0.2 mile east to a spring. ∎ *One may wonder why this canyon and other ones nearby don't have glacial lakes, for they were glaciated at least as much as the Sky High, Summit and Cliff lakes canyons. The answer lies in the rock—marble—which dominates your area. About ¼ mile before your trail reaches the Marble Valley Guard Station, you encounter an excellent outcrop of these rocks and can see why they can't hold lakes: water percolates right through them. Just east of the trail you can find a number of fissures and caves. This marble is just a 600-foot thick stratum out of a total of more than 10,000 feet of sediments deposited on the North American continental shelf during the Triassic period. Most of these sediments were volcanic in origin, for back then the continent's edge was a scene of intense volcanic activity. During a fairly long period of volcanic quiescence, coral reefs gradually built up a thick layer of limestone, which later was metamorphosed, along with the other Triassic sediments, and it became transformed into marble.* ∎

Beyond the marble outcrop you make a brief, steep descent to a creeklet, then climb 90 yards to the Marble Valley Guard Station, which is immediately west of a junction with the Canyon Creek Trail (5700–1.0).

*   *   *   *

Side route: A two-hour walk northeast down

this takes you to the wilderness' principal trailhead parking lot—the starting point for many weekend hikers. You might plan to camp in Marble Valley, for the next site, Big Rock Camp, has limited space.

*   *   *   *

From the junction you make a short climb north-northeast to a low ridge, then angle west-northwest up it for 200 yards to a junction with the Marble Gap Trail (5840–0.3), forking left. You fork right and cross the infant Canyon Creek in a couple of minutes. In a gully just north of this creek is a junction with a trail branching left. You now wind steeply north before starting a traverse around Black Mountain—the wilderness' most eye-catching peak. Hikers sometimes mistake it for Marble Mountain, which is hardly more than a high crest that one can pass without even recognizing. The PCT climbs northeast through a dense forest to Black Mountain's southeast ridge, traverses the mountain's glaciated east bowl, and then executes short switchbacks northwest up to some prominent trailside caves in a thick bank of marble. ∎ *On the opposite canyon wall, to the northeast, you'll see a continuation of this thick, gray band. Its thickness indicates the maximum depth to which any of the caves descend.* ∎

About 200 yards past these caves you pass under a vertical wall of loose, unstable marble, beneath which unsuspecting hikers have camped. Your route soon leaves its cover of hemlock, pine and fir to traverse northwest across a large, glaciated bowl. When the trail bends north, it enters forest cover again, then emerges in a smaller bowl.

In it you'll recognize Big Rock, on your left, which has broken off from upper slopes. Immediately beyond it a poor 100-yard-long trail (6640–2.2) descends down-canyon to Big Rock Camp, which can be packed with up to eight persons. Your trail next bends eastward, passing a second poor lateral down to the camp before reaching the Jumpoff (6650–0.4), a low point on a narrow crest. From here a trail starts east along the crest. Looking north from it you can see the twin summits of ultramafic Red Butte, which stands just northeast of Kangaroo Mountain and considerably west of Condrey Mountain, the highest peak on the

See map Q5

Paradise Lake and Kings Castle

horizon. In about four days you'll pass through that part of the Siskiyou Mountains and enter Oregon.

Starting northwest, you begin a long traverse above the headwaters of South Fork Kelsey Creek, cross a northeast ridge of Peak 7162, then make a minor descent ½ mile to a notch (6190–2.2) in the southwest end of Cayenne Ridge. From the notch a faint tread—the Rye Patch Trail—starts northeast along the ridge before making a 1¾ mile drop to Road 44N44. On the west side of the PCT's junction with the Rye Patch Trail is a spring, and you may want to get water from it rather than at nearby Paradise Lake.

The PCT leaves the notch and descends moderately northwest to the outlet of popular, murky Paradise Lake (6130–0.2). Just beyond the ford is a good-sized campsite by the lake's edge. Others can be found by taking the lake's loop trail to the opposite shore. All these camps are illegal since they are within 200 feet of the lakeshore. You're not supposed to camp in meadows either, and since the lake is surrounded by meadows, you're stuck. However, you should be able to find a site among red firs about 0.1 mile east of the lakes's outlet. This lake will be your last reliable water source un-til sometimes-polluted Buckhorn Spring 5.6 easy miles farther. Kings Castle, the first major landmark southbound PCT trekkers see in the Marble Mountain Wilderness, is the small marble block atop the high crest above the lake.

Leaving the lake, your trail contours, then makes an increasingly steep ascent to a ridge, from which it traverses northwest under the nearly vertical north end of the Kings Castle ridge. In ½ mile you descend the main crest north to a saddle junction (6580–1.6).

*　　　*　　　*　　　*

Side routes: From here two ducked trails descend steeply, one ⅔ mile east to very shallow Turk Lake, the other ⅔ mile west to slightly deeper Bear Lake. The latter is more inviting, and the drop to it is "only" 600 feet; the drop to Turk Lake is 750 feet.

*　　　*　　　*　　　*

You switchback north up the rocky crest, which is sparsely covered with Jeffrey pines. ❚ *Growing on soil derived from ultramafic rock, these trees seem to do better on such soil than do the wilderness' other conifers.* ❚ Upon ap-

See maps Q5, Q6

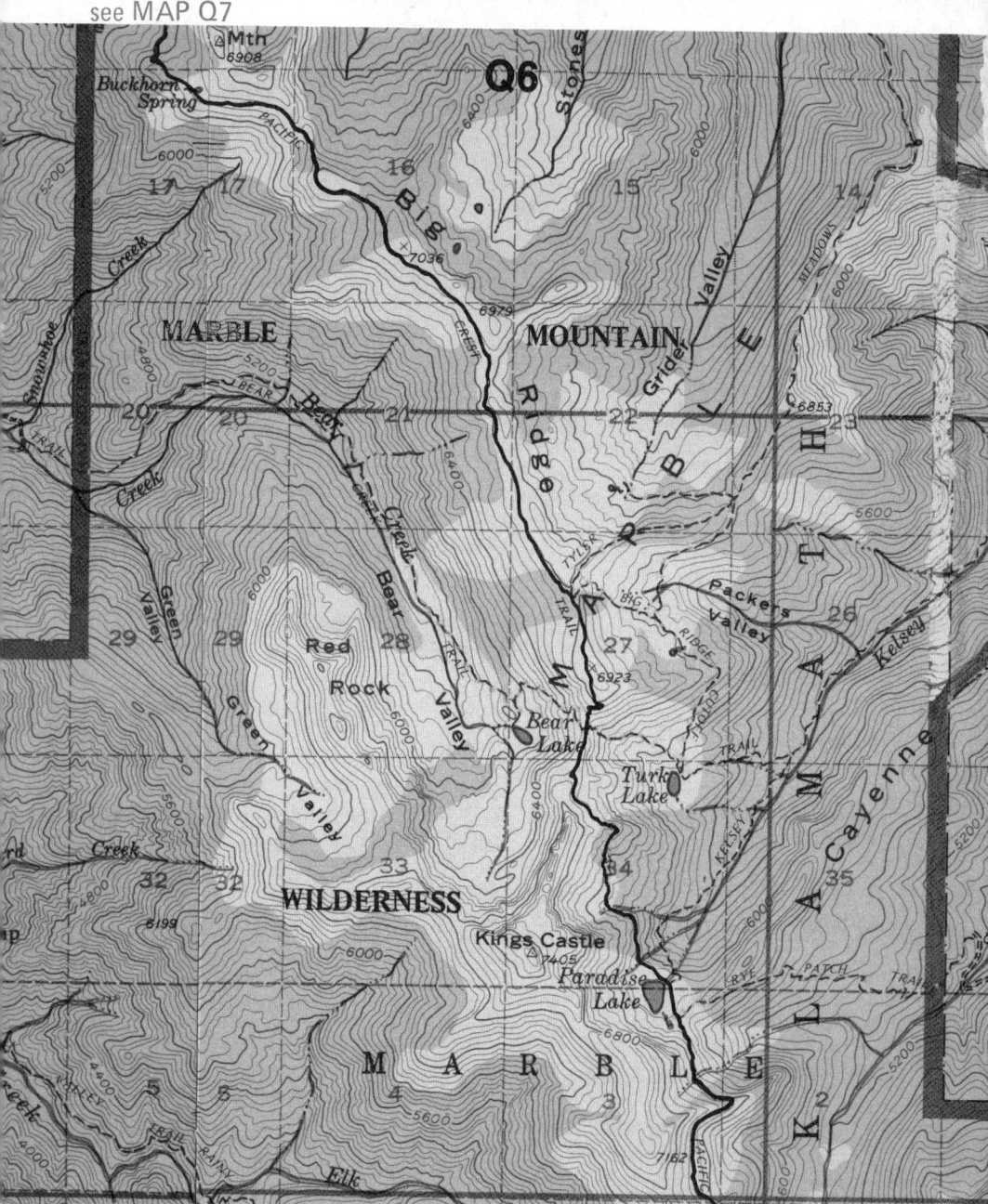

Q6

see MAP Q5

proaching Peak 6923 you get an excellent view back at Kings Castle, then onward you keep close to the crest and soon reach an open saddle with more views (6800–0.7). From here the Big Ridge Cutoff Trail drops east into Packers Valley, seen below, while the Tyler Meadows Trail starts a contour northeast to the wilderness boundary and the start of Road 45N77. Con-

tinuing along Big Ridge, you contour north, occasionally touching the actual crest and then finally descending its north end to a saddle below Buckhorn Mountain. Here you leave the last of the prominent outcrops of marble and traverse west across the mountain's open, south slope, cross its southwest ridge and immediately encounter Buckhorn Spring (6570-3.3).

See map Q6

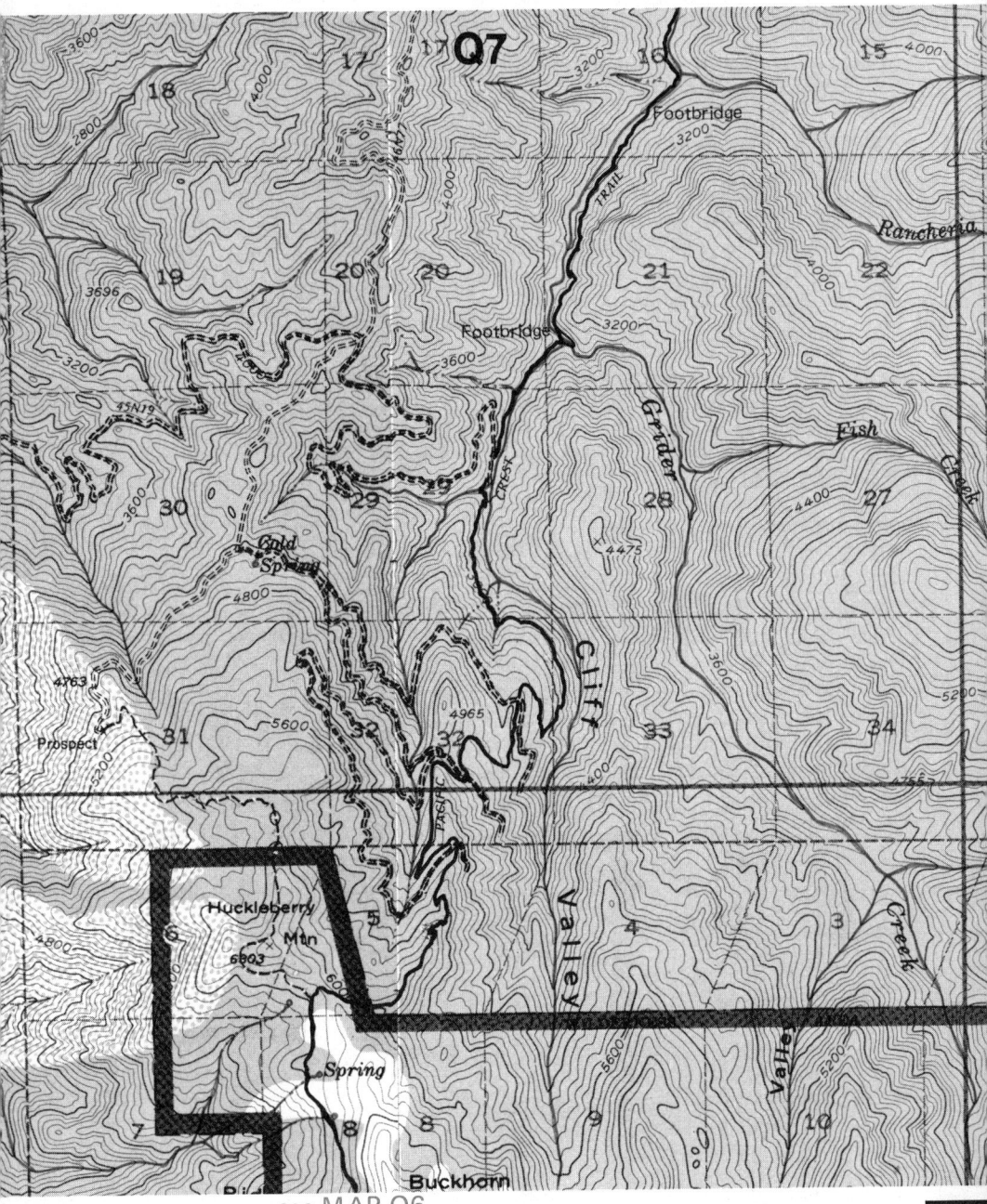

see MAP Q6

Your trail route, largely open for the last few miles, will now be mostly forested all the way to the Klamath River. Leaving the spring, you quickly enter a cover of hemlock and pine and soon descend to a small flat with a tiny pond (6300–0.3). Shasta red firs begin to give way to white firs and incense-cedars as you descend north and pass two springs that run well into August. After a ⅓-mile traverse from the second, your trail comes to a junction with the Huckleberry Mountain Trail (6020–1.0), which winds 2½ miles down to a road that goes to Cold Spring and Road 46N77. That road traverses many miles north on Grider Ridge before meeting Road 46N66, which descends east to Grider Creek Campground and Seiad

See maps Q6, Q7

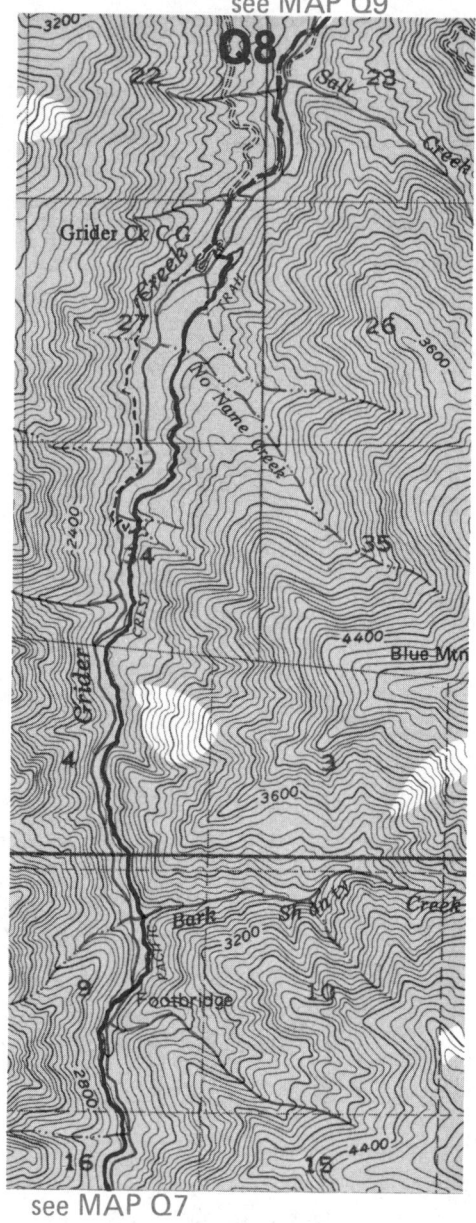

see MAP Q9

see MAP Q7

Valley—certainly not a shortcut to civilization.

After a two-minute walk northeast to a crest saddle, you start a 4400-foot, 13 ¼-mile drop to that campground. Among red firs, your well-graded trail starts a shady descent southeast, leaving the north boundary of Marble Mountain Wilderness as it turns east. You quickly reach a descending ridge and encounter white fir, Douglas-fir and even sugar pine. At a logged-over area midway along the first leg of your descent, you can look north down your **V** canyon and above it see the distant twin peaks, Kangaroo Mountain and Red Butte. In about two days you'll reach the crest of the Siskiyou Mountains in the notch between these two peaks. Cook and Green Pass is the deep gash to the east of Red Butte.

The first leg of your descent ends where you cross a good road (5300–1.5). From it you start north along the ridge on an abandoned road and follow it as it quickly switchbacks southwest into brush fields along a creek. You re-enter forest and parallel another good road, which curves around your descending ridge, and then your trail crosses the road (4800–1.0). You arc north, passing lots of trailside thimbleberries, which are indicative of your lower elevation, then soon descend southeast on a brush-lined, abandoned road (4820–1.0). In ¼ mile you turn north and descend through an old logging-scar to your last logging-road crossing (4370–0.9). Your trail starts north but quickly curves south, winding ⅓ mile in and out of gullies down to a switchback. Now you have a shady descent north in a virgin forest of Douglas-fir. You may hear Cliff Valley creek, a couple of hundred feet below you, but the slopes are too steep and vegetated to warrant a descent to it. After ¾ mile, you bend

See map Q7

Faint, distant Mt. Shasta above Big Ridge

Kangaroo Mountain and Red Butte: twin peaks above Grider Creek Canyon

southwest into the gully of an early-summer creeklet and then, a few minutes later near a second creeklet, you see your first madrones, with their rusty, slick bark. In ½ mile your trail bends west and momentarily crosses refreshing Cold Spring creek, then in 150 yards ends at the south tip of Road 46N72 (3200–2.0). Along this road you'll find spacious campsites.

After 150 yards of northward walking, you leave the road and parallel musical Cliff Valley creek down to Grider Creek, which you cross via footbridge (2870–0.8) immediately beyond the two creeks' confluence. A horse path first crosses Cliff Valley creek, then Grider Creek, then heads northwest to the footbridge. In this general area of upper Grider Creek you will see evidence of a former fire. Now above the east bank, your trail starts north down Grider Creek canyon and passes the first of many marble outcrops in ¼ mile. The trail stays fairly close to Grider Creek, but the canyon's slopes are so steep and the vegetation so thick that access to it is usually difficult. After a pleasant walk, you recross the creek on a second footbridge (2640-1.3). A campsite here is large enough to hold four tents. You now make a momentary climb, then traverse above a short stretch of marble-walled Grider Creek, which playfully cascades from pool to pool. Just ¼ mile past the bridge, you enter a small hollow in which a creek flows underground through an alluvial fan to nearby Grider Creek. Through the trees you'll see Rancheria Creek also joining your energetic stream.

In another ¼ mile you spy your first trailside poison oak, which is another indicator of your lower elevation. Douglas-firs still predominate, though you pass through a grove of madrones just before you cross your third footbridge (2330–1.7). Now along the east bank you gently descend to Bark Shanty Creek (2280–0.4), which is one of the most reliable tributary creeks in this canyon. Onward, you weave in and out of gullies, most of them minor. Over

Grider Creek

See maps Q7, Q8

see MAP R1

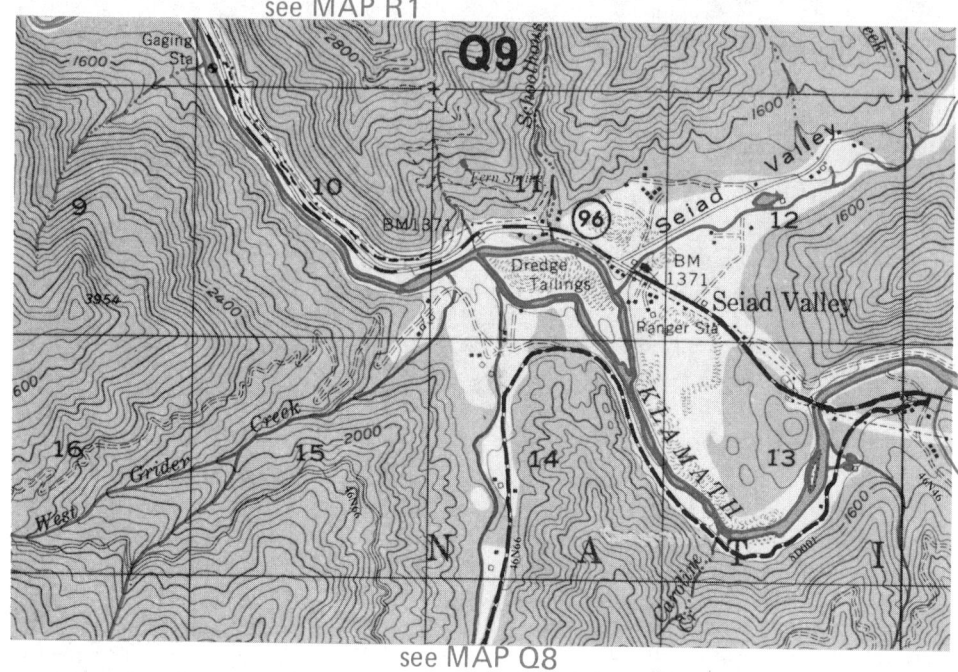

see MAP Q8

distance, Grider Creek gradually drops away from the trail, and access to it becomes increasingly more of an effort. Eventually the trail curves right briefly into a dry gully, but immediately before doing so it reaches a sometimes cryptic junction (1920–1.8) with the Old Grider Creek Trail.

*   *   *   *

Alternate route: Ahead, there are no camping opportunities or water availability along the PCT until Grider Creek Campground. For those wanting secluded camping, this narrow-treaded trail gives them several opportunities. It first winds rather steeply down to Grider Creek, where one or more downed logs should afford a bridge across it. The next ¼ mile of trail down along the creek stays close to it, but then over the next ⅔ mile it is mostly on a river terrace that is suitable for camping. Once you diagonal briefly northwest up across a seasonal creeklet, you leave camping opportunities behind. You climb to avoid a steep-walled stretch, then descend and soon reach the campground. You can leave the trail there or follow it to its end by the campground's entrance (1700–1.8).

*   *   *   *

From the Old Grider Creek Trail junction the PCT ducks in and out of the aforementioned gully, quickly ducks in and out of another one with usually trickling water, and then stays high, ready access to Grider Creek being thwarted by thick vegetation. Eventually the trail begins to drop, and you come to a switchback. If you are on horseback, continue momentarily ahead down to the creek, which you ford, and then head briefly up an old road to where PCT trail tread ends. If you are on foot, angle left and follow the PCT over to a nearby bridge that spans Grider Creek. Then in 40 yards you reach trail's end at the old road at the edge of Grider Creek Campground (1700–1.6). This has a pit toilet and sites with tables, but no trash collection and no piped water.

From here you face an all-road route to Seiad Valley. ▮ *For years the Forest Service tried to piece together a trail route to Highway 96, but private lands and the prohibitive cost of a massive horse-bridge across the Klamath River ultimately scuttled the project. Hence, you can consider the following route as permanent Pacific Crest Trail.* ▮

You walk past the small campground, which has most of its sites to the left and upstream of

See map Q8

you. To the right are facilities for equestrians. By the campground's entrance is the start of the Old Grider Creek Trail. You then take the campground's entrance road, 46N24X, north to Road 46N66 (1680–0.3), turn right, and take this well-used logging road downstream to your last bridge across Grider Creek (1520- 0.8). You continue downstream past private property, then curve east around a nose to a junction with a spur road (1400–1.5) on your left. After a few minutes' walk east on now paved Grider Road, you approach the Klamath River and see why a bridge across it would be expensive. Some hikers have attempted to ford the Klamath River in order to avoid the extra mileage on the roads.

Their comments in the Seiad Valley store's PCT register indicate that the mileage saved wasn't worth the stressful effort. You parallel the river, first southeast and then northeast, to Road 46N46, which parallels Walker Creek. Only 35 yards north on this road you meet Highway 96 (1435-2.4). On this you hike west, cross the Klamath River (1430–0.5) and continue to a store and post office in the sleepy settlement of Seiad Valley (1371–1.0). Immediately before the store is the Mid River R. V. Park, which for a reasonable fee lets you camp. It also has coin-operated showers and a laundry facility. Finally, it will hold parcels mailed to it. See "Supplies" in Section P.

See maps Q8, Q9

Q
Etna Summit-
Seiad Valley

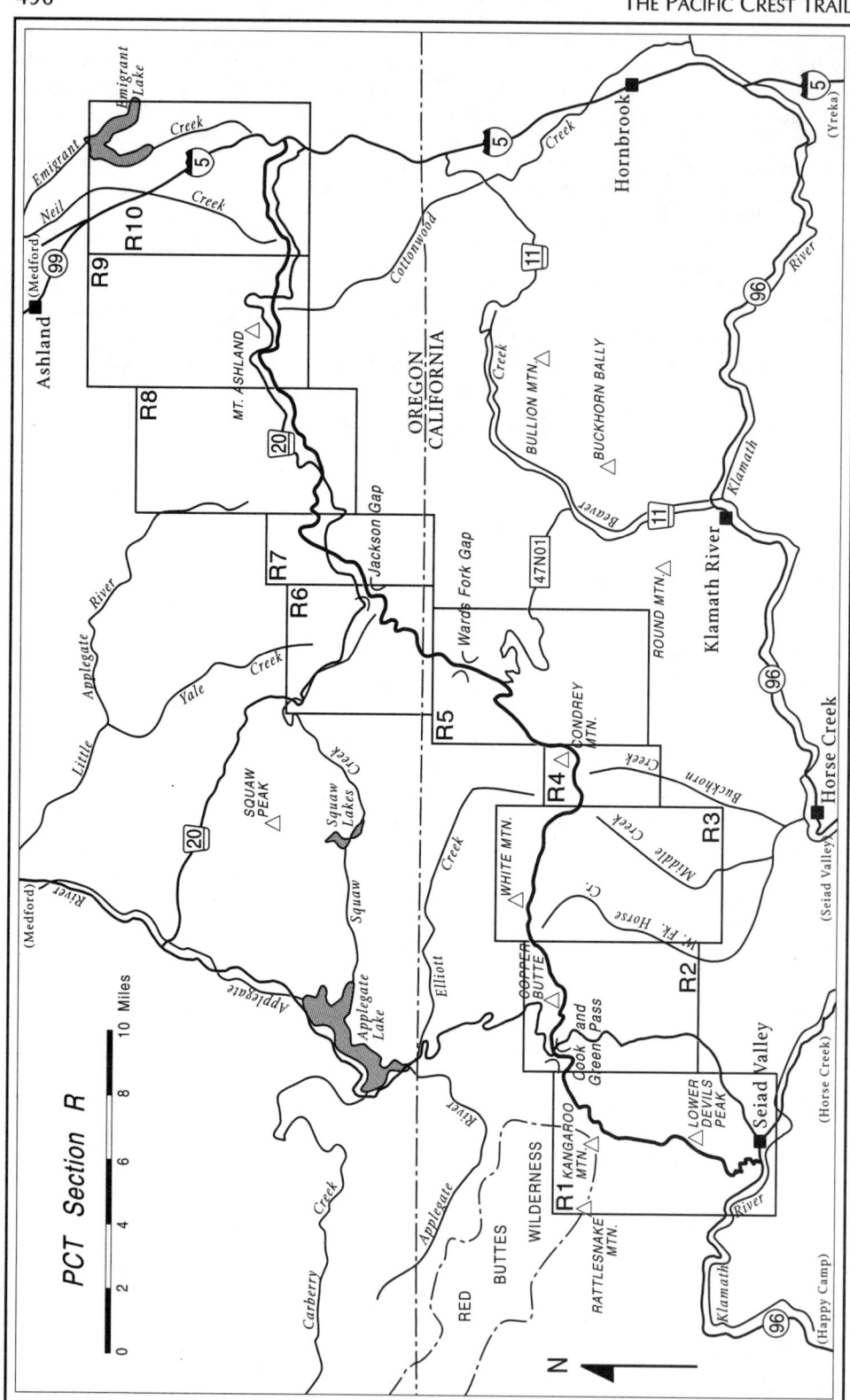

PCT Section R

Section R
Seiad Valley to Interstate 5 in Oregon

Introduction: In this section the hiker makes a long traverse east to get over to the Cascade Range. The long traverse west from Burney Falls to Marble Mountain was quite necessary, though inconveniently long, since a route going north from Burney Falls past Mt. Shasta would be a dry, hot one indeed. Before the Pacific Crest Trail route became final, this sun-drenched corridor was the one most hikers followed to the Oregon Skyline Trail—Oregon's section of the Pacific Crest Trail. Section R's route stays remarkably high for most of its length, dropping significantly only at each end. Although high, it has been only mildly glaciated, and because glaciers haven't scoured away the soil, thick forests abound. These, unfortunately, are rampant with logging roads. From Reeves Ranch eastward you are always paralleling one road or another, so you certainly lose the wilderness feeling this high-crest hike is supposed to offer. Views, however, are pleasing enough, and surprisingly few logging operations are seen from the trail. Before early July these roads are an advantage, for significant stretches of trail are still snowbound. The roads, being more open, are quite easy to follow, though they still have enough snow patches on them to stop motor vehicles. As you progress east on trail or road, you walk across increasingly younger rocks, first late-Paleozoic/early-Mesozoic metamorphic rocks, then mid-Mesozoic granite rocks of the Mt. Ashland area and finally mid-to-late Cenozoic volcanic rocks of the Interstate 5 area.

Declination: 17¼°E

Points on Route	S→N	Mi. Btwn. Pts.	N→S
Highway 96 at Seiad Valley	0.0		64.5
		6.5	
Lower Devils Peak saddle	6.5		58.0
		8.6	
Cook and Green Pass	15.1		49.4
		5.3	
Lowdens Cabin site spur trail	20.4		44.1
		7.5	
Alex Hole Camp entrance	27.9		36.6
		2.3	
Mud Springs spur road	30.2		34.3
		2.4	
Bearground Spring	32.6		31.9
		1.3	
Wards Fork Gap	33.9		30.6
		2.8	
California-Oregon border	36.7		27.8
		4.4	
Sheep Camp Spring	41.1		23.4
		2.3	
Wrangle Gap	43.4		21.1
		5.4	
Long John Saddle	48.8		15.7
		5.0	
Grouse Gap	53.8		10.7
		3.8	
Road 2080	57.6		6.9
		6.9	
Interstate 5 near Mt. Ashland Road 20	64.5		0.0

Supplies: No supplies are available once you leave Seiad Valley. Along this crest route virtually all roads south will get you down to Highway 96, which has a smattering of hamlets, and virtually all roads north will ultimately channel you down to the Ashland-Medford area. However, we don't think you should descend either direction since you would then be way off route. Even in an emergency situation, you're likely to get help from people driving along the near-crest roads long before you could reach any settlement. If you're continuing through Oregon, you'll want to end Section R in Ashland, and routes to it are described in this trail chapter. You won't find any more sizable towns within an easy day's walk of the PCT—other than Sisters—until you reach the Oregon-Washington border area, more than 400 miles beyond this section's end. If you think you'll need a new pack, a camera or a pair of boots, certainly stop in Ashland.

Maps: *Seiad Valley*   *Dutchman Peak*
       Kangaroo Mountain   *Siskiyou Peak*
       Dutch Creek   *Mt. Ashland*
       Condrey Mountain   *Siskiyou Pass*

The Route

You begin this section at the Seiad Store and post office (1371' elevation, located 46 miles west of Interstate 5 via Highway 96). Walking west along the highway, you immediately cross Seiad Valley Road, which heads northeast up to Horse Tail Falls and beyond to Cook and Green Pass. Not much farther on you reach School House Gulch (1380-0.5), from where the old PCT route once started. Following the road as it curves west, you quickly reach a newer trailhead for Lower Devils Peak Lookout Trail 12W04 (1380–0.3). Since it is an exhausting 4400-foot ascent to potential campsites by the Kangaroo Mountain meadows, one is prudent to start this strenuous trek in the cool shade of the morning.

Under a cover of madrone, Douglas-fir, incense-cedar and Oregon oak, your trail curves west and climbs moderately to reach a junction (1600–0.2) with a trail that parallels Highway 96 west for 1.4 miles before ending close to a stream-gaging cable that spans the mighty Klamath River. ∎ *The PCT was supposed to cross there, rather than on the Highway 96 bridge east of Seiad Valley, before this plan was abandoned.* ∎

See map R1

Seiad Valley, view east up the Klamath River

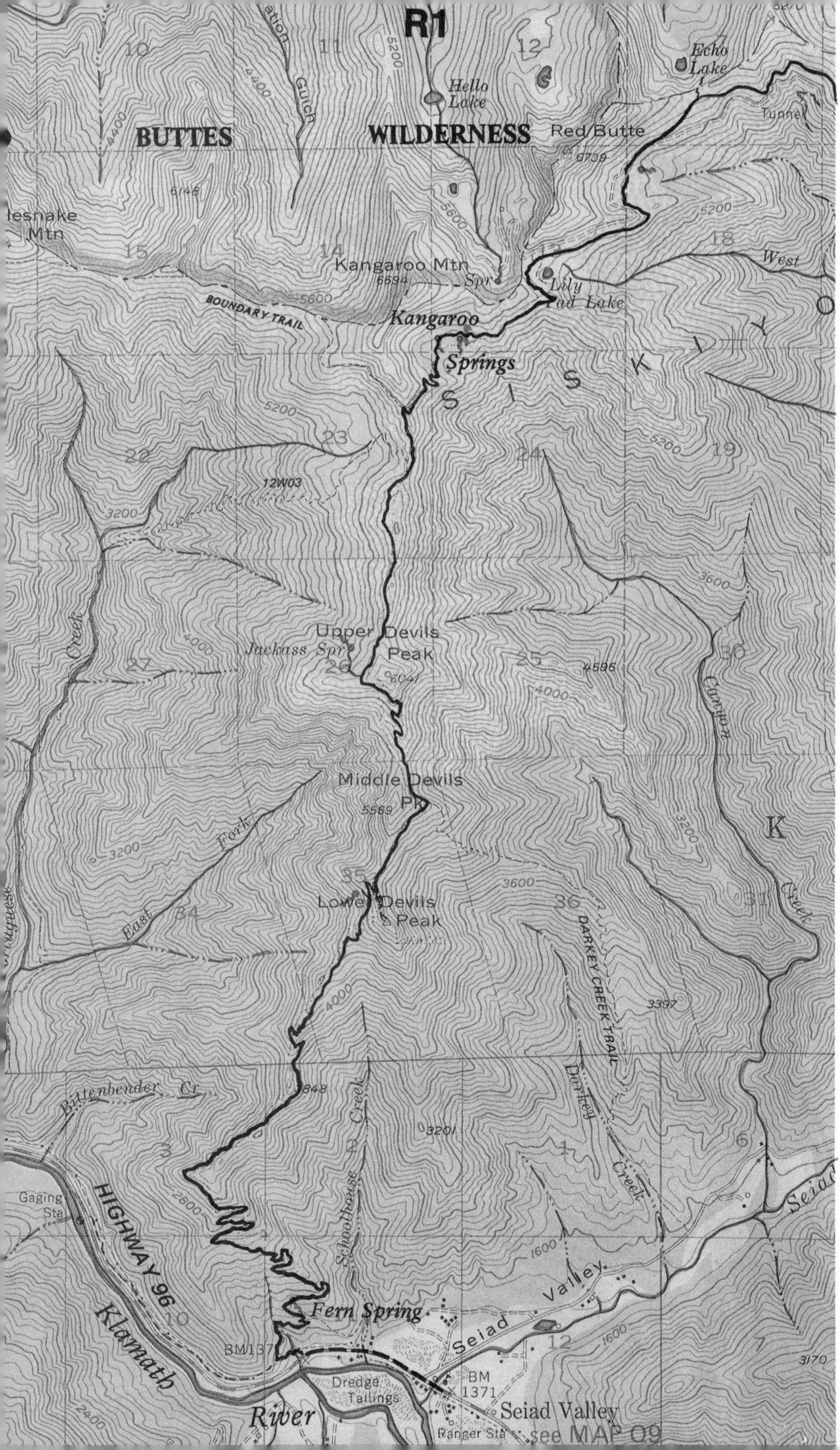

BUTTES

WILDERNESS

Echo Lake

Hello Lake

Red Butte
6739

Tunnel

lesnake Mtn

Kangaroo Mtn
6694

Lily Pad Lake

West

BOUNDARY TRAIL

Kangaroo

Springs

S I S K I Y O U

12W03

Jackass Spr

Upper Devils Peak
6041

4596

Creek

Middle Devils Pk
5589

Canyon

K

Creek

Fork

Lower Devils Peak

East

DARKEY CREEK TRAIL

3397

Darkey

Creek

Bittenbender Cr

3201

848

Schoolhouse Creek

Creek

Seiad

Gaging Sta

HIGHWAY 96

Fern Spring

Seiad Valley

BM 1371

Klamath

Dredge Tailings

BM 1371

Seiad Valley
Ranger Sta

River

see MAP O9

From the junction with the Highway 96 trail, where you cross under some minor powerlines, your trail heads north into a shaded gully with its poison oak, and you soon reach a junction with the original Devils Peak Lookout Trail, now abandoned. About ¼ mile beyond this junction you reach Fern Spring (1900–0.7), a small seep trickling from a pipe into a concrete cistern. You may find a trail register here.

Your well-engineered trail switchbacks up shady, though fly-infested, south-facing slopes, then follows a ridge system northeast up toward Lower Devils Peak. ▌ *Along this stretch you'll see some trees scorched in a widespread fire started by lightning in the summer of 1987. The damage here is minor compared to that north of Lower Devils Peak.* ▌ Where the ridge fuses with the peak's flank, you climb up some short switchbacks, then traverse north across west-facing slopes to a junction.

* * * *

Water Access: From here a 40-yard-long trail goes over to Lookout Spring. This trickling spring is usually reliable, though one has to marvel how any water flows at all, since the spring is so close to the Devils Peaks crest.

* * * *

From the junction you climb about 300 yards in a final push up to Lower Devils Peak saddle (5020–4.8), on the Devils Peaks crest.

* * * *

Side route: From the saddle you can follow a faint, rocky trail ¼ mile over to the remains of Lower Devils Peak Lookout, which was dismantled in 1976. The views you obtain from it are fine, but the many views ahead equal those from the lookout site. The lower room of the lookout still remains, albeit roofless, and it does offer a flat, fairly wind-free campsite.

* * * *

From the crest saddle you start across the first of several major burns you'll traverse before Lily Pad Lake. ▌ *Note the charred remains of knobcone pines here. These pines need a major fire, whose heat opens their cones, to release the seeds. These short-lived pines die in the process, but new pines soon sprout. Without periodic fires, the population would die out.* ▌ On the east ridge of Middle Devils Peak you meet the Darkey Creek Trail (5170–0.6), starting down the burned-over ridge. ▌ *As you traverse the northeast-facing slopes of Middle Devils Peak, you pass the first of several small groves of weeping spruce, spared from the conflagration. Note the trees' drooping "Douglas-fir" branches, their oversize "hemlock" cones and their scaly "lodgepole" bark.* ▌
North of the peak you reach a saddle, and from

See map R1

Lily Pad Lake

Upper Devils Peak (left) and Kangaroo Mountain, from Middle Devils Peak

here, as well as from short switchbacks above it, you have views of snow-capped Mt. Shasta (14,162') to the east and the Marble Mountain Wilderness to the south. Beyond the switchbacks you reach Upper Devils Peak's western arm (5820–1.0).

*　　　*　　　*　　　*

Water access: From here a spur trail once descended 330 steep yards past western white pines to seeping Jackass Spring amid a cluster of alders. The pines and the trail are largely gone, but if you bear about 330° downslope, you should have very little trouble finding the spring.

*　　　*　　　*　　　*

Your trail now makes a traverse north, and along it you pass the charred remains of a forest before you pass a small grove of weeping spruce. Just past it you descend briefly to a saddle, which has a junction with faint Portuguese Creek Trail 12W03 (5760–1.2).

*　　　*　　　*　　　*

Water access: If you need water, you can drop west about 300 vertical feet along this trail to the seasonal headwaters of Portuguese Creek and then follow the creek down another 300–600 feet to find flowing water.

*　　　*　　　*　　　*

The PCT next climbs north up to a quickly reached junction with Boundary Trail 12W47

(5940–0.3). ❚ *Before the creation of Red Buttes Wilderness in 1984, this was known as the Rattlesnake Mountain Trail. As you can see on this section's first map, the trail stays quite close to the south boundary of Red Buttes Wilderness. You'll likely have noted by now a high, often snowy peak along the western skyline, 7309-foot Preston Peak.* ❚

Now you head 100 yards southeast to a minor saddle on nearby Devils Peaks crest, which also happens to be the south ridge of rusty Kangaroo Mountain. The mountain's glaciated, broad-floored basin greets you as you start a short, switchbacking descent, and along it you may see two tiny ponds, each having a nearby campsite. ❚ *Heading north from the switchbacks, you discover a creek that disappears into a sinkhole dissolved from a layer of light-gray marble that contrasts strongly with the orange, ancient, ultramafic intrusives of this area. These rocks are likely the northern extension of the rock types one sees along the PCT in the Marble Mountain Wilderness, on the distant southern skyline.* ❚

Likely because of the often damp nature of the basin's floor, the basin was largely spared from the 1987 fire. The basin's western lands are drier, and if you need to camp, look for a site there. Heading east, you reach a spring (5760–0.8) in spongy ground. From this spring—the easternmost of the Kangaroo Springs—the trail soon reaches a southeast slope. This the trail traverses, and soon you reach Kangaroo Mountain's east ridge (5900–0.5) and leave burned, trailside vegetation behind, although you'll see burned slopes on lands south of you all the way to Cook and Green Pass.

See map R1

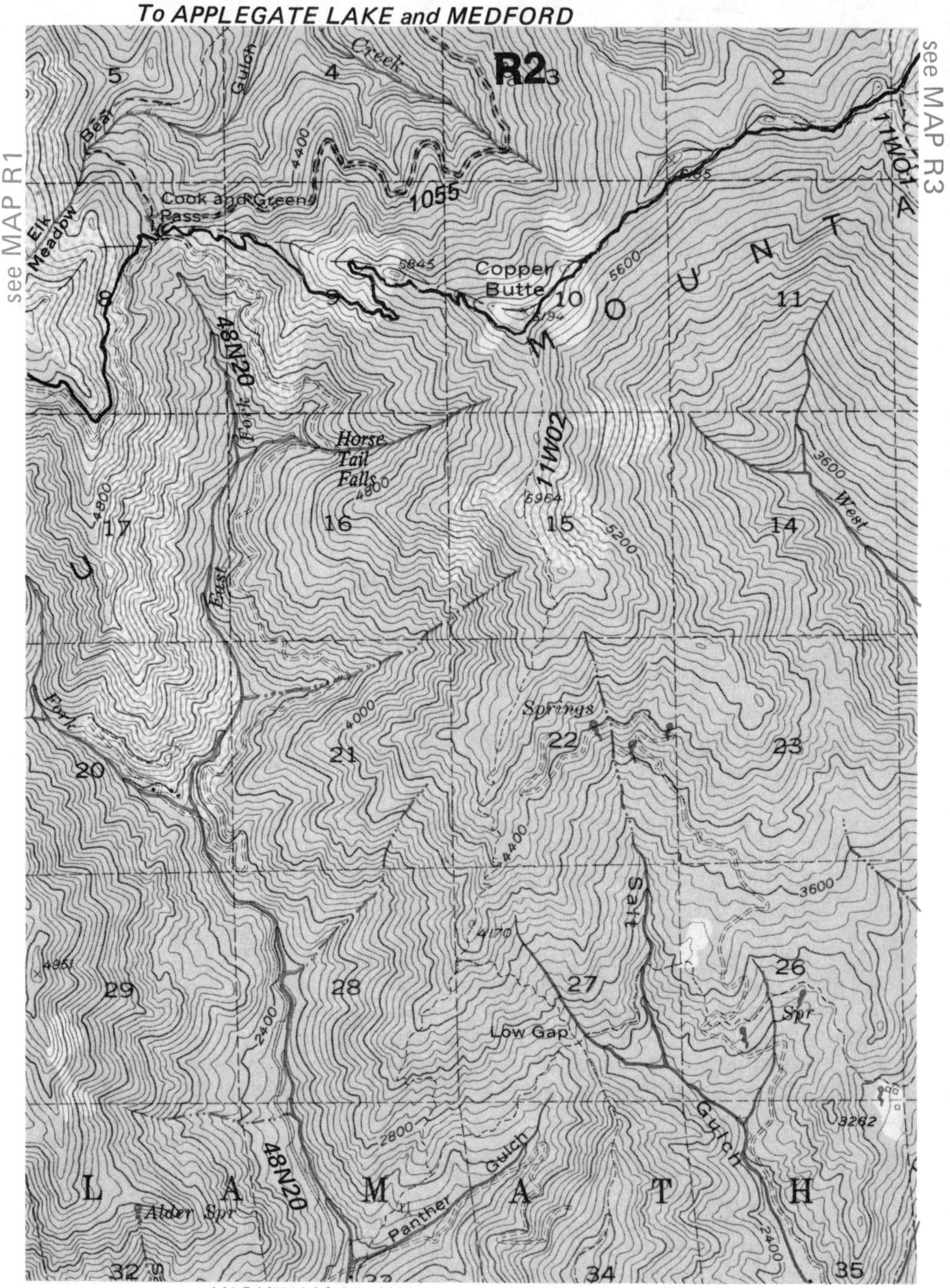

HIGHWAY 96 4½ MI.

From the east ridge you can gaze down at Lily Pad Lake, with its small, poor, adjacent campsites and its multitude of frogs. Your trail stays high above this lake and arcs northwest over to a narrow ridge, which is a small part of the Red Buttes Wilderness boundary. Along this ridge you may find a trail register, and just past it is a junction with a spur trail (5900–0.2). This goes 115 yards north along the boundary ridge to a jeep road, on which you could pitch a tent. Westward, within the wilderness, the jeep road is closed, but eastward it is still open and is

See map R1

definitely used. The PCT parallels it at a distance down to Cook and Green Pass.

With that goal in mind, you go but 200 yards northeast on the PCT before intersecting an old trail that starts from the jeep road just above you and drops to Lily Pad Lake. Now you descend gently east to a ridge that provides views down into the lake's glaciated canyon. From the ridge you circle a shallower, mildly glaciated canyon and cross the jeep road (5710–1.0) which has been staying just above you.

* * * *

Side route: Just several yards before this crossing a spur trail leads about 20 yards downslope to an excellent campsite. Hopefully the nearby spring will be flowing when you arrive here, but don't count on it.

* * * *

The PCT has kept below the road to avoid the Chrome King Mine, which lies just southwest of the road crossing. Next you traverse through a stand of timber, then climb past more brush to a junction on a crest saddle (5900–0.5).

* * * *

Side route: From here Horse Camp Trail 958 descends northeast toward nearby Echo Lake, whose environs provide camping superior to that at Lily Pad Lake.

* * * *

Leaving the saddle and the last outcrop of marble you'll encounter on your northbound trek, you make a long, mostly brushy descent, first east and then north, down to Cook and Green Pass (4770-2.5). There is room for at least several hiking parties on the forested, nearly flat crest immediately west of the road that crosses the pass.

* * * *

Water access: Get water by going along a trail that leads northwest from the pass. You'll reach a spring in 150 yards; if it's dry, continue another 225 yards to a creeklet. Here, along the crest border between Klamath National Forest to the south and Rogue River National Forest to the north, a major USFS road crosses the pass and then descends about 10½ miles to the start of this section's route, Seiad Store. The PCT route is about 4½ miles longer. Northbound from Cook and Green Pass, the USFS road snakes its way about 10 miles down to Hutton Campground, which is situated about a mile from a large reservoir, Applegate Lake.

* * * *

From this pass you follow an obvious trail east up the ridge toward Copper Butte. ∎ *On it you pass scattered knobcone pines in a vegetative cover that includes manzanita, western serviceberry, tobacco brush and Sadler's oak. Like tombstones, slabs of greenish-gray, foliated mica schist stand erect along the trail and, in the proper light, reflect the sun's rays as gla-*

See maps R1, R2

Deer on crest near Mud Springs

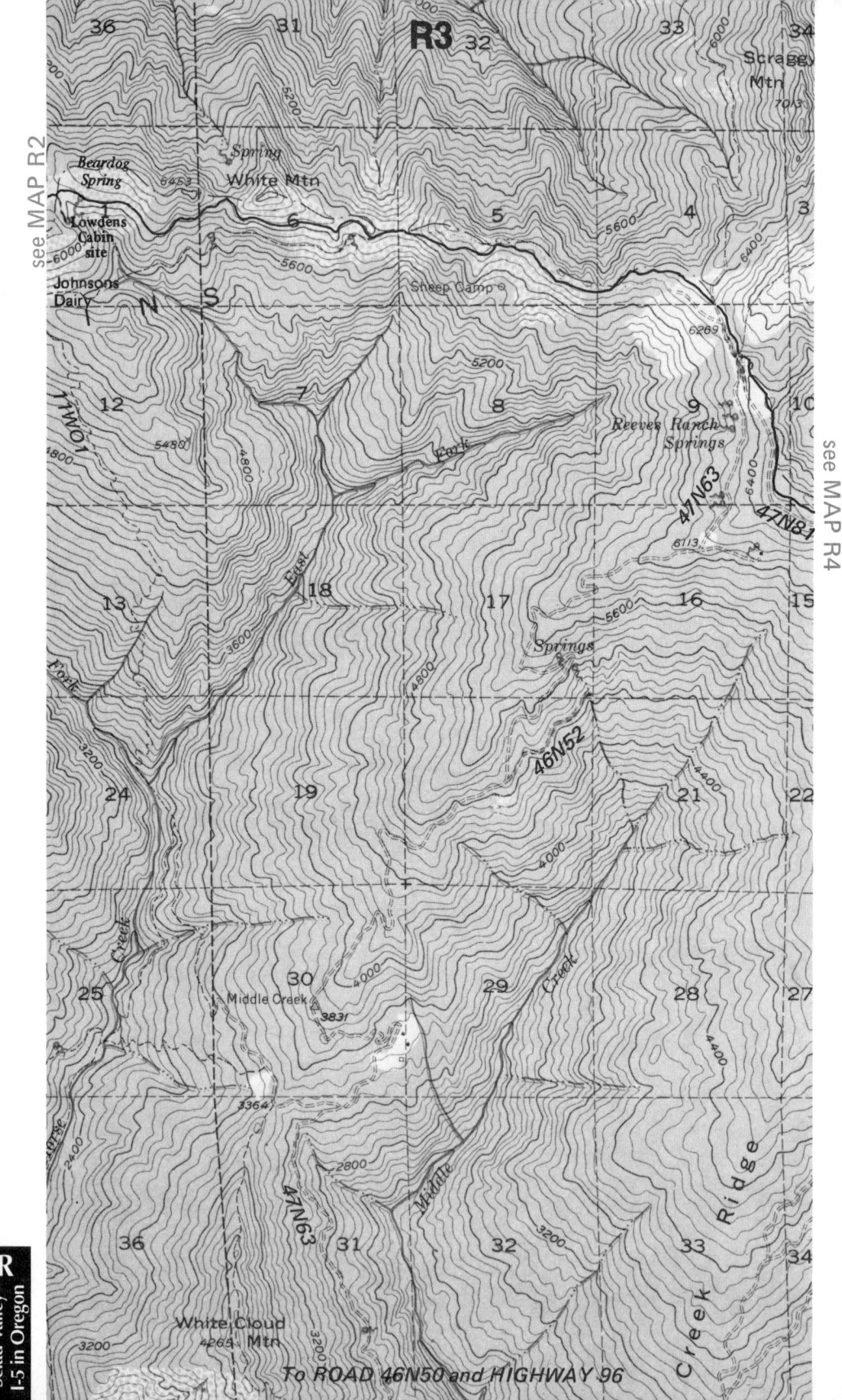

Seiad Valley-
I-5 in Oregon

R

To ROAD 46N50 and HIGHWAY 96

cially polished rocks do. ∎ Your trail makes a long switchback up to the crest, passing a clearcut in the process. There are other clearcuts to the south, on slopes east of Seiad Creek, and this patchwork landscape of forest and clearing contrasts with the burned slopes, which are mostly west of the creek.

∎ *Once back on the crest, the PCT enters a stand of white fir, red fir, mountain hemlock, Douglas-fir, ponderosa pine and knobcone pine—a combination you'd never see in the Sierra Nevada, where these trees are altitudinally zoned to a much greater extent. On the north slopes just below the crest, you'll also find weeping spruce.* ∎ Rather than struggle to the top of Copper Butte, as early PCT hikers did on the old trail, you make a slight ascent to its south ridge, on which you meet Trail 11W02 (6080–2.8), which descends south to Low Gap, Salt Gulch and Seiad Valley. Your course now becomes a northeast one and you keep close to the crest, crossing several forested crest saddles before arriving at an open one (6040–2.2), from which Horse Creek Trail 11W01 begins a brushy descent south to Middle Creek Road 46N50. This road descends southeast many miles to the hamlet of Horse Creek on Highway 96. You continue northeast to another saddle (6040–0.3).

* * * *

Side routes: Here you'll find a spur trail, hopefully marked, which heads 230 yards southeast to a small spring with an equally small campsite at the Lowdens Cabin site. It is better to camp at the saddle, where there is more room. Northward from it, Tin Cup Trail 961 descends 1.6 miles to Road 600.

* * * *

Leaving the saddle, you start a contour east and from brushy slopes can identify the spring area, across the meadow south of you, by noting a large log near the forest's edge. By Beardog Spring, immediately below the trail, your brushy contour becomes a forested one of Douglas-fir, Jeffrey pine and incense-cedar. Beyond a deep crest saddle, you soon start along the south slope of White Mountain. You cross somewhat open slopes again, reach its spur ridge, and then arc east across the upper limits of a meadowy hollow. At its east end is a junction (5950–2.0) with the old PCT.

* * * *

Water access: This trail will lead you to a seasonal seep near the hollow's west edge. Late-season hikers will have to descend the hollow a short distance to get their water.

* * * *

Just beyond this junction you reach another saddle and from it you climb east up to a higher crest. You stay close to it on a path that glitters with mica flakes before you eventually curve southeast and descend an open slope. Next you parallel a road across a long saddle, then almost touch the hairpin turn of Road 47N81 (6310–2.4).

See maps R2, R3

View northeast from Jackson Gap

*   *   *   *

Water access: You can take the lower road branch south ½ mile to Reeves Ranch Springs, located below the road. The northernmost spring is seasonal, but the two others appear to be perennial. Dense groves of alders give away their location but also make reaching them an effort.

*   *   *   *

The Pacific Crest Trail parallels the east side of the road's upper branch, climbing first south, then east, and eventually traversing the south slopes of Condrey Mountain before descending ¾ mile to a saddle (6630–3.1).

*   *   *   *

Side routes: From here a spur road leaves Road 47N81 to descend west-southwest 0.3 mile to Buckhorn Camp, a poor campsite beside a trickling spring a few yards farther east. Another spur road leaves the saddle, this one descending north ¼ mile to delightful Alex Hole Camp, located near a willow-lined spring. Here, where your far-reaching view north is framed by cliffs of mica schist, your only neighbors may be deer, chipmunks and mountain bluebirds.

*   *   *   *

On the PCT, you start to parallel ascending Road 47N81, then veer north away from it to climb the main Siskiyou crest. You almost top Peak 7043 before descending into a mountain-hemlock forest. Long-lasting snow patches can make the next mile to the Mud Springs spur road difficult to follow, but if so you can take the crest road, just east of you, to the same destination. If you encounter snow along here, you are certain to encounter more snow to the east. Just yards away from Road 40S01, the PCT crosses the Mud Springs spur road (6730–2.3).

*   *   *   *

Water access: You can continue northwest 0.2 mile down this road to its end, where there are several very refreshing clear-water springs. The campsites near the springs are small and sloping. You may prefer to camp by the PCT

See maps R3, R4, R5

near the start of the spur road down to the springs.

*   *   *   *

Past the spur road you have a wonderful, open, near-crest traverse that passes a prominent rock midway in your approach to less imposing, misnamed Big Rock. You descend northeast across its open, gravelly east slope of glistening mica, briefly enter a patch of firs, leave it, and head south back into forest as you descend to a crossing of Road 40S01 (6250–1.6). Your trail now enters an old logging area as it first continues southward, then turns northeast and descends to cross a road (5930–0.8), which lies immediately north of Bearground Spring. As you'll see, this is an area of several springs. In this vicinity, which in former days was heavily used by car campers, you should be able to find a decent campsite.

From the Bearground Spring road you start among shady Shasta red firs and make a steady descent northeast, crossing an abandoned log-

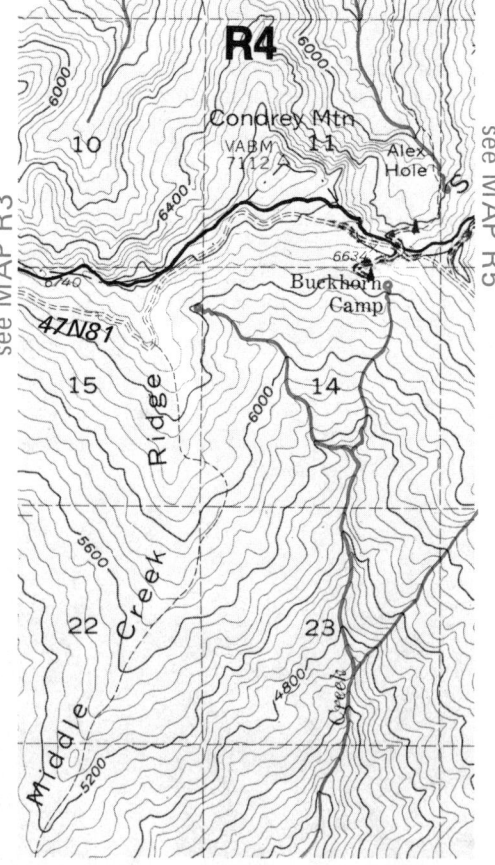

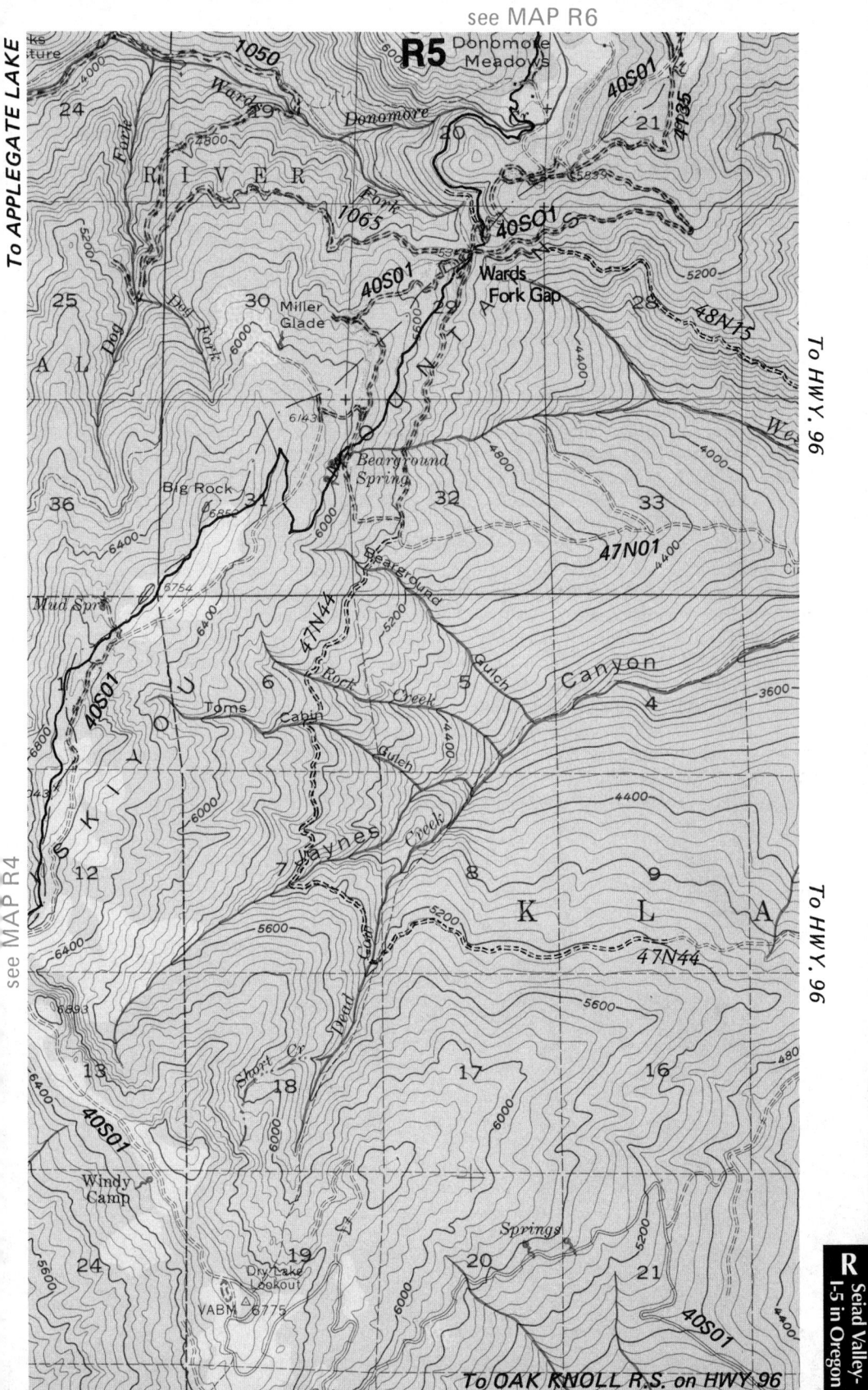

R5

To APPLEGATE LAKE

see MAP R4

To HWY. 96

To HWY. 96

Donomore Meadows

Donomore

Wards Fork Gap

Miller Glade

Bearground Spring

Big Rock

Mud Spr

Toms Cabin

Rock Creek

Bearground Gulch

Canyon

Short Cr

Windy Camp

Dry Lake Lookout

VABM 6775

Springs

1050

1065

40S01

49135

48N15

47N01

47N44

47N44

40S01

40S01

Haynes Creek

Dead Cow Gulch

To OAK KNOLL R.S. on HWY 96

ging road midway to a saddle. Nearing this saddle, you cross narrow Road 40S01 at its hairpin turn, immediately recross the road, and in a couple of minutes reach a 6-way road junction on the saddle, Wards Fork Gap (5317–1.3). Southbound Road 47N01 traverses over to Road 47N44, and from that junction both descend to Beaver Creek. Along the creek, Road 48N01 descends to Highway 96, reaching it just 0.7 mile northeast of Klamath River, a small community with store and post office. Road 48N151, descending east from the saddle, also will get you to Beaver Creek. Road 1065 traverses west from the saddle, but later drops to Road 1050, which makes a long, leisurely descent west to Hutton Campground and the nearby Applegate Lake area.

Between north-climbing Road 48N16 and east-climbing 40S01, the PCT starts to climb northeast from Wards Fork Gap. This short stretch can be overgrown and hard to follow. If you can't, then from the saddle head north briefly up Road 48N16 to a bend, from which a logging spur continues north. You'll see the PCT just above it, paralleling it first north, then west. Walk south up Road 48N16 midway to its second bend, and you should be able to find the northbound PCT without much trouble.

On it you make a short climb north before embarking on a long traverse that circles clockwise around a knoll to Donomore Creek. This you parallel east to within 100 yards of the Donomore Meadows road, then bridge the creek (5600–1.5) and wind northward up an amorphous ridge that may be crisscrossed with cow paths. In ½ mile you cross this road at a point about 80 yards east of a cabin, then parallel a jeep road, immediately below you, which follows the meadow's edge north. At the meadow's upper end, your trail curves east above it, then switchbacks west for a short, partly steep ascent northwest into Oregon, and soon veers north up to a logging-road saddle (6210–1.4).

Here you cross wide Road 2025, then climb east up a clearcut crest, and leave it to make a long, curving traverse northward to the west ridge (6750–1.6) of twin-topped Observation Peak. Kettle Lake, below you, immediately comes into view as you start an uphill traverse east. Unfortunately it lacks level land suitable for camping. You climb east to Kettle Creek, then climb north from it high above Kettle Lake before rounding the large northwest ridge of Observation Peak. A southeast traverse through stands of mountain hemlocks—snowbound until mid-July—gets you to Observation Gap (7030–1.2), a shallow saddle just west of and above 40S01.1. From the gap you go ½ mile on your crest trail, cross Road 40S01.1, traverse around the east slopes of Peak 7273, and then parallel the crest north to Jackson Gap (7040-1.2). Before reaching this gap you'll certainly notice landscape terracing in the Jackson Gap

See maps R5, R6

Sheep Camp Spring area

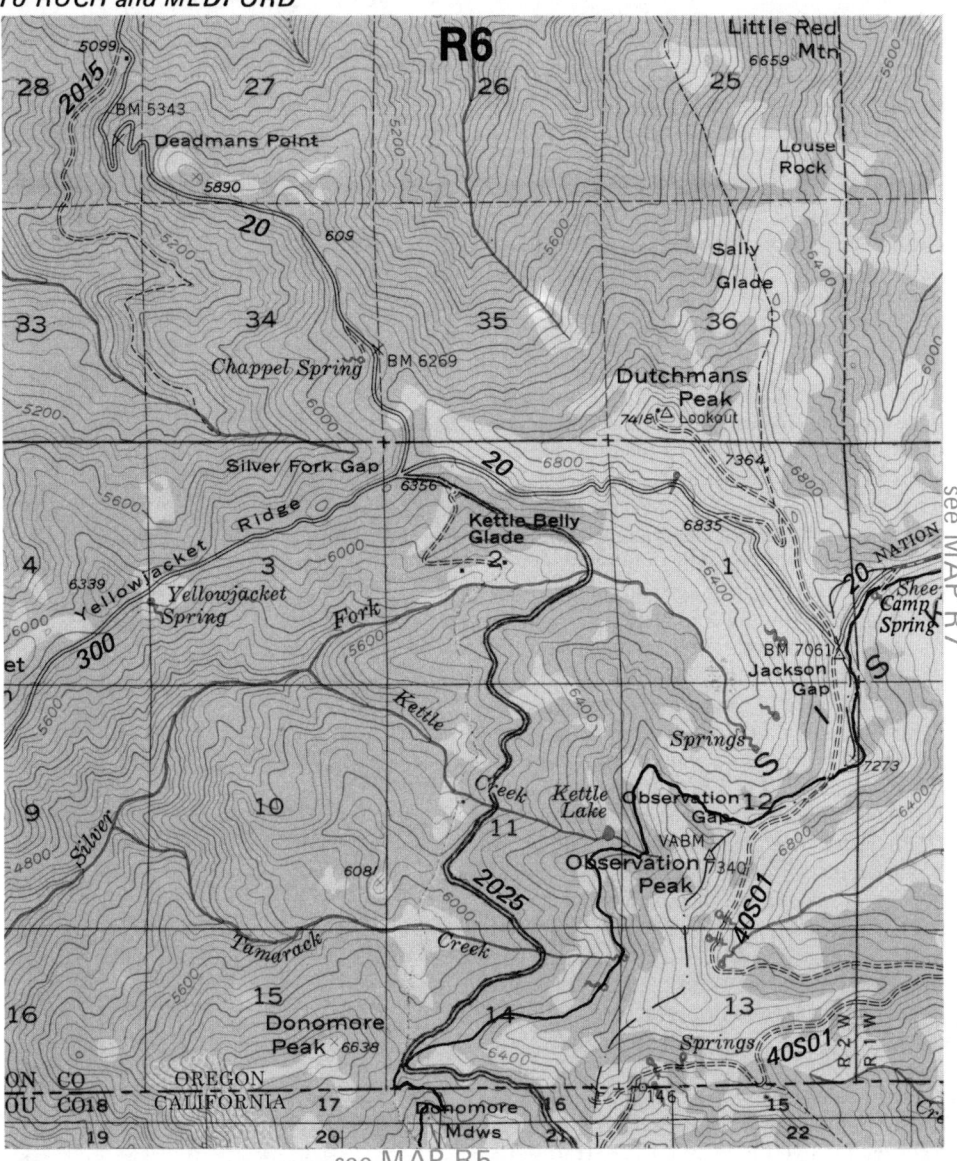

see MAP R7

see MAP R5

area, done to prevent erosion on the burned-over slopes. Crossing this gap just a few feet above you is broad Road 20, which you'll parallel all the way to the end of Section R. Before mid-July, snow drifts will probably force you to take this road rather than the PCT.

Leaving the cover of hemlocks and firs, you arc clockwise across the upper slopes of a huge open bowl, soon reaching a spur road (6920–0.3) to Sheep Camp Spring, located 10 yards south on it. Camp space is very limited, and since it lacks tree cover, you would probably

greet next morning's sunrise from a very wet sleeping bag. Departing east from the spur road, you gradually descend, with unobstructed views, to a spur ridge, then arc northeast to Wrangle Gap (6496–2.3), reaching it ¼ mile after you cross to the north side of Road 20.

* * * *

Side route: From here a spur road descends steeply west to Wrangle Campground. This little-used recreation site, nestled among Shasta

See maps R6, R7

red firs, has a large stone shelter complete with fireplace, two stoves and tables. In the '70s it also had tap water, and old-time hikers lament its loss. Unless the USFS decides to reinstate piped-in water, you'll have to get some from a nearby spring or lower down, from Wrangle Creek. The spring is at the upper end of a small bowl. To reach this spring from the shelter, head 210° for 150 yards.

*   *   *   *

From Wrangle Gap the PCT route could have gone east, but instead it makes a long climb north to the end of Red Mountain ridge and starts to wind southeast up it. The route does have the advantage of giving you sweeping panoramas of southern Oregon and its pointed landmark, Mt. McLoughlin—an Ice Age volcano. After crossing the ridge you contour south and then east, leaving Red Mountain's slopes for a winding, moderate descent to the west end of open Siskiyou Gap (5890–3.8), where you cross Road 20. ∎ *The northeast quarter of Section 34 lies in private land, and for many years the owner resisted attempts at building a direct trail, paralleling Road 20, over to nearby Long John Saddle. Finally in desperation, the USFS built a trail twice as long to that goal.* ∎ It first parallels Road 20 briefly over to its junction with Road 40S12, then parallels that road briefly over to a crossing (5800–0.3). Then it makes a long swing around a hill, offering you some Mt. Shasta views in partial compensation for your added hiking effort before finally reaching a 5-way road junction (5880–1.3) on forested Long John Saddle.

Road 20 traverses north across the level saddle and a minor logging road descends northeast. Between the two the Pacific Crest Trail starts to parallel Road 20 north, then climbs northeast through an old logging area. After a mile of progress, you come to a spur ridge and exchange this scarred landscape for a shady forest climb north. From a gully your gradient eases to give you a pleasant stroll northeast to an open crest saddle (6710–2.1). On it, your tread almost disappears as it parallels Road 20 for a few yards, then it becomes prominent again and climbs a short ½ mile up to a saddle just north of Siskiyou Peak. From this saddle you'll see chunky Pilot Peak on the eastern skyline—a guiding beacon for early pioneers

and for you. If you're continuing through Oregon, you should pass by it in a few days.

Your trail now winds ⅓ mile northeast toward a saddle on the main crest, crossing a spur road (6900–0.8) that is just 25 yards below its departure from crest-hugging Road 20. ∎ *The saddle is signed as the Meridian Overlook,*

See maps R7, R8

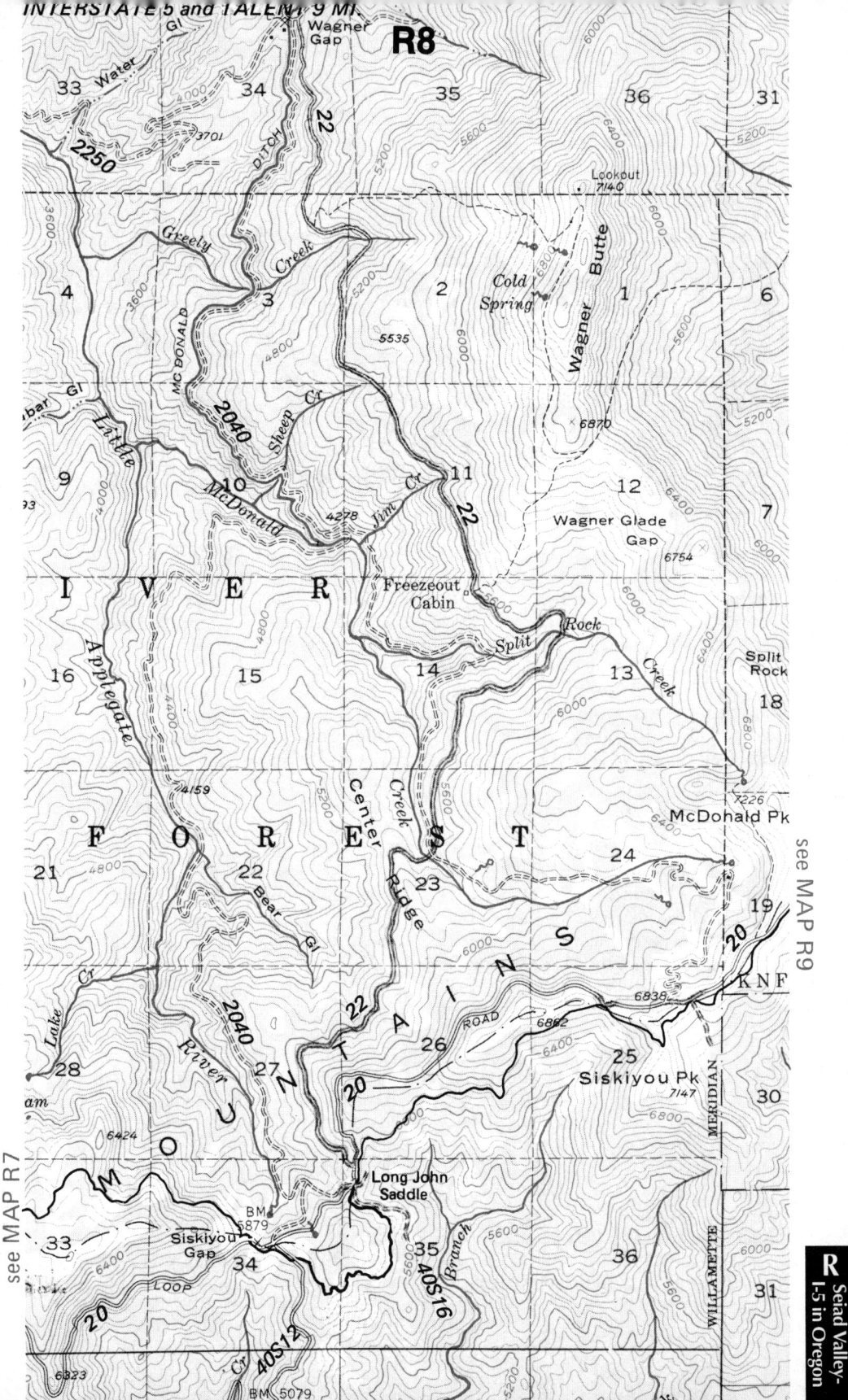

R8

see MAP R9

see MAP R7

Mt. Shasta, from Mt. Ashland Campground

since it is a viewpoint close to the Willamette Meridian. ∎

You parallel Road 20 northeast, sometimes below it and sometimes above it, to another saddle (7030–1.1) which is south of the main crest. Here the road bends north to descend, but you first go south briefly before switchbacking to descend northeast to reach Road 40S30 (6630–1.0) at its junction with Road 20 on expansive Grouse Gap.

*　　　*　　　*　　　*

Side route: This road takes you 0.2 mile south to a fork, from where you branch left on Road 40S30A for a minute's walk to Grouse Gap Shelter. Built in the mid-70s, it was finally fenced in two decades later (1994) to keep the local residents (cattle) out. The shelter provides protection from the elements and it offers dramatic sunrise views of Mt. Shasta. You can usually get water from the creeklet just northeast of and below the shelter, however, late-season trekkers will likely have to backtrack on 40S30A to 40S30, and then take that road ⅓ mile southwest down to an obvious gully with a spring-fed creeklet.

*　　　*　　　*　　　*

From Grouse Gap the PCT parallels Road 20 and passes several seeping springs before it gradually drops away from it down to a cross-ing of Road 40S15 (6480–1.9), which climbs ½ mile northeast up to this crest road. From their junction, Road 20 contours ½ mile northeast to the Mt. Ashland Ski Area, and eastward, the road is paved.

*　　　*　　　*　　　*

Side route: An alternative to camping at Grouse Gap Shelter is to camp at Mt. Ashland Campground, which straddles both sides of Road 20. To reach it, leave the PCT and follow Road 40S15 about 250 yards up to its bend left, from where you'll see an abandoned logging road that climbs directly upslope to the campground. The piped water isn't always flowing, and when it's not, get water in a little gully just above the campground's upper (north) sites.

*　　　*　　　*　　　*

From Road 40S15 the PCT contours southeast to the bend and then traverses northeast to an open bowl below the ski area. From this it traverses southeast to a saddle, where you cross Road 20 (6160–1.5). Continuing southeast down-ridge, you follow the PCT down to Road 2080 (6060–0.4).

*　　　*　　　*　　　*

Supply access #1: From your ridge you can take a supply route by following Road 2080 north down to Bull Gap (5500–2.8), where you meet Road 200, which climbs southwest up to the Mt. Ashland Ski Area. Continuing north, take Road 200, which in 3 miles rejoins Road 2080, all the way down to Glenview Drive (2200–8.5) in Ashland. Descend this road north, then descend Fork Street. You quickly reach Pioneer Street and follow it two blocks to C Street. The Ashland Post Office is one block southeast on it, at the corner of First and C streets (1920–1.1). To get back to the PCT, head southwest one block to East Main and walk southeast. It quickly becomes two-way Siskiyou Boulevard (1950–0.3), and from here you can continue southeast on it to Highway 66 (Ashland Street) (2010–1.1). Take this east past the Ashland Shopping Center to Washington Street, which has the Ashland Ranger Station at its end. Just east of this short street you reach Interstate 5 (1980–1.3–15.1). Since hitchhiking on freeways is legal in Oregon, you can hitchhike up it 9 miles to the Mt. Ashland exit. Alternately, you can continue on Highway 66, then go south up Highway 273 to that exit, about a 12-mile route. This route is described in the opposite direction at the end of this chapter.

Back at Siskiyou Boulevard you can also keep to East Main and follow it 1.0 mile east to the Pacific Northwest Museum of Natural History. It is a fitting introduction to your hike north through Oregon and Washington. From the museum, continue 0.9 mile east to Tolman Creek Road, and on it curve south ½ mile back to Highway 66, meeting it at the Ashland Shopping Center (supermarket, superdrug, bank, etc., etc.).

*   *   *   *

If you decide against the supply route, then continue east down the forested trail. The PCT stays on or north of the crest, but after 0.7 mile it crosses to its south side and in ¼ mile crosses a jeep road that climbs northeast back to the nearby crest. ∎ *Not until 1987 was the next stretch—through sections 23, 24 and 26—completed. Rights of way across private property held up PCT construction for more than a decade.* ∎

The PCT continues its eastern descent, first past grass and bracken ferns, and then mostly past brush. Soon the trail switchbacks and then quickly reaches the shady grounds of Mt.

Ashland Inn, a bed-and-breakfast establishment opened Christmas 1987. The rates are very reasonable, as such establishments go, but they are nevertheless far too high for the average long-distance hiker. However, the owners, Elaine and Jerry Shanafelt, do freely offer water to passing hikers.

A minute's walk below the inn you cross a saddle (5490–1.5), and then parallel Road 20 for a generally brushy traverse over to another saddle (5110–0.8). Next you make a similar traverse, this one to a saddle with 4 roads radiating from it (4990–0.8). Eastbound, the PCT is confined between an old crest road and Road 20 for the first ⅓ mile, then it parallels the latter as both descend east around ridges and across gullies. Three closely spaced gullies near the end of this descent provide spring-fed water before they coalesce to flow into East Fork Cotton Creek.

Because you are on private land, you aren't allowed to deviate from the trail's tread and aren't allowed to camp. Anyway, thick brush prevents you from doing either. About 0.4 mile past your last spring-fed gully, you cross a road (4610–2.5) that descends steeply southeast to nearby Road 20, which here turns southeast to cross a broad saddle. Then, after a short, steep descent of your own, you cross a road (4470-0.1) that climbs gently west up to a union with the first road at paved Road 20. Both dirt roads are private—off limits—as is a third road that you parallel east, then momentarily turn south to cross (4360-0.1). Now you parallel this road, staying just above it, dip in and out of a gully with a sometimes flowing freshet, then soon curve away from the road as you glimpse busy, nearby Interstate 5. Your path ends (4250-0.8) at an abandoned segment of old Highway 99, which you take for 140 yards around a hollow to a fork. Here you go left and descend an old, closed road 150 yards to trail's end on Highway 99. This trailhead is 250 yards north of where Mt. Ashland Road 20 ends at Highway 99 (4240-0.3), and that junction in turn is immediately north of where Interstate 5 crosses over the highway. Here, at the junction of Road 20 and Highway 99, your section ends. ∎ *The Mesozoic granitic rocks you've traversed across along the eastern crest of the Siskiyou Mountains are now overlaid by mid-Tertiary, thick, basaltic andesite flows; and the Shasta red firs and mountain hemlocks have yielded to Dou-*

See maps R9, R10

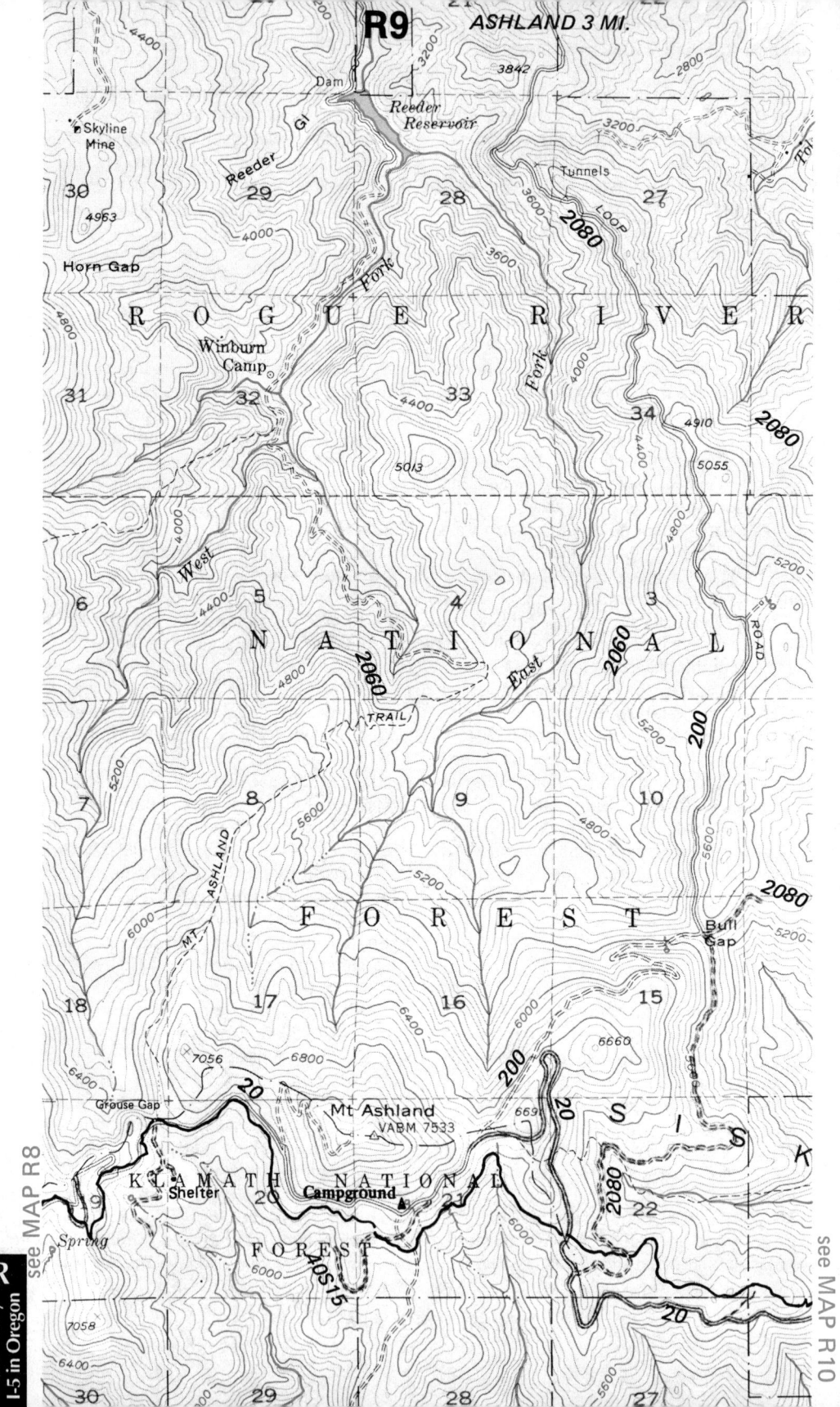

Dam
Reeder Reservoir
3842
3200
2800
Skyline Mine
Reeder Gl
Tunnels
LOOP
2080
30
29
28
27
4963
4000
3600
3200
Horn Gap
3600

R O G U E   R I V E R

West Fork
Winburn Camp
Fork
2080
31
32
33
34
4910
2080
4400
5013
5055

West
5
4
3
ROAD
6
2060
2060
200
N A T I O N A L
East
5200
TRAIL

7
8
9
10
2080
ASHLAND
5600
4800
Bull Gap
5200

MT
F O R E S T
18
17
16
15
6660
200

7056
6800
2080
Grouse Gap
20
Mt Ashland
VABM 7533
669
20
S I S K
9
Shelter
20
Campground
21
22
Spring
K L A M A T H   N A T I O N A L
2080
7058
F O R E S T
40S15
6000
20

30
29
28
27

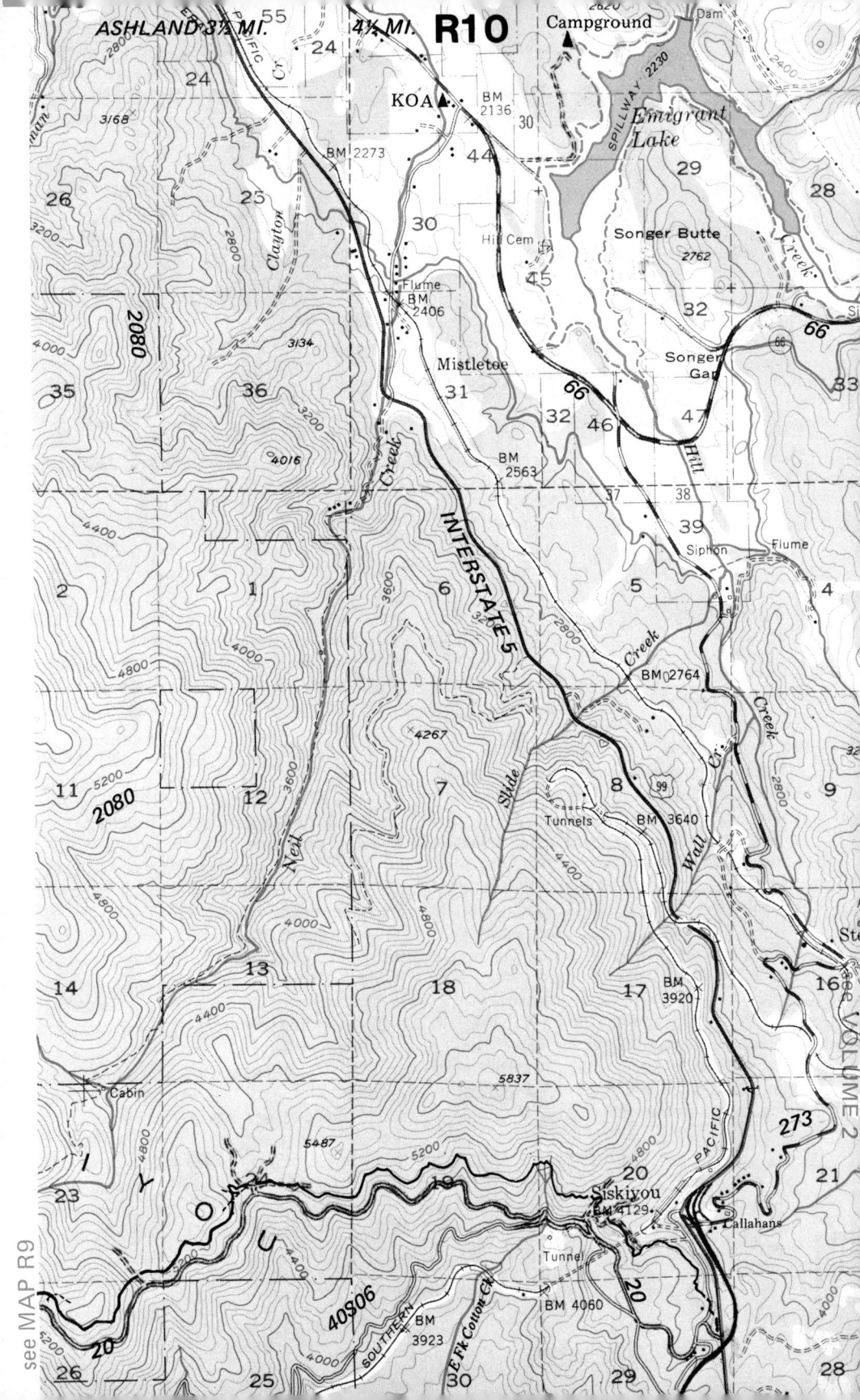

Ashland's Emigrant Lake, along alternate route

glas-firs and orange-barked madrones. ∎

*   *   *   *

Supply access #2: If you've hiked the PCT through much or all of California, you may want to celebrate your entry into Oregon by visiting Callahan's Restaurant. Go north on Highway 99 for ⅔ mile to Highway 273 and on it cross under Interstate 5 at its Mt. Ashland exit. The restaurant is just east of it. This ever-popular place, closed on Mondays, serves only dinners, and though Callahan's is expensive by backpackers' standards, it is one of the better dining places along or near the entire Pacific Crest Trail. If you've been starving these last few miles, you'll be glad to know that each of their dinners includes all the salad, soup and spaghetti you can eat. While the restaurant is closed, Callahan's Country Store, also on the grounds, usually is open. It has "emergency supplies": beer, chips, candy, more beer.

To resupply for another stretch of the PCT in southern Oregon, you can hitchhike 9 miles down Interstate 5 to the Highway 66 interchange and take the highway west into downtown Ashland.

*   *   *   *

Supply access #3: An old, temporary PCT route offers you another way down to Ashland. From Callahan's (3950–0.9 mile from end of

Road 20), you can go down tree-lined Highway 273 to a junction with Highway 66 (2290–6.7). Just east of it is the shallow upper end of Emigrant Lake, a popular fishing area; the deeper parts are relegated to water skiers, boaters and swimmers. Northwest, Highway 66 leads you to the main entrance to the Emigrant Lake Recreation Area (2150–1.8). Here a paved road heads southeast 0.4 mile up to a lateral dam, then curves north 0.6 mile to a public campground. Past the recreation area's entrance you'll come to fairly expensive but well-equipped Ashland KOA campground (2140–0.2) with showers and a store. It caters to backpackers as well as to car campers, and the larger your hiking group, the cheaper your per-person camp fee will be. Continuing northwest on Highway 66, you meet Dead Indian Road (1920–2.6) before your highway turns west and climbs to cross Interstate 5 (1980–0.7-12.9) at the outskirts of Ashland. Some backpackers prefer to celebrate in Ashland rather that at Callahan's, for there is quite a selection of good-to-excellent cafes and restaurants. In addition, more cultured backpackers take in one or more performances of Ashland's Oregon Shakespearean Festival, which runs most of the year. If the weather has been dreary or snow patches abundant, then perhaps a Shakespearean comedy will lift your spirits. Just north of the festival's grounds is the Ashland Hostel (150 N. Main), which welcomes PCT hikers and even has a PCT register.

*   *   *   *

See map R10

Recommended Reading and Source Books

Pacific Crest Trail

Clarke, Clinton C. 1945. *The Pacific Crest Trailway.* Pasadena: The Pacific Crest Trail System Conference.

Gray, William R. 1975. *The Pacific Crest Trail.* Washington, D.C.: National Geographic Society.

Green, David. 1979. *A Pacific Crest Odyssey.* Berkeley: Wilderness Press.

Holtel, Bob. 1994. *Soul, Sweat and Survival on the Pacific Crest Trail.* Livermore, CA: Bittersweet Publ. Co.

Jardine, Ray. 1992. *The PCT Hiker's Handbook.* LaPine, OR: AdventureLore Press.

Ryback, Eric. 1971. *The High Adventure of Eric Ryback.* San Francisco: Chronicle Books.

Schaffer, Jeffrey P., and Andy Selters. 1990. *The Pacific Crest Trail, Volume 2: Oregon & Washington.* Berkeley: Wilderness Press.

Sutton, Ann, and Myron Sutton. 1975. *The Pacific Crest Trail: Escape to the Wilderness.* Philadelphia: Lippincott.

Backpacking, Packing, and Mountaineering

Aadland, Dan. 1993. *Treading Lightly with Pack Animals: a Guide to Low-Impact Travel in the Backcountry.* Missoula, MT: Mountain Press.

Back, Joe. 1987. *Horses, Hitches and Rocky Trails: The Packer's Bible.* Boulder, CO: Johnson Books.

Darvill, Fred T. 1992. *Mountaineering Medicine.* Berkeley: Wilderness Press.

Drummond, Roger. 1990. *Ticks and What You Can Do About Them.* Berkeley: Wilderness Press.

Elser, Smoke, and Bill Brown. 1980. *Packin' In On Mules and Horses.* Missoula, MT: Mountain Press.

Fleming, June. 1994. *Staying Found; The Complete Map & Compass Handbook.* Seattle: The Mountaineers.

Ganci, Dave. 1993. *Desert Hiking.* Berkeley: Wilderness Press.

Graydon, Don. ed. 1992. *Mountaineering: the Freedom of the Hills.* Seattle: The Mountaineers.

Harmon, David, and Amy S. Rubin. 1992. *Llamas on the Trail: A Packer's Guide.* Missoula, MT: Mountain Press.

Latimer, Carole. 1991. *Wilderness Cuisine.* Berkeley: Wilderness Press.

Reifsnyder, William E. 1980. *Weathering the Wilderness; the Sierra Club Guide to Practical Meteorology.* San Francisco: Sierra Club.

Roper, Steve. 1976. *The Climber's Guide to the High Sierra.* San Francisco: Sierra Club.

Wilkerson, James A., ed., 1992. *Medicine for Mountaineering.* Seattle: The Mountaineers.

Winnett, Thomas, with Melanie Findling. 1994. *Backpacking Basics.* Berkeley: Wilderness Press.

History and General Natural History

Bailey, Harry P. 1966. *Weather of Southern California* (California Natural History Guide 17). Berkeley: University of California Press.

Brewer, William H. 1930 (1966). *Up and Down California in 1860–1864.* Berkeley: University of California Press.

Browning, Peter. 1986. *Place Names of the Sierra Nevada.* Berkeley: Wilderness Press.

Farquhar, Francis P. 1965. *History of the Sierra Nevada.* Berkeley: University of California Press.

Gunsky, Frederic R., ed. 1988. *South of Yosemite; Selected Writings of John Muir.* Berkeley: Wilderness Press.

Jaeger, Edmond C. 1965. *The California Deserts.* Stanford: Stanford University Press.
King, Clarence. 1872 (1989). *Mountaineering in the Sierra Nevada.* New York: Viking Penguin.
Reid, Robert L., ed. 1983. *A Treasury of the Sierra Nevada.* Berkeley: Wilderness Press.

Geology

American Geological Institute. 1984. *Dictionary of Geological Terms.* New York: Doubleday.
Bailey, Edgar H., ed. 1966. *Geology of Northern California* (California Division of Mines and Geology, Bulletin 190). Sacramento: California Division of Mines and Geology.
Hill, Mary. 1984. *California Landscape: Origin and Evolution* (California Natural History Guide 48). Berkeley: University of California Press.
Sharp, Robert P. 1994. *Geology Field Guide to Southern California.* Dubuque: Kendall/Hunt.
Shelton, John S. 1966. *Geology Illustrated.* San Francisco: W. H. Freeman.

Biology

Barbour, Michael, and Bruce Pavlik, Frank Drysdale, Susan Lindstrom. 1993. *California's Changing Landscapes.* Sacramento: California Native Plant Society.
Crampton, Beecher. 1974. *Grasses in California* (California Natural History Guide 33). Berkeley: University of California Press.
Dale, Nancy. 1986. *Flowering Plants: The Santa Monica Mountains, Coastal and Chaparral Regions of Southern California.* Santa Barbara: Capra Press.
Gaines, David. 1988. *Birds of Yosemite and the East Slope.* Lee Vining: Artemisia Press.
Grillos, Steve J. 1966. *Ferns and Fern Allies of California* (California Natural History Guide 16). Berkeley: University of California Press.
Hickman, James C. 1993. *The Jepson Manual: Higher Plants of California.* Berkeley: University of California Press.
Horn, Elizabeth L. 1976. *Wildflowers 3: The Sierra Nevada.* Beaverton, OR: Touchstone Press.
Jaeger, Edmond C. 1969. *Desert Wild Flowers.* Stanford: Stanford University Press.
Jaeger, Edmond C. 1961. *Desert Wildlife.* Stanford: Stanford University Press.
Jaeger, Edmond C., and Arthur C. Smith. 1966. *Introduction to the Natural History of Southern California* (California Natural History Guide 13). Berkeley: University of California Press.
Jameson, Everett W., Jr., and Hans J. Peeters. 1988. *California Mammals* (California Natural History Guide 52). Berkeley: University of California Press.
Keator, Glenn. 1980. *Sierra Flower Finder.* Berkeley: Nature Study Guild.
Niehaus, Theodore F., and Charles L. Ripper. 1976. *A Field Guide to Pacific States Wildflowers.* Boston: Houghton Mifflin.
Peterson, P. Victor. 1966. *Native Trees of Southern California* (California Natural History Guide 14). Berkeley: University of California Press.
Peterson, P. Victor, and P. Victor Peterson, Jr. 1975. *Native Trees of the Sierra Nevada* (California Natural History Guide 36). Berkeley: University of California Press.
Peterson, Roger T. 1990. *A Field Guide to Western Birds.* Boston: Houghton Mifflin.
Stebbins, Robert C. 1972. *Amphibians and Reptiles of California* (California Natural History Guide 31). Berkeley: University of California Press.
Storer, Tracy I., and Robert L. Usinger. 1963. *Sierra Nevada Natural History.* Berkeley: University of California Press.
Watts, Tom. 1973. *Pacific Coast Tree Finder.* Berkeley: Nature Study Guild.
Whitney, Stephen. 1979. *A Sierra Club Naturalist's Guide to the Sierra Nevada.* San Francisco: Sierra Club.
Whitney, Stephen. 1985. *Western Forests* (The Audubon Society Nature Guides). New York: Knopf.

Index

1995 UPDATE

The Valley Store (Section B, "Supplies") may be closed. If so, the next logical resupply point is thankfully quite close, and comprehensive.

From the junction of paved Terwilliger & Bailey roads in Terwilliger Valley (just east of the Valley Store), head due north 1.6 miles on Terwilliger Road to Kamp-Anza Kampground RV Park (3990'). This campground's staff is extremely friendly and helpful to Trailers. They boast pleasant, inexpensive camping, a surprisingly complete grocery (open 7 days a week), white gas sales, hot showers, water, telephones and laundry. Recently added are corrals and other equestrian accommodations—also quite inexpensive. They will also cash money orders and hold food parcels. For mail and package holds, please pre-contact:

> Terry & Marilynn Grant
> Kamp-Anza Kampground RV Park
> 41560 Terwilliger Road, Space 19
> "Attention PCT"
> Anza, CA 92539
> (909) 763-4819

Find the town of Anza 5.1 miles beyond Kamp-Anza, as described in more detail in the same "supplies" paragraph in Section B. It has a post office, restaurants, stores and other services.

The Pacific Crest Trail Volume 1: California
1997 UPDATE

Acknowledgments page. Photo credits of some photographers should read: Lyn Haber 238; J.C. Jenkins 230, 234; Ruby Johnson Jenkins 186, 189, 198, 205, 212, 220 221, 239, 240. Add to acknowledgments, with many thanks from the authors for updating input: Tony deBellis, Bruce Gilbert, Terry Astle, Chris Landa, Karl Duff and Rob Langsdorf.

p. 9, list of registers. There is one at the Tehachapi post office.

p. 16, col. 1. Sequoia National Forest headquarters were not moved; they are still at 900 W. Grand Ave., Porterville.

p. 27, last line. The word after "latitude" should be "is".

p. 61, col. 2, par. 1, l. 4-8. Emergency water is sporadically available 100 yards east of this junction down the road in a grove of Coulter pines, where a spigot jets out of a small cistern. If locked, there is a large cistern 10 feet up the hillside with an unlocked metal access plate. Don't count on it!

p. 112, par. 1. Water may not have been restored at Doble Trail Camp.

p. 116, col.2, par. 2. It should begin, "Just 300 yards after Holcomb Camp, the rerouted PCT climbs southwest on tread coincident with the Crab Flats Trail. In about another 300 yards steel pipes mark the junction where the PCT leaves the Crab Flats Trail. From there the PCT traverses west on fairly level tread while the Crab Flats Trail continues its climb to the southwest. Gently ascending, your way alternates in forest and high chaparral."

p. 118, col. 1, l. 2. The 40 yards of trail that were washed out have been corrected by the placement of a wooden bridge and the rebuilding of the trail.

p. 118, Map C13. The Deep Creek Campground shown in Section 18 no longer exists.

Also, the road shown arcing east from Section 13 to Section 18 along the top of the Mojave Forks Reservoir is no longer open to the motoring biker who is doing the PCT in sections.

p. 118, last par., to p. 119, l. 23. Substitute: "Upon reaching the spillway, walk southwest across the broken-glass-infested flat top of the spillway toward a paved ramp that leads north to the top of the dam. Walk steeply up to the top of the ramp, where you will see a PCT marker. Turn left here and stroll along the broad top of the dam 0.4 mile to where a wide, rutted dirt road goes steeply downhill southeast. Walk down this road adjacent to signs every few yards which set forth the water elevation behind the dam (if there is any water, which there almost never is.) At the bottom turn right and walk over the top of a cement structure, below which a small amount of water is being released through the bottom of the dam. Continue west down a steep grade on the other side of the cement structure and then angle left and cross the broad, usually dry West Fork channel. Scramble up the south bank and resume trail tread by turning right and proceeding west on an abandoned, torn-up road at the base of a cliff (3010-1.1)."

p. 119, col. 2, first full sentence: the path never comes to a jeep road.

p. 120, col. 1, last full sentence should read: "About halfway to Silverwood Lake you come to a flat area where an ascending jeep road from Highway 173 seems to terminate upon reaching the PCT (3480-2.6)"

p. 123, map C16. The black trail line was printed about one twelfth of an inch too low.

p. 132, col. 1, the first full paragraph should begin: "Soon the trail crosses the newer Southern Pacific Railroad tracks (3020-0.8) and swings to the right along a dirt access road for 30 yards, before bending southwest to wind...alluvium. At one point you amble south along a jeep road (keeping to the right where the road forks) for 100 years before trail tread resumes on the right side of the road."

p. 132, col. 1, last par., insert a second sentence: "Upon reaching the second powerline road, ascend south up the road for 150 yards before resuming trail tread on the right side of the road."

p. 138, col. 1. The Grassy Hollow Family Campground has been closed.

p. 145, last line. The next certain water is at North Fork Ranger Station in 5.5 miles. Water may also be found in early spring just before the PCT crosses Moody Canyon Road—1.4 miles from Messenger Flats Campground.

p. 149, par. 1. There may be no water in the streambed where the PCT crosses the Mattox Canyon stream. However, there may be a very nice flow a short way upstream.

p. 150, col. 1. Having emerged from your sometimes-wet ford of the river, the trail swings around to the right and empties you onto a flat maze of dirt roads, piles of debris and dirt, and other assorted scattered rubble. Don't dismay; simply head north to a dirt road adjacent to a barbed-wire fence, and follow the road a short distance east, to where you come to a break in the fence marked with PCT emblems which usher you left, north... (continue on p. 151).

p. 151, col. 2, middle par. The gap near the head of Bobcat Canyon is at an elevation of 2780, not 2980.

p. 151, col. 2, last par. After the first two sentences, substitute this description of new alignment: "Looking north, one sees the old PCT leading steeply up a hillside. However, the PCT continues to head downstream, crossing the creek six more times until finally turning west and heading up and over the southwest end of a ridge. After about 200 yards your trail drifts downhill a bit and comes to a four-way junction. An equestrian trail takes off to the left, but you follow the PCT to the

right, heading northeast up a very steep section of trail that deposits you on a little-used dirt road on the north rim of Escondido Canyon. Once on the canyon's rim,....Tiburcio Vasquez. Once on the rim you start a very gentle...junction (2535-0-9)...by a yellow pipe post. Head left down this dirt road for a short distance to another PCT marker. Turn right at this marker and follow a new section of PCT as it loops around north of a large grassy area, also passing north of the two most spectacular rock outcroppings. The trail eventually passes within 50 feet of a trailhead parking area and continues around half a dozen clifflets to strike Escondido Canyon Road (2510-0.9).

p. 152, col. 2. Camping is allowed at Vasquez Rocks.

p. 156. The mileages in the last column should be: 108.8, 107.0, 100.7, 98.5, 92.4, 86.1, 78.5, 71.5, 65.5, 61.2, 54.4, 47.7, 45.9, 42.4, 31.3, 24.7, 20.8, 8.6.

p. 160, col. 1, par. 2, the first sentence should read: "...then ascends moderately again, staying left at the first fork in the road, but going steeply uphill (next to a chain link fence) at the second fork in the road, to trail tread some 50 yards past a large steel electrical tower."

p. 160, col. 1, last par. should begin: "Leaving the saddle, one sees the old trail heading steeply up the spine of the ridge. You, however, start a traverse to the left of the ridge, gaining elevation gradually at first, and then more rapidly as you drift off to the northwest. Eventually you switchback steeply up almost to the ridge, where you switchback again back to the north. The climb moderates...on Sierra Pelona Ridge Road 6N07 (4500-2.7), ..."

p. 160, col. 2. Bear Spring is about 35 feet uphill from the trail, not the metal trough below the trail.

pp. 160-61, mileages at end of p. 160 and start of p. 161. The former should be 3785-0.6 and the latter should be 3340-0.9.

p. 164, col. 1. The San Francisquito Campground is no longer, but there is a trail camp near the ranger station.

p 177, col. 1, par. 3. There is probably water in Gamble Spring Canyon in the spring.

p. 183, Supplies. Tehachapi is now recommended for package pickups. To reach Tehachapi from the north end of Cameron Canyon, terminus of Section E, turn west (left) on the roadbed that parallels the railroad tracks, keeping well away from the heavily used tracks. Cross *under* the freeway in 2.0 miles, and then at the first opportunity, walk over to paved Tehachapi Road, which parallels the tracks and the freeway. You should be able to hitch a ride here. Continue west on the road 7.5 miles more to town and the post office, which is two blocks left on Green Street. You pass a Travelodge with gas station and minimart before you reach town.

p. 184, water, l. 4. There is now a series of springs in Sections F and G that has been upgraded in the 1990s to remove them from cattle contaminants: Golden Oaks (p. 189), Robin Bird (p. 192), Willow (p. 196), upper Yellow Jacket (p. 201), Joshua Tree (p. 213) and Fox Mill (p. 217). All have above-ground pipes for easy water collection, but all still need treating before drinking.

p. 184, Rattlesnakes, l. 7. The size should read 16-64 inches.

p. 187, col. 2, par. 2, l. 10. It should read, "Soon the PCT parallels the jeep road, crosses it again..."

p. 189, col. 1, l. 7. Begin the line with the word "Zond's".

p. 196, Water access. The BLM has upgraded Willow Spring and installed a special pump-action faucet for people. Next water is at upper Yellow Jacket Spring 0.7 mile up the side canyon.

p. 201, col. 1, 7 lines from bottom. The mileage figure should be 1/3.

p. 201, col. 2, Water access. The Forest Service has installed a new spring box and piping to the old trough at upper Yellow Jacket Spring. The other two springs nearby remain unim-

proved.

p. 202, bottom of page. It should say, "See maps F11, F12, F13."

p. 211, par. 3, l. 4. Numbers for the campsite should be (6190-2.1).

p. 213, col. 1, Side Route. This road in Cow Canyon has been closed to vehicles since becoming part of Owens Peak Wilderness.

p. 234, photo. It was inadvertently flopped, left to right.

p. 244. The mileages in the last column should be 175.8, 172.5, 167.2, 163.9, 155.9, 152.7, 150.4, 142.1, 135.0, 130.7, 125.5, 115.3, 112.0, 105.0, 100.4.

p. 245. The mileages in the first column should be 82.8 (unchanged), 87.6, 89.4, 97.0, 110.3, 117.3, 122.1, 128.4, 139.9, 147.7, 155.5, 158.7, 162.1, 166.1, 175.8.

p. 258-261. Campsites. Except for the spartan campsites at Wanda Lake, there are virtually no campsites between the 10,700-foot level on the east side of Muir Pass and those in the stunted whitebarks at the north end of Evolution Lake.

p. 261, col. 1, par. 3. Evolution Valley. The stream crossing below Evolution Meadow is dangerous, as deep holes have formed around large rocks there. The ranger directs hikers to a crossing near the head of Evolution Meadow.

p. 261, col. 2, par. 3, l. 4. Lateral trail to the Florence Lake Trail. There is no longer any evidence of this trail.

pl. 261, col. 2, par. 3, 11th line from end. Lou Beverly Lake junction. It's now signed *Three Island Lake*.

p. 261, col. 2, par. 3, 9th line from end. You bridge West Fork Bear Creek. It's no longer bridged.

p. 264, Resupply access. Vermilion Valley Resort. The owner, Butch Wiggs, and his family are very nice (even some freebies) to PCT hikers, and their resort is considered by many hikers to be the best rest-resupply stop along the entire trail. To get in touch: P.O. Box 258, Lakeshore, CA 93634; (209) 855 6558 (office); (209) 259 4000 (seasonal at resort—cell phone).

p. 264, col. 1, par. 4. Between Pocket Meadow and the meadow above the cascade on Silver Pass Creek the trail is exposed, loose, and rocky (very poor footing), and involves two hair-raising stream crossings.

p. 276, col. 2, l. 3. *southeast* should be *southwest*.

p. 310, col. 2, l. 5. The fraction is ¼.

pp. 363-87. The running head should have Highway 49 instead of Highway 40.

p. 272, col. 2, par. 1. No camping at Shadow Lake or between the trail and Shadow Creek where they are parallel.

p. 381, Map M10. The trail line was printed about one centimeter to the left of where it should be.

p.413, captions. The upper photo: A churning Hat Creek cascade; the lower photo: Subway Cave.

p. 493. The Grider Creek bridges are washed out.

Use these four pages for hitchhiking.

SOUTH

EAST

WEST